RESISTING HITLER

Resisting Hitler

Mildred Harnack
and the Red Orchestra

SHAREEN BLAIR BRYSAC

OXFORD
UNIVERSITY PRESS

2000

OXFORD

UNIVERSITY PRESS

Oxford   New York
Athens   Auckland   Bangkok   Bogotá   Buenos Aires   Calcutta
Cape Town   Chennai   Dar es Salaam   Delhi   Florence   Hong Kong   Istanbul
Karachi   Kuala Lumpur   Madrid   Melbourne   Mexico City   Mumbai
Nairobi   Paris   São Paulo   Shanghai   Singapore   Taipei   Tokyo   Toronto   Warsaw

and associated companies in
Berlin   Ibadan

Copyright © 2000 by Shareen Blair Brysac

Published by Oxford University Press, Inc.
198 Madison Avenue, New York, New York 10016

Oxford is a registered trademark of Oxford University Press

All photographs are from the Gedenkstätte Deutscher Widerstand
except for p. 15 (courtesy of Bercie Frohmann); p. 33 (courtesy of Neal Donner);
p. 91 (courtesy of Fred Sanderson); and p. 189 (courtesy of Rudolf Heberle).

Library of Congress Cataloging-in-Publication Data is available

1 3 5 7 9 8 6 4 2

Printed in the United States of America
on acid-free paper

To Karl,
partner on the quest

CONTENTS

I first heard of Mildred Fish-Harnack through a chance encounter more than a decade ago. The occasion was a dinner for a colleague who was researching a film on the tragic and futile July 20 plot to kill Adolf Hitler. As we talked, my husband, Karl Meyer, mentioned that his family had known an American who joined the German resistance and was beheaded in 1943. My colleague had not heard of Mildred. Nor had I, the unusual circumstances of her death notwithstanding. She was the only American woman executed on Hitler's orders during the Third Reich. She was killed in secret and in wrath. Her death came in the wake of the German defeat at Stalingrad, justly considered the turning point in World War II. The Nazi high command believed that she and her husband, Arvid, bore much of the blame for the disaster.

Karl in turn had heard of her from his mother, Dorothy, who was now in her nineties, and in questioning her, this is what I learned. Mildred Fish was born in Milwaukee of pioneer Yankee stock. In the 1920s she entered the University of Wisconsin and there befriended Dorothy and her husband, Ernest L. Meyer, a columnist for the Madison *Capital Times*. Strikingly handsome, Mildred was the belle of the campus literati when she met Arvid Harnack, a German student who had come to Madison to study labor history on a Rockefeller fellowship. They canoed and hiked around Lake Mendota with the Meyers, they sipped bootleg wine and took part in student dramatics, and they wed. In due course, Arvid returned to Germany and Mildred followed, for the first time meeting her scholarly and artistic in-laws: the Harnacks and their cousins, the Delbrücks and the Bonhoeffers who were a kind of academic royal family. The couple settled in Berlin, where Dorothy and Ernie visited them in 1932. Within a year, the Weimar Republic was dead and Hitler the unquestioned dictator of Germany. To the surprise and dismay of his American friends, Arvid became a civil servant, joined the National Socialist Party, and attained a senior post in the Ministry of Economics. When Mildred returned to America for a visit in 1937, it was generally assumed she had "gone Nazi." Only after the fall of Hitler's Reich did the truth become known.

But why, given the enormous interest in the Nazi era and World War II, did Mildred Fish-Harnack all but vanish from the history books? I began to visit West and East Berlin in order to find the answer. The Harnacks had belonged to the left-wing resistance. In West Germany, they were commonly viewed as little more than Soviet spies, whereas in East Germany, they were acclaimed as heroes, as harbingers of a future Marxist democratic republic. Fortunately, with the demise of the Cold War, it was possible to glean the far more complicated truth from long-closed intelligence archives and from interviews with Germans on both sides of the recently demolished Wall. In the pages that follow I hope to demonstrate that the Harnacks and the Red Orchestra—the name bestowed on their group by the Gestapo—belonged honorably to the anti-Nazi resistance, that the Harnacks risked their lives to provide vital information not just to the Soviet Union but also to the United States, and that they saw themselves as patriots seeking to oust from power an illegal despotism led by a fanatic and hateful usurper.

Many troves of new documents made this book possible. By filing under the Freedom of Information Act, I was able to have multiple documents pertaining to the Red Orchestra and the Harnacks—notably the so-called Gestapo Final Report—declassified, including those from the files of the CIC, CIA, FBI, and Military Intelligence. Following the turbulent events in the Soviet Union in 1991, the KGB made the Harnacks' own files available. German historians working on the trials of Red Orchestra members found new material in the military history archive in Prague. Two important caches of letters were discovered in attics. The first included nearly a hundred letters from Mildred to her mother, written in 1929–1935, recounting Hitler's rise to power and her own turn to the left. The second find was the correspondence of Martha

Dodd, the daughter of Roosevelt's ambassador to Berlin, sent after her death in Prague to the Library of Congress. Finally, with the generous help of a German diplomat, I was granted access to court records in Hanover documenting the futile efforts by survivors and relatives of the Red Orchestra victims to bring to trial their tormentor, Manfred Roeder.

I have chosen not to tell her story as a conventional biography but rather to convey it through documents and encounters with witnesses, some of them former intelligence agents, survivors who, for the most part, knew Mildred well. These witnesses sometimes disagree and offer conflicting interpretations of what they perceive as the truth. Their recollections have been filtered through a haze of half a century and the vicissitudes of Germany's occupation and division during the Cold War. Such reminiscences are often unreliable, for as Elizabeth Loftus, an expert on witnesses and their trial testimony, explains: "We interpret the past, correcting ourselves, adding bits and pieces, deleting uncomplimentary or disturbing recollections, sweeping, dusting, tidying things up." Witnesses may present things not as they were but as they should have been. Even though their accounts could not always be supported by documents, I have let them speak for themselves. Historians may desire a more critical view than I have brought to these encounters; however, I felt it important to include these firsthand recollections to convey more vividly the passions that shaped Mildred's life and times.

A NOTE TO THE READER

German speakers may wonder why I call the Rote Kapelle the Red Orchestra when a more literal translation would be the Red Chapel or Band. Because "Red Orchestra" has been used in previous books and articles on the subject, I opted for the name by which the group is commonly known in the English-speaking world. Likewise, the careful reader will also note that in the text of the book I have referred to Mildred as Fish-Harnack as she preferred to be known in Germany. However, it is Mildred Harnack Day in Wisconsin and the Mildred Harnack Oberschule in Berlin and, because it is easier to remember, that is how she appears in the title of the book.

The reader will find a list of abbreviations and a glossary of some common terms at the back of this volume.

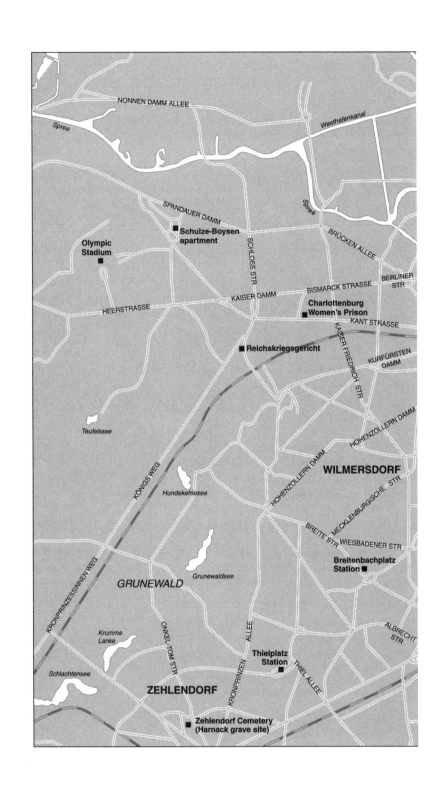

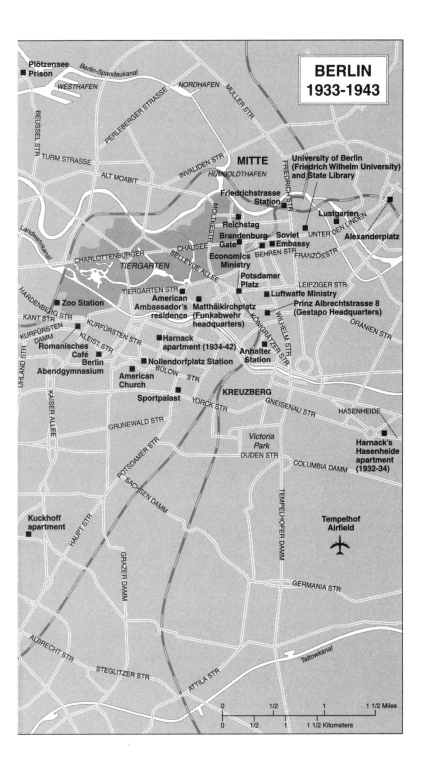

BERLIN
1933-1943

Plötzensee Prison

Berlin-Spandaukanal

WESTHAFEN

NORDHAFEN

MÜLLER STR

BEUSSEL STR

PERLEBERGER STRASSE

TURM STRASSE

INVALIDEN STR

MITTE

HUMBOLDTHAFEN

University of Berlin
(Friedrich Wilhelm University)
and State Library

ALT MOABIT

FRIEDRICH STR

Friedrichstrasse Station

Landwehrkanal

MOLTKE STR

Reichstag

Lustgarten

Brandenburg Gate

Soviet Embassy

UNTER DEN LINDEN

Alexanderplatz

CHARLOTTENBURGER

CHAUSEE

BELLEVUE ALLEE

Economics Ministry

BEHREN STR

FRANZÖS STR

TIERGARTEN

Potsdamer Platz

LEIPZIGER STR

Luftwaffe Ministry

HARDENBERG

Zoo Station

TIERGARTEN STR

KANT STR

KURFÜRSTEN STR

American Ambassador's residence

Matthäikirchplatz (Funkabwehr headquarters)

Prinz Albrechtstrasse 8 (Gestapo Headquarters)

KONIGRATZER STR

WILHELM STR

ORANIEN STR

KURFÜRSTEN DAMM

KLEIST STR

Romanisches Café

UHLAND STR

Berlin Abendgymnasium

Harnack apartment (1934-42)

Nollendorfplatz Station

Anhalter Station

American Church

BÜLOW STR

KAISER ALLEE

Sportpalast

YORCK STR

KREUZBERG

GNEISENAU STR

HASENHEIDE

GRUNEWALD STR

POTSDAMER STR

Victoria Park

DUDEN STR

COLUMBIA DAMM

Harnack's Hasenheide apartment (1932-34)

SACHSEN DAMM

Kuckhoff apartment

HAUPT STR

GRAZER DAMM

TEMPELHOFER DAMM

Tempelhof Airfield

GERMANIA STR

ALBRECHT STR

STEGLITZER STR

ATTILA STR

Teltowkanal

0   1/2   1   1 1/2 Miles

0   1/2   1   1 1/2 Kilometers

ONE

Plötzensee

Plötzensee

On February 15, 1943, sometime after nine in the evening, a green police wagon left Charlottenburg's Women's Prison in Berlin. Making its way to Plötzensee prison, it stuttered over the rough cobblestones, pockmarked from Allied bombs. It passed by the Charlottenburg Schloss, the former home of the Prussian monarchs where, only a few hours before, young mothers wheeled babies in carriages through the gardens. When it reached the gate of the prison, the handcuffed passenger rose from the wooden bench and stepped out of the van to meet the guards who led her through the dark prison to the first-floor death cell.

The room was small, cold, dimly lit. The radiators were set into the inner wall in order to prevent suicidal inmates from bashing their heads on them. Now, in winter they gave out little heat. One lightbulb burned throughout the night so the lone prisoner could be observed. It cast its faint light on the official, who appeared to tell her that the possibility of a last-minute appeal had been denied.

The next day, as she waited for the death sentence to be carried out, Mildred Harnack-Fish spent her time drinking corn coffee, reading, and translating some lines of Goethe into English. In a fine, clear hand, she wrote in the margins of her copy of his poems her rendering of "Vermächtnis" (Bequest):

> No being can to nothing fall,
> The everlasting lives in all,
> Sustain yourself in joy with life
> Life is eternal; there are laws
> To keep the living treasures cause
> With which the worlds are rife.

She was bent over Goethe when the prison chaplain entered her cell. During the twelve-year "Third Reich," Harald Poelchau witnessed more than 1,000 executions—among them Mildred's friends in the German resistance and the leaders of the July 20 plot to kill Hitler. Poelchau noticed how ill Mildred looked. Suffering from malnutrition, tuberculosis, and, some say, torture, she looked far older than her forty years. During the five months of confinement without visitors, she had visibly withered; her once thick blond hair was thin and white.

They discussed the Bible, then Goethe. They spoke about her work. Mildred told the pastor that "if one understood a writer completely as a human being," as she believed, "it was possible to translate even the most difficult passage."

Pastor Poelchau could give her little hope but he could comfort her by describing her husband's brave end. Until now, she had not been officially informed of his death. Arvid Harnack's petition to see his wife one last time before his execution had been denied. A few hours before his death he had written two letters: one to his family, the other to Mildred. His final wish was that she should be happy when she thought of him. Arvid had spent his last hours at Plötzensee calmly reading Plato's *Defense of Socrates*. During his last visit with the pastor he asked him to read from the Bible—the story of the birth of Jesus his father had recited every Christmas. He asked the chaplain if he could hear once more the prologue in Heaven from *Faust*. Poelchau recited it from memory.

Before his execution, Arvid asked Poelchau to join him in singing the chorale, "I pray to the power of love."

That winter hundreds of thousands of German and Russian soldiers died in the snow at Stalingrad. In Berlin, Arvid died believing that Hitler's war was lost. He had no doubt that their group had been right to oppose the Nazis; by doing so they had hoped to save Germany from this catastrophe.

Although she had suffered spiritually and physically, Mildred had never left his side until their arrest. Now she appeared resigned, cut off from those around her. She had built a wall to shelter herself from further emotional pain. Only when the pastor gave her the family photographs he had smuggled into the prison and her sister-in-law's gift of an orange did her composure change. Her eyes filled with tears when she saw the picture of her mother. She kissed the picture over and over, then wrote in pencil on the back: "The face of my mother expresses everything that I want to say at this moment. This face was with me all through these last months. 16.II.43."

She held the orange—a rarity in wartime Germany—turning it round and round, wondering at its shape and color before she reluctantly ate it. She was so intimidated, so mistrustful, that Poelchau dared not ask her for the ring with the Harnack crest that she wore, an heirloom he wanted to save for the Harnack family. He feared she would think he wanted to steal it. Finally, as he left, she accepted the warmth of his firm handshake.

She began to read from the English Bible that Poelchau had given her. Her tears marked the verses from 1 Corinthians 13: "Though I speak with the tongues of men and of angels, and have not charity, I am become as sounding brass, or a tinkling cymbal. . . . And now abideth faith, hope, charity, these three; but the greatest of these is charity."

The "shoemaker" entered her cell. He betrayed no emotion as he searched her mouth for gold fillings and exchanged her shoes for wooden clogs. He cut her hair, baring her neck for the guillotine's blade. Hands cuffed behind her back, she was led from her cell to the execution chamber between two guards. Their reward for this extra duty was a bonus ration of eight cigarettes.

The cortege crossed the courtyard to the execution chamber, which was divided in half by a black curtain. On the right, the representatives of the state sat at a table. After the identity of the prisoner was ascertained, the death sentence, "for helping to prepare high treason, showing favor to the enemy, and espionage, accused, the military court has sentenced you to death by guillotine," was read. The speaker turned to a man wearing a long black coat, white gloves, and a tall black hat, "Executioner do your duty."

The black curtain jerked open, revealing the spare white chamber. As it was winter, no light filtered through the two arched windows. In front, under the roof was the iron beam with eight meat hooks, the gallows on which Arvid had been hanged. A washbasin was attached to the left wall. On the right, barely visible in the light, was the brass and wood guillotine. At fifty-seven minutes past six o'clock in the evening, in the presence of the representative from the Justice Ministry, an official of the SS, and the chief guard, Frau Doctor Mildred Harnack-Fish, aged forty— wife of the late government official Dr. Arvid Harnack, instructor of English and American literature at the Foreign Policy Institute of Berlin University, and translator of Goethe—was beheaded. In seven seconds, as the Germans precisely determined, she was dead.

The curtain was closed. The official raised his arm in the Hitler salute and declared, "The sentence is carried out." Next to the number 2782/42 Mildred Harnack-Fish's name was entered in the *Bibliotheksbuch*, the book that recorded those executed at Plötzensee.

Meanwhile across town the prosecutor in Mildred Harnack's two trials, Manfred Roeder, caught the overnight express from the Friedrichstrasse Station. He was dispatched to Paris with orders to carry out the *Nacht und Nebel* decree against the French and Belgian resistance. Suspects were to be rounded up under the cover of night and fog, and handed over to the Gestapo; others were to vanish without a trace.

A handsome man in his early forties, Roeder was described as brutal and bereft of compassion—a man with few manners and no charm. Known by colleagues and enemies alike as "Hitler's bloodhound," he had warned the Harnack family against trying to save Mildred. He knew of her death and had no regrets. By his skillful supervision of the investigation and ruthless prosecution of the Harnack group, Roeder advanced a giant step forward in his career. In the waning years of the war he would become advocate general of the Luftwaffe. During the Third Reich, as the Austrian satirist Karl Kraus remarked, Germany, once the land of *Dichter und Denker*, poets and thinkers, had become the country of *Richter und Henker*, judges and hangmen. Yet in four years the death sentence in "the Mildred Harnack affair" would come back to haunt Manfred Roeder.

Recorded by Poelchau, Mildred's last words as the hour of her death approached were: "And I have loved Germany so much." There were no further rites. There would be no funeral. The guards put the headless body into the waiting wood basket, which was then delivered to medical students at the Anatomical Institute of Berlin University for dissection.

TWO

Transfiguration

Stamp issued by the German Democratic Republic in 1964

By summer 1942, Operation Barbarossa, the war against the Russians, was not going well for the Germans. The early successes of Hitler's army had been followed by the shock of the Russian winter and news of a clothing shortage so severe that the army collected coats on Berlin's street corners. Then came the spring thaw. Panzer tanks and trucks bogged down in the Russian mud. However, in this third year of the war, there was one lucky break. Nazi intelligence agencies broke a Russian military code and penetrated a large Berlin resistance group headed by an official of the Reich's Economics Ministry, Arvid Harnack; a Luftwaffe first lieutenant, Harro Schulze-Boysen; and their spouses, Mildred Harnack-Fish and Libertas Schulze-Boysen.

The Gestapo moved swiftly to arrest Harro Schulze-Boysen on Monday, August 31, at his office in the Luftwaffe Ministry. One week later they seized Libertas as she fled Berlin on a southbound train the day before the Harnacks were apprehended while vacationing at a seaside resort in East Prussia. By September 12, when officers appeared at the Barandov Studios in Prague to arrest another member of the group, Adam Kuckhoff, who was making a film, eighteen other suspects, including his wife, Greta, were in custody in Berlin. On September 16, Mildred's fortieth birthday, the Gestapo took her former pupil Karl Behrens into custody. He had been fighting on the eastern front near Leningrad. Back in Berlin, twelve more suspects were being questioned. On Saturday afternoon, September 26, the Gestapo arrested Harnack's stepnephew Wolfgang Havemann at the naval intelligence school in Flensburg while additional resisters were rounded up in Hamburg. By March 1943, there had been 139 arrests in connection with the "Red Orchestra affair." One by one they were photographed profile, front, and three-quarters for the "Gestapo album"—young and old, aristocrats, intellectuals and working-class, mothers, fathers, sisters, brothers.

The group had no name, but Hitler's investigators dubbed it the Rote Kapelle because the suspects stood accused of transmitting or "playing" to the Soviet Union hundreds of radio messages containing military secrets.

In the United States, the news of Mildred's death filtered slowly through the news blackout from wartime Germany. In April, the

New York Times carried a brief notice announcing the death of her husband under the heading "Von Harnack's Son Slain. Victim by Hitler's Order in Berlin Execution, British Report." The notice erroneously identified Arvid as the "son of von Harnack, noted German theologian and friend of the late Kaiser Wilhelm II." A subsequent article in May cited the official *Gazetter of the German Reich* as reporting that Mildred's estate had been confiscated: "Communistic activities are given as a reason. . . . The official announcement does not make clear whether Mrs. Harnack, wife of a German official hanged last February for treason, was also implicated in a sensational conspiracy that still awaits clarification."[1]

Mildred's hometown newspaper, the *Milwaukee Journal*, also reported on May 16 that Mrs. Harnack might be implicated in a "sensational conspiracy"[2] involving her husband and one or a dozen more Germans in an alleged plot possibly linked to a Mme. Kollontai, the Soviet ambassador in Stockholm. That day Mildred's sister Marion wrote to her twin brother, Bob, and her older sister Harriet:

> This morning while I was making the Sunday pancakes, one of our neighbors came in and I knew by the looks of her face that something was not just right. She had the *Milwaukee Journal* with her and showed us the enclosed article written about Mildred. It is too bad that Arvid is no more, and I am wondering what has become of Mildred. Tomorrow I am going to get in touch with the *Journal* and also the Red Cross and see if anything can be done to find out where and how she is.
>
> I thought I should let you know about this immediately so that if there is anything we can do, we can at least try to do it.

Mildred's sister Harriette sought the intervention of the Vatican in order to send a telegram to their "Precious Little Sister: Bob, Marion and Fred join me in assuring you the old home is waiting, and funds for your return passage when possible." In September they received a reply from the Apostolic Nunciature of Berlin stating " 'that Mrs. Mildred Harnack died in the beginning of this year and that at the apartment of Woyrschstrasse 16 there is no longer residing anyone of her family.' No other details are given in the report. I wish to express to you and the other members of your family my heartfelt sympathies on the death of your dear sister, which will be doubly hard to bear on account of the lack of any details concerning her demise."[3]

After the war, a melodramatic note was sounded in a 1947 article, "Harnack Deaths Covered Trail of German Hoard," in the *Washington Evening Star*: "When Hitler ordered the beheading of Mrs. Mildred Fish Harnack of Washington, and her husband, he sealed forever the lips of the two living persons who could bare the trail of $300,000,000 in hidden German assets in America," said a high Justice Department official identified as Harry LeRoy Jones, assistant to the alien property custodian. Arvid Harnack, according to this official, knew all the intricacies of the fabulous and far-flung I.G. Farbenindustrie, Germany's chemical giant, including its cartel arrangements and foreign investments. Jones added that the Treasury Department had looked forward to having Harnack appear as a witness at hearings to discover the wealth that Nazis had camouflaged abroad, particularly in the United States. When he and his wife were executed, the opportunity was lost: "Hitler's ghastly personal fear that hidden Nazi hoards might be bared by Mrs. Harnack was manifested when he personally ordered her guillotined after examining the record of her trial as an anti-Nazi and re-opening of her case."[4]

That same year, The *Washington Post* reported on a memorial service held by the Daughters of the American Revolution at Constitutional Hall. The then president general of the DAR, Mrs. Roscoe C. O'Byrne, eulogized their former member, the secretary of the Berlin chapter, describing Mildred with more enthusiasm than information as having typified "the sterner stuff of which Daughters of the American Revolution are made."[5]

Finally in December 1947, the most complete account of Mildred's death appeared in the University of Wisconsin *Alumnus*. The magazine described Mildred as "the only American-born woman to be executed by the Gestapo" and as "a patron saint of resurgent German liberalism." The story mentioned the Harnacks' visits to the United States in 1937 when acquaintances scorned the couple, interpreting their silence as pro-Nazi loyalty. The article refers to the anti-Nazi Red Orchestra by name, although nowhere does the article state that they beamed the transmissions of their secret radios at the Soviet Union. According to the magazine, the Red Orchestra numbered over six hundred members, including one sequestered in the wire room of Hitler's headquarters and another concealed among the Luftwaffe's top staff.

As described in the article, based on material provided by her German sister-in-law, Inge Havemann, Mildred Harnack was much more than the Red Orchestra leader's wife. For her husband she typed and distributed leaflets, maintained contact with other members, and arranged secret meetings. Using her position as literary advise to a Berlin book publishing firm as an excuse for her frequent travels, she maintained liaisons with the various branches of a nationwide resistance movement. So secret were the details that members of this network often did not know the others were anti-Nazi until they met in prison.

Further on in this account, we have Hitler thumbing through the court records, coming across Mildred's dossier, and immediately ordering her case reopened. Hitler set in motion the procedure that launched a second trial: "As the only American in his power" she became "the target for his hatred of this country."

At war's end, the U.S. Army Counter Intelligence Corps (CIC) began to investigate the case of Mildred Harnack-Fish and in November 1946, the Federal Bureau of Investigation (FBI) began its own file. Most of these documents were not declassified until 1998. The most interesting items are cross-referenced from the file of Martha Dodd Stern, the daughter of a former U.S. ambassador to Berlin. By 1948, the FBI had Stern under surveillance as a suspected Communist. In a letter intercepted by the FBI, Martha writes:

I have been sent some truly wonderful material about M[ildred] and A[rvid] and their calvary in Germany. I hope to make an article out of it. A. got thumb and joint screws and God knows what else. M. had to witness his slow death by hanging (they did it on a 12 inch rope) or some such horrible method of slow strangulation, practically a crucifixion. She had an ectopic pregnancy when she went to prison and got no medical care. They tortured her almost to death.

Her hair turned white, she became lame had tuberculosis and all sorts of other horrors before they decided to put her out of her misery on the chopping block.[6]

As the Cold War divided Europe and the Soviet Union strengthened its grip on Eastern Europe, the newly organized Central Intelligence Agency joined the pursuit. It hoped to identify survivors of the group who, having eluded capture or death sentences, might be still active in the Soviet intelligence services. The CIA kept a secret file on the Rote Kapelle, compiled in book form in 1973, based on captured Gestapo documents and allied postwar interrogations of German intelligence personnel. Under the Freedom of Information Act passed by Congress in the wake of Watergate, the government released the documents in 1976. The short entry on Mildred reads:

Mildred Elizabeth HARNACK nee FISH was born about 1902 in the United States. An American citizen, she was in the 1920s a student at the University of Wisconsin when she met HARNACK. She returned with him to Germany, where they both taught economics and philosophy. She was in sympathy with her husband's devotion to Communism. In 1939 she lectured at Berlin University and the Foreign Office. She participated in her husband's clandestine activities and was executed on 16 February 1943.

The rest of the file contains some information from a book, *Treason in the Twentieth Century*, by the German journalist Margret Boveri:

Louis LOCHNER [the Berlin correspondent of the Associated Press] . . . came into contact regularly at the meetings of the German-American Chamber of Commerce, of which he was president—with Arvid von HARNACK, who had the American desk at the Ministry of Economics and whose wife, Mildred FISH HARNACK, was one of the most prominent American women in Berlin society. She helped Martha DODD [Mrs. Alfred K. STERN] organize those now legendary tea parties which were such social events in Berlin in the 1930s. The assumption that one of the codes which

LOCHNER bore concealed on his person upon his return to the U.S. originated from the Rote Kapelle is far from fantastic.[7]

As early as January 1946, as the Nuremberg tribunal was convening, an official inquiry into the death of Mildred Harnack was opened by the War Crimes Group of the U.S. Army. File number 12-2262 was declassified in 1990. It reads: "February 21, 1946: Mrs. Harnack had dual German-American citizenship. It is quite possible that investigation will disclose the commission of a war crime and might develop considerable interesting information." What was the war crime Mildred's prosecutors were deemed to have committed? "O-27 = Denial of due process."[8]

Nine months later the army changed its mind.

On November 21, 1946, the army investigation determined that both Harnacks were "very deeply involved in anti-Nazi underground activities in Germany" and that "both were tried and found guilty of high treason and executed."

A further paragraph, in a letter to Captain Sloan of the War Crimes Group, elaborates:

> While Mildred HARNACK's actions are laudable and while she was an American citizen, she was plotting against the German government, was given a trial and there appears to be sufficient justification for imposition of the death sentence. Your advice is requested whether War Crimes Group has jurisdiction to try such a case. Upon receipt of your reply we will either forward our already rather extensive file to you or continue with the investigation.[9]

January 15, 1947. Lt. Colonel Ellis, chief of the evidence branch of the War Crimes Group, replies, "This case is classified S/R [special reference] and should *not have been* referred for investigation. Withdraw case from Detachment 'D' and *do not* continue the investigation."[10]

With this, the army closed its files.

THREE

Chum

Mildred, Washington, D.C., 1918

B etter not write but don't forget me," Mildred Harnack wrote on a last postcard from London to her friend and former classmate Clara Leiser. Clara Leiser never forgot Mildred Harnack. No one who knew her ever forgot her, as I quickly learned. Replying to my telephone call asking if she remembered Arvid Harnack's wife, Hazel Rice Briggs paused, thought back to encounters sixty-four years ago, and replied, "Mildred Harnack was the most beautiful girl I ever saw." Another classmate's memory was of a "brilliant student, very self-assured," with a "swanlike neck" who exhibited her individuality by "wearing long, straight hair when most of us were trying out permanents," a sort of pre-Raphaelite beauty. "Rossetti's *Beata Beatrix* combined with the movie star sexiness of Veronica Lake." A fellow aspiring journalist on the *Wisconsin Literary Magazine,* Mady Emmerling Knowles, broke the stillness of our late afternoon tea: "I can still hear her voice. Can't *you* hear her voice?" Nonagenarian Dorothy Meyer's face lit up when she described the dramatic effect that Mildred's braids produced against the black velvet robe she wore as a young housewife in Berlin. The Meyers' one visit to the Harnacks' apartment took place on a European trip in August 1932.

My biographer's query in the *New York Times Book Review* elicited a letter from Ann Arbor, Michigan. The four-line notice with Mildred's name at the bottom of a page stirred up Elizabeth Fine's memory of a spring day at the University of Wisconsin, when Professor Laird's beginning Greek class heard Mildred, then a graduate student, recite the first hundred lines of the *Iliad* by heart—in Greek. A former high school beau, emeritus Harvard geophysics professor Francis Birch, sent a picture, carefully preserved after all these years.

The Germans who knew her described a nobility of character and other steadfast qualities, comparing her to Gretchen from *Faust,* to the thirteenth-century sculpture Uta of Naumburg, and to Senta in Wagner's *The Flying Dutchman.* Unable to hold back her tears, Edith Reindl recalled the first time they met. "Mildred wore a simple blue dress. She had a radiant face and beautiful blond hair that she wore in a knot. As she entered on the arm of her husband, I said, 'this woman looks very charming. I would like to know her better.' " The two Berliners used to go for rides,

Mildred's loose hair blowing in the wind as she stood up, Isadora Duncan fashion, in the back of the Reindl's fast-moving open roadster. Rudolf Heberle met Mildred first in Wisconsin when she was *"the* campus beauty." He noted her strong gaze and proud bearing. "She strode while most women tripped," Heberle wrote in a 1946 letter to Ricarda Huch, which I found in a Munich archive. "We walked in the woods, wandered," he records, "and Mildred read us poetry." Professor Hugo Munsterberg confessed to staring at her from across the room: "Every young man was in love with her. I remember some lectures she gave on American literature at the American Women's Club . . . Mildred's husband was from one of Berlin's most illustrious families and she—she was a woman of extraordinary beauty—moved in literary circles."

In fact, the young Mildred yearned to be remarkable. She was theatrical: she loved to act, recite out loud, strike a pose, stand out in any crowd. She's the one girl who tilts her head in the high school pictures. She's the one coed photographed in profile for the 1925 Wisconsin *Badger Yearbook*. Even her last photograph, taken shortly after her arrest, number 228 from the Gestapo files, shows the now defiant eyes, the resolve around the mouth. Here is someone determined to go down in history boldly.

Those who knew Mildred well find it hard to believe she was a spy. "The Mildred I knew would have been in the resistance, she would not spy," says Dorothy Whipple Clague, formerly a Wisconsin radical and now a retired Washington pediatrician. How can this innocence, this boldness, this willingness to capture the attention of a room be reconciled with the traits necessary for a life of secrecy?

When Mildred Harnack returned to Germany after a 1937 visit to the United States, she left behind for safekeeping fragments of an autobiographical novel. These seventy-one pages, neatly typed in brown folders, survived the vicissitudes of World War II in the care of a professor of German, Friedrich Bruns. In an introductory passage, she describes her novel rhapsodically as one "of strong contrasts: It concerns resolution and will, age and bitter disappointment, deprived youth, and also youth in its mistakes and in its exquisite fulfillment of friendship." In her novel Mildred proposes to trace the "development of a family of the lower middle class in a city in the Middle West in the years 1915 to 1918."[1]

This midwestern city was Milwaukee, where Mildred Elizabeth Fish was born on September 16, 1902. Nowadays, Milwaukee is a blue-collar town fallen on hard times. Its tanneries have been boarded over and its breweries closed down. The aroma of leather and hops no longer permeates the air. It's hard to tell whether Mildred's old neighborhood is coming up or going down, since so many vacant lots have replaced her former haunts. The German-speaking families who lived immediately north of Wisconsin Avenue, where Mildred was raised, have been replaced by Southeast Asian immigrants. Her birthplace on Grand, razed long ago, has become the parking lot for the Marshall and Illsley Bank.

Yet in the closing years of the last century, migrants from Central Europe had transformed Milwaukee from a Yankee frontier town into a sophisticated metropolis, described by its boastful burghers as the "German Athens on Lake Michigan." In 1902, three out of four Milwaukeeans were of German descent; in the North and West End, where they settled, store advertisements read: "Hier wird Englisch gesprochen." Milwaukee's Germans established music academies, art institutes, and lending libraries. Fine public parks displayed statues of von Steuben, Goethe, Schiller, and a Teutonic-looking Robert Burns. The immigrants' interests were musical and literary. Irish maids dusted parlors with Steinways and Chickerings bedecked with plaster of paris or marble busts of Beethoven and Mozart. Yet these new Americans viewed culture ecumenically: colored prints of America's six great poets—Emerson and Whitman, Bryant and Whittier, Lowell and Longfellow—hung two by two over heavy carved-oak mantels. Masterpieces of Schiller and Shakespeare stood alongside *Der Hund von Baskerville* by Arthur Conan Doyle, translated by Georg Meyer, a local newspaper editor.

Weekdays, *Stammtisch* regulars—actors and painters, professors and doctors, brewers and bankers—assembled for black *Kaffee* and butter *Kuchen* around their reserved table at Martini's. The blackened wooden rack behind the huge glowing stove of the *Kaffeehaus* held the twelve Milwaukee newspapers, seven of them in the *Muttersprache*, German. One of them, the *Germania*, featured a column written by "Philip Sauerampfer" in the local dialect, Milwaukee-Deutsch ("Die Cow hat über die Fence geyumpt"). There were local features on the nearly one hundred *Gesangverein*, choral societies to which everybody belonged whether they could sing or not, and reviews of the Wednesday night performances of the German repertory company at the Pabst Theater. In summer, drinking songs echoed between *Biergartens* as steins passed hand to hand. In Schlitz Park, children played to the wheezy tunes of the carousel pulled by a brewery-wagon horse. Looking back on Milwaukee's halcyon years, Mildred's lifelong friend, columnist Ernest Meyer, wrote, "An indefinable easy-going gemütlichkeit flowed like a quiet stream through the life of the city."[2]

German immigration favored the west side: the Deutscher Klub was there, the Turner Hall, where Papa Brosius taught *die Jungen* gymnastics on Saturday morning, was there. During the nineteenth century, the aptly named Grand Avenue attracted Milwaukee's brewery aristocracy who built their palatial homes along it. However, by the time Mildred was born, the brewery barons—Pabst, Miller, and Schlitz—had begun to abandon their brick and stone mansions in the sixteenth ward for Rhenish castles along Lake Michigan. Then a thrifty new class of citizens, who did not mind the noise and danger of the streetcar, took their places. These middle-class burghers would rent out rooms and vote in socialist mayors.

Because Mildred Fish began her life in a city nearly as German as the city where she would end it, Berlin posthumous press accounts assumed that Mildred was German-American or Jewish. In fact, the Fish family came from old Yankee stock.

In her 1936 application for membership in Berlin's Dorothea von Steuben chapter of the Daughters of the American Revolution, Mildred traced her lineage back to one John Fish. This ancestor received wages as a private in Captain Christopher Manchester's company of Rhode Island Minutemen. John Fish was the great-grandson of Thomas Fish, who emigrated from England in 1642, becoming one of the earliest settlers and founders of the state of Rhode Island. The Rhode Island Fishes were the parvenus; the more illustrious Massachusetts branch, which intermarried with the Stuyvesants and Schuylers, came over on the *Increase* in 1635.

It was these Fishes, the most prominent among them, a member of New York's "Four Hundred," Mrs. Stuyvesant Fish, that produced generations of Hamilton Fishes, one of whom was the congressman who once headed the House Committee on Un-American Activities. While Mrs. Stuyvesant Fish was giving her celebrated parties—one featured a guest of honor announced as the Prince del Drago but really a monkey in full evening dress—other Fishes advanced north and west, becoming yeoman farmers in Wisconsin, Michigan's Upper Peninsula, and Canada. Charles Henry Fish, Mildred's grandfather, moved from Franklin, Connecticut, to Arcadia, New York, to Menomonee Falls, Wisconsin, where he worked as a blacksmith. His only son, Mildred's father, William Cooke Fish, was born in "the Falls" in 1856. William attended a normal school studying to be a teacher but, in a pattern he would repeat throughout his life, lost interest and dropped out.

Her mother's family, the Heskeths, were English Protestants. In later years, Mildred traced her own predilection for radical views to a nonconformist ancestor. This minister, against the custom of his time, took his daughter with him while he preached sermons alongside John Wesley, the founder of Methodism. Mildred's maternal grandparents left Lancashire in England's industrial north with a group of relatives, arriving in the United States in the mid-nineteenth century. When they reached Wisconsin, they joined the first wave of settlers in the town of Hartford near Milwaukee. Here her grandfather, William Henry Hesketh, served as schoolteacher and postmaster. He had one son and seven daughters, six of them by his English wife, Jane Hilton, the last by an American wife. Mildred's mother, Georgina, the fourth in line, was born on December 22, 1865.

Georgina was ambitious. While still a teenager, she taught school, learned typewriting and shorthand, and moved with two sisters to Milwaukee. There she fell in love with the handsome young man who wrote with a fine Spencerian hand. Looking through pictures in the family album years later, his eldest daughter Harriette described William Fish as a "dashing figure, with the waxed moustache affected by the blades of the period." With his fashionable clothes, his flashing eyes, and his confident pose, William "was no country bumpkin."[3]

In 1893, after a four-year courtship, Georgina and William

married. She was three months pregnant; a daughter, Harriette, was born six months later. It would be agreeable to say that William settled down. He did not. By reputation, he was a "sporting man," a lady-killer who liked horses. His story was the antithesis of the American Dream, in which material success rewards hard work. Lowering himself, as it were, by his bootstraps, he descended from profession to odd job: schoolteacher, insurance agent, salesman, clerk, horse trader. He objected to taking orders and was easily bored. A jack of no trades, his daughter put it bluntly, "He lacked persistence and application."

Georgina consoled herself with her four children: Harriette, the twins Marion and Marbeau (Bob), born in 1895, and Mildred who was born in 1902, when Georgina was thirty-six. She was an afterthought, probably an accident. Family legend says hers was an easy birth, which Georgina attributed to her study of Christian Science.

At a time when the young died before the old from now forgotten epidemics—polio, diphtheria, typhoid fever, smallpox—funerals for children were an everyday occurrence. A new religion, Christian Science, offered hope, the possibility of controlling the uncontrollable, the triumph of spiritual power over everyday feelings of impotence. Founded by an independent-minded woman, Mary Baker Eddy, "Science" avowed the sexual equality and duality of a Father-Mother God, which accounts in part for its appeal to many women and only some men. "Science" won large numbers of converts in the early years of this century, especially in Milwaukee. Georgina herself was an awed witness to two "healings"; nephew Charles recovered from polio and a friend's daughter survived "brain fever."

A strong and self-reliant person, Georgina became a lifelong adherent and sometime practitioner of Christian Science. She organized her week around her children, Wednesday night testimonial meetings, and Sunday services. Mildred and the twins—Harriette was already at university—struggled over their daily lessons with titles such as Ancient and Modern Necromancy alias Mesmerism and Hypnotism Denounced. They searched and found answers to questions like, Are Sin, Disease, and Death Real? At week's end, dressed up in beribboned hats and high-buttoned shoes, they made the long trip downtown by streetcar to Sunday school classes.

"She was a great pip, a pet of all the rest of the family. We were all very fond of her and played with her a lot," Mildred's oldest sister recalled. Her memories of Mildred, recorded in a 1987 interview, were decidedly sparse. Reading through the transcript, I remembered other lines of Harriette's that struck a decidedly discordant note. Harriette had written to Mildred's friend, Clara Leiser, "We ought not to sanctify Mildred. She never thought of anyone but herself!"[4]

From Harriette's diary we can reconstruct their childhood. Seasons were marked by the flooding of the yard for skating or bobsled rides down Booth Street Hill in winter, swimming in the Milwaukee River or outings in Mitchell Park rowboats in summer. On summer vacation visits to relatives on farms, Mildred gathered sweet corn in bushel baskets and watched while her aunt churned butter and her uncle played with the kittens on the back stoop. Fall was escorted in by the mounted police, who led the Labor Day parade, an event universally attended in this trade union citadel. For Milwaukee children, this was a time when following a horse-drawn fire engine or sighting the matched team of Percheron greys pulling the Pabst brewery wagon was worthy of a diary mention or a school theme. Real treats were going by Schuster's Department Store for school supplies and birthday presents, taking nickel elephant rides on Countess Heinie in the Milwaukee Zoo, lining up for the annual automobile parade, and setting off firecrackers on the Fourth of July.

It should have been a very pleasant life, but the depression that began in the 1890s climaxed in the panic year of 1907. Crops failed, murrain took the cattle, mortgages went unpaid, businesses bottomed up, and there was the ever-present threat of fires. Winters were cold and open fireplaces and stoves provided heat and oil lamps, light. Lightning struck granaries. William's insurance business should have flourished but in those days, when people set fires for profit as well as pleasure, he failed again and again to provide for the family.

The Fishes rented out rooms and took in boarders, but local directories show that they moved nearly every year to different houses in the same neighborhood when they could not pay their rent. The houses were all near Grand (now Wisconsin Avenue) so that William could stable his horses in the abandoned barns as the more affluent people acquired motorcars. Her mother, Mildred wrote, was wrinkled and worn by the time her last daughter was born. Gradually, she distanced herself from a husband who proved unfaithful and incapable of supporting his family.

An interesting thing about the Fishes is that there are no posed family photographs: no father in stiff white collar; no mother seated, baby on lap, in her Sunday satin dress, no boy in short pants, no girls with ribbons in their hair. Family portraits give an impression of solidarity that the Fish family never achieved. Certainly William and Georgina were mismatched. She quoted the Bible; he was devoted to Wild West stories. When Mildred was twelve, they separated. For a brief period in 1915, Mildred and her mother went to live in Madison, Wisconsin, with Georgina's sister, Laura. From Mildred's writings, it appears this was a bold attempt at independence that failed. Why they returned to Milwaukee is unclear, but return they did. Her parents, Mildred wrote, could not resolve their differences "between the man's world of the chisel, iron vise, and stable smells" and "a woman's world of longing."[5] Her mother's preoccupation with "Science" widened the gulf; her father was alienated by a religion that "cultivated tenderness instead of warmth," that emphasized the transcendence of Spirit over the earthly pleasures of the flesh.[6] William thought his youngest daughter strange and mistrustful. The objects of his gruff affection—and anger—were not his children but his horses and dogs. With the help of second daughter Marion, Georgina supported the downwardly mobile family with odd domestic chores. One day, it is not exactly clear when, William was finally "cast out."

If William was a common man, Georgina was an exceptional woman. She held the family together, supported her children financially, encouraged them in their ambitions, and saw that they were well educated. Georgina taught her children never to be afraid and her daughter felt that this deep-rooted attitude had much to do with shaping her later life. If there was something they wanted to do—attend college, for example—Georgina allowed no obstruction to stand in their way. Mildred attributed her own considerable strength of character to her mother, "the first and almost fundamental creative force" in her life. Georgina gave her daughter "truth, strength and delicacy of feeling" through "mutual love." From Germany, in the crisis year 1933, Mildred wrote that she had learned "how to use these qualities productively and not let unproductive forces destroy them."[7]

She would remember the awkwardness and desolation of family life together, which she characterized as "a certain materialization of tragedy." Still, although her literary reconstructions of her youth are often bleak, her recollections of her formative years in letters to her mother assume a rosy glow. In a 1931 letter to Georgina, Mildred writes about an encounter with a friend who remarked, "You are very fortunate, for you had a happy childhood. One can tell that from a certain quietness and trust in you." Mildred replied that her childhood had been very happy because of her mother, who, "in spite of her very difficult life had always remained inwardly quiet and strong."[8] Privately, however, Mildred became progressively doubtful about Christian Science. She described herself as an "unconscious unbeliever in Sunday School and religious names." Perhaps because she knew it was a source of parental conflict, she spoke of God and religion unwillingly. Nevertheless, her early exposure to Science left its mark. Ever inclined to view her fellow humans optimistically—often despite contrary evidence—she believed in their redemption once they learned the truth.

Mildred wrote her sketch for a novel in the 1930s. It portrays a sensitive, poetically gifted young adolescent, intensely aware of class distinctions. Her story is melodramatic; her heroines "ache," "dream," and "long," and one of them, Magda, dies of consumption. They have injured pride and are susceptible to the snubs of those "who have dreams of rising in the world." They, like Mildred, are isolated, outcast, keenly aware of being poor in a well-off neighborhood. Friends cannot be invited home because of shabby surroundings. There are crises of birthdays and other parties with no proper gifts. Even when called by different names— Dorothy, Eula—her heroines are all Mildred, thinly disguised, scantily fed, and clothed in hand-me-downs. Although she never longed to be rich, she despaired of being poor.

In her novel, Mildred writes of many girlfriends but has only one best friend. Intensely loyal, Mildred feels guilty when she abandons her first friend, an older girl who shares her poverty and literary interests, for another named Grace. Her lack of courage in standing by her chum haunts Mili, as Mildred's Milwaukee friends called her, and although she does not share her classmates' snobbery, she succumbs to Grace's physical beauty.

Grace and Mili become as close as only teenage girls can be. A year ahead in school, Grace inhabits a different social stratum. Mili loves the "simple luxury and harmony of Grace's home"[9] provided by the father who is a successful commercial traveler. Grace is beautiful, as tall and dark as Mili is tall and fair. Mili calls her the Egyptian princess. They imagine themselves Siamese twins and braid their brown and gold hair together on the way home from school.

Discussions of the naked Indian boy who wrote love letters in Maria Evans's books about the Hopi Indians arouse their sexuality. They flirt with the possibility of emulating the nude brown bodies, but the two girls only go as far as dancing in bare feet. On the great parlor sofa, they read the farm poems of James Whitcomb Riley, liking "the swing, the lilt of them, the easy way in which they ran along."[10] They talk about boys and school but are happiest when left alone together. Attending plays at the Pabst Theater, they wear roses not to attract the attention of young men but in the hope that some of the mystery and glamour of the flowers may rub off on them. In the idyllic future they plan, Grace is to play Galahad to Mili's Guinevere, one to paint, the other to write. "Old maids" together with cat, canary, and simmering teapot, they would live "in a white frame house on a green bank." Grace's mother said to Mildred, "If you had been a man, I know who would have married Grace." Years later, Mildred admitted, "She was right."[11]

Who was Grace? I wondered. Could she still be alive?

Margaret Emmerling Knowles answered my query in the New York Times Book Review. *She did not know if she could help as her memories were "somewhat misty." However, she wrote, "I can still hear her voice and see her face." I calculated "Mady" must be nearing ninety but her posture was remarkable. She did not wear glasses. Her hearing was good, her conversation free from complaints about the infirmities of old age. After college in Wisconsin, she had become a sports reporter on a Philadelphia newspaper. Mady Emmerling knew Mili in Milwaukee and was willing to tell me what she remembered, what remained:*

"I just remember her as an open-eyed, almost open-mouthed, eager, observing person, always taking things in. She had a lovely voice and liked to read poetry out loud . . . When I met Mili, I was in my teens. She and my friend across the street who were friends, real friends, went to the public high school. I didn't. But I used to walk around the block with them in the evening, that kind of thing. She was really a close friend of Grace Carlsruh's and that's how I got acquainted with her."

Mady kept up with Grace. They exchanged cards at Christmas but she had not heard from her in a couple of years and did not know whether she still was alive. She would look for her address.

Three weeks later Mady Emmerling sent a card with Grace's address in Florida. I wrote and a month later I received a letter from her daughter telling me that her mother had been moved to a nursing home in Cincinnati. She explained that in spite of physical problems, her mother's long-term memory seemed quite good. I telephoned the daughter and we agreed that I would send the story Mili wrote about Grace and some questions. The result was disappointing. At this distance, Grace could only remember that Mili was "brilliant and we skated a lot." This short, one-line theme would have many variations.

Nearly a year later a small gold-embossed green book, *Riley Farm-Rhymes*, arrived in the mail from Cincinnati. The daughter found it along with four snapshots of Mili when she was cleaning out her mother's house. Mili had dedicated it "To my chum, 'Gracious,' Christmas, 1918 from Mili." She underlined many passages in the book and on the last page penned a poem.

And this is the pledge that shall never grow old,
   and this is the Chum Song that silently sings
Through the now and the *then* and *what will be*—forever
   I love you, my chum, with a love that was never begun,
With a love that will silently live through—the always
   My love is the same through all space and a time,
For a love of a chum for a chum "endureth forever!"
                 —Mildred Fish (1918)

Mili began her literary apprenticeship on the school magazine and newspaper at West Division High. She competed for and often won literary prizes: a story, "Mein Kamerad," about "Christian love in war time" won first prize—an eight-dollar camera—in a national Christmas contest sponsored by the *Ellsworth* (Kansas) *Messenger*. This sparked her first appreciative review: the *South Bend* (Indiana) *Interlude* wrote that " 'Mein Kamerad' is worth more than an eight dollar Kodak."[12] Mili had chosen a career in journalism. She knew that two promising Wisconsin women had gotten their start on newspapers. One was Edna Ferber, whose book, *Dawn O'Hara*, about a young girl who becomes a successful reporter in Milwaukee, appeared in 1911. Her characters were taken from the "Front Page" offices of the *Milwaukee Journal*. Ferber's role model was another young Wisconsin reporter, later a novelist and Pulitzer Prize-winning playwright, Zona Gale.

An assassin's bullets fired in the obscure Bosnian city of Sarajevo ended Milwaukee's innocence. Within three years the powerful anti-Germanism of the World War I years would destroy its easy-going gemütlichkeit.

Many Germans had come to the shores of Lake Michigan because they did not wish to serve in the kaiser's army. Anarchists and Socialists did not believe in giving their lives for what they viewed as the kaiser's war. Although there were pro-German and pro-English camps, in Milwaukee the predominant sentiment was isolationist. Elected officials, including Milwaukee's Socialist mayor, Daniel Hoan, Socialist congressman, Victor Berger, and Progressive Republican senator, Robert M. La Follette, received strong support from those who wished to keep America out of the war.

The Senate Judiciary Committee investigating a connection between the brewing interests—heavy advertisers in the German-language newspapers—and German propaganda failed to find one, but nevertheless the Milwaukee German newspapers were censored. During the height of the war, the editors of the Socialist paper, the *Milwaukee Leader*, could neither send nor receive mail. In 1916, local Germans rallied to the cause of the fatherland, 175,000 attending a German relief meeting. But when, shortly after the United States entered the war on April 6, 1917, the *Milwaukee Journal* declared that it wanted "no more German-American banks or Deutscher clubs" it got its way. The statue of

Germania was removed from the Brumder Newspaper Building; the *Germania* became the *Herold*; the German theater was no more; the Deutscher Klub became the Wisconsin Club. Men shaved their Kaiser Wilhelm mustaches. Sauerkraut, a staple on local menus, became "liberty cabbage" and jelly rolls called bismarcks became "American beauties." The movements of Germans were circumscribed—bridges over the river were off-limits, as were areas around factories that might be sabotaged. Yellow paint was spattered over the homes of German-Americans on the west side as the citizens of "America's pinkest city" soon tried to outdo each other in protestations of loyalty to the United States.

Mili would never forget the experience of living through the war. At first, in 1914, there was a directive stating that the war could "only be of interest as a school study insofar as pertinent geographical and commercial problems automatically enter the children's daily recitations." No teacher should "indulge or permit a child to indulge in a condemnatory attitude towards any nation."[13] However, in May 1915, when the Germans sank the *Lusitania*, claiming hundreds of American lives, attitudes changed. Bismarck's countrymen had hoped that Americans would side with them, but they had forgotten his 1880 admonition that the most important political fact was that the North American continent spoke English. Now, teaching the language of Goethe was prohibited. School auditoriums rang with patriotic songs. West Side High School boys made flagpoles and bulletin boards. West Side High School girls sewed flags, knitted socks, and rolled bandages. Mili became the *Comet*'s war correspondent and she wrote the poem that could be said to prefigure her own fate:

Our Boys!

They saw the need—and went; their life
    Narrowed in a sterner living,
Stripped of its tinsel, leaving the bare intent:
    To fight and love.
Perhaps a nobler life is theirs in death—
    How little of the debt can we repay!
Even our gratitude they need not now!
    'Tis not enough to give our thanks,
Thanks that they justified our high ideal.—

Oh, God, is ev'n the fullest measure of our lives
Enough to justify the sacrifice.

(*The Comet*, 1917)

Friendship, love, sacrifice, a noble life: at fifteen she had announced her themes. In later years, Mildred would regret her patriotic zeal.

During January 1918, there were warnings about pneumonia
and flu, an epidemic that would sweep the world in the wake of
the war. In the Midwest there was a blizzard. In Milwaukee, the
heavy snowfall—twenty-one inches fell in thirty-six hours—was
the worst recorded in twenty years. Coal went undelivered and
garbage remained uncollected. Families went without their Monday milk and rolls. Shovels sold at a premium as residents became
trench diggers, fighting their way through waist-high snow. Behind
a five-foot drift in the barn, where he had been exiled by his wife,
William Fish was found dead. He was alone, having sold the
horses to pay bad debts. In his small office, the coachman's room,
the iron stove had gone out, yet the gaslight was still burning.

It was a shock. Some years later, Mildred wrote a story, "The
Death of Frank Burke," about it. She preferred to remember her
father as "still tall and straight." There had been "a hint of his
former overbearing and dramatic attitude in the way he held himself."[14] Mili called it "galloping consumption." His death certificate is more prosaic: "acute myocarditis," an inflammation of the
heart. On Wednesday, January 9, a notice appeared in the *Milwaukee Journal* of the eight o'clock funeral services for William
Cooke Fish, "aged 61 years, 10 months and 26 days." He was
buried in Menomonee Falls "among his family."

In retrospect, the family thought they could get along better
without him. Although his wife expressed regret that she had not
been kinder to William, she was now free to move to Washington
where there was a demand for workers in the expanding federal
government. No one recalls hearing Mili speak about her father,
and she never mentioned him in the scores of letters she wrote her
mother.

Her strongest feelings were evoked by her parting from Grace.
One July morning they met for the last time. Mili, dressed in a
deep green cape and holding her straw poke bonnet with a match-

ing green ribbon, looked back at Grace standing at the corner, her face "stormed by pain and grief."[15] With tears in her own eyes, Mili strode toward the train that would take her to Washington.

The four snapshots Mili sent Grace the next year along with the book of Riley's poems show a tall, narrowly built girl with an elegant long neck, sharp nose, generous mouth, and luminous skin, the head posed with its customary tilt. Not yet the beauty she was to become, she appears eager, self-confident, smiling, and, in the one picture in which she displays her voluptuous blond hair—it cascades well below the waist of her middy blouse—quite flirtatious.

In Washington, Georgina went to work as a stenographer in the Veterans Administration. With Harriette and Marion married and Bob struggling to make a living on a rented farm near Madison, Georgina focused on Mildred, who now bore the brunt of her dreams and ambitions. Harriette's husband, Fred Esch, gave them the brown-wallpapered front bedroom in the two-story white frame house on Brookville Road in Chevy Chase, Maryland. He planted an elm tree to remind them of home. Mili now had two young nieces, Jane and Marion, to care for. In her senior year, she made new friends at Western High, in Georgetown, a long trip by streetcar.

Western High was the public school of choice for Washington society; many members of Congress and diplomats sent their children there. Western High emphasized not only a solid academic preparation for university but also the "great educational force" of the lunchroom—"spotless linen, bright silver, china of gracious shape, and beautiful decorations." One of the boys who shared Mili's table was next-door neighbor Francis Birch. He became her confidant and sometime beau. Birch remembered Mili as "a very agreeable person." She was "introspective and concerned with things" he told me, but "her interest in social issues made her fair game to people that wanted her to become involved with things."

Both worked on the *Western Breeze*, the school newspaper put out by Margaret Merrill's journalism class, and both were editors of the yearbook, the *Trailblazer*. Miss Merrill also coached the drama club. Mili appeared as Princess Angelica before a packed house in the 1919 senior class play, Thackeray's *The Rose and the*

Ring. She went out for sports, earning a place on the basketball and baseball teams. Her classmates chose her as their class poet. The entry next to her yearbook picture, written by her classmates, recaptures the sixteen-year-old Mili:

> Her writings have that touch of skill,
> Which will yet lead to fame;
> And in the drama speaking
> Her ability's the same.

Records are scant for the two years following her graduation. It seems she spent the first working, probably at the Veterans' Bureau, where "efficiency meant that the efficiency experts tried to make every one work like a machine."[16] During her last year in the capital, she attended George Washington University. She disliked it. The school was not "business-like" enough. She was homesick. She was a Wisconsin girl and the family tradition was to attend a Wisconsin university. So, in the fall of 1921, with her savings and money from her mother—far too much according to Harriette, who felt Georgina was exploited—Mili returned to Wisconsin.

FOUR

Nonconformist

Mildred at the University of Wisconsin, 1926

Browsing through the papers of Louis Lochner, onetime graduate of Mildred's alma mater, Milwaukee's West Division High, and sometime Berlin bureau chief of the Associated Press (during the Third Reich), I came upon a multistanzed poem, "To and from the Guillotine," dedicated to Mildred Harnack. In 1947, the author, Clara Leiser, sent her verses to Lochner to enlist his help in establishing a Mildred Fish-Harnack Fund. "It is nearly incredible that this whole case has no attention here in America," Leiser wrote. Her finished poem would portray Mildred working in her death cell and recall the last lines of *Faust*: "das Ewig-Weibliche zieht uns hinau." The eternal feminine guides us on.

Clara Leiser was the recipient of the "better not write . . . but don't forget me," postcard, Mildred wrote from London in 1939. In fact, as I was to learn, not only did Clara Leiser never forget Mildred, but over the years she had become the self-appointed custodian of the legend and some letters. Long ago, she promised Mildred to bear witness, if necessary, to the Harnacks' anti-Fascist deeds, in case someone would accuse them of "being Nazis."

"She was a Communist, you know," Leiser said over the telephone, as if to discourage me in my search. Her own attempts at establishing a memorial for Mildred had been sabotaged, she claimed, by "that evil fellow Wisconsinite," Joseph R. McCarthy. Mildred's sister Harriette held a responsible position in the Labor Department and she feared exposure. At her request, Leiser dropped everything in the "McCarthy days." Although it was her "sunny, golden friend" she wanted to have commemorated, she did agree with Mildred's sister that "we shouldn't sanctify Mildred." Furthermore, if I intended to write a biography, she wasn't altogether sure she wanted to help. However, she occasionally called to ask me questions and ultimately warmed to my project. Finally after several postponements, I climbed the four flights of stairs to the top of a lovely old brownstone on New York's St. Luke's Place to see Clara and the box containing the materials she had been collecting since 1945.
Clara's feelings toward Mildred were ambivalent; her anecdotes began nobly but veered midthought to reflect badly on their subject. "Oh yes, Mildred was good-looking, but she was pretty

earthy. She had terrible table manners," she once told me. She claimed to be Mildred's closest friend, and there were visits—four in Berlin, one in New York—between 1933 and 1939. In 1935 they attended a mass trial in Berlin. Subsequently, Clara encouraged her to leave but Mildred replied ominously: "Some of us feel we have to stay to keep an eye on developments."

The last time she saw Mildred was in Berlin in August 1939. Mildred gave her a coin purse in which Clara smuggled out a diamond for a refugee. Clara wrote, edited, or translated three books on Germany. In 1941, the Nazis banned them "for the protection of the people and the State."[1] She spent her war years aiding refugees.

We talked about the poem she had written in honor of Mildred. The verses came to her suddenly. Late on a summer night in 1945, she was walking home from the post office after mailing a letter to Mildred's sister describing her last visit with Mildred during the war.

"The beginning was insistent. It had to be set down. The verses just poured out," she recalled. Her teacher, William Ellery Leonard, once remarked to her that "whether you ever amount to something will depend on whether something ever moves you enough." "Of course," she said, "that's what happened when I heard about Mildred's death."

"Madison is my home as no other spot of earth," professor William Ellery Leonard wrote in his autobiography,

> I needed these quiet inland lakes and bluffs, these wooded shores, these long coulees and sunny oak-openings, and these west winds of Wisconsin. . . . Madison was to me the peculiar City, a Capitol dome on one hill, a University dome on the other, and each dome, as in no other city, mirrored in water, and her homes and factories and stores, as in no other city, girdled with neighboring fields of corn and neighboring woodlands of wild flowers.[2]

Madison in the 1920s was the quintessential American town. Indeed, it was a model for *Our Town*, the play by Thornton Wilder, whose father, Amos, was the owner and editor of the *Wis-*

consin State Journal, one of two local newspapers. Like Athens, with which local boosters equated it, Madison was a city on a hill. The "Hill" was the site of the University. The student who climbed to the top floor of Bascom Hall, the Parnassus of the literary muses, looked down beyond the weathered bronze statue of the Great Emancipator, over the green of the lower campus, past the hot dog wagons and popcorn stands lining State Street, and across to the white granite Capitol, the seat of one of the most progressive legislatures in the country.

Madison was small but not provincial. Residents, if they are old enough, proudly tell you that there used to be a conductor on the old Northwestern railway line who would shout as the train pulled into the station, "Madison, capital of the World." There was something in the air, some called it the "hum of culture." There were musicales, bridge clubs, drama clubs, a science club, and a club that met together once a week to read Homer after tea—in Greek. Snobbery was intellectual; society was otherwise egalitarian. One social arbiter, Gertrude Slaughter, the wife of the chairman of the Classics Department, wrote in her memoir, "Nowhere have I seen less respect for the almighty dollar. When our only rich heiress married a poor man with brains, it was considered eminently suitable; not so when a member of one of the honored old families married a rich man without any intellectual distinction."[3]

There were many famous visitors. One of them, Horace Greeley, remarked that "Madison has the most magnificent site of any inland town I ever saw."[4] This was so not because of any remarkable foresight or careful planning by the city fathers, but because the town meandered through a cluster of beautiful lakes named after Wisconsin's Indian tribes—Mendota, Wingra, Monona, and Waubesa.

Madison's wide streets separated broad lawns. University buildings and some Langdon Street mansions were of the tawny local sandstone; most of the private homes and rooming houses that nestled in cul de sacs lining the campus were white frame. Bordering the tree-lined bays of Lake Mendota, the campus was bucolic: cows still grazed on the front lawn of Agricultural Hall. Year-round picnics, autumn bonfires, winter ice boating, serenades on spring nights in Sorority Alley, sunbathing on the fraternity piers and the idle drifting of canoes in summer figured far more prominently in campus life then than they do nowadays. Mildred's own memories of Wisconsin played against the backdrop of the natural beauties of Madison—Lake Wingra's Sunset Point and Lake Mendota's Picnic Point.

In 1921, when Mildred arrived on the Madison campus, suffragism was no longer an issue; the young women of Mildred's generation sprang from a new class. The turn-of-the-century campus feminist was an exclusive breed—she went to one of the "Seven Sisters" colleges and belonged to the uppermost regions of the middle class. After the war, women from the lower middle classes, even the poor, flocked to state universities like Wisconsin. Like Mildred, they paid for college by working their way through when they were not able to obtain scholarships.

During her first year at the university, Mildred worked for the *Wisconsin State Journal* as a drama and movie critic. This allowed her to enjoy tickets to many of the cultural events in Madison. Her *State Journal* reviews were unsigned but perhaps she was present at Fuller Theater when Richard Strauss accompanied Elizabeth Schumann in a lieder recital. Certainly, as she was "mad for dancing" she would have gone to see Anna Pavlova. And, like everyone else in Madison, she would have gotten tickets to the opening of *Miss Lulu Bett*, the Pulitzer Prize-winning play by Wisconsin's own Zona Gale featuring the original New York and Chicago cast. The *State Journal* promoted her to featured articles and then to society editor.

During the 1920s, Madison was in the throes of prohibition, an agony for a city justly proud of its breweries. The Eighteenth Amendment prohibiting the sale and manufacturing, the importing and exporting of liquor had swept in on the shirttails of peace. Now, proponents of sobriety claimed that a woman alone could walk safely down the State Street without being confronted by breweries and saloons. However, the clandestine nature of drinking made it an exceptionally attractive pastime for students. In 1921, the dean of women was denying charges in the national press of "drunken debauches," and that "girls" were "removing their garments and dancing almost naked at sorority houses."[5]

Such reports of wanton sex were undoubtedly exaggerated. The prosaic reality was that ten o'clock curfews were strictly enforced in dormitories, boarding houses, and sororities. Although Richard

Krafft-Ebing, Havelock Ellis, and Sigmund Freud passed from hand to hand, sex was more widely proselytized than practiced. Horace Gregory, a Wisconsin contemporary of Mildred's, wondered "if there had ever been a time when both students and faculty gossiped so freely about one another's private life—even the most innocent-looking of Madison's front parlors and music rooms took on a conspiratorial-confessional air whenever a tea-trolley, loaded with cakes and watercress sandwiches, came into view."[6]

The "Greeks," fraternities and sororities, dominated campus life. "He who cannot wear some kind of dingus on his watch chain is a very poor stick indeed," said one Greek. The "Greeks" ran the school clubs and the school paper, the *Daily Cardinal*. They were the homecoming queens and the football captains. As there were only two dormitories for girls, many coeds belonged to the sororities on Langdon Street simply to escape boarding houses and cafeteria food.

Mildred did not join a sorority. Working her way through college, she did not have the time or the money. She possessed her mother's strain of independence and appears to have had no regrets about her "barbarian" status. She lived, at first, on North Frances Street in Journalism House, a cooperative residence open to women interested in pursuing careers in Journalism. An additional benefit of residence was that journalists and authors, many of them women, like Zona Gale, came for talks. Some displayed contemporary prejudices. "Women journalists, in general are inferior to men especially as reporters," said one visiting journalist, Mrs. Frank B. Morrison. "There are certain things which a woman can do better than a man on a newspaper, but she can never do many of the things which a man does well, in the field of political news as an example." A successful newspaperwoman must rather be "a good judge of human character" and must "cultivate self-reliance instead of dependence upon other people."[7] Did Mildred feel the sting of such comments at the *State Journal*, where she labored in the traditional female ghettos of society and cultural news? Was it Mrs. Morrison's nattering or something else that changed Mildred's mind and then her major—first to humanities and then to English literature?

Leaving Journalism House, Mildred moved from rooming house

to rooming house. She joined a group of poets and radicals on the *Wisconsin Literary Magazine* who regularly expressed their contempt for the "Greeks." The "Lit" satirized the various campus types—the "tea hound," the "flippant flapper," the "intellectual"—in short, "the beautiful and the dumb." Mildred portrayed the shallowness of Wisconsin's students in two contributions: a sketch, "The Silver and the Gold," and a biting aphorism:

University Education

A monstrous caterpillar with five thousand heads,
ten thousand eyes, ten thousand legs crawls up the
hill every morning; tastes with no appetite the food
which others set for it; and then crawls down again.
In four years it is supposed to have spun its
cocoon and to burst forth a butterfly.[8]

She in turn came in for some ribbing from the *Cardinal*:

Mildred Fish's idea of University education seems to be
all wrong. Nobody ever told us that the Board of Regents recommended four years of college to make a
butterfly. . . . Some are born butterflies, some produce
butterflies and some (such as college professors and the
Wisconsin Literary Magazine) have butterflies thrust
upon them.[9]

The "Lit" was highly regarded and in this heyday of the "little magazine" it could be bought at newsstands as far away as New York. It was also chronically in debt and often criticized for being too "highbrow," too out of touch with the concerns of ordinary students. The rival *Cardinal* accused the "Lit" of being published for its writers, not its readers. During the war, the newspaper claimed, the magazine was in bad repute for its "harping on pseudo-liberalism" when some "intellectuals thought it a mark of advanced thinking to sneer at patriotism." A taint of bolshevism clung to the "Lit" well into the 1920s.[10]

Its writers, during the early 1920s—Kenneth Fearing, Margery Latimer, Horace Gregory, Stanley Weinbaum, Marya Zaturenska—were, in fact, an exceptional group though they are now nearly forgotten. Fearing, a radical poet in the 1930s and a regular contributor to the *New Masses*, is best remembered for his mystery classic, *The Big Clock*. Stanley Weinbaum, who died of cancer in 1935 at the age of thirty-three, was one of the early important American science fiction writers. Other "Lit" contributors who enjoyed better luck and long life, included the columnist Marquis Childs and the versatile *New Yorker* writer Emily Hahn. The most precociously gifted of the staff, Margery Latimer, published two volumes of short stories and two novels before dying in childbirth at thirty-three. Tall and sturdily built, Margery had red-gold curly hair, large china-blue eyes and a penchant for high-waisted Kate Greenaway calico dresses. A friend remembered seeing her stride down the campus "always quite alone, apart from the sleek boys and girls who tried to imitate at some distance what seemed to me a worldly attitude clipped from the latest issue of *The Smart Set* or *Vanity Fair*."[11]

Margery's beau, Kenneth Fearing, was quick-witted and adept at the cutting bon mot. "Young, cynical, adorable, precious—an observer of life, a guest," was how Margery described him.[12] She quoted his epigrams with relish. "Romance is a young man's conception of what life is going to be; realism an old man's misconception of what it was."[13] Margery overcame her aversion to Kenneth's messy hair, ragged trousers, and "that look of having-slept-in-clothes" although rumors persisted that she gave him his occasional bath.[14] Once, when she asked where he was going, Fearing announced, "To perform a public duty, get a haircut."[15]

Horace Gregory described Fearing, the son of a well-to-do Oak Park, Illinois, lawyer, as subscribing to "daredevil Communism with its undertones of sentimentality."[16] Gregory was a rival poet whose childhood tuberculosis of the bone had left him crippled and frail, something of an outsider. A serious classics scholar, he graduated in 1922 and rapidly moved on to a career in New York as a poet, teacher, and reviewer. He married Marya Zaturenska, who was the *Lit*'s "real Russian." A precocious poet, Marya published in national magazines while still in her teens. She often contributed poems on Russian themes—"elegies over John Reed" and a poem about the Russian writer and painter Marie Bashkirtsev. A decade later, her poetry won the Pulitzer and his, the Bollingen Prize.

By 1922, the year Mildred joined the staff, the passionate

editors of the wartime years had been replaced by "hairdresser, interior decorator types who wrote villanelles, ballades, ghazels, palinodes, rondeaus, chansons . . . without the remotest connection to anything that could possibly be happening to the authors."[17] In 1923, Fearing, whose own writing was hard and biting, became editor, and the "Lit" changed to reflect his and Margery's tastes. The editors met at four on Fridays in a smoke-filled room in the Student Union building overlooking Lake Mendota. Submissions were read: "His thoughts were apples tied to spiked branches with steel." Discussed: "Stop in the name of God! Do I have to listen to such rot as that?" Voted on: "Those in favor of this contribution will please raise their right hand." And rejected: "Poem is lost." Kenneth's usual charge was "sentimentality."[18] Although there was a pretense of democracy, Kenneth's vote was decisive. Meetings adjourned to a local restaurant where there were frequent intimations of revolt. Margery was the usual bearer of bad news; she fired editors, turned down submissions. Mildred and Marya had the thankless tasks of recruiting new staff and soliciting contributions. At one point, Fearing announced a competition with a ten dollar prize for the best single contribution; he, of course, was judge. Their efforts to broaden the appeal of the magazine seldom met with success because the natural tendencies of the editors were exclusive rather than inclusive.

Confronted with a decline in readership, in 1923, the "Lit" faced a crisis. Fearing in an editorial scornfully defended it against being "non-collegiate in character," for not representing the soil from whence they were supposed to spring, in short, "for not rivaling (those magazines designed for a child's consumption), *St. Nicholas* or *The American Boy*."[19] The *Cardinal* countered with gleeful derision: "Kenneth Fearing, editor-in-chief of the dusky long looks and melancholy air, puts forth a defense of last month's 'Lit' that ought to be preserved for the sake of one word alone— obfuscation."[20]

Professor Leonard, the maverick of the English Department, favorite teacher of the editors and frequent contributor to the "Lit," parried the thrust. In the *Cardinal*, he extolled the attempt by the "Lit" to be part of the literary movement of the day and called attention to a deeper problem: "The trouble is that students lack interest in the whole world of arts and letters, they have no humanistic interests. Not only do they not read the Literary magazine, but they do not read anything else. Students are not interested in opinions, ideas, or creative workmanship. The same lack shows in their reading and appears again in their conversation." He then invokes the eternal complaint of professors about their students: they are concerned with getting through courses rather than getting anything out of them; they think of college preparation in terms of jobs rather than richer living and of victories rather than sports.[21]

For her part, Mildred found the university wanting in "silver speech—something that flows between bountiful, creative minds" and "golden silence—to let thoughts creep through one's mind like smoke."[22] She detested glibness, writing in the "Lit":

> That woman terrifies me. When I talk to her I feel
> like a moth-eaten rug. With that shining cold nozzle of
> her mind; with that constant mechanical buzzing of her
> words, she runs over me as if she were a vacuum cleaner,
> and pulls the lint of my thoughts out, cleaning me until
> I am thread-bare.[23]

In the end, Fearing was forced to resign when critics complained that his editorial policy had been "irritatingly satirical and intolerably misanthropic, sour and biting." Called on the deanery carpet, Fearing announced: "I accept the resignation."[24] With his usual *esprit d'escalier*, he added, "At any rate, with a misanthropic editor out of the way, the university will be safe for democracy and morals."[25] The golden age of the magazine was over and most of the writers, including Mildred, lost interest; only Marya continued to appear.

For two years the "Lit" had been Mildred's creative outlet. As an editor, she contributed poems, aphorisms, and two sketches. It was here that she first received recognition as a writer. It was also her first experience of supporting an unpopular cause, of losing a heartfelt and hard-fought battle. She felt at one with this small brave band raging against the philistines.

William Ellery Leonard, the very model of nonconformity, was the professor who exerted the greatest influence over Mildred. It was under his grueling scrutiny that she attained intellectual independence, for he firmly believed in the Emersonian principle inscribed on the flyleaf of his autobiography: "Nothing at last is sacred but the integrity of your own mind." His classroom was the early testing ground, the place where Mildred learned to express her opinions honestly, for "Mr. Leonard" believed that one of the hallmarks of a good teacher was "the unconscious feel for a mind that isn't there yet." His remarks on themes were often cutting: "Get experience. Get honesty. Get over sentimentalism." In later years, Mildred recalled his lessons in the meaning of exactness: one assignment was to learn the exact meaning of words such as "propaganda," "socialism," and "radicalism."

He was the most vivid and controversial figure ever to grace the faculty table at the University Club. Now forgotten, Leonard achieved mythic status while alive—local newspapers ran front page stories recounting his escapades. Dropping in on Leonard, Ernie Meyer wrote, you were "as like as not to find him engrossed with a visiting Oxford don, or a German gestalt psychologist, or a Russian historian, or an archaeologist fresh from Asia Minor, or campus colleagues in astronomy, paleontology and in other fields of natural science of which he has more than a layman's knowledge, or an ex-I.W.W. (Wobbly) with hands still callused from the harvest-fields."[26]

He was a striking figure: over six feet tall, thin with flowing, prematurely silver hair, eyes black and piercing even behind his habitual glasses, his speech explosive. Like Mark Twain, he had a penchant for white suits; this he coupled with a Byronic predilection for lavender crepe ties. He was agoraphobic and unable to cross railroad tracks because, he surmised, the engine of a speeding train had frightened him as a small child. At home in a dozen languages and literatures, he gradually became a prisoner in his Murray Street apartment. Because of this phobia, his classes met at his home.

Leonard won the admiration of students for precisely the same reasons that parents and deans disapproved of him: he delighted in unpopular battles. He wrote poems in support of syndicalist Tom Mooney and socialist Eugene Debs. He refused to cheer the Allies during World War I. As he saw it, "the American flag became an alien symbol, not precisely as hoisted over the transports, but as wrapped around the political shysters, the profiteers, the sadists, and the nincompoops and ninnies now all-powerful in every village."[27] Although he was not exactly a proponent of free love, he vehemently disapproved of the university's restrictive sex codes.

Although the *Atlantic* named Leonard one of the six best living American poets, now he is remembered chiefly as a translator. Leonard's English rendering of Lucretius was credited with launching a fad for epicureanism that raged during Mildred's time throughout midwestern campuses. He also conducted his own life on epicurean principles. Of an amorous disposition, Leonard was married four times to three wives—two of them named Charlotte, all of them red-headed. His first wife, Charlotte Freeman Leonard, the daughter of a family with a history of insanity, committed suicide. The "Langdon Street aristocracy," or "Madison mob," as Leonard called them, blamed Leonard. Pouring his feelings into *Two Lives*, a multistanzed sonnet sequence, Leonard provided the campus gossips with material for four decades. Declaring it "a most secret and beautiful thrill," his student, Marya Zaturenska, gushed in the *Cardinal*, "To say that you have read it, to quote parts of it to sympathetic ears, is to have achieved the height of achievement. One can boast of it forever."[28]

According to Leslie Fiedler, one of Leonard's students who himself became a scholar and controversial critic, "Leonard came on more like a poet than a pedagogue." In a letter he elaborated,

> In all his classes he felt free to talk not just to the subject at hand but to anything that moved him at the moment. He didn't feel constrained by any kind of academic restrictions but did in the course of his class session quote dirty limericks and facts about old-time boxers. From him I learned (and still remember) what Bob Fitzsimmons' wife yelled through the ropes and what John L. Sullivan's last words were. It was from Leonard that I got the notion that a proper professional was a free soul, immune to contemporary taboos and interested in everything."[29]

After obtaining his M.A. from Harvard, Leonard studied at Göttingen and later Bonn, where he developed an abiding love for German culture. During Mildred's time, he held a firm and often articulated belief in Germany's innocence in the late war. Mildred shared not only Leonard's love of German culture, in particular the work of Goethe, but also his strong sense of social ethics and his devotion to Emersonian ideals. Susceptible as he was to female beauty, Leonard did not fail to notice Mildred. For her part, she stayed on after graduation to join him in the English Department and kept up this friendship throughout her life—writing to him in German.

One of Leonard's best friends was the German-born philosopher Max Otto, one of the university's most popular lecturers. His course, Man and Nature, packed Agricultural Hall, the largest room on campus. It was so crowded that he frequently pleaded with visitors not to come. A former cartoonist for the *Wisconsin State Journal*, he drew as he lectured. Though the class was large, one student remembered him as "speaking as though he were speaking to me especially." During his twenty-five-year tenure, fundamentalist clergy, editorial writers, and legislators attacked Otto for preaching atheism. Successive presidents came to his rescue, arguing that he had the "right to teach truth as he saw it." Philosophy as Otto taught it was a method to deal with the problems of ordinary life, not the problems of philosophers.

It is evident that Otto strongly impressed Mildred, imparting to her his belief in the necessity of moral activism in a world without an omnipotent deity. She had described herself as a child as an "unconscious unbeliever." She had not been comfortable with Christian Science. From now on—for example, on her applications for graduate school—she listed herself as a "nonbeliever."

Still, it was in the classics, and not philosophy, that Mildred excelled. She wrote her senior thesis on "A Comparison of Chapman's and Pope's Translations of the *Iliad* with the Original." She remained a favorite of the classics professor A. G. Laird. Sixty-five years later, a former beginning student of Greek remembered a tall graduate student with a blond braid around her head who was ushered into class by the professor. It was Mildred Fish. The class heard her recite in a clear "Greek voice" the first book of the *Iliad*, without a text, in Greek. The student, Elizabeth Bunting Fine, wrote of Mildred: "Her voice was lovely, her hexameters perfect, and, although as beginners we could not understand the words, we were absolutely mesmerized."[30]

It was in Laird's Homer class that Mildred met Clara Leiser. Clara envied Mildred's poise, the splendid ease and self-assurance with which Mildred could "slide in anywhere very gracefully." She was "awestruck" when Mildred asked her why she didn't come along to Mrs. Slaughter's little study group that met once a week to read the poet in Greek.[31] Subsequently, they took a graduate seminar in Meredith and Hardy together. They read Meredith's sonnet sequence *Modern Love*, compared themselves to his intrepid heroine, and vowed "to revolutionize poor woman's fate." Years later, on the margin of her last postcard to Clara, Mildred, alluding to Meredith's championing of "a dignified life of the spirit for women," penned, "I am not untrue to Meredith."[32] Clara interpreted this to mean that "women are virgins till men love their minds."

Mildred also felt a strong affinity with the transcendental philosopher Ralph Waldo Emerson. For her, Whitman and Emerson were the two great exponents of American literature, who expressed the essence of the country. One book of hers, heavily underlined with marginal notes, survived the war: Emerson's *Character and Other Essays*. When Mildred presented a Christmas gift of a book on Emerson to her sister-in-law, she wrote, "I especially like Emerson, because a shining power emanates from his soul."[33] Her own personal credo derived in particular from the much read and underscored aphorisms in the essay "Self-Reliance."

> Whoso would be a man must be a nonconformist.
> To be great is to be misunderstood.

These and other lines of Emerson would be the lodestars of her life.

Her friends did not remember any special man in Mildred's life but sometime in the fall of 1924 or spring of 1925, while she was struggling to complete her senior thesis, one appeared. Harry Turney-High, a southerner and a high Episcopalian, was a graduate student and an instructor in the Sociology Department when they met. Her family did not approve. "He was short and growing prematurely bald," Mildred's niece recalled with a grimace. "We didn't particularly like him. My mother described him as a runty little snit—a mama's boy." Whether or not he proposed marriage, Mildred considered herself engaged. She was devastated when he changed his mind, for "she had hoped that love was eternal."[34]

Mildred was in Madison; Turney-High was teaching in South

Dakota. If there was an explanatory March letter from Harry, it was lost. But in April, the *Cardinal* carried the announcement that Harry had married a secretary at the university, Ruth York. Fourteen years later in the midst of the European war, three lines in a letter to her sister, Harriette provid a clue: "I thank you Harriette, and him [her husband, Fred Esch] for the flowers which you sent when I was very sad in March 1926. They meant infinitely much to me."[35]

Harry Turney-High became an anthropologist. When he died, he left a legacy of books and articles on primitive warfare. He taught at the University of South Carolina and was remembered as a conservative. ("The United States has fought two civil wars—the American Revolution and the Civil War—both were a mistake.") Six years later, distilling her own recollections of the time, Mildred provides an answer as to what proved fatal in her romance with Harry. Turney-High admired James Branch Cabell, the southern author of novels dwelling on southern gallantry and courtly love "in which a perfect lady was hopelessly worshipped by a valiant poet-lover." But these ideals are unobtainable in real life, and Mildred observes that Cabell's "chivalrous heroes are in reality only ordinary men—which means that they are usually climbing rogues, cruel villains and deceivers."[36]

A friend helped Mildred get over Harry. Her work—she was teaching English at the university—and walks in the country helped too. "The sun and the sky and the trees reassured me gradually," she wrote, "then came Arvid's love, like sunshine too."[37]

FIVE

A Radical Marriage

Mildred and Arvid, Saalfeld, 1929

Arvid Harnack was born in 1901 into a Baltic German family in Darmstadt, the capital of the pro-English, pro-Russian, anti-Prussian Grand Duchy of Hesse. Born one year apart, Mildred and Arvid both came of age during the Great War. But while Mili wrote war poems and rolled bandages, Arvid Harnack experienced the conflict at closer range. German soldiers were billeted with the Harnack family and, during the last days of the war this patriotic seventeen-year-old ran away from home to join the kaiser's army. Underage and lacking papers, he was returned to his family only to join, after the armistice in 1919, the Freikorps, a right-wing paramilitary group. These were revolutionary times in Germany and Arvid fought the Communists in Upper Silesia, until he was taken prisoner. As the official story goes, his captors acknowledging his youth and not wanting to court trouble with his academically prominent family, released him on condition that he promise to give up fighting and return home or, as his friend Rudolf Heberle more mundanely recalled, they may have simply let Harnack escape.[1] But in 1921, during a hiatus in his legal studies at Graz and Jena, he was off again—this time traveling with a school friend through the newly created country of Yugoslavia—equipped with useful names but lacking proper visas or money. Once across the Austrian border, they continued their journey by raft down the Drava River, which formed the boundary between Yugoslavia and Hungary. Friendly Croatians gave the pair shelter for three nights. However, on the fourth night, delayed by damage to their raft, they were arrested by two Serbian soldiers who accused them of being Hungarian spies. Their plight was worsened by the bits and pieces of German and Austrian uniforms that they wore, articles of clothing banned in the former Austro-Hungarian province. While in detention, they amused themselves by playing the harmonica and studying a primitive map. Left alone with the wife of one of the soldiers, Harnack astonished his companion by suddenly falling on his knees and pleading with her in pantomime to let them go. However unheroic, the tactic succeeded; the kind-hearted woman obliged them by opening the door and pointing in the direction they should disappear. Afraid to give themselves away by changing their Austrian currency, they sneaked aboard an eastbound train, feigning sleep and ignoring the ticket controls. But as they left the train, they ran into the arms of a police patrol. Once again they were saved, this time by an invitation from a neighboring industrialist whose name they had been given. More close calls tempered by good luck followed as they visited Belgrade, Zagreb, and Sarajevo. The mosques and minarets of the Bosnian capital fascinated Harnack and soon he was off again, this time alone, penetrating deeper into the Balkans to Rumania. Traveling with arms smugglers, the born risk taker crossed the Black Sea by steamer to Turkey.[2] Back in Germany, having completed his legal education with a doctorate in 1924, Harnack moved on to postgraduate studies in Hamburg and at the London School of Economics before arriving in Madison, Wisconsin, as a Rockefeller scholar in 1926.

Family legend says Arvid and Mili met serendipitously. The newly arrived Rockefeller scholar confused Sterling Hall with Bascom Hall. When he appeared for a lecture, instead of the venerable Professor John R. Commons, Arvid saw instead a young instructor. Her radiant gaze and low mellifluous voice mesmerized him and he stayed to listen. It was remarkable, he recalled. "I felt as if Mildred was a member of my family."[3]

At the end of the hour, he apologized for the interruption and moreover for his poor English. She laughed and admitted that her German was equally poor. Charmed, he suggested that they might study these languages together. Intrigued, she agreed. He arrived for their next meeting "bringing a great bunch of thick, white odorous flowers." And so it was sometime in the spring that Mili recovered from her loss of Harry Turney-High and began what she called "the two happiest years of my life."[4]

The Harnack and Fish families, continents apart, were similar. In each there were four children whose mothers determined, despite straitened conditions, to see that they received the best possible education. Both Arvid, the eldest in his family, and Mili, the youngest, were their mother's favorites. Their fathers were both deeply troubled men who died while Arvid and Mili were adolescents. Financially, there was a significant difference. During the 1920s, while Mili's mother, newly employed by the government, prospered, Arvid's family, headed by his mother, struggled to subsist on her meager widow's pension, her savings wiped out by Germany's hyperinflation.

Arvid's nature fortunately equipped him for what would be a

spartan life. A teenage episode makes the point. He was trying to disarm a boy who had a pointed stick that he was using as a lance to strike the passersby. Instead, the boy shoved the stick at Arvid and broke his glasses. Nine shards of glass penetrated Harnack's eye. Instructing his twelve-year-old sister, Inge, not to cry, he walked stoically to the hospital, handkerchief pressed to the bloody eye, where a surgeon removed part of the iris in a long operation without anesthesia. Before the operation, he said to the surgeon, "Please, don't tie me down—I'll hold quite still." Which he did. After the operation, when the doctor led him out he asked in a fatherly way, "Now, my boy, is there anything else you'd like?" Arvid replied smartly, "Yes, please, sir, I'd like B[ülow]'s *German Politics*." As Arvid lay motionless on his back, both eyes bandaged, he comforted his mother: "The worst part is that you have to suffer again. If at least it were a sacrifice for the Fatherland! But there have been one-eyed men, haven't there, who've done great things?"[5] Harnack lost much of his vision in his eye but still completed his studies.

He was artistic. He drew well and wrote with unusual grace and feeling. He was also exceptionally hard-working. A motto that had adorned his workrooms since childhood was *Nutze die Zeit*— and use his time he did. He kept a diary so, like Goethe, he would be able to account for each hour of his life. Intensely ambitious, he displayed Olympian self-confidence and an arrogance bred from natural superiority; he won not one but two German Ph.D.s with highest honors, a feat rarely achieved in Germany. Possessed of a meditative mind, Harnack was a skilled debater. To some, he was too inclined to score a point, to badger his opponent, to drive him to the ground. A lifelong friend noted that this "evenness of temperament mixed with a kernel of scorn" was already present in his mid-twenties. His wisdom was apparent at this early age as well as "his gift for focusing on a political goal."[6]

Blond, blue-eyed and tall, Arvid was the physical counterpart of Mildred. She was aware of this. She wrote, with a trace of vanity, in her autobiographical story "Prothalamion," "They were both fair. This touched them always when they looked at each other. They both had very clear and open faces touched with poetry, but whereas he was sturdy, she was delicately built."[7] Initially, Mildred held back from a strong emotional commitment.

She wanted a comrade and a sibling, not a lover. Her landlady, a college professor's wife, promoted the match, saying, "It's clear what he wants bringing flowers like that—such beautiful flowers. Men from the North Sea [the Baltic] make very good husbands."

In her story, Mildred relates that in the early morning rain, they paddled across Lake Mendota and "delighted in their loneliness." The sun appeared and they beached their canoe and lay down on the pebbles. After a long silence, he struggled to speak, "This doesn't happen very often in my life." He asked her to kiss him. She, "thinking things over very carefully since the world had ended for her," and "not wanting the world to begin again in a trivial way," said no. She had loved someone. He was gone and would not return. She cried. He stroked her face and said he understood. There had been a woman in London. He had liked her as he liked "the trees and the earth in spring" but he would not have married her. In the afternoon, they went swimming. He disappeared and Mili remembered that "she was trembling."

As their relationship deepened, they spoke of having "one soul in two bodies" described by Goethe as "elective affinities." Their shared passions were nature and literature. Throughout the spring and summer they canoed out to Picnic Point, hiked to Palfreys' Glen, and danced under the moon to the sound of the saxophone on Lake Waubesa. She read to him from Whitman and Sandburg; he introduced her to Goethe. His English improved and so did her German. They shared cheap cafeteria meals and bootleg wine.

He wrote to her mother, asking for her hand. His proposal, with its self-conscious tone of bourgeois formality, reveals the stiffness of the writer's personality. "*Sehr verehrte, gnädige Frau,*" he begins his letter. So important was his proposal that he felt it must be conveyed in German. In personal matters, he was a prudent man and his caution shows throughout. It was clear to him the "second time he saw her" that they belonged together and "could bring out the best in each other." Mildred's nature was "so fine and delicate" he declared it could not be "other than good" when they were together. He believed she would also suit his family well, being very much like one of his sisters and his late father. After telling Georgina something of his personal circumstances and his family, he offers up his qualifications. He is a Doctor of Law and holds one of four German Rockefeller scholarships. After returning to

Germany, he hopes "to work in the German Ministry of Labor on international labor questions." His financial situation is such, he confesses, that he would only be able to support Mildred with difficulty so they have agreed that Mildred will continue to work. Because his work requires that he will have to be away from Madison at times, they would like to marry soon so they "can be together as fully as possible."[8]

Their engagement met with general approval and they were wed on Saturday, August 7, at her brother Bob's farm in nearby Brooklyn, Wisconsin. Bob's wife, Jane, and her mother prepared everything. Mildred's mother came from Washington, D.C., and her sister Marion with her laconic Norwegian husband from Evanston. The formalities were brief. Arvid wrote to his mother that he "just shook hands with my new relatives who said, 'well Harnack'—and that was the end of things."[9] The honeymooners bought a used Ford and made the pilgrimage, like other American newlyweds, to Niagara Falls.

Mildred was drawn to nature and was studying Hawthorne, whose essay on Niagara Falls she undoubtedly read. His description touched chords that readily resonated with Mildred: "I began to listen for the roar of the cataract, and trembled with a sensation like dread, as the moment drew nigh when its voice of ages must roll, for the first time, on my ear." The usual itinerary would have taken the Harnacks behind the Horseshoe Falls to Termination Rock. They would then pass behind the American Falls to the Cave of the Winds, descending the slippery staircase to the bottom. Soaked by spray and buffeted by winds, they would have crossed the rapids in the rising mist to Terrapin Tower. With luck, the reward would be, as it had been for Hawthorne, "a dazzling sunbow."[10] Custom required that they carve their initials on the trees on Goat Island or Table Rock. Did they take photographs? Did they collect a souvenir? If so, like so much in their lives, all traces have vanished.

Mildred was twenty-four years old. True to Meredith, she had found a man who loved her developing mind. During their courtship, Arvid had convinced her that while she was central to his being, she was to be not only wife but also a friend and comrade. In the coming years, Arvid would be absent for months at a time, so of necessity it became a marriage that granted Mildred a great deal of independence. Although the Harnacks defined their union as a marriage based on mutual autonomy (Mildred, for example, insisted on keeping her maiden name, using Fish-Harnack in the United States and Harnack-Fish in Germany), it bore elements of a traditional union as well.

Arvid Harnack was a man with strong familial instincts. When he was thirteen, his father died and he assumed the emotional burden of becoming a father to his younger brother and sisters. Unlike Mildred's feckless father, here was a man who took his responsibilities seriously. Arvid was disciplined and focused, Mildred malleable and loyal. Once Arvid set her life on its course, she never wavered. Friends admired and respected Arvid, but they loved Mildred. If Arvid was brilliant, it was Mildred with her sunny disposition and husky laugh who attracted people and forged alliances.

In later years, her relatives attributed Mildred's left-wing views to her university years in Madison. Questions of class and social problems engaged her. Sender Garlin, a Wisconsin radical and later foreign correspondent for the *Daily Worker*, remembered seeing her at the meetings of the Social Science Club. Garlin recalled that "she was attractive and lively, more than animated. She was, as we called it in those days, 'liberal minded' with a deep concern for social problems."[11] Critics would complain that the club was not an organization created "for the study of economic questions, but solely to spread propaganda of a radical and anarchic nature among the students."[12]

Campus organizations like the Social Science Club caused Calvin Coolidge in 1922 to attack the university as a "hotbed of radicalism," and this reputation lingered after World War II.[13] After the war, prompted by the Harnack case, the FBI opened files on the University of Wisconsin. And in the CIA files, declassified in 1989, is a 1949 article entitled "Hitler Sent U.S. Girl to Death" that appeared in the U.S. Armed Forces magazine, *Stars and Stripes*. From the file it appears that the innocuous tribute in the *Wisconsin Alumni Magazine* inspired an investigation of the university:

The "Stars and Stripes" article refers to a story glorifying Mildred FISH-HARNACK as an American woman who had died as a member of the German underground movement which was published in the WISCONSIN Alumni magazine. The recipient of the report at the University might offer a lead to further investigate pro-Soviet activities in the United States of former R/K [Rote Kapelle] members. Frau KUCKHOFF, possibly could have supplied the material for the aforementioned article, since she is a former student of the University of WISCONSIN.[14]

Frau Kuckhoff, then Greta Lorke, was indeed a graduate student in the 1920s. After the war she became a senior official at East Germany's Foreign Ministry and president of the Notenbank. Greta Kuckhoff would certainly have had much to tell a biographer about the Harnacks but she had died in the GDR in 1981. Before then, she offered a circumspect, government-vetted version of the affair in interviews, newspaper articles, and a 1972 memoir, *Vom Rosenkranz zur Roten Kapelle* (From Rosary to Red Orchestra). In 1976, she gave the dedicatory speech at the opening of the Mildred Harnack High School in East Berlin.

Greta Lorke (she later married German writer Adam Kuckhoff) was one of the German students invited to the United States on stipends. One magical winter night she met the Harnacks in Madison when they sailed ice boats and roasted pork chops over a wood fire on Lake Mendota. The friendship progressed on long cross-country hikes, when they were treated, according to the national origins of the farmers they visited, to waffles, doughnuts, pfannkuchen, cinnamon toast, or occasionally on one of the larger farms, to homemade ice cream. By tradition, as payment, they entertained their hosts with stories or songs.

"I liked Mildred," Greta wrote. "It wasn't friendship at first sight; our temperaments were too different. But I came to know her more quickly than I did the somewhat taciturn Arvid. I knew that Mildred loved the beauty of her midwestern home with its brightly colored fall. She also loved the exuberant language of the new American writers." According to Greta, Mildred also came to love Arvid's country and language, although it seemed to her that Mildred derived her notion of Germany entirely from her reading of the poetry, fairy tales, and histories of the Romantic period. This would all change when Mildred arrived in Germany, where "the swastika flag was already flying in various locations." The forests Mildred encountered in paintings and books were still there, but they were "soon to become the preserve of the Reich's hunting master," Hermann Goering.[15]

At home, the Harnacks held Shakespeare readings, their faculty friends taking the parts. Kuckhoff reports there were smiles when the two Germans, Greta and Arvid, attempted with their heavy accents the larger roles in *Lear, Coriolanus*, and *Henry IV*. However, Arvid "more than compensated for his German accent with his extensive historical knowledge" and "his ability to lead the participants in uncovering the meaning of the classical works."[16] Real or perceived treason plays a large role in Shakespeare's plays and the Madison discussions anticipated the themes of loyalty and betrayal that were to loom so large later in Germany.

Through the Harnacks, Greta was drawn into a remarkable circle of Wisconsin "radicals" that formed around Professor John R. Commons. Self-named the Friday Niters, its members met for thirty years for what one regular wittily described as "a transaction consisting in the transference of incorporeal intangible good-will value in economic philosophizing" (i.e., discussions).[17] Sometimes there were picnics—potato salad and hot dogs on paper plates—and occasionally there were lap suppers held west of Madison in the living room of the Commons' house on Middleton Road; more often there were dinners in the basement of the University Club. Most of the Friday Niters were graduate students of Commons. Sometimes other interested parties—including the outspoken architect Frank Lloyd Wright—also showed up on Friday nights. Although the discussions were serious, they included a lot of poking fun at pompous academics, parliamentary and legal procedures, and "John R.'s" golf game.

Central to these Friday meetings was the "Wisconsin Idea," which Adlai Stevenson once called the only unique twentieth-century American political idea. It had its origins in the special relationship between the university and the state of Wisconsin under Governor (later Senator) Robert M. La Follette, Sr., in which professors became consultants and their students researchers. Before and after World War I, Wisconsin served as a laboratory for the national Progressive movement, winning the state a reputation for innovation and liberalism that endured until the advent of Senator Joseph R. McCarthy. Commons and his students provided reasoned arguments for state unemployment insurance, workmen's compensation, a minimum wage, and a progressive income tax. In the late 1920s some Friday Niters worried that there was little more to be achieved at the state level. However, after the inauguration of Franklin Roosevelt in 1933, seventy-five of Commons's pupils and colleagues joined the New Deal Administration, playing pivotal roles in drafting the Social Security Act and launching the TVA, prompting one Milwaukee Socialist to remark that never had he seen "so many clear-thinking, socially-minded and all-round useful men and women."[18]

According to one Friday Niter, Dorothy Meyer, members of the Commons circle considered themselves "the crème de la crème of the University, the elite." Commons's secretary, Hazel Briggs Rice, added, "We were all liberals, very much so, but we were not at all way out. We were La Follette people. The Democratic Party was coming along much more strongly, but before that there were the Progressives. We were all Progressives."

"Mildred was beautiful beyond words," Hazel Rice told me. She was ninety-four and lived in a green-trimmed house in Shorewood, an upscale area of Madison. "I never spoke more than a half dozen words to her. She kept herself definitely aloof from the Communists entirely. I think she was not interested and they were not interested particularly in her. Arvid was a typically Prussian type. There was nothing as good as a German. There was no one quite as well-educated as a German. He was too philosophical, too historically minded to have really embraced the Nazis — they were an inferior bunch of thugs.

"I don't think Mildred at the time was outstanding as a person. Now what happened to her afterwards, under duress, is something I know nothing about. But I once said, 'He couldn't have chosen anybody who would be more dominated by him. She was definitely the passive type of woman. He called the tunes and she moved along. I wouldn't say she danced to them but she conformed. It was a step up for her. Everybody who knew Arvid or Mildred's background thought, 'Why, Mildred Fish comes from nowhere.' That was the attitude we all had.

"I always figured Arvid married her because she was outstandingly beautiful. She was a typical German maiden type — tall, slim,

exceedingly blond, with long, narrow features. She would come and pick him up at Sterling Hall and, of course, everybody was interested. Here was an American girl got herself engaged to a German student. This was of interest to us, you know, we were always keen on romance after all."

If Arvid annoyed some Friday Niters with his "Prussianness," Professor Commons saw through these defenses and made a special effort to draw him out. After World War II, John R. Jr. recalled his father's high regard for the intellectual and scholarly abilities of Arvid and his wife Mildred. His father was constantly aware of the advantages he derived from his friendship with Arvid, not only because of his comprehensive understanding and knowledge of German and European conditions in which he was rooted, but also "on account of the perceptiveness with which he could sum up ideas and facts into a clear and human philosophy."[19]

Harnack revered Commons, the mentor "who has decisively influenced me."[20] He wrote in 1929 to John R.: "My time in Wisconsin was one of the most beautiful in my life. You were there and I found Mildred there."[21] The academic fruit of his studies was a thesis, published in Germany in 1930, entitled "The Pre-Marxist Labor Movement in the United States" (Die vormarxistische arbeiterbewegung in den Vereinigten Staaten). It was not just an academic treatise, Harnack said, but "an expression of his ideals and a program of his further life."[22]

Besides his teaching, Commons wrote an autobiography disarmingly entitled *Myself*, a massive four-volume history of American trade unionism, and a multitude of articles that his students, including Arvid, translated. As his reputation grew, foreign students including Arvid and the political theorist Erich Voegelin made their way to Madison, as did another Rockefeller scholar, a sociologist from Kiel, Rudolf Heberle.

Heberle had met the Harnacks in 1927, and his estimate of the couple contrasted strikingly with Hazel Rice's. He wrote that the twenty-six-year-old Mildred "had a bold and noble profile, blue eyes, a radiant and strong gaze," and "a wonderful, melodic voice." Next to her, Arvid seemed "honest but somewhat insignificant." For Heberle, who had spent time in New York and Chicago without making friends, "the meeting with the Harnacks was a joyful and enriching experience." They walked in the woods, and Mildred read poetry. From this first meeting another followed. They met again in later summer and again the next winter at the Heberle home in Washington where the Washington Friday Niters gathered.[23]

"Arvid Harnack spoke about the Colorado coal strike of '27," Professor Heberle said, checking his guest book, more than sixty years later. "He had spoken with the strikers, I believe also with the leaders in prison—it was probably his first personal experience of these American working classes, and it apparently made a deep impression on him."[24]

Arvid and Mildred's heady encounters with the Friday Niters were, however, a preface to the climatic drama for many young radicals in Madison, the Sacco-Vanzetti case.

In 1921, a jury convicted two Italian anarchists, Nicola Sacco and Bartolomeo Vanzetti, of murdering two men in the holdup of a payroll truck in South Braintree, Massachusetts. The arrests came in the wake of the Red Scare of 1919–1920, a period of intense political repression in America. Judge Webster Thayer, who had presided at an earlier trial of Vanzetti, did not conceal his loathing for the defendants, a fish monger and a shoemaker. During a golf match, Thayer was heard to boast, "Did you see what I did to those anarchistic bastards?" As these details became known, many Americans concluded that the real crime of the defendants was not murder but their beliefs. Skillfully mobilizing the press and raising a substantial defense fund, their lawyers fought for six years to save the men but failed to win a new trial. When Judge Thayer pronounced the death sentence on April 9, 1927, someone in the court cried out, "It is death condemning life!"

The case became an international cause célèbre. Around the world, supporters rallied to the Sacco-Vanzetti Defense Committee, marched in protest, and signed petitions asking for their release. In Wisconsin, the *Daily Cardinal* noted that President Glenn Frank and faculty members William Ellery Leonard, John R. Commons, and one graduate student, Arvid Harnack, were among those petitioning the governor of Massachusetts "to appoint a committee of impartial citizens to conduct a public investigation of the entire case."[25]

No truly impartial committee was appointed. Instead, as Edmund Wilson wrote, the case "revealed the whole anatomy of American life with all its classes, professions, and points of view and all their relations, and it raised almost every fundamental question of our political and social system. It did this furthermore in an unexpectedly dramatic fashion."[26]

On May 3, the Harnacks joined hundreds of students and faculty members in a mass protest meeting at the gymnasium. Dane County District Attorney Philip La Follette, the younger son of "Fighting Bob," and Friday Niter Selig Perlman spoke.[27]

On June 4, Governor Fuller appointed a committee to investigate the case. Two college presidents, A. Lawrence Lowell of Harvard University and Samuel Stratton of the Massachusetts Institute of Technology, were on the panel selected to conduct an impartial inquiry. A few weeks later their report came out: Sacco and Vanzetti were guilty. In one of a series of columns in the *New York World*, Heywood Broun acidly remarked, "It is not every prisoner who has the President of Harvard University throw on the switch for him."[28]

During the summer of 1927, liberals, radicals, and dozens of journalists descended on Boston. "See you on the barricades," became the rallyng cry as Vanzetti began a hunger strike. A group of five hundred intellectuals—the Citizens National Committee for Sacco and Vanzetti—set up headquarters in the Bellevue Hotel across from the Massachusetts State House.

The Harnacks and their Wisconsin friends joined in the siege of Boston. The Friday Niters picketed the State House and attended mass rallies on the Common. Occasionally someone was arrested. Led by Elizabeth Brandeis, the Friday Niters tried to persuade her father, Supreme Court Justice Louis Brandeis, to intervene on behalf of the two anarchists. He shooed them away.

A huge rally coalesced the night before the execution. Sacco's wife, Rosa, and Vanzetti's sister, Luigia, appeared before the surging crowd. There were impassioned speeches by working men and women, most of them Italian, who vented their rage until tears ran down their faces. Rosa covered her face and Luigia Vanzetti stared stonily at the shouting assemblage. To one demonstrator, Katherine Anne Porter, "it was the most awesome, the most bitter scene I had ever witnessed."[29]

On August 23, the night of the execution, an even larger crowd gathered for the midnight vigil at Charlestown Prison. Armed with pistols, grenades, and tear gas, police on horseback sought to clear the space around the prison. All night the demonstrators stood silently, their faces turned to the light flickering in the tower. They had been told that "the extinction of this light corresponded to the number of charges of electricity sent through the bodies of Sacco and Vanzetti." At midnight the light winked on and off again; Katherine Anne Porter wrote fifty years later that her blood still chilled with the memory.[30]

Thousands of mourners filed by the open coffins at the Langone Funeral Parlor in the North End. They saw both men dressed in blue serge suits and noted the gray marks of the electrodes that had seared their brains. A funeral procession—mourners with black-lettered scarlet armbands—escorted the bodies from North End Park south through eight miles of Boston streets to Forest Hills Cemetery. On a gray, rainy day, 200,000 people formed a seemingly endless cortege.

For the Harnacks, as for so many other left-leaning idealists, the Sacco-Vanzetti trial was a profoundly radicalizing experience. For the Friday Niters it was a case of plutocratic Brahmins determined to teach a lesson to the immigrant poor. They noted that these self-educated Italians wrote letters of luminous eloquence. In his column in the Madison *Capital Times*, Ernie Meyer compared Sacco's simple good-bye filled with loving counsel to his son Dante with the frosty investment advice that Elbert Gary, board chairman of U.S. Steel, dispensed to his heirs. "No other cause would seem so pure; no other protagonists would glow so much like walking flames," wrote columnist Murray Kempton. "And no other end would come so clean and sharp and so utterly annihilating to the souls of those who cared. To have been in the Sacco-Vanzetti death watch was, for one time in a man's life, to have walked alone among the heights."[31]

One woman was heard to remark, "This is the beginning of the end—we have lost something we shall not find again." Illusions dissolved along with a certain credulous innocence. For the Harnacks the Sacco-Vanzetti case proved a foretaste of the shattering trials to come: the 1937 Moscow trials that would condemn their Berlin friends, true believers in the Soviet Revolution, and their own trumped-up trial in Hitler's Reich. All were theater, a farcical formality.

The Harnacks' gaze now turned eastward and Mildred assigned her freshman English classes the provocative topic "Russia's Part in International Anarchy." One of her students, Thomas Holstein, received an A+ on his paper. Mildred's note stated, "Worthy of praise, both for the effort to make more than a superficial study of a great question and for the clarity of organization." Holstein also received a gift from Mildred, G. Lowes Dickinson's book, *The International Anarchy, 1904–1914*, inscribed with a quotation from Tennyson's "Ulysses": "To follow knowledge like a shining star / Beyond the utmost bound of human thought."[32]

At the close of the spring semester 1928, Arvid's fellowship ended. He insisted, and Mildred agreed, that if she were not to assume the role of the traditional housewife, she must pursue a profession—teaching. As a student still working on his second doctorate, Arvid was unable to support a wife in Germany so Mildred accepted an offer to teach English at Goucher, a women's college in Baltimore. In September, after a trip to Chesapeake Bay to celebrate her birthday, they parted.

Baltimore in this period, as fellow Friday Niter Dorothy Whipple Clague wrote to Commons, was "the dirtiest, slowest, meanest, narrowest, ugliest, and most miserable city in America." She continued, "As for amusement, there is practically none, since people cannot laugh at themselves." On Sundays there were no movies, no theater, no open restaurants. "In short," Whipple concluded, severely, "Baltimore on Sunday has a remarkable resemblance to a graveyard."[33] For Mildred Baltimore had one evident virtue—its proximity to Washington and her mother, sister, brother-in-law, nieces, and friends, the Heberles and a few Friday Niters.

Mildred had difficulties adjusting to Goucher. Unlike Wisconsin's arcadian site, Goucher's urban campus was run-down, even ugly. One faculty member described the school as "a place for Southern girls who wanted to go to an eastern women's college but who wanted to stay below the Mason-Dixon line."[34] Sex discrimination was as pervasive as it had been in Wisconsin's English Department—women were assigned the lowly and monotonous task of correcting freshman themes and even female faculty members with Ph.D.'s were excluded from senior positions and received lower salaries. Yet Mildred had enjoyed the conviviality of her shared office on the third floor of Bascom Hall and the department's afternoon teas. At Goucher, because everyone came to school in the morning and left after classes, there was little of the camaraderie that Mildred had enjoyed at Madison.

Mildred began her teaching with a new course: New England Writers of the Mid-Nineteenth Century. She wrote her mother-in-law that she was lecturing first on Hawthorne: "his ethics, his aesthetics, and the conflict between them; then on Emerson and his philosophy of the Over Soul; then on Lowell and his criticism."[35] She also pursued her graduate work at Johns Hopkins with Professor Raymond Havens. Her theme, the "conflict of the aesthetic and ethical in Nathaniel Hawthorne" was one to which she would return. Unfortunately, she complained, all this left her little time for studying German.

Throughout her early life with Arvid, Mildred sought to define what an ideal marriage should be. Writing to her mother-in-law, she lamented that she had no one to lean on for nine months but added that this was a good thing as she needed to know how to stand alone. "A strong person makes a better *Kamerad*," she observed. "We have become so much one person that when one of us is gone, the other feels a little broken and lost."[36] In the Hawthorne essay/lecture, Mildred summed up what she thought the ideal of married love should be: "A fulfilled life implies not only the high development of ethical feeling, but also its harmony with a fully developed life of the body and the senses."[37]

Later that year, Mildred found time to steal the show in the faculty production of Bernard Shaw's one-act comedy, *Passion, Poison, and Petrification*. In her role of Phyllis, "the hysterical, affectionate, and modest lady's maid" who sweeps dead bodies into corners, she again displayed her comedic talents.[38]

During her year at Goucher, she applied for a D.A.A.D. (Deutscher Akademischer Austauschdienst—German Academic Exchange Service) fellowship. To be eligible, the applicant had to have "a working knowledge of German, two years of work in an American university, the ability to pursue independent study and research, a good moral character, and adaptability and good health." The applicant also had to be "willing to reside in

Germany for at least ten months." In his recommendation for her fellowship Professor Havens describes Mildred as an "unusual person: a mature, original thinker, unconventional and promising." He adds, "She writes well and might, I think, produce books that would arouse considerable interest."[39]

The term ended. In September, under the heading "Three Goucher Teachers on Leave This Year," the Baltimore *Evening Sun* announced that Mrs. Mildred Fish Harnack, an instructor in English, would study for a doctor's degree in Germany during the next scholastic year.[40] Full of hope and armed with her heavily underlined copies of Wordsworth and Emerson, she set off for Germany and a life of "plain living and high thinking." But she would soon experience the reality of the Concord poet's underscored couplet:

> Things are in the saddle,
> And ride mankind.

SIX

Scholar

The Harnack family at Jena. From left to right, Clara, Falk, Angela, Inge,
Mildred, Johannes Auerbach, Arvid. In front are Inge's two boys.

Nowadays the North German Lloyd docks in Manhattan are overgrown and abandoned, no longer witness to the noisy midnight departures that were an integral part of travel by sea. Imagine then a Monday night, June 2, 1929, when 2,000 travelers on the North German Lloyd liner the *SS Berlin* were jostled by a tidal 10,000 well-wishers seeing them off. On the Morton Street pier, under the arc lights, irritable parents sought lost children. Lovers parted with chaste kisses. Chauffeurs of first-class passengers hastened to round up porters for acres of leather trunks. Finally, stewards cleared the last visitors from the staircases, sailors hoisted the gangplanks, crowds cheered. The ship weighed anchor, blew its horn, and slid from the dock into the cool, clear night.

Imagine Mildred, as the *Berlin* passed out of New York harbor, standing on the deck alone. Most likely melancholy overcame her at the thought of leaving family and friends behind. While she looked forward to creating a new, improved Mildred—more refined and knowledgeable than the old Mili—by nature she was nostalgic and would look back. In the years ahead it was the lakes, the dells, and cornfields of Wisconsin, the friends from Milwaukee that she sketched in her writings.

Gertrude Stein wrote of Paris in the 1920s, "It became the period of being twenty-six. During the next two or three years all the young men were twenty-six years old. It was the right age apparently for that time and place." During the 1920s many literary Americans went abroad; for most of them, Paris was the goal. With the onset of the Depression many of them would return to America for good.

Looking back, one could say that Mildred, aged twenty-six in 1929, was at the right age but in the wrong place. Her final destination would be Berlin, a capital of exiles mainly from the East—Russians tossed up by the Revolution. If they had gold, jewels, or foreign currency, they could live cheaply in inflation-devastated Germany. Yet the voyage out was a positive act. A new, determined Mildred vowed to work hard, master German, take a doctorate, and devote her life to scholarly work. She would meld her "tender idealism" with Arvid's "pragmatic realism."

The America that Mildred was leaving in 1929 was undergoing a radical upheaval. That day's *New York Times* reported a slump in wheat prices. On the Chicago commodity markets, grain was selling at a record low. But there was good news from Germany. On the Berlin bourse, prices advanced as uncertainty about World War I reparations abated. A commission headed by an American, Owen Young, proposed new loans and the rescheduling of debt payments. There was a certain embarrassment in Berlin, however, over the *Graf Zeppelin's* failure to complete its first transatlantic flight. In Italy, Mussolini was lecturing the Catholic Church: instruct the young but leave the formation of their character to the state. Finally, from Russia, correspondent Walter Duranty filed another misleading dispatch about cheerful peasants on the Volga—one of the "success stories" of the Soviet collectivization.

It was on board the North German Lloyd liner that Mildred had her first look at that *rara avis*, the German professor returning to his native habitat. Arvid had alerted her to this Teutonic breed, so different from the American species. On German boats, passenger lists cited their obscure degrees and special honors. These privileged mandarins and their wives had the best seats at the captain's table; only royalty took precedence over them. At home, in small university towns like Heidelberg or Göttingen, their photographs appeared in shop windows like latter-day rock stars. Berliners liked to boast about the deferential treatment street car conductors displayed toward their professors. When the historian Theodor Mommsen returned from his classes at the university to his home in Charlottenburg, the conductor of the tram would slow it down almost to a halt when rounding the "Knie" so that the elderly professor could "leap" off the car between stops, a practice held over from his nimbler youth.

These academic keepers of the zeitgeist were engines of a scholarly industry: from their pens flowed a steady stream of books, memoirs, articles, and addresses. Most were prodigious correspondents. Generations of archivists have kept busy deciphering their handwriting and cataloguing their manuscripts. Dressed in silk robes, faculty members gave university events the appearance of convocations of Tudor princes. Like wine, they were assumed to improve with age. When they survived into their dotage, their absent-mindedness was forgiven. Their birthdays were commemorated by Festschriften and their retirements by public ceremonies. When they finally expired, they were remembered in memorial services. Even after death, there was transfiguration—they were reincarnated as streets, schools, and academic prizes.

Arvid Harnack assumed he would join these scholarly ranks. His stipends, fellowships, and academic honors, his two dissertations and two doctorates were preparation for joining the family business. His father and three Harnack uncles were professors. Soon, Arvid knew, Mildred would grow accustomed, as the other Harnack spouses were, to the title Frau Professor. It would only be a short time before she would master their tribal customs.

Arvid and Mildred were reunited dockside in Bremerhaven. The boat train took them on to Bremen, where a brass band welcomed travelers at the station. Mildred was struck, as generations of tourists have been, by the extreme cleanliness of German cities. Even the cobblestones were scrubbed until they shone. Red geraniums brightened every window box. Bicycles were everywhere, their bells making a cacophonous tinkling.

Their final destination was Jena, where Mildred met her German in-laws: Arvid's mother, Clara, his two sisters, Inge and Angela, Inge's two sons, Wulf and Klaus, and finally Arvid's sixteen-year-old brother, Falk. On her honeymoon trip, Mildred had written a postcard to Falk in which she wondered, "Will you like me even if I am not German?"[1] She need not have worried. She disarmed the family with her Greek, Goethe, improved German, and great looks. The Harnacks expressed amazement that Arvid, an impoverished student, had captured such a prize. Inge and Mildred soon became devoted to each other and talked daily when they were in the same city. Inge described the sensation the "blond Indian" caused that summer in Jena, when Mildred, dressed in a shiny blue bathing suit, her hair loosed from its customary chignon, dove from the five-meter tower in the Saalbad. Jenaites were astonished to see "this strange creature swimming with her long hair flowing loose without a cap."[2]

Her mother-in-law was equally captivated. Clara recalled, "We loved her from the first moment. With her thick blond hair and shining blue eyes, she was externally the counterpart to Arvid. She had his inner beauty—his goodness of heart, his love of mankind."[3]

One of the abiding puzzles about Mildred was her regretful last sentence, "And I have loved Germany so much." Since the years she spent there were the years that marked Hitler's rise, an answer to this question could shed light on her decision to remain in Berlin. What had prompted Mildred to move from her youthful nonconformism to the resolute altruism of her final years? In search of an answer on one late summer afternoon in 1989, I called on Arvid's younger brother Falk. He lived in a villa apartment in Dahlem in what was then the American sector of Berlin.

Retired and in ill health, Falk Harnack was cared for by his wife, the well-known actress Käthe Braun. Falk too had been an actor, then a theater and film director. During the war, he was a member of the White Rose, the Munich resistance group composed primarily of university students. During the period of his brother's arrest, he visited him in the Gestapo prison on Prinz-Albrecht-Strasse, arousing the suspicions of SS chief, Heinrich Himmler. However, in contrast to most members of the White Rose group, Falk Harnack escaped a death sentence and was released in the hope that he would lead the Gestapo to other members of the resistance. When this did not happen, he was sent to the Greek front where, warned that Himmler had ordered his rearrest, he went over to the partisans and fought against the Germans for the rest of the war. Given up for dead by his family, he made his way on foot back to Germany. Subsequently he worked for DEFA, the East German film company. When the East Germans banned a film he made from the Arnold Zweig novel, The Ax of Wandsbek, *he quarreled with them and from then on worked only in West Germany.*

Falk Harnack was a man whose sympathies were with the East but who found it impossible to conform to the constraints of Communist dogma. In turn, in the postwar era, Chancellor Konrad Adenauer's politics of accommodation, which permitted former Nazis to win good government jobs, appalled him. Although he never wrote more than a few lines about Mildred and Arvid, he spent much of his life talking and thinking about the resistance. He had told his story so often that he surprised me when he seemed overwhelmed by fresh emotion. He sometimes rose, at other times he raised his voice, to dramatize a point. It might have been the performance of an actor—staged for an American visi-

tor—but more than once, while he reviewed the events of the last fifty years, I feared for his frail health. His strongest emotions, I found on my two visits, were reserved for the Americans.

Tea and cake appeared. Then a book and a few photographs. He began our first interview by discussing Mildred's grave. On my Berlin map, he marked the Zehlendorf cemetery and told me how to find the simple granite marker.

"Since Mildred was buried there, no American official has visited her grave. No one! Mildred was a heroine, a heroine! It is important for the Americans to recognize that she was the only American woman executed by the Nazis in Germany. She was a fighter, for the Americans, for the Allies! Mildred fought for the Allied front. America owes her the highest honors and should not forget her."

Falk Harnack spoke about the events that devastated his family.

"There were these big scholarly families, four families—the Bonhoeffers, Dohnanyis, Delbrücks and Harnacks—all intermarried. We're all cousins. And the pride of these scholarly families is that they fought against Hitler, that they fought Nazi Germany. Arvid and Mildred, Hans von Dohnanyi, Justus Delbrück, Ernst von Harnack, Klaus Bonhoeffer . . . the pastor [Dietrich Bonhoeffer]. All have been executed. All of our elite. This is more important than anything else I can say. They all stood for a moral principle. They all had very good positions. They felt responsible for the moral principle and they fought to the last minute until they were executed by the Nazi criminals. And I am one of the few survivors—and Hitler wanted to murder me too. I am proud of these moral principles that the family stood for.

Who were these men, these members of these prominent German families, I wondered, who had so influenced Mildred and who had also resisted Hitler?

The Harnacks were among the most academically distinguished families in Germany. They were Protestants, Baltic Germans who migrated east, finding employment in the service of the Russian emperor. Born in St. Petersburg, Harnack's grandfather Theodosius rose from modest roots to become rector of the University of Dorpat (now Tartu in Estonia), a post formerly held by his father-in-law.

Arvid's mother too claimed professorial descent. Clara Reichau was the granddaughter of the founding father of German agricultural chemistry, Justus von Liebig, after whom the University at Giessen is named. Clara had trained as a teacher in Berlin and was fluent in French, English, and Italian. Rebelling against the restrictions of her Prussian family, she decided to pursue a career as a painter and she obtained a position as a governess in Florence. She met Otto Harnack at the Villa Borghese in Rome. He was twenty years older than his fiancée and already past forty when they married in 1889. What united them was a deep love of classical civilization manifested in a shared enthusiasm for Italy, a devotion to Goethe, and a common interest in nature and art, passions shared by their children. Upon their return from Italy, they lived in Berlin until 1896, when Harnack was called to the position of professor of literary history and aesthetics at the Technical University of Darmstadt.

Their oldest son, Arvid, was born in Darmstadt, the capital of the Grand Duchy of Hesse, from whose royal family the Romanovs chose their brides. Three years later, Otto Harnack transferred to the Technical University at Stuttgart. It was here that Arvid spent most of his childhood in an intellectually demanding environment that Greta Kuckhoff described as *"kulturdurchtränkt,"* saturated with culture. Otto Harnack was the author of various books, including biographies of Goethe and Schiller, and there was a large family library. Like his parents, Arvid would learn long passages from *Faust* by heart. Like Goethe, Arvid was the product of an older father from whom he inherited his scholarly nature and wanderlust and from his much younger mother his happy nature and protectiveness of others.

The family spoke of Otto Harnack as possessing a "Tasso-nature,"* a capacity for deep feeling and suffering. A "nervous disease," severe depression, tormented him and in 1914, on the eve of the European conflagration, he committed suicide by drowning himself in the Neckar River. As the eldest child, Arvid felt his father's death deeply. At ten, he had joyfully accompanied him on trips to the Black Forest and Lake Constance; at twelve,

---

*Torquato Tasso (1544–1595), great Italian epic poet, author of Jerusalem Delivered. Twice certified insane, he was the subject of a play, *Torquato Tasso* by Goethe.

he was fatherless. Years later, facing his own death, he wrote his family: "Lately, I've been thinking a lot about him and my mother who, in a deeper sense, fit well together. Strangely, I see both before me. . . . He's wearing a large bicycling coat and a soft black hat. His face is serious, his blue eyes look at me, and his mouth, surrounded by a blond beard, had its characteristic indescribable expression."[4]

"I am astonished at how much, after all, I am Papa's and your son," he wrote in a character-illuminating letter to his mother in 1929. "I'm reading rather a lot of Goethe. . . . Goethe is coming more and more to life in me and becoming my guide. Now I also understand how, as an admirer of Goethe, you were bound to come into conflict with your family. Sober and dutiful Prussian officialdom has little to do with the world-encompassing Goethe, lover of earthly beauty. Each has its virtues: Prussianism gives one a close sense of belonging to the state and to society, whereas Goethe releases [us] from both while connecting one to the world and shaping character. Life must have been very hard for Papa. On the one hand, he loved Goethe so much; on the other, he was, in his private life, in some ways a 'professor' in the negative sense."[5]

Otto Harnack was the youngest of four professorial brothers. His oldest brother, Adolf, assumed the role of paterfamilias to the young Harnacks who went to live with him in Berlin. For ten-year-old Inge, the discipline and exact scheduling of the elder Harnacks was a change from the "liberty and love" they were used to at home but she wrote that even though they "almost died from homesickness," they learned a lot. After some months, when the "wild Harnäckels" returned to their mother in Jena, Clara found some "young but well-formed characters."[6]

The impressionable young Harnacks could not have been in more competent hands. Adolf von Harnack (he was raised to the hereditary nobility by Kaiser Wilhelm) was one of the shining examples of the *Bildungselite*, the class that made the German universities and civil service the envy of the world. One of the most extraordinary men in Wilhelmine Germany, Adolf von Harnack was the preeminent Lutheran theologian and church historian of his day. An intimate and adviser of the last Kaiser's, he held the title of Geheimrat, or privy councilor. He was professor and subsequently rector at the University of Berlin, general director of the

Prussian State Library, founder and head of the Kaiser Wilhelm Society (now the Max Planck Society), a member of the Academy of Sciences and chairman of the Church Father's Commission, which he founded, and the Protestant Social Congress. On an American trip, the New York press eulogized him: "Professor Harnack is much more than a great scholar and critic, he is a great man."[7]

Soft-spoken, with great charm and a ready wit, Adolf von Harnack possessed an encyclopedic knowledge, in part due to a prodigious memory. He was once asked how long it would take him to memorize a page of Greek text that he had never seen before. He replied: "If I read the page slowly, I would know it by heart."[8] As a member of the *Briefadel*, the civil service nobility, Adolf von Harnack's presence was obligatory at a never-ending round of formal state dinners, court functions, and charity balls. A gifted speaker, he was called upon to commemorate anniversaries and open conferences. In his spare time, the professor penned scholarly articles and books, including the *History of Dogma*, seven volumes in its English translation. His bibliography contains 1,800 entries.

Adolf von Harnack believed in enlightened nepotism, helping his nephew Arvid financially and tugging at the sleeve of a colleague to ensure that his nephews, Arvid and Max Delbrück, and his pupil Dietrich Bonhoeffer, received fellowships to the United States. "The Balts are like the Jews," his grandson Adolf-Henning Frucht explained, "they are people of the Diaspora, they stick together."[9]

Mildred's introduction to the great man and his family came on a visit to Berlin in January. She was naturally apprehensive but the meeting, by her account, was "extremely interesting" and "successful." She made the beginnings of "real friendships" with Uncle Adolf and his daughters Elizabeth and Agnes von Zahn-Harnack. She observed that although he was not young, Uncle Adolf's mind was "deep and clear." He took her alone into his study where they talked for half an hour about philosophy, her former professor, William Ellery Leonard, and finally her work.

He cautioned Mildred: her graduate work in philosophy would be very difficult but worthwhile. "Do you know why difficulties are in the world?" he said, testing her.

"No, I don't know," she answered.

"For man to overcome them."

He asked about Arvid and their plans and offered his help. When their conversation was over, Mildred reported that she kissed his hand and was so overcome with emotion that tears came into her eyes.[10]

Within a week of her meeting, Professor Harnack saw to it that she met his powerful friends. She was seated at an official dinner between the ministers for state and culture. He presented her at tea at Harnack House, the home of the Kaiser Wilhelm Society. By the end of the week, the head of the German Academic Exchange told her he thought it would be possible for her to receive a fellowship from the Alexander von Humboldt Foundation. A month later she was awarded it.

In many ways, Adolf von Harnack was *sui generis*, the best example of his class; in others, he was a nonconformist. An unorthodox theologian, he was often at odds with the Lutheran clergy, which tried to prevent his appointment to Berlin's University. As a member of Kaiser Wilhelm's circle, he supported the monarchy. Yet he found himself pitted anomalously against church and crown. As a leader of the German pacifists on the eve of World War I, he argued, in a letter to the *Bayrischer Kurier*, against the "will to power." During World War I, he warned against the eastward expansion of the German empire. Once begun, he supported the war but publicly attacked Germany's nationalistic and materialistic war aims, and war profiteers. Subsequently, he abandoned the monarchy and, unlike most professors, welcomed the Weimar Republic. Together with pastor turned politician Friedrich Naumann, he drafted the parts of the new constitution that concerned the church and education. In a manner that would anticipate the thinking of his nephew Arvid, at a time when other scholars felt that they should disdain politics, he was an interventionist, believing his highest task was "to prepare his fellow men for right action in the present."[11]

Adolf von Harnack's brother-in-law, Hans Delbrück, the former tutor of Crown Prince Frederick, was Germany's leading military historian. In 1915, he organized a movement to oppose the Pan-German League. Before the war, the league, with its large roster of university professors, called for colonies and a large navy. During the war, it sponsored a petition calling for territorial annexation (of Belgium, for example), the creation of protectorates (Poland and the Baltic states), and unrestricted submarine warfare. Along with Harnack, Max Planck, and Albert Einstein, Delbrück sponsored a counterpetition urging a defensive rather than aggressive war, claiming: "The greatest prize that victory can bring will be the proudly achieved assurance that Germany need not fear even a whole world of enemies and the unprecedented testimony to our strength that our people will have given to the other peoples of the earth."[12] The counterpetition was ignored.

Delbrück was the editor and columnist of the *Preußiche Jahrbücher*, the most distinguished journal of its day. To see how government worked, he once got himself elected for a term to the Prussian parliament and one term to the Reichstag. After the war, he served on two parliamentary commissions: one investigating the origin of the war and the other, the reasons for Germany's collapse. Both commissions were unpopular and controversial. He fought against the rewriting of history by either right or left, against the "stab in the back" legend favored by General Ludendorff, who blamed the civilian government for the collapse of Germany, and against the Marxists, who blamed Germany's capitalists for starting the war. Together with Adolf von Harnack, Hans Delbrück fought against Adolf Stoecker, the demagogic Protestant preacher of anti-Semitism. Together they headed off Stoecker's attempt to introduce the "Jewish question" into the Protestant Social Congress and forced him to resign.

For more than forty years, Adolf von Harnack and Hans Delbrück met each Sunday with their wives, the sisters Amalie and Lina Thiersch. (The sisters were also first cousins of Clara Harnack, sharing a common grandfather, Justus von Liebig.) After a simple but hearty meal and small talk about family matters coupled with the good-natured teasing and testing of the children, there would be a short pause. Then Delbrück, according to one Harnack son, would start the discussion with, "What do you say about . . . ?" Everyone knew that the question was simply rhetorical: the moment had come for Delbrück to give his opinionated judgment, usually a preview of his column in the *Preußiche Jahrbücher*. Next, heads turned toward Harnack as the theologian proceeded diplomatically, "You are entirely right . . ." The elder Harnack never said "but," yet from his tone everyone knew it would be "an interesting discussion."[13]

Harnack's son Ernst wrote of these occasions: "Gradually I grew into the circle of ideas to which our fathers belonged and had the immeasurable luck to learn about national and world history as no history book can describe. . . . Behind all the great human institutions like the state, army, church, school, we learned there were people with their own wishes and goals, which made an indelible impression on me."[14]

The Harnacks and Delbrücks lived close to each other on the Kunz-Buntschuhstrasse in affluent Grunewald. Around the corner on the Wagenheimstrasse in a large yellow villa lived the Bonhoeffer family. Karl Bonhoeffer was the University of Berlin's leading psychiatrist and neurologist. After 1923, Adolf von Harnack recorded in his diary, Bonhoeffer joined the Harnack/Delbrück *Kränzchen*, the circle of prominent professors and politicians who gathered every Wednesday for a *Bierabend* at the Delbrück house.[15]

This bonding of fathers and mothers extended to sons and daughters where the closest friendships were forged according to age or interests. For example, one quartet—Arvid Harnack, Justus Delbrück, and Klaus Bonhoeffer, as well as his future brother-in-law, Hans von Dohnanyi—were all born within two years (1901–1902) and were all lawyers and civil servants. Max Delbrück, Karl-Friedrich Bonhoeffer, and the somewhat younger Adolf-Henning Frucht became prominent scientists. In some cases, youthful friendships blossomed into marriage.

The professors married late and had large families. This meant that the youngest children—born when their fathers were in their forties and fifties—were nearer the age of grandchildren. Amalie von Harnack, Lina Delbrück, and Clara Harnack had twenty-one children among them; Paula Bonhoeffer had eight children in ten years. The families were comfortably off before the war and even during the subsequent financial crises of Weimar Germany. There was adequate household help, including nurses for the children. With parents to help them over every difficulty, they grew up in what Dietrich Bonhoeffer called "a shameless security."[16]

Mildred was quick to observe (and adopt) the Harnack style. In spite of the comfortable circumstances of their parents, the younger generation lived modestly. When she went to dinner at the von Zahns she found Arvid's cousin Agnes living with her husband in an improvised apartment in Uncle Adolf's house.

"Yet," she remarked, "her husband has a high position in the government." She concluded that "the most educated and most interesting people live in the most modest way. No one loses class in Germany by living poor. Since the war, it is the common fate."[17] (It must be added, since it provided an example for Mildred, that during a period when Germans did not value higher education for women, two of Harnack's three daughters, Agnes and Elizabeth, nevertheless acquired Ph.D.'s.)

"When I think of Mildred," said her niece Jane Donner Sweeney, "I think of two streams coming together, the New England Transcendentalists (Emerson, for example), and the Harnack family tradition—what the Germans call *Dichter und Denker*, the people who were the writers and thinkers. Mildred and Arvid combined Emerson's 'plain living and high thinking' with the best examples of the German intellectual tradition of the nineteenth and early part of the twentieth century. They were a strain of Germany at the highest level. She felt it a privilege to be part of that."

In these patriarchal, inbred households, it was the professors who mattered. The standard biographies of Harnack and Delbrück include very little about the wives. Although they seem to have been exceptionally capable managers and mothers, they remain ciphers. In the first edition of her lengthy biography of her father, Agnes von Zahn-Harnack, one of Germany's early feminists, failed to give more than a genealogical glimpse of her mother. After World War II, she remedied this by adding a chapter on Amalie Harnack, in which she confesses that "it is easier for a daughter to describe her father than her mother. From the beginning the daughter sees her father's life in contrast to hers, his is the other world." His "daily life is drawn in strong broad lines"; her mother's day "is made up of countless tiny points and strokes," and the daughter herself "is inextricably woven into all of these minute details."[18]

Adolf von Harnack once described three types of happy marriages: "the congruent, the contrary, and the complementary marriage."[19] His own marriage fell into the second category. Amalie's father was a famous doctor and she made a fetish of cleanliness, causing her husband to joke that his wife had three passions: handwashing, opening the window, and taking things to the dry cleaners. Yet, according to her daughter, throughout her marriage to an important man, Amalie retained her full intellectual freedom, remaining independent. She "lived in him, but she did not become lost in him."[20]

Amalie was her husband's first and most important reader. Von Harnack read aloud much of what he wrote to his wife and was happy to take her advice, for she had an "extraordinarily fine sense of language" that allowed her "to recognize every false note in a sentence."[21] A second-rate effort would not survive her scrutiny. If his wife considered it good, Harnack was sure that his work would succeed with his public. But, as her daughter understood, "she was much more than his reader." She was "in the deepest sense his and all of our conscience."[22] From their mother, the children gained their "moral measuring stick for the true and untrue, pure or sullied, genuine or fake."

Even as children, the sons and daughters of the three families felt the burden of their illustrious ancestry. Academic standards were rigorous. Clara possessed a natural talent for educating her children, which she did when they were small. She recognized Arvid's intelligence but thought he lacked the ambition befitting a professor's son. Once, when she scolded him for falling to gain outstanding marks at the Stuttgart Gymnasium, he remarked charitably, "But the others also want sometimes to come in first."[23] Max Delbrück remembered his childhood as a "paradise," but he also wrote that although the girls worshiped their father, he resented him.[24] His sister Emmi Delbrück Bonhoeffer recalled that six-year-old Max, the future Nobel Prize winner, when told at a family gathering that unfortunately famous men rarely have famous children, tersely remarked, "Just wait."[25]

In this circle, Protestant but secular, the children were raised on "Goethe, Goethe, and more Goethe."[26] This special soil nurtured self-confidence, tempered with a sense of fairness and justice for the underdog. It was not enough to know what was right, they must act upon it no matter what the consequences might be. Along with this strong moral sense and pride in their splendid pedigree, colleagues also discerned a fair bit of arrogance: American friends remarked that Dietrich Bonhoeffer and Arvid Harnack both conveyed the impression that it was quite natural that they, as Germans, were superior.

The views of the Harnacks and their relations ranged over a

broad political spectrum—People's Party, Social Democrats, Christian Socialists, Communists—of Weimar Germany, though no one voted for the National Socialists. Even when parents had reservations about the politics of their children, family harmony prevailed. As Arvid's cousin Anni Frucht observed, "Hitler did one good thing. He brought everyone together [in opposing him]." Or, as one Bonhoeffer grandchild wrote, "The family had so much moral authority that it would have been far more difficult for the individual to become a Nazi or a Nazi 'fellow traveler' than to enter the resistance."[27]

Clara Harnack was a Socialist. As a sixteen-year-old in Berlin, against her parents' wishes, she heard August Bebel speak. He made an indelible impression. When her boys were born, she named Arvid and Falk after characters in the Strindberg novel *The Red Room*, which was fashionable among European leftists at the turn of the century. A pacifist, she was cofounder and later chair of the International Women's League for Peace and Freedom. Unconventional, she never cared for "one single moment what people would say."[28] She was impulsive and always spoke her mind, qualities that would prove troublesome after 1933. Even Mildred, who found her "interesting and exceptionally energetic," acknowledged that Mutter Clara was "excitable" and sometimes destroyed "one's peace considerably."[29] Even though the family was very poor, there was always room for needy strangers: hungry students, factory women with children sleeping in laundry baskets in the kitchen. Clara instilled a sense of social responsibility in her offspring: her daughters, Inge and Angela, were required to volunteer at Jena's local orphanages.

Mildred spent her first year in Germany in the small Thuringian town of Jena. Situated in the Saale valley amid pleasant hills and woods, Jena is the sort of place latter-day Germans have in mind when they speak wistfully of *früher*, a time in the past when things were less complicated. From a distance, it was the *Heimat* some Germans yearned for—a place where enlightened capitalism flourished before the war, before the greedy postwar years of the *Wirtschaftswunder*. In the old town, neoclassic buildings on the Market Square bear tablets that announce that Hans Christian Anderson and August Wilhelm von Schlegel lived there. A plaque on the *jugendstil* house at 20 Westendstrasse announces that Arvid Harnack, who was executed in 1942 as an anti-Fascist resistance fighter, was a student at the university from 1920 to 1923. There is also an Arvid-Harnack-Strasse near the planetarium and the Griesbach Garden, where Goethe and Schiller strolled.

There are three reasons for Jena's fame: its university, founded in 1548, where Schiller, Schelling, Fichte, and Hegel taught, and where some years later, Karl Marx received his doctoral degree; its world-renowned Zeiss optical works; and its proximity to the battlefield where Napoleon defeated the Prussians in 1806. During the last decades of the nineteenth century, Jena flourished as a model city between the poles of university and industry. The Zeiss Foundation concerned itself not only with commerce but also with social ideals and educational matters. Company profits were plowed back into the city and university. There was free health care, subsidized housing for workers, paid vacations, child care, adult education, low-cost loans—social benefits unique at the time. The foundation endowed university chairs, started the Botanical Garden, and built the Volkshaus and the world's first planetarium.

Arvid's family was at the center of Jena's cultural life in the 1920s when, during the Weimar cultural renaissance, it became a magnet for artists. After her husband's death, Clara moved to Jena and took a four-room apartment where she opened a studio. Here, to supplement her meager widow's pension, she taught art to students ranging in age from six to sixteen. During her years as a painter in Stuttgart, Clara had been commissioned to design a mural for the local hospital. In Jena, she joined the Kunstverein where members of the Bauhaus and the Dresden group *Die Brücke* exhibited their works. In 1920, Clara exhibited her paintings— mostly landscapes—at the society. The Kunstverein also sponsored literary and musical events, evenings of Expressionist literature, Dadaist presentations, film events, and photography exhibitions. Food on the table may have been simple but the Harnack children were expected to attend lectures of visiting scholars; and Clara found money for concerts and the theater. It was in Jena that Mildred developed an interest in modern art that culminated in the 1936 publication of her translation of Irving Stone's *Lust for Life*, a fictionalized biography of Vincent van Gogh.

The family closest to the Harnacks was Jena's "very modern-minded couple," Professor Felix Auerbach, a theoretical physicist, and his wife, Anna. Auerbach belonged to the circle of Jena professors who supported modern art and founded the Kunstverein.[30] Arvid's sister, Inge, married Auerbach's nephew, Johannes, a sculptor and graphic artist, one of the original Bauhaus students. And Walter Gropius, the head of the Bauhaus, designed the functional flat-roofed Auerbach house consisting of interlocking cubes. Edvard Munch painted the scientist's portrait. Mildred sent her mother a photograph of the Auerbach house, where she went regularly to read Goethe with Professor Auerbach's wife, Anna. "Now we are in the second book of Goethe's story of his life—*Dichtung und Wahrheit*," Mildred wrote. Frau Auerbach's "endless knowledge of the old customs of the time of Goethe" made the reading "twice as interesting" for her as it would have been otherwise.[31]

After a trip through the Black Forest with Arvid, Mildred settled into university life at Jena. They lived in a rented room in a house on the Landgrafensteig, where Inge noted that "everything was simple and clean." [32] Mildred wrote to her nephew that the house had a "fine view of the mountains." Every evening, accompanied by Arvid or sixteen-year-old Falk, she went walking over the mountains; every Sunday they went "to see a fine old castle or to have dinner in a little village nearby."[33]

She provided her mother with details of her first German Christmas: "The other day I brought home with me the funniest little Christmas tree you ever saw, all living with great dangling pine cones. It tickled me so to see it that I couldn't help buying it. We've invested in a new screen to cut off the sight of certain cooking implements etc. in the corner of our room; it is in orange and black . . . It is really quite a striking screen. We like it very much so we're going to call it your Christmas gift and put a pine bough on it and a card 'With dearest love' (from Mother)."[34]

Pursuing her doctorate at Jena, Mildred enjoyed more freedom than her American contemporaries. She was not compelled to attend lectures, nor were there required courses. Moreover, there was nothing to prevent her from changing universities. During the next two years, Mildred would spend semesters at Jena, Giessen, and Berlin. Her field was American literature, but as her courses did not follow any particular syllabus, she attended lectures in other subjects and listed two—philosophy and economics—as her minor fields for examination.

In Jena, Mildred found the professors kind but uninteresting. It was at Giessen, a small Hessian university with Harnack associations (Adolf von Harnack and Arvid's great grandfather, Justus von Liebig, taught there) that Mildred felt most welcome and where she later said that she received her most favorable impressions of German university life. Karl Viëtor, described by Arvid in a letter as "very young but gifted," was her guide to the study of German literature.[35] Only thirty-seven at the time when most German full professors were in their sixties, he had just become dean of the Philosophical Faculty. Mona Wollheim, a fellow student, remembers the Harnacks, who seemed older and more sophisticated than the other students in Viëtor's seminar. Arvid already "had something measured in his appearance and clothing" that gave him the air of a civil servant. Mildred attracted attention by her brightly shining hair "tied around her head unfashionably— the free forehead, the markedly regular features, the beautiful stride." Wollheim found that even Mildred's clothes "were individual in cut and style, but in a discreet way."[36]

At that time, even in the United States, scholars treated American literature as a poor relation of English literature. Americans still suffered from a kind of scholarly inferiority complex about their own writers. In Germany the development of American studies grew out of its experience in World War I, when Germans had failed to understand the culture and society of the United States. They had made an unfortunate assumption: because many Germans had settled the new world and had risen to positions of influence, they assumed that Americans would be just as inclined to be pro-German as pro-British during the war. But, as it would be noted, they had forgotten that most Americans speak English. One of Mildred's later colleagues, Friedrich Schönemann, returned in 1921 after an extended stay at Harvard to issue an influential manifesto calling for American studies: "We have lost the World War," said Schönemann, "because we did not know the United States well enough. We knew neither how to deal with its people nor did we understand its culture, its natural power, and its national strength."[37] Study American literature, he admonished, as the true reflection of American culture.

Mildred's *Doktorvater*, her Ph.D. supervisor, Walther Fischer, was the other significant figure in American Studies. Mildred assisted Fischer at one of his seminar courses at Giessen. He judged her "a convincing teacher and an excellent lecturer" and he wrote in a 1936 recommendation that he was "deeply impressed by the original and thorough knowledge of all the subjects she was interested in, by her industry and the great tact she showed under, sometimes, difficult circumstances."[38]

The "great tact" that Mildred displayed under difficult circumstances was undoubtedly related to the rise of student Nazis at Giessen, for it became one of the first universities to succumb to National Socialism.[39] By 1931 over half Giessen's students supported the Nazi student organization. This appalling statistic—Giessen students showed themselves twice as susceptible to the Nazis as the public in general—is partly explained by hard times. The British poet Stephen Spender graphically described this generation of German youth, "which had been born into war, starved in the blockade, stripped in the inflation—and which now, [1929] with no money and no beliefs . . . sprang like a breed of dragon's teeth waiting for its leader into the center of Europe."[40] Before 1933, the majority of students were from the educated upper or upper-middle classes, the *Bildungsbürgertum*. During the Weimar era these students crowded the universities because there were few jobs outside or, as they were fond of saying, "a few more semesters and we shall be unemployed." [41] Even as faculty positions and civil service jobs became scarce, students lingered in universities because an academic degree conferred exceptional status.

Mildred, always sensitive to poverty, blamed the chaos on the worsening economic conditions. Describing the appearance of the "downright poor in Germany," Mildred noted that there was "not so much open, dirty poverty here as in the U.S.A." Germans appeared in old but respectable clothing, "most carefully mended," which hid the fact that they were often hungry. "You can imagine why Germans scrape their plates clean," she explained to Georgina. It was no breach of manners in Germany; it was "an economic necessity." The young men in the universities too suffered from "economic fear." The trouble was "the war wasn't only against the kaiser. The people of Germany were half bled to death, and their hard times are not over."[42]

Whereas American professors of the period took part in the political debate—one of their contemporaries, Woodrow Wilson having just served as president—after the war, the German professoriate generally remained aloof from politics. The prevailing belief was that engaging in partisan politics did not mix with scholarly achievement. (Adolf von Harnack and Hans Delbrück were among exceptions to this rule.) Like the majority of the professional classes who were mostly right-wing, professors in 1929 were not necessarily National Socialists but showed little enthusiasm for the republic. Brought up under the old Reich, they were for the most part monarchists or nationalists. Apart from large urban centers, there were few Socialists, Social Democrats, pacifists, and Marxists among the professional ranks. Nor were they admirers of what is now called Weimar culture. Many considered it un-German, attacking it as decadent, Jewish, or Bolshevist.

By the time Mildred arrived at Giessen, many students had become the vocal and visible opponents of the few faculty members suspected of being socialists or pacifists. One target of the Nazis was Ernst von Aster, Mildred's professor of philosophy, who had been influenced by Marxism and who was a pacifist and supporter of the Social Democrats. His wife, Hildur Dixelius, a novelist, became a good friend and later Mildred's Berlin house guest. Another target was Arvid's *Doktorvater*, Friedrich Lenz, a member of the Giessen's "red faculty." Lenz, while not an orthodox Marxist, was an admirer of the Soviet planned economy, but he did not advocate it as a model for Germany which lay half-way between capitalism and communism. According to Lenz, Germany should be "independent both of East and West" and should adopt "the principle of total planning in an economy free from exploitation."[43]

In 1929, Arvid had joined a student group whose aim was "the spreading of socialism and pacifism within the student body through the scientific examination of all relevant questions." Later he signed up with the Social Democratic student group.[44]

Besides the Lenz seminar, Arvid created a discussion group that met at a local hotel every other Tuesday to discuss a topic presented by a speaker. This group, Mildred wrote, comprised professors of philosophy, literature, economics, and sociology, plus three or four clever students. Mildred found them "interesting and congenial people and was proud to be present "by virtue of the fact that I give lectures in an American university."[45]

One of Lenz's doctoral candidates was the Hessian crown prince. At one of these meetings, Arvid began describing how he would run the country as head of a socialist government in Germany. Suddenly the prince asked Arvid, "What would you do with me in that scheme of things?" Arvid replied, "If you would be in favor of my regime, I would have you work with me. If you were neutral and kept quiet, I would let you alone." He then added, perhaps half-jokingly but with a hint of chilling ruthlessness, "if you worked against me, I would shoot you!" Mildred reported to her mother that his royal highness took this well and promised to support Arvid's administration even though his grandfather had been the Tsar of Russia.[46]

It is 11:30 in the morning on June 15, 1930, in Berlin. A strong smell of linden blossoms hangs in the air as Mildred and Arvid gather with the Grunewald circle in the Goethe Hall of the Harnack House for a memorial service. Adolf von Harnack has died in Heidelberg, where he had gone to give yet another speech. His brother-in-law Hans Delbrück is missing; he succumbed the year before. As a string quartet plays the adagio from Haydn's G Minor Quartet, it is obvious to those present that an era has come to a close. There are eulogies from Friedrich Schmidt-Ott, the minister of state, and then Professor Hans Lietzmann speaks for the university faculty. Wirth, the minister of interior, is followed by Adolf Grimme, the Social Democratic minister of culture. Grimme, a future collaborator of the Harnacks, has just been introduced to them on this occasion. Grimme is already under attack by the Nazis.[47] Another speaker extols Harnack's years at the state library. Finally, a blond, powerfully built man wearing glasses rises. Twenty-four-year-old Dietrich Bonhoeffer pays tribute on behalf of Harnack's last students:

> Almost two generations separate us from this man, whose own students have become our teachers in their turn. We know him only as the venerable master to whose opinion the

entire cultural world listened attentively, a man who compelled in everyone he met reverence before a life of the mind spent in the struggle for truth, a man who, wherever he went, brought with him a world that left an indelible impression on all who were touched by it.

Bonhoeffer's manner of speaking is ponderous, almost hesitant, but it makes a strong impression. As the Bonhoeffers and the three widows, Amalie Harnack, Clara Harnack, and Lina Delbrück, look around the room, their grief is perhaps mixed with pride. Dietrich Bonhoeffer has just completed a year as lecturer in theology at the University of Berlin. He is preparing to go to America as a Sloan fellow at Union Theological Seminary. Klaus Bonhoeffer, considered by his father to be the brightest of his children, has been engaged to Emmi Delbrück since she was thirteen. They have just married. Klaus, a lawyer, has qualified for the civil service. A perpetual traveler, he too is about to set sail for America. Christine Bonhoeffer has married Hans von Dohnanyi, the son of the Hungarian composer Ernst von Dohnanyi. He is another rising young lawyer at the Reich Ministry of Justice. His sister Grete is married to Karl-Friedrich Bonhoeffer. Karl-Friedrich has worked in the laboratories of Max Planck and Albert Einstein at the Kaiser Wilhelm Society, and at an unusually early age he has been appointed full professor at Frankfurt. His close friend and protégé, Max Delbrück, has just completed a year's study in England and is preparing with a postdoctoral Rockefeller grant to study theoretical physics with Niels Bohr at Copenhagen. Justus Delbrück will follow his companions Klaus, Hans, and Arvid by first studying law and then opting for the civil service. Ursula Bonhoeffer has married her next-door Grunewald neighbor Rüdiger Schleicher. He plans to join the Air Force Ministry. Gerhard Leibholtz, the husband of Dietrich's twin, Sabine, has just been appointed to the chair of public law at Greifswald.

Ernst von Harnack has moved up from his position of vice president of Hanover and Cologne and is now the Social Democratic administrative head of Halle-Merseburg. His brother, Axel von Harnack, recently returned from Rome, is now a state librarian. Agnes von Zahn-Harnack has established herself as the leader of the German feminists with her book on the history of the German woman's movement. Arvid is preparing for his orals; in July, he will receive his second doctorate with the rarely given summa cum laude. Mildred and Arvid plan to move to Berlin in the fall, where she has won the Alexander von Humboldt Fellowship to continue her studies at Berlin University.

Bonhoeffer's speech draws to its end. "We saw him as a bulwark against shallowness, against atrophy, against any schematization of intellectual life . . . This is Adolf von Harnack's legacy to us: the true freedom to explore, to create and to live, and the deepest obligation to and dependence on that which is the eternal basis of thought and life itself."[48]

Von Harnack's heirs are prepared to serve the republic as professors, pastors, scientists, lawyers, and civil servants. Privileged, talented, proud, they seem poised on the threshold of exceptional careers. But within fifteen years, those who remain in Germany will be forced by a despotic regime to commit desperate acts. They will be hunted, trapped, jailed. Nearly all the men (and Mildred) will be executed. But on this June day, as the ceremony closes with the slow movement of Beethoven's Opus 135, Adolf Hitler is only an offstage presence. Klaus Bonhoeffer is among the prescient few. In a letter to his brother Dietrich in November, he will take a gloomy look at the "fond glances" cast in the direction of Fascism: "I am afraid that, if this radical wave captures the educated classes, it will be all over with this nation of poets and thinkers."[49]

SEVEN

Comrade

The Arplan group at the National Economic Institute of Kharkov (Ukraine).
Arvid Harnack is seated second from the right, Friedrich Lenz is seated fourth
from the right, and Ernst Niekisch is standing third from the right.

A well-timed spring cleaning is often the silent partner of biography. In 1992, forty-nine years after Mildred's death, her nieces, Marion and Jane, happened to clean out the attic of Marion's house in suburban Maryland, where Mildred and her mother had lived for two years after her father's death. Opening an old trunk, they found a hank of Mildred's blond hair and bundles of handwritten letters from Mildred to her mother. The envelopes bore German postmarks. The first letter was dated October 12, 1929; the last, Christmas Eve 1935, shortly before her mother moved back to Wisconsin. Here, in Mildred's own letters, was her firsthand account of the terrible final days of the Weimar Republic before its extinction by Hitler.

Against a background of deepening crisis in 1930, Mildred began her life as an American graduate student and teacher of English and American literature at the University of Berlin. Picture her scurrying by the grim beggars on the elegant Kurfürstendamm, the homeless sleeping cold and damp in the Tiergarten, taking train rides through the tent cities sprawled on the outskirts of Berlin. Picture her teaching the dirt-poor students at the university, appalled as she wrote her mother that "ninety-six percent of the German people possess no property and live from hand to mouth."[1] She reported to her brother that "times are very bad here and growing continually worse."[2]

In the early 1930s, the bottom fell out of the Western world. After the Great War, the dollar had become the world's fever thermometer. First came the Wall Street crash in 1929, then the tidal failure of credit as banks closed. Americans called in their foreign loans. Europe's most vulnerable economy, Germany, collapsed. What had been a crisis for the United States became a catastrophe for the Weimar democracy. Arnold Toynbee called 1931 the *annus terribilis* because it appeared then that "men and women all over the world were seriously contemplating and seriously discussing the possibility that the Western system of society might break down and cease to work."

"Look my dear," Hitler's muse, filmmaker Leni Riefenstahl, told an American interviewer in 1992, "the time was so different that it is impossible to speak of it if you were not there. Can you understand that you were living in a country that was very poor, almost kaput, with 6 million people out of work? It was horrible in Berlin."[3] The American journalist Dorothy Thompson, who was visiting Germany at the time, wrote "that every conversation I had in Germany with anyone under the age of thirty ended with this phrase. *'Es kann so nicht weitergehen. Es muß etwas geschehen.'*" (It can't go on like this. Something must happen.)[4]

Along with Arvid, Mildred witnessed these final agonies, the *Weimardämmerung* of the republic and, like many of their generation, they turned their eyes eastward toward the Soviet Union, then in the midst of a revolutionary economic experiment called the Five-Year-Plan. The Harnacks, like many others, believed that capitalism was bankrupt and looked with hope and interest to what they believed was an egalitarian system that promised jobs and dignity to all. They came to feel, as did the American writer Edmund Wilson, another sympathizer and certainly no fool, that the Soviet Union stood "at the moral top of the world, where the light never really goes out."[5] Step by step, Mildred and Arvid moved from sympathetic curiosity about Marxism to outright commitment, from opposition to the Nazis' "new world order" to clandestine resistance.

In summer 1930, Germany, led by Chancellor Heinrich Brüning, a beleaguered Catholic conservative and leader of the Center Party, was reeling from crisis to crisis. In July, unable to govern through the twenty-nine parties in the Reichstag, he tried to invoke Article 48 of the Weimar Constitution to rule by decree. When the Reichstag balked, Brüning made a fateful decision: he persuaded President Paul von Hindenburg to dissolve it. But in the September elections that followed, the National Socialists posted 6.5 million votes and the number of their deputies went from 12 to 107. Hitler promised "a gigantic new program behind which must stand not the new government but a new German people that has ceased to be a mixture of classes, professions, estates."[6] The Communists, who shared the Nazi contempt for Weimar democracy, captured 4 million votes and seventy-seven seats, mostly at the expense of the enfeebled Social Democrats.

When the new Reichstag opened, brown-shirted Nazi Reichstag members marched through the doors, gave the Hitler salute, and shouted "Germany awake! Death to the Jews!" (*Deutschland er-*

wache! Juda verrecke!) En route to the Reichstag, the delegates smashed the windows of Jewish department stores on the Leipzig-erstrasse. That evening the Nazi throng again gathered in the Pots-damer Platz. In a street drama that would be repeated endlessly, the Prussian police, mounted on horseback or shuttled about in wagons, attempted to disperse the mob with rubber truncheons. But in a pattern that would also be repeated (even though Prussia was governed by Social Democrats), no one was arrested among the "spontaneous demonstrators": no one was prosecuted. Instead the Nazi gutter press blamed the Communists for inciting the riot. Thus began a cycle of street brawls between Reds and Browns and monster demonstrations in the Sportpalast, where Hitler and Goebbels worked the crowd, inveighing against the "traitors" of Versailles and Jewish-Communist conspiracies. Those opponents who did not attend listened with horror and disbelief to the radio broadcasts.

"The elections were disturbing," Mildred wrote to her mother in October 1930, because a large group of Germans feeling the desperation of their situation thought it "would be a good idea to have a more absolute government again. . . . The group calls itself the National Socialists although it has nothing to do with social-ism and the name itself is a lie. It thinks itself highly moral and like the Ku Klux Klan makes a campaign of hatred against the Jews. The existence of this group, as well as the smaller one of the Communists, whose aims are finer, endangers the government in Germany. Neither group wishes to work through the Reichstag although both sit in it."[7]

Until 1930, Mildred and Arvid's life had been played out in the provinces against a background of small university towns. Berlin was not only the capital of Germany, it was proud of its reputation as a *Weltstadt*, one of the great cities of the world. Klaus Bon-hoeffer spoke for the younger members of the Harnack clan when he described the capital in a letter to his brother-in-law, Hans von Dohnanyi, as "perhaps intellectually the liveliest city in the world." And he added, "we are beginning to be the right age to enjoy it."[8] Berlin's Friedrich Wilhelm University was the greatest in Central Europe. Berlin's research institutes, glittering with Nobel Prize winners, were the world's finest. Berlin was an international press capital boasting more than one hundred newspapers. As a center of culture it had few peers. Its theaters equaled those in London; as a film center it rivaled Hollywood. Its museums were outstanding and its avant-garde galleries were on a par with Paris. In music it was preeminent. Yet it was said that its artists were rarely native Berliners but came from other cities in the Reich, for "no young actor, no new dramatist, no painter, sculptor, or architect in Germany could become great without having passed through Berlin, without having proved himself to the Berlin public."[9]

Berlin also had its critics. Hitler despised Berliners and thought Berlin more decadent than Rome. He dismissed Weimar Germany's cultural capital with one word: *ein Trümmerfeld* (a rubble field)! Others on the right sneered at Berlin's "cultural Bolshevism," which they blamed on the Jews and the Communists. Carl von Ossietzky, the editor of the prestigious left-wing periodical *Weltbühne*, sniped right back at the philistines: "*Kulturbolschewismus* is when conductor Klemperer takes tempi different from his colleague Furtwängler, when a painter sweeps a color into his sunset not seen in Lower Pomerania; when one favors birth control; when one builds a house with a flat roof; when a Caesarean birth is shown on the screen; when one admires a performance of Charlie Chaplin and the mathematical wizardry of Albert Einstein."[10]

Berlin was an amalgam of all those unsettling tendencies implied by the word "modernism." Its moral code was relaxed—too relaxed for visitors like Wyndham Lewis, who thought it a "sink of iniquity." Foreigners like Auden, Spender, and Isherwood went to Berlin to seek out the *Sonnenkinder* (children of the sun), the nude young aesthetes on the Wannsee Beach, the macquillaged boys in the glittering cabarets. Among heterosexuals there was a new promiscuity as hyperinflation wiped out the savings of middle-class families and they could no longer afford dowries. In the opinion of one Berlin journalist, as soon as this prerequisite for marriage vanished, so did the notion of premarital chastity.[11]

Arvid had taken a temporary job as a lawyer in the city administration of Saalfeld, and Mildred was alone during the week in Berlin. She spent her days at the university whose illustrious faculty included Albert Einstein and a sprinkling of Harnacks, Delbrücks, and Bonhoeffers. Mildred delighted in the prim manners of her fellow students who wore white collars and ties and used titles, addressing each other with the formal *Sie*. She was much amused by their midmorning and afternoon grand marches, sandwiches in pockets, around the domed precincts of the state library. It was a "rushing life" with both "duties and pleasures," she sighed, with Arvid's family, her studies, the theater, and music to keep her "running from morning till midnight."[12]

It is difficult to determine the exact number of American students in Berlin—estimates range from two hundred to a thousand—during the last days of the Weimar Republic. Most studied science, but a German Ph.D. in law, philosophy, or theology, or in newer fields like sociology or art history was also prized. Berlin, along with Vienna, was *the* place to study music. And before 1933, it was where Jewish students from the United States got around American religious quotas to gain medical degrees.

Mildred's friend, compatriot, and fellow student Warren Tomlinson in a letter home characterized the Yankees: "The church group, who are not a very first rate crowd; the students, who are a mixed-class group; and the 'embassy' group, who are the political, military, and wealthy commercialists supposed to be a snobby and high-living bunch with whom the rest of us don't associate! Then there are the Americans who are living practically German to get German language, views, and life; and there is the ever present pestilent tourist crowd. We are a great nation!"[13]

Although Mildred "lived German," mixing most often with the Harnack clan, she was also an active member of the American set, making use of the library at the Amerika-Institut, going to the picnics, boat cruises, and dances held by the American Student Association. And, more consequentially, the Harnacks were regular participants in the student and international forums of the American Church.

The pastor of the American Church, Reverend Ewart Turner, and his bride, Martha, also arrived in Berlin in the summer of 1930, when both were in their mid-twenties. But what was more unusual about the Turners' pastorate at the American Church was their concern for Germany's social and political problems. During his four years in Berlin, Turner made the church into a lively center for debate. The church forums hosted Nazis, monarchists, Jewish businessmen, Communists, and newspaper correspondents. By inviting guest speakers such as Hitler's press spokesman Putzi Hanfstaengl, Reichsbank president Hjalmar Horace Greeley Schacht, Ernst von Harnack (Arvid's cousin), and American correspondent Edgar Ansel Mowrer to the church for lectures followed by discussions, Turner hoped to foster a greater understanding of Germany's worsening crisis. After Schacht created a sensation by using his lecture in 1932 to announce his support for Adolf Hitler, curious Berliners flocked to the International Forum. An added draw of the Student Forum was the American-style Boston baked bean and apple pie supper provided at the modest cost of fifty pfennigs.[14]

Martha Turner remembered Mildred as a lively presence. "The Harnacks came to the meetings because they were interested in current events," she recalled. "I have quite a vivid memory of Mildred—very attractive, blond, full of life. Arvid was much quieter. We liked them both."

Yet already in 1930, Mildred was aware that she must tread cautiously in the heavily politicized atmosphere of Berlin. In a Christmas letter to her mother, she describes a meeting with a former minister of culture—the man who procured her fellowship. He was now out of a job but might assume a position of importance again: "In such situations I must act with the most extreme care, for one break would seriously endanger all my prospects. . . . What I do is to remind myself on the way to such teas that I am Mildred and that I am no more and no less than that." She resolves to bring out the best in people by remembering "that all people, whether they are exceedingly witty or exceedingly stupid and whether they have great titles or none, have no more and no less than these deep resources in themselves and hence deserve equally my respect."[15] (She succeeded, for it was this ability to stress the positive in people that is most remembered by her students and friends.)

In February 1931 she was invited to give a trial lecture on "Romantic and Married Love in the Works of Hawthorne" to faculty and students. This would be the first of many public lectures on American writers that Mildred would deliver. Proudly, if not entirely accurately, she reported to her family that she was "the first American lecturer ever appointed by the Prussian Ministry."[16] Yet she had reason to boast. She had begun her career at the university where most professors hoped to end theirs, and it was an unusual honor especially given the widespread resentment in these difficult times against the *Doppelverdiener*, families in which both wife and husband held jobs. For three semesters she gave lectures on American and English literature and language. Her pupils, Mildred wrote, were "comparatively clever and interesting," far more knowing than "my dear old American boys and girls at Wisconsin and Goucher." But Berlin's university students were unbelievably poor and hungry and therefore ready recruits for Nazi and Communist demonstrations. They were "weary and sad, for they had no future." Capitalist civilization, Mildred predicted, was approaching a "more and more serious crisis."[17]

The reference to capitalism's failure became a leitmotiv in Mildred's letters home. Like many German intellectuals, the Harnacks believed that the worldwide economic crisis and the rise of Hitler presaged the end of capitalism. Mildred saw no reprieve; only the Soviet Union appeared to offer hope. "Russia is the only country which tries to give all of her citizens work and food and to treat them all equally," she wrote. They were striving to learn all they could about Soviet Russia, "the scene of an enormously important experiment in loving your neighbor as yourself."[18] "It is interesting to know," Mildred continues enthusiastically, "that the Five-Year Plan in Russia is succeeding, and that it is capable of bringing greater good to the working class than has yet been known by them at any time."[19]

During this period Soviet Russia was relatively unknown, sealed off from the rest of Europe and, until 1933, unrecognized by the United States. Before 1930 there had been few visitors to the Soviet Union. Separated by a cordon sanitaire from the rest of Europe, Russia seemed a tantalizing, remote New Jerusalem. Various influential travelers sang its praises, generally after returning to the comforts of capitalism. The muckraking author Lincoln Steffens acclaimed it as a workable future, but added in 1926, while comfortably ensconced on the Italian Riviera, "I don't want to live there. It is too much like serving in an army at war with no mercy for the weak."[20] Mildred had little inkling of the darker side of Communism, of Stalin's profound distrust of the indigenous German left. Only later would he betray his willingness to execute foreign Communists, his own dictatorial savagery. And the few disquieting rumors that appeared occasionally in the Western press—the famine in the Ukraine, the betrayal of the Chinese Communists, and the stifling of dissent—were easily discounted as right-wing propaganda. In building the brave new order there were bound to be some excesses, the occasional mistake. Or to repeat the cant of the most influential of Stalin's Western apologists, *New York Times* correspondent Walter Duranty, "you can't make an omelet without breaking eggs."

As Stalin continued to consolidate his power in 1930, his regime perfected the guided tour that enabled more pilgrims to see less. But theirs was a predisposition to believe. The Harnacks' Hungarian-born contemporary, Arthur Koestler, was then a journalist with the Ullstein papers in Berlin. For young intellectuals in that time and place, Koestler recalled in his memoirs, Marxism

> was not a fashion or craze—it was a sincere and spontaneous expression of an optimism born of despair: an abortive revolution of the spirit, a misfired Renaissance, a false dawn of history. To be attracted to the new faith was, I still believe, an honorable error. We were wrong for the right reasons. . . . there is a world of difference between a disenchanted lover and those incapable of love.[21]

This longing for the arrow in the blue, for the absolute cause, the magic formula that would produce a golden age (to borrow Koestler's phrases), was felt with special passion by Arvid. He had gone to the United States to study the early utopian communities founded by Robert Owen and other dreamers, and he wrote of them admiringly in his doctoral dissertation on the pre-Marxist workers' movement. Again, Koestler defined the attitude: "The classless Communist society, according to Marx and Engels, was to be a revival, at the end of the dialectical spiral, of the primitive Communist society which stood at its beginning."[22]

"How does a German like Arvid become a Communist?" I asked Franz-Joseph Müller, a former member of the German resistance, who now directs the White Rose Foundation in Munich. For those born after the Great Depression, who have since witnessed the

*demise of Communism and the collapse of Eastern Europe's
"planned economies," it is difficult to understand the peculiar appeal of Communism, the fascination with five-year plans, and, finally, the breed of German Marxists to which the Arvid Harnack
belonged.*

*Müller gave an answer over drinks in a Munich hotel. "Because
they were idealists, they had hope. It came to nothing under the
Nazis." As to the appeal of Communism, the young were prepared
to regard Communism and even war as preferable to economic
chaos and Fascism. In the 1930s there were critical differences. "A
German Communist is not exactly the same as a Russian Communist. It's very different. How communistic is a German Communist? or a French Communist? You cannot compare them with
Stalinists. The old German Communists were idealists. In the
GDR, after they got money, that was something else. But after
'33, most of the German resisters who were killed were
Communists."*

The reservations Arvid assuredly had about the Bolshevik experiment were summed up in a phrase fashionable among German
leftists: "*Wir werden es besser machen.*" (We'll do it better.) Russia
had confounded Marx's own prediction that the new order would
arise in an advanced capitalist state like Germany, an anomaly that
had put untutored Russian peasants instead of skilled workers in
power, a wrong turn by the locomotive of history that Germany
would correct.

"Arvid was a great admirer of the United States," his nephew,
a British industrialist, stated. "In fact, it was in the United States
that Arvid picked up his left-wing views. He had his *Krisentheorie,*
crisis theory—which we all know is essentially true—that a boom
is followed by some form of depression and so forth. But Arvid
said it must be possible by applying Marxist principles to smooth
all of that out, employ productive capacity to the limit. He was
convinced that the greatest happiness for the greatest number lay
in the centrally controlled economy and he considered himself just
the sort of chap who could centrally control it."[23]

Another factor that made some Berliners especially susceptible to
Communism was their sheer proximity to Moscow. Everyone, it

seemed, traveling to or from Moscow sooner or later came through Berlin. Moreover, during the Weimar era, when Berlin's Russian colony grew to 320,000, it became in the words of one exile poet, V. F. Khodasevich, "the stepmother of Russian cities." Some, like Vladimir Nabokov, were hostile to the Soviet regime, but not all Russians were fleeing the revolution. Before 1934 it was still comparatively easy for Soviet artists like Ilya Ehrenburg, Boris Pasternak, El Lissitzky, and Sergei Eisenstein to come and go.

Both Red and White Russians settled in western Berlin, where Russian restaurants with balalaikas, blinis, borscht, and the inevitable gypsies were scattered around the zoo and in Charlottenburg (already baptized by them as Charlottengrad), so many of them, in fact, that the West End's main boulevard, the Kurfürstendamm, was nicknamed the "Nepski Prospect" for NEP—the New Economic Policy—in vogue at the time in the Soviet Union. The emigrants also practiced private capitalism. There were Russian publishers, theaters, and avant-garde art exhibitions and, most importantly, for the Harnacks there were Russian films.

This was the heroic era of the Russian cinema when directors like Eisenstein, Pudovkin, Dovzhenko, and Vertov were making masterpieces such as *Earth, Battleship Potemkin, Ten Days That Shook the World, Storm over Asia, Mother*, and *Man with a Camera*. All four Soviet directors were, in fact, more popular in Germany than in their own country, for it was in Berlin that they began to achieve their international reputation. Stephen Spender described the "long journeys to little cinemas in the outer suburbs of Berlin" where "among the grimy tenements we saw the images of the New Life of the workers building with machine tools and tractors their socially just world."[24]

Whenever she could, Mildred went to see these marvels. She wrote ecstatically to her mother that *Earth* was one of the "two most beautiful films" she had ever seen. The "fine manly fellow" who wanted to share all the land reminded her of her brother Bob, a struggling farmer in Wisconsin. "I wish you could have seen the wonderful pictures of the fields of grain and the clouds in the sky and the multitudes of apples and melons. It was so beautiful. . . . I wept and saw the film through twice."[25]

In fact, Mildred's letters after 1931 are full of Russia: Arvid is reading a magazine about Russia; she is reading a book, *Night over Russia*, by Vera Figner, a member of the secret terrorist organization People's Will (*Narodnaya Volya*), who was one of the plotters who assassinated Tsar Alexander II. Here was someone she could admire: "Finally she [Figner] was imprisoned with many comrades in the Russian Bastille for twenty years. One by one she bore the vanishing away of these comrades, who died of tuberculosis or killed themselves in despair—one poured oil over himself and burned himself—or went insane. Finally in 1903 I believe, she was freed, but could hardly adjust herself to living again. The book makes one wonder at the power of will in these people."[26] (A phenomenon of revolutionary life in Russia during the nineteenth century was the surprising number of and role played by women. Many of them were educated in Swiss universities; many of them were executed or exiled as terrorists.)

Mildred eagerly read everything she could about Russia "and the theories upon which the new system is being built."[27] At the same time, she was studying American history but, for Mildred, every comparison between the state of affairs in Russia and the West seemed to argue in favor of the former. These were not sentiments that Mildred's family could readily understand, much less approve. They found her letters tiresome, even condescending. Her sister Harriette resented Mildred's proselytizing. "Harriette accuses me of a didactic purpose and of course I have one," she confessed to her mother. "But so many new thoughts have come to me in the last few years and I like to feel that you share in them and understand them."[28]

These new thoughts were influencing her judgment of American writers. She admitted she was having trouble completing her proposed dissertation, her study of American literature based on the ideas of the philosopher Wilhelm Dilthey, a patriarch of the "history of ideas" school of literary criticism. Now, she confessed her work did not stand so clear before her: Dilthey, in the light of a newer generation of Marxist critics, seemed passé. Mildred read articles by Walther Mehring and Georg Lukács in *Linkskurve*, the leading Communist literary journal. It was they, not Dilthey, who now inspired her thinking and her teaching. Something of their proletarian didacticism can be sensed in Mildred's dismissal of Edith Wharton as someone "who writes mostly of the old elite in

New York" and of James Branch Cabell as an exponent of a "decadent southern 'aristocracy.' "[29]

Over the next few years, she was in great demand as a lecturer on the increasingly popular American writers. At the end of 1931, she gave a special lecture on Carl Sandburg at Marburg and Giessen universities. In the latter school, she reported with justifiable pride, "the hall was full to overflowing, the English Circle of professors' wives with whom I used to read sent me roses, and Professor Fischer, head of English there, told me it was the most successful lecture ever given under his auspices. Afterwards many old friends went to a café with us to talk until it was time for me to take the night train to Berlin. The nicest thing was said to me by Fraulein Gail (Professor Lenz's housekeeper). She told me, 'Your speech was you, just as you are.' "[30]

Mildred's growing self-assurance was palpable, and Arvid savored her achievements, remarking that she had grown very much in her ability to think things through clearly. Her husband, she wrote Georgina, "was very much pleased and very proud of his wife, which made his wife happy."[31]

During her first year on the faculty at Berlin, 1931, Arvid was in Marburg finishing his *Habilitationsarbeit*, the postdoctoral period of additional research and publication necessary for obtaining a professorship at a university. Mildred acknowledged that these separations occasioned by financial necessity and their shared goals of academic careers were difficult. They wrote daily—hundreds of "long letters about our business and pleasure" affirming that they were "each other's chief critics and advisers as well as lovers."[32] All of these soul-baring letters were lost in Gestapo searches and allied bombing raids. What remains are a few postcards to relatives attesting to holidays spent together.

She wrote her mother that they celebrated their fifth anniversary for two days with flowers, cake, candles, pineapple glacé, and a "beautiful excursion over the mountains and through the pine and beech tree forests." They seemed enviably happy: "The past five years are worth celebrating. We have grown to love each other more and more deeply, we have grown healthier, and our ideals have become clearer. We have grown more capable and clever. Our work has become more satisfying."[33] When they are alone,

In the fall Arvid and Mildred were together again in Berlin, where they moved to modern quarters ("a study and a little adjoining bedroom") in suburban Zehlendorf. These new rooms were in a brand-new garden housing estate, part of a planned community of three- or four-story apartment houses alternating with individual terrace houses constructed as a cooperative venture by building craftsmen and financed by the trade unions. Designed by the famous socialist architect Bruno Taut, the low-rise buildings with their austere lines and flat roofs, were the very epitome of modernism. The Harnacks were enthusiastic about their colorful new neighborhood adjoining a wood where they ran in the morning before breakfast. The neighborhood was nicknamed the *Papageien Siedlung* or parrot quarter because of the bright colors that the houses were painted. Mildred, always happier when surrounded by invigorating country air, sent a picture to Georgina of the new houses to give "a faint idea of what they look like—they are bright colored and gay and the tall pines with their funny tops harmonize in their straight long line with the purposely very straight line of the houses."[45]

Arvid was busy setting up ARPLAN (Arbeitsgemeinschaft zum Studium der sowjetrussischen Planwirtschaft), an organization of writers and scholars who met once a month to report on and discuss Soviet economic planning. For Arvid these discussions were a natural extension of the Friday night meetings of the Commons group or the "sociological evenings" at Giessen. When the first ARPLAN conference took place in January 1932, Arvid became managing secretary and Friedrich Lenz, his former economics professor from Giessen, became president.* Sergei Bessonov, a leading Soviet economist, later counselor of the Soviet embassy, who was at the time assigned to the *Handelsvertretung*, the Russian trade mission, and Alexander Hirschfeld, who later became Arvid's contact to the Soviet embassy, took care of technical matters.

---

*Other leading members of ARPLAN were the sinologist Karl August Wittfogel; Berlin University professor and former Reichstag member Otto Hoetzsch; Adolf Grabowski of the Institute for Social Research; the Hungarian literary critic and philosopher Georg (Gyorgy) Lukács; the economist Richard Oehring; the National Bolshevist Ernst Niekisch and journalists Ernst Jünger, Klaus Mehnert, and Paul Massing, who became a Rutgers University professor and, for a time, a Soviet agent.

Bessonov, who was a frequent lunch partner of Arvid's and a guest at the Harnack home over the next three years, was an exceptional man with an unusual mission: to recruit sympathetic economists, engineers, and scientists to go to the Soviet Union and to locate those who, although they preferred to remain at home, would supply the Soviet trade legation with information about Germany's technical secrets.[46]

A useful source for Soviet recruits or contacts were leftist professional groups like ARPLAN or the Intellectual Workers Union (*Bund geistiger Berufe,* or *Bund der Geistesarbeiter*), another Communist front group, to which the Harnacks belonged.[47] Its members were, as the name implies, intellectuals.[48] Officially, the Moscow line exalted the working proletariat at the expense of the intelligentsia, yet German Communists like the propaganda wizard Willi Münzenberg recognized the party's need for intellectuals, opinion makers, or "people of good will." Not necessarily party members, these sympathizers would become "agents of influence."[49]

The explicit purpose of the Bund, or BGA, in the words of Georgi Dimitrov, the head of the Comintern, the Communist International, was "to extend our ideological influence to those circles of the intelligentsia that for various reasons were difficult to reach through our other mass organizations." In late 1932 the BGA stepped up its activities: questions of interest to the intelligentsia were discussed in public meetings; individual sections for teachers, engineers, architects, and so on, were founded. "In general," Dimitrov wrote, "for tactical reasons, the appearance of known Communists was avoided; they appeared only rarely—and then only during the discussion—in the meetings that were open to everyone. The members of the Communist Party, the KPD, remained in the background. They helped those who were closest to us to develop the topics and the plan of work."[50]

ARPLAN also fit this description of a front group; its purpose, according to Dimitrov, was "to draw into our sphere of influence highly-qualified representatives of the intelligentsia with a correct outlook who were also supporters of a pro-Soviet orientation in German policy. Within ARPLAN there existed a Communist Party group. Its task was to steer the development of topics and the work of ARPLAN in the direction that was necessary in order to achieve the ideological influence we desired on this circle of the intelligentsia."[51] Münzenberg called these front groups "innocents' clubs," acknowledging that their members were not "witting," or knowledgeable, about the true purpose of the organizations.[52]

One member of ARPLAN, the Hungarian Marxist literary critic and philosopher Georg Lukács, found Arvid to be not only an outstanding economist but a thinker broadly interested in all theoretical and philosophical questions. When Lukács showed him an article on the young Hegel that he had written, Arvid read it with "much interest and understanding." The Hungarian praised Arvid as "very clever, diplomatic, and certainly energetic. He was a deeply convinced Communist." Lukács also remembered Mildred as being very intelligent, extremely well-informed, and exceptionally energetic, likewise "a very deeply committed Communist."[53]

An item recently declassified and obtained from the Soviet archives shows that during the halcyon days of ARPLAN the Soviets were keeping a vigilant eye on the Harnacks. Responding to a 1941 request for information on the couple from NKGB chief Pavel Fitin, Comintern chief Dimitrov forwarded the file that contained information from Lukács describing the Harnacks:

> Arvid Harnack belonged to an old well-known scholarly family. He was (not outwardly) a member of the KPD. In the beginning he was still encumbered by the remnants of bourgeois views, but he worked very earnestly to overcome these. He did a good job in ARPLAN and the Intellectual Workers Union, showing himself to be very adept at solving tactical problems. . . . His wife—reportedly an American by birth— taught English at the University of Berlin. She also participated in the work of the Intellectual Workers Union and in the seminars of the Union of Proletarian Writers. In the summer of 1933 she was in the Soviet Union. A conversation with her at that time left Comrade Lukács with the impression that she and her husband remained true to their convictions.[54]

In Germany at this time, the political situation was lurching from bad to calamitous. Christopher Isherwood wrote in *Christopher and His Kind*, his memoir of the period, that living in Berlin was "rather like living in Hell. Everybody is absolutely at the last gasp, hanging on with their eyelids. We are under martial law, and to all intents and purposes living in a Communist regime without any of the benefits of Communism. . . . Hitler and the Communists openly discuss plans for civil war and nobody can do anything."[55]

In January 1932, Mildred witnessed an encounter between the National Socialists and the Communists in front of the Karl Lieb-knecht House (where the Central Committee of the Communist Party was located). Indignant, she wrote her mother that "the po-lice openly assisted and protected the Fascists, struck at the pro-testing workers with their rubber batons, and put a great cordon about the whole square, allowing only Nazis to get through. A monster of an automobile—a kind of a tank in full armor, with little slits in it for shooting and an automatic gun which swung back and forth taking range at the crowd and the houses on either side of the narrow street—cruised up and down." The unem-ployed, the workers, Communists, and Social-Democrats walked in crowds up and down the street on the edges of the police cor-dons as a silent threat to the police and Fascists. Near the Alex-anderplatz the jobless workers shouted, "We are hungry." "Fight with the Communists for work and bread!" "Down with the Fas-cists." "Do not shoot, policemen! We are your brothers!"[56]

In May, Mildred unexpectedly lost her teaching position at the university. She had been lulled into a false sense of security since her classes had gone well and the number of her students had tripled. But the university was in financial straits; there was a prej-udice against foreigners and women because so many male German teachers were unemployed. There were also departmental intrigues. Professor Friedrich Schönemann, an ardent Nazi, re-turned from a leave in America to take charge of the American section of the English faculty. Mildred's leftist tendencies were scarcely a secret—she had written that she encouraged her stu-dents to study Marx as "a practical solution to the evils of the present."[57] Even though her students rallied around her, circulating a petition and collecting one hundred signatures, her appointment was not renewed. But the semester ended "beautifully." Her stu-dents presented her with a large bouquet of flowers and accom-panied her to her flat where they talked until midnight. She was sure that "one woman and one man in the class at least will remain my friends. . . . It would be my fault if the relationship ceased."[58] In fact the relationships with her students did not cease. Over the years they continued to visit and write her long letters. One of them, Paul Thomas, a one-armed war veteran, became an important participant in the Harnacks' discussion evenings and resistance work.

The Harnacks were also forced to move from their agreeable rooms in Zehlendorf. In June, Mildred wrote her mother that "the people with whom we live are National Socialists." She described them as Germans whose patriotic passions flared irrationally and who felt themselves morally superior merely on the grounds of being German. As the Harnacks did little to conceal their views (Arvid was then speaking a great deal in public), there were surely arguments. Therefore she wrote Georgina to "direct your next letter to the University of Berlin, English Seminar." They were about to move "quietly."[59]

The Harnacks' Berlin address for the next two years, 61 Hasenheide, is located at the borders of Kreuzberg and Neukölln. Before the Berlin Wall came down, Kreuzberg was the home of the *Alternativen*—students and bohemian artists—while Neukölln, the bastion of the Communist Party in 1932, has retained its working-class character. Partitioning apartments had become a necessity for middle-class families in Weimar Berlin and the Harnacks sublet rooms in a fifth-floor flat freshly decorated in soft modern colors, "dove tans, soft blues, and greens."[60] Mildred's own sunny room sported a view of vast avenues of green, steep roofs, and wide streets. She reported that "even in warm weather our rooms are cool and pleasant" and if it were not for "a bit too much music coming up from the *Konditorei* far below" it would be ideal.[61] A few weeks later she described their cheerful domesticity: "Our front room with its tower-like alcove looks lovely now with them (masses of lavender cosmos) loosely crowded in great vases against the soft yellow walls. Under the lamp on his desk sits my Arvid with his head on his hand reading the newspaper. I sit at my desk, writing by the yellow light of my shaded lamp and can see him through the wide doorway."[62]

The apartment was located near the Sportpalast and Tempelhof airfield. Below them were shops, and across the street a little house where they ate their "plentiful and good dinners." Behind a "church set in green in the center of the square" was a lovely park where she went walking and where the police practiced shooting. Radiating from the church square were streets leading in seven directions. One, the Fontane Promenade, a tree-lined boulevard, led over to the Spree River, a few minutes away. Sometimes at night, when lines of light made it look its most romantic, the Harnacks visited the harbor on the river.[63] "One can really work in these rooms," she concluded, "the light, the air, the pleasantness of the rooms" are all conducive to it. "We feel very happy about it." She felt friendlier toward Berlin: "It makes a great difference where you live, doesn't it!"[64]

In May 1932, Chancellor Brüning's government fell. He was replaced by a caretaker chancellor, the Center Party's duplicitous diplomat, Franz von Papen. Heading into the July elections, there were nearly five hundred brawls in Prussia alone. Living in working-class Neukölln, the "red center of Berlin" with its tradition of rioting and insurrection, the Harnacks witnessed firsthand the "ding-dong" battles between the Browns and Reds during that long stifling summer, described by Arthur Koestler.

"Hardly a day passed without one or two being killed in Berlin," Koestler wrote in *Invisible Writing*. "The main battlefields were the *Bierstuben*, the smoky little taverns of the working-class districts." Some of them served as meeting places for the Nazis, some were meeting places for his Communist friends. To enter the wrong pub was to cross enemy lines and from time to time the Nazis would shoot up one of the Communist haunts: "It was done in the classic Chicago tradition: a gang of SA men would drive slowly past the tavern, firing through the glass panes, then vanish at break-neck speed. We had far fewer motor-cars than the Nazis, and retaliation was mostly carried out in cars either stolen, or borrowed from sympathizers."[65]

Mildred reported home on the worsening situation. On July 3, she and Arvid witnessed a Communist rally in the Lustgarten, in front of the former kaiser's palace at the center of Berlin. A "new look of resolution" had appeared on the faces of the workers as they filed by the Harnack apartment on the way to the demonstration. "The procession took about fifteen minutes to pass." Although it was a "mighty crowd," Mildred added, "it was not so mighty as that of the National Socialists."[66] Her next letter home recalled how the years had slipped away: "Who would have thought that I should be living in Germany on the 12th of July, 1932, and hearing music coming up to me from the restaurants of Berlin, while Germany itself is full of unrest, of casual civil war."[67]

On July 17, in the Altona suburb of Hamburg, seventeen people were killed and several hundred wounded as the Nazis "spontaneously" paraded through the solidly Communist neighborhood to be met with sniper fire from rooftops. Papen seized on the killings to dissolve the Social Democratic Prussian government and Berlin's police force, claiming the takeover was necessary to restore order. The Socialists did nothing; the Communist Party's call for a general strike fell on deaf ears. The battle with Hitler, Koestler felt, was lost before it was joined. "It was evident to all but ourselves that the K.P.D., the strongest among the Communist parties in Europe, was a castrated giant whose brag and bluster only served to cover its lost virility."[68]

But Mildred was not so pessimistic. True, she reported on July 24, "the dictatorship of the right parties has come overnight here" and the "communistic press" has been taken over but there was room for optimism: "It is said by people who are capable of estimating the present situation that no such dictatorship as is in Italy can be erected in Germany. The reason is that the opposition of the left, i.e., of the workers, to the rule of property is far better organized and conscious of its own aims than it was in Italy." Therefore, she asserted, the conservatives will lose out "because the people are now really beginning to starve."[69]

Mildred proved to be overly optimistic. In the July 31 elections, the Nazis doubled their support again, winning over 14 million votes—37 percent of the electorate. The young, especially university students, voted disproportionately for Hitler. But the National Socialists still lacked a Reichstag majority; President Hindenburg still resisted appointing Hitler chancellor, citing his reluctance to hand Germany over "like a laboratory rabbit" to Hitler.[70]

When their Madison friends, *Capital Times* columnist Ernie Meyer and his wife Dorothy, visited the Harnacks they found them still sanguine: the Germans would never accept Hitler as their leader. In fact, Arvid was so convincing that Meyer, to his later chagrin, wrote a column home stating that "in a year the Nazis would probably fade, like the Ku Klux Klan in America."[71] Apologizing to the Meyers for their rushed hospitality, the Harnacks excitedly told them they were leaving the next day for the Soviet Union to have a look at the future.

EIGHT

Pilgrim

The Berlin Abendgymnasium Shakespeare group

In 1932, as the Great Depression continued to mock confident forecasts of imminent recovery, the Soviet Union was triply alluring to the West's alienated liberals. Here was a new society, seemingly immune to boom–bust cycles, that also had the appeal of the forbidden. As never before, Moscow became a magnet for pilgrims, the Mecca and Jerusalem of converts to a humanistic faith ostensibly rooted in reason and science. This claim seemed all the more credible since the global crisis appeared to confirm dire Marxist warnings about the insoluble contradictions of capitalism.

In 1932, Sergei Bessonov, the Harnacks' Soviet friend, arranged a study trip for twenty-three members of ARPLAN, starting late August. Mildred hoped to go with Arvid but she had to be back to begin a new job—teaching at a night school for adults—on September 1. Instead, she booked passage on one of the inexpensive tours for workers advertised by Intourist, the official Soviet travel bureau. It would be interesting to travel with workers, she wrote, and she was equally sure that it was good for a woman to travel alone, since "one becomes more active."[1] Her tour included both Leningrad and Moscow. In the Soviet capital she stayed with a friend, Stella, identified only as a "most humorous and kind-hearted" teacher.[2]

Fred Sanderson, then a student at the University of Frankfurt, met Arvid for the first time on the ARPLAN trip: "Harnack didn't give the impression of a hard liner. He was an objective guide. Only after the war did I learn that he had close connections with the Communist Party." Lenz, Sanderson felt, "was no radical and others in the group were essentially conservative but had become critical of the market economy because of the economic crisis." Asked if the trip was underwritten by the Russians, his answer was negative: "It was not a free trip. We were not invitees of the Soviet government. As I remember it cost five hundred marks. We went because we were interested and because it was the only economy that did not suffer a depression."[3]

More than once it has been alleged that during this trip Arvid was recruited by Soviet intelligence. In his 1953 book *Soviet Espionage*, David Dallin writes that the "study trip" of ARPLAN to Russia in 1932 was the "turning point" in Harnack's life: "In his contract with official agencies in Moscow his devotion and ability were noticed, and before his return to Berlin he was received by Comintern leaders Otto Kuusinen and Osip Piatnitsky. Harnack was asked bluntly whether he would work directly for the Soviet government. He consented."[4] Although Arvid's trip is well documented, no such meetings are recorded in his report of the trip or in recently opened KGB files. Still, writing in 1994, former KGB deputy director of Foreign Intelligence Pavel Sudoplatov repeats this version, claiming that Harnack worked for the Soviets "for a full decade."[5]

Even though they traveled by train through the Ukraine to Kharkov at the height of the Ukrainian famine, and despite their expertise as economists and engineers, Arvid's group seemed unaware of vast tragedy surrounding them—6 million people were starving to death at the rate of 6,000 a day. Arthur Koestler, who left Germany at the same time (July 1932) and went to the same place—Kharkov—recalled the train ride through the Ukrainian steppe: "At every station there was a crowd of peasants in rags, offering icons and linen in exchange against a loaf of bread. The women were lifting up their infants to the compartment windows—infants pitiful and terrifying with limbs like sticks, puffed bellies, big cadaverous heads lolling on thin necks." At the time these ravages were kept secret from the world. Koestler's official traveling companions took pains to explain that these wretched crowds were "kulaks, rich peasants who had resisted the collectivization of the land and whom it had therefore been necessary to evict from their farms."[6]

Why did the famine and the obvious failures of social planning go unnoticed by so astute an observer as Arvid Harnack? Koestler provides a plausible answer: "I reacted to the brutal impact of reality on illusion in a manner typical of the true believer. I was surprised and bewildered—but the elastic shock-absorbers of my Party training began to operate at once. I had eyes to see, and a mind conditioned to explain away what they saw. This 'inner censor' is more reliable and effective than any official censorship."[7] Koestler classified everything that shocked him as the "heritage of the past" and everything he liked as the "seeds of the future." By setting up this "sorting machine" in his mind he was able to live in Russia in 1932 and remain a Communist.[8]

In these days before the imposing public work projects of the

New Deal, the contrast between the gigantic engineering efforts of the Five-Year Plan—the Dnieper Dam, the White Sea Canal, the Turkestan-Siberian Railway—and the breadlines and Hoovervilles of the capitalist nations contributed to many liberals' predilection to credit the successes of the Five-Year Plan. Malcolm Muggeridge, then a British correspondent living in Moscow, marveled at the Intourist travelers who toured these wonders going from "strength to strength, continuing to lighten our darkness, and to guide, counsel and instruct us; on occasion, momentarily abashed, but always ready to pick themselves up, put on their cardboard helmets, mount Rosinante, and go galloping off on yet another foray on behalf of the down-trodden and oppressed."[9]

In Moscow, Mildred found that there was abundant food for visitors and other luxuries unknown in the rest of the country. She lacked the experience to discern "the living Moscow" that the disillusioned revolutionary Victor Serge described, "with its hunger rations, its arrests."[10] These were still the days before the Russians developed the "Moscow tic," people looking over their shoulders before daring to say anything about politics. Journeying from Berlin's despair, making her way alone, with "a few words of Russian" and pieces of papers with destinations written in Cyrillic on them, Mildred can be forgiven for the optimism that pervades her letters home. Moscow reminded her of "Washington in the days of prosperity at the end of the war." The streets are full of "busy, energetic human beings." She is greeted everywhere by "frank smiles." The air she breathes is permeated by "hopefulness and achievement."[11]

Arthur Koestler described the mentality of visitors like Mildred: "All foreigners whom I knew, and also the more mentally alert among the Russians . . . knew that official propaganda was a pack of lies, but justified this by referring to the 'backward masses.' They knew that the standard of living in the capitalist world was much higher than in Russia, but justified this by saying that the Russians had been even worse off under the Czar."[12]

His words capture with almost eerie precision what Mildred reported to her mother: "To be sure Russia is a land whose cultural level as a whole has been far below that of the U.S. and Europe, and, although immense improvement has taken place since 1917, there is very much still to be done. No one realizes this better than the Russians themselves. . . . The Russia of the Czars was a land of oppressed and backward people. It is an immense task to change the state of these people, to replace dirt and drunkenness with cleanliness and clean energy, to replace ignorance and superstition with such knowledge as will make every woman as well as every man able to manage the state."[13]

Mildred was looking for equality for women, and she found it. Women are "allowed to work in whatever fields they wish, according to their mental and physical capacity." Equal work receives the same pay. When women are pregnant "their work is made lighter for them" but not taken away. Instead they "receive two months vacation with pay, all necessary care before confinement, and two months after confinement." Women are not forced to bear children "but are encouraged to use birth control measures and are allowed to use abortion to a certain extent." If they are not treated well by their husbands, "they can leave them at any time and care for their children with the money which they earn, by some money which the husband is required to contribute, and by the help of the state." The husband also has "the privilege" of leaving his wife at any time. Money is not the bond between husband and wife; rather, they are each financially independent.[14]

Upon his return from the Soviet Union, Arvid wrote, mimeographed, and distributed the final ARPLAN report detailing the lectures they attended, the visits to model factories, model farms, the model Dnieper dam, and a model home for juvenile delinquents as well as cultural events that they attended.[15] He also began writing a handbook of the Soviet Union, describing the special character of Russia and its new system of planning. The book was to be published by Rowohlt and was set in galleys.

Mildred also returned to Berlin brimming with optimism to assume her new teaching position at the Berlin Abendgymnasium, a night school for adults founded in 1927 with the support of the Social Democrats. The BAG, as students called it, was the first institution in Germany to offer blue- and white-collar workers an opportunity to complete their high school education and thus have the chance to enroll in a university. It was coeducational, a novelty among German secondary schools of the time, and far less authoritarian. The faculty treated students as equals. Classes were inexpensive and the books were provided free. Before their evening classes, indigent students were treated to a subsidized warm meal at a neighboring restaurant.[16]

While prospective students sat waiting to complete their entrance exams, Mildred composed their portrait: "Men and women of my age, some older and some younger, answer the oral questions of the teachers. They are dressed in dark suits, shoes are well-shined; hair is well-combed; and the under-lip is not quite steady when they sit down to face the examiners. They have worked in offices for years. They have come here hoping to win more freedom and breadth in life."[17] But she believed the school was based on a false assumption "that it is possible for workers and clerks to rise to better positions in society through study. This is an unwarranted assumption in Germany today. . . . To a very large extent they are doomed to fall in the social scale rather than rise. There is little work to be had; they lose their positions; their unemployment insurance gives out after a time and they are thrown into the lap of charity, which means, when they have no other help, slow ruin and starvation by degrees." Mildred grimly judged that only a few lucky ones could succeed.[18]

Her teaching load of fifteen hours a week was daunting.[19] Coupled with this she also supervised the English Club, which hosted lectures on "economic, political and cultural relations" and gave an occasional performance of a Shakespeare play. She seems to have been an exceptional teacher as well as a congenial colleague. "As the only woman teacher on a staff of men," her principal wrote in 1936, "she had been agreeable to work with, and she has adapted herself excellently to the particular character of this school for adults."[20]

For many, "Miss Harnack" was their first introduction to America. After the war, several students wrote about her. What most remembered was her singing songs like "Old Folks at Home," "Clementine," and "John Brown" with them.[21]

Initially the singing embarrassed some of her pupils, as Maria-Dorothea Beck confessed in an article for a West German newspaper in 1967: "We were adults holding a wide variety of jobs: lawyers, bookkeepers and apprentices, actors and salesmen, laborers and clerks, journalists and office workers—all hungry for knowledge, all tired after the usual daily grind." But when Mildred sang "freely and naturally" before her class, instead of being "tired

and embarrassed" they became "alert and fresh," the gray classroom seemed "less cramped and oppressive."

Mildred entered the classroom in a very special way. "You never
heard her coming. No steps in the hall; no door opening or closing
behind her. Suddenly, there she was in the middle of the room.
Her walk like all her motions was light and deliberate. She would
have her books and notebooks down on the lectern before the class
could even stand up."

The last time Beck saw Mildred was at the graduation ball in
the banquet room at the zoo: "She was wearing a fine lace collar,
light on a dark background. This collar gave a timeless pictorial
quality to her beauty. I remember the graduation ball vaguely.
Only her image has stayed with me and the effect she radiated.
With her own magical blend of graciousness and restraint, she
transformed a sometimes awkward, never completely relaxed social event into something festive and gay."[22]

Mildred continued the practice she had begun at the university—socializing with students after class, which included walks in
the Tiergarten and conversation in the Romanisches Café, a famous gathering spot for Berlin's intellectuals.[23] Samson Knoll, although not a student at the BAG, was a member of her English
Club. Knoll, who later became an American professor, kept notes
on his weekly encounters with her. Sometimes they walked home
together. They always used the polite "Sie." "Yet," he wrote, "there
seemed to be absolutely no barrier between us. From the start
there was an understanding between us which we never discussed,
but which made the airing of ideas and sentiments easy and natural. . . . Our long conversations took place in an atmosphere of
complete mutual understanding and trust. Mildred's openness and
her genuine interest in people were important factors."[24] Mildred
was "a very quiet and calm type but this calmness was not somehow cold, but the opposite. She had a very warm personality."
Arvid was "quite friendly," he recalled, and "although they were
not particularly demonstrative toward each other, there seemed to
be an intimate understanding between them."

Fall 1932 was a period of cadres, cells, and study circles as
Communists and Nazis continued their "ideological struggle" to
win over Social Democratic workers in the November election.
There were Nazi camps and the Marxist evening schools. Maria-
Dorothea Beck remembered meeting with fellow students and

teachers at the Harnacks', where they studied Marxist topics—the crisis of capitalism and the planned economy of the Soviet Union. Arvid's brother Falk recalled a seminar conducted by Arvid in a restaurant close to the Alexanderplatz. In a letter, Mildred confirmed that Arvid "has been speaking a good deal in public lately on the present crisis."[25]

In a bizarre turn of events, shortly before the November elections, the Communists, with suicidal cynicism, joined with the Nazis in calling a transportation strike. In Moscow's view, the Social Democrats, not the NSDAP, were the true enemies; indeed, according to Ernst Thälmann, the leader of the German Communist Party, the Social Democrats were not even democrats; they were "social fascists." By now fully under Moscow's control, the KPD grievously underestimated Hitler, believing it could use him to destroy the last remnants of capitalism. "Not a single streetcar or subway train is operating in Berlin," Joseph Goebbels, soon to be the new propaganda minister, gloated in his diary.[26]

It appeared at first that the Communists had outflanked their adversaries when the Nazis received an unexpected setback in the November elections, losing 2 million votes and thirty-four seats in the Reichstag. The resurgent Communists gained 750,000 votes, capturing one hundred seats. On November 7 at the Soviet embassy, more than 1,000 guests celebrated their victory and the fifteenth anniversary of the revolution. The Harnacks, by now frequent embassy visitors, were very likely among them.

Mildred's improved morale was evident in her Christmas letter to her mother: "My life is proving more and more interesting and worthwhile as the months roll on. . . . the world unfolds swiftly and constantly [with] so many new and attractive—indeed, fascinating aspects—that I must feel that this time is the richest thus far."[27] She was even more optimistic on a note scribbled on a card dated January 29, 1933: "There's so much to work for in the world nowadays. Never have [there] been more glorious prospects. . . . I'm thirty years old and a free woman—I have the work I want, there are no insurmountable obstacles to advancing in it. . . . life is good."[28]

The very next day, Hitler came to power.

Communist election gains made the nationalist right more willing to take a chance on Hitler. When Franz von Papen failed to form a government, a last effort to block Hitler was attempted by the man who was the power behind Hindenburg's throne, General Kurt von Schleicher, the last chancellor of Weimar Germany. But Schleicher's attempt to form a coalition backed by the army failed. After two days of negotiations, on January 30, the doddering eighty-five-year-old Hindenburg appointed Hitler chancellor. The same afternoon Hitler met with his coalition cabinet, whose conservatives were supposed to restrain their headstrong leader.

With the password "Grandmother Is Dead" the Nazis launched their reign with a gigantic torchlight parade of SA and SS men up the Wilhelmstrasse. From their vantage point in front of the chancellery, Arvid and his stepnephew, Wolfgang Havemann, watched as the endless sea of brown and black uniforms passed with 20,000 blazing torches. The two men saw Hitler lean forward from the illuminated open window to bask in the adulation of his followers. They watched Hitler respond to shouts of *Heil* and *Deutschland Erwache* (Germany awake) with the salute borrowed from Mussolini. They heard the chorus of thousands of voices singing the German national anthem—*Deutschland, Deutschland über Alles*. Then standing behind Havemann, Arvid said quietly, "Look at them closely, those are butcher types. With their straps fastened and their daggers they are capable of anything. You'll see, with their torches they'll set first Germany and then Europe ablaze. Just wait, soon they'll have you in uniform." (Harnack was right. In May, while still a university student, Havemann was put into the first of a half-dozen uniforms that he was to wear during the Third Reich.)[29]

The entry for January 31 in Goebbels's diary was also prophetic: "In a conference with the Führer we lay down the line for the fight against the Red terror. For the moment we shall abstain from direct countermeasures. The Bolshevik attempt at revolution must first burst into flame. At the proper moment we shall strike."[30] The way was prepared for that moment four days later, when Hindenburg granted his new chancellor what had been refused to Schleicher—the dissolution of the Reichstag, so that a general election could take place on March 5.

Samson Knoll recalled the questions Mildred asked in the month after Hitler assumed power: "What do you believe? What can one do? What will you do if? What will Germany do?" "She was opposed [to the Nazis] from the very first day," Knoll remembered. "It was no accident that she got involved in the resistance." Knoll was Jewish and decided to leave. The Harnacks provided precious moral support. He kept up his visits until the end of May: "It was always a consolation to be with her . . . you had someone with whom you could talk without fear. It was very important."[31]

Unlike many of their class, the Harnacks, Delbrücks, and Bonhoeffers took Hitler's accession with deadly seriousness. As the psychiatrist Karl Bonhoeffer subsequently wrote: "From the start, the victory of National Socialism in 1933 and Hitler's appointment as German chancellor was in our view a misfortune—the whole family agreed on this. In my own case, I disliked and mistrusted Hitler because of his demagogic propaganda methods . . . his habit of driving about the country carrying a riding crop, his choice of colleagues—with whose qualities, incidentally, we in Berlin were better acquainted than people elsewhere—and finally because of what I heard from professional colleagues about his psychopathic symptoms."[32]

Arvid was quick to criticize those who saw Hitler as a harmless buffoon. "Gentlemen," he said, "this is not a comedy that is being prepared but a great tragedy, not only for Germany but also for mankind!"[33]

On February 1, 1933, Dietrich Bonhoeffer gave a talk on the Berlin radio entitled "the Younger Generation's Changed View of the Concept of Führer." He made no secret of his contempt for the narcissism of youth and the vanity of old fools, warning his listeners that "the image of the leader will gradually become the image of the 'misleader.'" Bonhoeffer did not finish; his microphone was abruptly cut off.[34]

On the evening of February 27, while Soviet diplomats watched from the windows of their nearby embassy, the Reichstag mysteriously burned.[35] Although historians still debate its political motives, the blaze indisputably gave Hitler the pretext he needed to eliminate the Communists. Within three hours, the flames were under control, but Hitler persuaded Hindenburg to issue an emergency decree. From that moment—in fact, until the German surrender on May 8, 1945—all the civil rights guaranteed by the

Weimar constitution were abrogated. Freedom of speech and press, rights of association and assembly, privacy of mail and telephone communications, and freedom from searches were suspended indefinitely. The decree made the betrayal of military secrets or even the spreading of false reports an act of treason. Treason now included the production, dissemination, or possession of writings that called for uprisings or strikes or that were "in other ways treasonable." A further decree allowed the government to carry out the death sentence by hanging, which many Germans viewed as a particularly dishonorable method of execution.[36]

Within hours of the fire, the police arrested 4,000 Communists, banned leftist newspapers, and ransacked their offices.

On March 4, the day before the general election, Hitler broadcast a final plea to the voters from Königsberg in East Prussia, which was heard on loudspeakers posted on streets throughout Germany. Still, despite a massive Nazi propaganda campaign and acts of terror directed against them, the Communists still captured 12 percent of the vote.

On March 9, the 288 seats won by the Communists were declared invalid. Their delegates were prevented from taking their seats and arrest warrants were issued, forcing the party leaders to emigrate or go underground.

On March 21, Munich newspapers announced the establishment of Germany's first concentration camp, at Dachau, approximately twelve miles from the Bavarian capital, for the Communists, Social Democrats, and trade unionists who had been rounded up. Although police records are incomplete, in Prussia alone during March and April there were about 25,000 arrests.

Near the Harnack apartment, across from Tempelhof Airport, a detention center known as Columbia House became notorious. One of the Harnack friends held there was Paul Massing, a member of ARPLAN, who was questioned about his Communist connections, beaten, and then sent on to Oranienburg concentration camp.

Another SA detainee would in years ahead become entwined in the lives of the Harnacks. He was Harro Schulze-Boysen, the twenty-three-year-old editor of a banned leftist periodical, *Gegner* (Opponent). Politically active since his gymnasium days, Schulze-Boysen had belonged to the Jungdeutsche Orden, a nationalistic utopian youth movement. He had developed into an outspoken revolutionary who, in his desire to unite activists on both the left and right of the political spectrum, held discussion meetings in restaurants.[37] Schulze-Boysen was arrested for the first time on March 3, 1933. On a postcard to his parents he wrote: "Just spent a day and night in jail. With no reason given, crammed along with fifty-five others into a dark, overheated cellar. Nasty tricks. Just got out. I met marvelous people during these hours. So: now more than ever!"[38] Schulze-Boysen named no coworkers, shunned political statements, and was released.

Schulze-Boysen and his friends planned to join the May Day parade, which the National Socialists proclaimed as "the first holiday of national labor." By carrying a large sign reading "*Gegner* Editorial Staff," the dissidents hoped to attract attention and new supporters. On April 26, probably tipped off by an informer, a squad of SS men interrupted the meeting of the *Gegner* staff and beat and arrested its participants.[39] They were thrown into "a diminutive cellar, rigged up like a police post," Adrien Turel, one of those arrested, later wrote. "There was straw on the bare floor and large republican flags served as bedclothes. We had to lie down with the lights on."[40]

Turel, a writer, philosopher, and Swiss national, was released, but Schulze-Boysen and a friend, Henry Erlanger, were forced between ranks of SA men who beat them with lead-weighted whips. Erlanger, a half-Jew, died soon afterward from the beatings. Schulze-Boysen, showing the defiant recklessness he would forever display, having passed three times through the gauntlet, returned a fourth time "naked, gasping, bleeding, desperate," for a "victory lap." He clicked his heels together and taunted his torturers: "Reporting for duty! Order carried out plus one for luck." This impressed his captors, who declared: "Man, you really belong with us."[41]

Schulze-Boysen was released through the efforts of his mother, who went to the police president, Admiral von Levetzow, a naval colleague and friend of her husband's. She recalled: "What a sight he was! Deathly pale, with dark shadows under his eyes, his hair hacked off by garden shears, no buttons left on his suit."[42] A friend who spent the night with Schulze-Boysen reported that his back was covered with whip marks and swastikas had been carved into his thigh with a knife.[43] Ernst von Salomon, who wrote for the *Gegner*, saw him shortly after his release and failed to recognize him: "He looked very different . . . he had lost half an ear and there were red cuts on his face that had scarcely healed." Schulze-Boysen told Salomon: "I have put my revenge on ice."[44]

In February, Mildred tried to reassure her mother about her recent trip to Russia. Afraid that her mother heard only "false news" in the American press, she promised to send "some real information" to her in English immediately. Her next letter, in March, aimed at reassuring her mother while cautioning her to be discreet: "Our curious ideas are not known here. We are not active politically. We are safe, very well, and happy. Who would bother himself about two students sitting off in a corner and thinking thoughts about the future of the world? So don't feel any worry about us at all. And best keep still. If any one asks you about us, we are not interested in the world from a political but from a scientific standpoint. That's all you need to say. You see, we are harmless and quiet people."[45]

In March, ARPLAN was disbanded and its membership lists destroyed. Many distinguished members, among them Germany's leading Soviet experts, fled abroad. ARPLAN's president, Professor Friedrich Lenz, came under sharp attack at Giessen, where the local SS (the *Schutzstaffel* or Black Shirts) condemned him as "a Communist closely tied to Moscow" and "a perpetrator of Marxist ideas." His house was raided and his lectures suspended. In September he was discharged "because of political unreliability" from the Hessian state service.[46]

Because of Gestapo raids, it was dangerous to have written anything that implied sympathy for the Soviet Union. Arvid's book on the Soviet Union, which had been completed and set into type by Rowohlt, was canceled and the printing plates destroyed.[47] According to Martha Turner, when Hitler assumed power, the Harnacks gave the Turners another manuscript to be hidden in their rooms at the American Church—Arvid's second book on the Marxist labor movement in the United States—the culmination of his work with John R. Commons, which he had written in hopes of obtaining a professorship. "They were very afraid," recalled Martha Turner. "The very fact that they gave us the manuscript meant that they were very careful. We felt the less we talked about it the better it would be."

By then, the church itself was closely watched. Martha Turner recalled that two Nazis attended every service and meeting. Among American parishioners, there was concern about the church's involvement in German politics. Pastor Turner's outspokenness, according to his successor, "in an inflamed situation, while delighting some, made others nervous." Although Turner had done "a magnificent piece of work," he was "too active, social, and prophetic for some of his parishioners."[48] He was recalled. When the couple returned to the United States in 1934, they brought Arvid's manuscript with them.[49]

Dicke Luft! is the expression Berliners use for situations in which it is wise to adopt a low profile. Arvid's political beliefs were too well-known in Berlin, and in March the Harnacks left town: "We have come to a little woods outside Berlin today where it is quieter."[50] They stayed in a small country hotel and Mildred devoted herself to writing. Things looked grim for the Harnacks. Arvid abandoned his academic hopes and took a job as a lawyer assisting Klaus Bonhoeffer, the corporate counsel for Lufthansa, while he prepared to take his second state examination to qualify for the civil service.

On April 1, Hitler called for a boycott of all Jewish stores and on April 7 he proclaimed the first Aryan law for the "reconstruction" of the civil service; Jewish administrators and lawyers were suspended. Subsequent decrees restricted the practice of Jewish doctors and limited the number of Jewish children admitted to schools. In the Harnack family circle, the talk was about Dietrich and Klaus Bonhoeffer's grandmother, then ninety-one, who imperiously walked through the SA cordon and violated the boycott of the Jewish-owned department store, the almost empty KaDeWe. Dietrich and Klaus met with an American visitor, Rabbi Stephen Wise, to discuss how to disseminate the truth about what was happening.[51] Dietrich, now teaching at the University of Berlin, began forming a circle that would become the core of a resistance group within the Protestant Confessional Church.

Those Jews who could prepared to emigrate. Mildred's friend Samson Knoll asked her to help a Berlin relative, a furrier. This furrier had a young partner named Alfred Futran, whose father had been a Communist journalist. One day Knoll appeared, explaining, "You have American contacts. Futran has to leave. Can you do anything?" Mildred listened but was completely noncommittal: she could not promise anything. She did not know what could be done, but she would talk to somebody at the American embassy. Suddenly Futran was gone, but Knoll saw him a few weeks later in Paris. He had gotten out. Knoll surmised that Mildred intervened on Futran's account with her friend, the U.S. Consul, George Messersmith. This would be the first of Mildred's discreet and timely interventions on behalf of those desperate to flee Germany.

The same spring, *Gleichschaltung,* the nationwide "putting into the same gear," descended on the school system. Persons of political unreliability and non-Aryan descent were *beurlaubt,* permanently suspended. Mildred waited anxiously as Easter vacation was prolonged while the BAG sought to preserve its future. During April, the traditional final exam period at the Abendgymnasium, half the faculty of twenty-four was dismissed, including four teachers who customarily prepared and supervised the graduation exams. The "great historical events" of 1933 had propelled the school into what was described by the new, accommodationist principal as a dynamic age of "powerful becoming." Mildred attended incessant conferences and was hurriedly assigned students. A special cell of the National Socialist German Student Association was founded to encourage students to "energetically follow the ideals of the new state." The "outspoken liberal-democratic tradition" of the founders of the BAG, deemed a "totally faded ideology," was exorcised.[52]

In a May letter to her mother, Mildred adopted a crude code— she meant the opposite of what she said—to praise events in Russia and condemn those in Germany. It illustrates the contortions to which she resorted before abandoning political comments entirely: "Yesterday there was an enormous May Day celebration here. How beautiful it was. Thousands, thousands, and thousands of people marched in order singing and playing through the majestic streets which radiate from our home. . . . there is a great impulse in masses of people which can be roused. . . . You know that I thought this impulse was directed rightly in the war and I think it is being directed rightly in the same way now. That is, it is being given the right motives . . . You remember what I said about the lonely lives in 'Winesburg Ohio'—that they need a society in which love is freer, not hindered by fear and selfishness." She writes that this love is expressed in the "sounds of marching feet," of a whole people moving collectively "towards the sun." But it could be "perverted like it is in Russia today." Mildred compared the false patriotism of Nazi Germany to what had occurred in America in 1917, concluding (again saying the opposite of what she means): "Here as in our country in 1917 it is being used rightly, as I have said: vs. the Jews, the radicals (especially those connected with Russia), against machinery; obedience of the wife to the husband, for the winning back of the old German colonies so that capital can expand. . . . Well, it is a very beautiful, serious thing—serious as death—and I hope it will never be perverted again! Think this over, for I want you to understand me."[53]

On May 10, the National Socialists staged a literary auto da fé in the large square facing the main building of Berlin University and adjacent to the State Opera House. Singing "students," 30,000 strong, carrying the by now familiar torches, marched down Unter den Linden where Dr. Goebbels, once a neglected author himself, oversaw the "cleansing of German literature of alien elements." On a gasoline-soaked log pyre, the "students" burned 20,000 works by Jews and other undesirables, books by Freud, Marx, Einstein, Tucholsky, Remarque, Heine, Thomas Mann and Heinrich Mann. Professors from the university, some wearing their caps and gowns, looked on at the blaze in the Opernplatz. The German Student Association had initiated the action, which won the support of the faculty, including Mildred's former colleagues.

In June, Mildred joined the National Socialist teachers' organization, the first of many compromises the Harnacks were forced to make. On June 9, the new principal addressed the faculty and students at the BAG graduation ceremony. Standing in front of the Nazi flag, he spoke of the "new recruits who were welcome replacements for the grown up troops," the graduates. The leaders of the German people, Professor Stecher stated, knew that it was in the schools that the "national and social destiny of the German people will be decided." With this in mind, they have laid a "massive hand" on all the places where "the German future" will be formed.[54]

NINE

Hostess

Heinrich-Maria Ledig-Rowohlt, Martha Dodd, Mildred
and Hans Fallada

T he reader may remember Martha Dodd from Mildred's intelligence files as the cohostess of "those now legendary tea parties that were such social events in the 1930s." With the discovery of Martha Dodd, my quest for Mildred took a sudden swerve. I hope the reader will forgive a long digression, for the story of Martha Dodd's friendship with Mildred deserves a special chapter.

October 30, 1941, Wolfsschanze, Hitler's East Prussian headquarters. The Führer is at dinner with his private secretary, Martin Bormann. Also present are Walter Hewel, the Foreign Ministry's personal representative to the Führer, Hitler's chief of staff, Field Marshal Wilhelm Keitel, and Vice Admiral Karl Jesko von Puttkamer, aide-de-camp to Hitler. The discussion concerns Hitler's requirements for an up-to-date foreign service, one that includes a half-dozen attachés able to seduce influential women.

Hitler says, "To think that there was nobody in all this ministry who could get his clutches on the daughter of the former American ambassador, Dodd—and yet she wasn't difficult to approach. That was their job, and it should have been done. In short, the girl should have been subjugated. She was, but unfortunately by others. Nothing to be surprised at, by the way: how would these senile old men of the Wilhelmstrasse have behaved in the ranks? It's the only way. In the old days when we wanted to lay siege to an industrialist, we attacked him through his children. Old Dodd, who was an imbecile, we'd have got him through his daughter. But, once again, what can one expect from people like that?"

Keitel inquires, "Was she pretty at least?"

Von Puttkamer answers, "Hideous!"

Hitler continues, "But one must rise above that, my dear fellow. It's one of the qualifications. Otherwise, I ask you, why should our diplomats be paid? In that case, diplomacy would no longer be a service, but a pleasure. And it might end in marriage!"[1]

From the *New York Times* morgue, a set of grainy clips. The first, dated 1979, shows a couple identified as the exiled Americans Mr. and Mrs. Alfred Stern. The sixty-something woman is the daughter of the controversial Ambassador William E. Dodd; the elderly man is a millionaire, Alfred Stern. The U.S. Justice Department has just dropped charges of espionage against the couple. Next, the flash-bulbs of photographers underscore the uncertain lighting at a press conference in 1957. The Sterns have just arrived in Prague from Mexico with their nine-year-old son, Robert, on Paraguayan passports, thereby escaping extradition to the United States to stand trial on three counts of espionage, the maximum penalty being death. They are happy, they say, to be in a haven safe from the prying eyes of the FBI. The article describes Martha as "a gay, vivacious, and still very attractive woman who once had a future; but now," the reporter says, "she has only a past."[2] Wanted by the Justice Department in connection with the Soble spy case, a minor sensation at the time, the Sterns have fled to Communist Czechoslovakia. Meanwhile Stern's former business partner, Boris Morros, a Russian spy turned FBI informant, is testifying before a federal grand jury and implicating the Sterns as participants in a Soviet spy network.

From another group of photos, one dated 1948 shows a smiling Martha at a fund-raiser for Henry Wallace, formerly Roosevelt's vice president, now the Progressive Party's presidential candidate. Others show the Sterns with likeminded prominent leftists of the postwar period—Lillian Hellman and Paul Robeson. Next we see a glamorous Martha standing next to producer Otto Preminger in Hollywood, where she has gone to make a film based on her best-selling memoir of Nazi Germany, *Through Embassy Eyes*. The last pictures show a Miss Dodd in Berlin during the 1930s: with her parents cozying up to the fireplace in the ambassador's residence, dancing with Hohenzollern Prince Louis Ferdinand, greeting Joseph Goebbels, captivating foreign correspondents William Shirer and Louis Lochner at the Foreign Press Ball.

October 1989, the Alcron Hotel. The biographer is in Prague hoping to see the now widowed Mrs. Alfred Stern. It is shortly before the "Velvet Revolution," which felled the Czech Communist regime. These are the heady days of glasnost. *During the summer, thousands of East Germans have fled west through Hungary. Now, Erich Honecker has persuaded the Czechs to close their border with Hungary. Consequently, hundreds of thwarted East Germans have climbed the walls of the West German embassy across the Moldau River in Prague, hoping to gain visas to the West.*

The voice on the telephone is softly southern, betraying Martha Dodd's Virginia roots. "No," she says firmly, she will not see me. I plead. I will call her several times over the next few days. She is "too sick," "too tired," and finally she "just doesn't want to talk about the old times in Berlin."

She does tell me that she met Mildred at the Lehrter train station in Berlin, "with the American Women's Club, she was a member. They met us when we arrived in Berlin. My father was arriving to take up his post as ambassador. I must have met her then."

Maybe she could solve one mystery. Mildred and Martha wrote a newspaper column together. It was signed Wesley Repor. Who then, I ask, was Wesley Repor?

"I was Wesley Repor. I used an alias. Mildred used her own name."

I ask about letters. Does she have any from Mildred? She did. But she has sent them all to East Germany. I will find them there. But where? She doesn't remember.[3]

"How did you find out what happened to the Harnacks?" I venture.

"After the war, I heard something. I must have gotten a letter. . . . really, I don't know anything about the Red Orchestra." Her categorical statement is disappointing but not unexpected.

As we are living through the tense final days before the collapse of Communism, the crackling on the line stimulates my paranoia— quite possibly the wires running from the Alcron Hotel under the Moldau to Martha Dodd Stern's suburban villa are tapped.

I telephone Martha Dodd again from Berlin in the summer of 1990. A close friend of hers has written ahead on my behalf. Maybe in the changed atmosphere since the demise of the Cold War she will see me. "No." She is adamant that she will not see me but she will answer my questions should I care to write.

When I return home I compose a long list of questions but before I can mail it, I pick up the New York Times *on August 29, 1990, and read the headline on the obituary page, "Martha Dodd Stern Is Dead at 82; Author and an Accused Soviet Spy."*

Nevertheless, her death results in an unexpected windfall: thirty volumes of her 10,400-page FBI file are released detailing the bureau's suspicions that the Sterns had funded Boris Morros's music publishing company to the tune of $130,000. This company, its

proprietor claimed, was a front behind which the Russians in-
tended to conduct an international courier operation, funneling
U.S. secrets to the Soviet Union. The restrictions on the Dodd
family's personal papers at the Library of Congress covering their
years in Berlin are also lifted. I phone Dodd's executor in Prague,
asking if she remembers seeing any papers about Mildred. By a
stroke of luck, she recalls that indeed there are two memoirs
locked away. She will send them. The first turns out to be the start
of a memoir about Mildred; the second, Martha's reminiscences of
a long-ago affair with a Russian diplomat.

Martha began her memoir of Mildred with the words: "The
years we knew each other were the most significant in my life.
Our work, our experiences, in those brave tragic years full of ac-
complishment and frustration are closely woven together. Every-
thing we thought about, loved, hated, fought for, we shared to-
gether. We, all of us, my husband, were in the German
underground from 1933 to 1943. I am the only one left."[4]

July 13, 1933. Mildred and other members of the American
Women's Club are gathered on the platform of the Lehrter train
station awaiting the arrival of the American ambassador-
designate, William E. Dodd, and his family. In newspaper photographs, the elder Dodds minus their son Bill—then driving the
family Chevrolet from Hamburg—stand in bashful discomfort.
Martha appears as she was—young, fresh, confident—smartly
dressed in dark traveling clothes, her hat cocked at a suitably
jaunty angle.

Aged twenty-four, Martha already had a "dark secret" (a de-
serted husband, a New York banker), and a stateside fan club
consisting of publisher Alfred Harcourt, professor and liberal activist Robert Morss Lovett, and writers Carl Sandburg and Thornton Wilder.[5] As the only daughter of Roosevelt's ambassador,
Martha was determined to capture Berlin—and she did. What
Alma Mahler Gropius Werfel, in her insatiable pursuit of famous
men, was to the dreamy years of *fin de siècle* Vienna, Martha
would be to the nightmare years in Berlin. Soon princes, the press,
members of the foreign diplomatic corps, and acolytes of three
secret services would be at her carefully shod feet.

Self-described in a letter she wrote to Otto Preminger, Martha was "attractive, blonde, high-spirited, romantic and vivacious, just out of college (the Margaret Sullivan type)."[6] A school chum and lifelong friend, Letitia Ide Ratner, recalled Martha as "the class Scarlett O'Hara . . . an enchantress—luscious and blonde, with luminous blue eyes and pale, translucent skin."[7] Martha was bright and talented. She was also impulsive and indiscreet and would acquire a Byronesque reputation of being mad, bad, and dangerous to know. Riding in the embassy car across the Spree River past the Tiergarten to the Hotel Esplanade on the Bellevuestrasse, she committed the first of what were to be many indiscretions. Passing the Reichstag, which had been partly burned a few months before, she blurted, "Oh, I thought it was burned down! It looks all right to me. Tell me what happened." The young protocol secretary chastised her, giving advice she would seldom follow: "Young lady you must learn to be seen and not heard. You mustn't say so much and ask so many questions. This isn't America and you can't say all the things you think."[8]

This habit of saying what they thought was a Dodd family trait, one that would get the ambassador and his two chronically garrulous offspring into situations embarrassing to the State Department. Dodd was a democrat with a small and large *d*, somewhat in the Jeffersonian mold, a distinguished historian and professor at the University of Chicago. But Berlin in 1933 was a difficult and delicate post, unsuited to Dodd's outspoken temperament. Dodd had courage but little comprehension of the tribal codes of diplomacy, and he lacked tact, a disabling flaw. His spontaneous gestures—heiling Hitler as well as George Messersmith, the U.S. Consul General, on the street—drove his staff to apoplexy.[9]

A self-made man determined to live on his $17,500 a year salary, he disdained protocol. His democratic instincts made him loathe pomp in most circumstances. He made an instant enemy of his deputy, Counselor George Gordon. A few weeks after his arrival, Dodd began sending letters home criticizing Gordon's spendthrift ways. (*En famille*, the Dodds called the State Department the "$ Department.")[10] Foreign embassies were not spared. Dodd's posthumously published diaries contain many shocked references to the extravagance of the representatives of Italy and France, whose governments were remiss in paying war debts to the United States. Even the proletarian officials of the Soviet Union came in for criticism, since dinners at their embassy on Unter den Linden were served on solid silver plates.[11] Dodd never learned that knotty political and economic problems might be more readily dispatched around the "white table" than at the diplomatic "green table." Often falling asleep or leaving early, Dodd seems to have gleaned little information on these official occasions, obtaining news instead from professorial cronies and friends in the press corps.

Martha and Bill also found the embassy crowd stuffy and they, in her words, were soon making "merry with newspaper people and a few stray counts and princes."[12] By hosting all-night parties soon after their arrival, Martha and Bill became the center of a hard-drinking, fast-moving international set. Agonizingly frugal and conscientious in his own conduct (Dodd bragged about his ability to give a reception for two hundred people with only one bottle of gin), the ambassador was indulgent of or indifferent to his children's excesses. Distaste and distrust were mutual and soon the embassy and consular staffs were reporting home on the escapades of the Dodd offspring.

The Harnacks naturally welcomed the New Deal, which provided so many of the Wisconsin Friday Niters with important administrative roles, and they welcomed the new ambassador. Like many Germans in his circle, Arvid, embittered by Versailles, distrusted both the French and the British, but his admiration for the United States and President Roosevelt never wavered. Ambassador Dodd, who would be faulted by his staff for preferring the company of German academics to diplomats, was immediately attracted to the couple bearing the distinguished Harnack name.

Dodd recorded in his diary that on August 18, 1933, "40 representatives of the American Women's Club of Berlin came to pay their respects and to listen to Mr. Gordon talk a little about the situation in Germany under Nazi rule."[13] It was probably at this reception that the friendship between Martha and Mildred began.

> I have tried earnestly and without success to recall the exact details of our first personal contact: the place, the time, and what we said or did (Martha wrote in her memoir of Mildred). What is important is that her fair strong face, her beautiful voice and deliberate thoughtful words are closely inter-

woven with those brave tragic days as to be inextricably a part of my own life and growth, to bring memories that are both saddening and strengthening. . . . I was drawn to her immediately. I knew intimately no other woman in Germany who possessed such sincerity and singleness of purpose. . . . Until I knew her I never really understood the frequent and often loosely applied phrase delicacy and strength. She was slow to speak and express opinions; she listened quietly, her large grey blue eyes serious (severe but warm), weighing, evaluating, trying to understand. She was never glib, never sarcastic at someone else's expense, never hasty nor bigoted. When she did speak she commanded attention. Her words were cautious, persuasive, charged with unobtrusive but incontrovertible logic.[14]

Martha, a fellow midwesterner, likewise intrigued Mildred. Soon she was writing to her mother about the ambassador's daughter. "She writes literary criticism and short stories; at bottom she is clear and capable and has a real desire to understand the world. Therefore our interests touch and we are going to try working together somewhat . . . I am very happy to find a woman who is seriously interested in writing. It's a hindrance to be lonely and isolated in one's work. Ideas stimulate ideas, and the love of writing is contagious. . . . I want to work hard now, having this stimulus."[15]

After she became bored and left college, Martha reviewed books for the *Chicago Tribune*. Her mentor and presumed lover, Carl Sandburg, urged her to write, to "make many notes in any humpty-dumpty style whatever what is useless can easily be sifted out later and the doing of paragraphs has a practice value . . . give way to every beckoning to write short things impressions sudden lyric sentences you have a gift for outpouring." He implored her to "find out what this man Hitler is made of, what makes his brain go round, what his bones and blood are made of." He told her that "before your eyes will pass the greatest pageant of crooks and gangsters, idealists, statesmen, criminals, diplomats, and geniuses. . . . Watch them, study them, dissect them."[16]

Thornton Wilder, who called Martha "my girl" and whose

picture she wore in a locket, told her to keep a diary of "what things looked like—the rumors, and opinions of people during a political time . . . Such a diary would 5–10–25 years from now be of the liveliest interest to you and—oh my God—to me." He cautioned against journalism: "I don't think (humbly offered) that you should engage in journalistic work not, I should imagine that signed or found out, it would shock people," but rather because, Wilder continued, "your concentration on your own stories would go to smithereens under hackwork."[17]

Nevertheless, two months later, Martha was writing Wilder that "Mrs. Harnack-Fish and I are going to edit a book column every fortnight on the *Berlin Topics*, the only English paper here. It is lousy. But we might be able to build up a little colony in the English-speaking group here. I mean following. Get people together who like books and authors. And then the books we would get too. I am taking it up with Alfred Harcourt. He sent me Gertrude Stein. Superb isn't it?"[18]

Their short-lived column "Brief Reviews" in *Berlin Topics* began with a review of two books, *Saturday Night at the Greyhound* and *O Providence*, by John Hampson, a male nurse who had become London's literary sensation. The minor Bloomsburyite had been a recent lecturer at the American Women's Club. Mildred's tastes ran toward proletarian writers like Albert Halper, the author of *Union Square*; Martha, using the pseudonym Wesley Repor, preferred the experiments of Kay Boyle.[19]

For Martha, the column was no substitute for writing short stories, which she continued with Mildred's encouragement. Martha was a stylish but undisciplined writer who stayed out all night and rose only in the afternoon. Mildred urges Martha to "write, write, write"[20] and suggests working holidays in a friend's house on a lake near Biebow in Brandenburg where they could be alone. Mildred described the small estate where she and Arvid spent occasional weekends as "very simple," its quiet rooms spacious "like those of a country palace," or "a hunting lodge of Goethe's time."[21] She suggested to Martha that they take typewriters and share the cost of the trip: "Do you still like Deutsches Beefsteak [hamburgers]? Do you like beer in old steins on a big scrubbed wooden table with wurst or frankfurters and flowers from the garden and candle-light shed from old hammered brass holders? Do you like tea under fruit-trees in the garden?"[22]

For Mildred, the column was an extension of the popular lectures on contemporary American writers she was already giving at such Anglo-American haunts as the Longfellow and the American Women's Club. She enjoyed the talks because they made her a quick study; she now read books with a new "intensity and swiftness." Her prose style was also changing, "becoming simpler and clear," she writes, which is "a blessing."[23] Mildred, less talented and lacking Martha's sure voice was adept, thanks to Arvid's prodding, at using her time well. She confides to Martha that she is thinking of pursuing creative writing, feeling "that the richness of life in the last few years ought, as you say, to be material for it." She shows Martha the sketches she has written about the "one most beautiful year" of her life in Wisconsin. "Arvid," she writes, "says we'll keep them for our grandchildren."[24] Martha's criticism, she assures her friend, helps her. "It shows a gift in you. I shall change the points you put your finger on and send it off as you say—to your literary agent. . . . What is her name and address?"[25]

Having children seemed to be very much on Mildred's mind and evidence suggests that around this time Mildred had an abortion, the first of several distressing experiences. During the Weimar era, the criminal code called for jail sentences for women who had abortions and for anyone aiding them. Even sharper measures prevailed after May 1933, and the number of abortions sank after laws preventing "acts of sabotage against Germany's racial future" were enacted. Birth control clinics were closed and *"Kinder, Kirche, Küche"* (children, church, kitchen) became the slogan of the thousand-year Reich.[26] A bachelor tax was enacted. There were loans to newlyweds, as well as allowances and child subsidies to parents with large families.

For "Aryan" couples like the Harnacks these incentives and proscriptions made abortion dangerous and illegal. When Mildred made a mysterious trip to England in the summer of 1933, her mother forwarded a check for the then considerable sum of $56 to a British doctor. She wrote her mother, "I am grateful for sending what you did to England. It's all right. Words about it are unnecessary. Please don't write anything more about it."[27] The precarious state of the Harnack finances, their dependence on Mildred's work as a teacher, and their doubts about their future in Hitler's Reich ensured that the Harnacks would postpone their family.

Mildred and Martha had many intimate conversations. In one of them, reported to her mother, Mildred characterized her attraction to and dependency on Arvid: "We [Martha and Mildred] recognized that there are personal contacts in life which, though dear, are destructive of one's creative force: such a one was mine with Harry [Turney-High]; but there are others which expand and strengthen one's ability to cope with life and understand the world more widely: such a one has been and is mine with my beloved Arvid."[28]

Throughout her years in Hitler's Germany, Mildred was an active, visible member of the American Women's Club, serving at one time as its president. Few groups were as active as the club, which was housed in comfortable rooms on the Bellevuestrasse near the American consulate. At its height in 1930, it listed over two hundred members.

It has now become fashionable to view women's clubs as elitist or, even more damning, foolish. The fashion shows, concerts, lectures, bridge, and teas that were regular features of every club-woman's life strike modern-day feminists as frivolous. But Berlin's club had a more serious side. In the early days of its creation, before the rise of Hitler, there was a committee charged with striving to promote peace that made "a serious and earnest attempt to bring the facts of the present needs and difficulties, particularly of the German people, to the attention of the folks at home."[29] By 1934, however, the main purpose of the club was to keep the ever more isolated expatriates in touch with their own culture. In later years, as more and more Americans left Germany, the club played an important and sustaining part in Mildred's life. As she became more and more threatened and isolated because of her resistance work, the American Women's Club would provide her with a refuge and a cover for her activities.

Members of the club paid only 1.50 marks for lunch and her lecture. Thus Mildred's pickings, added to the modest salary she received at the Abendgymnasium, were small. "Never, perhaps," she writes to her mother, "have I been so constantly busy, have had so many interests, have met so many interesting people . . . The only difficulty—and it is a great difficulty—is that for the present I receive practically no money for all this activity." In Germany because intellectual work had considerable status, it was so eagerly sought that "its market price was exceedingly low."[30] "Please excuse me for mentioning it," she pleads, "but I'm wondering whether anyone in the family has any clothes which she doesn't want and which I could have made over for me."[31] She had neglected appearance and felt at a disadvantage because she could not afford new clothes. She realized that the women in the club looked at her a bit "askance."[32] She reassures her mother that they are happy, adding that she is making ends meet by typing the manuscript of Ambassador Dodd's history of the Old South.[33]

Since Arvid's move to Berlin, the Harnacks had collected around themselves an informal circle that met in the two rooms of the fifth-floor Hasenheide apartment they sublet from a relative of the German writer Stefan Heym (who wrote in his postwar memoir, *Nachruf*, about meeting the "congenial but typical academic couple" who had "determined views on the mob which had come to power in Germany").[34] The regulars of the Harnack salon who came and went over the next few years consisted of several important publishers and editors—Samuel Fischer, Ernst Rowohlt, his son, Heinrich-Maria Ledig-Rowohlt, Max Tau, Ludwig Reindl and his wife, Edith; novelists and playwrights Ernst von Salomon, Max Mohr, Adam Kuckhoff, and Otto Zoff; translator Franz Fein; critic Erich Franzen; journalist Margret Boveri; and Mildred's students, particularly the young translator and writer Friedrich (Bodo) Schlösinger.[35]

Mildred left this description of one of her Saturday teas: "The lighted lamps and candles and flowers in the tower corner made our room lovely. We had a big tray of thin bread slices with butter and fine liverwurst, tomato slices, or cheese, brought up from the house where we eat, and it was supplemented by tiny cookies and a little dish of fruit." In a letter to Thornton Wilder, Martha described Mildred as "the kind of person who has the sense or nonsense to put a candle behind a bunch of pussy willows or *alpen rosen* [rhododendron]. Very poor and real and fine and not much in favor though the family is old and respected." In the same letter, Martha wrote enthusiastically about literary life in Berlin:

Rowohlt of Berlin is eager about my story so I think it will be translated into German and sold to some good magazine here. He has it, broodingly in his office. A lovely plump rosy cheeked Santa Claus of a man. Completely enchanting. His English reader [Ledig-Rowohlt] is surfacely shrewd and interesting. I meet the other important publisher, Fischer, on Monday by Arvid Harnack's. I have also met Max Mohr of whom you have heard if you don't actually know him. And at my last party I produced much to the astonishment (there was a little hushed gasping and whispering behind hands from the oh so proper gathering) of the diplomatic right set Ernst von Salomon! accomplice in the Rathenau murder and author of "The Outlaws." He is much worthwhile. Kurt Häuser is also about. But there is a sad lack of the old guard. However the Harnacks and I (since we have concluded we are the only people in Berlin genuinely interested in writers) conscientiously encourage all such free intellectual endeavor as there is left.[36]

There were several reasons for this salon, but the primary goal was very human: to get published. A second aim of these literary evenings was to forge the nucleus of a resistance network. If we look closely at the various circles to which Mildred belonged, they become the connecting links of a chain the Harnacks welded over a period of years into their resistance group.

Initially in Berlin, Mildred shared quarters with Arvid's congenial sister Inge, who was trying to eke out a living as a secretary. Then, divorced from her sculptor husband, Inge remarried Gustav Have-mann, a leading concert violinist and conservatory professor. It was in their home in Babelsberg that Gustav's son, Wolfgang Havemann, met Arvid and Mildred for the first time in 1931. The younger Havemann remembered Arvid quarreling with the violin-ist, "who was convinced of the mission of Hitler." (Gustav Have-mann had the dubious distinction of being listed in the Führer Lexikon, *the official handbook of prominent Nazis published in 1934.)*

Havemann, then a young lawyer, was a frequent visitor to the Harnacks, where after 1938, he participated in their "study eve-nings." In 1942, he was arrested and served a prison sentence be-cause of his resistance activities. After his release, he was wounded on the eastern front in 1943 and spent six years in Soviet prison camps. Interviewed in 1990 in Dresden, he added his observations on the subject of the Harnacks' friends:

"*Mildred knew several different circles of people. First there was the circle around the Berlin Abendgymnasium, that dated from around 1932—the circle that included Karl Behrens and Leo Skrzypczynski. Karl Behrens was a student of Mildred's at the Abendgymnasium whom they recruited for conspiratorial work. He followed them until the end. This was the group that Arvid built. Karl Behrens was a leftist, Leo Skrzypczynski was a businessman.*

"*The second circle was in the Hasenheide apartment. I was there once. It was a literary circle—editors, publishers, authors. It was a fixed day. In France it is called a salon. The idea was to become acquainted with new works. That was the second circle and it ended when the Harnacks moved.*[37]

"*The third circle was in Zehlendorf. There they had contacts with Greta and Adam Kuckhoff and the people around those two.*" *[Greta Lorke, the Harnacks' friend from Wisconsin had met and in 1937 would marry the dramaturge and playwright Adam Kuckhoff. In 1933, Greta returned to Berlin and from then on the Harnacks and the Kuckhoffs were closely linked.]* "*I didn't know that circle in Zehlendorf. In this system of work, there were very small circles. Our work in all these circles from the beginning was literary; it ended politically. And the more it became political, the more it became conspiratorial.*

"*Because Mildred was married to Arvid she also traveled in the expanded circle of his relatives in Grunewald, Zehlendorf, and in Neu Babelsberg, at the time Ufastadt [Berlin's Hollywood]. Gorky says, 'The poor and the rich have relatives.' But the poor Harnacks, Arvid among them, socialized with the rich Harnacks in the Grunewald.*

"*Finally, Mildred had the circle around the American Women's Club where she organized events. She also knew the American ambassador's daughter, Martha Dodd.*

"*There were other economic and political meetings conducted by Arvid. I met the president of I. G. Farben and business leaders from big corporations in Berlin. It was organized in the evenings. The work was divided and it served as a cadre school, a reservoir for gaining information.*

"*These were strong-willed persons, I was also one of them.*

When I was at Arvid's, I was a seventeen or eighteen-year-old student. Later, I was an officer. Through all this period, he led me and influenced me. Both the Harnacks were, if I may say it, Menschenjäger *people who hunt for other people. For example, when I got married, my wife was still in school. She was eighteen years old and immediately, Mildred contacted my wife. She influenced her as a student and, later on, politically. She was informed about contraception, for instance. They learned it from a Japanese professor. I don't want you to misunderstand, but it was their nature, loving people to attract others and to develop them. If they had had their own children, they could have invested this energy in their own family.*

"Mildred looked for people who were clean, ethical, noble . . . she looked for the worthwhile core in humans and she found it, even in me. One says in French les extrèmes se touchent — *opposites attract — but that's only half the truth. The other truth is that nobility attracts."*

Even with their salon, the Harnacks found meeting dissidents difficult because the persecution of the Jews together with *Gleichschaltung*—the policy of conformity introduced by the Hitler regime designed to eliminate opposition—had already made significant inroads into Germany's literary life. In 1933, a number of artists and writers were forced out of the Prussian Academy of Art, among them Henrich Mann and Käthe Kollwitz; others, among them Ricarda Huch, Alfred Döblin, Franz Werfel, and Thomas Mann, left willingly. Carl von Ossietzky and Erich Mühsam were arrested. When their books were burned, Bertolt Brecht, Ernst Toller, Kurt Tucholsky, and Leon Feuchtwanger emigrated. During these first years of the Nazi regime, the question of what to do—leave or stay and fight—and how and what to write was the preoccupation of many writers who were—more than artists and musicians—dependent on an untransferable language to reach and build an audience. Mildred experienced one author's dilemma firsthand in an encounter with Hans Fallada.

Fallada—the pseudonym of Rudolf Ditzen—was one of Germany's important writers, the author of an international bestseller, *Little Man, What Now?* Published by Rowohlt in 1932, it was made into a Hollywood movie. In the novel, Fallada examined the economic and political turmoil that beset ordinary Germans in Weimar Germany. Martha and Mildred were naturally eager to meet the author, "curious," as Martha observed, "to understand what was happening to a liberal writer who had seemed to understand at least a little of the struggle of simple people."[38] So when Fallada's editor, Ledig-Rowohlt, invited them along with Martha's beau, Boris Vinogradov, the handsome first secretary of the Soviet embassy, to meet Fallada on Sunday, May 27, 1934, they eagerly accepted.[39]

Fallada lived on a farm near the village of Carwitz in Mecklenburg, a beautiful district north of Berlin, to which he had retired after the Nazis seized power. The quartet made the three-hour trip in Boris's Ford cabriolet speeding along the chestnut-bordered roads, smelling the Maytime fragrance of acacias. Midway, as Martha wrote in *Through Embassy Eyes*, a sudden spring storm deluged them. Lightning turned the scene "wild and violent with color, intense electric green and violet, lavender and gray."[40]

The weather had cleared by the time they arrived at the lakeside cottage where Fallada lived with his wife and two children. Over coffee, Martha and Mildred spoke about America. Looking at the view over the North German lakes, they expressed a longing for their native cities—Milwaukee and Chicago—both situated along Lake Michigan. From Mildred's questions and Fallada's responses, Martha knew, even though her German was poor, that her friend was "gently probing his rationalization of his retirement." She reports in her unpublished memoir that he blushed, blustered, or maintained heavy abrupt silences.

Fallada's mood soon darkened when a heated discussion developed at lunch. Again the subject of emigration came up: was it necessary to leave Germany to write about it from an anti-Nazi point of view? After the meal, the women walked to the Bohnenwerder, the highest hill, while Fallada played chess with Ledig-Rowohlt. But to his publisher he seemed lost in thought. Didn't Mildred only repeat what Fallada had been asking himself lately? Can you adjust? Do you have to escape? Or is there a third way in the middle?

The two men discussed the public reception of Fallada's latest book. Not only had it not been confiscated but more than 20,000 copies were in print with new orders coming in. The foreword contained a "bow" to the SA, the "Brown Shirts, which might not have been necessary. The two Americans and Ledig-Rowohlt had discussed this in the car. Now Fallada reacted aggressively to Ledig's words. He resented the gossiping behind his back. It was easy for the women, one of whom was the daughter of the American ambassador, to talk. They had no idea what it is like for an author to await the possible banning of his book. Did the editor try to explain this to his friends? Ledig attempted to calm him. It was not meant that way. He was taking it too personally. The conversation ended. The women returned. As Fallada showed them his library and his sleeping infant son, his uneasiness and self-consciousness was apparent. It was time to leave. Boris took the ritual snapshots.

To Martha, Fallada seemed isolated, but apparently he was not a Nazi although she sensed "a certain resignation in his attitude." (Fallada remained in Germany, choosing the course of "inner emigration"—avoiding confrontation with the Nazis by picking politically neutral themes. After the war the Soviets made him the mayor of Feldberg but he died, shattered by his addiction to drugs and alcohol, in 1947.)

For her part, Mildred attempted to sound out Fallada. In her memoir of Mildred, Martha wrote that, although Mildred spoke of Fallada's cowardice and weakness that day on the way home, "she would not give him up; she never gave up any human being except for the minority of fanatic, brutal, hopeless Nazis. 'He has a conscience,' Mildred said about Fallada, 'and that is good. He is not happy, he is not a Nazi, he is not hopeless.' No matter how misled or ignorant a person he was, if he had any basic decency, she would cling to him and try to make him a better, thinking man. This approach to people was not only a result of the work she was able to do but was related to her infinite patience, love, and optimism. If such a thing were possible one almost might say that she was born to be a teacher. The meeting with Fallada made a permanent impression on me. I saw the stamp of naked fear on a writer's face—for the first time."[41]

During spring 1934, Arvid was often away. He was working in the law courts at Jena while studying for his state assessor's exam. On weekends in the spring and during the summer, Mildred joined him there.[42] It was in Jena that Mildred began, with her mother-in-law's help, to translate *Lust for Life*, Irving Stone's novelized biography of Vincent van Gogh for Universitas Publishers. Normally, translators translate into their mother tongue. Mildred was able to accomplish the rather unusual feat of translating into German with the help of her mother-in-law and her sister-in-law Inge. Explaining her method to her young Wisconsin nephew Bob, she writes, "I sit at the typewriter, the book beside me, she [Clara] sits close by so that she can see the book too. She is so witty and so quick that it goes much faster than when I work alone."[43]

Her own work also began to make its way before the German public. A Whitsuntide walk with Arvid through the Thuringian forests and meadows "deep purple with flowers or yellow with buttercups" inspired Mildred's impressionistic essay "Ripening Corn," one of the several that appeared in 1934 in a leading newspaper, the *Berliner Tageblatt*.[44] In it she reminisces about her childhood visits to her aunt's farm near an Indian reservation in Wisconsin, where she learned to love corn on the cob and popcorn. She uses this peculiarly American food as a symbol for the freedom, happiness, and hope which, she wrote, filled her homeland.[45] The theme of nature—the grass of New England, the cornfields of the Midwest—was one that Mildred would return to again and again. Regionalism was in vogue and her essays reflect this.

"Variations on the Theme: America" appeared in the *Tageblatt* in December 1934. Starting with a comparison of Hölderlin and Whitman, it is an essay on her personal pantheon of American poets—Whitman, Benét, Sandburg, and MacLeish. To Berliners unfamiliar with American literature, she expounded in effusive prose Frederick Jackson Turner's Frontier Thesis.* Whitman's song "was a conquering of the wild virgin soil." The War of Emancipation fed Stephen Vincent Benét's imagination: "the sober North, the gallant lost South . . . he took the landscapes, the cus-

---

*Frederick Jackson Turner (1861–1932), while a history professor at the University of Wisconsin, propounded his Frontier Thesis: "The existence of an area of free land, its continuous recession, and the advance of American settlement westward, explain American development." Turner maintained the frontier enabled Europe's underclass migrants to become independent property owners. During the 1930s, literary historians used Turner's idea to explain distinctive regional trends in American writing.

toms into his heart." Chicago poet Carl Sandburg loved the "vast prairie countryside of the Middle West" yet he lived in Chicago where in "the molten streams of the steel mills, the shoes of workers pock-marked with fiery cinders, in the specialized muscles of workers' shoulders, he saw the future."[46] From a relatively small capital of themes, husbanded carefully and loaned out many times in lectures, newspaper articles, and a doctoral dissertation, Mildred reaped some profit.

She was aware of her limitations as a writer. "My best field so far is literary criticism because I have experience there," she observed. "In the field of the article on things in general, or the story, I am not so good because I must learn two things: how to make other people live, and how to develop things to a climax and conclusion. I am a great egotist and always write about myself. This is an adolescent fault which I can now get over. I am old enough and experienced enough, am I not?"[47] "I am not a facile writer," she complained. "But practice will help me to become somewhat more so."[48]

Her Berlin life settled into a busy routine: lectures for journalist, literary critics, and university professors "under the patronage of the American Embassy," at the home of Klaus and Emmi Bonhoeffer, and twice a month at the American Woman's Club; teaching weekday evenings at the Abendgymnasium, afterward discussions and rehearsals for plays given by the English Club; Saturday there was the salon or the theater, concerts, or "bouts" of the movies. Sundays were spent in typical Berlin fashion, *draussen* (out of doors): long walks with Arvid, when he was in town, and friends in the many parks, woods, and lakes surrounding Berlin. Arvid was a master of train schedules. The Harnacks would take a train or S-Bahn to a chosen spot, get off, and walk to the next station.[49] As Wolfgang Havemann reported, they had developed an unusual pattern of walking where, interrupting their conversation, they would silently separate, each treading his side of the path, each partner careful not to disturb the other. Then, physically and emotionally refreshed, they would turn with clear heads and join their friends or return home.[50]

Martha Dodd described another lifelong habit of Mildred's: writing "unsigned postcards" from all over Germany. "In a delicate clear hand, as simple and pure as her personality, she wrote exquisite poetic lines as singingly lovely as her voice. She and Arvid were both nature lovers of the sort one finds only in Germany, not ashamed of the passion for physical beauty that was almost religious, at least reverent. . . . I prized these postcards and short letters written in sensitive prose. There was nothing studied or affected about them. Their feeling sprang simply from her full and joyous heart and had to be expressed."[51]

Initially, Hitler's Germany impressed Martha. Conditions had improved under the new regime. Her letters home, reflecting her father's initial optimism, were enthusiastic. "The youth are bright faced and hopeful, they sing to the noble ghost of Horst Wessel with shining eyes and unerring tongues. Wholesome and beautiful lads these Germans, good, sincere, healthy, mystic brutal, fine, hopeful, capable of death and love, deep, rich wondrous and strange beings—these youths of modern *hacken kreuz* Germany."[52]

Newspaper photographs showed Martha waltzing with Fritz von Papen, the foreign minister's son. World War I flying ace Ernst Udet, described by his date as short and chubby with a tubby tummy and a baldish head—but rakish and irrepressible—took her aloft in his private plane. Udet's boss, Reichsmarschall Hermann Goering, invited her falcon hunting at his estate, Karinhall. Louis Ferdinand, the son of the crown prince, entertained her at dinner at Cecilienhof. She regaled Hjalmar Schacht, the head of the Reichsbank, with off-color jokes.[53] Martha thought Joseph Goebbels had a great sense of humor and wrote her parents that she was sorry to have missed him when they were both in Hungary.[54] She cultivated gossip and lived on intrigue. As a friend, Sylvia Crane, remarked, "Martha was not a political theoretician. . . . She just liked sleeping with attractive men, and that's how she learned about politics and history."[55]

The snob in Martha enjoyed her conquests of the Nazi hierarchy: "It created something of a sensation when I sat between Graf von Bülow and Putzi Hanfstaengl—one fine, delicate, white haired, quiet-spoken with a slight lisp, gentle and shrewd and a little mysterious [Bülow], the other huge, loud-mouthed, good natured, joke-cracking (he told the prim Frau von Papen that girls opened his shirt to see if he had hair on his chest—otherwise he wasn't a good Nazi), hugely built, coarse, undependable, and almost broken down with his crazy genius and Hitler's love for him and his music. Playing them against each other was fun. . . . Politics absorb one completely here. You can't escape its fascination."[56]

Martha's one failure among the "newspaper men, bankers, princes and Nazi advisers" that she wrote she was "slaying with her fine proud cold eyes" was Hitler.[57] Putzi Hanfstaengl attempted to remedy this by being the intermediary and provided the introduction. He told Martha, "Hitler needs a young woman. Hitler should have an American woman. A lovely woman could change the whole destiny of Europe. Martha, you are that woman."[58] The Führer kissed her hand twice but the meeting was not a success: he spoke little English and Martha hardly any German. Later, Martha described him as a "frigid celibate" but she found his blue eyes unforgettable: "they overwhelm you."[59]

The embassy guest lists, which often included the Harnacks, were described after the war by one of the invitees, Ernst von Salomon, as composed of "the capital's *jeunesse dorée,* smart young men with perfect manners and an imperfect knowledge of languages," some in "the elegant black uniform of the Foreign Ministry, which so discouragingly resembled that of the SS." All were "smiling attractively or laughing gaily at Martha Dodd's witty sallies."[60]

Perhaps the most notorious member of Martha's dark-uniformed entourage was the "young, heavy-set, dark, deeply-scarred (from his dueling days in the 'Rhenania-Strassburg Corps' at the University of Marburg), brutal and repulsive" Rudolf Diels, head of Department IA of the Prussian Ministry of the Interior, later known as the Gestapo.[61] A hard-drinking man with "Mephistophelian manners," he silently slithered through a room usually ending at Martha's Chanel-scented elbow.[62] When she first arrived in Berlin, Diels and Martha were coupled on long drives and Sunday walks, at movies and in night clubs. By December 1933, he was also a jealous guardian, stalking the Dodd's Tiergarten residence as she melodramatically noted: "The snow is soft and deep lying here—a copper smoke mist over Berlin by day and the brilliance of the falling moon by night. The gravel squeaks under my window at night—the sinister faced, lovely lipped and gaunt Diels of the Prussian Secret Police must be watching and the gravel spits from under his soft shoes to warn me. He wears his deep scars as proudly as I would fling about a wreath of edelweiss."[63]

* * *

A more serious and lasting but equally dangerous affair, one that Martha confided to Mildred, was that with Boris Vinogradov, the tall, blond, blue-green-eyed Soviet diplomat with a "winning smile" who had been her escort on the Fallada visit.

The argument over recognizing the Soviet Union had played a part in the 1932 U.S. elections and in November 1933, the Roosevelt administration invited the Russians to open an embassy in Washington; William C. Bullitt, a Philadelphia millionaire, was dispatched to Moscow. Simultaneously in Berlin, Martha, who already saw herself as a leading player on the international stage, lost no time in normalizing diplomatic relations with the Soviet diplomat, adding him to her international entourage.

Boris had come to Berlin as press attaché in the embassy in 1931. By the time Martha met him, the thirty-one-year-old was first secretary. As Boris was the purveyor of press visas and letters of introduction on Soviet trips, most newspapermen remembered him favorably. William Shirer wrote to Martha that "even the most conservative American correspondents . . . hailed him as a friend although knowing that he was a dedicated Communist who believed in the greatness of the Soviet Union."[64] Shirer's boss at Hearst's International News Service (INS), Pierre Huss, however, would claim that "Benogradov" was the station chief of the NKVD, the Kremlin's secret service.[65]

Martha remembered being introduced to Boris at a dinner party given by Sigrid Schultz, the Berlin correspondent of the *Chicago Tribune*. "Schuli" (Count Detlev von der Schulenburg), a cousin of the German ambassador in Moscow and part-time employee of Sigrid's brought the Russian.[66] But it was at a nightclub, Ciro's, that it "took" a few weeks later.[67] Boris wooed her, "*gnädiges Fräulein, Fräulein Martha, seien Sie so lieb*" (gracious miss, Miss Martha, be so kind), he said in his accented, mellifluous baritone voice. "I am in the Sowjetischen Botschaft. . . . *Haben Sie Angst?*" ("I am in the Soviet embassy, are you afraid?")[68] When they finished bumping and stumbling around the dance floor—dancing was not among Boris's numerous skills—he sat her down, leaned over, and whispered, "*Ich möchte Sie sehr gern wieder zu sehen. Darf ich Sie anrufen?*" (I would like to see you again. Am I allowed to call you?)[69]

A protégé of Vyacheslav Molotov's,* Boris had, under Ambassador Leo Chinchuk, relative freedom to indulge his nonproletarian tastes. Martha invited him to join her friends, the American correspondents, at the Taverne *Stammtisch*. He took her dancing at Ciro's and to dinner at Horcher's, Berlin's most expensive restaurant. At the embassy—behind the famous rose windows that had been installed under the tsars—he entertained her friends with vodka, Crimean wine in costly crystal cups, and the finest caviar. He sent Martha orchids and presented her with his favorite record, Chaliapin singing "The Death of Boris" from the Mussorgsky opera, described by Martha as a portent of the future.[70] There were misunderstandings and with the help of a pocket dictionary, frequent quarrels. (She spoke no Russian; he no English. Their common language was German, which she barely knew.) Judging by his letters, he was genuinely in love, but there is always an undercurrent of doubt, reproachfulness, and mistrust. From the vantage point of middle age, Martha recognized his undying love, but at twenty-five she was naive politically and an irrepressible flirt.

(Armand Bérard, French diplomat—later U.N. ambassador—and competitor for Martha's affections and, according to Martha's memoirs, "Deuxième Bureau" [a member of the French secret service],[71] noted with malicious accuracy in his memoirs, *Un Ambassadeur se souvient,* that Boris had a wife and child at home in Moscow.)[72]

By March 1934 the affair had progressed to the point that it interested the Soviet intelligence services. Moscow wrote to the NKVD's Berlin station chief in a missive that appears in Martha's Moscow file:

> Let Boris Vinogradov know that we want to use him for the realization of an affair we are interested in . . . According to our data the mood of his acquaintance is quite ripe for finally drawing her into our work. Therefore we ask Vinogradov to write her a warm friendly letter [and] to invite her to a meeting in Paris where . . . they will carry out necessary measures to draw Martha into our work.[73]

*Chairman of the Council of People's Commissars who later replaced Litinov as Soviet foreign minister.

Martha would be drawn into working for the Soviets but it was the professional Dmitri Bukhartsev who would usher her in to the world of espionage, not the reluctant diplomat.

Martha's affairs shocked even the sophisticated diplomatic community. Fritz, the American embassy butler, was indignant, reporting to the wife of the military attaché that *"Das war nicht ein Haus, das war ein Maison."* (That was not a house but a house of ill repute.)[74] Fritz, according to Martha, was "almost surely an agent of the secret police." Like the operetta butler he resembled, he had the annoying habit of tip-toeing noiselessly on the soft carpets of the embassy library whenever Martha was entertaining gentlemen callers.[75] Eventually, the State Department was alerted to the ambassador's daughter's escapades. Raymond Geist, the acting consul general, revealed them in a confidential memo when he visited Washington. Geist reported that Martha was in the habit of publicly addressing the Gestapo's Rolf Diels, "this married man," as "dearie."[76]

As part of his job description for the Gestapo, Diels specialized in combating Communists and squired Martha to the Reichstag fire trial so she could see how effective and just the Nazi system was. Diels was also a master of espionage and Martha claimed it was he who ushered her into a world of tapped telephones, bugged rooms, and clandestine surveillance.

Mildred's admonitions, the Reichstag fire trial,[77] and Diels's subsequent revelations about the vast and complicated network of spying and terror anticipated two events that transformed Martha Dodd from an admirer of the German people into an enemy of the Nazi state and an enthusiastic convert to the Soviet cause: the Roehm purge and, a week later, a vacation trip to the Soviet Union.

During the first year of the Hitler regime, one journalist's wife remarked, "the window-boxes were just as gay," the "traffic continued to flow with the same admirable precision," and "trains arrived and left on time." Foreigners failed to notice anything out of the ordinary unless they were journalists who sought out the victims of the terror.[78] But gangs of Brown Shirts roamed the streets and journalists knew of their prisons and concentration camps for Communists, Socialists, and Jews. The street violence of the Brown Shirts and the widespread criticism it provoked provided Hitler with an important reason for destroying the SA, which had spearheaded the Nazi revolution of 1933. He achieved its destruction with the help of Himmler's SS and the tacit cooperation of the army.

The crisis was triggered on Sunday, June 17, 1934, with a sensational speech at the University of Marburg by Franz von Papen, the vice chancellor, who attacked the regime for its intolerance, for a lack of freedom of the press, and for the creation of a "false personality cult." Moving quickly, Goebbels, the propaganda minister, suppressed the rebroadcast of the speech and attempted to silence the newspapers but not before the *Frankfurter Zeitung* printed excerpts and von Papen had rashly distributed copies to the foreign press and diplomatic corps. But the expected support of the army never came and alarmed Berliners watched as military maneuvers increased.

"Bloody Saturday" fell on June 30, a beautiful day, perfect for the sunbathing that Martha and Boris had planned on the Wannsee beach. By lunchtime, however, truckloads of armed soldiers and SS men blocked the streets in central Berlin near Unter den Linden as police moved to occupy the Tiergarten residence of Ernst Roehm, head of the SA. Steel-helmeted SS men converged at Gestapo headquarters and sealed off Prinz-Albrecht-Strasse. Goering summoned the foreign press at three o'clock and told them that Roehm had been purged from the party and imprisoned.

At six o'clock, when Martha and Boris drove back to Berlin from Wannsee, they noticed the crowds of black-uniformed SS and green-uniformed Goering police but no Brown Shirts. As they neared the Tiergartenstrasse, they saw few civilians; all traffic seemed to have stopped. As Boris had diplomatic plates, they were allowed to pass through the cordons of police that surrounded the area. While Boris sped off to the Russian embassy, Martha made her way up the stairs of the embassy. Her brother greeted her nervously, "Martha, is that you? Where have you been? We were worried about you. Von Schleicher has been shot. We don't know what is happening. There is martial law in Berlin."[79] That evening, the "Night of the Long Knives," Ambassador Dodd received a formal note from Roehm declining a dinner invitation for July 6: Roehm was departing for "a rest cure."

Although little was published on Sunday, the news trickled out. Overnight it became apparent that Hitler had ordered the execution in Munich of several SA leaders, including Roehm and his homosexual entourage, the "Flying Circus," allegedly for plotting the overthrow of the Führer. Hitler went on to settle old scores with other prominent leaders, including a former chancellor, General Kurt von Schleicher and his wife, Elizabeth, General Ferdinand von Bredow, and leftist Nazi Party boss and sometime rival Gregor Strasser—all were massacred. Vice chancellor von Papen and his family were placed under house arrest and his two secretaries murdered. As this happened, Hitler nervously and hastily sought the support of President von Hindenburg.

Monday night Boris, Armand, and a few other friends gathered at a small dinner party hosted by Martha at the embassy. They gossiped about the rumors of a planned military coup. After dinner they retired to the ballroom to hear Goebbels's radio account of the last forty-eight hours. The propaganda minister accused "a foreign power" (which in context could only be Armand's chief, André François-Poncet) of backing Roehm and Strasser in the plot.[80]

On July 4, the Dodds hosted the annual embassy garden party. The Harnacks were listed among the several hundred guests. American jazz played softly as the Dodds stood at the entrance to the ballroom. Martha and her brother greeted visitors with the expression then current in Berlin, *"Lebst du noch?"* (Are you still among the living?). Outside on the terrace, people lingered in small groups; diplomats were jittery. No German dared mention the events of the past five days, but among journalists and Americans horrifying stories circulated.[81]

Although the official tally was eighty-five dead, other estimates range from 150 to 200 persons killed that week.[82] The Roehm purge not only marked the end of the SA but, together with President von Hindenburg's death on August 2, heralded the National Socialists' final consolidation of power. Whereas before violence was random—beatings by roving gangs of SA thugs—July 30, 1934, marked the ascendancy of the SS and Heinrich Himmler. Goering named Himmler chief of the Gestapo and turned the administration of the concentration camps over to the SS. Hitler was now chancellor as well as president; the routinization of terror had begun.[83]

After the Roehm killings, Martha feared she would have to cancel her holiday trip but left two days later, after a tearful familial farewell, on the first of several eastward excursions. Newspaper headlines over the pictures of Martha posing at the door of the Deruluft plane, "the daughter of the ambassador to Nazi Germany *chooses* to visit the Soviet Union," caused a "near diplomatic scandal."[84] The unusual vacation not only raised eyebrows at the U.S. Embassy but also took the Gestapo by surprise. (It believed Martha firmly in its camp because of her affair with Diels.)[85]

Although her visit to the Soviet Union was undoubtedly linked to her affair with Boris, they decided it was best not to go together. Left in Berlin, Boris at first consoled himself with the company of the German movie actress, Brigitte Helm, a rugged blond with languid eyes who had been the star of Fritz Lang's *Metropolis*. Then while Martha toured the Volga, he went to Moscow. She urged him to join her but he wrote that it was out of the question. Both parties were moving toward divorce, but their future was undecided. America, he said, was out of the question. He proceeded to the Crimea for a rest cure; she returned from Russia healthy and sunburned, a Caucasian cap on her head, to the waiting arms of her family in Berlin.

In her missing letters to Boris, Martha evidently criticized the Soviet Union. In his letters, which she saved, he scolds her, asserting that conditions were far worse before the revolution. Russia was not a paradise. She should understand that the Russians had a very difficult battle under challenging conditions, and their accomplishments from this standpoint were enormous.[86]

His arguments prevailed. In her book, *Through Embassy Eyes* (which she wrote in 1938 after returning to the United States), when she describes her first Soviet visit, the comparisons are at the expense of Nazi Germany. Having experienced Berlin's streets swarming with brown, black, and green uniforms, the "absolute lack of military display"—no parades, little evidence of the formidable Soviet Red Army—impressed her. She saw no sign of discrimination against the Jews or against other minorities. Food was plentiful, she wrote. The Soviets seemed to have a higher standard of living than the Germans.[87]

"She was absolutely wrapped up in the Nazis, and then she came back and was just as enthusiastic about the Communists," the wife of an embassy official remembers. "The attention turned her head completely. It was much more than she could handle. And of course, sweet Mrs. Dodd couldn't cope with it either. She couldn't cope with her daughter and she couldn't cope with the embassy."[88]

On August 7, 1934, as the ringing church bells announced the funeral of President von Hindenburg, Mildred wrote to her mother that "Arvid and I are now looking for other rooms, hoping to find some as nice as these again. These are too noisy. The traffic seems to us to have increased tenfold here in the last two years. Heavy trucks are continually going through to the barracks and places of detention [Columbia House] not far from here."[89] Because of their activities—frequent meetings and frank discussions with students and friends—Hasenheide had become too dangerous; Wannsee, although remote and inconvenient to her teaching, had the virtue of being far from the prying eyes of the Gestapo.

Mildred's once candid letters home were now devoted to pleasantries about the weather, holiday trips, the books she was reading, and the lectures she was giving. They are understandably frustrating to read since they conceal her covert life, the life she shared with Arvid. If there was important information, it was conveyed in a rather naive code. For instance, to deconstruct the following message, one must know (a) that it was illegal for German citizens to have money invested outside the Reich and (b) that while they were in the United States, they had invested their savings in Estonian bonds. Hard-pressed to know the status of their bonds, Mildred wrote on July 23, 1934, to her mother: "How is Esthonia? Is her health all right or have the hard times hit her too? We are thinking about her and hoping we shall hear about her in January. Dear old cat. She used to have kittens pretty regularly. How about this year?"[90]

After the Roehm purge Berlin changed overnight. The once free exchange between Germans and foreigners gave way to caution and mistrust. Ambassador Dodd's diary entry for July 13, 1934, records his impression of his final interview with Hitler: "I decided last Tuesday that I would never again attend an address of the chancellor or seek an interview for myself except upon official grounds. I have a sense of horror when I look at the man."[91] Dodd suspected that his mail was being opened, that messages in code were read, that even the diplomatic pouch was not safe.[92] Diels hinted to Martha that there were dictaphones concealed in walls, that could pick up conversations.[93] Berliners began to insert cotton plugs in telephones and made a habit of covering them with pillows as prevention against bugs when they were not in use. Trusted servants were now suspected; new acquaintances might be *agents provocateurs*. Secret files on diplomats grew; ambassadors used Berlin parks for private meetings.

German newspapers were heavily censored and Germans turned to foreign journalists for information. Most doors were open to them and in their presence tongues loosened. At their favorite bistro, the Taverne, journalists pooled information from Germans who risked their lives in covert meetings in public parks, railroad stations, and cafés. Because they risked expulsion if they ran stories critical of the regime, the correspondents became adept at sharing a story. Each would report one fact; if a reader combined all the accounts, he or she might have the complete story. Ambassador Dodd rated these American correspondents as the best information gatherers, far "cleverer than the French and British spies."[94]

When these candid stories appeared in American press, the Nazis raged at the Communists and Jews they accused of spreading "atrocity legends" abroad. An occasional reporter was expelled and a high-level official of the Foreign Office warned Orme Wilson, secretary of the American embassy, that "Germany would no longer tolerate the activities of spies. The People's Court would deal very severely with Germans whom it found guilty. Germany had been a center of espionage for the last fifteen years but hereafter every effort would be made to stop the disclosure of military information to other countries."[95]

Local papers carried articles on espionage. Mildred and Martha assuredly read with interest an article buried among recipes for welsh rarebit and chicken à la king entitled "Spying on the Increase—Tricks Many and Ingenious" appearing in the bible of the American colony, the *Continental News*. It alleged that there were 10,000 trained secret agents in Europe alone and described a *haus-*

fraulich technique used to send secret messages: hard-boiled eggs with messages and sewing stitches spelling out Morse code. One ingenious ruse was illustrated by a stamp collector's album: sets of stamps posted from a British port indicated, by the arrangement of the stamps and the date of the postmark, the different types of war vessels in the harbor. Thus three Montenegrin, two Peruvian, and four Chilean stamps meant "three battleships, two battle cruisers, and four light cruisers."

The article also detailed methods of carrying reports—with a small aluminum tube hidden in a nostril or in a shoestring—and cited a young American college girl, Marjorie Switz, who smuggled her messages in cigarettes. Unfortunately she was caught and, although she tried to smoke the evidence, she was arrested by the French as a Soviet agent.[96]

There was perhaps no one in Berlin with as much access to such excellent material and such high-level sources as Martha Dodd. So useful a source of information had not escaped the watchful eyes of the Gestapo and, after her Soviet visit, Martha became the target of an investigation. Their suspicions were not unfounded. By autumn 1934 she had apparently decided that, even though her father might earn nothing by his protests, she could fight the Nazis and in her own way, she did, boasting to Thornton Wilder:

> I know things about the Russian commercial agreements that France would give quite a lot of time and energy maybe money to know. I have heard [German economics minister] Schacht say not more than two weeks ago things that would make a roaring front cover headline and would probably bring the system crashing about his head (it will of course anyway). I bought jazz records for Molotov (including "Who's Afraid of the Big Bad Wolf"). I know some of the dirtiest tricks that are being played on the international chessboard mostly being played by the English who are swine from start to finish . . . My most loved of loves pronounces Hohenzollern Gogenzollern and almost I am sure (knowing him as I do) seduced Stalin's daughter this summer at a Russian home of culture and rest. My head is swollen with the snob-

bery I feel about being as successful as I am at balancing myself not less gracefully than the other 400,000 angels on the pin point of European security."[97]

Martha shamelessly bragged about her father's misplaced trust. She wrote, "We love each other and I am told state secrets."[98]

State secrets were exactly what the Soviets had in mind. While the lovers dallied with thoughts of marriage (Boris proposed a toast to "Martha, my wife," at a drunken luncheon at the Soviet embassy), Moscow decided somewhat prudishly to transfer him in December and bring in a more businesslike contact, a newspaper correspondent named Dmitri Bukhartsev.[99]

A memo in the Soviet archives reveals that Martha was indeed eager to help their cause:

Martha argues that she is a convinced partisan of the Communist Party and the USSR. With the State Department's knowledge, Martha helps her father in his diplomatic work and is aware of all his affairs. The entire Dodd family hates National Socialists. Martha has interesting connections that she uses in getting information for her father. She has intimate relations with some of her acquaintances. . . . Martha claims that the main interest of her life is to assist secretly the revolutionary cause. She is prepared to use her position for work in this direction provided, that the possibility of failure and of discrediting her father can be eliminated.[100]

"*Au fond*, Martha was not a heroine," says her friend, Sylvia Crane. Born for conspiracy and intrigue, she relished being the epicenter of an international power struggle, epitomized by three of her beaus, Russian Boris Vinogradov, Prussian Gestapo chief Rolf Diels, French diplomat Armand Bérard, and herself representing four great powers.

For her part, in a 1985 letter to William Shirer, Martha insisted that "despite rumors to the contrary," her affair with the young Soviet diplomat in Berlin "had nothing to do with later developments and faiths. These came from hatred of the Nazis, the (civil) war in Spain and deep respect for the Soviet Union as the biggest opponent of Hitler."[101]

* * *

By this time, in the wake of the Roehm purge, relations had chilled between Berlin and Moscow. The Germans boycotted parties at the once popular Soviet embassy. Martha learned that Gestapo agents were posted outside to report on all visitors. License plates of cars were reported as well as the number and lengths of visits. Followed on foot and by car, she recalled having "interesting experiences leading my 'shadow' into all sorts of tedious and ridiculous spots."[102] When she wanted to drop in on the Soviet embassy, she had the chauffeur let her off in front of the Adlon Hotel, a block away, and then she made her way on foot.[103]

December 1, 1934. Leningrad. An event occurred that was scarcely noticed by the foreign press. Sergei Kirov, Leningrad party boss and Politburo member, was assassinated at the Smolny Institute, party headquarters in Leningrad, under mysterious circumstances. Immediately Stalin instigated a massive pogrom. In mid-January, nineteen Communists, including Zinoviev and other members of the Central Committee who had opposed Stalin's leadership, were accused of the murder and tried. They were only the first of Stalin's victims. Encouraged by Hitler's example during the Roehm affair, during the next few years he would use the Kirov murder as a pretext to rid himself of his real or imagined enemies, ordering the great Moscow Trials, which would purge the leadership of the Soviet army, writers, and the other members of the intelligentsia. The so-called Show Trials would have severe consequences for Vinogradov, Bessonov, Bukhartsev, and others from the Harnacks' Soviet circle. The Great Terror had begun.

TEN

Literary Figure

Mildred, Arvid, and Martha Dodd

Nazi executions demanded a great deal of paperwork. During Mildred Harnack-Fish's last hours in prison, the authorities, with the punctilious thoroughness for which they became renowned, required her to fill out a *Fragebogen*, one of many questionnaires with which she was confronted during her last few years. Question 27 was "What do you think you will do after you are free? Will you take up your earlier profession or try to change to something new?" It's hard to know which was more incredible, the banal cruelty of the question or the mad optimism of her answer. "To further translate the best German writers like Goethe, in order to make them better known to the Anglo-Saxon world."[1] Yet this was how Harnack-Fish had conceived her mission from her first years in Germany and it looked for a brief moment as if she might succeed.

Sometime in April 1935, an invitation to attend a tea on May 8, 1935, engraved with the American embassy crest arrived in the Harnacks' mail. The guests of honor at the tea were to be Donald Klopfer, publisher of Random House and the magazine *Story*, and a recent conquest of Martha Dodd's, and American novelist Thomas Wolfe. The Harnacks arrive at 27a Tiergartenstrasse promptly at five in the German manner, and they are greeted by Martha and her mother, a small, wan, white-haired woman also named Martha Dodd. The family has been *en poste* less than two years but she looks extremely tired. Mrs. Dodd's straightforward simplicity contrasts with the formality of the white-gloved liveried embassy footmen who pass out mildly opalescent and mildly intoxicating cocktails along with the canapés—little slices of white bread covered with pale chopped vegetables and herbs.[2]

Some of the guests are the *Stammtisch* regulars, the twenty or so American journalists and their spouses who congregate after filing at the Taverne, an Italian restaurant, to discuss the stories of the day: Sigrid Schultz, the blond, vivacious, party-giving correspondent of the *Chicago Tribune*, the AP man "Louis B." and Mrs. Lochner—she represents the German-born dowager at full sail. In the corner, chatting with Wally Deuel of the *Chicago Daily News*, is Pierre Huss of the Hearst Press. Huss—slick, debonair, ambitious—is always on good terms with the Nazis, perhaps because he specializes in gossip and knows all the sexual innuendoes of the capital. Studious young Deuel has replaced Edward Mowrer, the former president of the hundred-member Foreign Press Association. Mowrer has been expelled. When told he'd have to leave Germany because the Führer had read his book, *Germany Puts the Clock Back*, and couldn't stand it, Mowrer replied curtly, "That's funny. I read his book, and I can't stand it either."[3]

The *New York Times* is represented by the sixtyish Guido Enderis wearing his trademark red necktie, Otto Tolischus, the "chief prop of the bureau," and the goateed Englishman Fred Birchall, European bureau chief. Surprisingly, there's the *Herald Tribune*'s John Elliot. A nonsmoker and teetotaler, he's seldom seen at parties. John Williams of the *Christian Science Monitor* is also present. There are two or three couples with British accents, among them Norman Ebbutt of the London *Times*, dean of the press corps, said to be the town's best-informed correspondent and the glummest; the beak-nosed woman of undoubted intelligence standing next to him is his colleague known to everyone simply as Mrs. Holmes.[4]

The German diplomatic set is noticeably absent. The American embassy is anathema to the Hitler regime. By now it is the better part of caution to avoid the Dodds and invitations are returned marked "out of town." Present among the German journalists are Margret Boveri of the *Berliner Tageblatt* and Bella Fromm, formerly the diplomatic columnist of the *Vossische Zeitung*.[5] Now that the paper has been aryanized, "Frau Bella" is covering the event for the *Continental Post*, the social organ of the English-speaking set. Bella is flush with gossip about Emmy Sonnemann's "crown princely wedding" to Hermann Goering. The Wagnerian-looking couple were married in the Dom under an arch of sabers drawn by a covey of doddering generals. Princely gifts have been "ordered" from every city, union, and factory in the Reich. Requisitioned paintings for the rapacious collector have arrived from Berlin's museums. A most unusual nuptial present was twenty-eight bombers from Germany's larger and more zealous cities. On a more personal note there was a yacht from a shipping firm and a car from Mercedes for commuting to Karinhall, the Reichmarschall's Mecklenburg estate.[6]

Huddled in the corner with Donald Klopfer (in Berlin on his way to the Soviet Union and Turkey) are the Rowohlts, *père et fils*. Rowohlt is Wolfe's German publisher and the son, Ledig-Rowohlt, has become the writer's chaperon and press agent rushing to and fro to collect his charge from the Hotel am Zoo.

Martha has charged Mildred and Greta Kuckhoff with inviting the German guests. She has dreaded asking these intellectuals for fear that the Nazis will observe, follow, or in other ways intimidate them.[7] Among the brave are Ludwig Reindl, the editor of *Die Dame*, who had been invited with his wife, Edith. He has commissioned Wolfe to write his impressions of Berlin. They stand chatting together with their friends, writers Otto Zoff and Richard Huelsenbeck. Zoff, who had been living at a safe distance in Italy, is in Berlin for a short professional visit.

"Don't you notice the danger, don't you know that the ceiling is caving in?" Huelsenbeck remarks. He is preparing to leave Germany as soon as possible.[8]

"Today you'll meet the Harnacks," Zoff tells Edith Reindl. "They'll be here. You'll have a close look at them. I have the feeling that you might understand each other well." Glancing over his shoulder at the door, he announces, "Look! Here they come."[9]

Mildred looks radiant in a simple blue dress, her blond hair knotted in a bun. Edith remarks, "That woman looks very charming, I would like to know her better."

Zoff replies, "That can be arranged."

Joining them are Greta Lorke and Adam Kuckhoff. Arvid has delegated Mildred and Greta to sound out opponents of the regime.[10] Mildred and Greta have invited John Sieg, the Detroit-born former editor of the *Rote Fahne* (Red Flag), the Communist Party newspaper. Sieg has links to the Communist underground. Immediately after the Nazis came to power, Sieg served four months in prison for his beliefs.[11] Now he is engaged in an earnest conversation with Ernst Niekisch. Niekisch, who accompanied Arvid on the ARPLAN trip to the Soviet Union, is the former editor of a monthly called *Der Widerstand* (Resistance) and a known opponent of Fascism. Arvid has warned Sieg that Niekisch is full of paradoxes. It will be difficult to enlist him in their group.[12] Nevertheless, Sieg is making an effort to win him over.[13]

Although this gathering seems completely innocent, in fact, Martha, Mildred, and Greta have assembled a not inconsiderable number of opponents of the regime. As the literary gathering evolves with the contrapuntal complexity of a Mozart finale *le tout Berlin* awaits the arrival of the American literary giant.

Suddenly the animated conversation is interrupted by the appearance of a gargantuan, embarrassed man who is introduced as the expected writer. Wolfe's dark head with its roached back hair towers above all the guests. He immediately becomes the center of attention as he roams the room modestly brushing aside compliments, endeavoring to be friendly.[14]

[Wolfe's first novel, *Look Homeward, Angel*, has just been translated and launched with a tremendous publicity campaign by Rowohlt. From America he has received a cable from his Scribner editor Max Perkins: his second novel *Of Time and the River* has received glowing reviews. Martha's note on embassy stationery, sent at Mildred's urging, has intrigued Wolfe. Tea is to be "from five till eight for a few fairly intelligent people." Martha assured him that like a "pack of maddened savage dogs" all of literary Berlin was "on his scent." She revealed she was also a writer; her brother, Bill, and her father were historians, "not diplomats in the common sense." She will be delighted to do anything for him, including taking him dancing, drinking, sunning, and motoring. Her father will arrange anything he requires as a tourist. Her concluding lines were calculating: "It is such an event when a writer comes to town that we become quite hysterical over it. I am tremendously anxious to see you, mainly of course because I admire your work so immensely."[15]]

Martha, drawn like a moth to the glow of literary fame, is at her seductive best. For his part, Wolfe is unaware that Mildred, Martha, and Greta have gathered together the literary opposition to Hitler. Rather, he assumes that the pleasant and interesting people to whom Martha introduces him are the glittering stars of the Nazi cultural firmament. The enthusiastic embassy crowd will transfigure all Berlin for him.

As most guests leave, a few, including Mildred, remain behind. According to one guest, the editor and writer Max Tau, Wolfe played a dangerous parlor game. Although he knew no one in the crowd, Wolfe, with Mildred translating, offered to characterize the guests. Neither money nor talent was important. "Only one thing is to be decided," Wolfe said, "are they reliable or not?" Late into the night, Tau stayed while Mildred read Wolfe's characterizations aloud. "This is a self-confident man," Wolfe said about one guest, "who is very friendly to everyone but then he curses those in power. I do not trust him; in the next moment, he could betray you as he has the powerful tonight." About another guest, "this small modest man with the generous, impenetrable face would sacrifice his life, never betray a friend, believe me." Wolfe's predictions both moved and unnerved the company. Later, according to Tau, they proved uncannily correct. (After the Kristallnacht pogrom in November 1938, when it became necessary for Tau, a Jew, to leave, Mildred engineered his escape to Norway.)[16]

Political events were hastening the decline and fall of the Harnack-Dodd salon. Emigration had left great gaps in the ranks of Berlin's literary establishment. Those who stayed in the capital were dispirited and demoralized. By 1935, all literary activities were regulated by the Reichskulturkammer, the president of which was Goebbels. The purpose of the cultural chamber, Goebbels declared, was "to unite all creative persons in a cultural uniformity of the mind."[17] Membership in the organization was de rigueur for German writers, critics, librarians, and book publishers. Only a writer who wrote fewer than twelve essays a year—hardly enough to live on—was exempt from becoming a member. Non-Aryans, of course, were excluded, as well as anyone considered "politically unreliable." There was a black list of works banned from public libraries. Walter Mehring, writing in 1936, remarked that Berlin had been a Weltstadt only as long as Tucholsky remained to write about it. He compared Berlin to a film running backward: the extraordinary artists who had descended on the city during the 1920s had all left by the mid-1930s.[18] As more and more German writers emigrated, were silenced, or were arrested, ironically, opportunities were created for the translation and publication of suitable works by foreign authors.[19]

Some American authors were banned. Dreiser and Dos Passos were forbidden because they championed the Soviet Union. Hemingway was also put on the index, although the Nazis admired his uncompromising masculinity, love for the heroic life, and devotion to "Anglo-Saxon ideals."[20] Sinclair Lewis became author non grata; books by Jack London and Upton Sinclair were burned. Still, in the mid 1930s, although his German list was diminished,

Rowohlt could publish Faulkner and Wolfe. Faulkner's rejection of industrialization initially found a natural resonance in the profoundly conservative cultural climate of the Third Reich, but eventually his books too were placed on the *Bücherkunde*—an advisory list published by the government—as "negative" and "translations not to be supported."[21] Wolfe however translated well and the Germans admired the honesty and vigor of his writing.

In their place a flood of mysteries and social novels appeared on the market to divert the German public. Agatha Christie, Somerset Maugham, and Margaret Mitchell, whose southern saga, *Gone with the Wind*, sold an amazing 300,000 copies in German, found a wide audience. Mildred's translation of Irving Stone's *Lust for Life* appeared in 1936, followed by her version of Walter Edmonds's *Drums along the Mohawk* in 1938.

Mildred also began to make her mark as a scholar, lecturer, and occasional essayist, activities designed to build a bridge between the younger American writers, particularly Faulkner and Wolfe, and German readers. If Mildred lacked in her fiction a first-rate creative imagination and deftness of phrase, her critical work displayed a genuine feeling for good writing and an ability to convey the author's personality.

In 1935, Mildred contributed an essay on Faulkner to Germany's most important critical journal, *Die Literatur*. Possibly because she had been helping Ambassador Dodd with his book on the Old South, Mildred had become fascinated by the race-haunted region. Viewed against the background of *Blut und Boden*—blood and soil (Nazi code words for racial purity)—her 1934 essay, "The Epic of the South," seems quite daring. Published in the *Berliner Tageblatt*, a once renowned but now merely popular newspaper, she wrote sympathetically that at the core of Faulkner's tragic view was "the question of the Negro."[22] In Nazi Germany, when criticism was no longer considered a private matter and when one influential critic could write that the cause of everything inferior and destructive in American literature resulted from the impact of "foreign races" (Jews and Negroes), this sort of "oversight" on her part could have ended her teaching career.[23]

Thomas Wolfe was the writer to whom Mildred felt closest. They were nearly the same age. On reading *Look Homeward,*

Angel, in 1933, she immediately sensed an important new voice. His ability to artistically shape material from his own childhood in order to "produce a deeper truth" was something Mildred sought to approximate in her own autobiographical novel.[24] She lectured on Wolfe in 1933 at the American Women's Club and again in 1934 before an audience of German academics and writers at the home of Emmi and Klaus Bonhoeffer. Later that year, she contributed an essay, "Three Young Writers from the United States: Thornton Wilder, Thomas Wolfe, and William Faulkner," to the *Tageblatt*.[25] Consequently, when the thirty-four-year-old North Carolinian arrived in Berlin in 1935, Mildred had already helped pave the way for his enthusiastic reception.

Immediately after his arrival in Berlin, Wolfe described in his notebook an appointment with Mildred at the St. Pauli bar on the Rankestrasse. This resulted in a two-part interview that appeared in the *Continential Post* and an essay in the *Berliner Tageblatt*.[26] The interview, probably the most revealing that Wolfe ever gave, was something of a literary scoop. In describing his work methods, Wolfe tried out on Mildred ideas that he would expound in a lecture at the University of Colorado and then edit into a three-part article in the *Saturday Review of Literature*. Finally, this account of his symbiotic working relationship with Max Perkins would appear in book form as *The Story of a Novel*.

In the Continental Post, Mildred described Wolfe as "the creator of an American epic-satirical novel of vast proportion," full of "the juice and meat" of life. In the same article she drew a vivid portrait of the six foot five inch author. "When a tall person stands with Wolfe, the young writer's great shape looms above him in the sunny May air. His brown eyes, meeting other eyes directly, sometimes shoot black lightning. At other times the almost childlike lips, the small nose and rounded cheeks are so quiet and natural that they express merely the power of the universal looking at things and unconsciously remembering them."

"Do you think the South is rising again?" Mildred asked, thinking of the desolation wrought by the Civil War, which "destroyed the might of the old plantation system."

"Yes, I do, but as a writer you can't stay in it. You'd get crushed. I haven't dared to go home to the South since I wrote my first book. When I finished *Look Homeward, Angel*, I received two criticisms . . . one was from a woman I had known in the South. She said if my great carcass was lynched, she'd look on with pleasure. The other was by a young woman writer, who has since married and died in childbirth. Her name was Margery Latimer." Margery Latimer was Mildred's friend and fellow Wisconsin "Lit" editor. In a 1929 review in the *Herald Tribune*, she had written that *Look Homeward, Angel* imparted an "intense shock" that gave "monstrous delight."

Wolfe said, "That criticism encouraged me to go on. I still keep that. I never met her, but I think she was fine. I'm awfully sorry she died."

In a passage that escaped Wolfe's biographers, he for the first time revealed his writing methods and acknowledged his debt to his editor: "Every time I'd get a hundred thousand pages piled up, I'd take them to my friend Max Perkins of Scribners. . . . And every time he'd say, 'that's good, that's the real stuff but it's only the knee joint.' Or, 'It's an arm.' As if the whole of the statue weren't there but had to be pieced together part by part . . . But one day I brought a pile to him and he said, 'Now you've got it. You've got all the parts.' I saw that but I felt I couldn't piece them together. So every day I wrote and every night I'd take what I'd written to Max and we'd talk it over. We'd go to a café and drink and work. That's how the second book was made."

They talked about other writers. Sherwood Anderson. Wolfe liked him. "But I believe he was hurt in his youth. So many Americans are hurt in their youth. . . . I was hurt, for instance. I don't know whether you grew up in a family. I did. And I was made to believe that whatever I did that didn't put money into my pocket was wrong. Even today I feel that if I didn't make any money on my books I'd believe I was a failure. But I know that isn't a good thing. The best things are not done for money. Don't you believe that?"

Like his editors, Mildred wondered how to order the thoughts that tumbled out of Wolfe's mouth: "I don't know how I'm going to make an interview out of this," she confessed, "but I'll write something. Is there anything special you'd like to say?"

"No." Then, after a pause, "there was an interviewer came to me in New York. And he went back and wrote things like my trousers were all unpressed and a milk bottle was standing outside the window of my room—I don't believe that's the important thing, do you?"[27]

The blizzard of publicity continued, also the favorable reviews; most of them came from critics hostile to the regime who could also indirectly express dissent by expressing their enthusiasm for Wolfe.[28] He wrote that his name "flashed and shone" and "fame shed a portion of her loveliness on everything about him."[29] Berlin intellectuals lionized the literary Jason who, like his character, George Webber, had "gone forth to seek the continental Golden Fleece." By night, German literary life temporarily revived as people emerged to meet Wolfe. According to Martha, Wolfe attracted people to the Romanisches Café who had not been seen since Hitler came to power. The Gestapo, aware of this, planted spies for weeks wherever the writer went, trying to "ferret out some free opinion that might have been less cautiously expressed after the sense of security and oblivion of terror that Wolfe's presence had given them."[30] For Germans, Wolfe was "the embodiment of the free world" that those in Hitler's prison were longing for.[31]

Wolfe was initially put off by Martha, whom he described in a letter to Perkins as "a little middle western flirt—with little shining stick out teeth, and a little 'sure that will be swell' sort of voice."[32] But soon he fancied himself in love with her. They plunged into a tempestuous affair and for all practical purposes he moved into the embassy.

They fought. Martha objected to his heavy drinking, the waste of his talent. She wanted to hear from his own mouth of his "loneliness and fear." Wolfe answered that he was neither lonely nor afraid. Even if he were, he would hardly talk about it to someone he had met only a week ago.[33]

Martha and her brother, with Ledig-Rowohlt and Mildred, chaperoned their guest around Berlin for what Wolfe described as "a wild, fantastic, incredible whirl of parties, teas, dinners, all night drinking bouts, newspaper interviews, radio proposals, photographers, etc."[34] Mildred and Wolfe went for walks in the Tiergarten, where the "wealth of the tall trees" and "the masses of pansies in full bloom, which the gardeners tore from the flowerbeds before they had time to fade," would forever remind her of

Wolfe.[35] Martha and Bill Dodd drove him to Weimar, the pleasant Thuringian town with its associations with Goethe and Schiller, and to the Wartburg, the castle where Martin Luther once sought asylum. Writing to Perkins, Wolfe declared the Germans to be "the cleanest, the kindest, the warmest-hearted, and the most honorable people I have met in Europe."[36]

A romantic and an anti-Semite, Wolfe was predisposed toward the National Socialists. Martha's friends "tried futilely to show him that all was not unconditionally superb in Germany,"[37] she wrote in *Through Embassy Eyes*. However, Wolfe resented Martha's lecturing and felt her opinions were suspect because "she was leaning toward the Communist side."[38] In the end, it was Mildred who changed his mind. As Martha recalled in her unpublished memoir, Wolfe had "great respect for Mildred's serious, patient and informed mind." It was Mildred who "developed Wolfe's later political understanding."[39] Six weeks after his arrival Wolfe left, having changed some of his ideas about the "noble spirit of freedom" in Germany.[40]

"He came over here and poured out the sense of his abundance and power, and thinking of him has been a fruitful thing since then," Mildred wrote to Perkins in a correspondence begun perhaps at Wolfe's suggestion. "Some time before knowing him I had felt great admiration for the way he could handle tragedy and comedy within satire in the creation of Gant in *Look Homeward*. . . . To my mind this ability is a kernel distinction of his—those slants which show the greatness in pettiness and the pettiness in greatness, and the vast humor and tragedy of it all. He caricatures humanity and humanizes caricature in an unusually rich and powerful way."[41] Perkins wrote back, she had "better defined that curious combination of elements in Wolfe's writing than anyone else."[42]

Wolfe's pocket notebooks from 1935 in Harvard's Houghton Library contain a short list that intrigued me: Berlin: Martha, The Old Man, Ledig, Rowohlt, Mrs. Harnack.

Besides Martha, the only person on the list alive in 1990 was Heinrich Maria Ledig-Rowohlt. My letter of inquiry yielded a message on my answering machine inviting me to come for a weekend visit to his chateau overlooking Lake Leman in Switzerland. Friends of his assured me that whether or not the trip to Lausanne produced new material for my book, I should not pass up the opportunity to meet a remarkable man. Three weeks later, he greeted me with a hug at the Lausanne railway station and drove me to Lavigny.

Switzerland has afforded sanctuary for countless refugees like Ledig-Rowohlt, who was living as an expatriate, having retired in 1983 from directing the German publishing firm that his father, Ernst Rowohlt, had founded. Not that he was alone in his "splendid isolation." There was the constantly humming fax, and our marathon three-day talk was frequently interrupted by the telephone.

During our sessions, Ledig-Rowohlt, a fit eighty-two-year-old, beamed at me from beneath the two bushy eyebrows that dominated his face—a feature that David Levine had captured convincingly in a caricature of the publisher that hung on the wall. Ledig-Rowohlt's love for, and devotion to, America's literature disposed him to fraternize with American writers, and he regaled me with tidbits selected from a vast repertory of literary gossip extending from Sinclair Lewis and Dorothy Thompson to John Updike.

He had known Mildred and Arvid slightly. Martha he knew better and Tom Wolfe, very well. Dodd and Ledig-Rowohlt were almost the same age in 1935: he was twenty-seven to Martha's twenty-six. As Wolfe had only a "cabdriver's German," they spoke English—Ledig-Rowohlt with a pronounced accent, now vanished that, much to his horror, the American captured with "phonographic exactitude" in a New Republic *article that grew into a book,* You Can't Go Home Again. *("I feel perfectly* dret-ful! *I have not efen been to bett! May I tell you something?")*[43]

Ledig-Rowohlt witnessed Wolfe's momentary passion for Dodd. Martha, Wolfe had confided to his friend, was "like a butterfly hovering around my penis." The publisher recounted one late-night fight. After many rounds of drinks at the Taverne, the two men returned to the embassy to look for Martha. When she descended the stairs, she was brandishing a copy of Wolfe's newest book, Of Time and the River. *She reproached Wolfe for wasting his talents drinking.*

"Wolfe got very angry. He stormed up the stairs and took the book out of her hands and tore its thousand pages with his bear's

paws and threw it out the window into the Tiergarten, like it was the phone book. And Martha threw herself on the couch, weeping. Wolfe stormed about, cursing and swearing. And I, it was very painful for me to watch that scene. I didn't know what to do but I started turning somersaults, backward and forward. She was weeping and he was storming. I was tumbling back and forth. Then they started to laugh. Tom embraced me, nearly crushing me in his arms, and they got over it. It was the very early morning, with the dawn just beginning to break above the trees in the Tiergarten and we went out to a place on the periphery of Berlin, to the Grunewald. There were the swans, the birds; Tom was in nature and he was happy again. We ate in a garden restaurant and he took the tablecloth and wrapped it around him and said, 'I'm Sitting Bull.'

We talked about the parties, Martha's and the Harnacks'.

"Martha was a little bit bourgeois, you know. She turned into some kind of bohemian but she had a petit bourgeois touch. Arvid was a very civilized man. And the main thing at his political center was obviously his hatred of Nazism."

I wanted to know if he had observed this at the time.

"I knew that I was moving with friendly, anti-Nazi mortals. That he was a Communist I knew from Martha. I knew that if he was a friend of Martha's—it was quite clear to me what she was— that he was anti-Nazi too. The main point was that they were anti-Hitler. And of course if you were anti-Hitler you would have helped the Russians. . . . Of course, one must say, if at that time you were friendly with the Russians and if you went to the Russian embassy, it was very likely that they would try to get you on their side, to help them.

"My father went to the Russian embassy. My old man, he understood himself as a Communist. He was a party member and his ideas were rather naive. We did quite a few books on Russia at this time and this was one of the reasons my father was very well received at the Russian embassy. They liked him. Ernst von Salomon also went to the Russian embassy. I never went. I wasn't invited. I was too unimportant at the time."

I asked about Salomon. In Fragebogen, Salomon's autobiography, he described the guests at the parties at the Harnacks' and *their friends as dangerously indiscreet, teacup revolutionaries, quite casually discussing things that could cost them their heads.*[44]

"No . . . the Harnacks, it was like a professor's home. . . . Ernst von Salomon was our author and an old friend of mine. His wife— she got to know him through me—said, 'Oh, I like that. There they stand with their little cups of tea and talk to everybody about what wonderful anti-Nazis they are.' But I can't believe that the Harnacks had such parties. I don't think that would fit Arvid's character. And I don't think it would ever fit with Mildred's. I can't believe it. But perhaps they may have been too open, you know. In a cocktail party you can talk too much. But you didn't get the impression that you were in a crowd of Communist traitors. It was Berlin society. You had a feeling of intellectuals opposing Hitler, nothing furtive.

"Of course, the people fighting Hitler, most of them were leftists. You know, most people from the outside, especially in other countries, they don't know how complicated everything was."

After the excitement of Wolfe's visit, Mildred felt a void, and her essays on Wolfe and Faulkner were to be her last. After 1935, she published no further literary criticism. Permission from nervous administrators was essential before publishing scholarly articles and it was seldom forthcoming. Nor did she write serious articles for newspapers. Since editors were held responsible for material damaging to the Third Reich, they became "rubber stamps for official views."[45] Even Goebbels candidly noted that "any person with the slightest spark of honor left in him will take good care in the future not to become a journalist."[46] Another literary visitor, the journalist Josephine Herbst, wrote that there was little to be found of interest in Berlin bookstores or newspapers. In a series of articles for the *New York Post*, in summer 1935, Herbst wrote that they contained "works about our animal friends, the birds and the bees, and pictures of Hitler smilingly accepting a nosegay from a little girl." Page one stories were devoted to thunder showers and "the butterfly is a major subject in the new Germany."[47] As if to illustrate Herbst's thesis that only the weather and nature were suitable subjects for journalism, after 1935, Mildred published only three articles—all in Reindl's *Die*

Dame, Germany's leading women's magazine. Two were picture stories, "In Arden's Wood" about women's colleges in the United States and "High School with Lasso," about a school for cowboys in San Antonio, Texas, and one was an impressionistic essay, "Summer Solstice."[48]

In 1936 Mildred began working as a freelance reader for various German publishing houses, scanning current American and British books with an eye to recommending works suitable for translation. In 1938, the Berlin publisher Rütten and Loening offered her a position advising them on American novels. But permission had to be obtained before a translation could be published from the "Promi," Goebbels's Propaganda Ministry.[49] Mildred informed Maxwell Perkins in 1936 that she was translating George Santayana's *The Last Puritan*.[50] It never appeared. That was also the case with her translation of Irving Stone's life of Jack London, *Sailor on Horseback*. In 1939, the Berlin publisher Universitas bought the German rights, and Harnack-Fish almost completed the translation when Goebbels's minions returned it marked "*Verboten*."[51]

Meanwhile, Hitler's "peace speech" on May 21, 1935, lulled the world into a false security even as the government made air raid shelters obligatory in public buildings. The first clear warning of the Third Reich's aggressive intentions came on March 7, 1936, when Hitler ordered 30,000 German troops into the demilitarized Rhineland, violating the Versailles Treaty and the Locarno Pact, which stipulated that remilitarizing this buffer between Germany and France would be a cause for war. Hitler's bluff worked; Europe's collective security system simply collapsed.

Mass trials were by now an everyday occurrence. Mildred's Wisconsin friend, Clara Leiser, visited the Harnacks in 1935. Because she held an official position in a New York court, Clara was permitted to visit two of these trials with Mildred accompanying her as an observer. One was a joint trial of seventeen boys and men for "high treason." They were accused of holding a meeting at which subversive sentiments were expressed and of distributing anti-Nazi literature. At another trial, eight Communists were accused of manslaughter for allegedly shooting a restaurant owner four years earlier.[52] Clara was also able to tour two prisons but was refused admission to a third, Plötzensee, where she asked to see Liselotte Hermann, a political prisoner awaiting execution.[53]

It was in late spring 1936 that Mildred saw Hitler at close range for the only reported time. According to her pupil Emil Kortmann, they were returning from an evening meeting of the English Club at the Berlin Abendgymnasium, walking along the Tauentzientrasse in the direction of the Zoo Station, absorbed in a conversation, when they met the Führer:

> Suddenly—we were scarcely a hundred meters from the entrance to the UFA Filmpalast—a great swarm of SS men appeared behind us as if they had sprung from the earth. They began pushing us, along with other pedestrians who happened to be passing by, toward the entrance to the theater. Everything happened so fast that we didn't have time to think, much less to talk. Nonetheless, we were convinced that we had been caught in a raid. However, it turned out to be something completely different. As we waited . . . the enormous double doors opened, and HE strode out, the greatest leader of all time, posing heroically, of course, waving to the left and right, accompanied by his ape-faced dwarf and other "dignitaries." Amid shouts of "Heil," Hitler climbed into a car and drove off, escorted by SS vehicles. As the two of us stood among the crowd, an older woman called out emphatically: "What an historic moment!" This sentiment was undoubtedly shared by others who were still standing around or, like Frau Harnack and myself, walking on. We said goodbye to each other at the Zoo S-Bahn with the thought: Given a mentality like that, we anti-fascists still have a lot to do![54]

By summer 1936, as Germany readied itself for the Olympics, the unemployment problem had been virtually solved and Hitler was assuring Europe of his peaceful intentions. German business was thriving, the Führer was at the crest of his popularity, and the Games gave him an ideal opportunity to show off the Third Reich's achievements. Railway stations were rebuilt, houses painted, and formerly empty stores let at artificially low rents; Berliners were urged to grow flowers instead of vegetables in their window boxes.

The streets thronged with tourists who saw the National

Socialists on their best behavior. Signs reading "*Juden uner-wünscht*" (Jews not welcome) were discreetly removed from public places; racks that held copies of the virulent anti-Semitic party paper, *Der Stürmer*, disappeared from walls; persecution was suspended for the duration of the Games.

The newness and neatest of things impressed visitors like Thomas Wolfe, who had returned to town to spend his blocked royalties. He wrote that "even the little cobblestones that paved the tramways were spotless as if each of them had just been gone over thoroughly with a whisk broom."[55] Along the entire ten-mile *Via Triumphalis*—running from the Alexanderplatz to the Olympic stadium—flags bearing swastikas and the five Olympic rings were hung out everywhere, giving the town the appearance of "a thrilling pageantry of royal banners. . . . such as might have graced the battle tent of some great emperor."[56] An enthusiastic Wolfe found the Art Deco stadium "the most beautiful and most perfect in its design that had every been built."[57] Hitler disagreed—he thought it too small. Never mind, the Führer decreed that after the 1940 Olympics scheduled for Tokyo, all future games would be held in Germany. A stadium seating 400,000 would be built in Nuremberg.

Mildred's interest in the Olympics had been sparked by a book on European sports by Carl Diem, the mastermind of the Berlin extravaganza, which she had translated for the 1932 Los Angeles games. Mildred found Diem's theme, the relation of sport to nationalism, "very interesting," though she deplored its "excessive patriotism" and the author's emphasis on "nationalistic aspects of sport."[58]

Martha invited friends to the embassy box at the Games, where they could observe the "Dark Messiah," as Wolfe called Hitler, at close range. They watched him beaming and slapping his thighs when his countrymen won and savored his humiliation over German losses to the great black American Jesse Owens. Once, sitting with Martha in the ambassador's box, Wolfe celebrated Owen's victory with a Native American war whoop. In a rage, Hitler twisted in his seat, spotted the offender, and punished him with a frown.[59] Owens was "black as tar," said Wolfe, but "what the hell, it was our team and I thought he was wonderful. I was proud of him, so I yelled."[60]

As the Games proceeded, to Wolfe, they were no longer "merely sporting competitions." Day after day, they became "an orderly and overwhelming demonstration in which the whole of Germany had been schooled and disciplined. It was as if the Games had been chosen as a symbol of the new collective might, a means of showing to the world in concrete terms what this new power had come to be."[61]

Entirely concealed from visitors and omitted from Leni Riefenstahl's subsequent film, *Olympiad*, was the wholesale transformation of German life. However, it was apparent to Berliners that by 1936, political, social, economic, and religious freedoms had vanished. The Nuremberg Laws enacted in 1935 deprived Jews of German citizenship and expelled them from public office and most professions. Sexual relationships and marriages between Jews and Aryans were forbidden. Although Hitler signed an agreement with the Vatican guaranteeing the freedom of the Catholic Church, it did not prevent the arrests of priests and nuns. A few months after the Games, the Protestant Confessional Church, which had broken with the official Lutheran Church over the so-called Aryan laws, came under attack and its pastors were arrested. Hidden from the tourists were the concentration camps that had sprung up all over Germany. Even the children's prayer "*Lieber Gott, mach mich fromm / Daß ich in den Himmel komm*" (Dear God, make me good / so I can go to heaven) was parodied: "*Lieber Gott, mach mich stumm / Daß ich nicht in Dachau kumm*" (Dear God, make me dumb / so that I don't to Dachau come).

"Only the horses are happy in Germany," was a cynical line of Ambassador Dodd's that Wolfe liked to quote.[62] Meeting with Shirer and Martha Dodd on his second visit, he confessed that he was somewhat conscious "of not being politically minded" at a time when most writers were and, they agreed, should be.[63] On his second visit more people unburdened themselves to Wolfe with tales of Nazi horror. "Both of these baffling experiences" Wolfe wrote in *You Can't Go Home Again*, "contained elements of comedy and melodrama but those were the superficial aspects." He began "to realize now the tragedy that lay behind such things:"

> There was nothing political in any of it. The roots of it were much more sinister and deep and evil than politics or even racial prejudice could ever be. For the first time in his life he

had come upon something full of horror that he had never known before—something that made all the swift violence and passion of America, the gangster compacts, the sudden killings, the harshness and corruption that infested portions of American business and public life, seem innocent beside it. What George began to see was a picture of a great people who had been psychically wounded and were now desperately ill with some dread malady of the soul. Here was an entire nation, he now realized, that was infested with the contagion of an ever-present fear. It was a kind of creeping paralysis which twisted and blighted all human relations. The pressures of a constant and infamous compulsion had silenced this whole people into a sweltering and malignant secrecy until they had become spiritually septic with the distillations of their own self-poisons, for which now there was no medicine or release.[64]

A terrifying episode occurred on the train to Paris when German police boarded Wolfe's train and arrested a Jew who had been sharing his compartment for attempting to smuggle money out of the country. This prompted a chastened Wolfe to write "I Have a Thing to Tell You." When the story appeared in 1937 in the *New Republic*, Wolfe's books—as he had been warned by Rowohlt— were banned in Germany.

Ledig-Rowohlt spoke to me about his own close brush with the Gestapo when Wolfe published his article.

"Martha called me to come over to the embassy one afternoon. She said, 'We'll be alone.' I was flattered. I thought, well Martha has her eye on me. So I went over and I must have been in the reception room because there were magazines there. She came in and picked up the New Republic, *which I hadn't noticed but which also was lying there. I read it and I got excited."*

"You knew you were in danger?"

"Absolutely, because it was a portrait of me. The title, 'I Have a Thing to Tell You,' was how I began all my atrocity stories about the Nazis. Martha advised me to leave Germany as soon as possible. She said, 'I'll give you a passport and you go to the States and then Tom will be responsible for you.' When I came to the office the same evening, my father was alone and I told him all.

First, he wanted me to translate the passage about himself—he was a bit vain. Then he said, 'Nobody will find out.' But then it began in the Berlin papers, in the Nazi papers. They wrote about Tom Wolfe with the title, 'Look Homeward, Devil,' and I got very worried. Well, the Gestapo showed up at the office. My father said I wasn't there. And they said, 'Oh ja, okay, Heil Hitler, we'll come back later.' When I heard that, I was sick. I thought they were after me. I was sitting in my room working and my father came back. My father was a great teaser, sometimes a little bit cruel to me. There was this kind of playing cat and mouse with me. I heard my father open the door to the Gestapo. 'You can come into my wonderful home, etc.' He was crazy! And then I thought if my phone rings, I'm in for it. And the phone rings. It's my father, who says, 'There are two gentlemen to see you, they want to talk to you.' Well, my knees were shaking but I went in. He was sitting there . . . they were sitting there. And then it came out. They wanted to know something about an author and a friend of mine. His name was Erwin Topf and he had written a book, Die Grüne Front, *attacking Germany's agricultural policy. And all they wanted from me was his whereabouts. But this chap was happily in the army, a major or something, and they couldn't touch him anymore."*

So nothing happened because of the Wolfe story. They never figured it out?

"They never accused me. They could have made it out. Tom described the view from our roof garden, our private home, very high up on the Kurfürstendamm. They could have found out by going to the publishing house and inquiring about it, and so on. But at the time [1937], they were busy with a lot of other things."

Rowohlt Verlag was eventually closed down by the Nazis for publishing the works of leftists, Jews (under pseudonyms), and other politically unreliable authors. Ledig-Rowohlt was drafted into the German army and fought on the Russian front.

"Those were terrible times, terrible, terrible times," he said. "Under Hitler, there was no justice. And immediately after, there was also no real justice. One was too much taken by the events, too much enraged by them, you know. Of course, the Germans don't like to see their evil side. . . . He was a joke, Hitler, absolutely mad. A joke and an evil genius but he made a lot of people rich.

"You know, I have something to tell you." I smiled, because of *the resonance of the phrase. "I feel a little ashamed because I am German." He then recited the ominous ending of "I Have a Thing to Tell You," which he memorized long ago:*

> 'Therefore,' he thought, 'old master, wizard Faust, old
> father,
> of the ancient and swarm-haunted mind of men, old
> earth,
> old German land with all the measure of your truth,
> your
> glory, beauty, magic, and your ruin; and dark Helen
> burning in
> our blood, great queen and mistress, sorceress — dark
> land,
> dark land, old ancient earth I love — farewell!'[65]

During the Olympic summer, a civil war erupted in Spain. Generalissimo Franco's Falangists, aided first by Mussolini and then by Hitler, rose up against a republic whose leaders, when rebuffed by the democracies, turned to the Soviet Union and to brigades of international volunteers. It was a proxy rehearsal for the greater conflagration. Hitler provided Stuka dive bombers and the Condor Legion; Mussolini supplied 75,000 troops already seasoned in Ethiopia; Stalin pitched in with 1,000 pilots, an equal number of planes and tanks, and more than 2,000 "advisers," including one young man who would come to play a pivotal role in the Harnacks' lives: Anatoli Gurevich, a Red Army captain recently arrived via submarine. Gurevich, at the time posing as "Victor Sukulov," was a blond twenty-five-year-old with glowing eyes and a vibrant personality who had a gift for languages and an as yet unrequited taste for "luxurious living and amorous entanglements."[66] In 1942, the Abwehr would identify him as "le petit chef," the second in command of the Brussels section of the Red Orchestra. But most often "Kent" was Gurevich's preferred alias, a name he borrowed from the British hero of a Russian spy novel: Edward Kent, an agent famous for his "astuteness, ice-cold nerve and incredible audacity."[67]

ELEVEN

Stranger

Mildred during her 1938 visit to the Heberles at the lakeside resort of
Gremsmühlen, Holstein

It is September 1988 and I am in Berlin. Germany's former capital is still a divided city, a lost metropolis more in need of exorcists than architects. Plötzensee, the favored execution spot for the Third Reich's opponents, lies in the French sector at the crossroads of two districts—where trendy Charlottenburg gives way to working-class Wedding. The neighborhood remains sinister: its main monuments are a juvenile detention center, Berlin's women's prison, and the Plötzensee Memorial. The memorial is all that remains of the prison and execution chamber where some 2,500 men, women, and children, many of them members of the German resistance, were guillotined or hanged during the Nazi era.

Plötzensee's main building contains two spare rooms. The first, with arched, leaded glass windows and fresh flowers, has a religious aura. Except for the meat hooks from which the men were hanged, it might be a Protestant chapel. Next door is an exhibition hall with memorabilia from the resistance: a few official documents, some protest posters, and photographs. Most of the pictures show the heroes of the July 20 plot to kill Hitler, men of military bearing with university dueling scars. The Plötzensee guillotine, one of the estimated nineteen employed in Germany in 1943, still featured as an illustration in the complimentary guide, has been removed. (The Nazis thought that the swift dispatch of the guillotine was more humane for women.) Nowhere is there a trace of the one American woman, Mildred Harnack-Fish, who was beheaded here.

However, in East Germany, sixteen stops east from Plötzensee on the maroon and caramel cars of the S-Bahn (that is, if the trains could pass uninterrupted through Friedrichstrasse Station in East Berlin) stands the Mildred Harnack School. This recently refurbished prewar building serves the community of Lichtenberg, a residential area favored by Communist Party bureaucrats and members of the Stasi, East Germany's secret police. Each year, the cleverest daughters of the KPD and Stasi are awarded Mildred Harnack prizes. The school had a *Heimatmuseum*, a special memorial room, and a hallway with a miscellany of photographs and uplifting newspaper clippings devoted to Mildred, including one that showed Greta Kuckhoff at the dedication of the school.

The exhibition is organized under a quote from Goethe: "Man

alone can do the impossible." As it transpired, among the main exhibits was a poem to Mildred, the "scout of the Red Army," the heroine of a song composed and set to music by a Russian in 1977:

> You came to us from across the sea
> to the silence of the brown morass
> you did not ask: what is Germany to me?
> Germany, the evil world
> that cries out for change
>
> In the dark night of Fascism
> your final words rang out:
> I have loved Germany so much
> the executioner himself drops the blade
> and Germany shouts its Heil, Heil, Heil
>
> Like the seas of the earth
> let us share your blood
> let us share your strength
> and know: this Germany will be
> the new time, this Germany will be
> the good world
> that we choose with you
> choose with you.[1]

There are some biographical details about Mildred's early life in Milwaukee and much about her final hours translating Goethe in her cell. But a great deal is left to the imagination. How did Mildred fight the Nazis? There are no descriptions about resistance activities; nothing to suggest what on earth it meant to be a "scout" for the Red Army. In 1970, she received the Order of the Fatherland War, First Class. For what? Celebrated in these school rooms—and put forth as a model for schoolgirls—is a Mildred who never doubted, never hesitated, never looked back; who was brave beyond belief and never broke under torture. Yet it is just these unremarked doubts and dilemmas that might give Mildred the human dimension and complexity that should appeal to students. To this visitor it appeared that if Mildred had not existed, the Communist Party myth-making machinery would have had to invent her—the useful sort of heroine after whom people could name their children, schools, or streets. But before I could make further notes we were shooed away by the principal, who was frightened because we were speaking English. The school was *verboten* to tourists. Mildred's courage was not evidently meant to provide an example for GDR school administrators.

Mildred belonged to the doomed generation of female radicals—one thinks of Tina Modotti, Olga Benario, Marina Tsvetayeva, Greta Buber-Neumann, and Milena Jesenská—who came of age during the "pitiless and cruel times" that followed World War I. Theirs was the generation, wrote one survivor, the Russian emigré writer Nina Berberova, "that was almost completely wiped out by war, revolution, emigration, the gulag and the terror of the 1930s."[2] They were, in W. H. Auden's phrase, "among the countless unmourned lives" who "silently vanished into History's criminal noise."

Contrasted to the romanticized chapbook portrayal of the heroic Mildred eulogized in the GDR is the real-life struggle she engaged in between 1936 and 1939. These were years of increasing isolation, doubt, and indecision for Mildred, years of conformity and capitulation in Germany. These were the years that produced the ubiquitous *Mitläufer*, the German who merely "followed along." It was a period of newsreels showing euphoric masses at Nuremberg Party days, cheering Hitler as he marched into the Rhineland and annexed Austria and the Sudetenland. And then, as if the Jews hadn't already endured enough (Aryan professions, German forests, German streetcars, and German benches), came Kristallnacht in November 1938. To the sound of broken glass hundreds and thousands of desperate Jews were pushed out of their homes into the streets. People who didn't submit lived in constant fear of being denounced by informers—strangers, family, and friends. Between 1933 and 1939, the pivotal dilemma for independent-minded people was whether to leave Germany or to stay. By 1936, many of the Harnacks' friends, relatives, and colleagues had left; many were to follow in the next two years. A scouting trip to the United States in 1937, an application in 1939 for a Guggenheim fellowship, and a boat ticket back to the United States in 1939 speak to Mildred's ambivalence. Her uncertainty is a point to which we will return. Here we need only mention the compromises and the dissemblings that were necessary for those

Germans who were out of step with the regime but chose to remain.

Max Delbrück's dilemma was typical. Introduced by Arvid to Martha Dodd in 1935, he became a close friend and sometime escort of the ambassador's daughter. By that time the future Nobel Prize winner was already a promising young scientist working at the Kaiser Wilhelm Institute for Chemistry. However, in May 1934, his habilitation essay, in which he was supposed to review his area of study and detail his own contribution to it, a work that was a prerequisite for a future professorship, had been turned down without explanation. His biographers speculate that it was probably because he failed to pass muster politically.[3] Like others who wanted to obtain a university position, Delbrück had to attend a *Dozentenakademie*, a three-week political indoctrination camp devoted to "free" discussions. He failed.

Another political test for Delbrück—one widely discussed in Harnack circles—was how to circumvent the customary closing to a letter, the obligatory "Heil Hitler." On official documents, especially job applications, this salutation was imperative. However, it was pointed out that "with great respect" was as great a lie as "Heil Hitler" so Max, Mildred, and others signed with the disagreeable closing.[4] Even such ordinary tasks as writing a letter or buying a railway ticket had become hateful because of the complicity of a bevy of bureaucrats who worked overtime registering people and searching strangers.[5]

Delbrück was saved in 1937 by the Rockefeller Foundation, which awarded him another fellowship (they had awarded him one in 1931). He spent the war years and the rest of his distinguished career in Pasadena, California. However, he felt lingering guilt about leaving Germany, and he strongly disagreed with those who criticized the Germans who stayed. Shortly before his death, he said that "the choices only seemed clear-cut to people who have no sense of reality of the situation."[6] In his opinion those who stayed—the Bonhoeffers; his brother, Justus; and the Harnacks—and resisted, deserved the greater credit.[7]

On January 26, 1937, a new civil service law gave Nazi officials the power to dismiss tenured employees whose loyalty was in doubt. This prompted a rush among civil servants to enroll in the

NSDAP. Nearly nine out of ten members of the Prussian civil service now belonged to the party. Only a few, like Justus Delbrück, resigned. But party membership could be deceiving. Arvid's boss at the Economics Ministry, Walther Funk, characterized some new converts as "Nazi brown outside, Moscow red inside."[8] In May, Arvid Harnack became one of Funk's "deceptive hamburgers"— Nazi Party member number 4153569.[9]

After Arvid completed his own habilitation work, he had vainly sought a university appointment. Instead, he continued the complicated process through which would-be lawyers rotated through the judiciary and civil service, the so-called Referendar stations. In 1935, he passed his last qualifying examination and, with the help of a friend of Greta Kuckhoff's, joined the Economics Ministry. As part of the Nazi *rites du passage*, Arvid's superiors had to certify that he was politically reliable, and like all new lawyers he had to be politically indoctrinated and physically toughened up at a National Socialist boot camp near Berlin. Adam Kuckhoff, noting the party emblem in Harnack's buttonhole and convinced that Harnack was an unprincipled careerist, boxed Arvid's ears on the street. Greta observed that "from Harnack's reaction I could see that he understood perfectly and was quite unperturbed."[10]

Close friends may have understood when Arvid joined the party but not the Harnack family. "Well, they were dead against it of course," said one cousin, Adolf-Henning Frucht. "They were appalled. You see it might be that Arvid was no organized Communist during '32 through '35 but he always said he was one. He never left any doubt that he was a Communist. He had Communist connections and no Nazi connections." Now family members reasoned that he had joined the Nazis chiefly to conspire against the party.

Another person who was not deceived by Harnack's Nazi Party membership was the Russian embassy official Sergei Bessonov, who had talent-scouted Harnack in 1932 during the heady days of ARPLAN. Always on the lookout for men on their way up, the NKVD had begun to concentrate on recruiting "young men from influential families" likely to rise to high positions in the establishment. According to intelligence procedures described by Soviet spy and defector Alexander Orlov, the Fifth Directorate of the Soviet Intelligence Service would have studied Arvid's life history beginning with his gymnasium years, analyzing his character traits, his weaknesses and vices, his friends and his family.[11] Exercising their characteristic patience, they waited until he was poised on the lower rungs of a promising ladder. On July 15, 1935, three months after Harnack joined the Economics Ministry, Moscow granted permission for an approach.[12] The solicitation was secured through a friend of Harnack's, the first secretary in the Soviet Embassy, Alexander Hirschfeld.

On August 8, 1935, Harnack met with Hirschfeld. According to KGB files, the first meeting lasted about three hours. Hirschfeld reported that although Arvid had agreed to provide the Soviets with information, he had "gone to great lengths to clarify the conditions of his cooperation with Soviet intelligence." Harnack explained how he "intended to combine it with his [Communist] Party and anti-Fascist activities." But Hirschfeld's mission was to inform Harnack that he should break off all ties with the illegal KPD; he would be more useful to the movement if he stayed away from the Communist Party. Hirschfeld explained that it would be dangerous to try to continue with his resistance activities. By "going underground, he could achieve far more in the struggle against Hitler." (Nevertheless, with his usual independence Arvid continued to engage in these activities.) According to his file, Harnack was given the code name Balt (perhaps because of his Baltic German ancestors) and an NKVD intelligence officer, Alexander Belkin, was assigned as his first Berlin control officer.[13] Notwithstanding, in the summer of 1936, the Comintern agent Alfred Kantorowicz, head of the Association of German Writers in Exile, reported that Arvid was in Paris, where he tried to make contact with members of the French Communist Party.[14]

Although he never considered himself a spy or an agent, merely a source, Harnack, by agreeing to help the Soviets in this manner, had taken the first step on the labyrinthine path that eventually would cost scores of lives.

What kind of information did Harnack provide to the Soviets? According to his KGB file, between 1935 and June 1938, Harnack supplied Moscow with "valuable documentary materials on the German currency and economy, secret summaries of Germany's investments abroad, and the German foreign debt." In addition, he reportedly provided the Russians with copies of Germany's secret trade agreements with Poland, the Baltic states, Persia, and others.[15]

Harnack's reports were not only passed to the Soviets, but accurate information—particularly on German rearmament—also found its way through underground circles into factories and to ministries in which many civil servants were not Nazis for, despite the Gestapo, there were many pockets of resistance in the ranks of the German bureaucracy.[16] A member of the Harnacks' resistance circle, the religious socialist and former Prussian cultural minister, Adolf Grimme, recalled that for those like himself the years of alienation had also been years of high integrity. Like-minded persons were in agreement about the regime, and far from being isolated, they supported each other, keeping their heads above the water by sharing their thoughts—as well as information.[17]

"Fanatic, rigid, industrious, conspicuously energetic and efficient, Harnack was not precisely a likable person, not a jolly good fellow; always serious, he had little sense of humor, and we, his colleagues, did not feel at ease in his presence," Reinhold Schönbrunn, one of Arvid's Communist friends, told David Dallin. "There was something of the puritan in this man, something narrow and doctrinaire, but he was extremely devoted."[18]

If Communists found Arvid puritanical, the NKVD had a very different opinion of Martha Dodd. After reading Martha's urgent love letter to Boris in which she wrote of a quarrel and farewell kiss she had given him on a visit to Bucharest in 1935 they wrote, "This amorality must be stopped."[19] Yet in January 1936, her contact Bukhartsev reported that Martha had told him about the "swinish behavior" of U.S. Ambassador to France William Bullitt during his visit to Berlin; in March she reported on a conversation between the German businessman Gustav Krupp and the American consul in Cologne. The Russian also reported several meetings with the ambassador's daughter in which she had again "frankly expressed her willingness to help the Soviet embassy." As reported by the agent, Dodd was studying the theory of communism with Arvid Harnack "to whom she goes often" but she was careful to conceal her convictions "due to her father's official status." When her father retires, she will be able "to conduct Communist activities more openly." The reporter cannot help ending on a salacious note: her father's position does not "prevent her from maintaining rather intimate relations with Louis-Ferdinand, the Crown Prince's son." As Martha explained to Bukhartsev, the crown prince was a perfect cover. The Germans and Dodd's colleagues who had viewed her affair with Vinogradov suspiciously "now consider her previous passion 'hearty' rather than 'political.' "[20]

In spite of Arvid's new government position, the couple continued their spartan ways. Mildred wrote about the concerts and plays they attended but they were frequently invited guests of friends and relatives. Although he bought himself a motorbike, Arvid continued to walk to work through the Tiergarten. Friends thought it perhaps a concession to his new status that Arvid joined the conservative Deutscher Klub, a successor to the equally exclusive Herrenklub. More likely, as senior government officials frequented it, the club allowed Harnack to cultivate new sources and it was certainly a reservoir for useful gossip.[21] Similarly, as protective coloring, Mildred joined the Berlin chapter of the ultraconservative Daughters of the American Revolution, becoming its secretary. The genealogical research she and her mother had carried out on a joint trip to England in 1930 helped trace her ancestry to the American Revolution and allowed her to prove to the Nazis that she was 100 percent Aryan.[22]

Although the Nazis shut down the Berlin Abendgymnasium, Mildred continued to see her students in private study groups. "If only the trust of a few was won, those brought their friends," wrote Greta Kuckhoff. "They loved it when Mildred discussed a newly published book from the United States with them in her home over a cup of tea. Because she only chose progressive works, the youth for the first time saw the current publications in Hitler's Germany with fresh eyes." The first helpless "what should one do?" had become we will get involved.[23]

In *Through Embassy Eyes*, which was published in 1939, Martha disguises Mildred as a "German married to an American" or "a lovely German woman—who detested the terror of Nazi Germany." In an interview she indicated that invariably this woman was Mildred. Mildred was the woman friend who would lead Martha into the embassy bathroom—as Martha remarked "a most difficult place to wire"—and "whisper some new event she had heard about."[24] The substance of these events, unreported in German newspapers, would end up in embassy cables.

In her book Martha gives the only contemporary account of some of the activities of the Harnack group as they were happening during the years between 1935 and 1937: "Speeches of Roosevelt and various statesmen all over the world were reprinted (speeches which are rarely reported in the Nazi papers or, if they are, so badly garbled they are unrecognizable), news of Spain, foreign opinion about Germany and the general European situation, comments about Hitler's policy, and information about labor movements in other countries. The speeches by Roosevelt and Churchill were translated by Mildred and Greta Kuckhoff. These leaflets were not at all incendiary but invaluable newspapers, offering information impossible to get in the German press."[25] Leaflets were also published by the Communist Party and passed around disguised as romances or other innocuous pamphlets. One underground classic was *The Brown Book of the Hitler Terror and Burning of the Reichstag*, which contained Dimitrov's famous concluding speech at the trial. This was disguised as a pamphlet with the title *Home Heating by Electricity* (Elektrowärme im Haushalt). Hired to translate *Mein Kampf* into English, Greta Kuckhoff confessed to using it to conceal the group's illegal writings.

How much Martha Dodd herself aided the Harnack group is uncertain. She may have assisted Mildred in getting visas to the United States for refugees or, with the help of her diplomatic passport, may have acted as a courier for the group. (In an interview, Katherine Smith, the wife of the military attaché, said that embassy personnel believed Martha went to Switzerland in 1935 on such a mission for the Soviets.)

The Harnacks' KGB files contain Liza's (Martha's code name) 1940 appraisal of the Harnacks:

They were intensely cautious in their technique of making contact, diplomatic in the extreme with other people, giving every impression of being highly trained and disciplined. Both of them maintained good contacts with Nazi women and men. Arvid was not suspected at the time and had an important post in the ministry. I am sure that, unless I have been profoundly deceived, they are completely reliable and trusted people from our point of view.[26]

And here is Mildred described in the prosaic jargon of the KGB files:

She is bold, tall, blue eyes, large figure, typically German-looking (although) a lower-middle-class American, intelligent, sensitive, loyal, very much the German *Frau*, an intensely Nordic type and very useful.[27]

The reader may wonder how Arvid Harnack, with his extensive contacts with the Soviets, escaped exposure. This obvious and important question becomes less mysterious on closer scrutiny.

To begin with, he was considered an expert on the Soviet economy, therefore a useful counselor during the vicissitudes of German–Russian relations. Harnack had a plausible cover for meetings with Russians, just as he later did for seeing Americans when he headed the American desk at the ministry. Equally important was his family's prominence, which gave Arvid a degree of immunity. It seemed unthinkable that anyone of his class and background might betray the fatherland. A similar caste blindness among the British protected the Cambridge spies, the KGB's "Magnificent Five": Philby, Burgess, Maclean, Blunt, and Cairncross.

Clearly, despite the recognition she received for her teaching and literary accomplishments, despite her network of friends and Arvid's family, these were not happy years for Mildred. Homesickness dogged her throughout her years in Germany. Her own family was in her thoughts and increasingly in her writing. In "The Preface to a Study of American Literature," Mildred injected this Proustian passage: "To think of the United States longingly from afar is to feel a rhythm in the mind and to scent a dust of remembered happiness. It is to remember how a frail mother whose life had begun in pioneer times sat in the woods in the fall . . . how her voice rose and soared in singing, 'Sweet land of liberty': how the tears swelled in her eyes in Hyde Park when a band of unemployed marched raggedly by playing the Star Spangled Banner."[28]

Mildred had not seen her mother since 1930, when she visited Mildred in Giessen and they traveled together to England for a short vacation. Now, in 1936, Georgina had retired from her government job and was living with Mildred's sister, Marion, in Milwaukee. She was also dying.

Homesickness impelled Mildred to write William Ellery Leonard, her former mentor on the English faculty at Wisconsin, in the hope of obtaining a position there as early as summer 1936. But the Depression and tight state budgets meant cutbacks at the university.[29] Circumstances were bad, Leonard replied, "no money, few prospects on our faculty." He attempted to let her down gently. "You have many splendid achievements as wife, as *Frau Professorin*, and as professor and introducer of American literature since you have mastered a foreign language and that wonderful culture; but we don't need this, in my opinion, unfortunately, in Madison in these wretched days."[30]

Clara Leiser was equally discouraging. She feared Mildred might think her "very cruel to point out the fact that all sorts of people who have been teaching the subject for years and are right on the spot couldn't get jobs," as Clara wrote Leonard. "But what foolishness it would be to say, 'Sure, come over. I'm sure you'll land something right away.'" Confidentially, she added, "Mildred and Arvid have to be very, VERY careful; they prefer not even to be mentioned. They're living in the most humble way, and live in danger of losing even that. More I'm pledged not to say."[31]

Nevertheless, within a year Clara informed Leonard: "Did I tell you that Mildred Fish wrote that she was coming over in January and asked whether she could stay with me because she couldn't take any money with her and didn't know where she would sleep? Martha Dodd (U.S. Ambassador to Germany's daughter) had already told me she was coming and I'd written inviting her to stay with me. I've not heard just when she's to arrive, and it might be that the latest edict forbidding any man over 18 to leave the country would change her plans, if she was hoping to look around for something for Arvid too."[32] A week later she reported that Mildred "arrives Friday, and meantime I wanted to rid my house of every scrap of anti-Nazi literature, for she was jittery even when I saw her in Berlin a year and a half ago."[33]

When the *Manhattan* docked a few days later, friends and

family found Mildred changed. The sunny, open, trusting Mili they had known had hardened into the superior, remote, self-conscious Frau Doctor Harnack-Fish. In Germany, Mildred had created an identity: a public persona as a confident lecturer, a popular figure in the American community, and an assimilated member of the distinguished Harnack clan. She had survived four years under the close scrutiny of Nazi colleagues as a teacher in Berlin and, like most Germans who opposed the regime, she took great care to conceal her feelings. In Germany discretion was the norm. But to her American friends, her reticence made her seem affected, odd, and somewhat schizophrenic. Compelled under the Nazis to lead a double life, by the time Mildred returned to America dissembling had become essential to her survival.

Mildred spent two weeks with Clara, prompting her hostess to fire off a letter of warning to Leonard in Madison: "I'm curious to know what you think of the 1937 Mildred Fish. I envy her will power, almost I envy a certain ruthlessness she's developed in pursuing her own interests & plans, no matter how rude part of the process may be." More critically, she characterized the changes she noticed such as "a certain condescension, long exercised by Europeans toward America & Americans" that has "taken hold of her, & amuses me." Mildred's "awareness of & references to her own facial beauty," annoyed her plainer friend, as did her "carefully adhered to *conviction* that she must dwell only on her strong points & never on anything approaching less than ideal characteristics (if indeed, they may be suspected to exist)," her "making a fetish of morning & evening exercises," and "her own assurance that anybody she approaches concerning a 'lecture' will be delighted & greatly benefited by the mere meeting with her." Although she insisted she was fond of Mildred, their two weeks together strained their friendship.

"Her German is more German than that of the *Deutschgeborene*. I asked whether the "r" had been specially practiced or was just acquired.

"It's really a Parisian 'r' was the reply.

"Have you been much in Paris?"

"Just once, ten days!!!"

Clara reported the final indignity to Leonard, himself a renowned translator: "I gasped (with indignation too) at her calm announcement that she had *rewritten* the entire first chapter of the Van

Gogh book [*Lust for Life* by Irving Stone, published in 1936] she translated without asking the author at all. To my protest that a translator ought to be a translator and not a re-*writer* she said, 'Well, I improved it.' That the author's approval might at least have been asked was a completely unimportant consideration."[34]

Mildred's high school friend Mady Emmerling had recalled that in New York, Mildred appeared "extremely frightened, cautious and reserved as if she felt there was someone looking over her shoulder all the time. At the same time there was a certain bravery about her. Under those perilous conditions she stood up for what she was. I recognized and admired that." But Mildred's necessary precautions led other friends to assume that she had become a Nazi. Clara hosted a large farewell party attended by many of Mildred's Wisconsin friends. Fifty years later, Dorothy Meyer recalled her final encounter with Mildred.

"Clara Leiser warned me that Mildred was going back to her husband, to a hostile country, and that anything she said could be held against her—therefore, we were not to discuss anything that had to do with Hitler. So we respected that. The only thing I said to her at the time was to ask her about her trip to Russia. And she said, 'We don't talk about that.' "

In fact, there was very little opportunity for private conversation in a large party of forty to fifty people. When the Meyers left, Dorothy asked Mildred if she would like to visit them.

"She kissed me and said, 'No, I might become too comfortable in your house.' When we were leaving I said to Ernie, 'I have the feeling, I've just been kissed by a Nazi.' But my husband said, 'Not unless I hear it from Mildred's own lips will I believe she is a Nazi.' "[35]

While in New York, Mildred sent a note to Thomas Wolfe. ("Will Triton ever blow his wreathed horn or Tom call me at Lex 2-8326? For I'm only able to stay here till Monday morning, yet there's a longing in me to know how you are.")[36] Although it's not known whether she saw him, according to Clara Leiser, they did chat on the telephone. She also sought out his former editor at Scribner's, Maxwell Perkins, to interest him in a book she was writing about American literature.

Armed with recommendations from Ambassador Dodd to his academic colleagues, Mildred embarked on a campus lecture tour that took her to Haverford College, New York University, Chicago, and Madison, where she undoubtedly made inquiries as to faculty openings. Her theme was the European reception of Carl Sandburg, Theodore Dreiser, Jack London, and Thomas Wolfe.

Leonard attended her Madison lecture, giving it a not altogether flattering review in a letter to Clara: "Her lecture was precisely what I'd expected it would be: she spoke with excellent platform voice and manner, and with a form in content methodical and scholarly, even writing names of books and people (Germans) on the blackboard (anent the German University professors' examination of the problem of 'Literature and Life') and yet got around to the topic for which people came to hear her only in the last ten or fifteen minutes, *The German Relation to Current American Literature* and then only superficially (aside from themes, political and social, which she naturally couldn't talk about). It was a simple fact that, even at this distance, I could have said far more to the purpose."[37]

The only items of importance that could be attributed to her stay in Germany and her literary contacts occurred in a private conversation between the teacher and his former pupil. "She did have data that might have made a good talk but she was under the compulsion to be distinguished." But what was he to do: "I'm tired of lying out of complacent good nature." Mildred had asked Leonard for a written recommendation but when he told her what was wrong with her lecture, it seemed not to have registered. Somewhat guilty, he wrote that "she seemed so genuinely glad to see me, so speedily responsive to G. [Grace, Leonard's much younger third wife], that I feel mean in all this. . . . for M. would doubtless stand up for me through thick and thin. And truly I wish indeed I could endorse her lecture, for, with all her pretentiousness, there is human warmth, human (in contrast to intellectual) sincerity, and a sort of bravery in the midst of misfortune, and pushing through mannerisms and affectations, a genuine regard for me."[38]

Professor Douglas Steere had never met Mildred and so was not put off by her newly acquired mannerisms. On hearing Harnack-Fish at Haverford College he offered a very different appraisal and wrote enthusiastically: "She discussed certain contemporary trends in European literature with a charm and a power and a vividness that I have rarely seen equaled. . . . She has the good sense to concentrate on a few significant features, to know what can be communicated in the brief span of an hour and what may be left undone. She has almost restored my ebbing faith in the function of the interpretative lecture along broad lines in a generation like our own."[39]

Mildred visited her Wisconsin relatives and for the first time went south to the land that was "awakening now in the pen of William Faulkner."[40] "After days seeing shacks and factories and magnificent homes—great extremes of riches and poverty—at Nashville," she wrote, "I am spending one day here to see the TVA. Then on to Washington."[41] There, her family urged her to leave Germany; once more they assumed the worst—that Mildred, once "a Red," had now "gone Nazi." Her niece Marion recalled, "The last time she was here Mildred was kind of strained, sort of roughened in her character. I guess she was hard-pushed knowing what course it was that she was on." Marion's sister Jane concurred: "When she came back to the United States, she conducted herself in a way that questions were not encouraged. She could not talk about Germany because, she said, 'I hold Arvid's head in my hands.' "[42]

Adding to the tension of the visit was the necessity of appearing to be a "good German," since her audiences included members of the American Nazi group, the German-American Bund. In Wisconsin, Mildred told her nephew she "was sure that she was being followed."[43]

Mildred called her high school friend Francis Birch, then a Harvard geophysicist, and sent him a recent photograph. She proposed a visit to Cambridge. They agreed on a date, and dinner and a bed were prepared for her. But when Birch went to pick her up at the train station, she did not appear. She never called, and Birch never heard from her again. "It was very strange, very unlike her," he said, "I assumed she was up to something."[44]

By this time, Mildred was engaged by necessity in "passing," a term commonly applied to light-skinned persons of African descent who pretended to be white. In order to survive during the Third Reich, many Germans and Mildred were engaged in wholesale "passing." At the far extremes, Jews tried to pass as Aryans,

Communist and Social Democrats joined the Nazi Party, homosexuals married. In normal times, social transactions depend on trust but the Third Reich was a society of impostors and fakes, the hallmark of which was a lack of authenticity. Whereas once she had enjoyed acting, now a great part of her life was devoted to posturing: at work as a member of a Nazi teaching organization, in society as a prominent member of the Daughters of the American Revolution. As Clara Leiser and Professor Leonard had been quick to point out, the new Mildred was a caricature of the old.

She returned to Germany in spring and accompanied Arvid on a tour of France while she awaited the arrival of her niece Jane. In Wisconsin, she had tried to convince her nephew Bob to return to Germany with her. He declined and she invited her niece, Jane Esch, her sister Harriette's younger daughter, for a summer visit. Jane eagerly accepted. Perhaps Mildred saw these younger relatives as possible recruits—she recommended that Jane read *Das Kapital* before she came to Germany. Or perhaps she merely sought to build a barrier against her loneliness. By 1937, save for diplomatic personnel, most of her American friends had left.

That autumn, Mildred led Jane and Charmetta Riebe, a friend from the American Woman's Club, on a week's walk through the Harz Mountains. Taking knapsacks and staying in hostels, they hiked from Quedlinburg through Thale, Bodetal, and Brocken, ending in Goslar.

A romantic and evocative region abounding in medieval cathedrals and squares, the Harz has many literary associations, particularly with Heine and Goethe. On a postcard to Falk, Mildred wrote that "the beauty of the mountains, the rivers and forests under the great sun is powerful. . . . Every evening we read *Faust I* together. It fits these surroundings."[45] Mildred particularly liked Quedlinburg, with its schloss and Romanesque cathedral perched on a sandstone cliff. But it was the wild grandeur of the valley of the Brocken, with granite slopes that bore names like the "Witches' Washbasin," "Devil's Pulpit," and finally the "Witches' Dancing place"—where each year on the Witches' Sabbath, Walpurgis Night, the spirits gathered—that formed the romantic backdrop for their nightly readings. "You can only appreciate the landscape of the Harz if you go by foot as Goethe has done," she enthused on a postcard to her mother-in-law.[46]

On September 15, 1938, the day before Mildred's thirty-sixth birthday, Thomas Wolfe died. A shattered Mildred wrote to his editor, Maxwell Perkins, that Wolfe's death left "a great emptiness in our generation." She was grateful, however, for his "abundance, passion and sting as a novelist," for "his quickening and satisfying joy as a person." She remembered him "as a friend giving armfuls of his love of the world we live in." Ending on an optimistic note she scarcely could have felt, Mildred wrote, "I hope the power of his genius will flow on giving rise to new genius quickly in our time. The world is changing very rapidly, but I do not think that its productive forces are leaving it. I hope that he was a sign that they are coming on."[47]

Another blow was the departure of Franziska and Rudolf Heberle. The Harnacks had been close friends of the Heberles since they met in Wisconsin, when Rudolf, also a Rockefeller scholar, had looked up John R. Commons. In 1935 Mildred became godmother to their daughter Antje. In a letter to Mildred's sister, written after the war, Franziska wrote that in spite of their daughter being born under the Nazi regime, they thought it "a good omen" to choose "such a courageous anti-Nazi" as they knew Mildred to be. "We could barely anticipate how much courage would be demanded from her later."[48]

Upon returning to Germany Heberle, a sociologist, published a study about the migration of farm workers to the city. His thesis was antithetical to the official line, thereby spoiling his chances for a professorship at Kiel. His position became more precarious when a student denounced him for teaching Marxism. Propitiously, he received an offer from the Sociology Department at Louisiana State University and in 1938 prepared to leave Germany. When he approached Arvid with the news, Heberle recalled that Harnack "got quite angry. He said something like, 'It's really a scandal that you have gotten yourself in a position that you have to leave the country.' So it appeared that he had also really counted on me." But characteristically, what reconciled Harnack to Heberle's departure was the fact that his friend was going to the South, where he could help Southern blacks.[49]

Heberle described Harnack as "somewhat donnish but essentially an activist. As such he had no sympathy personally with the more contemplative stand of sociologists who were not prepared for radical decisions. And he certainly was of the opinion, and with good reason, that such an attitude under the Nazis was untenable because this sooner or later must lead to a dead end from which one could escape only through emigration or spiritual subjugation. Only the determined anti-fascist fighter could keep his spiritual freedom. He was very unstoppable."[50]

Before they left in the summer of 1938, the Heberles invited Mildred to spend a final two-week holiday with them and their three children at a lakeside resort in Gremsmühlen in Holstein. "I've been to visit friends here," Mildred jotted on a postcard to her Wisconsin relatives, "where it is so far north that the twilight lasts till almost 11 o'clock at night. I am just finishing my translation of the novel, [*Drums along the Mohawk*] am teaching, lecturing, etc. A[rvid] has been away, as you know, so it has been a bit lonely."[51]

Franziska recalled that when the two women were together in the kitchen at Gremsmühlen, she wondered if Mildred were very poor because she had little luggage and only one white blouse: "At that time, I remember Mildred also told me—full of sadness—that she had a miscarriage and her sorrow astonished me because I believed that she intentionally had no children because of her political work."[52] Although this is the only direct evidence of what must have been a devastating event, we do know that the Harnacks wanted a family. Mildred was now thirty-five and perhaps the Harnacks decided against waiting for more propitious times.

In 1937, Ambassador Dodd declared that "four years' service is enough." His tenure, begun so optimistically with the idea that he "could have some influence in moderating the policies of the Nazi regime" and bring them "back to reason," had ended in failure.[53] As he explained to Bella Fromm, he had no delusions about Hitler when he was appointed to his post in Berlin. But he had "at least hoped to find some decent people around Hitler." He was thus horrified to discover that the whole gang was "nothing but a horde of criminals and cowards."[54] During his final years he became a near pariah. Increasingly isolated, often insulted—he seldom bothered to attend any but the most important diplomatic functions—Dodd had all but severed his relations with the Nazi regime. According to his daughter, the State Department, American businessmen, and the Germans all wished to have her father removed.

Meanwhile, Dodd's children added to his difficulties. Bill persuaded his father to help him solicit funds for the Communist-backed International Peace Campaign.[55] While his father was still *en poste*, Bill gave speeches at home attacking the Nazis. For her part, Martha's Moscow file indicates her eagerness to stay on in Berlin as an agent even after her father's term ended.[56] Martha prepared an extraordinary memorandum in March 1937 (months before her father's departure) for Abram Slutsky, the head of the NKVD's foreign department, which dealt with espionage and terror abroad and detailed the extent of the help ("my services of any kind and at any time") she was prepared to give the Russians:

> Currently, I have access mainly to the personal, confidential correspondence of my father with the U.S. State Department and the U.S. President.
>
> My source of information on military and naval issues, as well as on aviation, is exclusively personal contact with our embassy's staff. I lost almost any connection with the Germans except perhaps for casual, high-society meetings which yield almost nothing.
>
> I still have a connection to the diplomatic corps but, on the whole, it doesn't yield great results. I have established very close connections to journalists. . . .
>
> Is the information which I get from my father who is hated in Germany and who occupies an isolated position among foreign diplomats and therefore has no access to any secret information, important enough for me to remain in Germany. . . . ?
>
> I have done everything possible to make my father remain in Germany. I'm still going to do everything I can in this direction. However, I'm afraid he will retire this summer or fall. . . . He personally wants to leave. Shouldn't he arrange his resignation with a provocation once he decides the question of timing? Shouldn't he provoke the Germans to make them demand his recall or create a scandal, after which he could speak openly in America both orally and in the press. . . . To resign and to publish a protest? He could be convinced to do it if it had significance for the USSR.[57]

Martha also suggests that her father would be able to influence Roosevelt's choice of the next ambassador to Germany and offers to persuade her father to promote the Soviet Union's candidate for the post. Her offer to remain in Europe, return to the United States or go to the Far East as a journalist was considered important enough that it landed on Stalin's desk with a note from Yezhov, People's Commissar for Internal Affairs, asking for "instruction about Martha Dodd's use."[58]

After a nearly four-year off-and-on romance carried out in the capitals of Berlin, Paris, and Bucharest and now expedited by a discreet divorce, Martha was determined to marry Boris Vinogradov, then posted to Warsaw.[59] Her parents were not pleased.[60] Nevertheless she proposed a visit to Moscow via Warsaw in order to discuss her future with the NKVD. After their tryst in Warsaw in March, Boris wrote to his superiors that although she had established contacts with Earl Browder, the head of the American Communist Party, and with Comintern agent Otto Katz, he hoped that someone in Moscow with authority would "convince her to stay in Europe and work only for us."[61]

It was during this reunion in Warsaw that the lovers composed a joint letter to Stalin asking his permission to marry. Not surprisingly, they received no answer.[62] But in her file is an official "Statement to the Soviet Government," evidently written after her arrival in Moscow, which reads, "I, Martha Dodd, U.S. citizen, have known Boris Vinogradov for three years in Berlin and other places, and we have agreed to ask official permission to marry."[63]

As a result of her trip to Moscow, the lovers were ordered to stop using the post office and discontinue all telephone contact. Moscow informed its deputies that all correspondence between the lovers would be intercepted and in the future, Boris's replies would be dictated by the comrades in the NKVD. One wonders, if the letter from Boris to his "love," his "little Martotchka," was one of the products of the NKVD's scriptorium. In the first paragraph, he reassures her—"of course, I want to travel with you, not just ideologically but also practically." Further on he replies to her query, "anything new from our friend" (presumably the recipient of the memo, Abram Slutsky, the head of the foreign department of the NKVD and recipient of Martha's memo). The letter ends coldly: "I don't have to tell you that the work is the main thing and that everything, everything depends on your and my successful work."[64]

It seems there was no objection on the part of the NKVD to "Vinogradov's marriage to 'Liza.' However, this question will be resolved much later. For the present, in the interests of business, 'Liza' ceases even meetings with Vinogradov for six months . . . "[65] Nor was she to maintain any connection with anti-fascist friends like the Harnacks and Kuckhoffs or members of the Communist parties: "The connection will be maintained only with us."

As for her memorandum, the NKVD sanctioned her suggestion that her father provoke a public confrontation "in order to create strained relations between the American and German governments." Moscow also wanted to assist in the search for his successor. Meanwhile, Martha was to check her father's reports to Roosevelt and communicate short summaries of their contents. The NKVD's shopping list included reports she was to provide on Germany, Japan, and Poland. For her services, it is recorded that she received "200 American dollars, 10 rubles, and gifts bought for 500 rubles."[66]

What began as a grand passion in Berlin in 1933 had not withstood the distractions of distance and time, not to mention the prying eyes of the NKVD. Nor had the couple's handlers reckoned with Martha the indefatigable tease; her letters to Boris were littered with hints of amorous adventures, for example, December 8, 1936: "Armand is still here—but you must know that he means nothing to me now—as long as you are still alive—nobody can mean anything to me as long as you are alive."[67]

Boris was also experiencing doubts and, it appears, there was another, unknown woman, "Juliet #1." "Romeo" had demoted Martha to "Juliet #2" after their March meeting and, as he queried his superiors, "I don't quite understand why you have focused so much on our wedding. I asked you to point out to her that it is impossible in general and, anyway, won't happen in the next several years."[68] Six months later, he writes, he has again received a letter from Martha about marriage: "When she was leaving Moscow, I wrote you asking that you not give this type of promise. Nevertheless such a promise was given to her, and now she expects its fulfillment. Her dream is to be my wife, at least virtually, and that I will come to work in America and she would help me."[69]

As the Dodd family was preparing to leave in November 1937, Martha made a sudden visit to Warsaw. Boris reported that their rendezvous "went off well" and that a meeting had already been fixed with the local NKVD agent upon her arrival in New York in December. But she was still full of wedding plans "despite her parents' warning that nothing would come of it." However, as Boris related, the ever resourceful Martha was prepared to marry left-wing journalist Louis Fischer if her plans to marry the Russian fell through. By no means should the Russians leave her in "ignorance with regard to the real situation, for if we deceive her, she may become embittered and lose faith in us. Now she agrees to work for us even if it turns out that I won't marry her."[70]

Stalin had begun a political purge with the "Show Trials" growing out of the murder of Kirov, the Leningrad party chief. From 1935 to 1938, an estimated 5 million people were arrested, of whom 1 million were executed while unknown numbers died in camps.[71] No group was spared: old Bolsheviks, secret police chiefs, poets and scholars, party officials at every level, and nearly all the Red Army's senior officers. The world was asked to believe that Lenin's lieutenants were with few exceptions traitors, and that, with the encouragement of Trotsky, a Jew, they conspired with Nazi Germany to destroy the socialist motherland.

If the shock to Communists everywhere was profound, nowhere was consternation greater than in Germany, where many defendants in the Moscow trials once had direct links with their German comrades. Soviet diplomats who served abroad in Germany were especially vulnerable to charges of trafficking with the exiled pariah, Trotsky. Among those abruptly recalled was Arvid's close friend, Sergei Bessonov, the counselor in the Berlin embassy who helped found ARPLAN, and Martha's contact, the journalist Dmitri Bukhartsev.

Inescapably, during the roundup of former Berlin embassy attachés, Boris Vinogradov's name was added to the recall list. Boris saw Martha for the last time in December 1937. With the connivance of the Soviet ambassador in Berlin, he rashly left his post as chargé in Warsaw to be with her in Berlin. According to Martha, the German papers reported that, while he was in Berlin, the NKVD had raided the Warsaw embassy and Boris's office where they found incriminating documents. Accused of "collaborating with the Nazis," his making this final trip to Berlin without an official reason was tantamount to writing his death certificate.[72]

The last of Boris's Berlin friends to see him was the American journalist H.R. Knickerbocker. "Knick" was returning from covering the Sino-Japanese war via the Trans-Siberian Express. On learning in Moscow that Boris was serving in Warsaw, he arranged a stopover. They met at the Warsaw station, where Boris persuaded the journalist to stay overnight at the embassy. Years later, after both men were dead, Knick's wife, Agnes, wrote Martha that the two men discussed the Moscow trials and her husband asked the Russian, "If you are recalled to Moscow and if you have reason to believe that you have been falsely denounced, will you go back or will you choose exile in the West?" Although Boris surely knew that innocent comrades were already condemned, he answered that as a "loyal Communist," a youthful idealist who at sixteen had fought with the Red Army, he "would not be recalled and certainly not purged."[73]

The two men spent the whole night in conversation and argument, with Knick urging Boris not to return to Moscow and liquidation, and Boris steadfastly countering that "the Revolution was more important than one man's life."[74]

In January 1938 the French newspaper *Le Temps* reported that Boris Vinogradov had been recalled to Moscow from Warsaw.[75] It appears to be the sole published reference to his fate.

Boris's last letter to Martha, dated April 29, 1938, was written shortly before his execution, perhaps at the behest of the NKVD. Martha found it a moving document despite the gaps inflicted by the sharp scissors of the Russian censor. His final words to Martha were: "I love you, I'm full of you, I dream of you and of us."[76] As Martha recalled in a letter to Soviet journalist Ilya Ehrenburg that she wrote during a 1957 visit to Moscow, "It was a sad, sad letter and very loyal one (I still have it) and was his farewell I guess to me and to life. They say he was shot after this. I also wonder if his whole association with me, a foreign diplomat's daughter, could have helped destroy him in view of what we know of this tragic period."[77]

Years later, after World War II, Boris's execution was confirmed by Maurice Hindus, Louis Fischer, and friends in the State

Department.[78] In 1957, during the post-Stalinist era, Martha Dodd learned that her former lover had been "rehabilitated"—posthumously cleared of the charges against him.[79]

The Harnacks had their own reasons to be concerned over events in Russia. On March 2, 1938, in the pale blue and white columned ballroom of the former Nobles House in Moscow, before an invited audience that included foreign journalists, the first session of the so-called Great Trial of the twenty-one had begun. In the dock were the principal defendants: the senior Bolshevik and Lenin's favorite, pale, bearded Nikolai Bukharin; the former head of the Secret Police, Genrikh Yagoda; the former ambassador to Germany and former assistant commissar for foreign affairs, Nikolai Krestinsky; and Sergei Bessonov, formerly with the trade delegation in Berlin.[80]

At this, the most notorious of the Show Trials, defendant after defendant confessed abjectly to every imaginable crime, from espionage and murder to high treason and sabotage. Well rehearsed and having signed "confessions" extorted through torture or promises to take care of their families, the defendants were interrogated by Andrei Vyshinsky, a future U.N. ambassador, who reviled them as an "accursed generation of vipers" and a "putrefying heap of human scum."[81]

The first witness to be cross-examined was Arvid Harnack's luncheon companion, Sergei Bessonov. For ten months Bessonov refused to "confess" but now this "grim, gray-faced man with the air of an automaton," described in a deliberate manner how he acted in Berlin "as a link between Trotsky and Krestinsky." How, in 1933, he "arranged an interview between Trotsky and Krestinsky" and how together they "had plotted to betray the Soviet Union to the Germans."[82] Most of the defendants, including Bukharin and Yagoda, were condemned to death; three received prison sentences. Bessonov received the lightest: fifteen years. His colleague Bukhartsev did not fare as well. As her file indicates, Martha Dodd was informed of his execution in February 1937 as "a Gestapo agent."[83]

Stalin's terror had its consequences for Arvid Harnack. Five of the eight intelligence officers assigned to Berlin were recalled and executed for alleged treason. The decimation of the Berlin embassy, and the roundup of military and foreign intelligence operatives meant that Harnack was out of contact with Moscow from June 1938 through August 1940.[84]

In Berlin on November 7, 1937, the Soviet embassy invited guests to a celebration for the twentieth anniversary of the Russian Revolution. At a time when anti-Soviet feeling was at its height in Germany and shortly after an attack by Goebbels on the "Judaeo-Bolshevik world menace" in general and the Soviet Union in particular, Ernst von Salomon witnessed "a pale, distraught-looking" Arvid Harnack, together with two other Ernsts—the National Bolshevist Niekisch and the publisher Rowohlt—downing vodka and caviar and trout in aspic at the embassy on Unter den Linden. Besides the requisite diplomats, they were the only German guests. Noticeably absent was the assortment of generals and professors of former years.[85]

We do not know what the Harnacks, who were close to Bessonov and Vinogradov, made of the trials and confessions. In 1938, for many intellectuals on the left, Stalin still stood for a policy of not appeasing the Nazis. This caused many to close their eyes and mute their criticism. Rudolf Heberle recalled that Arvid was "very well-informed about what was going on in Russia, I remember that he explained to me for instance why Stalin executed so many generals: they were not reliable. Their relations with the Germans were too close."[86] Yet Martha Dodd, writing in 1979 to Greta Kuckhoff, recalled that Arvid "did not like what Stalin was doing to everyone everywhere. Even late in 1937, he spoke vehemently to me, and had agonizing doubts about the truth of the propaganda emanating from that source."[87]

Mildred's and Martha's paths had diverged since their salon days in 1934–1936. Martha made several long trips abroad; Arvid completed his legal apprenticeship and returned to Berlin and Mildred resumed her role as wife. More importantly, Martha spent more and more time with the snobbish embassy set while Mildred busied herself with her writing, teaching, and translating. They continued to see each other but less frequently. And as the Harnacks' illegal activities increased, Martha and Bill, outspoken and under surveillance by the Gestapo, were dangerous to know.

Martha wrote that the two women parted in the fall of 1937 at a busy restaurant: "We found an inconspicuous table and talked quietly for an hour, about books, ourselves, fascism and the future. We agreed to write each other now and then and later, when I heard from her, communications were mailed outside Germany. . . . But this last day I saw her she spoke only with grave pride of their growing effectiveness, hopefully of a new Germany in which we would enjoy the fruition of our work. Mildred was rarely demonstrative but this day she kissed me quickly before we left and I watched her move down the street without any premonition that she like so many of our friends had only five more years to live."[88]

The place is East Berlin. The year is 1991.

In Martha Dodd's correspondence intercepted by the FBI, I was surprised to see the name Jürgen Kuczynski, a name familiar to researchers in the field of espionage and someone—if he would talk—who might provide further clues to the mystery of Martha and Mildred. To my astonishment, I found his name in the Berlin telephone book and on two appropriately cold, rainy days in fall 1991, I visited him in the Weissensee section of eastern Berlin. As former Communist Party nomenklatura, the Kuczynskis lived in a large private house with 40,000 books, many of them rare editions.

Kuczynski is a name to be reckoned with among the world's secret services. For thirty years, Jürgen, his father, and siblings were the first family of Soviet espionage. Professor René Kuczynski, a former director of the German Statistical Office, a former fellow of the Brookings Institution in Washington, and a reader at the London School of Economics, passed on to Moscow information he had obtained from his friend and later British envoy to Russia Sir Stafford Cripps. His sister, Ruth, known in the covert world as "Sonya," was perhaps the most successful female operative ever. Klaus Fuchs was one of her assets.[89] Jürgen, "the dangerous Dr. Kuczynski" as he was dubbed by British journalist Chapman Pincher, also studied economics. During the 1920s he was also at Brookings, where he knew several Friday Niters and remembered meeting briefly with two German Rockefeller scholars, Arvid Harnack and Rudolf Heberle.

After a visit to the Soviet Union in 1930, Jürgen joined the

German Communist Party and became a contributor to the Rote
Fahne, *the party newspaper. During his years in Berlin, he was
recruited for Soviet intelligence by Sergei Bessonov, for whom he
had only the highest praise. Bessonov was the "perfect Communist," educated, cultured, intelligent, and a warm friend. Interested
in everything, he would hold a half hour's conversation about the
preparation of fish with Kuczynski's Alsatian wife, Marguerite.*[90]

*Kuczynski offered shorthand judgments on the other Russians
in the Berlin embassy. Boris Vinogradov . . . "very likely (KGB).
Alexander Hirschfeld"*[91] *. . . "He wasn't nice and he wasn't courageous. I didn't like him so much but he was assigned to be the
contact between the [Soviet Foreign Minister] Maxim Litvinov and
me."*

How was the material delivered?

*Once or twice a month Kuczynski saw Bessonov, Bukhartsev,
or the ambassador and submitted reports on the German situation
to be forwarded to Litvinov. I expressed surprise that during the
Third Reich, it was possible for a German national, a Communist,
and a Jew, to deliver reports to the door of the Soviet embassy
under the eyes of the Gestapo. Kuczynski replied that "the Gestapo didn't want to have any trouble with the Russians."*

*In 1936, when his work as an "illegal" in Germany became too
dangerous, he went to Moscow where the KPD party chiefs in
exile—Walter Ulbricht and Wilhelm Pieck—suggested he join his
family living in Britain. There, overtly, he represented the Comintern; covertly, he continued to send his reports evaluating the
military, economic, and political situation in England to Moscow.
He also organized fellow German Communist exiles, and he
helped British and American intelligence recruit KPD members for
undercover detail in Germany. (According to his American contact, Joseph Gould, Kuczynski together with his sister supplied the
Americans with seven German Communists who were parachuted
behind the lines in Germany. Three disappeared. The four who
survived provided the Americans with a great deal of useful information.) Kuczynski himself became a colonel in the OSS (Office
of Strategic Services), the predecessor of the CIA, but as he admitted to me, "Of course, I shared everything I learned with the
Russians." (OSS chief William Donovan condoned the practice of
hiring known Communists: "I know they're Communists; that's*

why I hired them." Later, he elaborated, "I'd put Stalin on the payroll if I thought it would help defeat Hitler.")[92]

In spite of what he called his "illegal activites," Kuczynski had been occupied for most of his eighty-seven years in scholarly writing—more than one hundred books, including a forty-volume history of the working class. An erudite man with courtly manners and a proclivity for Cuban cigars, he had the patrician face of a Russian wolfhound.

Jürgen maintained a fifty-year friendship with Martha Dodd. He visited her in Prague and in the 1960s accompanied her on a trip to Dresden. "Martha Dodd," he laughed. "We called her the anti-Fascist nymphomaniac—a wonderful woman. She should have written her memoirs. She once said to me, 'Jürgen, you're the only resistance fighter I haven't slept with.'"

Kuczynski hadn't known Martha Dodd in Berlin: "But Dodd I knew before he became ambassador. I knew the Dodds through my father. Dodd gave two lectures at the Brookings Institute. I visited Ambassador Dodd in Virginia and met [his son] Bill there. I met Martha in the United States when we went there to collect money for the party in '38." Alfred Stern, Martha's beau and future husband, gave him some money. "Martha wanted to know whether she should marry him."

I asked his opinion of Ambassador Dodd. "Nice, yes, that's it."

"Not effective?"

"He was a naive liberal. He was a very useful ambassador from the point of view of the Nazis because he was so harmless."

"Dodd couldn't do much about the Nazis. He was ineffectual but Martha, you are saying, decided she could help?"

"Yes quite, and she did," he replied elliptically. "Yes, she was very effective if she wanted to help." This was as close as I got to his confirmation that Martha Dodd was indeed a Soviet spy.

We talked about reports that Martha, at Mildred's urging, had gotten diplomatic help for people, especially visas to the United States. Kuczynski replied by recalling that he had been interned in England as a German alien at the onset of the war in 1939. On learning of this, Martha wrote to the British ambassador in Washington, Lord Lothian, a personal friend of her father's. She also pressed President Roosevelt to intervene. According to Kuczynski, this brought about his release.

He had just missed a 1935 meeting with Bessonov in Copenhagen, which he believed spared his life. In view of this, I asked about the Moscow Trials. In spite of his friendship with Bessonov and other members of the embassy, had he believed them guilty of being Trotskyites?

"I will tell you how difficult it was. I believed in them. My father didn't believe in them—that these people were guilty. But then came the treachery of Flandin and Daladier, who surrendered France to Hitler. My father came to me and said, 'Now I believe in the trials.' It was so fantastic to him that the leaders of France would betray their country in favor of Hitler that he then thought it was possible in the Soviet Union too."

The Kuczynskis are the last of the breed of idealogical "spies" recruited during the heyday of Hitler, Mussolini, and Franco. They did it not for money but to oppose Hitler and support the Communist cause.

Had he felt betrayed by present-day events: the breakup of the Soviet Union and the reunification of Germany? Had the risks of the "illegal work" been worth it?

"Yes, yes, you see firstly I was excluded [in the GDR] from all important political activities. That is I was mostly active as a scholar, and therefore I could write. I mean I had my difficulties and punishments from the party but I could publish quite a bit. You know the [West German] paper the Frankfurter Allegemeine Zeitung, a very conservative newspaper. When I was eighty-five, they wrote a congratulatory article and the headline was 'Ein Querdenker und fröhlicher Marxist' (A dissident and happy Marxist). There you have the story. I will tell you another thing. I wrote a book, Conversations with my Great-Grandson. It was a great success; 260,000 copies were sold also in West Germany. And his first question was, 'Are you happy about this country?' And I wrote definitely yes, because I think the system is very useful and then I said at the same time, definitely not, because there were so many mistakes we made. Today I would say just the opposite. I would say definitely not because the system couldn't work but definitely yes because a great number of good things have been done."

The visit concluded with a discussion of spy novels. He had the large red English paperbound edition of John LeCarré's The Perfect Spy *on the table. Kuczynski confessed to being a fan of the form but read them in English—"the only language for espionage." He had the largest collection (3,200) of English* Spione *and* Krimis *in Germany—no inconsiderable feat, since they couldn't be legally imported into the GDR. He took me downstairs where he stored his large collection of Havana cigars, and offered me three volumes by P. D. James. It was an offer I could not refuse.*

TWELVE

Resister

Libertas and Harro Schulze-Boysen

In the wake of Hitler's defeat, the world found it hard to believe that there was a German opposition to National Socialism and that there were "good Germans" who tried to get rid of the German leader. The British historian A. J. P. Taylor even insisted that "the German resistance was a myth."[1] This was hardly surprising since the extent of internal resistance was hidden from the German people for a decade and the outside world with one notable exception, the July 20 bomb plot. Gestapo and police records confiscated by the Allies in 1945 were only selectively available for decades. Only recently have scholars begun to examine the classified British, American, and Russian diplomatic and intelligence archives, which reveal a more complicated truth relating to the German resistance.

In 1939, according to a secret Gestapo report, the number of Germans in prisons and concentration camps under "protective custody" for political reasons, awaiting trial, or under sentence was 302,535. Other data show that between 1933 and 1945 some 800,000 Germans were imprisoned for active resistance.[2] These figures undoubtedly include some Jews and disaffected Nazis, but the sheer numbers counter the idea that the German resistance was a "myth." Recent books drawing on German and British sources have thrown new light on the frustrated attempts of the German opposition—military, political, and clerical—to unseat the regime.[3] Some scholars now believe that if these overtures to the British and Americans had been pursued, World War II might have been prevented, or at least shortened.

Former German chancellor Willy Brandt, a Social Democrat who fled Germany to combat Nazism, defined a resister as a person who "takes serious risks to act illegally in a world where right has become wrong." By that definition both Harnacks were resisters. They took risks: they rescued Jews and other dissidents, and they translated, printed, and disseminated illegal literature. Their task was immeasurably more difficult than that of resisters in occupied Europe who could count on the support and protection of the population. The Harnacks faced a homegrown dictatorship that enjoyed considerable popularity. Yet while other German resisters are viewed by some as heroes, the Harnacks, by contrast, are perceived in the West as Stalin's agents rather than as persons of conscience seeking the destruction of an illegal regime. They are relegated to the category of spies.

In the Harnack case, as in a world where right becomes wrong, historians have relied on captured Gestapo documents or the postwar testimony of Gestapo interrogators and Nazi judges to assess the group's motives and deeds. The Gestapo was determined to find a Soviet spy group, and that was what it found. The story of the Harnacks' search for American allies has never been told. The possibility that Arvid assisted the United States as well as the Soviet Union has never been investigated. Only an oblique hint from Arvid's brother Falk ("you should go into the archive of President Roosevelt because it was top secret at the time") pointed toward the missing piece in the Harnack puzzle: an American diplomat named Donald Heath.

Ambassador Dodd was supplanted in Berlin by a career diplomat, Hugh Wilson, who liked to quote Talleyrand's advice to a young colleague: "Above all, not too much zeal." To this dictum, Wilson appended his own corollary: "We do not love, we do not hate, we do not judge, we do not condemn; we observe, we reflect, we report."[4] During the few months of his tour—he was withdrawn in protest after Kristallnacht, the infamous 1938 pogrom against German Jews—he was faithful to his precepts. Joining Wilson as the first secretary at the end of 1937 was Donald Heath, another career foreign service officer. Heath and his sociable wife, Louise, became welcome additions to Berlin's dwindling diplomatic set.

American expatriates remember Heath as a short, good-looking, extroverted Kansan who liked to play the piano at parties. An embassy colleague, Jacob Beam, recalled him as a careful listener who spoke good German but had one peculiar characteristic: "He didn't look you in the eye. He looked down at his desk. He was listening but in order to concentrate on what you were saying, he couldn't see you."[5] A Harnack relative described Heath as "one shrewd cookie . . . with a good perception of people and things. He was the original lateral thinker. He was always coming up with different answers to questions. You asked him a question and he'd give an answer which you didn't realize was related to your question. Then he would scratch his head and move on."[6]

A former newspaper reporter, Heath had served as an army

lieutenant in World War I. After a stint as White House correspondent for the United Press, he joined the State Department and moved slowly through the ranks. When it appeared that he did not possess the requisite independent income for the expensive Berlin posting, the Treasury Department came to Heath's rescue.

Secretary Henry J. Morgenthau felt he "imperatively needed" a special Treasury attaché in Berlin to ferret out economic information.[7] However, a special posting conflicted with government cost cutting. So Heath, nominally attached to the State Department, acquired additional duties as an intelligence officer in the Office of Coordination, a predecessor of the Office of Strategic Services. As "Morgenthau's man," he was given additional pay and in 1939, a further special entertainment allowance.[8]

Heath arrived in the wake of a 1937 cable from the Berlin embassy reporting a German warning to German citizens "against treasonable acts involving the delivery of economic information to foreigners." Traitors would be executed.[9] In light of this, Heath's initial attempts at obtaining information were understandably futile.

Mildred's friend George Messersmith, a former consul general in Berlin and subsequently assistant secretary of state, recalled a dinner conversation with Secretary Morgenthau in which he again deplored the lack of vital information from Berlin.[10] In a confidential message to the Berlin embassy, Messersmith conveyed Morgenthau's disappointment.[11] In particular, the Treasury desired "full reporting on the position and operation of the German Treasury, Reichsbank, money market, debt, gold and exchange position, *et cetera*, that it is receiving in Paris and London."[12]

These topics were precisely within Arvid Harnack's area of expertise. In the Economics Ministry, he worked on balance of payment and foreign exchange questions.[13] As a colleague wrote, "His duties put him in direct contact with all the various country desks; and his position as chief of a basic desk [trade policy] allowed him to participate in all decisions that were made. His position of responsibility brought him into almost daily contact with the Foreign Office, in the economics department of which the corresponding country desk chiefs worked. He systematically acquired a reliable overview of our current economic capacity, our production and our reserves, and he evaluated our foreign trade situation at any given time. In this way, Harnack became one of the persons most knowledgeable about the state of the economy."[14] Moreover, in his new post as government counselor (he was promoted in 1938) he could plausibly meet with his American counterparts.

After Heath met Harnack, the "circumstances beyond his control" that prevented Heath from obtaining information were "removed."[15] Arvid, who was never named in order to protect his identify, is identified by internal evidence corroborated by Heath's son successively as a "confidential source," an "authoritative German source," a "well-placed source," or a "high official of the Economics Ministry" in long-neglected State Department documents.[16]

Initially Harnack responded cautiously to Heath's overtures. Under Dodd there had been security breaches that had threatened the embassy's intelligence sources. A German economist had supplied the American embassy with a confidential analysis. Carelessly left lying around, it had fallen into the hands of Goebbels's spies. Nevertheless, in 1939, Harnack met periodically with Heath, apparently without arousing suspicion.[17]

Occasionally, the Harnacks were guests of the Heaths. More often Mildred and Louise Heath met at the American Women's Club. When Mildred became the tutor to the Heaths' son, the two couples began regularly to spend weekends and ski vacations together. Invariably, these social encounters were followed by weekly yellow cables to Washington, "From Heath for Treasury": on the "armament boom," the decrease in real wages of workers, foreign exchange statistics, gold imports as a portent of war, I. G. Farben's foreign trade balances, and so forth.[18] With Arvid's help, Heath's career was substantially advanced in Berlin.

In 1938, Harnack introduced Heath to another important source, Otto Donner, the German husband of Mildred's niece Jane. Donner had become a friend of Max Delbrück when, for political reasons, both failed their university habilitation accreditation. Through Delbrück, Donner met Harnack and subsequently Mildred's niece. Jane and Otto were married that same year when Donner was working for the Research Office for Military Economics. The two men developed a close personal relationship and the German passed the American information.[19]

In the Morgenthau archives in the Roosevelt Library at Hyde

Park, an important letter from Heath to the treasury secretary, dated May 2, 1939, and catalogued merely as a thank-you note, contains Heath's comments on these "useful sources," the "highly educated" civil servants who now had become members of the National Socialist Party:

> It is indeed a practical necessity for them to be members if they are to advance or even retain their positions in the government. . . . The attitude of these young Liberals is that, given the strength of the National Socialist Movement, there is no possibility of combating from without. The only alternative, they say, is to strengthen their position in the government and attempt to modify the movement and wait until a favorable internal or external event will bring about its downfall.

Further on Heath amplifies Arvid's views:

> It may be said here that the majority of this group are inclined to be moderately Socialist in their views. They do not disapprove of the increase of state intervention and the control of industry and commerce under the National Socialist regime. What they object to is the restriction on personal liberty, freedom of thought and the present policy of military aggression, instead of international cooperation, which they feel will eventually lead to a European war.[20]

After the war, Heath acknowledged to his family and the Harnacks that Arvid was his source and had provided "very useful inside information about the true state of things in Germany."[21]

Further corroboration of Harnack's help comes from an unusual quarter: an inventory in Harnack's KGB file, information Harnack supplied the Russians before his contacts were cut off by the Soviet purge trials. Although the list ends in June 1938, soon after his contact with Heath begins, the material is strikingly similar to the substance of the American reports: information on German currency and economy, investments abroad, and foreign debt and trade agreements.[22]

By late 1937, it was clear there was little prospect for a popular uprising against Hitler. Few knew this better than Arvid Harnack, who had close family and civil service connections to members of the German resistance. During this period, Arvid carefully cultivated these anti-Hitler sources, many of whom believed that the only realistic possibility of overthrowing the regime lay with the Army. Nevertheless, Ernst von Harnack remarked: "The opposition must spin their web through the whole machinery of the regime," and implored, "and at the same time try to make contact abroad."[23] Arvid's strategy was similar: penetrate the ministries, find accomplices, search for allies abroad, and prepare to take over after the overthrow of Hitler.

Here a brief digression is needed to describe the resistance in the armed forces, which culminated in the July 20, 1944, plot to overthrow Hitler. From the moment Hitler seized power in 1933, the senior military viewed the Führer with a mingling of ambivalence, distrust, scorn, and hatred. They approved of Nazi plans to rearm Germany and flout the Versailles Treaty, and for the most part they were indifferent to the movement's anti-Semitism and its dictatorial methods. But Hitler was an upstart, a nobody, an amateur at strategy, and an adventurer. His thuggish Brown Shirts were an embryonic rival to the Wehrmacht. Three times from the first stirrings of the National Socialist movement until 1933, at every point when Hitler tried to seize power, there appeared a general, "a bemonocled figure in field grey and claret-coloured trouser stripes, with uplifted hand, crying 'Halt!' "[24]

In 1934, Hitler launched his blood purge and eliminated the Brown Shirts and their commander, Ernst Roehm. He followed up with a psychological masterstroke. That August, after the death of Hindenburg, Hitler assumed the presidency and compelled his army officers to take an oath of personal fealty: "I swear before God to give my unconditional obedience to Adolf Hitler, Führer of the Reich and of the German people, supreme commander of the Wehrmacht, and I pledge my word as a brave soldier to observe this oath always, even at peril of my life."[25]

The oath notwithstanding, Hitler's deadliest enemies still wore army field gray and claret-colored uniforms. On November 5, 1937, in a meeting with his senior commanders, Hitler disclosed his intention to subdue Austria and Czechoslovakia, by force if necessary. An adjutant recorded his saying that, "every generation needs its own war, and I shall take care that this generation gets its war." But Field Marshal Werner von Blomberg, his minister of war, and General Freiherr Werner von Fritsch, the commander in chief of the army, objected that Germany was still too weak. Both men were then framed and purged; Fritsch was charged with homosexual acts.

Fritsch was vigorously defended by Hans von Dohnanyi at the Ministry of Justice, one of the few departments struggling to maintain a degree of independence. As a young man, Dohnanyi had frequently accompanied the Delbrücks on their Sunday visits to the home of Adolf von Harnack. In 1925, Dohnanyi and Arvid Harnack had been colleagues at the Institute for Foreign Policy in Hamburg, where both were members of the circle around Professor Albrecht Mendelssohn-Bartholdy. As a result of his defense of Fritsch, Dohnanyi caught the attention of General Ludwig Beck and Colonel Hans Oster of the army intelligence staff, the Abwehr. They drew Dohnanyi into the so-called Generals' Plot.

In September 1938, alarmed by Hitler's plans for *Lebensraum* for Germany at the expense of Czechoslovakia, Poland, and the Ukraine, Generals Beck, Erwin von Witzleben, and Franz Halder conspired to arrest Hitler if and when he ordered the army into the Sudetenland. The chancellery, key ministries, and the headquarters of the SS and Gestapo were to be occupied. Some plotters advocated assassinating the Führer while others wanted to put Hitler on trial. At the Ministry of Justice, Dohnanyi had been secretly collecting evidence of Hitler's crimes, the so-called chronicle of shame.[26] Because of this secret dossier, Dohnanyi was asked to prepare the prosecution. Dohnanyi also advocated bringing Hitler before a panel headed by his father-in-law, psychiatrist Karl Bonhoeffer, that would declare the Führer mentally ill.

In fall 1938, at the time of the Sudetenland crisis, General Beck told a coconspirator who happened to be heading for Britain, "Bring me back certain proof that England will fight if Czechoslovakia is attacked and I will put an end to this regime."[27] Prime Minister Neville Chamberlain ignored this message from the German high command, and his cabinet on August 30 decided not to issue an ultimatum to Hitler. Interrogated after the war, General Halder, the sole survivor of the plot, maintained that a successful *coup d'état* was prevented by Chamberlain's arrival in Munich in September. In the notorious Munich Pact, Britain and France accepted a compromise proposed by Mussolini and allowed German troops to occupy the Sudetenland. For the military conspirators, as well as the Harnack group, Munich was a devastating blow.[28]

As civilians were drawn into the military resistance, Oster and Dohnanyi bridged the two groups. They were joined in 1937 by pastor Dietrich Bonhoeffer. Like Harnack, Bonhoeffer participated in family discussions in which resistance strategy was argued. Thus Bonhoeffer, though a clergyman, moved from passive resistance to practical action. Other Harnack relatives joined the circle of those known as the July 20 conspirators. Through Dohnanyi, Justus Delbrück was recruited into the Abwehr and the resistance in 1940. In the back of the office managed by Arvid's cousin Ernst von Harnack, who had been dismissed by the Nazi as the Social Democratic president of the council in Halle-Merseburg, and Klaus Bonhoeffer met for the first time with Dr. Carl Goerdeler, the disillusioned former mayor of Leipzig, who had resigned in protest in 1937 when a statue of the Jewish composer Felix Mendelssohn was removed from its position in front of Leipzig's Gewandhaus Hall. Through Goerdeler contact was established with Wilhelm Leuschner, the leader of the illegal Socialist Trade Union. Ernst von Harnack also had ties with other Social Democrats, among them former Reichstag deputy Julius Leber. Now Ernst von Harnack's informal chamber music evenings became resistance meetings in disguise.

Given his personal ties to these key figures, Arvid was most probably aware of their plans. He would doubtless have approved any move to rid Germany of the Nazis, although a strike against the Führer himself seems not to have been discussed in Harnack's own circle. According to Otto Donner, Harnack's plan in early 1935 was "to gather around himself a group of oppositional individuals who had insight into the situation and, if possible, occupied key positions." All were to remain in their jobs to try and "penetrate into the Ministries."[29] Harnack's KGB files verify this agenda:

CORSICAN [Arvid], after losing contact with us in 1938, continued his proselytizing work among the intelligentsia along the established lines of the BGB [*Bund geistiger Berufe*], the Intellectual Workers Union, avoiding any connections to the KPD. With the assistance of his wife, he has personally vetted old acquaintances from the Union, carefully selecting and drawing in new recruits. At present, within the larger circle, centers have been formed, each of which is dedicated to the education and training of a small group. Although CORSICAN himself cannot personally vouch for every person, every one of these sixty people, the whole network of people who have the same background, think alike and come from the same social strata.[30]

The files also record the way in which the group camouflaged its operations:

While not all the members of the circle know one another, something of a chain exists. CORSICAN himself tries to remain in the background although he is at the heart of the organization. The aim of them all is to prepare personnel to occupy administrative posts [in the German Government] after the [military] *coup d'état*. CORSICAN himself has had no contact with the Communist Party.[31]

Arvid and Mildred's most significant contacts were with Harro Schulze-Boysen, the young man we met in 1933 in the SA cell, and his wife, Libertas. Rudolf Heberle recalled how, in 1935, he acted as an intermediary between Harnack and Heberle's wife's second cousin, Schulze-Boysen:

"I visited Harro during the period he was in the Air Ministry," Heberle told me, "and found that he was definitely opposed to the regime, which didn't surprise me at all because I had had a long correspondence with him while he was still publishing *Gegner*. So I arranged that Harro would come over to the Harnacks' one evening and, of course, it clicked immediately. They found that they shared the same ideas. But after Harro left, Harnack said, 'Tell your cousin that I appreciated meeting with him. I was very interested but I don't want to see him again because it's too dangerous.' "

Arvid, preternaturally cautious, was perhaps initially put off by Schulze-Boysen's reckless temperament. However the alliance between the Harnacks and the Schulze-Boysens began five years later, in 1940, as a result of a meeting between the Kuckhoffs and the Schulze-Boysens.[32] Adam and Libertas shared an interest in films. He wanted a job as a director, and in 1941 she would become a scriptwriter in Goebbels's Propaganda Ministry film center. The Kuckhoffs were impressed by the Schulze-Boysens, who were young, good-looking, and brimming with patrician self-confidence.[33] Most importantly, they shared the Kuckhoffs' political views.

The Kuckhoffs sensed a logical partnership. Harro's military intelligence, gleaned in the Luftwaffe, would supplement Arvid's economic information. The Kuckhoffs sensed an affinity of opposites, a synergy between the two. Arvid, the consummate bureaucrat, could teach Harro caution, direct and discipline him, channel his energy. Harro could bring his bravado and a sorely needed sense of fun and renewal to the group.

As often happened when much was at stake, the approach was made through Mildred. Greta arranged for Mildred and Libertas to meet on a week's holiday in Saxony, anticipating the meeting of the two husbands. Mildred and "Libs" sat in the narrow kitchen, protected from other eyes and ears. Because the kitchen had a special entrance, Greta gave Mildred the key and when she closed the door behind her, she pressed her small son close to her. "I saw it clearly before my eyes," she writes in her memoir. "From then on our work not only implies the risk of losing our freedom, from now on death was a possibility."[34]

Mildred was readily drawn to the blond, blue-eyed, twenty-seven-year-old Libertas, who had the kind of beauty, animated and sensual, that cannot be captured in photographs. Lawyer Rudolf Behse, who later defended her, declared that he had never seen such "a beautiful woman, with such sex appeal."[35] Never alone, Libertas was a "decided flirt" whose musical and athletic talents made her the center of attention.[36]

At their first meeting, Greta Kuckhoff was annoyed when Libertas passed around pictures of Schloss Liebenberg, her ancestral home. The imposing estate would be overrun by the advancing Russian army in the final days of World War II and then used by East German Communists as a rustic playground for the new party elite, but in the Thirties, Liebenberg's manicured gardens, princely rooms (including a library with 30,000 books), and hunting preserve still belonged to the family. Libertas loved the schloss of her grandfather, Prince Philipp zu Eulenburg-Hertefeld, where she spent her childhood.[37] An architect by avocation, the prince acquired his title from his close friend and confidant, Kaiser Wilhelm II.[38] A self-taught writer, musician, and composer, Eulenburg bequeathed the name Libertas to his granddaughter. She was named after the heroine of her grandfather's "Tales of Freedom."

In 1933, shortly after she graduated from finishing school in Zurich, Libertas, impressed by the German youth movement joined the Nazi Party. She was working for Metro-Goldwyn-Mayer in Berlin as a press aide[39] when she met Harro Schulze-Boysen. They were married in 1936 in the chapel at Liebenberg underneath a painting by Guido Reni (later "liberated" by Soviet soldiers).[40] Her mother-in-law, Marie-Luise Schulze, did not entirely approve of Libertas, whom she found naively optimistic, too ready to gossip, too easily influenced, not sufficiently domesticated, and too immature to be a steadying influence on her charming but reckless son.[41] Her offer to teach Libertas to cook was refused by her son, who didn't want to continue the "middle-European sentencing of the wife to the kitchen" tradition. Instead, he wrote his parents that it was much more important that Libs use the day in order to help him in his work than to work in the kitchen, go to the market, or dust. Having said this, he continued to send his laundry home from Berlin to Duisburg.[42] Like Mildred, Libertas seldom cooked, since it was "cheaper, more plentiful and healthier" to eat in a restaurant.[43]

Like Arvid, Harro insisted that Libs be independent—"to become accustomed to surviving as her own person even when separated from me." Once when she complained that she couldn't live a day without him, he insisted that her lack of independence was intolerable. "Libertas is my closest companion and confederate," he wrote his parents. "Should fate ever choose to separate us by force (and for people like us there is no assurance that this won't happen), it is precisely then that she must be able not only to 'live a day without me,' but also if need be—and everything depends on this—to work and function one-hundred percent."[44] Nevertheless Libertas continued to suffer under the critical gaze of her mother-in-law. From this distance, it is hard not to sympathize with Libertas, who was "so unfortunate as to fall in love," as she wrote, in "this rotten country."[45]

Once married, Libertas also became an opponent of the regime. In 1937, while others rushed to enlist in the Nazi Party, Libertas asked permission to leave. Her explanation was cleverly disingenuous:

> The prerequisites for my political engagement as a woman have fallen away since my marriage. For reasons of time and health I believe that I am today no longer in the position to satisfy all the demands of Party work. For me, it goes against the grain to be only a paying and not at the same time a working member. I am naturally, like every other German comrade, prepared to make sacrifices fully and completely for the support of the movement—but I must only—so have I also understood the Führer—perform these actions in the frame of my household and my remaining duties which are to my husband and family.[46]

Harro Schulze-Boysen's ancestry was military rather than princely. During World War I, Harro's father, Commander Edgar Schulze, a nephew of Grand Admiral von Tirpitz, served as chief of staff to the German naval commander in Belgium. The commander was stationed at the German naval base at Kiel in 1909, the year of Harro's birth. Thus Harro was exposed from childhood to the naval traditions of his family, though he was too young to fight in World War I. And like Arvid Harnack, smarting from Germany's humiliation at Versailles, as a teen Harro joined the Jungdeutscher Orden (Young German Order), a conservative nationalistic organization. In moving left in the 1930s, the editor of *Gegner* also shared Harnack's vision of the future.

Working-class Communists were surprised that heirs of patrician families like the Eulenburgs and Schulze-Boysens were drawn to their movement. One survivor, the East German historian Heinrich Scheel, recalled his first visit to the couple's apartment ("already in enemy territory") in the Altenburger Allee in Berlin's West End. "This neighborhood! This apartment! And there was a woman's fur coat hanging in the hallway!"[47]

Yet Harro was no conventional Communist, according to his mother, "My son's goal was to overthrow the dictatorship. To him every means and every ally was acceptable, regardless of whether they stood to the right or to the left . . . he found his best companions in arms primarily on the Communist side—probably because the most active, uncompromising, and courageous resistance fighters were in their ranks."[48] As Schulze-Boysen, writing from Geneva to a French friend in 1935, observed, it appeared impossible to escape right or left dictatorships but in Germany "the Fascist dictatorship gives the Marxist new arguments. They are the martyrs." This gave them an advantage.[49]

When *Gegner* was banned in 1933, he continued his covert political opposition. As a cover, in April 1934, Schulze-Boysen began his "extraordinary energizing and interesting activity."[50] Departing from his family's naval tradition, he joined the intelligence staff of Goering's Luftwaffe Ministry. According to Field Marshal Erhard Milch, Goering's deputy, the personnel chief of the Luftwaffe had initially turned Schulze-Boysen down for a commission because of his suspected Communist sympathies. However, Goering, pressured by Prince Eulenburg, a shooting companion, overruled his deputy and disregarded what he probably viewed as Schulze-Boysen's youthful indiscretions.[51] Being nouveau riche himself, Goering was undoubtedly flattered that someone from a distinguished family would want to enter his ministry. But the lieutenant's career really advanced when Libertas charmed Goering during a fall hunt at Liebenberg. Fluent in five languages, Schulze-Boysen thereafter summarized articles on foreign air forces for Goering. Eventually he also processed intelligence reports from German air force attachés abroad. He was thus able to obtain and disseminate newspapers, photographs, and secret documents from his ministry.

Schulze-Boysen appeared to be the Nazi *beau ideal*, the very personification of a German officer.[52] Yet not everyone was favorably impressed. Interrogated after the war, a judge at his trial, Alexander Kraell, claimed that Schulze-Boysen was "a complete adventurer, intelligent and clever, but impulsive and unrestrained, reckless, given to exploiting his friends, ambitious in the extreme, an innate and fanatical revolutionary."[53] Former OSS operative and Director of Central Intelligence Allen Dulles, who never met Harro, nevertheless described him as "always wearing a black sweater," someone who "went around with revolutionaries, surrealists and the ragtag and bobtail of the 'lost generation.' "[54] Yet Ernst Niekisch, who kept his contacts to Schulze-Boysen (until his own arrest in 1937), remembered him as "an outstanding gifted man, enterprising, courageous, human, absolutely unsullied."[55]

Harro and Libertas were leaders of a bohemian circle. Among its members were sculptor Kurt Schumacher and his wife Elisabeth, a photographer; journalists Walter Küchenmeister, John Graudenz, and Walter Husemann, whose wife, actress Marta Wolter, had starred in Brecht's film *Kuhle Wampe*; author Günther Weisenborn and his wife Joy; Dr. Elfriede Paul; dancer Oda Schottmüller; a young dentist, Helmut Himpel, and his fiancée Maria Terwiel, who was unable to practice law or marry Himpel because she was half Jewish. By the end of the decade the group also included two friends and former members of a Communist youth group, Heinrich Scheel and Hans Coppi.

Unlike the Harnacks' no-nonsense study groups, the Schulze-Boysens' twice-monthly Thursday gatherings of thirty-five to forty people in their Charlottenburg atelier were fun. Harro described them to his parents as "nice picnic evenings." After an hour and a half of something good to read—Ernst Jünger, Plato, Machiavelli—there was music and dancing until twelve.[56] Marxist discussions and resistance activities were interspersed with parties, picnics at Liebenberg, and sailing on the Wannsee. Every Whitsun the group met for a holiday reunion. Cauldrons of corned beef were consumed while political arguments raged. Günther Weisenborn told tall tales of his adventures as a farmer, teacher, and postman in South America. Libertas and Walter Küchenmeister read poems. Everyone sang to Libertas's accompaniment on the accordion. After the war, Weisenborn recreated these outings in his play *The Illegals*. In particular he memorialized "the laughing, dancing, flirting" Libs: "comrade of secrecy, bride of long shadows, pal of the hidden, whisperer's friend, courageous sister of secret heroes."[57] Another comrade, Werner Dissel, wrote that "it was simply great to meet with them. . . . We made our jokes and fooled around. For us it was always like some carnival."[58]

But the same bohemian gatherings also gave rise to the licentious picture of the Red Orchestra that persists in spy literature and films. In West Germany, sensationalized magazine and newspaper accounts, based on interviews with Gestapo and Abwehr agents, Nazi judges and lawyers, began to appear in the 1950s.

As a result, long after their deaths, the lifestyle of the Harnack/ Schulze-Boysen group would be controversial.

In his book *The Red Orchestra*, French journalist Gilles Perrault quotes an unnamed source as asserting that there were wild parties at which the guests engaged in "wholesale adultery." Recruits to the resistance cause were gained through sexual seduction, which was made the more titillating in that Libertas and Mildred were said to be lesbians and Schulze-Boysen a homosexual.[59]

Far more credible is the recollection of Hugo Buschmann, a close friend of the Schulze-Boysens, who told *Spiegel* editor Heinz Höhne: "I was present on one occasion. If that was an orgy, then young people today [1949] who drink Coca-Cola and dress in beatnik rags, are also engaged in an orgy. Of course people were merry; they were, after all, living dangerously and probably wanted some outlet. But it was certainly no orgy."[60]

Undoubtedly, a certain heightened sexuality sprang from the shared danger, particularly in the group around Schulze-Boysen. There was also an appreciation for the few joys possible under the swastika and, not unnaturally, a sense of living on the edge. Clandestine activities weakened family ties. Conversely, bonds were strengthened among conspirators. The line between lover and comrade was not easily drawn. Further confusing the issue for biographers is the fact that members described clandestine meetings as merely lovers' assignations when they were interrogated by the Gestapo.

The Civil War in Spain was the event that galvanized the international left and some key members of the Schulze-Boysen's inner circle. "If you are anti, must you not actually do something against it?" Kurt Schumacher demanded at one meeting.[61] A plan was then hatched to take advantage of Schulze-Boysen's position in the Luftwaffe Ministry, where a "Special Staff W" was directing Germany's aid to Franco. Harro gathered together confidential details of numbers of men, planes, tanks, arms, and munitions that the Luftwaffe was carrying to Spain, as well as plans for a putsch that was to bring Barcelona under control of the Fascists. A new recruit, a distant relative of Libertas, a journalist employed by United Press, Gisela von Pöllnitz, shoved the report through the mailbox of the Soviet embassy. But she had been observed by the Gestapo and was arrested.[62]

Members of the group panicked. Küchenmeister left for

Cologne, and Weisenborn and Schulze-Boysen planned to escape to Holland. Schulze-Boysen's atelier was searched by the Gestapo, but they found no clues and his superiors in the ministry supported him. Pöllnitz was released—she had not betrayed anyone.[63]

Beginning in 1937, in the Wilmersdorf waiting room of Dr. Elfriede Paul, the group began copying and disseminating leaflets containing material on the Spanish war obtained through Schulze-Boysen. They targeted friends, acquaintances, and politically important Germans and mailed them leaflets, only a few of which survived. The hope was that these people might be persuaded to join the resistance if they only knew the truth about the "animalistic behavior" of the Fascists. Secrecy was essential: to avoid suspicion only a few stamps would be bought at any one post office. Even getting paper was a complicated. According to police regulations, every private citizen had to explain to a shopkeeper why the purchase was needed. Under the guise of making house calls, Dr. Elfriede Paul would drive around and mail carefully disguised anonymous leaflets from distant post boxes.[64]

"The whole world is aware that we did not eliminate Hitler; did not overthrow Goebbels; did not kill Goering," wrote one resister. "But few people know why none of these things happened."[65] Resisters were unarmed. Danger was omnipresent. Many members of the Schulze-Boysen group had spent time in the hands of the police, SA, or Gestapo; some spent years in prison or concentration camp. Harro himself, as already noted, was arrested and badly beaten by the SA in 1933; his Jewish friend was killed before his eyes. In 1937, as the Spanish Civil War was being fought, Harro was summoned to the Gestapo and confronted with Werner Dissel, who had been arrested for "subversive activities and Communistic demoralization." Fortunately, he managed to slip the friend a cigarette package. Underneath the silver foil he had written, in tiny letters, *Fontana Terra Incognita*. Thus his friend was not to reveal what the Gestapo did not know—that he had given Schulze-Boysen information about the changes occurring in the fifth and sixth panzer (tank) companies and their deployment in Spain.[66] In 1939, Libertas was also briefly arrested in East Prussia as an espionage suspect.[67]

In 1934, Walter Küchenmeister was released from a year's "protective custody" at Camp Sonnenburg, where he had contracted tuberculosis. Nineteen-year-old Karl Böhme, arrested in 1933 for "preparing high treason," was released from a youth prison in 1935. In 1936, he was charged with "making remarks hostile to the state." Six months later, he was acquitted. Eighteen-year-old-Hans Coppi was arrested in 1934 for "preparations for undertaking high treason" and sentenced to two years in a juvenile prison. Undeterred, Coppi was again arrested just after his release for "preparing forbidden publications" and sentenced to four weeks in prison. Another Communist youth group member, Fritz Thiel, was detained in 1936 on suspicion of "high treason" but was released for lack of evidence. Also in 1936, Walter Husemann was detained without trial in Sachsenhausen. After spending additional time in Buchenwald, he was released in 1938. *Rote Fahne* editor Wilhelm Guddorf was released after five years in prison, where he shared a cell for a time with the sinologist Philipp Schaeffer. Guddorf was arrested again in a police sweep after a planned coup against Hitler was discovered.[68] Thrice-arrested Schaeffer remained permanently under the eyes of the Gestapo.

In the Harnacks' own circle, another *Rote Fahne* editor, John Sieg, was rounded up in a sweep of suspected Communists and spent four months in an SA prison in 1933. In 1936, Wilhelm Utech was picked up and questioned about illegal leaflets; he was jailed for a year.[69] Utech, together with another of Mildred's students at the Abendgymnasium, Karl Behrens, was accused in 1937 of "preparations for high treason." Their actual crime was distributing leaflets.[70]

Arvid had his own brush with the Gestapo in 1940 when he was turned in as a result of an anonymous tip, probably from a jealous colleague at the Economics Ministry, identifying him as a Communist. Because he had access to secret files and was known to be a special favorite of his boss, State Secretary Friedrich Landfried, who often confided in him, a nasty investigation followed, but Harnack had the firm support of his superiors and the allegations were dismissed.[71]

Recruiting under these conditions posed grave difficulties. Greta Kuckhoff recalled that there were more stool pigeons and informers than likely recruits among those dissatisfied with the regime: "The harvest of those honest beings won to resistance was so small and insignificant that it could never justify the great dangers of this trust."[72] Utech, later a member of the central committee of the East German Communist Party, described how these approaches were made: "As a tactic from which to proceed, Harnack advised us to first speak in conversations as if we ourselves were National Socialists or close to the NS movement. The object was to lead the other person to reveal his political attitude toward National Socialism. This 'testing' was to be carried out very carefully, so that we did not reveal ourselves prematurely and thus endanger our work. It would also be helpful, Harnack said, to lend books to the people whom we were seeking to contact in this way. In initiating contact we should take care that the persons to be won over met certain prerequisites of intellect. In Harnack's words, 'Naturally, such people should not be won over to whom one first has to teach the ABCs.' "[73] Harnack could be very tough at meetings. Utech remembered that he strongly criticized Paul Thomas for a superficial report on "the economic development of the last thirty years." To Harnack economics was the key to understanding the present situation: "the economic section is the most important part of the newspaper for a Marxist." For the most part, they studied the forbidden classics of Marx and economists such as Sombart, Mill, and the French theorists Gide and Rist although Mildred led a discussion of Kipling's *Kim* to aid in their understanding of colonialism.[74]

Fearing wiretaps, the Harnacks refused to own a telephone. Monthly meetings were no longer held at the Harnacks' home. They were moved to the less conspicuous apartments of the Behrenses or the Thomases in working-class areas under the guise that they were birthday parties or English lessons. As war threatened, participants huddled around radios, listened to broadcasts from Moscow and London and discussed current events.[75]

Some segments of society engaged in spying on others: *V-Leute or Vertrauensmänner*, formerly used to identify a trusted confidant, now stood for informants, those persons enlisted by the Gestapo to infiltrate groups by passing themselves off as opponents of the regime. To aid it in capturing "enemies of the state," the Gestapo enlisted the services of these *V-Men* and *agents provocateurs*, some of them former leftists. When these informers infiltrated resistance groups, Gestapo arrests followed, and defendants were often tortured and induced to betray others. Friends learned to avoid comrades recently released from prison who might have been "turned."[76] Utech recalled that once after his release from prison, he sought out Mildred after a lecture she gave at the Volkshochschule in 1937. When she questioned him about his prison stay, he assured her that he had given no "statements about the group around her husband."[77]

Discipline was relentless. Possible recruits, including wives, were closely vetted. "Everyone knew that arrest might mean death," recalled Wolfgang Havemann. "We didn't talk about such things. The circle of those who knew about our work had to be kept very, very small—no questions were asked about the work that anyone did. We often didn't know the true names of people. We used aliases so that even if you were arrested, you could only tell them you were 'with Kurt.' Then they couldn't find him."[78] The observance of these rules of conspiracy meant that the group was never infiltrated.

Even though the state might be effective in arresting resistance fighters, it was, in the case of the members of Harnack/Schulze-Boysen group, unable to break their will. Their prison experiences merely tended to harden their commitment and gave them the additional benefit of a wide network of contacts with fellow inmates.[79] Still, as Jürgen Kuczynski has written, while working underground may have trained better fighters, it did not necessarily make them more lovable. Harnack and Schulze-Boysen had little time for the faint-hearted. Although less harsh than Harnack, Schulze-Boysen once mocked his pacifist friend, Hugo Buschmann: "You have the overresponsive tear gland of the *petit bourgeois*."[80]

Another person who testified to Arvid's hard-heartedness was Adolf von Harnack's grandson, Adolf-Henning Frucht, the son of Arvid's cousin Anni. The first time I saw Frucht's name was in the Hamburg archives of Der Spiegel. *Frucht was the subject of the magazine's 1978 series "Espionage: The Secret V-Substance." The director of a prestigious East German medical research institute, he had betrayed to American intelligence the Warsaw Pact's Alaska Plan—an offensive scenario designed to take out the U.S. personnel manning the early warning radar in the Aleutian Islands with a special poison gas effective at below freezing temperatures.*

The article was full of spy story staples: Berlin treffs, wristwatches with microphones, high-speed car chases, and a final border arrest. The CIA was sharing intelligence with the West Germans and Frucht had in turn been betrayed by an East German mole burrowing in West German BND files. "Eastern Europe's greatest atomic traitor" was rewarded with a life sentence in Bautzen II, East Germany's most notorious prison for spies and political prisoners. After ten years, through the efforts of his wife, his cousin Max Delbrück, by now a Nobel Prize winner, and others, he was exchanged in a Menschenhandel or "body swap," for a Chilean Communist in 1977.

Frucht's motive for betraying state secrets was not money, nor was it political—after a stint in a Soviet prisoner of war camp, he had returned to the Russian sector of Berlin "because they needed qualified doctors." Rather, he had acted as a scientist concerned with saving mankind from the dreadful specter of chemical warfare, and "the public matters [read resistance] with which my family has been concerned with for 150 years."[81] I made a note of a quote I liked by Frucht's mother, Anni von Harnack, referring to the fate of the Harnacks, Delbrücks, and Bonhoeffers: "Our family is like the potato, the best ones are underground."

After a decade in Bautzen, the then sixty-five-year-old Frucht was reported to be very ill and I assumed that he had died. Then I found letters in two archives: those of Max Delbrück and Martha Dodd. Since it was clear from the Spiegel article he had known the Harnacks, I decided to write him at his last known address in Cologne. Six weeks later I received an excited telephone call from Berlin. It was Professor Frucht.

We exchanged calls and faxes over the next few months. He was eager to help and urged me to come to Berlin because his health was failing. His value to me, he explained, was that he was one of the few people who "knew the inner workings of the various secret services without ever directly being in their employ." He often chided me for my naïveté: "You need to know more about secret service techniques to understand Mildred. I would like to give you a crash course." Finally in October 1991 I visited the seventy-eight-year-old Frucht in a Wannsee hospital.

Frucht had his own pet theories that he tried out on me: that Arvid was the control, Martha Dodd the Soviet agent, and Mildred *the safe contact. He recalled that Max Delbrück, then working on nuclear fission in the Berlin laboratory of Lise Meitner and Otto Hahn, was invited, at Arvid's instigation, to the American embassy in 1936 where Martha, according to Frucht, had tried to recruit Max. The attempt failed but the two cousins had joked about it when they were reunited in California in 1979.*

Frucht had strong opinions on both Harnacks. In the 1930s he had participated in a Reichstag fire discussion group with Arvid and had seen the couple intermittently after that. While he admired Arvid's courage, he had deep reservations about him personally: "What was the personality of Arvid really? He was a Communist. He was a member of the Nazi Party. He was an organizer of a spy group—a very bad one I have to say. And he was a scientifically interested man, of course. Now what was he really? I think he was first of all enormously ehrbegierig*—ambitious, extremely ambitious, and not eager to ask too much, where and how. I think he saw all his personal connections from this angle, including his marriage to Mildred. Mildred was another way for him to get somewhere. You see I have the worst impression of him."*

(I wished later that I'd argued with Frucht, defended Arvid. If he impressed some people as a ruthless fanatic, there were many others who had loved and admired Arvid. During and even after the war, when it was known what he had done, several friends named their sons for him.)

Frucht viewed Mildred as a victim of circumstance.

"I see her now as a girl from the country, from the Midwest drawn by dint of love into a field where she was absolutely overwhelmed. They asked too much of her; it was too difficult for her to do it. It's a terrible story. She did what he told her to do. Mildred was drawn into problems that were just too complicated for everybody and especially for her. She was desperately unhappy. Unhappy is not the right word. She was in a situation that was insoluble."

I agreed that she was desperately unhappy but allowed at the same time that I felt she was incredibly courageous and that she had certainly inspired the devotion of friends and family.

"Falk very much adored Mildred," he continued, "and he wanted his brother to be seen as a typical hero of political . . ."

Resistance? I volunteered.

"Be careful with Widerstand *(resistance); say* Verfolgt *(persecuted). "Persecuted" because in all totalitarian states you can be arrested without having done anything. Falk wanted Arvid to be seen as a typical victim of persecution. He always tried to protect Mildred too against accusations. Thereby he closed his eyes to reality of his espionage. So also toward Communism."*

People now make the distinction between Communist and Marxist. Would you call Arvid a Communist or a German Marxist? I asked.

"After 1933, the distinctions were unimportant. It looked like the only ones fighting the Nazis were the Communists. You see the group you're researching, the Prussian civil servants, was very homogenous and exclusive. Whether they were Communists, Christians, or Socialists, there was not much difference. You had to do your work and not talk much about it. After the war, people asked if Arvid was a Communist. If so, was he a good one? How very ridiculous to try to describe a real person in real times this way. This is sheer nonsense.

"It might be said that Arvid made a wrong decision to go with the Communists. I read somewhere that in small circles, he was very anti-Stalin and very distraught about Stalinism but you see it didn't last very long. And, of course, I felt if he had ever survived to see the Communists as victors, he would have gotten into the most serious difficulties."

Frucht's own foray into the resistance was brief: in 1939, he acted as a courier between his uncle, Ernst von Harnack, and the former mayor of Leipzig, Carl Goerdeler. And he drove through Saxony looking for Social Democrats and Communists "to discuss with them what should be done in the case of a military coup against Hitler."

Frucht's experience speaks to the wider ordeal of resistance survivors who assumed, all too credulously, that their past would be a commendation to the new rulers of the German Democratic Republic: "When I was imprisoned in East Germany, I told them I was anti-Fascist before the Russians came. I believed that it would give me a better standing in the interrogations. But it didn't help. The opposite happened. They reasoned that if you were able to resist the Nazis then you would certainly be capable of resisting the Communists too."

In 1939, just before the outbreak of the war, the tension and tempo of clandestine struggle increased. Members forged documents to smuggle opponents of the regime, vulnerable Jews, and money abroad. One survivor, Elfriede Paul, described her trips to Paris and London to speed preparations for the emigration of persecuted Jews. In August 1939, Kurt Schumacher, an excellent mountain climber whose sculptural medallions still adorn Berlin's Schleusenbrücke and who also made decorative motifs for Goering's Karinhall, hid for two weeks and then spirited the Communist Rudolf Bergtel, who had escaped from a concentration camp, across the Swiss border.[82] These adventures were not always successful. In 1939, Mildred's former student Karl Behrens was arrested for forging exit papers for his Jewish brother-in-law, Charly Fischer.[83] Fischer was captured and executed at Sachsenhausen.[84]

In his reminiscences published after the war, the author and editor Max Tau credits Mildred with arranging his escape to Norway in 1938.[85] Inevitably, the Harnacks' business and vacation trips to Norway, Copenhagen, Paris, and London began to have covert purposes. And the KGB's Corsican file states that with Mildred's assistance, one member of their circle from the Bund der Geistesarbeiter days, an old member of the KPD, obtained an American visa.[86] Because she was now a reader—a scout for English-language books for the Potsdam firm of Rütten and Loening—her work provided "cover" for these trips. It would appear natural to meet with strangers in foreign countries. At home, she could use her work as a translator to procure rationed ink and paper for clandestine publications.

Throughout her stay, Mildred kept her American and German passports. In spite of her excellent diplomatic and governmental connections in Berlin, she was always careful to renew passports and obtain visas abroad in Paris or in Brussels, where she was unknown. A letter that turned up in 1992 in an archive describes a strange encounter which suggests that she may have been using one or both passports for trips throughout 1938–1940 to obtain residency permits abroad for refugees.

Mona Wollheim, formerly a fellow student with Mildred at Giessen, recalled an unnerving episode in Paris around 1938. Although Wollheim was living in France, she still had a German passport. Suddenly she received a summons from the German consulate. Near the consulate as she was on her way home a woman, in halting French which betrayed her as a foreigner, asked for directions to the consulate. Wollheim told her but couldn't suppress the remark, "Surely you are Frau Harnack." Mildred was very surprised but understandably did not recognize Wollheim since they had hardly spoken to each other and had not seen each other since 1929. After a few harmless words they separated, but Wollheim never forgot the strange encounter.[87] One can imagine how Mildred, who frequently suspected she was shadowed by the Gestapo, felt about this chance encounter.

Another sorry meeting—this time with the British author, Rebecca West—took place while Mildred was in London in 1939. West reported this encounter in a letter she wrote in 1963 to Allen Dulles, then former head of the CIA. (Dulles had just published *The Craft of Intelligence*, in which he mentioned Mildred Fish.) It shows how Mildred's desperate attempt to obtain translating work resulted in a surreal misunderstanding:

> I have the oddest recollection, and an unpleasant one of Mildred Harnack Fish. She turned up with an introduction from an English writer now dead, at my flat in Orchard Court, and gravely told me that Hitler adored my books. She was empowered to tell me so, and bore the message gladly, because she and her husband were trying to civilize the Nazi state by working for it in the cultural sphere. She went on to say that every book I had written would be published in a beautiful German translation if I would only sign a declaration that I had no Jewish blood in me. At which I asked her to go. She went on, telling me the advantages I would secure if I did this little, little thing, even telling me that if I didn't people might think I had Jewish blood. I explained that I certainly hadn't, but that I would rather die than do such a thing as sign a declaration to curry favor with Hitler, and I threw her out of the front door, and as I did so, I made the uncharitable remark, "I hope Hitler does to you the worst thing he ever did to a Jew."[88]

In 1949 when West was in Hamburg, someone showed Pastor Poelchau's book *Die letzten Stunden* (The Last Hours) to West and she opened it to the page where there was "the blond and vague face of Mildred Harnack Fish beside a text which showed that Hitler had done that very thing." West felt "considerable remorse," until a friend who was an ex-Communist said, "Let me suggest to you, dear Rebecca, that she was not merely disguising her real convictions when she came to England on this mission. She was also engaged in a typical Communist attempt to tie bricks around the necks of all conspicuous anti-Communists."[89] (By 1963, West had become a virulent anticommunist and, as we shall see, Mildred's story was now being viewed by Dulles and others through the prism of Cold War ideology.)

Mildred continued her barrage of postcards to friends in the United States. Her last postcard to Clara Leiser, dated January 12, 1939, was mailed from London and signed M: "Here for a few days. . . . I think of you, and often think of you, thanking you at heart for your warming kindness of two years ago. An interesting woman psychologist may bring greetings. Better not write but don't forget me and don't be angry. *Power* to you. I cherish your gift of the Dreiser [*American*] *Tragedy* and I'm not untrue to Meredith dear Clara."

Friends and family struggled to understand this need for secrecy. Clara wrote to William Ellery Leonard that "the other day came a card, the first in about two years, from Mildred Fish-Harnack, who was in London for a few days. Just asked me not to be 'angry' to see a woman psychologist she was sending to me, and above all, not to write her! I could wring her neck for not taking the chance of writing me a letter . . . during her days of freedom."[90]

Greta Kuckhoff wrote that Mildred needed to observe a number of conspiratorial measures which ran counter to her innate honesty: "She also lacked the recklessness which, in spite of all the danger, enjoys the excitement of an encounter, an unexpected incident," recalled Kuckhoff. Yet "convinced by the necessity of the smallest, seemingly insignificant detail in the service of a good deed, she conscientiously carried out all her tasks."[91] Greta and Mildred met to discuss these assignments in the Tiergarten: "Mildred and I, we had become real Tiergarten monument experts. It is easy to point out on the basis of the history of those crumbling heroes [mostly old Prussian nobility] a clarifying word about our time. But no one should believe that everything we did had a political aim. No one should think that we had no walks where we forgot war heroes in the face of our affection for each other. We made boat trips on artificial lakes. We observed the small girls playing hide-and-seek. But it grew increasingly difficult to be happy. Swastikas were painted on benches, more often there were signs reading, 'Jews not wanted.' It wasn't meant for us but it affected us."[92]

Mildred had written to Clara Harnack in November 1937, shortly after her trip through the Harz with Jane, that her niece wanted to marry "a nice economics lecturer" Otto Donner, at the university and earn her doctorate. It was a great joy for Mildred that she would remain in Germany, "although for her family at home, it will be painful."[93] (In fact, in view of subsequent events, Harriette never forgave her younger sister.)

After the war, Otto Donner observed that both Harnacks "were in a tremendous nervous strain all these years, for they knew the danger hanging over them." They sacrificed a private for a political life. Arvid sadly remarked that they had "renounced children because they thought they should not hamper their political work by family interests, and because they always had to keep ready to fold their tents and to flee." Mildred suffered from the lack of privacy and comfort associated with this kind of life.[94]

Mildred's trip to Denmark in the spring of 1939 with Arvid and the Donners was followed by a trip alone through Norway, the subject of a piece she wrote for *Die Dame*. "Through Norway" is a melancholic paean, a testament to her longing for her beloved Midwest. At the end of the piece, she tells of an encounter with a young Norwegian woman whose fiancé is a sailor. When they parted, Mildred had an urge to tell her something and took her hand: "If you should once lose your faith in God, don't lose your faith in the goodness of people."[95]

As Hitler moved from victory to victory—the Anschluss with Austria and the dismembering of Czechoslovakia in 1938—it was obvious to most Germans that they were headed toward war. But the French and British persisted in appeasement; the Americans continued to maintain their "splendid isolation." Harnack and Schulze-Boysen, like other opponents of Hitler, didn't share the general euphoria after Munich. At the height of the Czechoslovakian crisis, Schulze-Boysen wrote to his parents predicting war: "I now say that in 1940–41 at the latest, but probably even next spring, there will be world war in Europe with class warfare as its sequel. I state unequivocally that Austria and Czechoslovakia were the first 'battles' in this new war."[96]

A clear statement of the resistance's position is expressed in Donald Heath's letter to Secretary Morgenthau, dated May 2, 1939. Up to Munich the group "believed that a firm stand would be made against Hitler." If France and England had stood up to Hitler, he "would have been afraid to go to war and the check to his prestige would have been sufficient to bring down his regime." Heath reported that most of them profoundly distrusted Chamberlain. They regarded the prime minister as being "secretly very sympathetic" to the National Socialists and "still under the delusion that Hitler's aims were definitely limited to Eastern Europe and that the Führer could be 'appeased.'" Heath continued, "Their one hope is in President Roosevelt, in whose democratic ideals and ability they have a very considerable belief."

The letter concludes with an analysis of Hitler's aims and character:

> They point to the program and psychology as exemplified in *Mein Kampf* and his actions since he has been in power. They think him obsessed with the idea of dominating Europe and with putting Germany in the position occupied by the British Empire in the first half of the Nineteenth Century.
>
> The limitations of education, experience, judgment and tradition which restrained Bismarck after the Franco-Prussian War do not exist in the case of Hitler. They declare it is only too obvious that he sees history as a sheer battle of force in which one race or country for a time battles its way to primacy knocking down its predecessors on the way up. They think that he judges that now or never is the time for Germany to make this effort because with further delay opponents will gain strength faster than she will.[97]

According to his son Donald, in May 1939 Heath took a holiday walk with Arvid, identified circumspectly in his letter to Morgenthau as "a man in the second rank of officers of one of the most important ministries." Arvid believed that only punitive economic measures and a firm stand by England and France on the Polish question, even to the point of sending troops, might restrain Hitler and bring down the regime. Arvid remarked that "as a German he thought that the return of Danzig and the corridor to Germany must eventually be conceded; but he said that such concessions at the present time, without exacting a firm commitment to disarmament, would be fatal." Heath cites this conversation as "an interesting example of the undercover opposition that still exists against this regime among German officials."[98]

In mid-August 1939, Arvid returned from a summer's working visit to Washington. This was the second extended tour he made as the Economic Ministry's American expert in charge of dealing with German industrial property in the United States. His mission, in which he was successful, was to secure German copper and aluminum supplies before the war, which now appeared to Arvid inevitable.[99] During this trip, before the outbreak of the war, probably on the recommendation of Heath, Arvid met with officials of the Treasury Department. Arvid warned them, according to Falk, that war was imminent and urged the necessity of "hitting the economic nerve of the Nazis." He also detailed hidden German assets, like I.G. Farben's, that should be seized in the event of war.[100]

These secret meetings remain unconfirmed. We can assume that Harnack's reception paralleled that given another member of the resistance, the former German Rhodes scholar and Foreign Ministry official, Adam von Trott zu Solz, when he met with Americans in 1940. The Americans thought him, at best, an "impractical idealist" and, at worst a "Nazi agent" and "spy."[101] They assumed it was impossible for a "good German" to visit the United States in an official capacity. Yet it was difficult to counter these suspicions by openly professing an anti-Nazi position. As a senior British official remarked, "There is always something suspicious about 'anti-Nazis' coming to this country in fear of their lives, especially if they get away with it."[102]

If we know little about Harnack's reception by government officials, we do know how Mildred's family viewed him. Mildred's sister Harriette wrote to Clara Leiser in 1947: "Neither of them

[Mildred and Arvid] ever gave us an inkling of their political activities though Arvid spent most of the summer of 1939 in our Chevy Chase home. In fact, my brother-in-law still has difficulty in believing that Arvid was not a Nazi, as he was always convinced he was."[103]

On August 21, 1939, a late-night music program on German radio was interrupted by an announcement that the Minister for Foreign Affairs, Joachim von Ribbentrop, was flying to Moscow to sign a pact between Germany and the Soviet Union. Germany and Russia agreed to desist from attacking each other while a secret protocol defined their spheres of influence in Eastern Europe. Latvia, Estonia, and Lithuania fell to Russia. Poland was divided. Hitler now had access to Russia's vast supply of raw materials. In exchange Stalin was to receive airplane engines, naval blueprints, torpedoes, and mines.

All over Europe, "gaining time" was the justification invoked by Communists as they scrambled to rationalize the abrupt dissolution of the anti-Fascist Popular Front. Inside Germany, party members could not understand how Stalin could ally himself with their Nazi tormentors. Exiled German Communists now naïvely believed Hitler might tolerate the German Communist Party. In reality, in the most shameful sequel to the pact, exiled German and Austrian Communists, and even Jewish refugees, were turned over by the NKVD to the SS at the River Bug at Brest-Litovsk on the Polish border, to face certain execution.

According to accounts written long after the war and reflecting the official party line, the Harnack/Schulze-Boysen group sought to put a favorable interpretation on the pact: Stalin knew best and was buying time. Greta Kuckhoff remembers that as soon as the pact was announced, she and Adam visited the Harnacks. Arvid discounted the prospect of German–Soviet friendship, saying, "It is absolutely clear that Hitler will now prepare even more determinedly for war against the Soviet Union. Economically, he is not yet ready. So he will try to gain control of the raw materials and productive resources of other nations as quickly as possible." The primary role of the group, Arvid said, now must be to gather information.[104]

Mildred's student Wilhelm Utech recalled a discussion meeting in the Grunewald forest led by Harnack in late August shortly after he returned from the United States. In a clearing in the woods, Harnack elaborated his thesis that war was imminent and that Hitler was bound to attack the Soviet Union. He presciently argued that the Wehrmacht would strike in the direction of Baku in the Caucasus, since "this would solve Germany's oil problem."[105]

During the last week in August, as the crisis over Danzig escalated, rumors flew through Berlin. Private cars were requisitioned and antiaircraft guns installed on the roofs of strategic buildings along Unter den Linden. Troops and armored vehicles moved through the city on their way to the Polish border. Hitler canceled the annual Nuremberg rally scheduled for September 2. On August 25, 1939, all communications—radio, telephone, telegraph—with the outside world were temporarily cut off.

On August 26, the embassy advised Americans to leave Germany for the United States. Later that week, they chartered two special trains to take American women and children to Denmark. During the crisis, Chargé Alexander Kirk showed reporters the camp bed he had moved into his office. As the hot, sultry weather continued, the reserves were called up, and Berliners stood in line for ration cards. A strident headline in the Sunday edition of the Party newspaper, the *Völkische Beobachter*, announced:

Whole of Poland in War Fever! 1,500,000 Men Mobilized!
Uninterrupted Troop Transport Toward the Frontier!
Chaos in Upper Silesia![106]

The British ambassador, Neville Henderson, met continuously with Hitler as the Führer dictated his Polish ultimatum. All talks ended on Friday, September 1. At dawn Hitler hurled his army against Poland. Polish cities and villages were bombed as the Polish cavalry quixotically charged German tanks. At 10 A.M. in a speech to the Reichstag, Hitler justified the invasion by saying that a Polish "attack" on a radio station in the border town of Gleiwitz had occurred. The "attack" had been faked by the SS using prisoners impersonating Poles.

That same evening, in the midst of a blackout and to the accompaniment of air raid sirens, friends of the Schulze-Boysens met in Grunewald. They were celebrating Harro's thirtieth birthday and, so they thought, the end of Hitler. Recklessly, accompanied by Libertas's accordion, they first sang the "Marseillaise," then "It's a Long, Long Way to Tipperary," and finally Harro taught everyone the words to the Polish national anthem, "Poland Is Not Yet Lost."[107] One guest, Hugo Buschmann, described the scene: "What illusions those people had! They were all convinced that the end of the Third Reich was in sight; indeed, most of them thought it was imminent."[108]

On September 3, Britain and France reluctantly honored their pledge to Poland and declared war on Germany. A week later, Schulze-Boysen wrote his parents: "This war will bury the old Europe with all its former civilization and thereafter, when the air has drifted away, the atmosphere will be purer. Our own life does not seem so important to me. *Vivere non est necesse.*"[109]

Two weeks later Stalin's armies marched into Poland to seize their allotted share under the pact. Earlier in the same year Stalin in a speech to the Eighteenth Party Congress, assailed the British and the French for failing to stand up to Hitler. Buried in his five-hour speech was an announcement that the trials, the purge of "spies, murderers, and wreckers" of Soviet institutions had run its course: the army and intelligence services would "no longer have their sharp edge turned to the inside of the country but to the outside, against external enemies."[110]

Meanwhile, a Polish-Jewish exile and former Zionist, Leopold Trepper, a graduate of the GRU military intelligence school in Moscow, took over a Soviet network of agents in Brussels. Working under the cover of a trading company known as the Foreign Excellent Trenchcoat Company with branches in Belgium, France, Holland, and Germany, Trepper employed as deputies two of the Soviets' best agents: radio operator Mikhail Makarov, now masquerading as the Uruguayan Carlos Alamo, and Captain Anatoli Gurevitch, also known as "Kent," Victor Sukolov or Vincente Serra. The two agents had been tested and hardened in Spain. Another operative stationed in Brussels was an East Prussian radio expert, Johann Wenzel, nicknamed "the professor" for his considerable technical skills. Wenzel trained recruits, extending his circuits into Holland.[111] When Hitler invaded Poland, the group went into action. But because of the pact, there were "no concrete in-structions about directing their work against Germany." Instead, their work would be aimed at England.[112] Moscow's blunders and the fate of these agents, for the moment offstage in our story, would tragically impact the group in Berlin.

THIRTEEN

Spy?

Alexander Korotkov around 1940

The Berlin winter of 1939–1940 was one of the coldest in memory. For eight weeks the overnight temperature consistently fell below freezing. Thick ice covered the lakes in the Tiergarten. Deep snow draped public buildings; no trucks were available to cart it away. Arvid wrote his mother that he and Mildred skied in the Grunewald while they waited for the western offensive to begin. Every weekend uniformed hordes—SS, SA, Wehrmacht officers, Hitler Youth, or German Maidens with red "Winter Aid" buckets—badgered passersby for "voluntary" contributions. Berliners were wise to the ruse: money requested for "the poor" was transformed into guns, tanks, and airplanes.

Food had become scarce. Mildred could not find coal for the porcelain stove that heated their apartment and was obliged to sit and work in crowded cafés or in the university library to keep warm. Hot water was irregular, and all but weekend baths were forbidden. After evening classes, Mildred groped home through the blackout along the frozen Landwehr canal, wearing a glowing phosphorus button on her coat. Private cars and taxis were banned. Only an occasional ghost of a bus, with a small blue lamp burning in the ceiling, lit the snow-covered streets.

Train travel was an ordeal. Switches froze. Trains were late, the stations unheated. There were so few trains that passengers had to arrive hours early to get a seat. When the Harnacks traveled to Czechoslovakia, they brought back gifts of flashlights and blankets, which would be handy in air raid shelters.

At a time when truth was severely rationed, Germans relied on BBC broadcasts from London. Code words came into use. "Now we have to go to prayer," meant that the 10 P.M. BBC news in German was about to begin, a Bonhoeffer relative recalled. Another phrase indicated that a person had been arrested: "By the way 'x' received visitors yesterday." Those arrested were said to be "in the hospital."[2]

Carelessness could have dire consequences. Arvid and Mildred experienced this firsthand when Arvid's mother was arrested during the *Sitzkrieg*, the eight-month "phony war." Clara Harnack overheard some children singing Nazi songs. She asked them if they knew that there were better songs, German *Volkslieder*, for example, to sing. A vigilant passerby reported her to the Gestapo. Only by appealing to the Nazis' understanding of the problems that "the bombings" of Poland had wrought on an old woman's mind, could the family explain her rash statements. After some time in prison, Clara was released on condition she leave Jena. The family then decided for her own safety to confine her to a sanatorium.[3]

"People's ears were honed to catch any insinuation," said Stanley Herman, then an embassy official and pastor of the dwindling congregation of the American Church. "In private and public circles, the whole atmosphere became electric as soon as politics came into the picture. You were always listening to what a person was really saying between the lines. You had a system of government where your very life was at stake. Your career depended upon what you said and to whom you said it. You were super cautious."[4]

It was during these early stages of the war that Mildred finally, after a decade's work, completed her doctorate. Although teaching and translating occupied much of her time, the delay was more likely the result of her strong dislike for the conditions under which she labored. The Nazis had succeeded in suppressing all serious research and scholarship. Her dissertation, "The Development of Contemporary American Literature with Some Main Representatives of the Short Story," was an abbreviated version of the book she had been working on for some time.[5]

Harnack-Fish seems to have chosen this particular moment to finish her doctorate because she was again thinking of returning to the United States. In October 1939, she applied for both Rockefeller and Guggenheim fellowships for the next year with the idea of completing research on her book in America. Mildred's efforts failed; the Guggenheim committee's files reveal they judged Harnack-Fish, by their high standards, "a beginner."[6] The Rockefeller Foundation also turned her down. Because she knew Arvid's career would suffer if she appeared to be angling to leave Germany, Mildred had American correspondence sent care of Donald Heath at the U.S. Embassy.

Earlier, in 1937, Arvid had hoped to persuade the Rockefeller Foundation that since his work concerned America, his effectiveness would be greatly increased if he could have a further period of work in the United States. Rudolf Heberle, now in America, interceded on Arvid's behalf with the Rockefeller Foundation. But

Harnack failed to win a further stay. The foundation bureaucrats informed Heberle of the difficulty in making social science appointments in Germany in view of the risk that "foreign experience might decrease the willingness of the beneficiary to adjust himself to German conditions on his return."[7]

Practically, Mildred knew she should return to the United States since, despite a lull in hostilities after the fall of Poland, a world war appeared inevitable. Yet, emotionally tied as she was to Arvid, as well as his family and friends, she had little choice. She would go with Arvid or she would not go at all, and Arvid would not leave. As head of the Harnack family, he had his mother and siblings to consider. More importantly, he told his mother, "We have to stay in this country: here is where our biggest enemies are. If we go, who will remain?"[8] If Mildred alone left, Arvid's position and his work, both in the overt and covert spheres, would be compromised. He would come under close scrutiny and be suspected of disloyalty to the Third Reich. Furthermore, she loved the language of Goethe and Schiller. Finally, an overwhelming consideration was her commitment to the Harnack cause, the pull of which was stronger than her sense of survival. She would stay.

Nevertheless, Arvid was tormented about subjecting his wife to an ominous future. During one of the couples' weekend walks, Arvid implored Heath, without success, to persuade Mildred to leave. Perhaps sensing the danger he was in, Arvid booked passage for her on an American ship, good at any time, so that she would always have the possibility of leaving Germany.[9]

During this "Twilight War" of 1939–1940, when, despite their declarations of war, Britain and France seemed unwilling to engage the enemy, Arvid and other dissident Germans searched for allies abroad. Harnack continued to provide Donald Heath with information about Germany's war economy. Carl Goerdeler, the former mayor of Leipzig, and the Foreign Ministry's Adam von Trott had been traveling to England and the United States on business trips, where they hoped to encourage support for the efforts of the German opposition. The Abwehr's Hans von Dohnanyi, Dietrich Bonhoeffer, and Hans Oster, made a futile attempt to initiate peace negotiations with the British through the Vatican.

The British wanted the resisters to oust Hitler; the members of the German resistance wanted assurances that the allies would not take advantage of the resulting turmoil. Regrettably neither side was prepared to act first.

Not only did these hopes for a peace fail, but Hitler enjoyed new successes—the invasion and occupation of Denmark and Norway in April 1940—which reinforced the perception among the German opposition that only the military could carry out a coup. However, the only military figure prepared to leap into action and commit "treason" was Hans Oster, the deputy to the Abwehr chief Admiral Canaris. During the winter, as the attack on the West was repeatedly postponed, Oster again and again informed his friend, the Dutch military attaché in Berlin, Gijsbertus Sas, of Hitler's ever-changing orders which the attaché forwarded to his Belgium colleague. On April 3, Oster warned the attaché that the invasion would occur the following week. The attaché urged that the information be passed to the British. Dutch intelligence officers ignored the request, perhaps because Oster had cried wolf too often, and the Dutch commander in chief denounced Oster as a "miserable fellow" for his trouble.[10]

Oster's rationale for this "treason" was that Hitler was preparing to invade neutral neighbors to whom he had given guarantees of inviolability. "People may well say that I am a traitor but in reality I am not," Oster said to Sas. "I regard myself as a better German than all those who are trotting along behind Hitler. It is both my purpose and my duty to liberate Germany, and with her the world, from this plague."[11] Dietrich Bonhoeffer, who approved Oster's actions, contended that under the National Socialists "treason" had become true patriotism and "patriotism" had become treason.[12] Oster was not the only "traitor" whose motives would be slandered.

"Operation Yellow," the attack on Holland, Belgium, and Luxembourg, actually began on May 10. Within the week, Churchill replaced Chamberlain as prime minister. Holland and Belgium fell. German tanks thrust through the "impenetrable" Ardennes Forest, trapping the British and French armies. In June Mussolini entered the war, France fell, and the Germans drove the British across the channel.

* * *

Due to Mildred's covert existence during wartime, letters and diaries—core materials for biography—are for the most part missing. In the crucial years from 1939 to 1942, we experience her life not in her own words but in the stilted language of bureaucracies. Still we are fortunate in one respect: the collapse of communism has enabled us to obtain Soviet intelligence files never meant to become public. They offer a remarkable glimpse into the lives of the Harnacks and their circle, particularly in the crucial period of the Nazi-Soviet Pact.

The Harnack files underscore, on the one hand, the pressures on the Soviet operatives and, on the other, Arvid Harnack's insistence on charting a course independent of Moscow. The result was a pragmatic modus operandi between an exceptional agent runner, Alexander Korotkov, and his German sources. The files also offer an insight into Stalin's obsessions and the sycophancy that pervaded his intelligence services. In the end, the most precious material the Harnack group provided—information on the imminent German invasion—was not only ignored but scornfully rejected by Stalin.

Thanks to the KGB files that became selectively available in 1993–1994 through the efforts of British journalist John Costello and former KGB agent Oleg Tsarev, a much fuller story can be told, one that contrasts sharply with the accounts of the Red Orchestra published before 1993, but one that is consistent with the character and psychology of the Harnacks and their principal collaborators, the Schulze-Boysens and the Kuckhoffs.

On Tuesday, September 17, 1940, a tall, thin, thirty-one-year-old man appeared at the door of the Harnacks' fifth-floor apartment. Mildred was away. The day before she had celebrated her thirty-eighth birthday alone in Marienbad, a spa where she had gone to take a cure and escape British bombs.[13] The caller bore greetings from Arvid Harnack's old friend from the Soviet embassy, Alexander Hirschfeld. Speaking impeccable German with only a faint accent, he identified himself as Alexander Erdberg and said that he needed the Harnacks' help.

Erdberg was in reality Alexander Mikhailovich Korotkov. The highlights of his career follow, summarized as you might find them revealed in his KGB dossier under his code name, Stepanov. Alexander Mikhailovich Korotkov was born in 1909. As a nineteen-year-old he came to the attention of Veniamin Gerson, the secretary of Genrikh Yagoda, the head of the NKVD. In seven years Korotkov rose from the position of elevator operator in the Lubyanka, the OGPU (later NKVD) headquarters in Moscow, to become an operative in the foreign intelligence service. He learned German and the Soviets posted him to Austria, France, and Switzerland. A protégé of the famous spymaster Alexander Orlov, whose deputy he had been in France, Korotkov became a skilled agent runner. In 1936–1937, he worked in the Soviet trade mission in Berlin. Recalled to the Soviet Union in 1938, he was dismissed from the NKVD during Stalin's purges, the pretext being the alleged treason of his in-laws. But in a highly unusual occurrence—he appealed directly to his chief, Laurentia Beria—the resourceful Korotkov was reinstated, and he returned to Berlin as deputy in the *rezidentura*. As a "legal," he had the benefit of diplomatic cover as third secretary in the Soviet embassy.[14]

Korotkov surveyed the Harnack's three-and-one-half room apartment with professional acumen. Located on the Woyrschstrasse, now Genthinerstrasse, the flat was typical of the Tiergarten quarter: large rooms with high ceilings and a *Kaiserzeit* charm. He knew from their file that they were a scholarly couple so he was not surprised to see a number of bookcases and two large desks. A scattering of oriental carpets and Clara Harnack's paintings—mostly landscapes of Thuringia and a few still lifes—completed the decoration. The most interesting feature of the apartment was the state-of-the-art Blaupunkt radio, selected by Falk Harnack, the better to monitor foreign broadcasts.

Korotkov noted approvingly that the Harnacks had chosen the top floor with security in mind. A firewall separated them from the next building and protected them from eavesdropping. There was no telephone. Would-be callers were screened through Arvid's office at the ministry. Conveniently close to the Tiergarten, the Russian visitor observed, the flat would be convenient for *Treffs*.

Suspecting an *agent provocateur*, Harnack was wary of the uninvited guest. He had been out of touch with Moscow for more than two years. During that time he was perhaps aware that several of his Russian contacts, the so-called residents formerly assigned to the Berlin station, had been executed or had "disappeared" in the purge trials.[15] For some time there had not even been a Soviet ambassador at 7 Unter den Linden.

To convince Harnack that he was not a decoy, Korotkov did not question him but proposed a second meeting. With Moscow's assent, he secretly transported Harnack by car to the Soviet embassy.[16] Even there, Korotkov found he had a hard sell. Only reluctantly did Arvid agree to help the Russians.

Practitioners of espionage have grouped motivations for spying under the mnemonic MICE: money, ideology, compromise (which includes blackmail), or ego. We cannot know precisely why Harnack agreed to help the Russians, but four theories have been advanced:

1 Money was the motive, asserted Harnack's prosecutor, Manfred Roeder. However, even though the Russians were usually unstinting in buying help, no significant money passed through Harnack's hands until the eve of the Soviet invasion several months later, when Harnack received 20,000 Reichmarks (about $8,000). This he appears to have shared, distributing it to cover the expenses of the group. This small amount of money would hardly have been an inducement to risk their lives.[17]

2 He was ideologically driven. Nazis debriefed by the Americans and British, who hoped to gain a sympathetic hearing, said that Harnack was a "fanatic Communist." However, according to the verdict in Harnack's trial, suppressed for forty years by the East Germans, Harnack was "not a [Soviet-style] Communist by conviction. He believed in a planned national economy because of scientific considerations. This was the explanation for all his actions."[18]

3 Harnack was blackmailed by the Russians, according to one postwar investigator Dr. Finck.[19] Because he had provided the Soviets with information between 1935 and 1938, he was possibly entrapped in what CIA counter-intelligence chief James Jesus Angelton has called "a subtle web of irresistible compromises."[20]

4 Harnack felt himself "morally bound to assist the agents

dispatched to him." According to a witness at his trial, Harnack said that he had only spied for the Soviet Union in wartime because of his personal pledge to Erdberg.[21]

A revealing statement by Korotkov in the KGB's Corsican file (after 1940, when Arvid was reinstated, his codename was changed from Balt to Corsican) provides a clue to Harnack's motivation: "He considers it his duty to inform us about what his acquaintances tell him, not because he sees himself in the role of an agent with us as his chiefs, but rather first and foremost as representatives of the Soviet Union, of a country with whose ideals he feels connected and from which he awaits support."[22] Korotkov tells Moscow that Corsican impresses him as "an honest person, a truly moral person, who says what he means."[23]

Korotkov recognized that Harnack was not motivated by money: "To suggest money to Corsican right now would not be appropriate." However, he continues, "it would not be a bad idea to make a gift of food (packed without Soviet labels) and perhaps a coat for his wife. The second is perhaps too sensitive. Such a gift from a highly placed person in Moscow should in no way appear like a payment but rather appear in the way of a comradely relationship."[24]

Disinterested idealism is a rare motive, and Arvid Harnack appears to be an anomaly in the annals of espionage. He was not a paid agent, nor was he, like the Cambridge Five, an ideological spy whose primary objective was to help the Soviet Union. Disillusioned by Versailles, disappointed by the appeasement policies of English and French politicians at Munich, Harnack was finally dismayed by the collapse of France. He had helped the Americans for three years; perhaps he was disillusioned with Roosevelt's evasive public statements on the European war. He viewed his aid to the Russians primarily as a way to defeat Hitler. Harnack never regarded himself as an agent of a foreign power, nor did he follow Soviet orders. Rather he saw himself as an equal partner with the Soviets, and the surviving KGB documents show that was how Korotkov treated him. Harnack proved supremely resourceful and courageous, but there would continue to be concern in Moscow "that Harnack was primarily building his network as a secret anti-

Fascist conspiracy and only secondarily exploiting it as a source for Soviet intelligence."[25]

Reluctantly, Harnack made the leap into action and under the eyes of German law he was now a traitor. But was he? The Nazis, in a mockery of legality, used force majeure to rewrite German laws and abolish elections, and so by these standards theirs was an illegal regime, therefore there could be no question of betraying it. Hitler was the traitor. These arguments prevailed in a landmark libel case in West Germany against General Otto Remer, who in 1952 had defamed members of the July 20 as "traitors."[26] In 1953, a law was passed including resisters among those indemnified as victims of Nazism. Yet, in 1956, when the KPD was outlawed in West Germany, veterans of the Communist resistance became ineligible for compensation.[27]

Traditionally, historians of the German resistance have drawn an ethical distinction between *Hochverrat*—treason by internal revolt—and the greater crime of *Landesverrat*—espionage or betrayal of one's country to foreign enemies. This has resulted in a curious double standard by which some resisters—such as those who would after the events of 1944, be called the July 20 conspirators—inhabit the high moral terrain of *Hochverrat*, of genuine resistance, while the Harnacks and Schulze-Boysens are consigned to the darker realm of espionage and their group used to illustrate the "dangerous propinquity of resistance and treason."[28]

For years, the orthodox Western view held that Harnack and Schulze-Boysen "cannot be included in the ranks of German resistance." As West German journalist Heinz Höhne opined, "The fact that they worked for the Soviet Secret Service has fixed a great gulf between them and the rest of the German resistance, a gulf which will probably never be bridged; for the majority of German anti-Nazis, Schulze-Boysen and his people were just traitors, clandestine minions of a power which would have suppressed liberty in Germany as effectively as National-Socialism succeeded in doing." They were merely "cogs in the machine of a foreign espionage organization."[29] By contrast, Oster, who also passed military secrets to the enemy, was a hero who "wished to induce the enemy to take counter-measures, thereby checking Hitler's warlike adventure in its infancy."[30] Yet Oster, Friedrich Werner Count von der Schulenburg—the German ambassador to the Soviet Union who warned his counterpart of Hitler's imminent strike—and Harnack and Schulze-Boysen were *all* prepared to betray their country, to commit what the Nazis would term *Landesverrat*.

Arvid believed, in his brother's words, "that he had to actively counter injustice and crime." He thought that "whoever has convincing knowledge about a planned crime has the binding duty to warn the one against whom the crime is directed. The Fascists, the German National Socialists, were leading a barbaric war. This was a barbaric crime and the Harnacks saw it as their moral obligation to warn the Russians and the Americans. If there is any treason, then it was the National Socialists who betrayed the Germans by starting the criminal war."[31]

Harnack thought himself a German patriot. According to Egmont Zechlin, he saw a future alliance between Germany, Russia, and China. This bloc would be "economically and militarily impregnable."[32] In fact, an alliance between Germany and Russia had been part of mainstream German political thinking since Bismarck, and Harnack's belief in the "planned economy" was in fashion not only in the Soviet Union but in the United States, where Keynesian ideas were ascendant. In Germany, Arvid's associate Hjalmar Schacht, in his tenure as economics minister, was a successful practitioner of centralized controls.

Harnack thought socialism would acquire a unique form in Germany. Schulze-Boysen also told a colleague that only if Germans had their own brand of socialism could they become independent of the Soviet Union.[33] In their naïve view, Stalin would not insist on a Soviet Germany but instead would content himself with a peace-loving Reich.[34] A fellow conspirator, Adolf Grimme, remembered Harnack's telling him that "we need a fist in order not to become a puppet of Moscow."[35]

On September 26, 1940, as the Battle of Britain reached its final stage, bombs battered London and the British attacked German ports in the hope of stalling the impending invasion of Britain. Arvid Harnack provided Moscow with his first intelligence report. He reported that an attack on the Soviet Union was in the planning stages:

An officer of the supreme command of Germany (OKW) has told CORSICAN that by the beginning of next year, Germany will be ready for war with the Soviet Union. A preliminary step will be the military occupation of Rumania, which is planned for the near future. The objective of the campaign will be to occupy western European Russia along the Leningrad-Black Sea line and to create on this territory a German vassal state. The remainder of the USSR is to be constituted into a state which is friendly towards Germany. At a conference of the Economic Warfare Committee, its chairman, Rear Admiral Gross, dropped hints that the general operations against England are being postponed.[36]

What was extraordinary about the information Harnack provided the Soviets was not its prescience—the occupation of Rumania was indeed a prelude to the invasion—but rather that it went against current thinking. At that time—at the height of the Hitler-Stalin pact—few believed that Hitler would be so irrational as to fight a two-front war, in the East as well as in the West.

Because of Arvid's new role as an illegal agent, Mildred endured two years of terror—fear that she sublimated by intense activity. Her customary cheerfulness underwent a change, according to Wolfgang Havemann, who said she was "constantly tense" and "always under stress, as if on duty."[37] Falk said that she was in "a state of panic."[38] In the second winter of the war, because of wartime rationing, fuel and food were scarce. Mildred prowled the streets and waited in long queues for potatoes and other starches. In Berlin, no coffee could be found, meat and fresh green vegetables were seldom obtainable, and even salt and pepper disappeared from the dinner table. It was the year of the "Eins": *Einheit* (unity) soap, *Einheit* toilet paper, and *Eintopfgerichte*, often just a Sunday soup made from the week's leftovers.

The redemptive bright spot for Mildred during a year of increasing hardship was the birth of Jane and Otto Donner's son, Andreas, on September 31, 1940 amid exploding British bombs. Mildred reported to her family that the two couples were spending the evening together with friends, the "usually stately and beautiful" Jane sitting "with an added measure of serenity." The women had gone off by themselves and "were discussing the new books on women's health and babies." From time to time, Jane looked at her watch and made notations in her calendar. When it was time to leave, Jane casually remarked, "Well, I think I'll go right over to the clinic just in case the baby might come. I've been keeping track, and the pains are coming every seven minutes now." They headed by foot (no taxis were available) for the hospital. Arvid continued the story in a letter to his mother, providing a good-natured aside amid otherwise stressful times: "We were not allowed to stay in the hospital. This was just as well because at 11:30 P.M. the air raid sirens went off. Against the thunder of guns, the little thunder ["Donner" means "thunder" in German] was born. Otto had gone home to fetch Jane's things. He almost didn't make it back because at the first checkpoint personnel wouldn't believe his story about the baby. Andreas arrived around one o'clock." Mildred brought a bouquet of "pink roses, big white cyclamen looking like butterflies, and lilies of the valley" to Jane, and she read her sonnets from Shakespeare celebrating her maternal state.[39]

In December, Arvid reported to his mother that, although their neighborhood escaped harm, they were spending a lot of their time in a bomb shelter: "caution is the mother of procelain cups." Theirs was in a large office building so sturdy that it seemed "humanly impossible that anything could happen there. The people who gather there are nice. One older, quite agreeable woman thinks it is disgraceful to go to sleep at such critical times. So she talks constantly. This doesn't prevent us from sinking into the arms of Morpheus, however, albeit on chairs [that have been] pushed together."[40]

Preoccupied with her new baby, Jane was increasingly out of touch, but there was one witness who saw Mildred on a daily basis, whose memories are still vivid after fifty years. Donald Health Jr. was thirteen when he saw the Harnacks for the last time in 1941. Our telephone conversations were replete with the jargon of the intelligence agent he later became:

"In 1939, I was on a farm in Pomerania, on the Baltic, and when I came back suddenly all I heard was, 'Arvid, Arvid, Arvid.' My mother and father were fascinated by Arvid and Mildred. The

American School had just closed and Mildred's niece Jane, who had taught U.S. history there, continued to tutor me in that subject. Mildred became my tutor in English and American literature. My mother welcomed this arrangement as it gave them a reason to see one another.

"We started out with Gulliver's Travels, Beowulf, *then went on to John Donne and the Elizabethans. She wrote out a reading list in her own hand. I took to reading in part because of her. I got in trouble for reading books that I shouldn't be reading—*Anthony Adverse—*in the American Women's Club. I read a lot of German books. She discussed the Wobblies and the history of the American labor movement, but I don't remember her discussing communism.*

"She was like Julie Christie in Dr. Zhivago, *really very interesting. I was very attracted to her. She was very Germanic and wore out-of-date clothes. People would look at her. You noticed her across a crowded room. She was a man's woman. Very striking. A total presence, vocal, visual, thoughtful, she told you what's what.*

"I began going to school at the Harnacks in November and December of '39. By the end of 1940, Mildred was too busy. I went twice a week to her apartment with my briefcase. I took the U-Bahn or the S-Bahn to Nollendorfplatz. I was told to look around carefully before walking to Mildred's. I walked past a burned-out synagogue [this was after Kristallnacht]. A man sold hot chestnuts in the street and I would take them up to the apartment. Another man would play hurdy-gurdy music in the street and Mildred and I would throw down ten-pfennig pieces. My briefcase was filled with food for Mildred. [Diplomats could obtain butter and cheese from Denmark or a rare orange through the embassy commissary.] She would admire the fruit and then take a deep inhalation of the apple or orange."*

Every day young Donald carried a message to Mildred from his mother, or from his father to Arvid. He described himself as the "trotteur conventus"—*the go-between. He paid close attention to all that he saw, excellent training for an intelligence officer.*

"You came in the door of the apartment into a hallway and then entered the dining area where there was a porcelain stove. In the living room were bookcases, a table with writing materials,* *and a couch. There was a picture of Mildred's mother on the table, and paintings on the wall. I went back in '46 but the street was all rubble. All of it was gone—bombed.*

"It was about this time that our cook, who worked for German intelligence, was discovered on the carpet photographing my mother's diary. The Gestapo wanted to get diplomats in compromising sexual or black market scandals. One German intelligence officer tried to recruit my father, but he was very sensitive to 'elicitation techniques.' My parents warned me before every outing with the staff. 'You don't know where we went or whom we talked with. No talking to strangers.' I was debriefed when I came home and I'd tell them what I'd been asked and what I'd said.

"On the weekends my parents would take their car around Berlin and meet the Harnacks in one of the parks. Once when Falk was on leave, he also came.

"It was in 1941 during a walk in the Spreewald, a wood near East Berlin, that Arvid told my father that he worked for the Russians. It was probably in May or June of that year. Arvid said in an oblique manner that he was working with the Russians. Arvid had very specific views and was very defensive about the Soviets when my father tried to argue with Arvid against the Soviet Union.

"Arvid didn't know that my father was a Treasury intelligence officer; he thought he was merely State Department. For that matter, neither did Alexander Kirk, the American chargé. My father was part of a Berlin-Rome-Tokyo group that worked for Morgenthau.

"Arvid was provocative, and my father could get bright red when he was angry. Arvid got information out of my father, and my father got information from Arvid. But he frequently had to tell Arvid to control himself. Arvid saw the future in socialism and the need for order. But it was a strong friendship. When Arvid was in the U.S. before the war, he had written a secret memo to the State Department, offering his help against the Nazis.

"In April 1941, I went over to the Harnack's apartment. Mildred had asked to 'borrow' me on Thursday. Mildred and I met and took the S-Bahn to Potsdam to the city park and began walking. Mildred said, 'A lady will join me and walk ahead and you fall behind. Do keep your eyes open.' A handsome woman arrived carrying a briefcase—Mildred also had a briefcase. She and Mildred could have exchanged documents."[41]

Shortly after taking up contact with Harnack, Korotkov was recalled to Moscow. He received orders and a ten-point plan for his work with Corsican. Korotkov was to discover the role of the opposition within Germany, confirm details about Hitler's plans in regard to the USSR, and sniff out information about the German economy in the event of war. He himself was to be the link with Corsican and his group. Korotkov studied the points and signed his name beneath the words "read, understood and carried out."[42]

Treffs were to be set up by slipping a letter into Harnack's mailbox. "I am back in Berlin," the message was to read. "Came to see you and didn't find you there. I'd be very pleased if you would visit me." The rendezvous was to take place one week after the date of the letter, at eight A.M. at the telephone booth at the Fasanenplatz. The Russian was to approach Harnack with the question, "How do you get to the Woyrschstrasse?" Harnack was to answer that he lived there.[43] According to the files, further meetings were to be held in the former Lithuanian House (then a consulate), in a cafe or automobile, or, as a last resort, in the Harnack apartment. Korotkov would note that Mildred was sometimes present.[44]

On January 17, 1941, Korotkov met again with Harnack in his apartment and reported that his reception was "very warm." At this meeting Harnack appeared to have overcome the mistrust and tenseness he had exhibited earlier and was completely forthcoming. Harnack insisted, however, on a single point: he did not want to reveal surnames for fear that a loss or theft might occur, even though he was sure that the Russians "probably handle secret documents better than the Germans." At this meeting, Harnack outlined the organization of his group. His circle included around sixty persons whose work was primarily intellectual—writers, state officials, engineers, and technical workers. Some had previously belonged to the Bund der Geistesarbeiter. Others formerly had contacts with the Communist Party. Korotkov confirms that after 1938, when Harnack had lost contact with the Russians, he resumed his ties with members of the BGA and had found some new recruits. "His wife helped him with this," says Korotkov.[45]

Mildred also appears in subsequent KGB files. In a message dated March 10, 1941, Korotkov says she was "completely in the picture about Balt's [Harnack's] connections and work. She herself carried out work for the Communist Party and in 1933 or 1934 was in Moscow twice with a special visa [one that was separate from her passport, enabling her to disguise her visit—probably made by transiting through a third country—from the Germans] for talks with Comrade Kuusinen [a Finn who was a powerful member of the Comintern secretariat] who, at the suggestion of the German comrades intended to use her for Comintern work in Finland, since in addition to a German passport she also has an American one. Currently, the wife of Balt heads the American Women's Club in Berlin and is admitted to the American embassy as an American citizen. She has a valid American passport. At the same time, as Balt's wife she is considered a German citizen by the German authorities."[46]

From these files and her relatives' recollections, it appears that Mildred made a second trip to the Soviet Union, probably in fall 1933. Little is known about this trip aside from a brief mention in a letter from Hungarian Communist Georg Lukács, who met her in Moscow ("on what business she was there for, I naturally cannot say, she didn't speak about it and I didn't question her") and the reference in the KGB files released only in 1994.[47]

Harnack's most important informants, according to the Soviets, included two former members of the Bund der Geistesarbeiter: Hans Rupp, head economist for I. G. Farben (code name Turk) and Dr. Tietjens (or Titzien), a wealthy White Russian emigrant who had become a Communist and was a marketing psychologist and de facto head of Leiser, a large shoe chain. His code name was Albanian.[48] Baron Wohlzogen-Neuhaus (code name Greek) had been introduced to Arvid by his former professor Friedrich Lenz. The baron worked in the technical department of the OberKommando der Wehrmacht, the army's supreme command. Four former students of Mildred's appear in the KGB files: Paul Thomas, a one-armed World War I veteran and sometime tutor of young Donald Heath, code named Armless;[49] Mildred's former students Karl Behrens, who was now working as an engineer in the design department of the German electrical giant AEG, who became known as Beamer,[50] and his wife, Clara, who was a stenotypist at the OKH; Wilhelm Utech, a.k.a. Worker; and a young man identified only as one of Harnack's closest associates and a translator in the Air Force Ministry, who probably was a private English student of Mildred's named Herbert Gollnow. A friend of Behrens, Leo Skrypczynski, also appears with the name Teacher, and Adam Kuckhoff is Old Man. Finally, the KGB lists two Harnack relatives: Wolfgang Havemann, Harnack's stepnephew, code named Italian, and his nephew by marriage, Otto Donner, who became chief of the Research Office of War Economics under General Thomas and a member of the Committee for the Four-Year-Plan, who emerges as Anonymous. From time to time, it also appears that Harnack's friend Egmont Zechlin provided information.[51]

In an American military intelligence interrogation conducted in 1947, Otto Donner did not deny that he had supported Harnack's illegal work, yet he was careful to distinguish his views from those of the Harnack group: "This group was Communist. I was not a member because I didn't want to devote myself to communism. But in terms of the negative, in our rejection of Nazism, Harnack and I were completely united. I helped Harnack whenever I could, not just with information but, for example, by turning over my apartment for secret meetings."[52]

Donner typified several Harnack informants, many of them who were not Communists but were identified as members of "Corsican's agent group." Thus the term "agent" and also the number of members of the Corsican group, reckoned by the KGB as sixty, must be treated with caution. Moreover, in his January meeting Harnack told Korotkov that "in this circle, smaller 'centers' have formed . . . so that CORSICAN no longer knows personally all of those belonging to these circles." Harnack declared his intention "to remain in the shadows," although Korotkov noted that "he is the soul of the organization." The goal of the organization was "to prepare cadres who would be able to take over command positions after a coup. For this reason, problems of socialism are worked on and discussed and individual topics even assigned . . . an exchange of information takes place . . . and new people are drawn in and educated."[53] In fact, most of the educating was accomplished by Mildred since, as one member recalled, Arvid was seldom at the meetings.[54]

During their first secret embassy meeting, Korotkov had grasped the need for exceptional caution to protect Harnack's informers in key agencies. When Korotkov informed Moscow Center of

Harnack's demand that his resistance activities be given priority over his intelligence activities, Moscow protested. If Harnack's group were picked up because of its resistance work, the whole network would be blown. In the end, however, the Center accepted Harnack's terms. Korotkov had convinced Moscow that Harnack would never agree to abandon his crusade against Hitler simply to become a channel for the transmission of secrets to the Soviet Union.

Harnack's value to Moscow greatly increased when he persuaded Harro Schulze-Boysen to join in helping the Russians in December. Senior (Starshina), as he was code named, had excellent sources in the Air Ministry and a sharply analytical mind. Korotkov had been pressuring Harnack to introduce him to Schulze-Boysen, but the Luftwaffe had transferred him to the operations staff engaged in planning the attack on the Soviet Union. Stationed at Wildpark Werder near Potsdam, he could come to Berlin only on weekends. As he was usually in uniform, meetings must occur "accidentally" on neutral ground.[55] However, Korotkov would not be put off. He had important questions for Senior and on March 27 the three met face-to-face for the first time.

Harnack had coached Korotkov in the fine art of handling "the fiery Decembrist," as he called him. Schulze-Boysen "should not be left with the feeling that his party work, which he values so highly, should degenerate into mere espionage."[56] Schulze-Boysen's contacts with members of the Communist underground were a serious breach of the conspiratorial rule that agents and party members should not mix. His "party work" would continue to vex the Russians, sparking an exchange with Moscow when Korotkov discovered he still had ties to the Communists.[57]

Briefed by Harnack, Schulze-Boysen knew the true nature of the work of the embassy secretary. In a message to headquarters, Korotkov reported that Senior "gives the impression that he is fully prepared to tell me everything he knows. He answered my questions without evasion or the intention of concealing anything." Moreover, Schulze-Boysen had prepared for the meeting by putting down on a piece of paper "certain points to pass on to us." Korotkov adds that there were small things that he wished to bring up at the meeting, but he demurred. He did not want to give the impression that Soviet intelligence had "found a victim from whom they will try and squeeze every available morsel."[58] Senior clearly impressed Korotkov, who astutely remarked that while Harnack was a dreamer who made great preparations for the future—for a time when the Communists would come to power—Schulze-Boysen, by contrast, was an energetic person who concentrated on the need for action.[59]

According to KGB files, Kuckhoff (Old Man) assumed responsibility for a third Berlin network when he met with Korotkov in April. Moscow's instructions were to isolate the agents, meaning that Kuckhoff should be distanced from Harnack, "using an appropriate pretext" and "without wounding Arvid's sensibilities."[60]

In an interview, Greta Kuckhoff described their initial meeting with the sympathetic Russian: "He had read *Till Eulenspiegel* [a play adapted from a sixteenth-century German book] by my husband and we spoke quite a lot about architecture . . . Erdberg [Korotkov] told us about personal family things—that he had previously been in Paris [in the early 1930s as the assistant to Alexander Orlov] and that he had two daughters and would like to have a son. After the war [he proposed] we would exchange apartments in order that I could become acquainted with Moscow and they with Berlin."[61]

This display of tact and understanding toward the group suggests the high regard in which the Russians held them. It conflicts with the CIA view of Soviet agent-running practices contained in the agency's report on the Harnack/Schulze-Boysen group: "Moscow made little allowance for field problems or for the personalities of the various agents."[62]

During this period, Harnack also continued to share information with the Americans, informing Heath of Germany's belligerent intentions. Otto Donner confirmed that he gave Donald Heath, whom he had met through the Harnacks, numerous pieces of information. The most important was that in the end of 1940 or the beginning of 1941, Donner informed Heath "of measures that made it appear that Hitler was preparing an attack on Russia to occur soon."[63]

"I had become aware of certain facts," Donner reported, "because the Research Office had had to prepare a statistical analysis concerning Russia and because I heard from friends in other offices that similar subjects were being worked on where they were. I took this as a pretext to go over to the OKW, (Thomas's office)* and get into a conversation with a captain who told me a lot of things he shouldn't have. Mr. Heath passed my information on to Washington." The State Department in turn informed Moscow.[64]

In January, Schulze-Boysen reported that the Luftwaffe was planning reconnaissance flights over Soviet territory to photograph Russian defense lines and the city of Leningrad. He informed Moscow Center of the posting of Russian experts to Goering's staff.[65] In March, he reported that these flights over Soviet territory were "proceeding at full pace." Taking off from Bucharest, Königsberg, and German-occupied Kirkenes in northern Norway, the Germans had been especially careful to photograph the Russian naval base at Kronstadt. The intelligence section of the Luftwaffe was archiving the photographs.[66] Operational plans targeting the Soviet Union were confirmed, as well as troop concentrations on the Soviet border.[67] Two field marshals informed Egmont Zechlin that the attack was now set for the first day of May, when the Russians would be unable to burn their green wheat, making it possible for the Germans to harvest it. Another message read: "By occupying the Ukraine, the Germans will deprive the Soviet Union of its main industrial base. The Germans will move east to occupy the Caucasus. The Urals, according to their calculations, can be reached in twenty-five days."[68] This confirmed an earlier message that had quoted General Halder, chief of the general staff of the army. Halder was "convinced of the success of a blitzkrieg" attack on the Ukraine and the Baku oil industries, which yielded most of the Soviet Union's aviation oil, kerosene, and gas. If the attack were a surprise, the Red Army would be left reeling from the shock and could not destroy the supplies they left behind in the overrun area.[69]

In April, Schulze-Boysen revealed that the Luftwaffe had completed preparations for the air attack on the Soviet Union. Designated targets were the railroad junctions in the western Soviet Union, the electric power stations of the Donetsk coalfield in the

---

*General Georg Thomas (1890–1945), the head of the Economics and Armaments branch of the German army (OKW). After 1938 he was in contact with the opposition formed around General Beck and Goerdeler. In preparation for February 1941 he warned Hitler against the Soviet invasion because of the inadequate armaments preparation.

Ukraine, and Moscow's airplane factories.[70] In April, Korotkov reported that an anti-Soviet campaign would be launched in the German press "attributing malevolent intentions to the Bolsheviks." At the same time the transit of German goods to the Soviet Union was to be suspended.[71]

Other useful items followed in May: the American military attaché in Moscow was a German agent; German cryptologists had the Persian codes.[72] The crisis in the Balkans delayed Hitler for a crucial six weeks, and it became clear that the Russian offensive would begin in June.

In early June, Schulze-Boysen reported that bases in Poland were being equipped to receive aircraft; Harnack provided the list of quartermasters who were to manage occupied territory in the Soviet Union.[73] Goering was transferring his headquarters from Berlin to Rumania. Schulze-Boysen reported that documents he had seen showed that the Germans planned to capture the Red Army in a pincer movement south from West Prussia and north from Rumania.[74] Amiak Kobulov, the NKVD station chief in Berlin, in an attempt to persuade his bosses of the importance of this message, added that it was not meant as a "provocation" but came "straight from the heart."[75]

On June 16, Schulze-Boysen presented Korotkov with the Luftwaffe order of battle. His report ended with a warning: "All German military measures for the preparation of an armed attack on the Soviet Union have been fully completed and the blow can be expected to fall at any moment."[76] This final message was immediately forwarded to Stalin by deputy NKVD chief Vsevolod Merkulov. Stalin's penned response, now written in history's marginalia: "To Comrade Merkulov. You can send your 'source' from the German air force staff to his much fucked mother! This is not a 'source' but a disinformer. J. Stalin."[77]

The Soviet leader immediately summoned Merkulov and the inexperienced head of foreign intelligence for the NKVD, Pavel M. Fitin, to a private meeting. Stalin's first words were to Fitin: "Chief of Intelligence, there's no need to repeat the special report; I have read it closely. Tell me what sort of sources are reporting this, where they work, how reliable they are, and how they are able to obtain such secret information." Fitin fumbled some explanations. Stalin had the final word: "Look here, Chief of Intelligence, there

are no Germans who can be trusted, except for Wilhelm Pieck.*
Is that clear?"[78]

That Stalin, who had once been overheard to state that "a spy
should be like the devil; no one should trust him, not even himself,"[79] failed to heed his Berlin informants, and at least one hundred other warnings, constitutes a suggestive footnote to the annals of espionage.[80] Leaders do not welcome intelligence that
conflicts with their strongly held views.

Recent disclosures divulge that party leaders and the general staff
were informed that an estimated 191 divisions, or more than 3
million men, had been deployed along Soviet borders. Both the
GRU, the military intelligence department of the Ministry of Defense, and the NKVD obtained thousands of ciphered messages,
including those brought by diplomatic courier from Berlin, warning of an impending attack. Messages were delivered to Stalin,
Molotov, and Marshal Timoshenko. Many of them originated
from the Berlin *rezidentura*. However, in studying this information
a flaw is apparent, a fatal weakness inherent in the Soviet's syco-
phantic secret services—its chief analyst and final reader, Stalin.

The information landing on the dictator's desk tended to confirm what Stalin wanted to hear—that war might be avoided and
Hitler appeased. But if a political settlement with Germany was
not feasible and war was inevitable, it might at least be postpon-
able. In April, Merkulov presented Stalin with a report from
Schulze-Boysen. It seemed to support Stalin's tactic of delay and
appeasement by suggesting a breach between Germany's military
and political leadership that might promote a political settlement.
According to Israeli scholar Gabriel Gorodetsky, Schulze-Boysen's
report "depicted in lively colors the clash between Goering and
Ribbentrop, a clash that had 'gone so far as to sour their personal
relations.' "[81] Harnack's report that the four-year planning committee thought that Germany "stood to gain much more" from
trade than through the occupation of the Soviet Union served to
further encourage Stalin's stance.[82] In May, Schulze-Boysen reported that there was resistance both among the majority of

---

*Wilhelm Pieck (1876–1960) was one of the German Communists who survived
the purges. In 1949, he became president of the German Democratic Republic.

German officers and some circles of the Nazi Party to a war with the Soviet Union, which could "lead to Hitler's downfall."[83]

The motto current among the Stalin's subordinates was "sniff out, suck up, survive" (*ugadat, ugodit, utselet*), even if this meant suppressing inconvenient but accurate information.[84] However, the espionage hierarchy feared being accused of dereliction of duty, with the attendant consequences. Officials struck on an ingenious solution: unpleasant information was not so much concealed as delivered raw, without analysis. Notations to the "Military Leader of all Times and Peoples" were qualified by phrases like "this report looks like disinformation" "it would need to be checked out," "it comes from unreliable sources, etc."[85] This approach worked well with Stalin, who preferred raw material to analyses, which he described as "dangerous guesswork." "Don't tell me what you think, give me the facts and the source!" he admonished his intelligence chiefs. What Stalin wanted were "facts and figures hidden in the secret vaults of foreign governments." Informants preferably should be "of the caliber of foreign ambassadors and general staff officers."[86]

Key warnings about Operation Barbarossa came through the GRU, military intelligence, headed (thanks to the purges) by the relatively inexperienced Lt. General Filip Golikov, who habitually divided his agents' information into two categories: material "from reliable sources" and "from doubtful sources."[87]

Falling into the doubtful category was Leopold Trepper, "the grand chef" of the GRU's Brussels–Paris network. Trepper wrote that General Golikov informed him on March 20, 1941, that "all documents claiming that war is imminent must be regarded as forgeries emanating from British or even German sources." The next day Golikov sent Stalin an update on the rumored surprise German attacks. In his conclusion he wrote, "Rumors and documents to the effect that war against the USSR is inevitable this spring should be regarded as misinformation coming from the English or perhaps even the German intelligence service."[88] When Trepper tried to hand the Soviet military attaché in Vichy information on Operation Barbarossa, the attaché patted him condescendingly on the shoulder and said, "My poor fellow, I will send your dispatches, but only to make you happy."[89] As late as June 21, when Trepper hurried to Vichy to warn the attaché that the attack was coming the next day, he was again rebuffed: "You are completely mistaken. Only today I met with the Japanese military attaché, who just arrived from Berlin. He assures me that Germany is not preparing for war. We can depend on him." Trepper insisted that the message be sent. Ironically, he did not receive Golikov's reply until a day after the invasion on June 23: "You can tell Otto [Trepper's code name] that I have passed on information on the imminence of the German attack to the big boss. The big boss is amazed that a man like Otto, an old military and intelligence man, has allowed himself to be intoxicated by English propaganda. You can tell him that the big boss is completely convinced that the war with Germany will not start before 1944."[90]

When the GRU's best agent, Richard Sorge, sent a warning from Tokyo in May that the German ambassador in Tokyo had been informed that the attack on the Soviet Union would begin in June and that "nine armies consisting of 150 divisions will be concentrated against the U.S.S.R," Stalin remarked that Sorge was "a shit who has set himself up with some factories and brothels in Japan."[91] The GRU's reply to their agent was brief: "We doubt the veracity of your information."[92]

Stalin's preferred intelligence service, Beria's NKVD, fared no better. After 1939, when only two of the sixteen members of the most important foreign intelligence post—the Berlin *rezidentura*—had survived the purges, Vladimir Dekanozov, former deputy to Beria, became ambassador to Berlin in November 1940.[93] Short, with a beak-like nose and a few strands of black hair combed over a bald head, Dekanozov earned the moniker "the hangman of Baku" for the many death sentences he prescribed in the Caucasus following the Russian civil war.[94] Although a diplomatic novice, he possessed impeccable intelligence credentials and he should have been the ideal person for the job. But on the eve of the war, Ambassador Dekanozov had barely succeeded with the help of Korotkov in rebuilding his network. He was undermined both by his former chief, Beria, and his deputy Amiak Kobulov. Differences arose because Dekanozov was providing his information to his present chief, Foreign Minister Molotov, who passed it on to Stalin without informing Dekanozov's former boss and patron, Beria. Dekanozov's deputy, Kobulov, was exceptionally inexperienced, moody, and quarrelsome and, in time-honored bureaucratic tradition, worked hard at exacerbating the differences between Dekanozov and Beria.

Another serious problem for Stalin and his intelligence services was the successful disinformation campaign mounted by the Germans. In February, the Abwehr set in motion a detailed plan to confuse Moscow. They used neutral diplomats—of the sort favored by Stalin—to leak information to the Russians that Barbarossa was a "deception diversion" designed to cover up the invasion of Britain. The Russians were told that the massive transfer of German troops to the Soviet borders was designed to mislead the British. Special maps of Great Britain were printed and distributed. English-speaking interpreters were added to units, and strategic areas of the English Channel and the Norwegian coast were declared off-limits.[95] When Germany's ambassador to Moscow, Count Werner von der Schulenburg, warned his shocked counterpart Dekanozov at a private lunch of the coming invasion of the Soviet Union, Stalin's response to the news was to inform the Politburo that "disinformation has now reached the ambassadorial level!"[96]

Stalin believed another rumor spread by German intelligence: Hitler's flexing of his military might on Russia's borders could be a prelude to a new German ultimatum demanding concessions in the Ukraine. Even Harnack succumbed to this ruse, reporting in April in a message that was forwarded to Stalin and Molotov: "At a meeting of responsible officials of the Ministry of Economics, press representative Kroll declared, 'The USSR will be asked to join the Axis and attack England.' As a guarantee, the Ukraine will be occupied and possibly the Baltic [states] also."[97] In early May, Schulze-Boysen developed the ultimatum theory: "Germany wants to present the U.S.S.R. with an ultimatum in which more extensive export privileges will be demanded as retribution for Communist propaganda. In order to guarantee these, German emissaries are to be stationed in the industrial and economic centers and the factories of the Ukraine. Some areas are to be occupied by the Wehrmacht. A war of nerves, aimed at demoralizing the Soviet Union, is to precede this ultimatum."[98]

Stalin and his intelligence chiefs had a surfeit of information from too many sources—secret intelligence, newspaper stories, embassy rumors, and street gossip. Overwhelmed with information, the Soviets failed to analyze and use it. The instructions that Korotkov received in April support the hypothesis that perhaps Harnack and Schulze-Boysen supplied too much information. "Recently," Moscow complained, it had been receiving "such an abundance of agent reports about Germany's 'secret' preparations for an attack that—if one also considers the speculation in the Anglo-American press—the question arises of whether a deliberate disinformation campaign is being conducted."[99] According to Gorodetsky, a summary document "calendar of information obtained through 'Corsicanets' and 'Starshina' from September 6 1940 to June 16 1941" reached Merkulov just before the German attack. Rendered moot by subsequent events, it was returned by Fitin to the head of the German section and subsequently was buried in the archives.[100] In spite of Moscow's intransigence, in the months to come Harnack and Schulze-Boysen continued to provide information that would contribute to Hitler's ultimate defeat by the Red Army.

Stalin's failure to act on the warnings of his intelligence services may have had an additional cause: his greatest fear was not of an invasion but having to fight Hitler alone. Harnack's intelligence played into this fear, reinforced by the swift surrender of France: that Hitler and Churchill would negotiate a separate peace and unleash the full power of the Wehrmacht on the Soviet Union. Gleaned from his Herrenklub sources, Harnack's report, which reached Moscow in January 1941, stated that "the opinion grows that Germany will lose the war [on the western front] and, in the light of this, it is necessary to come to terms with England and America in order to turn its weapons against the East."[101]

In December 1940, Pavel Sudoplatov, the deputy director of foreign intelligence, outlined a ten-point plan for Corsican's group for Beria. According to the list, which was brought to Berlin by Korotkov in January, Arvid's principal task was to ferret out military information—but an equally important assignment was to inform Stalin about the German opposition to Hitler.[102]

Unlike his British and American counterparts, Stalin took a serious interest in the German resistance. Not, it must be said, in order to support them, but because he feared that they might negotiate preemptive peace treaties with the Americans and British behind his back, enabling Hitler to unleash a one-front war against the Soviet Union. In fact, during a key period from January through May 1941, Arvid—who had many contracts with the Social Democratic and conservative resistance around Goerdeler and Julius Leber principally through Ernst von Harnack—provided Stalin with an overview of the resistance and at the same time reinforced his paranoia about an Anglo-American-German rapprochement:[103]

> January 20, 1941: "CORSICAN informed us that one of his sources working on the aviation staff as an adviser [Schulze-Boysen] said that Goering is more and more inclined to conclude a peace agreement with England and America. This attempt to come to an understanding with the Americans was clarified by close associates of the [Luftwaffe chiefs], Goering, Mil[ch] and Udet by the American air force attaché Paton. Over breakfast, Donald Heath, the secretary of the American embassy in Berlin, informed CORSICAN that the German generals wanted to come to an agreement with the U.S.A."[104]

> February 26, 1941: "Carl Goerdeler, the former Reich commissar for price monitoring, made an attempt to reach agreement with the Wehrmacht leadership on the elimination of Hitler and the formation of a new regime. The talks were carried out on an extremely high level. As a whole, the representatives of the generals argued against Goerdeler's proposals, although the director of the military-economic staff of the Supreme Army Commander, General Thomas, and the commanding troop general, Hoepner* supported Goerdeler's ideas fully. Currently the supreme command of the Wehrmacht shares the ideas of Hitler and approves his militaristic plans. Goerdeler's group is holding fast to its Anglo-American orientation."[105]

> April 11, 1941: ". . . A member of the Luftwaffe staff, Holzhausen, stated that Germany's total war against England and the United States cannot be won. A peace treaty with them

---

* General Erich Hoepner (1886–1944), at one time Count Klaus von Stauffenberg's commandant, belonged to the July 20 conspirators.

is therefore necessary. So that the English will listen and in order to offset their unfulfillable desire for colonies, the Ukraine is to be separated from the USSR. The conquest of such an important source of food and raw materials as the Ukraine will wring concessions from the English in reaching a peace treaty with Germany."[106]

This report was forwarded to Merkulov, Stalin, Molotov, Timoshenko, and Beria, suggesting the importance that was attached to its contents. Moscow also evidenced interest in Ernst von Harnack and Adolph Grimme, a religious socialist and the former Prussian culture minister, who was a friend of the Kuckhoffs and Harnacks.

> May 5, 1941: "... Center is extremely interested in A. Grimme, hereinafter NEW. See to it that OLD MAN [Kuckhoff] activates the relationship and comes close to him. We hope this will be a way to obtain information about what happens in the group around Carl Goerdeler, which has extensive connections with the country's political and military circles. . . ."[107]

Playing to Stalin's paranoid psychosis was his deep distrust of Winston Churchill, who had led an anti-Bolshevik crusade during the Russian Civil War. Thus the bizarre defection to Britain of Hitler's deputy Rudolf Hess, ostensibly on a personal peace mission, on May 10, 1941, could be viewed in Moscow as corroboration of Schulze-Boysen's split-at-the-top theory, and it certainly played to Stalin's fear of an Anglo-German peace treaty. Furthermore, as Gorodetsky has suggested, the archives reveal that the British Foreign Office and British intelligence, in an attempt to forestall what they believed to be a rapprochement between Hitler and Stalin, manipulated the Hess affair to promote tensions between the two.[108]

Hess had been a student of the eminent geopolitician Karl Haushofer, the architect of Germany's Lebensraum policy, whose calling card he was carrying to Britain. Haushofer's son Albrecht* was

---

*Albrecht Haushofer (1903–1945) was professor of political geography in Berlin and a distinguished playwright and poet. He was acquainted with both Harnack and Schulze-Boysen and had many contacts within the resistance with the group around Goerdeler, the Kreisau Circle, and the Red Orchestra. He was ar-

thought to be the inspiration behind the flight. The younger Haus-hofer was acquainted with the Duke of Hamilton, the premier peer of Scotland and a member of the Cliveden set, the aristocratic clique of appeasers. Haushofer had evidently suggested to Hess that the duke might act as an intermediary in a peace initiative. Reports leaked from Kim Philby and others to Moscow immedi-ately after Hess's defection caused the NKVD analysts to conclude that "the Hess flight was not the act of a madman nor an attempt to save his life from an intrigue but the realization of a secret conspiracy by the Nazi leadership to strike a peace with Britain before opening the war with the Soviet Union."[109] Further, the Hess flight was viewed by the Kremlin as confirming the split be-tween the top Nazi leadership: Hess, with the backing of Goering, was thought to be "making a personal attempt to conclude peace" in order to interfere with the German-Soviet understanding.[110]

By reinforcing his anxieties about an Anglo-German alliance against the Soviet Union, the Hess flight made Stalin doubly anx-ious to avoid actions that might appear provocative to the Ger-mans. So as not to antagonize Hitler, Stalin continued to scrupu-lously observe the letter of the pact. He delivered all raw materials on schedule, sometimes even exceeding the promised quotas. In April, for example, additional Soviet trains delivered 2000 extra tons of raw rubber, further aiding the German war effort.[111] No wonder that Goebbels compared Stalin to a rabbit mesmerized by a snake.[112]

In June new means of summoning Harnack were devised. Contact was to be established by throwing a financial newspaper, the *Börsen-Zeitung*, in Harnack's mailbox. One week from the date on the newspaper was to be the date of the meeting. A red line through the date on the first page meant that the meeting was for the same day. *Treff*s were usually at eight o'clock in the evening; the meeting place was the Tiergarten S-Bahn station at the exit furthest from the Charlottenburger Chaussee. The agent would approach Harnack with the question of how best to come to Woyrschtrasse. In an emergency, Harnack could be approached at home between 8:30 and 9:00 in the morning or 7:30 and 8:00 in

---

rested as an accomplice of Adam von Trott's for his participation in the July 20 conspiracy and was shot by the SS in the closing days of the war.

the evening when the concierge was away. Korotkov notes that Coriscan's wife "is fully informed about our contact."[113]

Sometimes Mildred would be called upon to summon Arvid from the office when an important visitor or message arrived. But most of the Harnack/Schulze-Boysen/Kuckhoff material was passed directly to Korotkov in a café, an auto, or an outdoor setting like the Tiergarten. It was vital to ascertain whether your partner arrived at these assignations "clean," without a shadow. Thus Berlin's parks and woods were favored because it was easy to determine if you were being tailed. Greta, Mildred, or Libertas often covered these meetings, walking innocuously behind their men as they talked in the Tiergarten.

As the deadline for Barbarossa approached, the group despaired of impressing the Russians with a sense of urgency. And, despite his warning to Moscow that he was reluctant to press for written materials because with this it would be possible to frighten Coriscan, "headquarters kept pressing Korotov for documents " 'complete with stamp and signature.' "[114] Yet, as Greta indignantly complained, "We were not people who could crack safes and steal documents."[115]

Almost as an afterthought, in mid-April, Moscow instructed Korotkov to provide for radio contact with Berlin in the event of war. Harnack was to become the resident "illegal" and select a radio operator.[116] Harnack initially refused the radio contact, but he did agree to continue supplying the Soviets with information. In the end, he took responsibility only for collecting and enciphering the material which was to take place in the Harnack apartment. The transmitting would take place elsewhere.[117]

Moscow notified Berlin that they were sending "a portable transmitter-receiver mounted in a suitcase, with a power supply via accumulator and anode dry batteries. The device is meant for Corsican." They were including a diagram and instructions. The radio could reach up to six hundred miles and operate from "a field, forest, or farmhouse, etc." As it was battery powered, it would not work for more than two hours but Moscow was sending a reserve power source with instructions for how to hook it up by the next post. Establishing contact was to be done through call signs: "D6" was Corsican's radio, "A1" was the Soviet station (probably located at Minsk). Moscow added a word of caution:

in the event of discovery by the police or Abwehr, the radio must be destroyed—tubes first.[118]

Finally, in May, two "music boxes" (in Soviet espionage jargon) arrived by diplomatic pouch. Both were short wave transmitters. One was battery powered and the other, when dismantled, could be fitted in a suitcase but needed electricity to operate.[119] It was decided that Kurt Schumacher, code named Tenor, would become the radio operator. When he was drafted into the army, Schulze-Boysen suggested that the job be given to the inexperienced Hans Coppi, described by Schulze-Boysen as a former "young Communist,"[120] though "unfortunately he had no idea whatsoever of the technical side of things" and would probably first "have to learn the essentials, such as the Morse alphabet" and the elementary rules of radio use.[121] When Coppi suggested bringing into the group an expert who was a party comrade, Moscow objected, recognizing the danger of exposure: "We have categorically forbidden anyone being brought into this matter and have reiterated this to 'Starschina' as well."[122]

Sándor Radó, the Hungarian head of the Soviet "Lucy" network in Switzerland, characterized radio communication "as the Achilles heel of intelligence activity." Radio communication with Moscow, which could have been the Berlin group's greatest strength, would become its greatest weakness.[123]

In order to pick up the radio, Greta was designated to meet Korotkov at the entrance of the Thielplatz subway station. She remembered wearing—contrary to the usual admonitions of anonymity—a bright yellow raincoat. Korotkov came up the steps carrying the eight-pound radio concealed in small suitcase of rubberized fabric. As she recalled, "It wasn't light."

Korotkov volunteered to carry the bag as they walked to the Breitenbachplatz. As there were a lot of SS men around, Greta's heart was pounding particularly hard when Korotkov clumsily dropped the suitcase.[124]

"What happens to the suitcase?" Greta inquired.

"Innocuous, isn't it? The best thing is to store it with your air raid kit, so you can grab it when the alarm sounds."

As they parted, Korotkov said that he'd take the play Adam had written, *Till Eulenspiegel*, with him to Russia; maybe it could be staged. (*Till Eulenspiegel* was to become the Berlin group's recognition signal with which they could be approached by couriers from Moscow in the case of an emergency.)[125] Greta hurried home with the suitcase. When the Kuckhoffs tried the radio, however, it failed to work. Hearing nothing from Korotkov, Greta consulted Arvid. They agreed on a plan whereby Greta took the radio to her friends near Spandau, where they hid it in a shed. Eventually, Korotkov came and retrieved the malfunctioning equipment.[126]

On Saturday, June 21, only hours before the German attack, Ambassador Dekanozov received instructions to hand the German government yet another note offering to discuss the deteriorating German-Soviet relations. But calls to the Foreign Ministry failed to rouse Ribbentrop or his deputy. As the weather was pleasantly warm, Dekanozov gave everyone the weekend off and ordered a staff picnic on the Baltic.[127] The Soviet ambassador still had not replied to Fitin's request for "clarification" of Schulze-Boysen's last message about the imminent attack. Nor was he aware that Beria in his report to the "highest name," demanded his recall: "I again insist on recalling and punishing our ambassador to Berlin, Dekanozov, who keeps bombarding me with 'reports' on Hitler's alleged preparations to attack the USSR. He has reported that this attack will start tomorrow . . . But I and my people, Joseph Vissarionovich, have firmly embedded in our memory your wise conclusion: Hitler is not going to attack us in 1941."[128]

Acting on the code word Dortmund, overnight the German army crossed the Soviet frontier. In spite of myriad warnings from the largest foreign intelligence network in history, the operation caught the Soviet military by surprise. On the first day, more than 1,400 Soviet aircraft were destroyed on the ground. Many Red Army officers were on vacation at Black Sea resorts. Only the Soviet navy was on alert.[129]

In Berlin, on returning to their embassy, Soviet diplomats found it surrounded by SS units. Telephone lines had been cut; there was no way to contact Moscow. Fearing an SS assault, the Russians proceeded to the top floor, where, behind steel doors and windows, they destroyed documents and codes in special quick-burning ovens. Because intelligence warnings had been ignored, wives and children of Soviet diplomats had not been sent home and along with all other Soviet citizens in Germany were rounded up and taken to Gestapo headquarters. That afternoon they were shifted to an SS camp outside Berlin.[130]

In the next few days, some 1,500 Soviet citizens awaited exchange for the 120 Germans in Moscow.[131] The diplomats within the embassy still could not contact the outside. Only the first secretary, Valentine Bereshkov, was permitted to leave but, even on his official visits to the Foreign Office, he was accompanied by an SS officer, a man named Heinemann. However, it was apparent that somehow Korotkov had to contact his sources.

By skillful wining and dining, Bereshkov enlisted the help of the talkative Heinemann. Over breakfast, Heinemann hinted that he had money problems. Bereshkov offered him 1,000 marks that he had "saved to buy a music box." Cash, he subtly assured Heinemann, that he would be unable to take out of Germany. To Bereshkov's relief, Heinemann accepted the bribe. Later, over a lunch of Russian delicacies, cognac, and beer, Bereshkov brought up the sad case of an embassy employee, "Sasha," and his German fiancée who would now not be able to see each other again. Heinemann offered, in the guise of accompanying Bereshkov to the Foreign Office, to smuggle "Sasha" Korotkov out for a last visit with his girl. They drove the embassy Opel to the Wittenbergplatz subway station where they dropped off "Sasha," arranging to pick him up two hours later at the Nollendorfplatz.[132]

On the train, Korotkov accidentally saw his putative fiancée, Greta Kuckhoff. She recognized him but could not understand why he was not at the embassy like the others under heavy guard. His sudden appearance and the fact that he was able to move so freely alarmed her, particularly when, to her surprise, Korotkov failed to follow her off the train. Nor did she encounter him when she walked to the square where they had sometimes met. In fact, the overcautious Korotkov made no attempt to contact her.

A day or two later, Korotkov was again dropped off at the subway by Heinemann. This time he called the Kuckhoffs from a public telephone. A meeting was arranged at the Rudesheimerplatz. Concerned for her safety, only Adam went. He returned home upset and irritated. Moscow had insisted that in addition to their "information work" they should also strengthen the internal resistance work in Germany itself by carrying out a bizarre sabotage mission: the group was exhorted to strew nails on roads leading from Berlin so as to prevent military vehicles from heading East.[133]

Korotkov's final July 24 report states that two radios had been turned over and safely hidden.[134] Korotkov gave the battery-powered radio to Coppi in the apartment of the Schumachers. However, its short range and frequency proved inadequate to the task, so the Kuckhoff's set, which had been repaired by the Russians, was handed over to Coppi at the Eichkamp S-Bahn Station.[135] Two copies of the codebook *Der Kurier aus Spanien* (The Courier from Spain) were alleged to have been distributed, one to Moscow and the other to Coppi.[136] Korotkov briefed them on ciphering, explaining they were to destroy all enciphered transmissions, and Harnack was given 8,000 marks to distribute to his group for expenses.[137]

On June 26, Coppi successfully tapped out the words *"Ein Tausend Grüsse an alle Freunde"* (a thousand greetings to all friends) on the appointed frequency.[138] Moscow replied: "We have received and read your test radio message. The substitution of letters for numbers and vice versa is to be done using the permanent number 38745 and the codeword *Schraube*."[139]

At around midnight on July 1, 1941, Korotkov and his 1,500 countrymen boarded a special train that spirited them to the Russo-Turkish border. As a parting gift, Korotkov took with him a memorandum from Arvid describing the "strengths and weaknesses of the German armaments industry."[140]

FOURTEEN

Prey

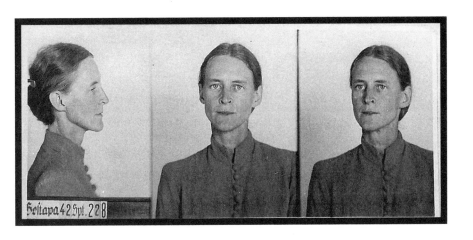

Gestapo photograph of Mildred, 1942

Klk from ptx . . . klk from ptx . . . klk from ptx 2606. 03. 3032 wds. No. 14 qbv," began the first Red Orchestra message intercepted by the duty officer of the Wehrmacht's Funkabwehr radio monitoring station at Cranz, a resort town on the Baltic seacoast north of the East Prussian city of Königsberg. The opening call letters were followed by a message containing thirty-two five-figure cipher groups. A Morse signature followed: "AR 50385 KLK from PTX."[1]

It was 3:58 A.M. on June 26, 1941, only four days after the commencement of Operation Barbarossa, the largest military assault in history, and the German army had already penetrated well into the Soviet interior. Three weeks later a three-pronged attack would leave German panzers only two-hundred miles from Moscow. The fury of the first German assault left the Russian front broken, weak, and wavering. As a consequence, the Soviet military radio service was in disarray. The Russians abandoned normal precautions governing security against German intercepts; closing gaps and coordinating an orderly retreat took precedence over the possibility that the enemy might benefit from overhearing the radio traffic.[2]

A few hours later the intercepted message was forwarded to the Funkabwehr Radio Signals Security, headquartered on the Matthäikirchplatz only a few blocks from the Harnack apartment in Berlin. Because Signals Security's direction finders were inadequate, the Germans could only surmise that the PTX signal was from North Germany, Belgium, Holland, or France. In fact, the PTX signal originated in Brussels. This intercept proved to be only the first of hundreds of "concerts" of radio signals emanating from Russian transmitters working in German-occupied Western Europe and the Soviet Union, known collectively as the Red Orchestra signals, which were as yet indecipherable to the Germans.

The Abwehr habitually designated radio networks as "Kapelle," variously translated as chapels, bands, or orchestras so that Ardennen-Kapelle, or Ardennes Orchestra signified a radio ring operating in the Bastogne region of France. The designation "Rote" referred to the "red," or Communist, network. The organizers of these orchestras were called "conductors," the short wave transmitters "pianos," the operators, "musicians."[3] During the year 1941, some five hundred radiograms from secret transmitters were picked up in the West by the Funkabwehr and the Orpo (*Ordungspolizei*).[4] However, locating the "pianos" proved difficult and solving the messages, impossible. The Red Orchestra was an intelligence coup for the Russians—or so the legend goes. But the truth is far more equivocal, their work more often riddled with failure than success.

According to the legend, during the 1920s and 1930s, Soviet intelligence established a net that stretched from Tokyo to Paris and even to London and Washington. At the center of this net, so the prevailing story holds, was the Berlin radio operation with several transmitting stations, its hundreds of messages, its penetration into the highest ranks of the Third Reich. Although the story is still incomplete, since the Russians have not released all relevant Soviet files, the truth, as it now appears, is that after the initial five-word greetings to their friends, the most important of the Berlin transmitters fell silent.

Mildred Harnack knew nothing of the extent of the Soviet radio networks in western Europe, nor was she aware of the battle being fought between Russian intelligence and German counterintelligence radio services, but it was on their scales that her life was now delicately balanced. This battle of wits between agents lasted little more than one year. Ultimately, Berlin's amateurs would be driven to ground by Berlin's professionals.

In May, puzzled by Alexander Korotkov's inexplicable indifference to matters of technical training, the Harnack group concluded optimistically that in all probability there were already trained radio personnel in place. In fact, as a critical Greta Kuckhoff succinctly concluded, their own technical preparation was "extraordinarily inadequate."[5]

We have already met twenty-five-year-old Hans Coppi, described by the Gestapo as "a machinist, former deliveryman, houseservant, and handy man,"[6] the radio man for the group. A Communist, Coppi had previously been arrested and jailed several times for preparing illegal pamphlets. When Coppi's first battery-operated short wave transmitter had insufficient range for the tasks at hand, Korotkov, as already noted, supplied him with a new model but failed to instruct him in its proper use. The transmitter was designed for alternating current. When Coppi tested it by plugging it into direct current, he blew out the transformer and the tubes.[7]

Moscow instructed Coppi to send his messages in Morse code at a predetermined wavelength and time. Normal Soviet practice was for the "musician" to instigate contact. Moscow Center would then reply on its own fixed wavelength. Both would then switch to another wavelength with a different call sign for the evening's work.[8] But Coppi misunderstood times and dates of transmission: Moscow's instructions were to transmit at set hours and days of the month, in multiples of four and seven. However, the first month, July, had thirty-one days. Instead of waiting until August 1 to start over, Coppi continued. Often he was sending when he should have been receiving Moscow's queries. After their positions in Brest and Minsk were overrun by the Germans, Soviet technicians waited in vain at listening stations in their London and Stockholm embassies for Berlin's signals, but Coppi's messages were lost in the ether.[9]

According to Korotkov's plans, there was to have been a second operator for Harnack but Karl Behrens never served. This meant that by the end of July 1941, during the first critical days of the Soviet invasion, the Berlin station went "dead."

Meanwhile, there was the sorry tale of the peripatetic radios.

Accounts vary as to the number and the location, but we know that Korotkov had provided two. Initially one radio was located in Coppi's house in the Tegel woods, but it was later moved. The Harnacks hid one for a while. Arvid pressed Zechlin, who lived in Wannsee, and Havemann, who lived in Babelsberg, to hide a transmitter. They refused. Sometimes a radio was moved for transmission purposes to a rooftop apartment where escape was possible or to a hut in one of Berlin's numerous community gardens. At one point, Schulze-Boysen hit upon the ingenious idea of hiding a transmitter in the studio of modern dancer and sculptor Oda Schottmüller and, as an alternative, with Countess Erika von Brockdorff. Both women were bohemians who would not be suspected of knowing military secrets. Thus the informational and technical parties would be separate; should one side be picked up, they would not be able to incriminate their opposite numbers. Because artists were known for irregular hours, late-night guests would not be considered unusual. Another ingenious idea was for the women to wheel transmitters in baby carriages. But as air raids intensified, hiding transmitters became increasingly dangerous. Greta Kuckhoff remembered spotting Erika von Brockdorff, whom she had not yet met, with a telltale suitcase in a bomb shelter they shared.[10] "At the time, we were all going about with pieces of luggage—everyone carried his special treasures or favorite items with him—a suitcase attracted no attention," Kuckhoff remarked in an interview. "Storing it in an empty attic would have been more dangerous because no one except the air raid warden had any business up there anymore."[11]

From early 1941, when he became a member of the operations staff of the Luftwaffe, Schulze-Boysen had been stationed in Wildpark Werder, a few miles southwest of Berlin near Potsdam. Although this posting gave him access to the secret diplomatic and military reports from German consulates and embassies and information about the Axis air forces, it also meant that the burden of the enciphering and deciphering fell to Arvid. As yet unaware that Coppi's messages were not reaching Moscow, Harnack spent evenings enciphering messages at home to the point of nervous exhaustion.[12] Karl Behrens passed them to Hans Coppi. After Behrens was drafted in 1942, Rose Schlösinger became the conduit.[13]

Using the key word "SCHRAUBE" ("screw"), the KEY book—probably *Der Kurier aus Spanien* (Courier from Spain)—Arvid probably enciphered the messages with numbers replacing letters of the alphabet in the classic Soviet checkerboard pattern devised by pre-Revolutionary conspirators. Such enciphering involved two stages: the first involved converting the original message into numerical form using a table with coordinates at the top and left. The second stage itself had two stages: the encipherer chose a passage from the key book and converted it, like the message, into numerical form; he then added the two sets of numbers using non-carrying addition ($8+6=4$, not 14). The sum became the cryptogram that was transmitted. Arvid would most likely have indicated somewhere in his transmission the page and line of the key passage so that the receiver would be able to decipher the cryptogram. Usually this indicator was disguised by, for example, adding the date of transmission to it. Because the key did not repeat and thus approached randomness the system made the cryptogram extremely difficult to solve. Even seizure of the key book would not assure a solution.[14]

By mid-July 1941 the Wehrmacht had conquered Riga, Pskov, and Minsk and was already approaching Moscow. When reports of the disarray of the Soviet army reached the Harnack group, its leaders were stunned. Having given Korotkov specific information—the names of towns on the route of the main thrust—they were devastated to learn that those very places were overrun with little opposition.[15] Nevertheless, in the coming months, Harnack and Schulze-Boysen made contacts and forged alliances, and, despite initial setbacks, their optimism revived as the Soviets defenses improved and their most active period of resistance activities began.

Schulze-Boysen and Harnack believed that by 1943 they could bring about the rapid collapse of the Third Reich, and, according to one friend, they still wanted to blanket Germany with a network of opposition groups. Building on a base of Harnack's family contacts, ARPLAN friends, and Mildred's past and current students, they added a considerable group from the Schulze-Boysen and Kuckhoff circles. Through Wilhelm Guddorf, John Sieg, and Walter Husemann, all old-line Communists, Arvid and Harro were able to overcome their reputation as "salon Bolshevists" and establish connections with cells in Berlin factories. Through Guddorf, there were contacts with the Hamburg waterfront group led by Robert Abshagen, Franz Jacob, and Bernhard Bästlein. Eventually Falk Harnack would befriend the White Rose students in Munich.

An important associate was neurologist John Rittmeister. A student of Freud and Jung, Rittmeister was a humanist and radical socialist who based his opposition to Hitler on moral grounds. Affiliated with the German Institute for Psychological Research and Psychotherapy in Berlin, he offered practical assistance to Jewish and homosexual patients. In 1939, he married Eva Knieper, a nurse, and the couple formed a political discussion group.[16]

Rittmeister founded the newspaper *Agis*, named for the highminded but unrealistic Greek king Agis IV, who reputedly burned mortgages and divided the land among the citizens of Sparta. One *Agis* pamphlet was a call to action entitled *"Die Sorge um Deutschlands Zukunft geht durch das Volk"* (Distress about Germany's future runs through the nation). A February 1942 police report described the history of this mimeographed six-page pamphlet in which the author, most probably Schulze-Boysen, contended that the war was lost. The author writes: "A final victory of National Socialist Germany is no longer possible. Every day that the war is prolonged brings only new, unspeakable suffering and victims. Each further day of war means that in the end a larger bill will have to be paid. . . . Hitler will go under just as Napoleon went under." The final paragraph exhorts the reader to send the pamphlet "out into the world. Give it to friends and colleagues! You will not be alone! Fight first with your own fist, then with a group. TOMORROW BELONGS TO GERMANY!"[17] Group members mailed it from various post boxes in Berlin to two hundred influential people—Catholic priests, Protestant pastors, judges, professors, and members of the diplomatic corps. A Gestapo report earmarked for the attention of Goering, Goebbels, and Martin Bormann warned that this article was being distributed throughout the Reich.

Another publication of the group was supposed to be a twice-monthly newspaper in six languages, *Die innere Front* (The home front), intended for foreign workers and soldiers. Herbert Grasse, a printer, achieved the not inconsiderable feat of obtaining the needed printing press and paper. In two years of existence, they published around twenty issues.[18]

Adam Kuckhoff and John Sieg wrote "Letters to the Eastern Front" meant to incite passive resistance among Germans on the Russian front.[19] Arvid's analysis of German Fascism, "*Das national-sozialistische Stadium des Monopolkapitalismus*" (The National Socialist stage of monopoly capitalism) described by the Gestapo as a "tendentious and antigovernment economic treatise," reached groups as far away as Hamburg and Munich.[20]

Nevertheless, as Greta Kuckhoff acknowledged, the propaganda campaign was not especially effective. Associates often returned home with their pockets still stuffed with leaflets. As repression tightened, fear overcame whatever receptivity most Germans might have had to the idea of resistance.[21] When the anonymous material arrived in mailboxes, the recipient usually turned it over to the Gestapo. It must have seemed that only the Gestapo took these pamphlets seriously.

To those who questioned the value of propaganda work that diverted scarce energy from vital intelligence activities, Schulze-Boysen offered a pointed answer: "We have got to do it. If the Russians come to Germany (and they will come) and if we are to play some role in Germany, we must be able to show that there was a meaningful resistance group in Germany. Otherwise the Russians will be able to do what they want with us."[22]

The group approached foreign workers in hopes of inciting them to revolt, particularly the French laborers who gathered at the Bärenschenke. (This seedy pub on the Friedrichstrasse was still operating as of 1989; it had survived under the East German regime partly because of its association with Berlin resistance.) Cato Bontjes van Beek and her sister would wait in the crowded anonymity of the S-Bahn station and pass out cigarettes, matches, soap, medicine, and warm gloves which they put, along with messages, in the coat pockets of the foreign workers. But the efforts to recruit foreigners failed. According to Werner Krauss, "The psychological difficulties were very great: readiness to collaborate [with the Nazis], or at any rate political apathy, was widespread, particularly among the French workers."[23]

The response was better among German factory workers. Sympathetic doctors among the group wrote medical excuses for resisters who wished to hinder production. Translators produced documents with deliberate errors in the hope that they would cause misunderstandings. Günther Weisenborn, a broadcaster on German radio, made intentional mistakes, adding zeros to make statistics appear ridiculous, when transmitting the news.

Most important, the group gave urgent priority to collecting documentary evidence of Nazi war crimes. Schulze-Boysen filled a cabinet with clippings from party newspapers in which the Nazis boasted of their crimes. He would show them to potential recruits.[24] Libertas, with the help of Adam Kuckhoff, who was working in Poland on a film, gathered evidence—letters and reports of eyewitnesses—about the mass murder of Jews and civilians in the East. As part of her propaganda work at the German Cultural Film Center, Libertas pored over film from the front. She enlisted a colleague to help make copies of the most damning pictures with a Leica camera. Strangely, many of the people who committed atrocities requested their own copies of the pictures. Libertas interviewed them and started a card file that she hoped would identify and convict them.[25] Like Hans von Dohnanyi, whose "chronicle of shame" documented the miscarriage of Nazi justice, the group's aim was to build archives for what they assumed would be postwar trials. Their attempts to pass this information to the Allies through their personal contacts in Switzerland and Sweden met with indifference. Nevertheless, it would be one of the counts held against the group during their Gestapo interrogations.

Caught up in unrelenting stress, Mildred and Libertas yearned for a more normal life. Libertas confided to Günther Weisenborn that for five years she had loyally worked for Harro but, with each of their deeds risking a death sentence, she could not bear the fear any longer. She "wanted to live, simply to live. She wanted love and peace."[26] Yet both women continued to work and the risks heightened as the months passed.

In spring 1942, Goebbels's Propaganda Ministry launched an exhibition to build support for the war against the Soviet Union, prompting the group's most audacious act. Because Arvid was especially interested in the German reaction to *The Soviet Paradise*, displayed in the Lustgarten, the Harnacks and Kuckhoffs spent half a day at the exhibit. Everything displayed was gray and colorless, as if the sun never shone on Communist countries. Captured pictures of Stalin and Lenin and half-empty liquor bottles decorated the exhibition rooms meant to show the filth and squalor of peasant communes. Photographs of punishments dealt the partisans by the SS and Wehrmacht were also shown.[27]

In May, Schulze-Boysen and some nineteen other men and women, mostly members from the Rittmeister circle, roamed five Berlin neighborhoods, pasting handbills over the original exhibition posters with the message

Permanent Exhibition
THE NAZI PARADISE
War, Hunger, Lies, Gestapo
How much longer?

Although Schulze-Boysen's friends escaped notice, the Gestapo arrested another mostly Jewish group led by Herbert and Marianne Baum. Acting independently, they were attempting to set fire to the exhibition. Although damage was negligible, most of the Baum group were executed.[28] Mildred and Arvid did not participate in this exploit. There had been an argument about it. Some felt that the action was pointlessly dangerous, but Schulze-Boysen and his circle believed they must do something about the exhibition. It was precisely this kind of reckless act that made Arvid despair of his co-leader. Save for the occasional pamphlet and the illicit discussion meetings, the Harnacks steered clear of anything that might compromise their carefully maintained cover—that of a hard-working government official and his scholarly American wife.

Because of the war, there was obviously scant demand for English-language fiction, so Mildred's translating work declined precipitously. Teaching occupied most of her time. Besides lecturing at the Volkshochschule, she became, in 1941, an English-language teacher in the Foreign Studies Department (Auslandswissenschaftliche Fakultät) of Berlin University. Designed primarily to train SS and SA members for the foreign service, this department had many women enrolled in language classes, expecting to become interpreters or translators.[29] Although headed by SS Major Dr. Alfred Franz Six,[30] the institute had faculty and students actively engaged in the resistance. Schulze-Boysen and Egmont Zechlin taught there, and three students were to become important members of Harnack/Schulze-Boysen group: Eva-Maria Buch, Horst Heilmann, and Herbert Gollnow.

Eva-Maria Buch graduated to become an assistant language teacher on the Foreign Studies Department. As a result of her friendship with Wilhelm Guddorf, she translated the The Home Front (the illegal newspaper the group was distributing) into French and made contacts with foreign workers.

Horst Heilmann was a favorite pupil of Albrecht Haushofer. As a seventeen-year-old Hitler Youth member, Horst also caught Schulze-Boysen's attention in a seminar with a well-written paper, entitled "The Soviets and Versailles." Under Schulze-Boysen's influence, the former NSDAP party member's unconditional acceptance of National Socialism wavered.[31] Heilmann introduced Schulze-Boysen to Haushofer, and despite the latter's antipathy to communism, a friendship sprang up between them. They discussed the possibility of cooperation between the "West" and "East" oriented opposition, and it was through Haushofer that Schulze-Boysen and Harnack learned of the planned military coup against Hitler.[32] In 1941, the mathematically gifted Heilmann enlisted in the Wehrmacht and was sent to intelligence school. After his graduation, with the help of Schulze-Boysen, Corporal Heilmann became a cryptanalyst for English, German, and Russian radiograms at the Funkabwehr's Radio Signals Security headquarters at Matthäikirchplatz.[33]

Little is known about Herbert Gollnow. In Gestapo and CIA files and in books written since the war, he appears as the alleged lover of Mildred Harnack and is portrayed either as a naïve young man or an infatuated dupe. This much is certain: by degrees Harnack and Schulze-Boysen weaned the lieutenant from National Socialism and he appears to have supplied them with military secrets.[34] Only one photograph of Herbert Gollnow has been found. In the Gestapo triptych taken at the time of his arrest, he appears as a dark-haired, square-jawed thirty-one-year-old. Just four years before, Gollnow had answered Jane Donner's ad in a Berlin newspaper offering to teach English, her mother tongue. *Studentin unterrichtet Englisch, ihre Muttersprache.* Gollnow hoped that proficiency in English might further his career in the diplomatic service, but when war broke out he became an air force lieutenant. When Mildred's niece, now married and teaching at the American school and working toward her doctorate, became too busy, she passed Gollnow on to Mildred. At first, according to Jane Donner, he had been reluctant to exchange the young instructor for her older aunt. But when he met Mildred, she gained a student and then a recruit for the Harnack study circle.[35]

At Arvid's suggestion, in summer 1941, Gollnow resumed his studies at the Foreign Studies Department. Through Schulze-Boysen's connections he was reassigned, on October 12, 1941, to the Abwehr, where he organized sabotage operations in the southern sector of the eastern front.[36] His military superiors described him "as an officer of impeccable character and above-average intelligence who performed well in his area of specialization and displayed good military appearance and proper military bearing."[37]

Over four years, the relationship between Mildred and Gollnow may have grown into a love affair. Gollnow found much to admire in his instructor, who impressed him as "the ideal perfection of womanhood."[38] According to one judge, in conducting the affair "she had acted more out of loyalty to her husband than of her own volition."[39] That she lured the hapless Gollnow into bed to question him about Abwehr operations, as alleged, seems wholly out of character. When asked whether Mildred could have carried on an affair with Gollnow, Arvid's brother was categorical: "only if her heart were engaged" and "only with Arvid's knowledge."[40]

A more probable explanation than sexual enticement is that an intimidated Gollnow sought to impress the Harnacks with his extensive knowledge of the military situation. When Arvid expressed pessimism, Gollnow poured out figures, facts, and details he heard at the office on how well the Russian campaign was going.[41]

According to the Gestapo, Gollnow admitted telling Arvid about a sabotage mission against England that was to start from Portugal. Furthermore, in the spring of 1942, he told Harnack that the people living in the Caucasus were willing to fight the Russians and that the Germans would employ them as airborne troops. He hinted that disloyal Caucasians would deliver the Soviet oil industry—one goal of the Maikop summer operation—into the hands of the Germans. From Gollnow, Harnack thus learned about the planned invasion of the Caucasus and about air landings and commando operations behind the Russian lines aimed at preventing the destruction of the oil fields. Gollnow seems to have bragged to Mildred that in the fall of 1942, he himself would take part in a sabotage operation originating in Norway in which two Irishmen would be air-dropped into England. He also revealed a Wehrmacht plan to use Russian prisoners of war in the assault on Moscow. Furthermore, he told Arvid about the structure of the Abwehr infiltration behind enemy lines, reporting that the Germans were seeding a well-organized network of informers throughout Russia. He even named Kubishev as the exact location for air-dropping German agents.[42] However, most of this information, which was included in the judges' verdict, appears not to have reached Moscow.

Naturally, Mildred did not mention her covert activities in letters to relatives that were, as might be expected, very circumspect and concerned mostly with the difficulties in procuring decent food in Berlin. Early in December she wrote Arvid's mother, who was living in a small German town: "Could you send us [more] potatoes. It is a disturbing feeling not to know whether hunger weakens to a large extent. We eat potatoes now each evening. This evening we had a costly small potato—it tastes like a miracle after chestnuts. They were really tasty. We scraped together radish with salt and a salad from parsley root."[43] Her Christmas letter to her sister-in-law mentions an invitation to a private screening of *Broadway Melody* for the American seminar at the university. It proved to be a welcome antidote to the war restrictions she had been experiencing. Fred Astaire's face was not handsome, she wrote, "but he had something imaginative and unpretentious and understanding about him, and was so given to his art that one had to respect him and truly like him. There was also a wonderful lightness and carefreeness in the dancing and large lighted spaces and lively, shimmering baroque surfaces, so that one left the show feeling happy and pleasantly excited, wonderfully relieved."[44]

These letters assume a surreal quality in light of the December 7 Japanese attack on Pearl Harbor, and Hitler's declaration of war on America four days later. After burning their papers, the U.S. Embassy staff members were escorted to the railway station en route to an internment camp at Bad Nauheim.[45] Surely Mildred must have felt distraught and abandoned as the last Americans left Berlin; thus it is frustrating to read in her correspondence that she was passing the time with her students discussing Emerson and Faulkner and translating two German stories.[46]

Mildred's concerns at the moment were private. During the winter of 1941–1942, she had an ectopic pregnancy and she was devastated by the loss. She was operated on at a Nikolassee clinic, but her recovery was slow. Several months later, she wrote to her American family, "I was very sick for a long time. At first we had hoped that we would have a child, but that was lost." Naturally, this *still* makes me sad.[47] She was thirty-nine, subjected to enormous stress, and, like most Germans, undernourished. For her, the two happiest events of the war years had been the birth of babies to her niece Jane and to Wolfgang Havemann's wife, Ursel. A delighted Mildred wrote Ursel that she was "very proud as a woman that it is a girl, the daughter of such a capable forward-striving mother. In my family I admire the inner courage and love and fineness but also the enduring energy of my mother very much. Also, the example of my oldest sister, who was active, independent, and helpful and who supported me when I was little has meant much to me. I believe that for women a great future is impending, greater than anybody dares to suspect. Even though great obstacles persist, she will learn to come into her heritage."[48]

In March, there was a last family occasion, her nephew's confirmation. In April, still unwell, she went for an extended rest cure to Bavaria.

Nestled in the beautiful alpine valley of the Wetterstein Mountains near Garmisch-Partenkirchen, Schloss Elmau had rich Harnack associations since Adolf von Harnack summered there. Founded by the theologian's great friend, the religious philosopher Johannes Müller, Elmau combined the attributes of sanitarium, religious retreat, and art colony for a clientele of academics, civil servants, and their families. There were lectures by distinguished professors and nightly concerts by world-famous musicians. Folk dancing and the continuously changing seating arrangements at dinner encouraged the intermingling of guests. The "convalescents" were supposed to rest "body, soul, and spirit" and to "let things grow." The minimum month's stay was devoted to "the creative development of one's nature."

Mildred was elated to be away from Berlin where, in spite of Goering's boast that he would call himself Meier if even one British plane bombed the capital, bombs rained day and night. At the end of her six-week stay, Arvid came for a visit. His wife observed that he also benefited from the "peace and friendliness that was due in part to the excellent organization of the household staff." From their window they saw the alpine weather change from "pearl colored early morning to the evening that was sometimes as pale pink as a flower." On May 1, it snowed, but in spite of that, she wrote, they took a long walk to Garmisch. "The woods and the mountains looked wonderful in this unexpected winter magnificence." Most welcome was the plentiful food, after Berlin's spartan diet. They looked forward to meals because the food, "despite the limited fat and meat, was always tasty."[49]

Once home, Mildred continued her twice-weekly visits to the doctor for treatments and shots. On May 24, together with the Havemanns, they celebrated Arvid's forty-first birthday with a rare bottle of red wine. For the first time, Wolfgang Havemann recalled, Arvid appeared desperate. He used the occasion to make an impassioned statement about the war and the destruction of Germany's old cities by Allied bombers. Referring to the rolling back of the eastern front, he predicted Hitler "would expend every last young German along this blood route." Finally, he put the question to the group: "What else can be done to ward off this overwhelming misery?"[50]

Things had already begun to unravel months before, when a blunder occurred that would shatter the Berlin group. On August 26, 1941, when it had been more than two months since Moscow had heard from Korotkov's friends, Moscow sent orders to Anatoli Gurevich, the GRU's agent in Brussels. Showing how desperate they were to restore contact with Berlin, the respective heads of the foreign intelligence section of the general staff of the Red Army, the military intelligence service, the GRU and Fitin, and the head of the foreign intelligence service of the NKVD all signed the message. The enciphered directive instructed Gurevich, alias Kent:

Go to see Adam Kuckhoff at 18 Wilhelmstrasse,[51] telephone 83-62-61, the second stairwell on the left, top floor, and tell them that you have been sent by a friend of "Arvid" and "Harro," whom Arvid knows as Alexander Erdberg. Mention the book of Kuckhoff that he gave him [Erdberg/Korotkov] before the war and the play *Ulenspiegel* [*Till Eulenspiegel*]. Suggest to Kuckhoff that he arrange a meeting for you, KENT, with "Arvid" and "Harro." If that is impossible, then clarify through Kuckhoff:

1) When will the radio connection be made and why isn't it working?
2) Where are all the friends and what is their situation? ITALIAN [Havemann], BEAMER [Behrens] LEO, KARL, and the others.
3) Get detailed information for transmission to ERDBERG.
4) Suggest that someone immediately be sent as a liaison to Istanbul, who will personally contact the [Soviet] trade representative, or to Stockholm, who will personally contact the consul, in both cases in the name of BEAMER.
5) Prepare a [safe] house for receiving people.

If Kuckhoff cannot be found, contact the wife of "Harro," Libertas Schulze-Boysen, at her address 19 Altenburger Allee, telephone 99-58-47. Say that you come from someone whom she met together with Elisabeth [Schumacher] in Marquardt.[52] These instructions also hold should you meet up with Kuckhoff.[53]

Moscow had committed the unforgivable error of radioing names and two addresses, thus compromising Corsican, Senior, Old Man, and their friends all in one message. When Kent's boss, the GRU agent, Leopold Trepper, heard of the security breach, he exclaimed, "It's not possible. They have gone crazy!"

Gurevich has been described by a member of the Gestapo who knew him well, as of medium height, well-proportioned with dark hair, a high forehead, and thick lips punctuating a long, narrow head. He constantly smoked a pipe, and because he ate and drank to excess, he was prone to gain weight. Gurevich patronized expensive restaurants in Paris and Brussels, where he sometimes re-ordered the main course three times. When buying clothes—leather shoes, for example—he ordered them in masses. Thus, violating all conspiratorial rules, Gurevich succeeded in attracting attention to himself. Waiters and store clerks remembered him.[54] The story of his Berlin visit can be reconstructed from an interview he gave Hans Coppi, the son of the radio operator, in 1992 and from his 1942 Gestapo interrogation.

Gurevich reached Berlin on October 29. Following orders, he first made contact with Kurt Schulze, a GRU radio operator. The best radio man in Berlin, Schulze was servicing the Arier network, whose leader was Ilse Stöbe, a former journalist, then working in the information department of the Foreign Office. To his surprise, Gurevich discovered that Schulze, through Walter Husemann, had already been in contact with Hans Coppi and had tried to repair the radios. When this failed, Schulze used his own radio to try to reach Moscow without success.[55]

Next, Gurevich called Schulze-Boysen at the number listed in the Center's message. Libertas answered the telephone and the Russian spoke of "meeting Elizabeth at the bathing resort," which satisfied Libertas, who agreed to meet him at the Zoo underground station. There he inquired about the others whose names and addresses Moscow had sent to Brussels and that were "in part garbled." She replied that "all of the people in question were well."[56] He asked her how Choro was doing and she told him he would have to speak to Choro himself. (Choro, as Schulze-Boysen's biographer speculates, does not refer to Harnack, Corsican, but was rather the garbled Russian transcription of Harro.)* He asked why Moscow hadn't heard from Berlin. Libertas answered that their radio was defective. She agreed to a meeting with Harro the next evening (October 31) at the same station. During his interrogation, Gurevich recalled encountering Libertas at the U-Bahn station and then walking a short distance until they met a man whom Libertas introduced as Choro. The three proceeded to the couple's apartment on the Altenburger Allee. During the brief walk, Gurevich recalled speaking about "very general topics." At their apartment, he spent another four hours with Schulze-Boysen. According to Gurevich, who wrote down key words in a notebook, Schulze-Boysen volunteered the following information:

1) The coming winter (1941/42) will, in the view of experts, be very harsh. He was referring to cold and snow.

2) No attack on Moscow is to be expected; rather, the German military leadership intends to conduct an offensive against the Caucasus. As grounds for his information, CHORO stated that enough oil to conduct the war was not available in Germany or would be available only a short time longer, so that an offensive against the Caucasus would be required to deal with this oil shortage. In this connection, he also spoke of the offensive in the direction of Maikop. And there was more concerning the destruction of the oil fields by the Russians were Germany to draw near to these areas. He also spoke of the quantities of combustible fuel available and similar things.

3) In connection with the taking of Petsamo a Russian "Talmud" [codebook] had fallen into German hands.†

*Gurevich recalled that Libertas used the designation CHORO only after he had first used the word himself. Members of the group did not know the code names. In Russian, the *H* is sounded in the throat so that Harro would sound like Choro.
†This codebook, which the Finns captured from the Russian embassy in Helsinki, was turned over to the Germans and eventually, after the war, to the Americans. The Russians had failed in their attempt to burn it and the charred codebook

4) The Germans had uncovered an English spy organization in the Balkans; in that regard, the Russian agents who are working together with the English should take care.[57]

Gurevich recalled that he had asked Schulze-Boysen, "Where are the Führer's headquarters? What equipment do the aircraft have for the use of poisonous weapons?"

Schulze-Boysen answered all questions and asked how the information would be sent to Moscow. The visitor said he intended to radio Moscow immediately upon his return to Brussels that evening. Gurevich recalled another detail: Schulze-Boysen warned him that it would be dangerous to write, telephone, or visit him directly because it was possible he was being watched and Gurevich's foreign accent would betray him. Schulze-Boysen gave Gurevich a different address for written messages. In turn, he supplied Schulze-Boysen with an address in Brussels and promised to provide a further address in Paris. Mail would go through the military postal service. Gurevich provided two backup addresses: the Soviet consulate in Stockholm and the trade office in Istanbul.[58]

Hereafter, crucial details begin to blur. According to the Gestapo, Kent gave the "Arvid group" a transmitter and the address of one of his operators in Brussels should they fail to establish working contact with Moscow.[59] But Kent's own interrogation protocol does not mention giving any radio to Schulze-Boysen. Instead, the two discussed only two radios, Coppi's, which was defective, and that of an unidentified man, probably Kurt Schulze. Gurevich gave them his own cipher system.

Mildred's role in all this remains obscure. Gurevich confessed only to meeting the Schulze-Boysens, never Arvid Harnack. Yet the Maikop material came from Gollnow and, although the evidence presented at Mildred's trial gives a different date (August) for Gurevich's visit, it suggests she was the go-between:

Frau Schulze-Boysen came to her one day in August 1941 and asked urgently to speak to her husband, saying that a man had come from Brussels, she [Mildred] at least suspected

was helpful in deciphering the so-called Venona traffic, the telegraphic messages collected by Americans in the United States from NKVD, GRU, and other sources, which exposed the Rosenbergs, Klaus Fuchs, and Martha Dodd. Only in 1995 was some of the material released by the National Security Agency.

that the stranger's visit was connected to the secret radio link. At the request of Frau Schulze-Boysen she immediately fetched her husband from his office, without, however, being present during his discussion with Frau Schulze-Boysen.[60]

Gurevich returned to Brussels from Berlin with material for seven messages.[61] The Moscow file reveals that the Harnack/ Schulze-Boysen group provided Gurevich with information that the chief of German military intelligence, Admiral Canaris, had for a large bribe recruited General de Gaulle's chief of staff as an agent. With the French officer's help, de Gaulle's espionage network in France had been uncovered and a number of French officers arrested. Schulze-Boysen also reported that the Germans had solved the greater part of the telegram sent by the British to the Americans and had obtained the key to cryptograms sent by the Yugoslavs to Moscow and England.[62]

On November 23, Gurevich relayed Schulze-Boysen's information to Moscow on the whereabouts of the Führer's headquarters, "Wolfsschanze," and also Goering's headquarters in the area of Insterburg; on losses of German parachutists in Crete; and on the transfers of troops. On November 24–26, Gurevich sent reports on Germany's chemical warfare preparations. Next, GRU Center received a report that the alliance between the Soviet Union and the United States had demoralized not only the German civilian population but also the commanders of the Wehrmacht so that, in the personal opinion of Harro, an attack on Leningrad was not expected to continue: "the city presumably is to be forced to surrender by a total blockade and being cut off from the rest of the country." The German thrust would unfold toward the Crimea and the oil regions of the Caucasus. A last report, sent November 27, contained information on the German Luftwaffe production and its losses. Kent had agreed on a way to be "in contact with the group by mail, and if necessary in Germany. The entire group is healthy and has great opportunities to work."[63]

"You have only to kick in the door," Hitler had announced to an army commander on the eve of the Russian invasion, "and the whole rotten structure will come crashing down." At the time of Gurevich's Berlin trip in October 1941, the Führer's optimism seemed justified. The Germans had penetrated deep into Russian territory. The fall of Kiev gave them access to the Ukraine's grain, Leningrad was besieged, and the capture of Smolensk had opened the way to Moscow. However, in October, Richard Sorge, a GRU spy operating in Tokyo, informed Moscow that Japan (then preparing for Pearl Harbor) would not use its Manchurian army to attack the Soviet Union. This freed fresh Russian divisions in Siberia that were now thrown against an exhausted German army.

One of the most important of the encouraging messages that the Harnack group forwarded through Gurevich informed the Soviets that the Germans were running out of fuel and supplies as winter was approaching and that the German air force had experienced severe losses. Confidence in a quick German victory had evaporated.[64]

By early December, just ten miles from the city limits of Moscow, the German army was halted by the onslaught of the Russian winter. Liquid mud turned to solid ice. German troops were ill clad because munitions had been given priority over clothing. Now exposed to temperatures of -30 to -50 degrees (F), they suffered from frostbite and despair. They abandoned tanks, trucks, and artillery as the oil froze, rendering them useless. In early December, the Russians launched a massive counteroffensive.

Harnack and Schulze-Boysen's messages also provided Moscow with details of the coming German summer offensive: army Group B's Voronezh offensive and army Group A's thrust in the direction of the Caucasian oil wells. According to the Gestapo, "this intelligence offered the Russians the opportunity to repel the first German Voronezh offensive."[65]

All this is fodder for the persistent legend that the Red Orchestra contributed to the Soviet victory at Stalingrad in February 1943 and cost 250,000 German lives.[66] One of Schulze-Boysen's associates even asserted that but for the Red Orchestra, the Germans would have succeeded in Operation Barbarossa.[67]

Undoubtedly, the Berlin group provided valuable information. However, an NKVD memo dated November 25, 1941, demonstrates the difficulty the Russians had in making use of Berlin's intelligence. All reports were sent to NKVD chief Beria, but instructions as to implementing these reports were not received.[68]

Consequently, the Russian army failed to respond to them, suggesting that Stalin's minions disregarded the reports.[69] Stalin wanted documents: operational dates and plans, minutes of top-level meetings at the Führer's headquarters at Wolfsschanze—the kind of details that Schulze-Boysen was unable to provide. Based on what we now know, Berlin's reports made no difference to Soviet military strategy.

Colonel Joachim Rohleder, head of the counterespionage section of the Abwehr, offered an interesting evaluation. Asked after the war if Schulze-Boysen and his coworkers had done treasonous harm to the Wehrmacht, Rohleder said that the group caused no "significant military damage."[70] In startling contrast to the wild postwar claims of members of the intelligence community, lawyers, judges, and Gestapo officers, is his description of the group as carrying out their "espionage activity in a hopelessly amateur fashion."[71]

> As the proven facts show, Schulze-Boysen and his helpers did not shrink from military espionage on behalf of Russia. However, all of these people saw their principal task as that of enlightening the German people politically in the spirit described, doing everything possible to get rid of the Hitler regime in Germany.[72]

The Gestapo final report covering the investigation of the Red Orchestra alleges that from June 14, 1941, to August 30, 1942, the Berlin group sent five hundred radio messages to Moscow.[73] It could be that the messages were picked up by the Germans but not by the Russians. However, if the files of the KGB are to be believed, it appears that these five hundred messages from the elusive band of operators reporting to Center were a mirage.

In a further irony, when Gurevich returned to Brussels to begin sending his material, the sheer volume meant that he had to flout the established rule of tradecraft: in order to avoid being picked up operators should be on the air for only short periods of time. Because he obtained so much material in Berlin, Kent's operator was on the air seven days in a row, five hours every night, always from midnight to 5:00 A.M. This blunder allowed the Germans to home in on the signal.[74] With the aid of signal-locating vans and direction finders with aerials concealed in a suitcase, they narrowed the search to the Etterbeck section of Brussels. At 2:30 A.M.

on December 13, thirty-five men with heavy woolen socks over their boots raided the villa at 101 Rue des Atrébates, where the transmitter was located. Kent's Polish encipherer, Sophie Poznanska, who was decoding dispatches, threw her papers into the fireplace but the Germans arrested her along with Rita Arnould, the housekeeper and courier. Another agent injured himself while attempting to escape. The Germans seized the still-warm transmitter and fished half-burned papers with telltale columns of figures from a stove. They also found a secret door that led to a darkroom lit by a red bulb: a forger's workshop, crammed with false documents, rubber stamps, chemicals for the manufacture of invisible ink, and other espionage paraphernalia.[75] Trepper, who had been expected, was delayed, and Gurevich was not at the villa. Both fled to France, where both were arrested, Gurevich on November 12 and Trepper on December 5.

After Gurevich's Berlin visit, Moscow had tried to reestablish contact with Berlin via the Stockholm resident. When nothing happened, the GRU ordered another agent, code named Adam, to Berlin from Stockholm, where he was to contact Kurt Schulze, the radio operator of the Arier network, and provide him with additional funds. In June 1942, Moscow received confirmation that Adam had made contact with Schulze. He had also buried 500 marks in a brown bottle with a black stopper under a tree approximately 130 yards from the Brandenburg Gate.[76] Schulze sent a message to Moscow through Adam and Stockholm: "We have no anodes. I am trying to get batteries. Hans [Coppi] called you with no result. We are trying to do all we can."[77]

Berlin needed a new, more powerful transmitter and Moscow recklessly parachuted agents with radios behind German lines. In May, the Russians parachuted German refugees Erna Eifler and Wilhelm Fellendorf into northern Germany. They were to make contact with Ilse Stöbe, chief of the Arier network in Berlin, but she was working at the time in Dresden. Then the frustrated operatives contacted the Bästlein resistance group in Hamburg. But within days, the Gestapo was on their trail, even though they possessed false papers, food coupons, and money. In July the two were arrested.

On August 5, 1942, two German POWs, technicians trained by the NKVD—Albert Hössler and Robert Barth—were dropped in the region of Briansk with at least one radio for the group and made their way to Berlin as soldiers on furlough. Although alerted to their arrival, the Berlin group, not surprisingly, had difficulty finding volunteers to hide the parachutists. That August, the Harnacks had rented comfortable quarters in Bad Saarow, about forty miles from Berlin, where there was a large garden and pleasant company. Here Mildred prepared a shelter for the parachutists but it was deemed unsuitable. Schulze-Boysen suggested bringing them to a camping site on the Teupitzsee, but eventually the men stayed with the Schumachers.[78]

Hössler reported via his radio to the NKVD: "Arrived safely. I have met with Tenor [Kurt Schumacher] and have spoken with 'Harro.' All goes well. The anti-Fascist group has grown considerably and is actively working. Their radio apparatus is functioning but for some reason cannot make contact. After the reception of this radio message I will supply additional information from Corsican and Senior. At the moment my quarters are secure."[79]

It was the last news Moscow would receive from the Berlin group.

Since December 1941, at their headquarters on Berlin's Matthäikirchplatz, a team of cryptanalysts headed by a high school math teacher, Wilhelm Vauck, had been studying the intercepted messages on the charred paper from the fireplace in Brussels, but cracking the Russian cipher required seven months and a lucky break.

From the scraps, the Germans determined that the Russians were using a checkerboard system based on a so-called book key. From the frequency of the vowels, they deduced that the book was in French. By mathematical analysis, they deduced that a key sentence contained the name "Proctor."[80]

Meanwhile, the Russian agents captured in Brussels behaved courageously and remained silent; the cipherer Sophie Poznanska preferred suicide in Saint-Gilles prison to revealing her secret. However, the housekeeper, Rita Arnould, began to talk. She recalled that the three agents frequently read books that they left on the tables. And she remembered seeing the titles of some on Sophie's desk. (Through an oversight of the Germans, who failed to confiscate the books, Trepper had been able to send someone to recover them.) In Paris, the Germans scoured secondhand bookstores. On May 17, 1942, they located the book on which the

Russian code was based: *Le Miracle du Professor Wolmar* by Guy de Teramond.[81] Written in 1910, it fulfilled the requirements of the Soviet secret service: it had a limited distribution and had never been marketed but had been offered as a free supplement to newspaper subscribers of *Le Monde illustré*.[82]

Then luck favored the Germans again. On June 30, they arrested another Soviet radio operator. Johann Wenzel was captured after a gunfight in a suburb of Brussels. After being severely tortured, he was escorted to Berlin in July. Versions differ as to whether Wenzel gave them help or whether the codebreakers of the Signals Security team had already succeeded in independently breaking the cipher. But by mid-July, the Germans had deciphered the August 26, 1941, transmission from Moscow Center to Kent that gave the names and addresses of the Berlin network.[83] In the hope of arresting a whole network, the Abwehr waited, watched, and monitored visitors and telephone calls. According to one source, during late summer, more than fifty persons in Berlin alone were under surveillance.[84] Unscrambling the radio traffic, the Germans became aware of the depth of penetration that Harnack and Schulze-Boysen had achieved into the political, economic, and military hierarchies of the Third Reich.

In a KGB interrogation conducted after the war, one of the Gestapo officers described the surveillance technique and the circumstances surrounding the group's arrest:

> Through the police presidium of Berlin we obtained photographs of these persons and ordered them to be kept under careful visual observation, which showed that these individuals were in contact with one another and that Schulze-Boysen was also in contact with the sculptor Schumacher. Of special interest was the contact of Schulze-Boysen with a young member of the deciphering department of the OKW. I have forgotten this man's name. A final circumstance forced us to begin the arrests prematurely because any continued investigation was threatened with failure due to the fact that Schulze-Boysen could have been warned by his acquaintance in the deciphering department.[85]

The young man who forced the Gestapo's hand was Horst Heilmann, a member of the Signals Security decryption team.

Following a weekend sail on the Wannsee in Schulze-Boysen's boat, *Duschinka*, in August, Schulze-Boysen confided in his former student. It was at this moment that Heilmann claimed to have become aware that Schulze-Boysen worked for the Russians and that even if Harro "were not himself in direct contact with Moscow, he was nonetheless in direct contact with people who were."[86] Heilmann agreed to help his mentor and volunteered the information that the Brussels messages had been deciphered and that most of the radio keys and the names of some Russian agents were known. Heilmann also agreed to pass along the deciphered messages. The next day when he went to work, Heilmann looked for the messages that contained the names of Kuckhoff, Harnack, and Schulze-Boysen. He then realized that his friends, the Schulze-Boysens, had been exposed.[87]

According to one version, Heilmann immediately called Schulze-Boysen but he was not home. Leaving an urgent message with the maid, Heilmann asked that Harro call him back as soon as possible.

Schulze-Boysen returned the call late that night, but it was Dr. Vauck, the head of the cryptoanalytical team, who answered Heilmann's telephone.

"Schulze-Boysen here. You wished to speak with me?"

Vauck, astonished that he had the prime subject of his investigation on the line, could only respond, "Hello? I'm sorry . . . I didn't quite hear . . ."

"Schulze-Boysen. My maid has just given me your message. I was to call you as soon as possible. What can I do for you?"

This was too much for Vauck. He could only ask whether his caller's name was spelled with a *y* or with an *i*.

Schulze-Boysen replied, "With a y. Of course, I think I must have the wrong number. You didn't call me?"

"Well—no—I don't think so . . ."

"Obviously a mistake on the part of my maid. She mixed up the number. Do forgive me."

"Not at all."

"Yes," said Schulze-Boysen.

After hanging up, Vauck called the Gestapo. Clearly, Heilmann had attempted to warn his comrades. The Gestapo realized that they had to act quickly and they arrested Schulze-Boysen on Monday, August 31, at his office.[88]

* * *

In August, as she was scouting for quarters for the Russian para-chutists, Mildred wrote to her family in Washington (in a letter smuggled through Switzerland) that she and Arvid had taken a small place on an isolated lake at Bad Saarow.[89] Arvid was work-ing hard, she reported, "day and night" his "whole life is given to his work." She was giving lectures on the literature of the fron-tier,[90] enjoying the works of Lincoln and Whitman and translating the works of Goethe for a publishing house. The final lines of the Mildred's letter sound a farewell:

> H[arriette] you had a birthday a few days ago and I thought so much about you. I would like so very much to see you, my dear, dear big sister. I thank you for all the love in the past.

> May we all remain as healthy as possible so that we may see each other again with great happiness. Despite our being sep-arated, let's not be worried and anxious. We can all be hap-piest by maintaining ourselves, prosper and flourish and leave worry and anxiety out of our hearts.[91]

A final glimpse of Mildred comes from Inge Havemann, who vividly recalled their last visit at Inge's house on Lake Hundekeh-len:

> We sat on the small dock—the boys dived, only appearing occasionally on the water's surface, and Mildred drank in the sky, water, the summer air like it was her first experience. We said little. She appeared so tired but slowly her inner tension dissolved and her light laugh resounded. Later, she lay in the small house at the open window and spoke with cautious words about the unrest, the fear which filled her life, also of the longing for her distant homeland, and her mother. She appeared exhausted but composed. Here, outside, was peace. Then came the night and sleep. Not for Mildred. I managed to reach her just as she was carefully opening the entrance door of the house. I could not hold her. That was how it always was. Her place was at Arvid's side.[92]

On August 23, "a day never to be forgotten," Stalingrad became an inferno as the Luftwaffe began to carpet bomb in relays. One thousand tons of bombs were dropped. Nearly 40,000 residents were killed; the Sixth Army would soon claim 26,500 prisoners. When the petroleum storage tanks on the Volga received a direct hit, the blazing oil spread across the Volga. The German high command not surprisingly expected Stalingrad to fall within the next few days. Falk met his brother in Berlin the following day. He had come from Chemnitz, where he was stationed in the army. Usually composed and calm, Arvid seemed nervous. Together they searched the apartment for microphones. Finding nothing, they nonetheless moved from the study into the bedroom. They discussed whether the leadership of the group could be headquartered outside Germany. Arvid felt this was impractical: political events had to be followed firsthand. They also talked about a name for their organization. Although this hadn't been an issue during the preceding years, Arvid now felt that this could be an important recruitment tool, a rallying point for a broad spectrum of anti-Fascists.[93]

The Harnacks had planned a two-week vacation together with the Zechlins at Preil, a seaside resort on the Kurische Nehrung near Königsberg in East Prussia. Together they rented a blue-shuttered fisherman's cottage between the sea and the brackish lake. Although they saw each other almost daily in Berlin, Arvid and Egmont looked forward to "quiet discussions." At this stage, fourteen months after the invasion of the Soviet Union, according to Zechlin, they agreed that an end had to be made to the senseless war. Since the Allies would not negotiate with Hitler, the war could be ended only by people who had a legitimate right to do so, ergo the opposition.[94]

During the winter they had discussed the situation over daily lunches, Arvid prophesying that everyone would "one day have to decide whether we wanted to live east or west of the Elbe." Arvid felt that Stalin would prefer an understanding with the Germans to one with the Anglo-Saxons, who stood to profit from the continued German–Russian conflict. Harnack was sure that in order to prevent this "Stalin would make concessions." Zechlin, who was working with Haushofer, and Adam von Trott, whose contacts were with England, continued to act as a liaison between the men and Harnack in order to promote the common goal of eliminating Hitler. He had recently brought Haushofer together with Harnack for this purpose. Both men agreed that negotiations with either the East or the West should begin as soon as possible while Germany was still undefeated.

Walking in the privacy of the Nehrung's elk marshes far from Berlin, Harnack and Zechlin planned to discuss how to end the war and topple Hitler while preserving German sovereignty. However, the holiday on the Nehrung would not be the restful retreat they had hoped for.[95]

The Harnacks arrived at Preil on September 5, a day before the Zechlins. Dressed in short pants and wearing a rucksack on his back, Arvid met the Zechlins at the boat landing at nearby Nidden. In the evening the two couples strolled down Preil's main street, the women walking in front. To the accompaniment of rustling trees and the roar of the distant sea, the men began to talk. An unbridled horse running home passed the strollers, prompting Arvid to remark how beautiful it was to be free, alone with nature and away from all of the city's intrigues. He was looking forward with pleasure to their few days of vacation.

Arvid appeared eager to talk but was interrupted by a gust of wind that announced an approaching thunderstorm. Running to their cottage before the downpour, they had no chance to finish their conversation.

The next morning, when Zechlin appeared in the yard, he saw Arvid in shirtsleeves talking to a stranger. Other men were waiting at the gate. Arvid spoke quietly, his voice betraying a certain irony. "The gentlemen have a breakfast date with a lady and have forgotten in which house she lives."

At this moment the man produced a badge and announced: "We're from the police alien registration office. We've come to search the town." Zechlin was not suspicious until the man said, "We have also been ordered to tell Oberregierungsrat Harnack that he is needed in his ministry."

An indignant Anneliese Zechlin declared, "They could have just sent a wire!"

The police asked whether the Zechlins had planned to meet anyone. Zechlin answered, "Yes, naturally, the Harnacks."

Following the exchange with the police, Zechlin went to the Harnacks' room and opened the door. Surrounded by three men, the Harnacks were packing.

Arvid stepped toward Zechlin and murmured in a low voice,

"We're going with these gentlemen to Berlin. I am needed in the ministry." After a pause during which he strove to suppress his anger he continued, "It's a shame what in Germany you . . ."

At this moment, one of the men stepped between them. Everything now became clear. Zechlin sought to approach Arvid to whisper something, but the men prevented it. When he tried to help Mildred pack, another agent said that he would be "delighted to help her." The man even offered Mildred a cigarette with the words, "Go ahead, take it. It'll buck you up."

Pretending to believe that Arvid was really being recalled to the ministry, Zechlin suggested coffee. Arvid replied, "The gentlemen are very friendly. They haven't had their coffee either. You go ahead, and we'll follow." The Zechlins returned to the cottage and came back with their coffeepot. When they returned, they found the Harnacks, who were continuing to pack. As Mildred was led to the table, Zechlin watched as she broke down. Putting her hands over her face, she groaned, "What a shame! Oh what a shame!"

Arvid and Zechlin continued to speak in the presence of the policeman who stood next to them. Zechlin tried to assure Arvid that it was only a misunderstanding. He would meet with the officials of the university's Foreign Studies Department and the matter would be cleared up.

Mildred finished her packing, and made the beds. Finally, with a characteristic gesture, she took a vase that she had filled with flowers and thoughtfully looked around the room before placing them carefully on the table. She straightened the tablecloth before casting her eyes once more around the room to be sure everything was in order. Then the Harnacks left.

The Zechlins tried to go with them, but the senior Gestapo officer, who had been treating them with extreme courtesy, addressed them curtly, using Zechlin's title for the first time: "Professor, I believe that you are too intelligent not to know what is going on here. I am under orders to handle this matter as quietly as possible. Due to your presence, this has not been quite successful. I hereby inform you that you are to remain silent about everything you have seen and heard; otherwise we'll have to arrest you."

He then turned to Frau Zechlin, "Madame, the same applies to you."

Zechlin tried to sustain his dignity: "These two people are faculty colleagues of mine. You shall not prevent me from notifying the department about the matter as soon as possible."

The officer informed them that they would not be allowed to do that—any telephone calls would be intercepted. Yet when he turned around, Zechlin managed to signal to Arvid that he would do all in his power to help them.

As they left the room, Zechlin kissed Mildred's hand. In bidding farewell to Arvid, he looked straight into his face. Deeply moved, Arvid said, "Dear Egmont, I thank you for everything, also for today." It was the first time he had called his friend of ten years by his given name.[96]

The place is Selent. The year is 1990.

Falk Harnack described Egmont Zechlin as Arvid's "most faithful friend." The Zechlins' last address was in Selent, a small town near Kiel in Holstein. My telephone call from Hamburg brought an immediate invitation.

After the war, Zechlin returned to teaching at the University of Hamburg. During our conversation, I was frequently reminded that he was a historian as well as a biographer of Bismarck. Cautious about the unreliability of memory, he did not want his recollections—or speculations—confused with the facts he reported in 1945. I had to plead with him to allow me to tape-record our conversation. As the interview was in German, I was afraid that I might not remember our conversation precisely and my quotes would be inaccurate. Finally, he relented but insisted on reading part of his article "In Memory of Arvid and Mildred Harnack" into the record.

Dr. Anneliese Zechlin's personal recollections contrasted vividly with her husband's "official" version. She was a country doctor whose offices adjoined the couple's comfortable house.

We began with their first impression of Mildred.

"I can't remember, but she was beautiful," Zechlin recalled. His wife added the word besinnlich: *"She was a serious, thoughtful kind of person, a very sensitive, tactful, artistically gifted woman. When she visited us in Wannsee, she once quoted Goethe's poem, 'Über allen Gipfeln ist Ruh.' She said the words in English and I thought to myself, wonderful, now we're going to have the poem*

in English in her translation. It was a premonition of her death. How did it start, the poem? . . . 'Über allen Gipfeln ist Ruh? . . . Calm is over all the hilltops . . . You feel not a breath.' I still see her in front of me while she recited that. 'Wait, soon you will be calm too.'

"She was fanatically against Hitler," continued Frau Zechlin. "In all other respects, she was an American. As a wife she followed her husband. Arvid happened to be with us when war broke out between Japan and America, and Pearl Harbor infuriated him. Both were very, very angry."

Before their vacation on the Nehrung, Anneliese Zechlin recalled visiting Mildred in the clinic at the Nikolassee after her ectopic pregnancy. "Mildred confided that she had many 'worries about her husband. He was always away at night.' And I was so dumb I didn't understand that he was meeting with people in the resistance. He was in the underground. Arvid always came home very late at night and Mildred feared for him. I was so stupid, I thought he was being unfaithful. So I asked her, 'Do you believe he's got a girlfriend?' And she said, 'No, that isn't it.' But I didn't shift gears. I was so naïve. I was a medical student and I didn't think about it any further. So I said, 'Come with us to Kurische Nehrung, we want to go there in a few weeks and take a bit of a rest there.' The Harnacks quickly agreed."

Had they any idea about the resistance activities of the Harnacks?

"No," Anneliese answered emphatically.

Her husband disagreed. "I must see that quite differently. This word 'resistance' only came up after the war. It was not pronounced because it was too dangerous but all of us talked about the situation all the time and, of course, about Hitler. And, of course, no one was allowed to hear this."

Did they spend other vacations with the Harnacks?

"No, but they visited us frequently in Wannsee and stayed overnight. In Marburg we were together a lot. But you can read all that in my memoir; it's all there."

Anneliese gently interrupted. "Now I want to tell you something personal about Mildred Harnack. The two of them visited us in Wannsee. We spent a nice evening together and had a bit to drink. They were so relaxed that they didn't want to go home. They lived *in Berlin Mitte and we lived in Wannsee, and the S-Bahn was running still and I was quite surprised.*

"'Oh no, I can't go home,' she said. 'Haven't you got a bed for me?' Of course, we had a bed for them. So they stayed the night with us just as they were, without a toothbrush or anything else. They crawled into bed and slept happily just as they were—quite unbourgeois. She was quite happy and relaxed the next morning. This was probably due already to the fear that at home she might get arrested, and this way she had vanished and was therefore safe."

We discussed the last time the couples had been together on the Nehrung.

"We went for a walk the night before she was arrested," Anneliese continued. "We said at that time that the Harnacks must have known on the way to the Nehrung that they might be arrested—they made a very quick decision to come. They had been warned, and they wanted to deposit themselves in Sweden. We discussed whether they didn't want to go to Sweden by fishing boat."

Arvid had received a card warning them that they were being followed. He had eagerly accepted the Zechlins' proposal for a vacation on the Nehrung and it had been Zechlin's suspicion that the Harnacks had perhaps intended to cross to Sweden in a fishing boat.

"But that is pure hypothesis. I discussed it the other day again with Falk Harnack," he told me.

"Falk also had the suspicion because of the fact that Arvid introduced him to [Vladimir] Semenov [then a diplomat in the Berlin Embassy], who was later in the embassy in Sweden.

"There was Erdberg [Korotkov] and there were two other people in the Soviet embassy with whom I often lunched: Bessonov and Hirschfeld about whom one doesn't know exactly. Hirschfeld was the press spokesman. In the time before the war with Russia, I was very often together with the people from the Russian embassy. It was arranged by Harnack.

"In the embassy there was also an official, whom I also got to know slightly, Semenov, same name as up to five years ago, the big Soviet ambassador, identical with the person in Bonn. I wrote him a letter about Arvid. I asked him some things but the Russians

don't tell you anything. Even if you've been a historian for twenty years, you still get a stupid answer. Semenov was in Stockholm when the ambassador was Aleksandra Kollontai. And in this letter, I wrote that we went for a walk the night before but a storm interrupted our conversation and in the morning they were arrested. I often thought about this later. I knew that Arvid had connections with Stockholm . . . Where, when, and how?"

Before the war with Russia?

"Yes, before the war. But after the war, I learned, but only as a historian, that Semenov was at the embassy in Stockholm during the war and that the area he covered was the German desk. And from this I draw the conclusion that Harnack had still wanted to tell me something about his connections with Stockholm. But nothing came of that. As a historian, I tried to research connections. I looked into a lot of Swedish archival material about this Semenov and Kollontai, and there were lots of stories that Kollontai wanted to arrange a separate peace between Germany and Russia. But Semenov never responded. Falk Harnack is always asking me about this."

I asked about Mildred's alleged affair with Herbert Gollnow.

"I was also interested in a statement which allegedly says that in the Gestapo files—'Dass dieses Verhältnis so weit gegangen sei.' ('That this relationship had gone so far.') I can't remember it word for word. Allegedly, even employees of the Gestapo blushed about this sort of thing and therefore it would have been terribly important if anything like this was written in trial files on the record. It's important to know first of all how this rumor could have arisen. To learn if Gollnow didn't want to justify himself at the last moment by saying that it wasn't his fault. She seduced him. She was beautiful; she could have seduced me too. She was a beautiful, sensuous, sensitive, well-educated, literary woman with whom it was a pleasure to have a conversation. Every conversation with her was unusually deep. It made you feel personally involved with her. If you're writing a biography it would be important to trace this rumor . . ."

What was the Harnacks' marriage like?

"They seemed like two people in love. If there is any truth in this story, she may have had an affair, but not in the way it was described. Arvid's fanaticism was such that he could have said to

his wife, 'Why don't you start something with this man so that you can find something out.' That's the only way I could think of it. They were definitely in love with each other."

Our afternoon's conversation was interspersed with walks in the backyard garden. Egmont Zechlin, who was then ninety-three, had poor circulation. He ended our talk by protesting that he was worn out. "It's too long ago, and we've taken up too many subjects."

FIFTEEN

The Woman in Cell 25

Solitary cell of the prison at Prinz-Albrecht-Strasse 8
at the end of the war

America's declaration of war and the Soviet Union's military recovery had given the group reason to be optimistic. They were convinced that when the war started to go against the Germans, entire sections of the population would rise up and the war would end. The group had also been lulled into a false sense of security by their well-placed military informants such as Heilmann, Schulze-Boysen, and one of his sources, Colonel Erwin Gehrts of the Luftwaffe Ministry. Consequently the arrests caught them unprepared.[1]

After Schulze-Boysen was arrested at his office on August 31, 1942, Heilmann and Libertas frantically tried to warn the others. Radios were hidden, compromising documents burned. But it was too late. Within the week, Heilmann and the Harnacks were arrested; Libertas was dragged off a train as she was fleeing south. By September 12, the Gestapo's cellar housed eighteen more suspects, including the Coppis, the Kuckhoffs, the Schumachers, and the Graudenzes. On Mildred's fortieth birthday, her former pupil, Karl Behrens, was arrested on the Russian front; twelve other suspects were seized in Berlin. By the third week the Gestapo had caught up with Arvid's stepnephew, Wolfgang Havemann, and members of John Rittmeister's group. Although totals vary, it appears that there were 139 arrests in connection with the "Red Orchestra affair."[2]

The Gestapo imposed maximum security, warning that whoever spoke about the matter "risked his life." So secret was the affair that weeks passed before family members became aware of the arrests. Some relatives were also arrested—spouses, the mother and father of Hans Coppi, the father of Cato Bontjes van Beek, the daughters of John Graudenz. (It is noteworthy that neither Arvid's mother nor his siblings nor any of Libertas's or Harro's family members were detained; among the Nazis, rank had its privilege.) There were two reasons for this secrecy. If it became known that so large an organization had penetrated several ministries, it would have a demoralizing effect on the populace, shattering the myth of Nazi infallibility.[3] Even more important, the Abwehr had decided to engage the Russians in a *Funkspiel*, a radio disinformation game, in which Russian agents captured in Germany (Hössler and Bart), Belgium (Wenzel), and France (Gurevich and Trepper) were "played back" to elicit further information about suspected agents from Soviet intelligence.[4] If it became known that the Berlin group had been picked up, the game would be over.

Those arrested were first taken to the most dreaded address in Nazi-occupied Europe, Prinz-Albrecht-Strasse 8. In happier times, when the former palace housed an art school run by her father, Libertas had played on the stairs in the huge entry hall. Under Hitler it became Gestapo headquarters. In the same rooms in which Libertas had taken drawing lessons, the *Schreibtischmörder*, the murderers who labored behind desks, composed memoranda in punctilious bureaucratese that disguised the orders' real purpose.[5]

Two weeks after Mildred handed over her valuables, shoelaces, and belt (the latter in order to prevent suicide), she was brought to a large, dark room and fingerprinted. Then she was led to a large revolving stool that was adjusted to her height. After she sat down, she was told to look toward an old-fashioned wooden box camera. Then the lights were extinguished save the special reflectors. As she peered forward into the dim light, she could see little. The guard, following the photographer's orders, moved toward her, pressing her head rigidly against the neck brace. She was photographed three times: front, profile and three-quarter. She looked straight into the camera without a trace of fear, as if she were determined to go eyes blazing into history.

Initially, the Gestapo held prisoners in basement cells, the *Hausgefängnis* of Prinz-Albrecht-Strasse. When the cells became overcrowded, some men were moved to Spandau. But Arvid Harnack, Adam Kuckhoff, and Harro Schulze-Boysen remained behind, occupying three of thirty-eight solitary cells. Most of the women were taken to the Alexanderplatz prison, but Mildred and Libertas also languished in the *Hausgefängnis* until December, when they were transferred to the women's prison located on Kantstrasse in Charlottenburg. At first the prisoners remained under so-called protective custody—without an indictment, without lawyers, and without contact to the outside world.

Initially members of the Sonderkommission Rote Kapelle, a special commission of the RSHA set up to counteract and investigate the Red Orchestra,[6] conducted the interrogations. Its head was SS Colonel Friedrich Panzinger, a cold and sober technocrat who specialized in communism, sabotage, and opposition. Panzinger concentrated on furnishing information to the investigators and compiling reports on the affair for Reichsführer Heinrich Himmler. Although he sometimes met with family members of the prisoners, Panzinger seldom intervened in the investigation. Ex-chemist and beer hall brawler SS Major Horst Kopkow, the head of Section IV A2 (counterespionage), directed day-to-day operations. Kopkow assigned Johannes Strübing, Hans Henze, K. K. Büchert, Alfred Göpfert, and Walter Habecker as interrogators.[7] The first group arrested included the Schulze-Boysens, Harnacks, Kuckhoffs, and Schumachers. Strübing was given the assignment of interrogating Schulze-Boysen, while the Harnacks were interrogated by Habecker and Henze.[8]

In the Prinz-Albrecht-Strasse cellar, prisoners sat on boxlike seats arranged in a long row along one wall, each in a separate niche so they couldn't see their neighbors. SS men paced back and forth in front of the seats or sat and watched their charges, making nasty remarks. Under the harsh light, the prisoners remained, day and night, without food or drink, before the interrogations and after the interrogations, usually for several days, until finally they were transported to other prisons.[9] For those persons lucky enough to leave Prinz-Albrecht-Strasse, the "grüne Minnas," the police vans, where familiar faces could be seen and prisoners could hug and talk, provided the only "moments of comfort—unless your blood had already run cold for fear of what was to come."[10]

"*Mitgegangen, mitgefangen, mitgehangen*" goes an old German saying. "Marched together, caught together, hanged together." Once Werner Krauss and John Rittmeister had discussed what they would do if they were arrested. Krauss's view had been that one was under no obligation to tell the Gestapo the truth. The only thing that mattered was somehow to talk oneself out of the mess without getting other comrades in trouble. To this Rittmeister replied, "I'll stick to the truth and tell them to their face what I think of them, even if it costs me my head."[11] Most of those now in custody, however, had not allowed themselves to think the unthinkable. Picked up, one by one, at their apartments, at work, or on vacation, they were unprepared for prison. Caught unawares, they had not agreed on cover stories.[12]

To date, no copy of any of the Harnacks' interrogations has

surfaced. But in 1994, Hans Coppi (the son of the radio operator) was working in a Russian archive and discovered an interrogation of Wolfgang Havemann dating from 1944, when Arvid's step-nephew was in a prisoner of war camp in the Soviet Union. As Havemann's memory of the events of 1942 was still fresh, it is the nearest thing we have to a contemporary document and it reveals something of the Gestapo's methods.[13]

On the last Saturday in September, a team from the Gestapo and Abwehr arrested Havemann in Flensburg, where he was sta-tioned as a naval intelligence officer. On the way back to Berlin, they began questioning the unsuspecting Havemann. When one of them began a discussion of radios, he knew how "the hare would run."

"Have you any interest in radios? Have you tinkered with them?" . . . and so on.

When Havemann arrived at Prinz-Albrecht-Strasse, he noted in passing the two small leather suitcases and furled umbrella of the Harnacks.

On the next day, he filled out a questionnaire. After he was fingerprinted and photographed, he began to be interrogated by the Gestapo's Büchert.

Havemann asked if the agent could explain why he was arrested.

"No," answered Büchert.

"Well, it must be for some serious reason when it is the Gestapo and not the police who are bothering with me."

"I don't know," Büchert replied. "It's so easy to get into trouble with all of these laws. But perhaps, if you're quite sure you're clean, maybe you know someone who might be suspect?"

Havemann ran through a list of possible suspects in his mind. Who might interest the Gestapo? Perhaps some relatives? He had some half-Jewish stepbrothers and sisters [Inge Havemann's chil-dren], but they had been brought up not by their birth father but by his own father, who was a well-known Nazi sympathizer. Any-way, the Gestapo was not interested in children.

"Among your relatives, has anyone spoken about the war?"

"Yes, certainly, but not in any antigovernment sense: everyone has their own personal concerns."

"What concerns?"

"Well, business ones, especially."

"Do you have relatives in business?"

"A brother in Hamburg is a businessman, and my father-in-law is with a bank."

"Is that all?"

"All of my closest relatives . . . otherwise there is only a former relative of mine, a brother of my former stepmother, who works in the Economics Ministry."

"What's his name?"

"Dr. Harnack."

"What does he think about the war with the Soviet Union?"

"Does he want a German victory? Isn't he in favor of drawing closer to Russia economically and politically? You needn't cover for your uncle. He is already so incriminated that you can't save a single hair on his head. You know very well Harnack is a Marxist. Why didn't you say so right away?" The game had begun.

Havemann was questioned about his own life: "Did you visit foreign countries? Didn't you once go to Italy? Do you know any Italians? Are you unaware that you are also known as Italiener?"

Although Havemann, like the others in the group, had never heard the codenames, he realized that he could not feign complete innocence. But how much to tell them?

His second interrogation started with questions about Mildred. He had to describe her life and work, and then the conversation turned to the Americans whom he had met through his stepaunt. With relief, he expanded on this topic for the entire evening because he knew it wasn't dangerous. He spoke about his acquaintance with Mildred's niece and her husband, Otto Donner, Thomas Wolfe, Donald Heath, the American Women's Club and the American Church, Ambassador Dodd and his family.

The third interrogation dealt with the Harnacks' circle of German acquaintances, particularly Skrzypczynski and Behrens. Then Büchert confronted him with reading material from Harnack's economic study group and posed further questions about Harnack's political position and what sort of advice Harnack as an older lawyer had given the young jurist.

Of course, Harnack was interested in a planned economy, said Havemann, but he denied that Harnack was taken in by Communist ideas. Arvid did believe that the nationalization of the most important industries and banks in Germany was unavoidable, as it had been in Russia. In the summer of 1942, Havemann remembered, Arvid had once asked him to a meeting to discuss such questions with interested intellectuals but Havemann had declined. In his trial, he gave the reason for this: in such meetings you start by discussing poetry and then you end up on the gallows. As he left, he was told to think about the Harnacks' Russian acquaintances.

The following week Walter Habecker took over the questioning. In photographs Criminal Inspector Habecker looks as if he stepped from a George Grosz painting. Günter Weisenborn remembered that Habecker, a native Berliner, "was short and broadly built, with a primitive gray bald head and a Hitler mustachio under his sweaty nose, a face such as one sees in typical illustrations of a criminal." Weisenborn described the "gray, unhealthy color of the inspector's face, his two dull but sinister sharpshooter's eyes, and the hardness of his broad jaw."[14] Habecker would become notorious for his brutal interrogations of the Harnacks and members of the July 20th resistance.

The inspector had a habit of cutting a cigarette into two halves, lighting one of them, and organizing his papers and pencils meticulously before he picked up a file. Then he was ready.

By way of introduction, Habecker stated that he was a former navy man and knew all about Flensburg and the naval intelligence school. What did Havemann know regarding the White Russian acquaintances of his family and his stepmother's brother-in-law Günther Auerbach, who had been living in the Soviet Union since 1932? What did he remember about ARPLAN and Arvid's leftist activities, which the Gestapo had investigated at the time of his entrance into the Nazi Party?

The following day, Habecker showed Havemann the Gestapo photo album of those arrested in connection with the Red Orchestra proceedings.[15] Havemann recognized not only the Harnacks but Skzypczynski and Behrens as well. Other faces looked familiar but he was careful to conceal this. Habecker attempted repeatedly but unsuccessfully to link Havemann with Schulze-Boysen. Then the interrogator came to a picture of a man about thirty-five years old—fairly square head, gray eyes, short hair—and remarked, "You see people like this drop from heaven, just come out of nowhere." Habecker showed him further pictures of the Russian paratroopers, saying, "We looked for them and found them all over Germany."

When Havemann remarked that he had "never seen nor suspected so much activity" at his uncle's, Habecker answered, "He tried to give us that impression too, at first. But after we worked on him, tortured him, he was very shaken up. But he soon got a hold of himself."

Habecker read the names in the photo album to Havemann several times. Havemann was to indicate which names he recognized. Finally Habecker confronted him with the telegram summoning Kent to Berlin containing the names and addresses of the Berlin group. The telegram had been sent from Moscow, and his interrogator maintained that Havemann was indeed Italiener, which the naval officer again denied. Havemann told the Soviets that only later, when they read Arvid's actual testimony to him, did he understand that the message in the telegram referred to him. Harnack's exact words were: "As for Italiener, I have already said that this is my nephew by marriage, Wolfgang Havemann. He is an assessor and lieutenant in the OKM (Oberkommando der Kriegsmarine). I don't know in which department he works. He was always extraordinarily close-lipped about duty-related matters. In March 1941, the embassy official Erdberg [Korotkov] asked me what persons from my circle of acquaintances would be possible candidates for future cooperation with the Soviet Union. I mentioned my nephew, among others. But I referred to him using this cover name because if possible I did not want my family drawn into these matters."

It was now clear that the Gestapo had the names of Harnack's circle as well as those of the Russian paratroopers. The subject of the third day of Habecker's interrogation was Havemann's activities in the OKM. Habecker sought to elicit evidence proving that Havemann had given Harnack material for the Russians. The effort failed when after several hours Havemann "burst into tears of moral indignation over the suspicions," so impressing Habecker that he left with an abrupt "Heil Hitler."

Büchert now replaced Habecker, and he tried a different tactic: he took Havemann outdoors for the first time since his arrest for a walk in the garden. The conversation at first seemed to be about trivial matters. Büchert remarked that he had "never worked on such an interesting case." It would "make a wonderful novel if it weren't so sad and forbidden." He continued along this indirect line of elicitation, remarking that "it was very appropriate" that Gestapo headquarters was housed in the former Academy of Art "because studios and artists played a large role" in the Red Orchestra matter. But Büchert's indirect approach to Havemann fared no better than Habecker's line of questioning.

After a two-week pause, Havemann was questioned again, this time by Alfred Göpfert, who asked what the naval intelligence officer knew about Anglo-American escort convoy traffic to Murmansk and Archangel. When he had nothing to say, Göpfert pursued a line of questioning leading to the Abwehr lieutenant Horst Heilmann. On the third day of this cycle, Havemann admitted he had met Heilmann on the occasion of a family holiday at the Harnacks.

Referring to Havemann's specialized intelligence training, Göpfert asked what he thought about an encrypted key organized like a book, in which the recipient replaces the text occurring next in the book? Havemann interrupted him: "Oh you mean like in the Bible, where one person uses Luke 5:15 and the next person picks up at verse 16?" When he said yes, Havemann told him that the key system was "completely obsolete" and in his view "would not be secure." Havemann assumed correctly that Göpfert was angling to find out what advice he had given Arvid on encryption.

Several days later, the Gestapo accused Havemann of taking part in meetings with Harnack, Skrzypczynski, and Behrens that resulted in highly treasonous activity. Göpfert claimed that Arvid had admitted showing his stepnephew anti-Nazi leaflets now in the Gestapo's possession. Havemann was thus maneuvered into confessing that he knew of three leaflets. In his trial, Havemann realized from Harnack's testimony that the Gestapo had used the elicitation technique of playing one person's testimony against another. He had been tricked with respect to Harnack's statements. Harnack actually said, "It is true that I also occasionally showed my nephew Havemann leaflets. Which individual ones, I can no longer say, but I remember clearly that Havemann did not agree with their contents; each time there was a heated debate between us." From Harnack's initial words, "it is true," Havemann concluded that it was his own confession that the Gestapo had read to Harnack.

During his trial Havemann also learned what Harnack had said about the radios: "In May 1941, I discussed the makeup of the radio organization with Erdberg. We also discussed the necessity of a backup station in Berlin. Erdberg suggested that this be established at my nephew's in Potsdam since, after all, he was a master radioman. I rejected this categorically because, as I have said, I didn't want to have my family involved in these things. Furthermore I didn't consider Havemann's overall outlook ready for this."[16]

The Gestapo restricted communication among prisoners, keeping most of them in solitary cells. Male prisoners wore handcuffs, and one of the few opportunities for talk came when they met in the toilets where the sound of running water could drown whispers. Occasionally they exchanged *Kassiber*, minute written messages passed on stairs or left in books. By this means they spread information about the direction of interrogations and rumors about torture and the fate of fellow members of the group—many of whom had never met before their arrest. Prisoners exchanged news while they were waiting together at the Prinz-Albrecht-Strasse or were being transported in the police vans. More information came from the interrogators themselves. In an effort to pressure her into confessing, an interrogator told Greta Kuckhoff, "Since your husband and Arvid Harnack have contributed nothing toward clearing up this case, we have now employed the necessary methods to loosen their tongues." Greta asked, "Are they still alive?" The interrogator replied, "Yes, but it depends on you whether they get by next time."[17]

Some prisoners preferred taking their own lives to betraying friends and relatives. In spite of the Gestapo's preventive measures, John Sieg succeeded in hanging himself in his cell. Hermann Schulze and Herbert Grasse also committed suicide while in Gestapo custody. During an interrogation, Walter Husemann shattered a window in an office on the top floor and tried to jump to the courtyard, nearly taking Habecker with him. Hans Kummerow smashed his spectacles and swallowed the glass. When this did not succeed, he slashed his wrists. Stanislas Wesolek suffered severe internal injuries after trying to hang himself with a rope. Albert Hössler died in Gestapo custody, allegedly murdered during the preliminary investigation.

At first, Harnack, Schulze-Boysen, and Adam Kuckhoff had resisted saying anything incriminating. Even when shown the decoded messages, Schulze-Boysen refused to talk. But, as Habecker was fond of remarking, they had "other methods" by which prisoners could be "softened up."[18] When information was not forthcoming, this required "intensified interrogations" (*verschärfte Vernehmungen*), as they were called in euphemistic bureaucratese. In October, Arvid Harnack and Adam Kuckhoff were introduced to the "Stalin room."[19] There they were stretched between four beds, and calf clamps and thumbscrews were applied. Then they were whipped.[20] Believing he had given members of the group four weeks to escape, Adam Kuckhoff confessed, implicating John Sieg and Adolph Grimme.[21]

The most cunning torture was reserved for Libertas Schulze-Boysen. She was treated to an "open cell" and a special friend—a beautiful, flame-haired Gestapo secretary named Gertrud Breiter. In Breiter, Libertas believed she had found a woman hostile to her superiors—not an agent *provocateur* but a loyal friend. Libertas trusted her to carry letters to her mother, copies of which reached the Gestapo. Libertas naively told Breiter details of her resistance work and asked her to warn those members of the group who were still at liberty. Breiter also led her to believe that when the investigation was concluded, she would be released. Then the Gestapo informed Libertas that her friends had been arrested because of her statements.[22] When she became aware of the extent of Breiter's betrayal, she was overwhelmed with remorse, writing to her mother, "I had to drink the bitter cup for now I learn that a person to whom I had given my complete trust, Gertrud Breiter, has betrayed me (and you): '*Now eat the fruit of your deeds, for whosoever betrays will himself be betrayed.*' Out of egotism I too have betrayed friends; I wanted to be free and come back to you—believe me, though, I would have suffered from inutterable guilt."[23] As her mother-in-law lamented to Höhne, "Very many people went to the gallows as a result [of her betrayal], very sad."[24]

After the war the prosecutor, Manfred Roeder, was to claim

that "since the officials had known everything already," Libertas had betrayed no one. In his unpublished postwar interview with historian David Dallin, Roeder added a tantalizing footnote: none of those arrested had betrayed others or given new names. The Germans received the necessary clues directly from Moscow, for which Roeder credited the *Funkspiel*. When the "turned" radio operators demanded more information, Moscow transmitted the names and addresses of other members of the group.[25]

The Nazis rewarded Breiter with the War Service Cross Second Class plus 5,000 Reichsmarks for her efforts. She was promoted and received a special letter of commendation from Himmler.[26] The men fared even better. They were rewarded with promotions and part of the 100,000 Reichsmarks set aside by Goering for "especially meritorious officials."[27] Besides receiving an additional 5,000 Reichsmarks, Kopkow was allowed to purchase for a mere twenty marks the confiscated household goods of the Schulze-Boysens, whose assets had been seized and "recycled" by the senior finance president in Berlin.[28]

The Gestapo raids uncovered at least one radio. When they arrested Helmut Roloff on September 17, the Gestapo confiscated the first, nonfunctioning, radio. This was most probably the battery-operated one that Korotkov had originally left with Hans Coppi and Hannelore Thiel wheeled in a baby carriage to Roloff's studio and hid under the piano. "Today we're finally in luck and found the thing," commented the Gestapo.[29]

Yet in some accounts, meant to exaggerate the role of the Berlin group, the Gestapo was alleged to have confiscated as many as fourteen radios.[30] In fact, there probably were no more than four: the two delivered by Korotkov that were nonfunctioning, the one in Schulze's possession (according to the Gestapo report, he had three but only one that was available to Coppi) and the one brought by the paratrooper Hössler in August 1942 and left with the Schumachers. Along with the radios, the Gestapo confiscated some 40,000 marks; a multitude of forged documents, including identification papers as well as false ration cards for travelers; two copying machines; and an extensive apparatus for photoenlargement and photoreproduction used in the production of the illegal writings.[31] More mundanely, the Gestapo noted that when they arrested Hannelore Thiel, they found besides an amplifying device for a Volks radio-receiver an "agitational article: 'Organize the Revolutionary Mass Struggle against Fascism and Imperialist War,'" a box of books that included three Russian textbooks, Marx's *Capital,* a notebook, and a bag of snapshots.[32]

On November 9, 1942, five French policemen acting on behalf of the Abwehr arrested Gurevich and his companion, Margarete Barcza, at his home in Marseilles.[33] At the end of November, the Gestapo brought him to Berlin. Interrogated by Strübing, who played first on his vanity and then on his fears, Gurevich filled in the missing blanks, providing details on Soviet intelligence operations in western Europe, Czechoslovakia, and Berlin. He was forthcoming about his Berlin trip in October 1942, picking out Libertas, Harro, and Kurt Schulze and his wife from the photos in the Gestapo album. With near total recall, he gave the dates, times, places, and specifics of his meetings with Libertas and Harro. He could not say who Arvid was, nor did he know who Italiener, Beamer, Leo, or Karl were. When confronted with the file of radio messages, he identified those that came from the Berlin group. Gurevich's hands shook and his eyes betrayed anxiety as he concentrated on Strübing's questions.[34]

Gurevich's loquacity owed much to the fact that the Gestapo held Barcza, his common-law wife, and he feared for their young son. As a plaintive footnote to his nearly total confession, the "petit chef" (Leopold Trepper was the "grand chef") said that he became an agent "out of the fear that something could happen to my parents if I refused. . . . Anyone who knows the conditions in the Soviet Union knows that I could not refuse. I am not a Communist; rather, I have always considered myself simply a Russian."[35]

Rumors persist that Mildred was tortured—and even that she was forced to watch Arvid's execution—but there is no official record to confirm the former and Falk Harnack said the latter allegation was untrue.[36] What is verifiably certain is that she received no visitors and was forbidden to write except for two notes, one with instructions for the cleaning woman and the other requesting vitamins.[37] Falk Harnack testified after the war that the Gestapo forbade visits and letters, first because Mildred was ill and second, on Roeder's instruction, "because she was an American."[38]

Maria Grimme, arrested on October 12 and confined to the women's prison at Alexanderplatz, remembered seeing Mildred at Prinz-Albrecht-Strasse while awaiting interrogation:

> Someone was carried into the waiting room on a stretcher, hardly breathing. The stretcher was placed so that the person's head was right next to me. I looked over and was startled by the remarkable expression in the person's eyes. . . . shortly thereafter two Gestapo officers came in, pulled this individual up by the arms and said, "So, Frau Harnack, feeling better?" Frau Harnack was then taken out; some time later, however, she was brought back in again on the stretcher. Although she complained of being cold, none of the prisoners dared to give her a blanket from those on hand. After a while she tried to fetch one of the blankets herself but collapsed.[39]

The Gestapo beat and slapped women as well as men during interrogations. Since Mildred's health was poor and she appears to have developed tuberculosis, it is impossible to say whether her condition was worsened by the brutality of the Gestapo or simply by the poor conditions in the prison.

"Cruel days and more merciful nights" punctuated by screams was how Mildred's fellow inmate Marie Luise von Scheliha described the prison. (She and her husband, Rudolf, a diplomat, had been arrested in late October in connection with the Red Orchestra affair.) Shortly after the war she set down her impressions of prison life:

> People allowed ten minutes of fresh air in a prison yard are like withered leaves. . . . towards evening fear steals through the corridors. Heavy iron doors close, open, then morning comes, comes again, is recorded in small marks on the wall. One group stands for a week. It is a sinister sign language of the times. In the prison yards we walk slowly in fours. Some women lift their arms as if drowning. Their cells are so cramped they can hardly move; [now they] spread their arms like dancers towards the fresh air and the open space.

Nameless mute suffering has changed these people into shadows of themselves. A fine narrow face attracts my attention. Its gaze is turned inwards. Suddenly in passing a whisper: "Preserve yourself. I am here without a name so that no one can find me. I am in cell 25. Don't forget me when you get out. My name is . . ." I did not catch the name. A policemen [tells] me quietly, "We wash our hands of what goes on here. You are not permitted to talk." And sadly he looks away.[40]

Years later, from photographs, Marie Luise von Scheliha identified Mildred Harnack as the woman in cell 25.

Mildred's situation improved when she was moved to the Charlottenburg women's prison on the Kantstrasse in December. The prison director, Anne Weider, was a former Social Democrat and social worker who was filling this post because she was forced to by the Nazis. This was the first time that such a large number of political prisoners had been brought to her prison. At registration, as Greta Kuckhoff recalled in a postwar interview, "a certain sympathy was detectable—very reserved, but nonetheless effectual." There was a library and although "it was no paradise," the days of the prisoners being strictly regulated, the treatment in contrast to the Gestapo prison "was more impartial and open-minded."[41]

According to Roeder, Mildred attempted suicide and supposedly injured a guard during the ensuing struggle.[42] The circumstances, however, were never completely clarified. Contained in the East German Communist Party (SED) archives is a terse note stating that she swallowed some pins. We are left to wonder how she got them.[43] In 1946, Greta Kuckhoff wrote Martha Dodd that Mildred "knew that there was no way out, so she tried to commit suicide so as not to be made weak by torture. She failed and the result was that she received a particularly severe treatment: nobody was allowed to see her, to write to her, or to send some extra food. She must have suffered terribly."[44]

Strübing gives another hint of the reasoning behind the harshness shown Mildred: "About four or five weeks after the first arrests, instances occurred in the house prison of secret messages being passed between persons who had been arrested in connection with the Red Orchestra. Because of these events, the department chief of Section IV banned the prisoners from writing or speaking."[45]

Joy Weisenborn remembered that when she arrived in January in the Charlottenburg women's prison, she heard from other prisoners that compromising notes had passed between Mildred and Libertas and that one was discovered under a hay mattress.[46] Kurt Schumacher had been caught in a similar situation while attempting to deliver a note to Harro by slipping it in the slot through which food was passed. He wrote that he was now deprived of everything: "My own books from here, all writing material, even the picture my beloved Elisabeth drew of our two faces. It is so good that its destruction would be a real pity. Even the poor little walk I can no longer take; I cannot receive any mail or packages."[47]

In the face of what he knew was overwhelming evidence of their guilt and the probable outcome of their trials—death sentences for most—Schulze-Boysen tried one last ploy. He hoped to save group members' lives by stalling in the belief that the disastrous German defeat at El Alamein and the ominous counteroffensive of the Russian army around Stalingrad in November would provoke the military opposition to get rid of Hitler. He told the Gestapo that he had smuggled some sixty highly secret and incriminating documents of the highest political and military importance to Sweden. If his friends were condemned to death, the documents—containing revelations of Nazi crimes—would be published by the British or Soviet government. As one of Schulze-Boysen's contacts was alleged to have been Aleksandra Kollontai, the Soviet envoy to Sweden, the threats were taken seriously and the deception temporarily succeeded—even Kent was queried about the Stockholm connection.

Kopkow and Panzinger summoned Schulze-Boysen's father, Captain Edgar Schulze, then serving as chief of staff to the German naval command in Holland, to Berlin. The Gestapo offered the son a deal: divulge everything in return for a pledge of leniency for his friends. However, after the Gestapo applied torture, it became clear there were no documents and that Harro contrived the story in order to save his comrades.[48]

Not until late September did the Harnack family officially learn that Mildred and Arvid had been arrested. The Gestapo summoned Arvid's cousin Axel von Harnack to Prinz-Albrecht-Strasse, where Panzinger questioned him about a relative bearing the same last name who was active politically. Axel froze. He immediately thought of his brother, Ernst von Harnack, whom the Nazis had dismissed from the government of Halle-Merseburg. Panzinger then steered the conversation to Arvid. How did his cousin stand with him?

Axel was surprised and replied truthfully that he was not particularly close to Arvid and saw him infrequently. Panzinger shouted, "I am telling you now, we have him!"

Axel learned that Mildred, with whom he sometimes lunched in the cafeteria of the Berlin state library, was also in custody. Panzinger warned that the matter was serious and must remain absolutely secret; nobody except the nearest kin must know of the arrest; nobody must talk about it. Retaining a defense attorney during the investigation was not permitted. Friends and colleagues were to be told that the Harnacks were on an "official trip abroad of indefinite duration."

As Falk was serving in the army in Chemnitz, the couple had requested that Axel be allowed to take charge of their affairs and he accepted the power of attorney that enabled him to deal with the post office, bank, landlord, and other matters. At the end of the conversation, he ventured to tell Panzinger that there must be some mistake. It was very likely, Axel suggested, that in the course of his official duties Arvid had been "placed in a false light and awakened some suspicion." Mildred, he knew, "kept away from all German political affairs and devoted herself entirely to her profession."[49]

During the next few weeks, Axel answered mail from Mildred's students wanting to know when she would return and he tried repeatedly but vainly to speak with Mildred. Mildred's case at first looked promising and the family hoped that the Gestapo would let her go. However, Panzinger, possibly armed with knowledge gained from the compromising *Kassiber*, told Axel that as Mildred had "lied so much and denied things that she was bound to know," she had to be "deeply implicated in the conspiracy."[50]

The Gestapo allowed Falk two visits with Arvid. His first meeting in mid-October was deeply upsetting because his brother, whom he had seen just two months before looking very strong and energetic, appeared suddenly very old. It became clear that Arvid had had no fresh air in six weeks. They "embraced tightly and tenderly," Falk wrote his mother and sister, and "fought against the softness and emotion that threatened to break out." They sat down in two chairs with a table in between. Arvid began the conversation: "I have done certain things. I have admitted it." Falk gave him cake, cigarettes and matches, and Cebion (vitamin C). Arvid was visibly pleased by the gifts. Sitting straight and upright, Arvid "radiated great warmth" but—"you could see that he had gone through a great deal inwardly."

"How do you spend your time?" Falk asked.

"The first week, I lived, turned inward in a Buddhist fashion, letting everything flow by me," Arvid replied. "I am now working on my book."

Then Arvid inquired about his mother's health. Falk assured him that he should not worry but that she was "healthy and brave." Falk's letter continued:

> Everything is taking place in a sphere that is too far above us. But what can be done is being done, this you can believe. He thinks of us each evening at nine o'clock. I told him we'll do this too. Because the matter has become more complicated for Mildred—so I was told—I was not permitted to see her, but I have hopes for the next time. To me personally it seems impossible that M. is involved in the affair. After all, she lives with her head in the clouds, caught up in literature and art.[51]

After a discussion of business matters, Arvid broke off the conversation. They stood up and embraced and Arvid was led away.

Next, Falk Harnack and Zechlin strove desperately to save the Harnacks. Defying the Gestapo's warning at the time of the Harnacks' arrest, Zechlin had immediately telephoned to the Foreign Studies Department in Berlin and confirmed that Dean Six was in town. Overnight, Zechlin returned to Berlin and contacted Six, who promised to make inquiries. Falk now sought out State Secretary Landfried, Arvid's superior at the ministry, whom Harnack respected, although he had not let him in on his political plans.[52] He visited Landfried in his private apartment shortly after being briefed by Zechlin. After Landfried had assured himself of Falk's identity by checking his passport, he informed him that he was not supposed to discuss the case. When Falk responded by telling him that he had discussed the case with the Gestapo, they had a brief conversation. Landfried described Arvid as "the best horse in the stable" but said he was unable to help him. Falk asked him if he didn't think Harnack's contacts would be invaluable to Germany if in fact the war took an unfavorable course? Landfried answered, "That is not for me to say." He then stood up and terminated the conversation, saying: "Please give my condolences to your mother."[53]

Falk's second visit to Prinz-Albrecht-Strasse occurred on Sunday, November 15, at 11:00 A.M. Panzinger, who had met Falk the first time, was not there and Kopkow received Falk "extremely coolly, icily, and correctly." Falk gave Arvid food, a new photograph of his mother, and a report on the family. Arvid asked his brother for a picture of Mildred. Then Falk asked Arvid to describe his life:

> My cell is about so big [wrote Falk quoting Arvid]. (With his arms he indicated a size of approximately 1.5–2 meters by 3–4 meters.) When I stand on the chair, I can see a bit of sky. There is a bed in the cell that folds up during the day, a chair, and a small table. The day begins at 6 A.M. . . . Washing up; then there is black coffee and two pieces of bread spread with either margarine or marmalade. Lunch at noon, cabbage or red beets. Once a week there is a slice of bacon; on Sundays, some meat. At 6 P.M. we have the evening meal—black coffee and some bread. The food is abundant but poor and lacking in vitamins.

As he was only allowed to walk in the yard every other day, Arvid tried to compensate for his confinement by doing calisthenics. Most important was to stay calm. "People who cannot preserve an inner equilibrium find it especially hard," he told Falk.

There was a stir and an interruption as someone came to drop something off. Falk used the moment when they were unobserved by the guards to ask Arvid through sign language if he had been beaten. Arvid leant slowly across the table and whispered: "They have tortured me." Then he said: "Greet all of my friends warmly for me." As Falk noted, the greeting was not meant casually but rather constituted his brother's clear-cut instructions to warn everyone he knew.

Lawyers were not allowed to be present during the investigation period. But when the conversation turned to Arvid's trial, Falk reported that everywhere he turned, lawyers declined to defend him out of fear. Arvid put his case tersely: "I believe in principle I did the right thing and acted correctly. The war is lost and salvation lies in the way I began. Some of the means I used were wrong, but I believe that the world will still need us."

Falk described his visit to Landfried and proposed to go to the head of the Gestapo. Arvid replied that it would be useless. "We don't want to be sentimental. Things are as grave as they possibly can be."

Arvid had been repeatedly questioned about their cousin Ernst von Harnack's resistance activities but had explained away the meetings of Ernst's group as "an innocent encounter of old fraternity brothers."

Falk asked the waiting official if it would be possible to visit Mildred: "The family is worried about her." The official would only say that "her nerves are in order." He told Falk that Mildred had been ill but had recovered. Falk seized on this to ask whether letters and food could be sent to her. The official nodded. Falk left some food and a letter from Clara Harnack and he received permission to write Mildred a note: "Dear Mildred, I was just with our beloved Arvid. We both send you heartfelt greetings and kisses. Your loyal brother-in-law, Falk."[54]

"The discovery of a spy ring on such an unprecedented scale, in which members of various ministries played leading roles, struck Berlin like a bombshell," recalled Alexander Kraell, the principal judge in the Red Orchestra trial.[55] Although few people were supposed to know about the "secret affair of the Reich," the Gestapo's blanket of silence had many holes. Schulze-Boysen's cousin by marriage Ambassador Ulrich von Hassell stated, in a version of his diary that appears in translation in the CIA's files: "In the salons, in the antechambers of ministers, in the corridors of the headquarters, there was talk of this abscess, the stench of which was polluting the air of the Third Reich. Each professed to know it all; what one did not know, one invented. The affair became a myth and suspicions knew no bounds."[56] Gestapo chief Heinrich Müller reported the progress of the affair to Goering, Himmler, and

Hitler. They were furious because "the accused were neither Jews nor persons of low mentality nor social failures. On the contrary, they were members of the elite."[57] According to one aide, an enraged Goering expressed himself excitedly about the espionage case "in which officers and aristocrats played principal roles" because Schulze-Boysen had been his protégé, and Libertas's family had entertained the field marshal at Liebenberg, the affair particularly humiliated him.[58] According to Himmler's appointment calendar, on October 2, the Reichsführer was present at the interrogation of Schulze-Boysen; on October 8, 21 and on December 14, there were further calls from Himmler to his deputy, Müller, concerning the Red Orchestra affair.[59]

Meanwhile, far from the Gestapo cells, the fate of the prisoners was hostage to a battle raging around the besieged city on the west bank of the Volga. What happened at Stalingrad pulled the trap on the scaffolds in Berlin. From September 1942 to February 1943, almost the exact period covered by the investigation, trial, and execution of Mildred Harnack-Fish, the Red Army hammered the German Sixth Army at Stalingrad.

Lying on the Volga River, Stalingrad had become the objective of one of two spearheads of the 1942 German summer offensive. The Germans aimed to cut the Red Army's communications and supply lines along the Don and Volga Rivers and then push on to the Caucasus oilfields. By August 23, General von Paulus's Sixth Army had arrived at Stalingrad's northern suburbs. Stalin was determined to defend his namesake city. Hitler was equally obsessed with taking it. The Russians, just in time, realized they could redeploy their forces defending Moscow. By late November, the Germans and their allies were encircled. When it became apparent that Goering's Luftwaffe was unable to supply the army, Hitler, to the consternation of his field commanders, forbade a breakout and retreat. Instead, he ordered the German army to fight "to the last soldier and the last cartridge."[60] The result was the bloodiest military debacle in history. The Russians killed or captured nearly 250,000 Germans and their allies, including nearly all of the Sixth Army. By the end of the siege in February, 1,000 tanks, 1,800 artillery pieces, and a fleet of transport planes had been obliterated. More than any other battle, Stalingrad changed the course of the war. No military defeat has so deeply impressed itself on German memory.

In his diary, Ambassador von Hassell blamed the "vast Communist conspiracy" on the Spree for the colossal disaster on the Volga. How was it not possible "to establish a link of cause and effect between the poison at Berlin and the deadly paralysis that seized the Wehrmacht?"[61]

A setback of this magnitude, so it seemed to the regime's defenders, could not be blamed on the general staff or on the commander in chief. Nor could it be blamed on Goering, though he had failed to deliver on his promise to supply Stalingrad by air. It was more tempting to fix responsibility on the "Soviet agents," the group of resisters in Gestapo custody.

So widespread was the belief that the Berlin group contributed to the loss of Stalingrad that Field Marshal Keitel, chief of the German high command, in his posthumously published memoir made the astonishing claim that the group had betrayed the German plan of attack to the "newspapers of the Western powers." These papers, claimed Keitel, reproduced at least one sentence of the Führer's basic directive "so accurately that there could be no doubt that there had been treachery somewhere along the line." According to Keitel, Hitler, growing ever more obsessively suspicious, became convinced that the general staff was the source of this betrayal. The Führer believed, Keitel asserts, that "the guilty party was a renegade officer in the air force operations staff who had established contacts with the enemy's espionage network." Only when the trial of the Red Orchestra established that "a major organization of traitors and spies had been uncovered in Berlin" did the Führer stop abusing his general staff. Keitel gave it as one of two causes for the defeat at Stalingrad; the second occurred when a German plane was shot down, allowing the attack orders to fall into Russian hands.[62]

When Admiral Canaris, the chief of the Abwehr (who himself fed secrets to the Allies), was called as a witness at the principal Red Orchestra trial he offered this startling (and inflated) estimate: "This spy network has cost Germany the lives of 200,000 soldiers."[63] It now appears from the KGB files that little of the information intercepted by the Germans arrived in Moscow. It was Hitler's own folly, not the Harnack-Schulze-Boysen group, that caused the debacle at Stalingrad.

* * *

When the Gestapo ended its investigation in mid-October, Müller proposed bringing the case before the civilian People's Court, where members of the group were certain to be swiftly tried and executed.[64] Karl Jesko von Puttkamer, Hitler's aide, recalled the Führer's order that "the Bolshevists within our own ranks" were to be treated without mercy.[65] But the Wehrmacht's legal department contended that only a military tribunal was competent to try the case because various principals—Schulze-Boysen, Heilmann, and Gollnow—were members of the armed services and the most serious charges involved military espionage.[66] Goering approvingly conveyed their arguments to Hitler. The Führer ultimately agreed to have the "Red Orchestra criminal case complex" assigned to the Reich Court Martial, the highest military court.

When judge Alexander Kraell was asked why civilians and women appeared before a military tribunal, he replied that it was impossible to split the complex and give part of it to the People's Court. Even though the majority of the defendants were civilians and there were many women among them, the sentences by a military court were "an optically unpleasant by-product, but—unfortunately—this could not be avoided."[67]

The court was divided into four senates, or chambers. The decisions of the Reich Court Martial Court did not automatically become law unlike those of other German courts, but required confirmation by a senior military commander. An exception was made for the Red Orchestra trials—the confirmation of the sentences was reserved for Hitler himself.[68]

Representing the state was the prosecuting attorney Manfred Roeder. Born in Kiel, the son of a court clerk, Roeder had volunteered for service in the field artillery in World War 1. He was gassed, earning the Iron Cross Second Class. Like Arvid Harnack, Roeder joined the Freikorps army engaged in fighting after the war. Later he studied law and passed through the successive qualifying rounds for a legal career. In April 1935, as Arvid entered the Economics Ministry, Roeder joined the Luftwaffe legal service.[69] Looking far younger than his forty-two years in his Luftwaffe colonel's uniform, Roeder's official photograph betrays no trace of the cruelty for which he became notorious. With the dark and dashing good looks of a film star, his unlined face gives an impression of calmness and benevolence, two characteristics that he notably lacked.

By 1942, he had proved himself an able if entirely ruthless investigator. Hans von Dohnanyi, who also fell under Roeder's purview, used words such as *Bluthund* (bloodhound) and *Blutrichter* (blood judge) to describe him.[70] Rudolph Behse, one of the lawyers opposing him in the Red Orchestra trial, said that cynicism and brutality were at the core of his character. His "limitless professional ambition" was matched with "innate sadism."[71] Even Roeder's own judicial colleagues found him "harsh, inconsiderate, and even unscrupulous."[72] When asked why Roeder had earned the hatred of so many, Judge Eugen Schmitt said, "There was something lacking in his temperament; he did not possess the normal man's sympathy for the sufferings of others, so that he did not mind witnessing an execution or undertaking unpleasant tasks such as informing a colleague of his impending arrest on homosexual charges."[73] Arvid's cousin Axel von Harnack, who visited Roeder in his Luftwaffe office on behalf of the Harnacks, observed, "Never since have I experienced so pronounced an impression of brutality as I did from this man. He was a creature surrounded by an aura of fear."[74]

The Gestapo provided the evidence; Goering ordered Roeder to concern himself only with drawing the indictments. By early November, Roeder had received more than thirty volumes of Gestapo reports. After studying the files, he conducted further "short concluding interrogations."[75] In late November, Roeder prepared an eight-hundred-page indictment and proceeded to prosecute the band he described as "professional gamblers, Communist fanatics, disoriented introverts and drug addicts, disillusioned bourgeois, anarchists in principle, people whose sole motive was a passionate desire to live it up, Communist outlaws acting as couriers, agents and saboteurs, deserters and émigrés."[76]

Such was the man who had the power not only to snuff out the lives of Mildred and her friends but also to tarnish their memory.

After a pretrial visit to Roeder, Falk Harnack reported to the family that the charges were indeed serious: "high treason and, regrettably, espionage."[77] Falk and Zechlin tried to engage Klaus Bonhoeffer as the Harnacks' defense lawyer. However, Klaus declined to serve, pleading that he was already compromised by his own resistance activities.[78] Ultimately, only four lawyers were accredited to the court. They had to serve approximately eighty defendants in the more than twenty trials that took place between December 1942 and September 1943.[79] Inge Havemann persuaded one of them, Dr. Schwarz, to take the Harnacks' case. But as the lawyer was suspected of sympathizing with the defendants, he was allowed to see only part of the closely guarded Harnack files.[80]

Although matters of life and death were involved, Mildred may never have known the charges against her, since the attorneys were not supposed to show them to their clients. Another defendant, Günther Weisenborn, wrote that his lawyer approached him for the first time in the courtroom: "I'm your official defender, I know your files. Don't worry unnecessarily. You know that the worst that can happen is the death sentence. We'll see each other later." These were the sole words he spoke to his startled client.[81]

There were no more visits to Arvid. On December 5, Falk wrote his mother that the apartment and its contents had been seized. On December 7, he confided, "Still no news from M; the authorities are annoyed with her. The entire matter will soon be decided, and we must steel our hearts!"[82]

A few days before he was tried, Arvid was dismissed from the civil service. According to German law, civil servants could be discharged only if they were sentenced to death or prison,[83] but Hitler was determined, even before the trial, that Harnack should lose his state counselor status. All formalities were meticulously observed. Harnack first had to resign, which he did by signing a "voluntary petition." Only then could he be dismissed by order of Hitler and Economic Minister Funk.[84]

On December 14, the eve of their trial, Arvid wrote a last letter to Mildred. In it he reminded her of their happy days in Madison, when they just met and he was living at the University Club:

My dearest love,
    If I have had the strength over these past months to remain inwardly calm and composed, and if I look ahead calmly and with composure to what lies ahead, this is be-

cause I feel part of all that is good and beautiful in the world, and because I share the feeling of which the poet Whitman sings toward the whole earth. Insofar as human beings are concerned, those close to me, especially you, were the incarnation of this.

Despite everything, I look back gladly on my life. The darkness was outweighed by the light. And this is largely because of our marriage. Last night, I recalled many of the beautiful moments we shared. And the more I did this, the more I recalled. It was like looking at a starry sky wherein the number of stars grows and grows the more closely one looks. Do you remember Picnic Point, when we became engaged? I sang for joy the next morning at the club. And before that: do you remember our first serious conversation at lunch in the restaurant on State Street? That conversation became my guiding star, and so it has remained. How often during the sixteen years that followed did I lay your head on mine, at night, when life had made us weary? And then everything was all right. In my thoughts I have done this during the past weeks and will do it again in those to come. I also think of you and all my loved ones each morning at eight and each evening at six. They think of us at the same time. Do this, too; then we'll know that the love in the world flows among us.

Our intense work meant that life was not easy for us, and the danger of being overwhelmed not slight. Nonetheless, we remained living human beings. This became clear to me during our time on the Grossglockner,* and again this year, as we watched the great elk emerge before us. Earlier you had risen like a goddess from the sea.

You are in my heart. And you must always stay there: *"Du sollst immer darinnen sein"*! My greatest wish is for you to be happy when you think of me. I am when I think of you.

Many, many kisses! I am holding you close,
Your A.[85]

---

* The Grossglockner is the highest peak in southern Austria in the eastern Alps on the border between the Tyrol and Carinthian provinces. The Harnacks vacationed there in September 1941.

SIXTEEN

Stalingrad's Scapegoat

Courtroom of the Reichskreigsgericht

One of the ironies of Mildred's fate is that the stations on her personal *via crucis* survived the war: the fisherman's cottage on the Kurische Nehrung where the Nazis arrested her, now a last Baltic outpost of the former Soviet empire; Prinz-Albrecht-Strasse 8, where the Gestapo imprisoned her, its ruins now a highlight of Berlin sightseeing tours; the Kantstrasse women's prison, now serving a more benign purpose as a land registry office; Plötzensee Memorial, where she was beheaded; and the building on the Witzlebenstrasse that housed the Reichskriegsgericht—the courthouse where she was tried.

A crowned Prussian eagle grasps a snake in the pediment over the copper doors of the block-long, four-story courthouse. Underneath, the stonemason has chiseled a blindfolded head of Justice and the words "Reichskriegsgericht." Before the demise of the Wall, a provisional wood tablet memorialized the place where the Reich Court Martial sentenced more than five hundred men and women to death. However, the role of the court in Nazi times and the recognition due its victims is still controversial: in 1989, an irate West Berlin judge had the wooden sign torn away. Now a bronze tablet again reminds us that "this building, Witzlebenstrasse 4–10, housed the Reich Court Martial from 1933 to 1943. Here the highest court of the Wehrmacht judicial system condemned countless conscientious objectors and resistance fighters to death for their stance against National Socialism and war."

Early on Tuesday, December 15, 1942, a green police van collected nine men and four women from prisons throughout Berlin and deposited them in the cobblestone courtyard of the courthouse. Around 9:00 A.M., the principal group of the Red Orchestra, so-called because it included the Harnacks, Schulze-Boysens, and Schumachers, as well as Horst Heilmann and Herbert Gollnow, assembled before the second chamber.[1] Some members of the group met for the first time. For others, husbands and wives, it was an overdue reunion.

The sign on the door of the courtroom read "Secret Trial, Public Not Allowed." Two uniformed military policemen flanked the two defense lawyers, Drs. Behse and Schwarz. Other soldiers with fixed bayonets stood motionless before the windows and doors. Near the door, a Gestapo commissar sat at a folding table, preparing to take notes. The spectator's row in the back of the room was empty—no family members or visitors had been admitted to the courtroom.[2]

Five judges—a vice admiral, two generals, and two professional judges—entered the room.[3] Everyone, save the defendants, gave the Hitler salute. Official solemnity pervaded the room as the judges sat down at a horseshoe-shaped table on the dais of the wood-paneled room. The faint winter light fell through the four large windows illuminating an enormous bust of "the supreme judicial lord," Adolf Hitler. Presiding over the court was its president, Judge Alexander Kraell.[4] The prosecutor, Manfred Roeder, sat in a high-backed chair to the left of Kraell; across from him, on Kraell's right, was the recording clerk.[5] A railing separated the twelve wooden chairs for the defendants who sat across from the judges. In front of the judges was a table that served as a witness stand.

One by one, flanked by soldiers, the defendants were summoned before the court. As in all such cases before the Reich Court Martial, the prosecuting attorney led the proceedings. Roeder had submitted the evidence along with separate written indictments for each defendant to the chamber. The indictment contained a complete history of the circumstances, the recorded evidence, and a juridical estimation of the case.[6] There was no jury. Certainly there were no peers, no fellow German civilians. When Mildred's turn came, she was ordered to step to the bench. The charges were read aloud. The questioning was peremptory; she was told to answer with a simple yes or no. There were no witnesses for the defense. Schwarz was not permitted to consult or instruct his client.[7] Instead, there were witnesses for the prosecution, most of them Gestapo agents. Although obtained in a large part by means of torture, the Gestapo protocols would serve as the basis for the judgment. In presenting their defense, neither lawyer criticized the proceedings, nor, as Dr. Behse, the lawyer of the Schulze-Boysens, would subsequently admit, did they bring up the question of torture because "it did not influence the truth of the investigation results."[8]

Mildred did not hear the evidence; she was sent from the room during the questioning of these witnesses. After her hearing concluded, she was allowed to remain in the room, joining the Schulze-Boysens and Arvid, so that as the sessions progressed each of the chairs was filled. During intermissions, the defendants filed out to the waiting room, where they ate and smoked whatever they brought with them from their meager prison rations. And it was there in the smoke-filled room that she was reunited with Arvid for the first time in three months.

On the trial's final day the prisoners spoke their "last words." Arvid was composed. For twenty minutes he described his political and economic views, his fierce words contrasting gloomily with his low, tired voice. He repeatedly declared his hostility to the Third Reich. He gave his reasons for joining the opposition, which he said was the only means by which Germany could be saved from disaster. When Schulze-Boysen rose to speak, he admitted his deeds proudly but was silenced when he attempted to give his motives. Kraell refused to hear political propaganda.[9]

After the defendants had spoken, Roeder demanded twelve death sentences and the judges retired to their chambers. In a last gesture of defiance, the defendants rose and rushed into one another's arms.

On December 19, the defendants heard the verdicts. The court sentenced Arvid, Harro, Libertas, Kurt and Elizabeth Schumacher, Hans Coppi, Kurt Schulze, John Graudenz, and Horst Heilmann to death for reasons that included "preparation for high treason, war treason, undermining military strength, aiding the enemy, and espionage." Herbert Gollnow received the death penalty for "disobedience in the field and disclosing state secrets to the enemy." Mildred, however, received only six years in prison and six years' "loss of honor." Erika von Brockdorff received ten years.

When Mildred's sentence was pronounced, Arvid looked radiant. He smiled at her; her life has been saved. Schwarz's successful legal strategy had been to plead that Mildred, like any good German wife, had simply followed the orders of her husband. How could she have been duty bound to denounce her own husband and deliver him to a certain death?

The judges were clearly sympathetic to this "highly educated American" and they blamed Arvid for introducing Mildred into the "world of socialist ideas." She "had shown great understanding for German literature and, by translating important German books into the English language, she had served the German

cause." As an American who came to Germany only in 1929—
and who remained a foreigner, the judges condescendingly added—
she could hardly be expected to understand Germany's political
development or her husband's views about them.[10] "As a result,"
they concluded, "she raised no objections to her husband's illegal
activity, which she became aware of despite his definite attempt to
keep her out of it, and which took place, in part, in their shared
apartment."[11]

As to whether Mildred acted from her own beliefs or only met
her husband halfway, the judges felt this question was "clearly
answered in favor of the latter." Mildred's lawyer had succeeded
in convincing the judges that she had been primarily occupied with
her professional and literary activities and her household tasks.
Her criminal actions "objectively and subjectively did not go beyond the framework of assisting" high treason and espionage. Her
deeds were not, the court found, undertaken independently, but
stemmed from a wish to help her husband. For these reasons, the
court hesitated to impute to her "any traitorous intent in the questions she put to Gollnow." They therefore sentenced her only as
an accessory to espionage, not as a conspirator.[12]

The court also sympathized with Lieutenant Gollnow. The verdict described him as "a decent character who had originally also
been a completely convinced National Socialist." Harnack and
Schulze-Boysen, who concealed their views and plans from him,
led him astray. Gollnow was "in no way to be considered a Communist." Nevertheless, he was condemned to death and "to the
loss of military honor" because of "disobedience in the field and
the surrendering of state secrets."[13] Yet ambivalently, the court
petitioned the Führer to commute the sentence.[14]

Interestingly, in view of the postwar legends subsequently spun
by Kraell and Roeder, the verdict does not mention any love affair
between Gollnow and Mildred Harnack-Fish. Surely the court
would not have treated her as favorably if they had believed she
was an adulteress and seducer. Instead, Gollnow was judged to
have "become the victim of his eagerness and the determined ma-
nipulation of the codefendant [Arvid] Harnack."[15]

After the trial ended on December 19, Axel sent Falk a telegram
that read, "*Buch nicht lieferbar aber sechs Bilder*" (book not deliverable, but six pictures). The family had prearranged a code:

Book = Arvid
Picture = Mildred
Not deliverable = death sentence
Numbers = years of the prison[16]

The next day, Inge, who had been waiting outside the court-room for the verdict, wrote her mother:

> Although we all had secretly anticipated this, it was still a blow. Again I want to *earnestly* entreat you to not give up hope. The sentence must still be confirmed at the highest level (the supreme commander) and, in the meantime, the plea for clemency will be submitted. There is a time limit of 3 months, according to the attorney. The poor woman got 6 years. A[rvid] received the verdict with complete composure and exemplary bearing. On one of the previous days he had been able to speak in his own defense, so as to clarify his motives. This was his greatest wish and will have been a great relief to him. For his wife it is *dreadful*. How nice that they were together again for these five days.[17]

When the court pronounced its verdict, Roeder and the chief of the Wehrmacht legal department went immediately to Goering. The Reichsmarschall wanted to know if other members of the Luftwaffe were entangled in the "treason complex." The lawyers said no. They next spoke about the two women who had been sentenced to prison. The lawyers favored prison terms, since the women "had been drawn into this treason by their husbands in the most irresponsible fashion." But Goering exploded when he heard the words "prison term." He had been ordered by the Führer "to cauterize this sore." The Führer, Goering said, would never approve the light sentences.[18]

Nor did he. When Hitler received the verdict, dispatched by courier to his headquarters, both he and army chief Keitel signed the document dated December 21, 1942, confirming the death sentences. However, Hitler refused to confirm the judgment of December 19 against Mildred Harnack and Erika Gräfin von Brock-dorff. A new trial would be held under another chamber of the court.[19]

Hitler and Goering were determined to have one defendant hanged publicly at his place of work. They also wanted to publish the sentences against the Harnacks, Schulze-Boysens, and the rest. The plan was set aside, however, when Himmler's deputy Müller pointed out that if this happened "the lines to Moscow [the *Funkspiel*, or "radio game" with which they were trying to entrap further Russian agents] that have been built up will be broken off again. It will then require long preliminary work to achieve once more such a chance of double agent activity."[20] In order to preserve the disinformation effort, there were no public hangings and the sentences went unpublished.

On December 19, the final day of the trial, Katyusha regiments began their artillery barrage signaling the beginning of Operation Uranus, the climatic Russian counterattack on Stalingrad, which Hitler insisted on calling the *Schicksalstadt,* the "city of fate." Thirty miles away, troops were awakened "because the ground trembled."[21] In the view of one judge, Hitler ordered the executions shortly before Christmas because of the worsening situation at Stalingrad; "Hitler declared that these traitors should not go to the gallows with the hope of a Soviet victory."[22]

On Tuesday, December 22, Berlin was overcast and buffeted by a freezing east wind. At Plötzensee in the afternoon, Arvid wrote a last letter to his family:

> My dear ones,
>
> In a few hours I shall leave this life. I would like to thank you again for all the love you have given me, especially in these last days. The thought of your love has made all that is difficult easy for me. So I am happy and calm. I am also thinking of Nature, so immensely powerful, to which I feel so connected. This morning I recited out loud: *"Die Sonne tönt in alter Weise"* [the first line from the prologue in Heaven of Goethe's *Faust*].
>
> Above all, I am thinking of the fact that humanity is moving forward. These are the three roots of my strength.
>
> It was a special joy for me to learn that an engagement is expected soon in the family. I would like very much for my signet ring, which belonged to my father, to go to F[alk]. His signet ring can then go to L.* My ring will be given to you

---

* Lilo Ramdohr, a member of the White Rose resistance group, who was Falk's fiancée.

with my things. This evening I will hold a small pre-Christmas celebration for myself, reading the Christmas story aloud. And then comes the moment of parting.

I would have liked to see you all one more time; unfortunately, this is not possible. But my thoughts are with you all, I am not forgetting anyone. Each of you must sense this, especially Mother.

Once again, I embrace and kiss you all.

Your Arvid

P.S. You must celebrate Christmas properly. This is my last wish. And sing *"Ich bete an die Macht der Liebe."* ["I pray to the power of love."]

Günter Weisenborn had seen Schulze-Boysen a few days before holding his head high, his blond hair shimmering in the light. He wrote, "Here he stood in the Gestapo cellar, young, talented, clean, a tortured messenger from the future world."[23] Harro wrote in his farewell letter to his parents:

The time has come. In a few hours I shall abandon this *Ich*. I am completely calm and ask that you accept this with composure. Such important things are at stake today all over the world that one extinguished life does not matter very much. What has happened, what I have done—I do not want to say any more about this. Everything that I did was done in accordance with my head, my heart, and my convictions, and, in this light, you as my parents must assume the best. I ask this of you! This death suits me. Somehow, I have always known of it. It is "my own death," as Rilke once said. . . . If you were here—as you are, invisibly—you would see me laughing in the face of death. I have long since overcome it. It is common in Europe for spiritual seeds to be sowed with blood. Perhaps we were simply a few fools; but when the end is this near one perhaps has the right to a bit of completely personal historical illusion.[24]

In her final letter to her mother, Libertas wrote, "So, my love, the hours strike: first Harro goes [to his death] and I think of him. Then Horst goes, and I think of him. And Elisabeth will think of me."[25]

Passing the prison, the Protestant pastor Harald Poelchau

learned from a guard there that a group of "high-level political prisoners" was scheduled for execution that evening. Although he was prison chaplain, Poelchau had not been informed. When he complained, Roeder said cynically that "no participation of the clergy was planned!" Ignoring the prosecutor, the pastor immediately visited the prisoners in their cells, staying with them until their sentences were carried out.[26]

Usually a firing squad carried out sentences in military trials, but for the leading male members of the Red Orchestra a more degrading method, hanging, was chosen.[27] Before the trial, Hitler had already decided on the method of their execution: a large T-beam with eight meat hooks on rollers spaced along the ceiling of the execution shed.[28]

It was an overcast day with a chilly wind blowing from the east. That afternoon it grew dark early and one by one the lights were switched on in the cells. Singly, the handcuffed prisoners were led into the shed. Arvid remained "upright and calm."[29] Roeder was present at the executions, glittering in his dress uniform with silver armbands, his Heimat sword at his side. Starting at 7:05 P.M., at intervals of five minutes, Schulze-Boysen, Harnack, Kurt Schumacher, and John Graudenz were hanged.

The executions took place in a single room in separate compartments divided by curtains. The hangman stood on a stool. The prisoner was hoisted up, and the hangman placed the thin noose round his neck. The noose tightened as the stool was pulled away and the prisoner, strung from the meat hook, slowly strangled to death.

Other prisoners were executed by the "more humane" guillotine.[30] At 8:00 P.M. the blade fell first on the neck of nineteen-year-old Horst Heilmann and then on Hans Coppi, Kurt Schulze, Libertas Schulze-Boysen, and Elizabeth Schumacher. Only Libertas cried out: "Let me keep my young life!"

The guards departed, and Roeder and the other witnesses left the shed. The duty officer walked down the long corridor jangling his keys. He shut the doors of the now empty cells and turned out the lights, one after the other. Soon it was completely dark.[31]

Because a military court sentenced the defendants, its procedures were unfamiliar to civilians. Normally weeks elapsed after a trial between sentence and execution, and the families hoped to appeal the sentence. In the week following the end of the trial, Germany's administrative offices closed down for the Christmas holidays. Even so, Falk and Egmont Zechlin made a desperate last effort to save Arvid. On December 22, Falk sought an interview with Professor Jens Peter Jessen, a member of the conservative resistance and a friend of Colonel Oster in his office at the Wehrmacht high command in the Bendlerstrasse. Falk and Zechlin hoped to persuade the "West-oriented" opposition that it needed to save Harnack in order to negotiate with the Russians.

Jessen said cautiously, "Our conversation must remain strictly confidential. The eastern front is collapsing. Do you believe that Harnack and his friends would be in a position to start negotiations with the USSR?"

Falk answered tentatively, "To the extent I could learn about what has gone on at the trial, I believe that I can answer yes to that question."

"I've received the same information. We'll have to keep this group in reserve at all costs. I'll go to Funk immediately with Oster. Funk is the only one who could still obtain a delay."[32]

It was a futile dream. It was already too late.

On Wednesday, December 23, Thora Eulenburg, Libertas's mother, made the rounds of all the Gestapo prisons in Berlin with a Christmas package for her daughter. Searching for her daughter, she went first to Alexanderplatz, then to Prinz-Albrecht-Strasse, to Kaiserdamm, and finally to the Lehrterstrasse prisons. Though prison officials knew that her daughter was already dead, they cruelly sent her scurrying from place to place. Finally, she went to Goering, for whom she had sometimes played the piano. He too put her off. Only after the new year did his adjutant inform Libertas's uncle, Prince Eulenburg, that Libertas had been executed on December 22.[33]

That same stormy day, just after 11:00 A.M., Falk's cousin Elizabeth von Harnack called to tell him Arvid had been executed. Her friend, the chaplain, Poelchau, had telephoned the news. Late in the afternoon, Elizabeth, Inge, and Falk met at the train station and went to the pastor's apartment, where he described Arvid's last hours.[34] At noon the next day, Falk Harnack went to visit

Roeder at his Luftwaffe Ministry office in order to intervene on Mildred's behalf, only to have Roeder declare, "They are both lost."

"Why?" Falk said disingenuously. "There is still the possibility of an appeal for mercy for my brother. For Mildred Harnack, it will be a hard time but with energy one can survive six years of prison."

Roeder answered, "Your brother was executed yesterday. He died like a man. Forget your brother, you have never had a brother! But if you make a word about this trial public, as a soldier, you will be shot according to martial law. The affair must remain secret."

After a long silence, Falk asked for the return of his brother's body.[35]

Roeder replied, "You'd like that. We are not creating martyrs! What is *your* attitude, anyway, toward the National Socialist state?"[36]

Falk went silent and then, finding his voice, deflected the question: "What do you mean, 'Mildred is lost'? The highest German court has just sentenced her to six years' prison. The sentence cannot be changed, since it was handed down by the highest court. It can only be lightened by an appeal for mercy."

Roeder concluded the interview brusquely. "On orders of the Führer there will be a retrial."[37]

That evening at 8:00 P.M., as the Zechlin family was preparing to light its Christmas Eve candles, the telephone rang. It was Falk. Both parties knew the telephone was tapped; Arvid's brother gave the prearranged signal: "The book is finished."[38] Falk then boarded a Heidelberg-bound train, almost empty because of the holiday, to perform the terrible duty of telling his mother.

Axel von Harnack, cousin and counselor, set off to plead once more with Roeder. He found the prosecutor in a malevolent mood. When Axel spoke of his cousin who had "passed away," Roeder screamed, "Because of his reprehensible activities he suffered a shameful death. He was one of the greatest criminals that has ever existed in Germany; he has committed the worst treason in this war!" When Axel asked about Mildred, Roeder raged, "I strongly urge the Harnack family not to undertake anything whatsoever on behalf of this woman! You are to assume the attitude that this woman had nothing whatsoever to do with you. She no longer belongs to your family!"[39]

They never saw or heard from Mildred again. Nor did they hear from the officials until they received a bill for fees for the death sentence, room and board charges for Prinz-Albrecht-Strasse and Charlottenburg prison, court costs, and executioner's fees. There was even a twelve-pfennig charge for the stamps used to send the bill.[40] The personal effects of the Harnacks were not returned to the relatives but they were able to buy back a few mementos from the Finance Ministry.[41]

On December 20, the day after Mildred was sentenced, the warden on duty asked a fellow prisoner, young Communist Gertrud Lichtenstein, if she would care to become Mildred's cellmate. Gertrud knew why the orders came that ended Mildred's solitary confinement: "the murderers feared that Mildred might harm herself—she had probably said something to this effect." Even though they had never exchanged a word (they had only glanced at each other in the prison yard), they "spontaneously fell into each other's arms once the guard closed the door." Once together, they became "extremely close."[42]

After their frugal breakfast of dry bread and ersatz coffee, the two women talked or taught one another songs and poetry. There were no books, but Mildred possessed one great treasure—a pencil. With it she wrote out the poems of Goethe for her cellmate. She also taught her American songs. They had much to talk about: Mildred spoke of Arvid and of her constant anxiety about him, of their time together as students, of her work in Germany, and about how she was drawn into the illegal work. In short, they "talked about everything under the sun."

After lunch they napped, and then it was time for their walk, the "bear dance," as the prisoners called it, in the prison yard. Mildred received no mail and she was very worried about how she would survive the six years in prison. Christmas came and went with Mildred at times "close to despair." Early in January she was informed that her case was being reopened. "I can still recall how agitated Mildred was and what hopes and fears this reopening of her case raised in her," Lichtenstein recalled. "I encouraged her hope that her sentence might be reduced, although in my heart I was not convinced this would happen."

In a final gesture, before her second trial Mildred gave Gertrud the final December letter from Arvid and begged her to safeguard it. Even though she had carried it for only a few weeks inside her dress, Mildred had read it so often that it was almost illegible. On January 15, Mildred's companion carried the letter with her as Gertrud was put on the transport to the concentration camp Ravensbrück.[43]

In Spandau prison, when the male members of the Red Orchestra heard that the sentences against Mildred and Erika von Brockdorff had been voided, pandemonium broke out. Returning from an interrogation at Prinz-Albrecht-Strasse, Karl Böhme brought back the news. Usually news was telegraphed from cell to cell by knocks on the heating pipes. Now agitated prisoners shouted across the entire floor of Block 9: "They have voided the sentences against Mildred and Erika in order to be able to murder us all!" One prisoner recalled later that "those in their cells hammered with their fists against the doors, throwing the wardens into flurries of agitation, and shouted aloud questions and answers to one another. Only very slowly did this storm ebb and give way to the depressing sense of being delivered helplessly to despotism."[44]

On January 12, in far-off Morocco, the Casablanca Conference began. It was there that Roosevelt and Churchill declared—with the approval of Stalin—that the alliance sought Germany's "unconditional surrender," thus undermining the military opposition to Hitler. Officers who might agree on bringing Hitler down were not prepared to contribute to their country's total defeat.

Mildred and Erika's four-day ordeal before the third chamber began on Wednesday, January 13, at 9:45 A.M., as Berliners were beginning to learn of the unfolding debacle at Stalingrad. In November, the Führer had given strict instructions: the encirclement of the Sixth Army was to be kept from the German people. The Christmas post now arriving from the front would be the last many families would receive from their sons, brothers, and fathers. In the concurrent trial of other members of the Red Orchestra before the second chamber, there was, for the first time, the ominous reference to the "struggle of the German Volk for its life."

When Hitler refused to confirm Mildred's sentence, the Wehrmacht legal department faced the dilemma of finding grounds for a new trial. New accusations carrying the death penalty were fabricated. They cited paragraph four of the Regulation on Violent Criminals, which read: "A punishable attempted crime or offense or abetting of the same is generally punishable by the penalty permitted for the crime itself." Thus the lesser crime of aiding in the preparation of espionage was also made punishable by the death sentence.[45]

After the war, Admiral Bastien, who headed the court, tried to invest the preordained verdict with a veneer of legality. He said that it was "out of the question" that the retrial chamber was placed "under pressure" by the repeal of the first sentence by the Führer. He was "not aware of any pressure by the Führer on the chamber" to hand down a death sentence. Of course, Bastien confessed, "in individual cases" Hitler did sometimes present his opinion about the "appropriateness of the death sentence for certain crimes." He added that the chamber "was not influenced by such expressions of opinions."[46]

Since the records of Mildred's second trial have not yet surfaced, our only account of the evidence is the questionable postwar testimony of one of the judges, the president of the third chamber, Dr. Karl Schmauser.[47] Giving his self-vindication the gloss of fairness, Schmauser claimed to have stayed up late the night before the trial working through a large number of publications and translations that the defense counsel had submitted "to demonstrate that the defendant Harnack was not only an extremely educated woman but also an unusually valuable individual in human terms."[48] In her first trial, Mildred was "to a great extent under the influence of and in the thrall of her codefendant husband. He had not only obviously tried to protect her as much as possible, he had also sustained her through the example of his own character. This influence was missing in the new trial." As a result, Mildred was not only "considerably less sure of herself," she "also admitted significantly more in the new trial."[49] Now it appeared that Mildred was not merely an accessory to treason, but a traitor herself. In Schmauser's opinion, "instead of the charge upheld by the second chamber of simple aiding and abetting in the preparation of treason, insofar as such an offense even exists, the charge should have been that of preparation of treason committed in conspiracy with the other defendants." Schmauser raised a further objection: to the original verdict of six years when, he maintained, the court had itself laid down the fundamental legal rule that the only rightful penalty against a German for "preparation for treason committed after the outbreak of the Russian campaign [in a] struggle on behalf of Bolshevism and communism" was either life imprisonment or death.[50] Schmauser never addressed the obvious question of how Mildred, as an American citizen, could be sentenced to death for aiding the enemy when the enemy was, at the time, an ally of the United States.[51]

Schmauser frequently invoked the specter of Bolshevism. Mixing fantasy with fact, he asserted that Arvid "had been bent ever since his return from a one- or two-year stay in Moscow [he thinks around 1936] on working for the establishment—with the help of Russia and, if necessary, with violence—of a Soviet Germany." Nevertheless, there may be some truth in his statement that Mildred not only knew of his contacts with Moscow but "during the war, she herself helped to pick up new radio transmitters." But he stretched the evidence in saying that not only was she informed about the radio traffic but she "also probably assisted in the encoding herself." In one case, when an agent or parachutist had arrived with a radio message, she went immediately to the Economics Ministry to tell her husband "that he should report sick and come to their apartment right away." Meanwhile, "she had hidden the radio message in a book." Schmauser recalled that it was brought out in the second trial that Libertas and Mildred provided cover for their husbands during walks in the Tiergarten in order to allow the men to discuss their plans undisturbed.[52]

According to Schmauser, Mildred was also aware that Arvid questioned his nephew Wolfgang Havemann about military secrets and that this information was sent to the Russians via an illegal transmitter. For example, Havemann told Harnack where the German U-boats were deployed outside of Murmansk in order to block American munitions transports to Russia. This made it possible for the Americans to avoid the blockade by taking a different route.[53]

The court found Mildred guilty. Schmauser reported that the defendant Mildred Harnack "was convicted beyond the shadow of a doubt by virtue of her own statements as well as the evidence of having committed not only continued treason on behalf of the belligerent power Russia but also, probably, continued espionage within the meaning of the law." For both offenses, the only permissible sentence was death.[54]

What was new in the second trial was the allegation that Mildred carried on adulterous relations with Abwehr Lieutenant Herbert Gollnow "with the knowledge, at least, of her husband."

Gollnow had been separated from the others after their December trial and sent to the Lehrterstrasse military prison on January 21. He was kept alive presumably to be a witness against Harnack-Fish. Did he believe he would be set free if he testified against Mildred? Did he sign documents? Give false testimony? The extent of his collaboration can only be surmised because Herbert Gollnow was shot on February 12 at Tegel prison.

The presiding judge from Mildred's first trial, Alexander Kraell, testified after the war that in this trial the judges did not consider it completely proven that she had deliberately questioned Gollnow. "It then turned out," said Kraell, "that Frau Harnack had had an adulterous relationship with Gollnow which, after the trial, as I recall, was investigated more closely." At Mildred's second trial the judges came to the conclusion "that the questioning of Gollnow had been committed deliberately for the purpose of treason."[55] "The assessment of the conduct of Frau Harnack concerning these things," Kraell maintained, "was decisive for the question of her sentence." The judge stated that "Frau Harnack denied it but the statements by Gollnow were believable."[56] The court stressed "that Mildred Harnack also approved, on the basis of her own worldview and political stance, of the endeavors pursued on behalf of Russia, and made these endeavors her own."[57]

According to Schmauser, Gollnow gave Mildred information concerning planned sabotage missions "in about twelve cases," whereupon Arvid, using the illegal radio transmitter, passed directly to Moscow or to Kent. About ten of these sabotage units of paratroopers were captured or killed, Schmauser states. Thus he concludes "the reports given by the defendant Harnack to her husband resulted not only in the death of Gollnow but also in the deaths of an estimated two or three dozen German soldiers. There was no doubt that the defendant Harnack not only could have been and would have been aware of these consequences in advance but that, in fact, she was."[58]

It seems likely that the judges, fearful for their skins, lied to officials at Nuremberg and subsequently in the postwar proceedings against Roeder about the evidence against Mildred. None of the specific allegations about the dead German soldiers or an affair with Mildred appear in the charges against Gollnow at his trial. Instead, during a 1953 interview with David Dallin, Manfred Roeder asserted that it wasn't until after Mildred's execution that it was revealed that she had betrayed the German parachutists dropped on Soviet territory. Roeder claimed instead that he had been reprimanded by Hitler for hurrying her second trial because Mildred and Gollnow had gone to their deaths before "certain matters could be investigated."[59]

In her second trial, according to Judge Kraell, Mildred had not "made a complete confession in subjective terms, but by and by she admitted the objective events," which showed her knowledge of the work of her husband was "so encompassing that given her personal intelligence, her subjective guilt could not be doubted."[60]

About the conduct of the prosecutor, Roeder, the judges offered no reproach: "There is nothing to say about Dr. Roeder's conduct in the trial," said Schmauser. "To my knowledge, he asked five or six questions, principally in connection with the Gollnow charge. I had no reason to intervene against the content or manner of these questions or his closing argument."[61]

When Erika heard Schmauser declare that the court had "wavered for a very long between 'life in prison or the death penalty' " she wrote to her husband: "This was all so comical since I knew that the death sentence had been passed on us when our first one wasn't confirmed. Then when he said that it had been difficult for them because women were involved, I had to smile slightly. That must have made him mad, and he shouted: 'Have the defendant Brockdorff taken out!' As I went out, he called after me: 'You won't be laughing for long.' Upon which I stopped, turned around and said: No. I'll still be laughing when they cut my head off." [62]

We don't know if Mildred made a final speech but Erika did make one:

I was arrested four months ago and came here with the usual ideas about the Gestapo. I knew: now it's all over, the Gestapo torments and tortures people until they say what the Gestapo wants to hear. But during the interrogations the commissars said they weren't monsters, that they were there to separate guilt from innocence. This reassured me, my faith in justice was restored, and I was happy when I heard that our trial would be soon and before the Reichskriegsgericht. Because I said to myself: there are people of such stature there, who certainly have enough knowledge of human nature to judge correctly. The ten years in prison was very hard for me, but I wanted to try to make up for my offenses through work. But this new trial has robbed me of the last thing I had left, my belief that there is justice in Germany. And this is what was hardest and most bitter. Especially since I really did not know that there was a transmitter, and this transmitter did not even work, as I learned in my interrogations.

At this Schmauser jumped up and told Erika that "in such circumstances something like that could cost the lives of 10,000 soldiers."[63]

The collusion among Mildred's accusers to portray her as a seductress is consistent with an old tradition. In the Middle Ages, women like Joan of Arc, who were anomalies in a patriarchal culture, were tried and martyred by decollation or burning at the stake. This persisted through the Reformation, when Protestant Europe (and America) burned witches, who were often credited with demonic sexual allure. In our time, heresy against the church acquired a new guise as treason against the state. Mata Hari became the archetype of a spy as disciple of Venus as well as of Mars. As Hitler realized, executions created martyrs. Admiral von Puttkamer recalled that when he presented Mildred's first sentence for confirmation, the Führer had raged against creating "another Edith Cavell."[64] Defaming Mildred thus served this purpose as well.

On February 3, a special bulletin from Führer headquarters interrupted the programming on German radio. Unlike the usual fanfare that preceded such announcements, there was instead the ominous slow beat of a drum followed by the second movement of Beethoven's Fifth Symphony. Finally a funereal voice spoke: "The supreme command of the Wehrmacht announces that the battle of Stalingrad has come to an end. True to its oath of allegiance, the Sixth Army, under the exemplary leadership of Field Marshal Paulus, has been annihilated by the overwhelming superiority of enemy numbers . . . The sacrifice of the Sixth Army was not in vain . . . They died so that Germany might live."[65]

After the debacle at Stalingrad, Germany's total defeat became imaginable. With an eye to the future, judges and lawyers had every incentive to tarnish the character of all members of the Red Orchestra. The men were accused of betraying their country for gold, and in Schulze-Boysen's case, for a leather jacket, sailing boat, and small plot of land.[66] The women became harlots. Roeder showed Harro's mother nude photographs of Libertas that the Gestapo had found in the studio of the sculptor Kurt Schumacher. Although they were of the kind that artists use to model from, Roeder claimed that they were proof of the orgies that the group had held. With prurient glee, he inquired if she knew that her daughter-in-law had had sexual relations with three or four men, "not even all of her own class."[67] By not-so-subtle insinuations, Mildred Harnack-Fish, who had impressed her judges in her first trial as a "highly educated American," the chaste symbol of a noble wife and helpmate to her husband, now became a seducer of young officers, a murderer of German soldiers, and an adulteress whose husband cynically manipulated her love affair. And incredibly, if cruelly, this stain on her posthumous reputation proved nearly indelible.

Gestapo Commissar Strübing's testimony in the postwar investigation of war crimes charges against Roeder typifies the slander and illustrates the helplessness of the relatives of the defendants who were ignorant of the charges when they were invited to "enlighten" the inquisitors of Prinz-Albrecht-Strasse.

Strübing testified that the "entire behavior of Herbert Gollnow was personally unintelligible" to him. When reproached, Gollnow told him bluntly that "his relationship to Frau Harnack was one of sexual bondage." Not content with maligning Mildred, Strübing added that when he interviewed Gollnow's mother, she said that she had never been able to understand why her son had no relationships with women. She had already come to the conclusion that her son had homosexual inclinations.[68]

What is interesting about the alleged affair is not whether it happened but its exploitation in postwar magazine articles, books, and films. In later years, veterans of the Red Orchestra case—prosecutors, judges, and Gestapo investigators, often hiding behind a cloak of anonymity—would further embroider the story of Gollnow's recruitment. A principal theme of the Gestapo—the promiscuity of the women of the Red Orchestra—is luridly amplified in the book *The Red Orchestra* published in France in 1967. The author, journalist Gilles Perrault, quotes an unnamed Gestapo source: "As soon as the other learned that Gollnow was pliable, things happened very fast. In other words, Mildred slept with him. So did Libertas, Schulze-Boysen's wife. In fact, they were both lesbians, so Gollnow was treated to some pretty titillating experiences. . . . Just think of it! Two women, one of them at least—Libertas—a real dazzler, and both of them cultured aristocrats to their fingertips. And there they were, offering themselves to him—showing him pleasures he had never even dreamed of!"[69]

Allegations of sexual misconduct followed a pattern. About Erika von Brockdorff, who received the death sentence for hiding a radio, Strübing stated, "She came from a petit bourgeois family. Her father was a minor postal official. This woman did not have a good reputation, due to her alleged earlier employment as a bar girl. [In reality, she was briefly a model and then, from 1934 to 1941, a stenotypist in a government office.] There was talk in the Schulze-Boysen circle that she had married Cay von Brockdorff for sexual reasons only . . . I myself did not interrogate Frau von Brockdorff. However, one of my comrades who had to conduct discussions with her once told us in one of our daily meetings that while being questioned Frau von Brockdorff had said to him, word for word: 'If I ever get out of here, I'll teach you how to fuck.' "[70]

Strübing continued the slander: "A few times, if I remember

correctly—in at least three cases—she offered her apartment for radio transmitting and for the repair of the radio equipment. There were also paratroop agents among the men who used her apartment. Those men, I think without exception, used the opportunity to sleep with the Countess Brockdorff. The first chamber [*sic*] was of the opinion that in putting her apartment at their disposal the woman was particularly interested in the opportunity for intercourse and possibly she was not seriously interested in the radio transmitting."[71]

The Gestapo final report abounds in such details. What its authors left out of the report, the judges added to the Lüneburg files: Oda Schottmüller, Erika von Brockdorff, Elizabeth Schumacher, and two stenographers were "intimate" with Schulze-Boysen.[72] In a newspaper article, Roeder accused the Countess von Brockdorff of having "intimate relations with four Soviet agents in a single night."[73] Libertas's power as a seductress was such that two Gestapo agents allegedly had to remain in the room at all times during her interrogations.[74] Nor was she spared a final indignity—an autopsy was performed to see if she was pregnant. (She wasn't.)

On a note smuggled to her mother, Libertas wrote, "If I may ask one thing of you, tell everyone, everyone about me. Our death must be a beacon." The Gestapo's purpose in introducing salacious slander into the case was to ensure that history would regard those in the Harnack's circle as libertines, totally "enslaved" by their leaders.

The Red Orchestra trials resulted in death sentences for nineteen women. Although most of these women were not engaged in espionage—many were only engaged in distributing leaflets—they chose to fight against a state that was both atavistic and repressive. From the outset, the Hitler regime strove to limit the role of women to that of wife and mother, restricting their rise in the civil service and most professions. Women were routinely discouraged from academic achievement. Yet almost all the women in the Red Orchestra were professionals: doctors, college teachers, journalists, translators, script writers, librarians, nurses, lawyers, dancers, actresses, artists, photographers, writers, stenographers, and fashion models.

Unlike the conservative resistance in the German military that evolved into the July 20 group, in which women were kept mostly in the dark about the conspiracy, the women of the Red Orchestra were participants. Of the 108 individuals pictured in the Gestapo album, 90 were listed as "active members" (excluding 18 unknown and marginal figures): 54 were men and 36 were women.[75] However, it is also true that the men excluded the women from real decision making. Their leaders, Harnack and Schulze-Boysen, were males; they made the strategic decisions. "Sometimes it was the one, sometimes it was the other," wrote Greta Kuckhoff. "There were often conflicts of opinion, questions that were intensively argued, but there was no struggle for authority, no hard feelings."[76]

In the Red Orchestra the roles were distributed by gender. Women were recruiters, gatherers of information, and translators of texts. They arranged and held illicit meetings. And the women, it must be said, often ran the greater risk, acting as couriers, transporting radios and duplicating machines—often in baby carriages, and, later, concealing illegal radio transmitters. As another female socialist recalled: "The organizational tasks always fell to us women: duplicating and distributing leaflets, carrying messages, hiding illegals, etc. When operations were debated, the situation discussed, pamphlets planned, we were usually not there." [77] Thus the wives, sisters, mothers, and lovers were not consulted even on matters of life-and-death.

No doubt the men believed they were protecting their women by marginalizing their roles, for example, when Adam told the Gestapo that he, not Greta Kuckhoff, had picked up the transmitter from Korotkov. Yet Greta probably spoke for most of the female resisters when she wrote: "I was not told the whole truth, this was uncomfortable—but I was used to not asking."[78]

Mildred's death sentence was confirmed, and she was executed on the evening of February 16. A colleague of Mildred's, a librarian at the Foreign Policy Faculty, preserved a last impression of Mildred.

A coworker had denounced Irmgard Kamlah for subversive remarks. After the Gestapo arrested her, she became Mildred's fellow prisoner at Charlottenburg. In a letter to Axel von Harnack four years later, Kamlah wrote that she could "still not speak about my feelings at that time." She first saw Mildred on the daily "constitutional," the circular walks in the prison yard. The guards excluded Mildred from the common circle and kept her under close observation. Kamlah overheard the matron, with a glance at Mildred, instruct the supervising guard: "You know, no talking, and have her walk alone at all times."

So Mildred walked alone while the others walked in pairs. For half an hour, around the wall of the rectangular prison yard they walked in a circle while Mildred walked on a diagonal path between them. Dr. Kamlah provides a haunting glimpse: "Mildred looked terribly sick and frail, as if she were able to remain upright only with great effort. Nonetheless, she stumbled in great strides from one corner of the prison yard to the other, as if hunted, always looking past us with a fixed stare. She wore a gray hooded coat with some sort of green trim. She had pulled the hood low over her head, so that I could not see her hair. All this remained the same for the next three days, except that during our next walk I knew what it was all about. She was the first *Todeskandidatin* [death candidate], or T.K., whom I had ever seen." (Death candidates wore a special armband with TK sewn on it.)

On Monday, February 15, Berlin schools held memorial services for the soldiers who had fallen at Stalingrad and Goebbels prepared his Sportpalast speech. Calling for "total war," he would ask for the full support and devotion of the German people in their death struggle against their enemies. On that rainy windy night, sometime around nine, a van pulled into the prison yard. When the lights were out and the prisoners in their wooden bunks, Kamlah's cell door opened and a matron brought in a young woman who was crying violently. The woman was half-dressed and carried her belongings and a blanket and a towel over her arm. Blinded by tears, she was pushed along by the guard. She was ordered to put her things on a stool and assigned to a bunk shared by one other person. The cell door clanked shut and the light was turned off. After some time, she had a whispered conversation with the newcomer, who had been Mildred's cellmate until this evening, when Mildred was taken away for execution. The newcomer thought that a request for pardon must have been submitted, since Mildred had spoken of this. But the request must not have been considered. "Mildred had said that not enough time had passed for a decision." I believe I recall the young woman saying that Mildred had not reckoned with her execution occurring so soon. She had thus been stunned when she was taken away to Plötzensee.[79]

"Five months earlier," as her sister-in-law wrote, Mildred "had been forced to exchange the richness of life for the solitude of a dark cell; she had been beautiful then, with shining blond hair. She went to her death as a bowed and white-haired woman. What suffering befell her during those five months? No one will ever know."[80]

In her last hours in Plötzensee, Mildred traced in her neat small hand the words of Whitman's elegy on the death of Lincoln, "When Lilacs Last in the Dooryard Bloom'd," which she called the "most gentle, finest of his long poems.[81] Although Mildred had applied herself to Marx and Lenin, it was the American radicals Whitman and Emerson to whom she now returned. She cherished nature, love, and Goethe. A stanza from her translation of Goethe's "Wanderer's Nightsong" might serve as her epitaph:

> Every bough
> Is at rest
> Now.
> Every crest
> Is in stillness deep.
> The birds are still,
> Wait, for you will
> Also sleep
> death.

As a final gesture in the room where she had to change into a sleeveless, open-necked smock, she gave away a treasured book soaked with her tears, *A History of the Ancient World* by Michael Rostovzeff, a former University of Wisconsin professor. It was inscribed to the prison guard: "To Miss Klaing in memory of Feb. 16, 1943 in the room where you can see this beautiful tree through the window." Before she was led to the guillotine, she spoke her final words to Pastor Poelchau: "And I have loved Germany so much." They sound now as a terrible rebuke.

SEVENTEEN

Epilogue: A Life in the Files

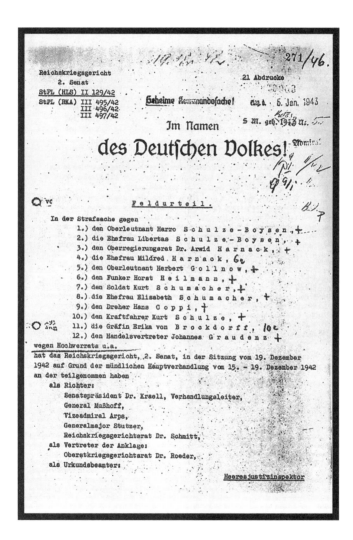

Sentencing document from Mildred's December 1942 trial

A whitewash," the archivist exclaimed, adding that the boxes of files he was about to hand over were a national shame. We were seated in the anteroom of the modern, green-carpeted reading rooms of the State Archives of Lower Saxony in Hanover. The fifteen volumes of files had been closed to the public until the mid-1980s, when a handful of scholars were permitted to see them. An additional favor was granted: the privilege of seeing the two-volume summary by the state attorney Hans-Jürgen Finck, not generally available to researchers. The "Files of the State's Attorney Lüneburg (I Js 16/49) Judicial Inquiry against the former General Judge of the Luftwaffe, Dr. Manfred Roeder, with the Statements of Witnesses," contain more than 2,800 pages of testimony—of wives, parents, friends, Gestapo interrogators, judges, and lawyers—along with newspaper articles and pamphlets collected between 1946 and 1951.[1]

It was indeed a whitewash—Roeder had not been brought to justice—but the investigation must be seen against the background of a quickening Cold War. From this vantage point, it is a revealing case study of "mastering the past" in postwar West Germany, by both Allies and Germans.

In nineteen separate trials between December 15, 1942, and July 1943, the Nazi military court convicted seventy-seven members of the Red Orchestra. Of these, forty-five men and women were sentenced to death and twenty-nine received jail sentences. Some soldiers were ordered to "front probation." Only two defendants were acquitted on grounds of insufficient evidence.[2] The Nazis had cast a wide net; almost everyone connected to Harro Schulze-Boysen was arrested. If they had been picked up only for resistance activities, the sentences might have been lighter, but in the context of a "spy network" engaged in passing secrets to the Soviets at the time of Stalingrad, death sentences were predictable. Among those executed was a nineteen-year-old woman who had merely participated in a poster-pasting action and distributed leaflets. Another twenty-two-year-old female death candidate had simply helped Jews, befriended French prisoners of war, and distributed leaflets.

Days after the fall of Berlin, in the ruins of Prinz-Albrecht-Strasse, a poem by Harro Schulze-Boysen was found jammed in the floorboards of his Gestapo cell. The last stanza expressed what he hoped would be his testament:

The rope and blade
Are not the final arguments
And our judges today
Are not the Last Judgment[3]

The Harnacks, the Schulze-Boysens, and their comrades died clinging to the belief that they would be vindicated. They collected evidence of Nazi war crimes believing that the SS and Gestapo would be brought to justice; they assumed their inquisitors and judges would face not only legal prosecution but also the sterner judgment of history. It was not to be.

Immediately after the war, a group of survivors of the so-called Red Orchestra trials, including playwright Günther Weisenborn, former Prussian culture minister Adolf Grimme, and Greta Kuckhoff, banded together to demand a trial for Manfred Roeder, whom Grimme called "one of the worst criminals to make a travesty of justice in those years."[4] In 1945, they submitted a brief to the International Military Tribunal at Nuremberg, charging that Roeder had committed "crimes against humanity" by treating relatives of the defendants with brutality and extorting testimony by torture.[5] A central element in the case was Roeder's treatment of Mildred Harnack-Fish. He had not allowed her to write or to receive visitors; he had approved torture; he had forced her (it was said) to watch the execution of her husband; he had pressured Goering and Hitler to secure a death sentence against her; he had forbidden the return of her body to her family. Most of these accusations came from Falk Harnack, who, in his testimony at Nuremberg, called Roeder "one of the bloodiest and cruelest persecutors of the German anti-Fascists."[6]

A call for witnesses was published in the press, and the VVN (*Vereinigung der Verfolgten des Naziregimes*), an organization of the victims of fascism, began collecting evidence. The war was over and resistance members expected to be honored. Initially, they were candid: in March 1947 Greta Kuckhoff, for example, acknowledged her links with the Soviets.[7] Meanwhile, for their part, the Americans arrested Roeder at the end of the war. Although they were aware of the role he had played in the Red Orchestra trials, he survived by shrewdly rationing his insights into Soviet intelligence networks, first for the British and then for the Americans. In 1948, having pumped him dry on the subject of the "Bolshevist high treason and espionage organization in the Reich and Western Europe,"[8] the American occupation authorities found no justification for trying "Othello," as they code-named him, for "crimes against humanity." Instead, after refusing a Russian request for custody, they released him to the German authorities in the western occupation zone, who were supposed to look into the charges against him.[9]

Erhard Heinke, a Nuremberg prosecutor, was assigned the case. In June 1948, the following short item appeared in the Nuremberg *Telegraf*:

> In the persecution of the members of the Schulze-Boysen/Harnack resistance group, the then judge advocate Colonel Manfred Roeder, presently in the Neustadt internment camp, played a particularly evil role. Roeder is to be charged with crimes against humanity. All members of the resistance movement are hereby urged to submit reports on Roeder's actions. Photostats of documents which may support the case against Roeder are also solicited. All material is to be addressed to Attorney Dr. Heinke, Nuremberg, Palace of Justice, Room 355.[10]

However, by 1949, the year when the two Germanys came into being (and coincidentally the year Roeder was released from detention) it was already apparent that in the Federal Republic, preferment went to those Germans who could prove they hated the Communists more than the Fascists. Resisters who had survived the trials of 1943 and who, like Grimme, chose to settle in the West, prudently chose to distance themselves from colleagues in the East. In 1949, Grimme, now head of Northwest German Radio in Hamburg, told an official visitor that he wanted "nothing to do with Frau Kuckhoff politically." He disassociated himself from a 1947 article in the Communist daily, *Neues Deutschland*, in which Greta said that the survivors "would not rest until the stain left by men such as Roeder was erased from the face of Germany."[11] Others declined to testify because they feared having their relatives' names listed along with so-called traitors. By December 1949, Kuckhoff, by then a senior official in East Germany, had given up hope for a Roeder trial because, she wrote, "conditions in West Germany are such that no equitable outcome can be expected."[12]

After his release Roeder returned to his wife's home in Neetze, near Lüneburg, where a local prosecutor, Dr. Finck, pursued the inquiry on behalf of the Germans until November 1951, when the investigation was suspended. Finck's two summary volumes ("the whitewash"), abundantly confirm the distaste of lawyers, whether American or German, for trying their own, for executing the law, even in Hitler's Germany. One researcher, on examining Finck's report, concluded that Finck had dismissed the charges against Roeder as "Communist intrigues."[13]

It is chilling to read the Lüneburg files, for in them Roeder and his Gestapo colleagues are the accusers and not the defendants. It is the Red Orchestra members who are being retried—this time by history. As the dismayed and critical West German diplomat Ulrich Sahm has written, Roeder's behavior "not only appears justified but desirable in terms of national interest."[14]

In a 1951 letter to Weisenborn, Schulze-Boysen's mother, Marie-Luise, spoke for the disillusioned relatives: "Perhaps we'll see one another in a trial in Lüneburg again, but it is also possible that nothing will come of it. The important thing is that Roeder is finally silenced."[15] Meanwhile, the focus of all this attention, former General Judge Manfred Roeder, shrugged off these accusations as attempts by survivors and relatives to "make themselves appear as martyrs."[16] In 1952, he published his version of the events in a book, *Die Rote Kapelle*. (Roeder ended his days in Glashütten, a small town in the Taunus.)

The fate of the members of the Sonderkommission Rote Kapelle was best summed up by resistance scholar Johannes Tuchel: "No German court has ever opened proceedings against the Gestapo who participated at the RSHA in the torture of Red Orchestra inmates. No German court has ever investigated whether this did not constitute accessory to murder."[17]

The indulgence of the Third Reich judiciary was not confined to the Red Orchestra trials. In the entire postwar period, beginning with de-Nazification trials under Allied occupation, not a single judge or prosecutor was ever convicted for involvement in the judicial travesties that characterized Nazi courts.

After the war, resistance survivors expected to be honored. This was not to be the case in West Germany: in the early postwar years resistance members were sidelined and their pensions went unpaid. Meanwhile the Americans and the British recruited former Gestapo members for the newly formed West German intelligence services. After the Cold War began in earnest in 1947, the families of the men and women who had given their lives resisting Hitler were suspect. Hence the particular bitterness of survivors like Falk Harnack.*

Falk witnessed the resurrection of high-ranking Nazis in the Adenauer years even as Western intelligence agencies suspicious of his left-wing views kept him under surveillance.

"The Americans copied the system [of phone taps and surveillance] that the Gestapo had," Falk told me. "The Gestapo developed a very good system of entrapment and the Americans took it all over—instead of directing it against the Nazis, they directed it against the anti-Fascists after the war. The Americans employed all these National Socialist criminals . . . in the CIA! They all worked for the CIA and defamed us [the resistance] after the war. When I was in Munich, I became acquainted with some very good American officers. They were the first people to come after the war. They were Jews—German or Austrian refugees. They could distinguish between a German anti-Fascist and a Nazi. Even then they warned me, 'Be careful, the next group will work together with all these Nazis.' And then came the German secret service, recruited by General Gehlen.† He hired all these people from the Gestapo and the SS. All of this is very, very dark, very dark. A disgrace for the United States that it cooperated with these people,

---

* Falk Harnack, stationed in the army at Chemnitz, became an important link to the White Rose group led by Hans and Sophie Scholl. Composed of university students at Munich, the group distributed leaflets calling for passive resistance against the Nazis. After the defeat at Stalingrad, the sixth and final leaflet was distributed—the Scholls dropped some from the staircase of the main building of the university on February 18, 1943. A janitor saw them and detained them and summoned the Gestapo. The group was arrested and the leaders were executed. Falk, who was not present, was tried with other members of the group by the People's Court but was not convicted.

† General Richard Gehlen served during World War II as the head of the Foreign Armies East (FHO). The Allies recruited him after the war to run the Bundesnachrichtendienst (BND), the West German Intelligence Service similar to the CIA.

these mass murderers. And the people that knew the truth, they were left on the outside. They were not considered."

In his condemnation of Americans, Falk excepted Donald Heath, who returned to occupied Germany as the director of the Office of Political Affairs for the American military government (OMGUS). Heath was notably helpful to the Harnack family, assisting Jane Donner and her husband, then in Allied custody, to resettle in America. In an interview before his death, Falk Harnack recounted a dramatic reunion in 1947, when Heath asked him to describe precisely the events leading up to the arrest and trial of Mildred and Arvid. "We were both alone in the garden room," Falk recalled. "When I finished, I'll never forget how all of a sudden he burst into tears and got up and went out into the garden unable to talk anymore."[18] According to his son, Heath's career was clouded by his contacts with the Harnacks, though he did serve in Bulgaria (and was expelled as a spy). Later he was posted to Indochina and Saudi Arabia as ambassador.

Thus in the West, the members of the Red Orchestra were written out of history, their politics caricatured and their personal courage only backhandedly acknowledged. In the East, at least initially, they were all but invisible for a different reason: the Soviets had no wish to draw attention to their intelligence operations, especially in Germany. Only years later, in East Germany, when the winds had shifted, were survivors like Greta Kuckhoff permitted to publish reminiscences of the Berlin underground, and then only in a sanitized form. The GDR also issued stamps commemorating the Harnacks, Harro Schulze-Boysen, Adam Kuckhoff, and the Coppis. In January 1970, the Russians summoned Falk Harnack to the embassy of the Soviet Union in Berlin where they gave him the posthumous orders they had awarded the Harnacks. Arvid received the Order of the Red Banner, the highest order of the Red Army, and Mildred, the Order of the Fatherland War, First Class, its highest civilian award.[19]

In the United States, Mildred was forgotten. At first there was a burst of local pride when, in 1947, the alumni magazine of the University of Wisconsin published the first full account of her fate (but omitting any reference to the Red Orchestra's links with Soviet intelligence). One alumnus, Richard Lloyd Jones, the conservative editor of the *Tulsa Tribune,* wrote the university's Board of Regents to suggest that "somewhere on the campus there should be a memorial on which is inscribed 'don't write—never forget me.' " Regent William Campbell replied, "Certainly she is the Nathan Hale or Edith Cavell of the university." Campbell assured the newspaper editor that everyone was enthusiastic about the idea of honoring Mildred Fish Harnack: "It will not be allowed to die out."[20]

To be sure of their ground, however, a university official asked Wisconsin's senior senator, Alexander Wiley, to initiate an investigation in Washington.[21] The senator looked into the matter and replied that an army investigation had found no official records "pertaining to underground activities" (here he means resistance as opposed to espionage) of the Harnacks.[22] That the university declined to honor Mildred Fish, Class of '25, suggests that Senator Wiley warned the university that their heroine was surely a Red and probably a spy.

In fact, in January 1946, the War Crimes group of the U.S. Army opened an official inquiry into the death of Mildred Harnack-Fish. But by November, Americans were distancing themselves from the case. A war crimes officer wrote that "although the evidence uncovered to date tends to indicate that these persons were tortured in order to secure evidence upon which they were tried, it has also been determined that considerable of the evidence connecting Mildred Harnack with the underground activities came from letters and notes written by and to her from other members of the underground."[23] In December, after interviews with surviving members of the Red Orchestra, the investigators concluded that "Mildred Harnack was in fact deeply involved in underground activities aimed to overthrow the government of Germany; that the trial (although secret), was conducted before five judges of the highest state military court and that this court, in view of the activities in which she had been engaged, was justified in imposing the sentence which was imposed."[24] The case was closed.

Ponder the remarkable implications of this judgment: one set of lawyers working for the U.S. Army upholds the judgment of another set of lawyers working for Hitler's Reich and concludes that "the highest state military court" was "justified" in ordering the beheading of Mildred Harnack-Fish. What the army lawyers did not note is that the "highest state military court" tried her twice, the first time sentencing her to six years of hard labor. Thus under their own harsh rules, Nazi judges did not initially find enough evidence, even after torturing the defendants, to justify a capital sentence. Only after Hitler's direct intervention and his refusal to confirm that prison sentence was she retried and convicted of seducing a German officer to obtain military secrets. In these proceedings, she did not have the rudimentary right of counsel in secret trials whose transcripts have been conveniently lost. The witnesses against her were Gestapo agents whose testimony is contained in their final report.

That Mildred was aware of Arvid's resistance and espionage activities is not in dispute: of course she was. The real question is whether her own involvement in espionage was sufficient to justify her execution. Here the evidence consists entirely of the lost and suspect testimony of Herbert Gollnow, the German officer who was her student. It is far more believable that she was beheaded because Hitler wanted a blood sacrifice, because her trial coincided with the Nazi debacle at Stalingrad, and because she was a despised American and left-winger.

Mildred's politics are likewise not in dispute. Her politics evolved from Emerson, by way of the Wisconsin Progressives, to Marx. Her radicalism was reinforced by the shock of the Great Depression and her hatred of Hitler. If she deluded herself about the realities of Stalin's Russia, her offence was surely no greater than that of Neville Chamberlain and his circle of appeasers, who gullibly believed that Hitler could be trusted when he said that the Sudetenland was his final territorial demand. Invariably left out in the reckoning of the Harnacks' politics is their abiding commitment to the America of Franklin Roosevelt, as tangibly shown by the risk Arvid took in purveying economic intelligence each week to Donald Heath, the U.S. Treasury's agent at the Berlin embassy.

But the matter goes deeper. Consider, for example, the consensual Western view about the July 20 conspirators, whose courage was unquestionable but whose politics were a bundle of contradictions. Some were conservative monarchists, and most wanted to preserve the greater Germany of 1939, which included Austria and the Sudeten region of Czechoslovakia. Repelled by Hitler, many hoped that Allied help in eliminating Hitler would be forth-coming, although it was fundamentally up to the Germans them-selves to eliminate a criminal regime.

Still, so obvious was the sincerity of these resistance heroes, so manifest their courage in hideous circumstances, that their political lapses have been excused or overlooked. In the case of the Red Orchestra, the reverse is true. Their political sins are kept in the foreground while their moral courage is allowed to fade into the background. When they are remembered, it is to recall that they wanted to substitute a Red dictatorship for a Brown one, even though the facts contradict this view.

What might be called the orthodox Cold War judgment on the Red Orchestra is summed up in a Central Intelligence Agency study commissioned by the Nixon administration in 1973. U.S. Document 0-7708 deals with the question of treason from a rigidly Cold War viewpoint: "A number of German and some non-German writers have grappled with the problem of whether those Germans who worked as spies for the Soviets were heroes or trai-tors. For the most part these ruminations bog down in legalisms (*Landesverrat vs. Hochverrat*), abstractions, or emotionalism. In no case could those who opposed the Nazis and actively sought their downfall be considered traitors to the German heritage or peoples. But there is a clear moral distinction between those whose goal was the restoration of a representative indigenous German Government and those who sought to exploit anti-fascism for the benefit of the Soviet Union."[25]

Falk Harnack wrote in 1963 that there was

a fundamental, worldwide difference between high treason and espionage committed in a democratic state or in a bestial dictatorship. In a democracy, the opposition has legal meth-ods and can work for a change in national politics. Counter to this is a dictatorship, where all opposition to the govern-ment is brutally suppressed and (the facts speak for them-selves) stamped out. The Hitler dictatorship killed 100,000 of its opponents, millions of others were eliminated on racial grounds, countless friendly nations were invaded, all had to be destroyed in the interests of the German people. But Hit-ler's dictatorship had at its disposal limitless power; it had extraordinary means of support. Only the most extreme measures had any real chance of success. The (resistance) acted from moral duty. Above all, the people had to be torn from the criminal path that Hitler's leadership had trodden, and a national catastrophe had to be avoided. That was the opinion both of the right as well as the left resistance.[26]

That so few citizens did challenge a criminal regime remains a source of shame and bafflement in Germany. Yet only too slowly has the world become aware of the courageous minority, the "other Germany," ranging from the poor and powerless to the well-born and affluent, who did resist. If most German universities too readily succumbed to Nazi purges, some of the greatest academic families did not bend. Three members of the Harnack family were executed for treason. Besides Mildred and Arvid, Arvid's cousin Ernst, the son of Adolf von Harnack, was hanged for his part in the resistance. At the time of his imprisonment, Arvid had sent him a message through Axel urging Ernst to leave Germany immediately. Arvid's cousin failed to heed the warning. After the events of July 20, 1944, Ernst sought refuge with various friends and family members, but he was arrested September 29 and executed on March 5, 1945, at Plötzensee.

Other members of the extended Harnack family, many of whom had been present at the 1930 memorial ceremony for Adolf von Harnack, also paid for their role in resistance activities. On almost the same day that Karl Bonhoeffer received the Goethe Prize, Germany's highest academic honor, his son Dietrich was arrested. Karl Bonhoeffer was to lose two sons and two sons-in-law to the Gestapo. On the night of April 9, 1945, as the Russians were fighting their way through the outskirts of Berlin, the chief of the Gestapo's fourth division, Walter Huppenkothen, ordered the execution at the Flossenbürg concentration camp of Dietrich Bonhoeffer, along with Hans Oster and Admiral Canaris. Bonhoeffer's brother-in-law Hans von Dohnanyi met a similar fate at Huppenkothen's hands at the Sachsenhausen camp. On April 23, 1945, a week before Hitler's suicide in a Berlin bunker, guards took Albrecht Haushofer, Klaus Bonhoeffer, and Bonhoeffer's brother-in-law, Rüdiger Schleicher, from their cells at Berlin's Moabit prison and shot them in the back of the neck, dumping the bodies in the rubble of a nearby park.

Since 1933, wrote Agnes von Zahn-Harnack, the Harnacks had been asked countless times,

> What would your father, what would the great university professors of the turn of the century say to what is happening now in Germany? The question has been asked about the fathers, and it has been answered by the sons and daughters, unreservedly and in one voice. Erwin Planck,* Klaus and Dietrich Bonhoeffer, Rüdiger Schleicher, Hans von Dohnanyi, Arvid and Mildred Harnack, Ernst von Harnack: they fought and died for the ideals which their fathers handed down to them by teaching and example, for justice and truth, for the necessity of man once again becoming a *res sacra*, a sacred thing, to his fellow man; they fought this battle in shared conviction with their wives and children, all equally prepared to make the final sacrifice should it be required.[27]

These were the ideals that Mildred shared and for which she gave her life. They represented the Germany that Mildred loved. Her sacrifice has been indifferently reciprocated. Wisconsin ignored her existence until 1986, when a Milwaukee lawyer, Arthur Heitzer, commandeered support for an Assembly Bill designating her birthday, September 16, Mildred Harnack Day, a special observance day for the Wisconsin public schools. Heitzer also shored up the faltering legislators when the American Legion attacked them in 1987. State Commander Lloyd A. Wagener charged that "It is inconceivable that our school children have been legislated to observe a day in remembrance of a woman who, by her own activities, renounced the free, democratic society that now honors her while school children are not allowed to recognize their God in a classroom."[28] In East Germany, her memory was belatedly recalled when her name was bestowed on a secondary school in 1976. After unification in 1990, when the City of Berlin School Act was extended to the east, the school was compelled to give up its former name. Over the protests of parents and staff its name was changed to the politically antiseptic Comprehensive School Number 5. The principal then led a campaign to restore the name. After all, she said, Mildred Harnack's deeds were not discredited

---

* Erwin Planck (1893–1945) was the son of the physicist Max Planck and a Grunewald neighbor of the Bonhoeffers, Harnacks, and Delbrücks. He was executed at Plötzensee as part of the July 20 Plot.

by a regime that exploited her memory. A member of the local school board went further: "Some of these people," he said, "would have risen from their graves had they known how their names were being used."[29] On February 16, 1993, the fiftieth anniversary of her death, her name was once again restored to the Mildred Harnack school.

In reliving her life and delving for six years in archives east and west, I could find no reason for denying her that honor. Her obscurity, though unjust, is somehow appropriate, for her life suggests how an ordinary person can rise to extraordinary circumstances, and acquit herself with remarkable courage and dignity. Her body, after her execution, escaped oblivion only because an anatomy professor, Dr. Stieve, charged with its dissection recognized her remains. He had them cremated and returned the urn with her ashes to the Harnack family after the war. They are buried in a simple grave, with two pine trees as sentries and a granite rock with a bronze inscription: "Arvid Harnack, Ph.D., Mildred Harnack, Ph.D."

Clara Harnack in front of the former Gestapo headquarters in 1945.

A final note on Martha Dodd. When she returned to the United States in 1937, she determined to pursue her political and literary causes. In a letter to Boris Vinogradov, which arrived in Moscow in July 1938, after his death, she confessed that she had fallen in love again and recently married. On June 16, wearing a black velvet gown, she was wed to Chicago millionaire Alfred Stern on her father's Virginia farm. Having the means to resume her literary career, she wrote a memoir about her halcyon days in Berlin. *Through Embassy Eyes*, published in 1939, became a best-seller. She joined with her brother Bill in editing her father's diaries, *Ambassador Dodd's Diary* (1941) and wrote two novels, *Sowing the Wind* (1945) and *The Searching Light* (1955). She flirted with Hollywood and Otto Preminger in the hopes that her books about Berlin would be made into a movie following the success in 1943 of *Mission to Moscow*, a pro-Soviet film based on Joseph Davies's adventures as a credulous American ambassador in the Russian capital.

During the 1940s, the Sterns presided over a salon whose guest list featured prominent leftists like Lillian Hellman,[1] Paul Robeson, and, during his campaign for the presidency in 1948, Henry Wallace. One guest characterized the Stern set as *"la très haute société communiste."*[2] Among those in attendance were the third secretary of the Soviet embassy (and NKGB station chief), Vassili Zubilin (also known as Zarubin), and his wife, Helen. Zubilin introduced the Sterns to Boris Morros, Hollywood producer turned Soviet agent, who later metamorphosed into an FBI informant. The Sterns gave this "charming counterspy" $130,000 for a music business, which he was to operate as a Soviet cover for agents and couriers. Although Alfred was the financier, Martha's forte, Morros claimed, was talent spotting. She recruited new volunteers including the most useful Jane Foster Zlatovski, a painter and former member of the OSS in Indonesia, who was willing to pass along information including names, photographs, and biographies of U.S. agents, to the Soviet Union.

By 1947, thanks to information provided by Morros, the FBI had the Sterns under continuous surveillance. The couple's 10,400-page FBI file contains verbatim transcriptions of telephone calls and mail intercepts, including letters from Greta Kuckhoff and Jürgen Kuczynski in Berlin. Tipped off by a gossip column item that a daughter of the former ambassador to Germany was being summoned before the House un-American Activities Committee and alarmed by the death sentences in the Rosenberg "atomic spy" trial, the Sterns fled with their adopted son Robert to Mexico in 1953.

Four years later, Jack and Myra Soble and Jacob Albam, all friends of the Sterns, were indicted for espionage, and in Mexico, the Sterns were served with a Federal Grand Jury subpoena. They accepted $936 in travel expenses for their return to New York for questioning in the Soble case. Fearing extradition proceedings against them, the Sterns instead bolted first to Amsterdam and then to Prague. When they failed to appear in court, they too were indicted. Of the six counts in the charge, one—conspiring to transmit U.S. defense information to the Soviet Union—carried the death penalty. Among the familiar names in the indictment were the Zubilins, Jane Zlatovski and her husband, George, a former interrogator with U.S. military intelligence in Austria, and General Alexander Korotkov, the Harnack's Soviet contact, who was running the KGB's networks in the West.[3]

In 1957, the Sterns began their peregrinations through the Soviet bloc. At one point they tried living in Cuba, but they settled in Prague. In the 1970s, Martha decided to write another memoir of her days in Berlin and contacted journalist friends who had known Boris Vinogradov and the Harnacks. It developed that the Soviets too remained interested in the lovers. Former *Chicago Tribune* correspondent Sigrid Schulz wrote Martha that her assistant, Detlev von der Schulenburg, while a prisoner of war in Russia, had been repeatedly questioned about Boris. "The main interest of the questioners centered on the problem of whether your friend had given us [the American press] any information."[4]

In 1979, a reluctant Justice Department dismissed the indictment against the Sterns, explaining that two witnesses essential to the prosecution had died. It would have been possible for the Sterns to return to the United States but they owed a considerable sum to the IRS in back taxes as well as a fine of $50,000 for contempt of court. The Sterns remained abroad. Alfred died in Prague in 1986 and Martha in 1990.

Thanks to KGB files and the so-called Venona* decrypts, in which she appears, we now know that Martha Dodd was more than a gullible fellow traveler. Certainly her efforts on behalf of the Soviet Union in the postwar era cannot be attributed to "anti-Fascist sentiments."

Among those members of the Red Orchestra who survived the war was Greta Kuckhoff. She rose to prominence in East Germany as the vice president of the Peace Council and director of the Central Bank. After some difficulty with the German authorities, who presumably did not want her to reveal Moscow's intelligence blunders, she published her memoir in 1979.

Anatoli Gurevich, the Soviet intelligence agent whose arrival in Berlin and return to Brussels was the unwitting cause of the fall of the Red Orchestra, survived the war in German hands. He aided Heinz Pannwitz, the head of the special commission "Red Orchestra" in France in the radio playback game (*Funkspiel*), the object of which was to get Moscow to divulge Soviet operatives in the West, an operation that met with some success. In May 1945 Gurevich allowed himself to be arrested by French troops on the Austrian border. He was returned to France and turned over to the Soviet military mission in Paris. Upon his return to Moscow in June, he was arrested by the NKGB. A military court sentenced him to twenty years in the gulag for collaborating with the Gestapo. After the amnesty that followed Stalin's death in 1955, he

---

* Venona was the codename given by the U.S. Army Signal Intelligence Service to the project that decrypted intercepted Soviet diplomatic telegrams. The resulting messages revealed how the Soviets had penetrated various U.S. government agencies and had stolen military secrets. The Venona decrypts were used most famously to convict the Rosenbergs.

was released. But after protesting his treatment to Khrushchev, he was again arrested in 1958. He was released in 1960 on condition that he remain silent about his Red Orchestra activities. (Upon their return to the Soviet Union, Trepper and Wenzel were also arrested. Stalin wanted no witnesses to his failure to act on intelligence warnings of Operation Barbarossa, in which 100,000 Soviets were taken prisoner in the first hours of the invasion.) Gurevich was "rehabilitated" in 1991 and lives at the time of this writing in St. Petersburg, where he is reportedly at work on a memoir.[5] In 1996, Hans Coppi, the son of the Red Orchestra's radio operator and biographer of Schulze-Boysen, hosted a documentary, *Verlorenes Leben* (Lost Life), on Gurevich for German and French television.

Alexander Korotkov left Berlin in June 1941 and reappeared there in 1945 as the KGB's principal resident. A year later, he returned to Moscow as the head of the KGB's illegals directorate, which oversaw operations directed at foreign countries such as the United States. In 1957, he was once again stationed at Karlshorst (Berlin) as the intermediary between the KGB and the Ministry for State Security (Stasi). Due to increasing tensions between Korotkov and KGB Chairman Alexander Shelepin, he was recalled to Moscow where he died of a heart attack after a tennis match in 1961. Markus Wolf, chief of East German foreign intelligence, delivered his eulogy.[6]

GLOSSARY AND ABBREVIATIONS

Abwehr   German military intelligence specializing in espionage, counterespionage and sabotage for the German high command
ARPLAN   Arbeitsgemeinschaft zum Studium der sowjetrussischen Planwirtschaft
BA   Bundesarchiv Koblenz
BAP   Bundesarchiv, Potsdam
BGA   Bund der Geistesarbeiter; sometimes called Bund geistiger Berufe
BND   Bundesnachrichtendienst; German Foreign Intelligence Service, similar to the CIA
Brigadeführer   SS equivalent of major-general rank
CIA   Central Intelligence Agency
CIC   Counter Intelligence Corps
Comintern   Communist International
FBI   Federal Bureau of Investigation
FOI   Freedom of Information
Funkabwehr   Radio counterespionage or signals security
GDW   Gedenkstätte Deutscher Widerstand, Berlin
Generalrichter   Roughly equivalent to Judge Advocate
GDR   German Democratic Republic (formerly East Germany)
Gestapo   (Geheime Staatspolizei) Secret State Police—later Branch IV of the RHSA
GRU   Glavnoye Razvedyvatelnoye Upravlenie; military intelligence of the Red Army
GU   Justus-Liebig University, Giessen
HU   Humboldt University Archives
IfZ   Institut für Zeitgeschichte (Institute of Contemporary History), Munich
IML   Institute for Marxism and Leninism of the Central Committee of the SED
KGB   Komitet Gosudarstvennoye Bezopasnosti; Committee for State Security
KPD   Kommunistische Partei Deutschlands; the German Communist Party
LOC   Library of Congress
NA   National Archives
NKVD   Narodnyi Kommissariat Vnutrennikh Del; People's Commissariat of Internal Affairs (1934–1943); after 1943, the NKGB

NSA   National Security Agency

NYPL   New York Public Library

Oberregierungsrat   High rank of the German civil service equivalent to lieutenant colonel

Obersturmbannführer   An SS rank equivalent to lieutenant colonel

OGPU   Obyedinyonnoye Gosudarstvennoye Politicheskoye Upravleniye, Russian state political administration, forerunner of the NKVD (1923–1934)

OKH   Oberkommando des Heeres; High Command of the German Army

OKW   Obercommando der Wehrmacht; the High Command of the German Armed Forces

OSS   Office of Strategic Services; forerunner of the CIA

RC   Russian Center for the Preservation and Study of Records of Modern History

Regierungsrat   The most junior rank of the higher civil service

Reichsführer   Himmler's title as head of the SS

Reichskriminaldirektor   The rank held by Heinrich Müller as head of the Gestapo

RFIS   Russian Foreign Intelligence Service Archive

RK   Rote Kapelle

RKG   Reichskriegsgericht; Reich Court Martial, Germany's senior military court

RSHA   Reichssicherheitshauptamt; the combined Security Police (Gestapo and Criminal Police)

RWM   Reichswirtschaftsministerium—the German Economics Ministry

SA   Sturmabteilung; the Brown Shirts, who acted as a paramilitary group during the rise of Hitler

SD   Sicherheitsdienst; the intelligence service of the SS

SHSW   State Historical Society of Wisconsin

SLD   Sächsische Landesbibliotek, Dresden

SS   Schutzstaffel; originally Hitler's body guard. Under Himmler it became a state within a state. It included the Gestapo.

UWA   University of Wisconsin Archives

VVN   Vereinigung der Verfolgten des Naziregimes; a postwar association of the victims of the Nazi regime

NOTES

CHAPTER ONE

The description of Mildred Harnack-Fish's final hours was recreated from several sources. After the war, Pastor Poelchau published two books on the events at Plötzensee, *Die letzten Stunden* and *Die Ordnung der Bedrängen*. A further article about the prison pastor, "Der Mann, der tausend Tode sah," appeared in the *Schweizischer Illustrierte Zeitung*, April 4, 1948. A report by the director of the Berlin Anatomical Institute, Professor Stieve, appeared in the *Frankfurter Rundshau* (December 31, 1945). Other details of the death chamber at Plötzensee are from Gostomski and Loch, *Der Tod von Plötzensee*, and Haase, *Das Reichskriegsgericht und der Widerstand gegen die nationalsozialistische Herrschaft*, pp. 137–43. Vols. 1, 8, and 12, of the *Case against Manfred Roeder* in the archives of Lower-Saxony (Hanover) contain further material. Mildred's translations of Goethe are in the Humboldt University Archive (Berlin). Her death certificate is in the files of the Stadtamt Berlin-Charlottenburg. Falk Harnack's report, "Mildred Harnacks letzte Stunden" (Gedächtnisprotokoll nach dem Bericht von Pfarrer Poelchau, February 1943), is reproduced in Brüning, *Mildred Harnack-Fish: Variationen über das Thema Amerika*. "Mildred Harnacks letzte Stunden" is in the Falk Harnack archive at the GDW.

CHAPTER TWO

1 *New York Times*, April 11 and May 15, 1943.
2 *Milwaukee Journal*, May 16, 1943.
3 A. G. Cicognani, archbishop of Laodicea, to Harriette Esch, September 25, 1943.
4 *Washington Evening Star*, December 4, 1947.
5 *Washington Post*, April 19, 1947.
6 Martha Dodd Stern, February 16, 1948, FBI file no. 100-57, 453-333.
7 "The Rote Kapelle," 2:340 (RG 319 ZA 020253), NA. I have corrected the CIA's mistakes. In copying information from p. 352 of Boveri's book, the CIA identified Louis Lochner as Louis LECHNER and Martha Dodd as Mrs. Alfred K. STEIN. Also reproduced in CIA, *The Rote Kapelle*, p. 290.
8 Memorandum dated February 21, 1946, to Lt. Col. Bruton from D. P. Hervey, Attorney Prosecution Section, RG 153, file 12-2262, NA.

9 Memorandum to Captain Sloan, RG 153, 7708 War Crimes Group, from Albert R. Perry Jr., Crimes Liaison Officer, November 21, 1946, file 12-2262, NA.

10 Lt. Col. Ellis to Lt. Col. Herte, Chief Investigation Section, January 15, 1947, RG 153, file 12-2262, NA.

CHAPTER THREE

1 MH-F, "Outline of a Novel," pp. 1, 4, Mildred Harnack Papers, HU.

2 Meyer, "Twilight of a Golden Age," *American Mercury*, August 1933. For turn of the century Milwaukee, I also relied upon Meyer, *Bucket Boy* and *Making Light of the Times*; Gregory, *The House on Jefferson Street*; Ferber, *Dawn O'Hara*; the *WPA Guide to Wisconsin*; Still, *Milwaukee, The History of a City*; and Austin, *The Milwaukee Story*.

3 Arthur Heitzer interviewed Harriette Esch in 1987. Her daughters, Jane Donner Sweeney and Marion Potter, also provided access to her childhood diary and their genealogical research.

4 Marion Potter interview with Arthur Heitzer.

5 MH-F, "A Turn of the Tide," p. 2, HU.

6 MH-F, ibid., p. 7.

7 MH-F to GF, December 11, 1933. (Unless otherwise noted all of Mildred's letters are from the Jane Donner Sweeney collection.)

8 MH-F to GF, January 22, 1931. The friend was a Swedish writer, Hildur Dixelius who was married to Mildred's philosophy professor, Ernst von Aster.

9 MH-F, "Journal of Memories," p. 2, HU.

10 MH-F, ibid., p. 13.

11 MH-F, ibid., p. 14.

12 Although no copy of the story has been found, "*Mein Kamerad*," is described in a campaign flyer "Hear Ye, Hear Ye." The announcement proclaims the candidacy of Mildred Fish for the Comet editorship along with her qualifications: "Vote for Mildred Fish because she is entirely fitted to make the next year's Comet a record-breaking one." Collection of Jane Donner Sweeney.

13 Milwaukee Public Schools, *Our Roots Grow Deep*, p. 29.

14 MH-F, "The Death of Frank Burke," p. 1, HU.

15 MH-F, "A Journal of Memories," p. 19, HU.

16 MH-F to GF, September 20, 1932.

CHAPTER FOUR

1 "Nazis Ban Sheean Works," *New York Times*, January 18, 1940.

2 Leonard, *The Locomotive God*, p. 257.

3 Slaughter, *Only the Past Is Ours*, pp. 111ff.

4 Quoted in the *Daily Cardinal*, February 16, 1924.

5 Curti and Carstensen, *The University of Wisconsin*, 2:531.

6 Gregory, *The House on Jefferson Street*, p. 106.

7 *Daily Cardinal*, May 7, 1922.

8 *Wisconsin Literary Magazine*, October 1923, p. 3.

9 *Daily Cardinal*, October 6, 1923.

10 *Daily Cardinal*, November 13, 1921.

11   Gregory, "In Memoriam: Margery Latimer (no date or citation), Toomer Papers, Beineke Library, Yale University.

12   Latimer to Mildred Hergenhan, June 1923, Toomer Papers, Beineke Library, Yale University.

13   Latimer to Blanche Mattias, Fall 1924, University of Wisconsin–Madison, Library, Microfilm 7416.

14   Latimer to Blanche Mattias, February 1924, University of Wisconsin–Library, Microfilm 7416.

15   Rakosi, *The Collected Prose of Carl Rakosi*, p. 91.

16   Gregory, *The House on Jefferson Street*, p. 121.

17   Rakosi, op. cit., p. 100.

18   Latimer, *Guardian Angel*, pp. 181ff.

19   Fearing editorial, *Wisconsin Literary Magazine*, April 1923.

20   *Daily Cardinal*, November 13, 1923.

21   *Daily Cardinal*, January 19, 1924.

22   MH-F, "Silver and Gold," *Wisconsin Literary Magazine*, February 1923, pp. 112–13.

23   MH-F, "Mechanism," *Wisconsin Literary Magazine*, October 1923, p. 25.

24   *Daily Cardinal*, March 20, 1924.

25   *Daily Cardinal*, March 21, 1924.

26   Meyer, "William Ellery Leonard," *American Mercury*, July 1934, p. 340.

27   Ibid. For the description of Leonard, I have also consulted Leiser, "Wisconsin Writers IV: William Ellery Leonard," *Wisconsin Journal of Education* February 1926; "William Ellery Leonard: Some Memories and New Poems," *Tomorrow Magazine*, May 1, 1949.

28   *Daily Cardinal*, September 28, 1924.

29   Fiedler to author, March 27, 1991.

30   Elizabeth Bunting Fine to author, February 6, 1990.

31   Leiser to MH-F, July 31, 1932.

32   Leiser to Selma Waterman, September 4, 1946 and MH-F to CL, January 12, 1939.

33   MH-F to Inge Havemann, Christmas, 1930, Falk Harnack Collection, GDW.

34   MH-F, "Prothalamion," p. 1, Harnack Papers, HU.

35   MH-F to Harriette and Fred Esch, June 1, 1940.

36   MH-F to GF, July 13, 1931.

37   MH-F to GF, February 24, 1929.

CHAPTER FIVE

1   After the war, Arvid's brother Falk told Greta Kuckhoff another version of the story ("Einige Stichpunkte über Arvid Harnacks Leben entsprechende Ausprechen mit Falk"). During his Freikorps time—approximately two years—Arvid was wounded and spent nine months in a military hospital. Together with a friend, he had been "arrested by the 'Reds'" but had escaped. His good treatment resulted in his conversion [to communism]. Arvid had witnessed a group of Communist workers who, at great danger to themselves, had saved a library. When these events occurred, Falk was eight years old. His account of the story, however, which appears in Greta Kuckhoff's archives (BA, Potsdam), was written at a time when Falk was interested in proving what a great and early Communist Arvid was.

2 Rascher, "Meine Freundschaft mit Arvid Harnack (1901–1942) im Jahre 1921."

3 Clara Harnack, "Unermüdlicher Streiter für die Menschenrechte: Die Mutter Arvid Harnacks über ihren Sohn und die Schwiegertochter Mildred," *Neues Deutschland*, December 1977. Other biographical material comes from Ingeborg Havemann, "Mildred Harnack, Eine Erinnerung," *Heute und Morgen*; and a chapter from an unpublished dissertation by Jürgen Danyel.

4 MH to Martha Dodd, n.d. LOC.

5 Clara Harnack to Arvid Harnack, December 11, 1942, GDW.

6 Kuckhoff, *Vom Rosenkranz zur Roten Kapelle*, p. 53.

7 In Mildred's story "Prothalamion" about their courtship, she gave the suitor Arvid's middle name, Rudolf. The title is from Edmund Spencer, who coined the word from the Greek meaning a song celebrating a marriage (pro— meaning before + *thalamos*—the bridal chamber).

8 AH to GF, February 16, 1926, Falk Harnack Collection, GDW.

9 AH to CH, August 8, 1926. Falk Harnack Collection, GDW.

10 Hawthorne, "My Visit to Niagara," in *Miscellanies: Biographical and Other Sketches,* p. 247.

11 Garlin to Brüning, October 12, 1980, quoted in Brüning, "Mildred Harnack-Fish als Literaturwissenschaftlerin," p. 7.

12 Letter to *Daily Cardinal*, November 16, 1921.

13 Coolidge, "Enemies of the Republic," *Delineator*, June 1922.

14 CIC Files, Rote Kapelle RG 319, ZA 020253 (Boxes 59, 60). Declassified February 14, 1989. Harnack FBI File.

15 Kuckhoff, pp. 50ff. The "Reich's Hunting Master" was Hermann Goering's favorite title. He felt it added to his reputation as the "last Renaissance man." He kept a hunting lodge and pursued his quarry in a variety of costumes. Joachim Fast in *Plotting Hitler's Death* (p. 47) recounts a conversation between Sir Eric Phipps, the British ambassador, and Goering following the Roehm purge. When Goering arrived late for a dinner given by the diplomat, he excused himself by saying he had just returned from hunting. The ambassador replied testily, "For animals, I hope."

16 Ibid., p. 49.

17 "The Principles of a Juristic Philosophy as Applied to a Transaction." Parody in the John R. Commons papers, SHSW. For John R. Commons and the Friday Niters, see Commons, *Myself*; Curti, *University of Wisconsin*; Voegelin, *Über die Form des amerikanischen Geistes*; David R. Myers, "The Wisconsin Idea: Its National and International Significance," *Wisconsin Academy Review*, Fall 1991.

18 Oscar Ameringer, *Milwaukee Leader*, April 27, 1931. Commons' pupils were a substantial component of the Roosevelt "brain trust." A short list would include Arthur Altmeyer, assistant secretary of labor; David Lillienthal, TVA director; George Matthews, Securities and Exchange commissioner; Edwin Witte, director of The Committee on Economic Security, which drafted the model Social Security law; Ewan Clague, director of the Bureau of Labor Statistics; Katherine Lenroot, chief of the Children's Bureau; William B. Leiserson, head of the Labor Conciliation Board; Summer Slichter, NRA official. It is worth noting that among these fellow Friday Niters

were an unusual number of remarkable women: Elizabeth Brandeis, economics professor and drafter with her husband, Paul Rauschenbush, of Wisconsin's Workman's Compensation law; Evelyn M. Burns, one of the creators of Social Security; Dorothy Whipple (Clague), pediatrician and later Georgetown University professor; Elsie Gluck, one of Commons's best students whose promising career ended in suicide; Anna May Campbell Davis, lawyer and economics professor; Marion "Clinch" Calkins, English faculty member, Harry Hopkins' speech writer and investigative reporter, poet, and author of *Some Folks Won't Work*, about the unemployed, and *Spy Overhead*, on the hiring of private police to infiltrate labor unions; Hazel Briggs Rice, Commons's secretary, novelist and poet.

19 Letter from John A. Commons to John B. Schwertman, field director, American Red Cross, Raleigh, N.C., June 29, 1945. Harnack Papers, HU, German translation (the English has disappeared).

20 Arvid Harnack's résumé dated July 7, 1930, GU.

21 Arvid Harnack to John R. Commons, February 19, 1929, Commons Archives, SHSW.

22 Otto Donner to Harriette Esch, September 5, 1945, in Harnack War Crimes File, 12-2081, declassified June 6, 1990, NA.

23 Rudolf Heberle to Ricarda Huch, October 12, 1946, Munich, IfZ.

24 Rudolf Heberle interview with author.

25 *Daily Cardinal*, April 20, 1927.

26 Edmond Wilson, *The Twenties*, p. 389.

27 *Daily Cardinal*, May 4, 1927.

28 Heywood Hale Broun, ed., *Collected Edition of Heywood Broun*, p. 198. My additional sources for Sacco-Vanzetti were Felix, *Protest: Sacco-Vanzetti and the Intellectuals*; Francis Russell, *Sacco and Vanzetti: The Case Resolved*; Meyer, *Making Light of the Times*.

29 Katherine Anne Porter, *The Never-Ending Wrong*, p. 39.

30 Ibid., p. 44.

31 Murray Kempton, *Part of Our Time*, pp. 45ff.

32 During WW II, Holstein served as a U.S. Army officer in Europe. Upon hearing of Mildred's death in 1947, he felt he had "helped a little to avenge her death at the hands of the Nazis." Nora A. Holstein to author, May 12, 1990.

33 Letter of Dorothy Whipple Clague, Ewan Clague et al., John R. Commons Archives, SHSW.

34 Marjorie Nicolson, oral history interview, MS Division, Butler Library, Columbia University.

35 MH-F to CH, September 28, 1928, Rote Kapelle Collection, GDW.

36 Ibid.

37 MH-F, "Romantic and Married Love in the Works of Nathaniel Hawthorne," in Brüning, "Mildred Harnack-Fish als Literaturwissenschaftlerin," p. 52.

38 *Goucher College Weekly*, February 28, 1929.

39 R. D. Havens to the Germanistic Society of America, Institute of International Education, February 13, 1929, Harnack Papers, HU.

40 *Baltimore Sun*, September 15, 1929.

CHAPTER SIX

1 MH-F to FH, August 20, 1926, Falk Harnack Collection, GDW.
2 Inge Havemann report. Rote Kapelle Collection, GDW.
3 Clara Harnack, op. cit.
4 AH to CH, December 10, 1942, Falk Harnack Collection, GDW.
5 AH to CH, February 20, 1929, Falk Harnack Collection, GDW.
6 Inge Havemann report.
7 *New York Daily News*, quoted in von Zahn-Harnack, *Adolf von Harnack*, p. 294.
8 *Christliche Welt* 44 (1930): 728.
9 Adolf-Henning Frucht, interview by author.
10 MH-F to GF, January 1930.
11 Lietzmann, *Gedächtnisrede auf Adolf von Harnack*, p. lviii.
12 Craig, *Germany*, p. 362.
13 Ernst von Harnack quoted in von Zahn-Harnack, op. cit., p. 140.
14 Ibid., p. 139.
15 The *Kränzchen* included, besides Harnack, Delbrück, and Bonhoeffer, philosopher Ernst Troeltsch, historian Friedrich Meinecke, and sociologist Heinrich Herkner, and occasionally, Theodor Heuss, the future president of the Federal Republic.
16 Bethge, *Dietrich Bonhoeffer*, p. 9.
17 MH-F to GF, February 1, 1930.
18 Agnes von Zahn-Harnack, op. cit., p. 218.
19 Ibid., p. 224.
20 Ibid.
21 Ibid., p. 219.
22 Ibid., p. 224.
23 Clara Harnack, op. cit.
24 Fischer and Lipson, *Thinking about Science*, p. 20.
25 Ibid., p. 20.
26 Bucholz, *Hans Delbrück and the German Military Establishment: War Images in Conflict*, p. 21.
27 Renate Bethge, "Bonhoeffers Familie und ihre Bedeutung für seine Theologie," p. 4.
28 Inge Havemann report.
29 MH-F to GF, October 31, 1929.
30 Wahl, *Jena als Kunststadt*, p. 95.
31 MH-F to GF, October 12, 1929.
32 Inge Havemann report.
33 Postcard dated Jena, October 4, 1929, a copy of which was in the collection of Clara Leiser.
34 MH-F to GF, December 21, 1929.
35 AH to John R. Commons, February 19, 1929, John R. Commons Archives, SHSW.
36 Wollheim, "Gießen zu Beginn der dreißiger Jahre," GU.
37 Quoted in Brüning, *Mildred Harnack-Fish*, p. 200, n59.
38 Walther Fischer, June 8, 1936, GU Archives.
39 Already at Giessen in 1929, a year before their breakthrough in the national

elections, the Nazis controlled the student governing organization, the AStA (*Allgemeiner Studentischer Ausschuss*). By 1931 well over half of the student body supported the Nazi student organization, while Nazi support among the electorate stood at approximately half that level.

40 Spender, *World within World*, p. 107.
41 Mosse, *The Crisis of German Ideology*, p. 193.
42 MH-F to GF, February 1, 1930.
43 Arvid Harnack's words from Günther Weisenborn's personal files, quoted in Höhne, *Codeword Director*, p. 114.
44 Anderhub, "Die Gießener Studenten in der Schlußphase der Weimarer Republik oder wie Mildred und Arvid Harnack zu Gegnern des Nationalsozialismus wurden," in *Mitteilungen des Oberhessischen Geschichtsvereins*, vol. 65. Arvid Harnack's membership card from 1930 for the Socialist student group is in the Falk Harnack Collection, GDW.
45 MH-F to GF, November 2, 1929.
46 MH-F to GF, November 15, 1929.
47 According to Adolf Grimme, who became a member of the Harnack group and was arrested in 1942, this was the occasion when he met Arvid Harnack. Grimme, interview by David Dallin, Cologne, February 1, 1953, p. 169, D Papers, Dallin Papers, Ms. Division, NYPL.
48 Dietrich Bonhoeffer, *Gesammelte Schriften*, 3:60.
49 Klaus Bonhoeffer to Dietrich Bonhoeffer, November 11, 1930, quoted in Bethge, *Dietrich Bonhoeffer*, p. 123.

CHAPTER SEVEN

1 MH-F to GF, February 13, 1931.
2 MH-F to Bob Fish, November 6, 1931. Clara Leiser Collection.
3 Schiff, "Leni's Olympia," *Vanity Fair*, September 1992, p. 260.
4 Thompson, *Saturday Evening Post*, May 23, p. 193. Quoted in Furth, *American Cassandra* p. 156.
5 Wilson, *Travels in Two Democracies*, p. 321.
6 Hitler, *Mein Kampf*; quoted in Kershaw, *Hitler, 1889–1936: Hubris*, p. 330.
7 MH-F to GF, October 18, 1930.
8 Quoted in Bethge, op. cit., p. 12.
9 Italiaander and Haas, eds., *Berliner Cocktail*, p. 11.
10 Quoted in Deak, *Weimar Germany's Left-Wing Intellectuals*, p. 2.
11 Friedrich, *Before the Deluge*, p. 127.
12 MH-F to GF, November 13, 1930.
13 Quoted in James Lee Colwell, *The American Experience in Berlin during the Weimar Period*, p. 34. Ph.D. diss., Yale University.
14 For accounts of the American Church I am indebted to Mrs. Turner, who sent clippings and personal memoirs of the period and her husband's book, *The American Church in Berlin: A History*.
15 MH-F to GF, n.d. [December 1930].
16 MH-F to GF, January 29, 1931. In fact Agnes Smedley had previously taught English at the university. See MacKinnon, *Agnes Smedley: The Life and Times of an American Radical*, p. 102.
17 MH-F to GF, April 24 and July 25, 1931.

18 MH-F to GF, December 26, 1930.

19 MH-F to GF, April 24, 1931.

20 Quoted in Caute, *The Fellow-Travellers: A Postscript to the Enlightenment*, p. 3.

21 Koestler, *Arrow in the Blue*, p. 274.

22 Koestler in Crossman, ed., *The God that Failed*, p. 16.

23 J. A. interview by author.

24 Spender, op. cit., p. 120.

25 MH-F to GF, January 15, 1931.

26 Mildred probably read a German translation (*Nacht über Russland*) of Figner's autobiography, *Zapechatlennyi Trud*. The much-abridged English translation published in 1927 was called *Memoirs of a Revolutionist*.

27 MH-F to GF, April 16, 1931.

28 MH-F to GF, June 25, 1931.

29 MH-F to GF, April 24, 1931.

30 MH-F to GF, December 3, 1931.

31 MH-F to GF, April 24, 1931.

32 MH-F to GF, January 29, 1931.

33 MH-F to GF, August 9, 1931.

34 MH-F to GF, April 24, 1931.

35 MH-F to GF, December 31, 1931.

36 MH-F to GF, November 22, 1931.

37 Fitzpatrick, *The Russian Revolution*, p. 78.

38 Clements, *Bolshevik Feminist: The Life of Aleksandra Kollontai*, pp. 226–27.

39 MH-F to GF, August 16, 1931.

40 MH-F to GF, July 25, 1931.

41 Schneider, *Marburg, 1933–45*, pp. 16ff. for an analysis of the NSDAP tilt from 1925 on. Marburg's economy was based on the university. Most of the people living there were either employed by or dependent on the university. A great number were pensioners.

42 MH-F to GF, April 13, 1932.

43 "In Memory of Arvid and Mildred Harnack," by Zechlin, document in the Rote Kapelle File (RG 319, ZA 020253), NA, declassified December 17, 1991. English translation of "Erinnerung an Arvid und Mildred Harnack," an earlier version of "Arvid und Mildred Harnack zum Gedächtnis."

44 Ibid.

45 MH-F to GF, February 28, 1932. She also describes the apartment in her letter of December 20, 1931.

46 The era of close Russo-German military and political cooperation began in 1922 with the signing of the Treaty of Rapallo. This agreement between two outcasts enabled the Germans to circumvent the terms of the Versailles Peace Treaty that specifically prohibited the acquisition of advanced weapons such as tanks and airplanes in exchange for their technical and monetary support for the new Soviet regime. Following the agreement, Germans and Russians began to manufacture arms jointly in factories in Kharkov and Moscow. Moreover, many Russian officers came to study at Berlin's Technical University. By the end of the decade German engineers vied with Americans in

providing technical assistance for the projects of the Five-Year-Plan—Stalin's vast industrialization effort. As the German economy failed and the Nazi threat grew, the Soviets were able to step up the recruitment of skilled workers who were attracted by the promise of highly paid jobs in Russia. The Russians, through the auspices of the Handelsvertretung, also engaged in industrial espionage. In fact the trade mission's quarters, a large building on the Lindenstrasse, exempt as it was from police searches due to a unique diplomatic arrangement that granted it extraterritoriality, housed a "nest of spies." Particular targets were the chemical, iron, steel, electrical, and aviation industries. In spite of help from the police and the Abwehr, Germany's counterintelligence agency, large corporations like I. G. Farben were only minimally successful in warding off Soviet penetration. The problem for the Germans was that the illegal trade in arms was also handled through the Soviet military–staffed "Engineering Department" of the Lindenstrasse mission. See Dallin, *Soviet Espionage*, pp. 71ff.

47 Sometimes *Bund der Geistesarbeiter* appears as the *Bund geistiger Berufe*.

48 In a letter from Pavel Fitin, the director of Foreign Intelligence of the NKGB, to Georgi Dimitrov, chairman of the Comintern, dated March 12, 1941, Fitin inquires about several former members of the BGA: Professors Friedrich Lenz and Rudolf Heberle, Johannes [*sic.*, Arvid] Harnack, Social Democrats Ernst von Harnack and Julius Leber, Heinz Tietjens, director of the Leiser Shoe Company, writer Adam Kuckhoff, Hans Rupp, who was an employee at I. G. Farben, journalists Harro Schulze-Boysen, Ernst Jünger, Karl Behrens, an engineer for AEG, Wolfgang Havemann, and Baron Wolzogen-Neuhaus, who was employed in the technical section of the OKW. Dimitrov File, Comintern Archives, Moscow, no. 495-74-141, pp. 36ff.

49 Gross, *Willi Münzenberg: A Political Biography*, p. 133; quoted in Stephen Koch, *Double Lives*, p. 19.

50 Georgi Dimitrov to Pavel Fitin, April 12, 1941. Dimitrov File, Comintern Archives, Moscow, no. 495-74-27, pp. 27ff. Quoted in Coppi, Danyel, and Tuchel, *Die Rote Kapelle im Widerstand gegen den Nationalsozialismus*, p. 119.

51 Ibid.

52 Quoted in Koch, op. cit., p. 14.

53 Georg Lukács to Renate Dörner, October 11, 1965, Harnack Papers, HU. In a 1941 letter from G. Dimitrov to P. M. Fitin in the Soviet Archives (Russian Center for Preservation and Study of Records of Modern History, Moscow, Dimitrov Archive, 495-74-141), Lukács states that "in the summer of 1933 she stayed [*weilte*] in the Soviet Union." He encountered Mildred for the last time in fall 1933 in Moscow: "On what sort of business she was there for, I naturally can't say. She didn't speak about it and I didn't ask her." From a conversation with her, Comrade Lukács had the impression that she and her husband would be supportive (to their cause).

54 Georgi Dimitrov to P. N. Fitin, April 12, 1941. Quoted in Coppi, Danyel, and Tuchel, *Die Rote Kapelle im Widerstand gegen den Nationalsozialismus*, p. 119.

55 Isherwood, *Christopher and His Kind*, p. 127.

56 MH-F to GF, January 23, 1932.

57 MH-F to GF, February 14, 1932.
58 MH-F to GF, August 8, 1932.
59 MH-F to GF, June 18, 1932.
60 MH-F to GF, July 3, 1932.
61 MH-F to GF, July 20, 1933.
62 MH-F to GF, August 24, 1933.
63 MH-F to GF, September 18, 1933.
64 MH-F to GF, July 3, 1932.
65 Koestler, *Invisible Writing*, p. 23.
66 MH-F to GF, July 3, 1932.
67 MH-F to GF, July 12, 1932.
68 Koestler, *Invisible Writing*, p. 24.
69 MH-F to GF, July 24, 1932.
70 Macgregor Knox, "Conquest, Foreign and Domestic, in Fascist Italy and Nazi Germany," *Journal of Modern History* 56, no 1 (March 1984): 37. Quoted in Stern, *Dreams and Delusions: The Drama of German History*, p. 125.
71 Meyer, "Through Europe on One Museum," *Capital Times*, October 1932, Karl E. Meyer collection.

CHAPTER EIGHT

1 MH-F to GF, August 13, 1932.
2 MH-F to GF, October 17, 1932.
3 Fred Sanderson telephone interview with author.
4 Dallin, op. cit., p. 236. He cites Reinhold Schönbrunn as an interview source (Dallin Papers, XYZ 85–86). The interview is not in the Dallin papers now in the New York Public Library.
5 Sudoplatov and Schechter, *Special Tasks*, p. 137.
6 Koestler, *The Invisible Writing*, p. 51.
7 Ibid., p. 52.
8 Ibid.
9 Muggeridge, *Chronicles of Wasted Time*, part 1, *The Green Stick*, p. 244.
10 Quoted in Enzensberger, *The Consciousness Industry*, p. 137.
11 MH-F to GF, September 3, 1932.
12 Koestler, *The Invisible Writing*, p. 53.
13 MH-F to GF, September 3, 1932.
14 Ibid.
15 ARPLAN Report, collection of author. See also Niekisch, *Erinnerungen eines deutschen Revolutionärs*, 1:216ff.
16 The BAG was founded by Dr. Peter Silbermann, who had spent a year studying evening high schools in the United States. Mildred succeeded her friend and fellow American Warren Tomlinson as the English teacher when he returned to the United States in 1932. Through Tomlinson's efforts—he pioneered a conversational method and authored two textbooks—English became the most popular foreign language.
17 MH-F to GF, May 2, 1933.
18 MH-F to GF, September 29, 1932.
19 During 1932–1933 she was also teaching English at the Berlin Handelshochschule.

20 Dr. Gotthilf Stecher, May 15, 1936, HU.

21 Rudolf Holberg to Clara Leiser, May 15, 1949, Leiser Collection.

22 Maria-Dorothea Beck, "Erinnerungen an Mildred Harnack," *Die Andere Zeitung*, September 14, 1967.

23 Kortmann, "Zusammenarbeit mit Mildred und Arvid Harnack." Rote Kapelle Collection, GDW, Berlin.

24 Samson Knoll in several conversations provided the author with information about Mildred and the BAG. I have also used a copy of his diary entries for the period and a transcript of the talk he gave to the Mildred Harnack School in Berlin (Wallgora Archiv, Staatsbibliothek, Berlin), which he amended in a letter to the author in November 1992.

25 MH-F to GF, June 18, 1932. Richard Lowenthal, a journalist with the London *Observer*, in an interview with David Dallin told of being present at a meeting of an "organization of intellectual professions" (probably the BGA in February 1933, where Arvid Harnack lectured on economic questions (Dallin Papers). According to Wilhelm Utech, Harnack also gave a lecture early in 1933 to the students of the Abendgymnasium on the Soviet planned economy. Utech Protocoll, Rote Kapelle Collection, GDW.

26 Goebbels, *Tagebücher*, Vol. II, p. 709.

27 MH-F to GF, December 12, 1932.

28 MH-F to GF, January 29, 1933.

29 Wolfgang Havemann, "Über die notwendige Einheit von Theorie und Praxis bei der Anwendung des Marxismus-Leninismus (Erinnerungen an Arvid Harnack aus den Jahren 1931–1942), p. 7, Rote Kapelle Collection, GDW.

30 Goebbels, *Tagebücher*, Vol. II, p. 759.

31 Brüning, *Mildred Harnack-Fish*, p. 168, and information provided by Samson Knoll to the author.

32 Karl Bonhoeffer, *Lebenserinnerungen*: quoted in Bethge, op. cit., pp. 191–92.

33 Clara Harnack, op. cit.

34 Bethge, op. cit., p. 193.

35 The circumstances and blame for the fire have been debated by generations of historians. See, for example, Tobias, *The Reichstag Fire* and Hofer et. al., eds., *Der Reichstagsbrand: Eine wissenschaftliche Dokumentation.*

36 See Müller, *Hitler's Justice: The Courts of the Third Reich*, pp. 29ff.

37 For a discussion of Schulze-Boysen's politics, see Coppi, *Harro Schulze-Boysen—Wege in den Widerstand.*

38 S-B to his parents, card dated March 4, 1933, quoted in Coppi, op. cit., p. 120.

39 Coppi, op. cit., pp. 126–27.

40 Turel, *Ecce Superhomo*, Vol. I, p. 219; quoted in Höhne, op. cit., p. 105.

41 Marie-Luise Schulze, "Warum ich im Jahre 1933 Parteigenossin geworden bin." Quoted in Höhne, ibid.

42 Ibid., p. 106.

43 Coppi, op. cit., p. 128.

44 Von Salomon, *Fragebogen*, p. 397.

45 MH-F to GF, n.d. [between February and March 1933].

46 Gundel et al. eds., *Giessener Gelehrte in der Ersten Hälfte des 20. Jahrhundert*, Vol. II, p. 602.

47 Ledig-Rowohlt in an interview with the author.

48 Herman, *The American Church in Berlin*, p. 51.
49 Unfortunately, this manuscript has been lost. After Mr. Turner's death, Mrs. Turner disposed of it.
50 MH-F to GF, March 8, 1933.
51 Bethge, op. cit., p. 201.
52 Speech at the close of the sixth school year by Dr. G. Stecher, student adviser and acting leader of the BAG, June 9, 1933, *Handbuch des Berliner Abendgymnasiums*.
53 Mildred refers here to her "Winesburg, Ohio" letter (October 16, 1932) in which she discusses Sherwood Anderson's biting sketches of small town life: "They are stories of very lonely people—people who are hoping to make connections of love and sympathy with other people or with God . . . and (those) that cannot. She quotes from Matthew Arnold's poem, "Dover Beach": We are here as on a darkling plain. Swept by confused alarms of struggle and flight. Where ignorant armies clash by night. . . . She concludes significantly: "Since I have been to Russia I think that a society is possible in which people are united in a common aim of good for all and therefore love and understand each other better, a society in which the effort is intelligently persistently made by all to take away unnatural, unloving restrictions from women and men as well, and to give all people the time to become gentler and better friends. Much work must be done to bring it about, but it is possible." MH-F to GF, May 2, 1933.
54 Stecher speech, BAG, June 9, 1933.

CHAPTER NINE

1 Trevor-Roper, ed., *Hitler's Table Talk*, 1941–1944, p. 102.
2 David Burke, *New York Daily News*, September 1, 1957.
3 Some letters from Mildred to Martha are in the William E. Dodd papers in the Library of Congress. Other letters from Martha to Greta Kuckhoff are in the (East) Berlin Akademie der Künste. At one time there was a "Dodd Archive" in the Humboldt University Library that required the permission of Klaus Fuchs's nephew, Klaus Fuchs Kittowski, for viewing. However, when the "Dodd Archive" arrived, it consisted of one innocuous letter from Martha Dodd to Emil Fuchs, Klaus Fuchs's father. It would appear that, since the fall of the Wall, the "Dodd Archive" has been purged.
4 Martha Dodd Stern, "In Memory," unpublished, Martha Dodd Stern papers, LOC. Martha Dodd was hardly in the German underground from 1933 to 1943. Since she left Germany for the United States at the end of 1937, if she helped the resistance, it was clearly from abroad.
5 Martha Dodd, *Through Embassy Eyes*, p. 41.
6 Martha Dodd Stern, treatment for a film based on *Through Embassy Eyes* and Ambassador Dodd's diary, Martha Dodd Stern Papers. Martha Dodd's correspondence is at the Library of Congress and is filed either with the Dodd Papers of her father or, more frequently, under Martha Dodd Stern.
7 Vanden Heuvel, "Grand Illusions," *Vanity Fair*, August, 1991, p. 225.
8 Dodd, *Through Embassy Eyes*, p. 22.
9 Jacob Beam, unpublished ms., p. 40, Beam papers.
10 Mrs. W. E. Dodd to William E. Dodd Jr., December 15, 1937, William Dodd

Papers, LOC. The State Department compounded Dodd's displeasure by dispatching two rich young men, John White, brother-in-law of Jay Pierrepont Moffat, head of the Division of Western European Affairs at the department, as Gordon's successor, and Orme Wilson as the new second secretary. Their mission was to counter the ambassador's penury and to prop up the standards of American diplomacy. Soon Dodd was boring Roosevelt and Secretary of State Cordell Hull with handwritten letters criticizing the waste and indolence of these "wealthy staff people." Men who "want to have cocktail parties in the afternoon, card parties in the evening and get up next day at 10 o'clock" and who "think more of wearing good clothes than doing good work"; men who make themselves "ridiculous imitating Louis XIV." (WED to Hull, October 4, 1933, State Dept., quoted in Dalleck, *Democrat and Diplomat: The Life of William E. Dodd*, p. 206.)

11 These criticisms of the Soviet embassy were excised from the East German edition of the book, which was published after the war.

12 MD to TW, July 1933, Wilder Papers, Beinecke Library, Yale University.

13 Martha Dodd and William Dodd Jr., eds., *Ambassador Dodd's Diary*, p. 24.

14 MD, "In Memory," unpublished, Martha Dodd Stern Papers.

15 MH-F to GF, November 12, 1933.

16 Carl Sandburg to MD, quoted in Phillip Metcalfe, *1933*, p. 17.

17 Wilder to his family, June 26, 1933, quoted in Harrison, *The Enthusiast: A Life of Thornton Wilder*, p. 131; and TW to MD, n.d., Dodd Papers.

18 MD to TW, September 25, 1933.

19 See MH-F and MD (Wesley Repor): Brief Reviews (John Hampson, *Saturday Night at the Greyhound; O Providence*), November 12, 1933; (Albert Halper, *Union Square*) November 26, 1933; (Kay Boyle, *Gentlemen, I Address You Privately*) February 4, 1934; (Hervey Allen, *Anthony Adverse*) February 18, 1934; Book Nook (Aldous Huxley, *Uncle Spencer and Other Stories*) February 18, 1934. Between January 1933 and February 1934 the paper was called *Continental Post and Berlin Topics*. After that it was called *Continental News and Berlin Topics*. Mildred translated a short story of Kay Boyle's, "Your Body Is a Jewel Box" ("Dein Leib ist ein Juwelenschrein"). It is included in Kurt Ullrich, ed., *Neu Amerika: Zwanzig Erzähler der Gegenwart*.

20 MH-F to MD, Sunday night, n.d. Dodd Papers.

21 MH-F to GF, August 1, 1933.

22 MH-F to MD, May 14, 1934, Dodd Papers.

23 MH-F to GF, November 12, 1933.

24 MH-F to MD, n.d. The sketches Mildred referred to were probably "Prothalmion" and "Der Mond und das Saxophon."

25 MH-F to MD, May 4, 1934, Dodd Papers.

26 Bridenthal, et. al, eds., *When Biology Became Destiny: Women in Weimar and Nazi Germany*, p. 68; and Focke and Reimer, *Alltag unterm Hakenkreuz*, p. 124.

27 MH-F to GF, August 1, 1933. State Department records show that Fred Esch, Mildred's brother-in-law, had sent an inquiry to the American consulate in Berlin asking them to find her. She had not written since her summer trip and the family was concerned. In 1942, Mildred had an ectopic

pregnancy. The injury to her fallopian tubes might have occurred during this earlier abortion.

28 MH-F to GF, December 11, 1933.

29 *The (Paris) Herald*, July 30, 1931, quoted in Colwell, op cit, p. 80.

30 MH-F to GF, November 29, 1933.

31 MH-F to GF, November 12, 1933.

32 MH-F to GF, May 5, 1934.

33 MH-F to GF, November 29, 1933.

34 Heym, *Nachruf*, p. 74. Heym emigrated and fought in the American army. In 1948, he wrote *The Crusaders* about his army unit, which was hailed as one of the best books on World War II. As a Communist, he feared becoming a target of McCarthyism. Subsequently, he emigrated to Czechoslovakia, then Poland, and finally to the GDR, where he gained a reputation in the West as one of East Germany's careful dissenters. After reunification, in 1994, he became the senior member of the Bundestag.

35 Samuel Fischer, the son-in-law of the founder of S. Fischer Verlag, published many of Germany's leading authors. The Fischer list included Thomas Mann, Hermann Hesse, Stefan Zweig, and Gerhart Hauptmann. Ernst Rowohlt made a specialty of American authors, among them Sinclair Lewis, William Faulkner, Ernest Hemingway, and Thomas Wolfe. After Kristallnacht, in November 1938, he emigrated to Brazil but returned during the war to Germany. Heinrich-Maria Ledig-Rowohlt was the illegitimate son of Ernst Rowohlt. After his father's emigration he took over the publishing house. After the war, he continued as head of one of the most successful publishing houses in Germany. He shared his father's predilection for American authors. (See chapter 10) Max Tau was the chief editor of Cassierer. Ludwig Reindl was the editor in chief of *Die Dame*, the leading women's magazine for which Mildred occasionally wrote. After the war, he became the editor of the newspaper in Constance. Ernst von Salomon was an accomplice to the political assassination of Walther Rathenau in 1922. During the period of Mildred's salon, he was a Rowohlt author and reader. In 1951, Rowohlt published his sensational autobiography, *Die Fragebogen*, in which the Harnacks appear. Max Mohr, a playwright, author, and doctor, died in exile in Shanghai in 1937. Adam Kuckhoff was a theater director, playwright, and dramaturge whose 1937 novel, *Der Deutsche von Bayrencourt*, was published by Rowohlt. He met the Harnacks' Wisconsin friend Greta Lorke in 1930 at a theater conference and married her in 1937. Through her, he met the Harnacks. He was also a member of the BGA. Otto Zoff, at one time a reader for Fischer, was a novelist, playwright, and director. After Hitler's takeover, Zoff, an Austrian citizen, left for Italy, where he continued to publish. He emigrated to the United States in 1941. Franz Fein was the German translator of William Faulkner. Margret Boveri was the foreign editor of the *Berliner Tageblatt*. After the war she wrote *Treason in the Twentieth Century*, which includes a chapter on the Harnacks. Mildred's student Friedrich (Bodo) Schlösinger became a translator of Russian and English during the war. He committed suicide on the eastern front after hearing the news of his wife's death sentence. Some of these names were included in a letter to Martha Dodd dated May 15, 1934; others were in an undated card, H File Dodd Papers.

36 MD to Thornton Wilder, December 14, 1933, Wilder Papers, Beinecke Library, Yale University.

37 As the common denominator of the Harnack salon was literature, not politics, conservatives and Social Democrats, Communists and liberals were represented. Although only those who opposed the regime were invited back, only a few members of the Harnacks' literary circle—the Kuckhoffs, the Schlösingers, and Havemann—would become active members of the resistance; some—Rowohlt, Tau, Franzen, and Zoff—would emigrate. Many guests did not learn until after the war that the Harnacks were engaged in illegal activities.

38 Martha Dodd, "In Memory," Martha Dodd Stern Papers.

39 Composite scene based on participants' accounts: Martha Dodd, *Through Embassy Eyes*, pp. 83–85; H. M. Ledig-Rowohlt interview by the author; MD to HM L-R, letters in Dodd Papers, two letters from Hans Fallada to MD, dated June 8 and June 18; the memoir of Mildred Harnack by Martha Dodd all in the LOC; and the Fallada diary in the Fallada Archive, Neu Brandenburg, Germany. A version of the conversation between MH-F and Hans Fallada is reconstructed in Crepon, *Leben und Tode des Hans Fallada*, pp. 188–94.

40 Dodd, *Through Embassy Eyes*, p. 84.

41 MD, "In Memory," unpublished, in Martha Dodd Stern Papers.

42 MH-F to GF, February 20, 1934.

43 MH-F to Bob Fish, May 16, 1934. Clara Leiser Papers.

44 MH-F to GF, May 22, 1934.

45 MH-F "Reifender Mais," *Berliner Tageblatt*, August 23, 1934.

46 MH-F, "Variationen über das Thema Amerika," *Berliner Tageblatt*, December 2, 1934.

47 MH-F to GF, August 30, 1934.

48 MH-F to GF, February 20, 1934.

49 Jane Donner Sweeney, interview by author.

50 Wolfgang Havemann, "Erinnerung an Mildred und Arvid Harnack." Havemann Archives, Städtische Bibliothek, Dresden.

51 MD, "In Memory."

52 MD to TW, December 14, 1933, Wilder Papers, Beineke Library, Yale University.

53 Fred Oechsner, telephone interview by author.

54 MD to parents, postcard in the Dodd Papers.

55 Vanden Heuvel, op. cit., p. 248.

56 MD to TW, December 14, 1933, Wilder Papers, Beinecke Library, Yale University.

57 MD to Thornton Wilder, September 25, 1933, Wilder Papers.

58 Dodd, *Through Embassy Eyes*, p. 63.

59 Shirer, *Twentieth-Century Journey: The Nightmare Years*, p. 127.

60 Von Salomon, *Fragebogen*, p. 167.

61 Metcalfe, *1933*, p. 87.

62 Dodd, *Through Embassy Eyes*, p. 52.

63 MD to TW, December 14, 1933, Wilder Papers, Beinecke Library, Yale University.

64 Shirer to MD, May 1969.

65 *New York Journal American*, N. D. Huss calls him Benogradov, probably confusing the Russian *V* for a *B* on a document.

66 MD to Agnes Knickerbocher, July 16, 1969. Sigrid Schultz's diary doesn't record that she gave any Christmas party in 1933. She wrote Martha (March 14, 1970) that if they met at her house, it was at a party on January 20, 1934 (LOC). However, her diary shows that it was January 19, 1934, Schultz Archives, SHSW. In her memoir, "Bright Journey into Darkness," Martha suggests that perhaps she first spotted Boris at the Nuremberg party day in September 1933.

67 MD to Agnes Knickerbocher, July 16, 1969.

68 MD; Martha's unpublished memoir of Boris, "Bright Journey into Darkness," is in the Martha Dodd Stern Papers, LOC.

69 Ibid.

70 Ibid.

71 Dodd, *Through Embassy Eyes*, p. 41.

72 Bérard, *Un ambassadeur se souvient: Au temps du danger allemand*, p. 236. (In fact, in "Bright Journey into Darkness" Martha says that Boris's daughter lived with him in the Berlin embassy while his wife remained in Moscow.)

73 Dodd NKVD file 14449, 1:13; quoted in Weinstein and Vassiliev, *The Haunted Wood*, p. 51. The ellipsis is theirs.

74 Katherine Smith, interview by the author.

75 MD, "Bright Journey into Darkness."

76 Wilbur Carr confidential memo, June 5, 1935, Wilbur Carr Papers, Box 12 (LOC).

77 Boris Vinogradov would also play an enigmatic role in the Reichstag fire trials. In Steven Koch's book on the espionage role of the Comintern, *Double Lives*, "Comrade Vinogradov" appears as the Soviet agent who was ordered by Karl Radek in Moscow to find information connecting SS Oberführer Kurt Daluege, at the time acting on behalf of the SA, to the fire. Koch uses the telegram to support his theory that Stalin and Hitler collaborated to use the Communist propaganda campaign and London countertrial, the brainchild of Comintern agent Willi Münzenberg, to discredit the SA, thus preparing the way for the Roehm purge (pp. 360 ff.).

78 Mowrer, *Journalist's Wife*, p. 289.

79 Dodd, *Through Embassy Eyes*, pp. 142–43.

80 Ibid.; Bérard, op. cit., pp. 236ff.

81 Dodd, *Through Embassy Eyes*, pp. 157–58.

82 Kershaw, op. cit., p. 517.

83 Bracher, *The German Dictatorship*, p. 239.

84 Dodd, *Through Embassy Eyes*, p. 170.

85 Diels was removed from the Gestapo but survived the war and testified for the prosecution at Nuremberg. He later published his powerful recollections of the Nazi years, *Lucifer Ante Portas*. He died in 1957 when a hunting rifle discharged accidentally.

86 BV to MD, July 11, 1934, Martha Dodd Stern Papers.

87 Dodd, *Through Embassy Eyes*, pp. 169ff.

88 Mrs. John C. White, interview by author.

89 MH-F to GF, August 7, 1934.

90 MH-F to GF, July 28, 1934.

91 Dodd and Dodd, *Ambassador Dodd's Diary*, p. 126.

92 Dodd, *Through Embassy Eyes*, p. 275.

93 Ibid., p. 53.

94 Ibid., p. 162; and von Salomon, op. cit., p. 107.

95 Orme Wilson memo, November 9, 1934, Box 59, Dodd Papers.

96 *Continental News and Berlin Topics*, January 20, 1935. See also Dallin, op. cit., p. 64, for Switz case.

97 MD to TW, November 10, 1934, Wilder Papers, Beinecke Library, Yale University.

98 MD to TW, September 25, 1933, Wilder Papers, Beineke Library, Yale University.

99 Agnes Knickerbocker to MD, n.d., LOC; and Weinstein and Vassiliev, op. cit., p. 51.

100 File 14449, p. 25, quoted in Weinstein and Vassiliev, op. cit., p. 52.

101 Shirer, *Twentieth-Century Journey: A Native's Return, 1945–1988*, p. 286.

102 Dodd, *Through Embassy Eyes*, p. 275.

103 MD, "Bright Journey into Darkness."

CHAPTER TEN

1 MH-F Papers, 40, 8, HU.

2 Salomon, op. cit., p. 167.

3 Fromm, op. cit., p. 127.

4 Descriptions of the press are from Shirer, *Berlin Diary*, pp. 40ff., and Fromm, op. cit. A list of guests was published in the *Continental Post*, May 26, 1935.

5 She was opposed to Hitler, and after the war she wrote a book, *Treason in the Twentieth Century*, dealing with some aspects of the German resistance. Yet Boveri admired some of the Nazis and was reluctant to abet the defeat of Germany, a stance that would separate her from many of her colleagues. Greta Kuckhoff mentions seeing Bovery (*sic*) at the tea in her book, p. 179 (1986 ed.).

6 Fromm, op. cit., pp. 194ff.

7 Kuckhoff, op. cit., pp. 177–78.

8 Kuckhoff, op. cit., pp. 177ff. Kuckhoff has the wrong year. She has confused two parties: one for Wolfe and Donald Klopfer that took place in May 1935, and that for Charles Lindberg and the Olympic team, which was on September 4, 1936.

9 Edith Reindl, interview by author.

10 Kuckhoff, op. cit., p. 178.

11 John Sieg wrote under the pseudonym Siegfried Nebel. He was arrested in 1933. After a period of unemployment and low-paying jobs, he obtained, in 1937, a signals position on the Reichsbahn, the German railroad. In this capacity he was later able to sabotage trains, sending military transports to the wrong siding or assisting them in going the wrong direction. In 1941, he was one of the editors of *The Inner Front*, an illegal newspaper. Regina

Griebel et al., *Erfasst*, pp. 192–93, and Alexander Blank and Julius Mader, *Rote Kapelle gegen Hitler*, pp. 72ff.

12 Ernst Niekisch founded *Der Widerstand* in 1926. In its pages, he campaigned against reparations, characterizing them as capitalistic blackmail. Like Harnack, a champion of the "eastward orientation" in foreign policy and a world revolution against capitalism, Niekisch preferred the appellation "National Bolshevist." Key members of the resistance would meet in his apartment, left-wing opponents in one room and right-wing in another. In 1937, Niekisch was arrested, accused of treason, and sentenced to life imprisonment. He was released in 1945. (See Peter Hoffman, *The German Resistance*, pp. 19ff.)

13 Kuckhoff, op. cit., p. 178. In his memoir, *Erinnerungen eines deutschen Revolutionärs*, Vol. I, p. 247, Niekisch mentions meeting "enemies of the state" at the Dodd embassy.

14 Ledig-Rowohlt, "Thomas Wolfe in Berlin," *American Scholar*, Spring 1953, p. 186.

15 MD to Thomas Wolfe, n.d. Wisdom Collection, Houghton Library, Harvard University. See also MD to Elizabeth Nowell, May 2, 1949.

16 Tau, *Das Land, das ich verlassen mußte*, pp. 251ff.; Tau, *Ein Flüchtling findet sein Land*, p. 175; and *Auf dem Weg zur Versöhnung*, p. 84. Just how Mildred managed to help him leave, however, is not revealed.

17 Goebbels radio broadcast quoted in Engelmann, *In Hitler's Germany: Daily Life in the Third Reich*, p. 64.

18 Mehring quoted in Grunfeld, *Prophets without Honour*, p. 206.

19 Focke and Reimer, *Alltag unterm Hakenkreuz*, Vol. III, p. 23ff.

20 Effenburger, *Umriss der amerikanischen Kultur und Kunst*, p. 157; quoted in Springer, *The American Novel in Germany*, p. 83.

21 Springer, op. cit., p. 87. Also Pusey, "William Faulkner's Works in Germany to 1940: Translations and Criticism," *Germanic Review*, October 1955.

22 MH-F, "Three Young Authors from the US: Wilder, Wolfe, Faulkner," *Berliner Tageblatt*, August 5, 1934.

23 Effenberger, op. cit., p. 37; quoted in Springer, op. cit., p. 27.

24 Quoted in Brüning, *Mildred Harnack-Fish*, p. 91

25 MH-F, "Drei junge Dichter aus USA. Thornton Wilder, Thomas Wolfe und William Faulkner," *Berliner Tageblatt*, August 5, 1934.

26 MH-F, "One of the Greatest of Younger American Authors in Berlin," *Continental Post*, May 12, 1935 and May 19, 1935; "Thomas Wolfe," *Berliner Tageblatt*, February 17, 1935.

27 MH-F, "One of the Greatest of Younger American Authors in Berlin." This passage refers to an unhappy encounter Wolfe had on February 18, 1935, with Sanderson Vanderbilt of the New York *Herald Tribune*. Vanderbilt began his interview: "With a good two inches of blue shirt separating the bottom of his rumpled vest from the top of his unpressed pants . . ." Magi and Walser, ed., *Thomas Wolfe Interviewed, 1929–1938*, pp. 21ff.

28 Donald, *Look Homeward*, p. 322.

29 Wolfe, *You Can't Go Home Again*, p. 623.

30 Dodd, *Through Embassy Eyes*, p. 91.

31 Ledig-Rowohlt, op. cit., p. 192.

32 Donald, op. cit., p. 323.

33 Wolfe to MD, n.d. photostat in LOC.

34 Kennedy and Reeves, eds., *The Notebooks of Thomas Wolfe*, p. 748.

35 MH-F to Maxwell Perkins, September 19, 1938, Archive of Charles Scribner's Sons, Princeton University Library.

36 Wolfe to Perkins, May 23, 1935, in Nowell, *The Letters of Thomas Wolfe*, p. 460.

37 Dodd, *Through Embassy Eyes*, p. 92.

38 Wolfe to Frank Wolfe, May 27, 1935, quoted in Donald, op. cit., p. 324.

39 Dodd, "In Memory."

40 Wolfe to Perkins, May 23, 1935, quoted in Nowell, op. cit., p. 459.

41 MH-F to Perkins, March 21, 1936, Archive of Charles Scribner's Sons, Princeton University Library.

42 Perkins to MH-F, April 7, 1936, Archive of Charles Scribner's Sons, PUL.

43 Wolfe, "I Have a Thing to Tell You," *The New Republic*, March 10, 1937.

44 Von Salomon, op. cit., pp. 289ff. Salomon quotes his wife as describing another Harnack party: "They stand about there, well-dressed, decent-looking people and they talk about 'cross-channels of communication.' . . . They describe Hitler and Himmler and Rosenberg and Frick as utter fools, and they tell me, me who've never even met any of them before except the Harnacks and the Schulze-Boysens . . . They say to me, 'Do you know, dear lady, I have heard from an absolutely sure source, because you see I have a direct link with Zurich . . . of course we exchange our information . . . ' And then, his wife says, "he suddenly catches sight of another man and says, 'Excuse me for a moment, dear lady,' and gives the other man a yellow envelope, saying: 'Strictly confidential' and winks . . . And there I sit on the sofa and can hardly breathe. So I ask who the decent-looking old man is and who is the one he spoke to, and they tell me that one's a ministerial Councillor and the other's an adjutant, and that one over there is in the SS and this one here is a diplomat."

45 Time-Life, *The Third Reich: The New Order*, pp. 59–60.

46 Ibid., p. 62.

47 Josephine Herbst in the *New York Post*, quoted in Langer, *Josephine Herbst*, p. 191. Herbst came to Berlin to seek out members of the German underground. Meeting opponents of the regime surreptitiously on train platforms and park benches and shunning the telephone, she collected stories of illegal strikes, of underground pamphlets announcing "Down with Hitler," of resistance in factories, all evidence reported back to America of opposition to the regime. Herbst's biographer reports that it was Hede Massing, still an active Communist but then living in the United States, a friend of the Harnacks from the ARPLAN days, who gave Herbst leads. Herbst was also acquainted with Ernie Meyer, then a columnist for the *New York Post*, who could also have put her in touch with the Harnacks. As Herbst was careful not to keep notes of names, telephone numbers, and addresses that might endanger her sources, one can only speculate that she contacted Mildred. The stories were subsequently reprinted by the Anti-Nazi Federation in New York as "Behind the Swastika."

48 MH-F, "Im Wald von Arden," *Die Dame*, Vol. 26 (1938): 12–13, 68; "Sommersonnenwende," *Die Dame*, Vol. 12 (1939): 56; "Hochschule mit Lasso," *Die Dame*, Vol. 19 (1939): 8–9.

49 Time-Life, op. cit., p. 82.

50 MH-F to MP, March 21, 1936. Archive of Charles Scribner's Sons, Princeton University Library.

51 After the war the Allied government gave Universitas permission to publish it. Dedicated to Harnack-Fish, it was said to be the first American book published in postwar Germany. *Washington Post*, June 24, 1946. (I was unable to verify that it was ever published.)

52 Clara Leiser, "The Atmosphere of Terror," unpublished ms. Clara Leiser Papers, Anita Leiser Collection.

53 Clara Leiser, "Just Try Prison Visiting in Naziland!" Ms in Clara Leiser Papers.

54 Emil Kortmann, "Zusammenarbeit mit Mildred und Arvid Harnack." Rote Kapelle Collection, GDW.

55 Wolfe, *Story of a Novel*, p. 287.

56 Wolfe, *You Can't Go Home Again*, p. 626.

57 Ibid.

58 MH-F to GF, June 12, 1932.

59 Dodd, *Through Embassy Eyes*, p. 212.

60 Quoted in Donald, op. cit., p. 386.

61 Wolfe, *You Can't go Home Again*, pp. 625ff.

62 MD to Elizabeth Nowell, February 18, 1957, LOC.

63 Shirer, *Berlin Diary*, p. 67.

64 Wolfe, *You Can't Go Home Again*, pp. 630–31.

65 Ibid., p. 704.

66 Heinz Höhne, *Codeword Direktor: The Story of the Red Orchestra*, p. 43.

67 Gilles Perrault, *The Red Orchestra*, p. 44.

CHAPTER ELEVEN

1 The German version of the song is in the Mildred Harnack Papers, HU.

2 Berberova; quoted in Fraser, *Ornament and Silence: Essays on Women's Lives*, p. 22.

3 Fisher and Lipson, op. cit., pp. 72ff.

4 Ibid.

5 For a discussion of the effects of mass conformity, see Lüdtke, "The Appeal of Exterminating Others: German Workers and the Limits of Resistance," in Geyer and Boyer, eds., *Resistance against the Third Reich*.

6 California Institute of Technology oral history; "Max Delbrück—How it Was," *Engineering and Science*, 23.

7 Fischer and Lipson, op. cit., p. 97.

8 Fromm, op. cit., p. 203.

9 In the DDR, scholars maintained that the idea of joining the party came from Moscow. The directive, they argued, was Dimitrov's "Trojan Horse" speech at the Seventh Conference of the Communist International in 1935. However, since Arvid did not join the Nazi Party until it became all but mandatory in the civil service professions in 1937, he seemed to arrive at

this decision independently of Moscow's directive. The May 1937 date was important in the de-Nazification process after the war: those who had joined the party before May 1 could not hold a job in the civil service or business. A particularly low number identified one as either a dedicated Nazi or an opportunist.

10 Kuckhoff, Lüneburg, Vol. VIII, folio 131; quoted in Höhne, p. 118.

11 Orlov, *Handbook of Intelligence and Guerrilla Warfare*, pp. 15, 108ff.

12 Corsican file no. 34118, Vol. I, p. 12; quoted in Costello and Tsarev, *Deadly Illusions*, p. 75.

13 Ibid., p. 75.

14 Corsican file, document 10, letter from G. Dimitroff to P. Fitin, April 12, 1941; quoted in Coppi, Danyel, and Tüchel, *Die Rote Kapelle im Widerstand gegen den Nationalsozialismus*, p. 119.

15 Corsican file, Vol. I, p. 37; quoted in Costello and Tsarev, op. cit., p. 77.

16 Kuckhoff, "Rote Kapelle," *Aufbau* (Berlin) 1 (1948): 31. In Arvid's own ministry, Minister Hjalmar Schacht, while working miracles with the German economy, was himself working against the regime—help that was recognized in 1946, when Schacht was acquitted of war crimes at Nuremberg.

17 Grimme, pp. 79–81; quoted in Rosiejka, *Die Rote Kapelle*, pp. 30–31.

18 Dallin, op. cit., p. 236.

19 File 14449, Vol. I, p. 27; quoted in Weinstein and Vassiliev, op. cit., p. 54.

20 Ibid., Vol. I, pp. 17–18; quoted in ibid., p. 53.

21 Costello and Tsarev, op. cit., pp. 75–76.

22 Information from the DAR. According to the *Washington Post* (December 3, 1947), Mildred became the secretary of the Dorothea von Steuben Branch. The genealogical research that Mildred and her mother carried out on a joint trip to England in 1930 helped her trace her ancestors back to the American Revolution. The Fish family tree, officially filed in May 1936 with the U.S. consul general, Raymond Geist, also enabled Mildred to prove her 100 percent Aryan roots. U.S. State Department document dated May 13, 1936, Harnack papers, HU.

23 Kuckhoff, op. cit., p. 187.

24 Dodd, *Through Embassy Eyes*, pp. 276–77.

25 Ibid., pp. 279–80.

26 Corsican file, Vol. II, p. 77; quoted in Costello and Tsarev, op. cit., p. 76.

27 Ibid.

28 MH-F, "Preface to a Study of American Literature," Harnack Papers, HU.

29 MH-F to William Ellery Leonard, April 5, 1936, Clara Leiser Papers.

30 William Ellery Leonard to MH-F, February 29, 1936, Leonard Papers.

31 Clara Leiser to William Ellery Leonard, January 5, 1936, Leiser Papers.

32 Clara Leiser to William Ellery Leonard, January 11, 1937.

33 Clara Leiser to William Ellery Leonard, January 18, 1937.

34 Ibid. In Mildred's translation of *Lust for Life*, she omits the first thirteen pages of the original and abridges the rest of the novel. Even making allowances for conditions in Germany, which made the omission of a sympathetic Jewish character in the original mandatory, Mildred made many other

changes. Perhaps most interesting for what it reveals about the translator, Vincent van Gogh emerges as a hero of the working class. Clearly, Mildred felt she understood the painter better than the author. Her translation, *Vincent van Gogh, Ein Leben in Leidenshaft*, is still in print in Germany.

35 Dorothy Meyer, interviews by Eva Mekler and author.

36 MH-F to Thomas Wolfe, January 29, 1937, Wisdom Collection, Houghton Library, Harvard University.

37 William Ellery Leonard to Clara Leiser, March 22, 1937.

38 Ibid.

39 Recommendation, Mildred Harnack Papers, HU.

40 MH-F, William Faulkner lecture, September 5, 1934, at the Longfellow Club, Berlin. Mildred Harnack Papers, HU.

41 MH-F to Bob and Jane Fish, March 1, 1937, Leiser Papers.

42 Marion Potter and Jane Donner Sweeney, interviews by author.

43 Robert Fish, telephone interview by author.

44 Francis Birch, telephone interview by author.

45 MH-F to Falk Harnack, October 1, 1937. Falk Harnack Collection, GDW.

46 MH-F to Clara Harnack, n.d., Falk Harnack Collection, GDW.

47 MH-F to Maxwell Perkins, September 19, 1938, Archive of Charles Scribner's Sons, Princeton University Library. It appears from the letters in the archive that Perkins sent Mildred a copy of Wolfe's last letter to him. See Thomas Wolfe to Maxwell Perkins, August 12, 1938, in Elizabeth Nowell, ed., *Letters of Thomas Wolfe*, p. 777.

48 Franziska Heberle to Hariette Esch, December 21, 1943, author's collection.

49 Rudolf Heberle, interview by author.

50 Rudolf Heberle to Ricarda Huth, October 12, 1946, lfZ.

51 MH-F to Bob and Jane Fish, June 7, 1938. Arvid spent the summer in Washington working on behalf of the Economics Ministry.

52 Franziska Heberle to Renate Dörner, March 28, 1965. Falk Harnack Collection.

53 Dodd, *Through Embassy Eyes*, p. 16.

54 Fromm, op. cit., p. 132.

55 William Dodd Jr., whose Berlin Ph.D. dissertation Greta Kuckhoff translated into German, (Kuckhoff, op. cit., p. 181) was probably a courier for the Soviet Union intelligence services. In 1936, the International Peace Campaign (*Rassemblement Universel pour la Paix*), a Comintern front, was employing him in Brussels and sending him to Shanghai via Warsaw (where Boris was then chargé) and Moscow (William Dodd Jr. to Martha Dodd, August 10, 1936). When Dodd returned to the United States, he became one of the officers of the left-wing American League for Peace and Democracy. He made an unsuccessful run for Congress from Virginia in 1938. According to Weinstein and Vassiliev (op. cit., p. 67), he became an NKVD source providing them with information "gathered from his discussions with leading Washington Congressmen, Senators, and government officials." In 1943, Dodd, then in a federal post, was called before a House committee where his political convictions cost him his job. In 1945 he went to work for Tass,

the Soviet press office in New York, but was fired when Martha complained that it interfered with her ability to pursue covert work.

56 Weinstein and Vassiliev, op. cit., p. 54.
57 Memo to Slutsky from Martha Dodd; quoted by Weinstein and Vassiliev, pp. 56–57.
58 Ibid, p. 55.
59 Trips stamped in the diplomatic passport of Martha Dodd, Stern Archives.
60 Even before she announced her intention of marrying "this man," her mother had written: "The news of your future plans impacts us [sic]. I had hoped that you could in all your acquaintances find some one save a combination of the two things [probably married and a Soviet citizen] which may bring you sorrow later." Mrs. WED to MD, January 3, 1936.
61 Weinstein and Vassiliev, op. cit., p. 55.
62 MD to Ilya Ehrenburg, October 18, 1956, LOC.
63 Dodd File, pp. 33–34, quoted in Weinstein and Vassiliev, op. cit., p. 55.
64 Boris Vinogradov to MD, May 15, 1937, LOC.
65 See Weinstein and Vassiliev, op. cit., p. 58.
66 Ibid., p. 58. Ambassador Dodd had intended to stay on in Berlin until March 1938. But after a contretemps with the State Department over his replacement's attending the Nazi Party Congress in Nuremberg, which Dodd had traditionally boycotted, was leaked to the press, he was recalled in November. He set sail from Germany on December 31, 1937. He appears not to have had any hand in the appointment of his successor, Hugh Wilson. Upon his return Dodd gave a series of anti-Nazi speeches and, perhaps influenced by his children, joined the American Friends of the Spanish Democracy.
67 Ibid., p. 53.
68 Ibid., p. 58.
69 Ibid., p. 59.
70 Ibid.
71 Volkogonov, *Stalin: Triumph and Tragedy*, p. 307, says that "between 4.5 and 5.5 million people were arrested, of whom 800–900,000 were sentenced to death." However, Christopher Andrew and Oleg Gordievsky state in *KGB: The Inside Story* (pp. 139ff) that in a response to a secret request from the Politburo in 1956, the KGB "produced a figure of about 19 million arrests for the period 1935 to 1940, of whom at least 7 million were shot or died in a gulag. Robert Conquest in the first edition of his book, *The Great Terror*, estimated the figure at 7–8 million arrests in 1937–38. In the latest edition of his book (1990) he gives a figure of 20 million dead for the Stalin period.
72 MD to Ilya Ehrenburg, October 29, 1957.
73 Agnes Knickerbocker to MD, July 29, 1969.
74 Agnes Knickerbocker to MD, June 4, 1969.
75 Ibid.
76 Boris Vinogradov to MD, April 29, 1938.
77 MD to Ilya Ehrenburg, October 29, 1957.
78 Agnes Knickerbocher to MD, June 4, 1967.

79 llya Ehrenburg to MD, January 31, 1957.

80 Maclean, *Eastern Approaches*, pp. 83ff.

81 Leonhardt, *Child of the Revolution*, p. 58.

82 Maclean, op. cit., p. 86. For Bessonov's refusal to confess see Fischer, *Men and Politics: An Autobiography*, p. 520.

83 Weinstein and Vassiliev, op. cit., p. 54.

84 Costello and Tsarev, op. cit., p. 78.

85 Von Salómon, op. cit., p. 167.

86 Rudolf Heberle, interview by author.

87 MD to Greta Kuckhoff, June 19, 1979.

88 Dodd, "In Memory," p. 4.

89 Ursula, the most celebrated of the Kuczynski siblings, lived in a village outside Oxford. Her career began in 1930 in Shanghai, where she belonged to a group that included Gerhard Eisler, Agnes Smedley, and Richard Sorge. During the 1930s, she trained in Moscow. After settling her children in England in 1939, she moved on to Switzerland, where she founded the Rote Drei, as it was called by the Gestapo. (Britons and Americans preferred the name "Lucy Ring.") The information gleaned via the Lucy Ring was shared among the British, French, and Soviet Intelligence services. During the war, Sonya was posted by the GRU to Britain. She became the contact (after Jürgen had recruited him) for the atom spy Klaus Fuchs. Sonya's network penetrated the British War Cabinet, the RAF, and the Supreme HQ Allied Expeditionary Force (SHAEF). Her father provided her with confidential information from high-level friends like Sir Stafford Cripps, the Labor politician. Sonya spent the war years transmitting secrets to the Soviets from a farm outside Oxford. (She hid the transmitter parts in her children's teddy bears.) Now a "retired" great-grandmother, she lives in eastern Germany. See Williams, *Klaus Fuchs, Atomic Spy*, pp. 50ff.

90 Kuczynski, *Memoiren*, p. 257.

91 Alexander Hirschfeld was Boris's successor as chief of the press department in Berlin and later first secretary. After he left Berlin, he became chargé in Königsberg.

92 Williams, op. cit., pp. 49ff.

CHAPTER TWELVE

1 Quoted in Walter Laqueur, "Nazism and the Nazis," *Encounter*, April 1964, p. 43.

2 Hoffmann, *The History of the German Resistance*, p. 16. According to the Gestapo report of April 10, 1939, 162,734 Germans were held in "protective custody" for political reasons; 27,369 were awaiting trial for political misdemeanors and 112,432 were under sentence for political misdemeanors.

3 See Hoffman, op. cit.; Lamb, *The Ghosts of Peace*; Deutsch, *The Conspiracy against Hitler in the Twilight War*; Meehan, *The Unnecessary War*; Von Klemperer, *The Foreign Policy of the German Resistance*; and Joachim Fest, *Plotting Hitler's Death*.

4 Washington, D.C. *Star*, December 3, 1938.

5 Stewart Herman, interview by author.

6 J. A. Interview by author.

7 Confidential memo from George Messersmith to Hugh Wilson, June 8, 1938, State Department Documents RG 59, 123 H 353/216, NA.

8 Hugh Wilson to George Messersmith, June 20, 1938, State Department Document RG 59, Confidential file 123 H 353/217, NA.

9 State Department cable from Ferdinand Mayer, chargé d'affaires to the secretary of state, August 13, 1937. State Department Documents RG 59, 862.50, NA. Attaché's report on espionage, September 16, 1937, quoting the *Völkischer Beobachter*.

10 George Messersmith to Herbert Feis, June 4, 1938. State Department Documents RG 59, 123 H 353/214, NA.

11 George Messersmith to Herbert Wilson, June 8, 1938, RG 59, Confidential file 123 H 353/216, State Department Documents, NA.

12 Ibid.

13 A detailed list of the activities of Arvid Harnack in the American section of the Economic Ministry from the years 1935 to 1942 is to be found in the Russian Center for the Preservation and Study of Records of Modern History, in Moscow, Collection RWM, Working division plans from the years 1939 to 1942 (1458-53-5) and the files from the American Division (1458-23).

14 Quoted in Falk Harnack, "Vom anderen Deutschland," GDW.

15 Herbert Feis to Wayne C. Taylor, assistant secretary of the treasury, May 12, 1938, State Department Documents RG 59, 862.5151/1884a, NA.

16 Because the anonymity of Heath's informants was preserved, it is sometimes difficult to distinguish what information was provided by Harnack or by other sources, notably economics minister Hjalmar Schacht, whom Heath recruited, and Reichsbank director Emil Puhl. However, Puhl is named and Schacht was not recruited until 1940, when Summer Welles was in Berlin. Thus Harnack appears to have been the prime source of the 1938–1940 reports.

17 Ambassador Jacob Beam, formerly a secretary in the Berlin embassy under both Dodd and Wilson, in an interview with the author confirmed that Arvid's official contact in the American embassy was Donald Heath.

18 See Heath reports 1939–40 State Deptartment Documents RG 59, NA.

19 Otto Donner, interrogation April 1, 1947 by Paul Katscher, Summary no. 1755, RG 238, NA.

20 Heath to Morgenthau, May 2, 1939, Morgenthau papers, Roll 49, pp. 284–88. Franklin Delano Roosevelt Library, Hyde Park.

21 Heath, July 1946. Collection of Sue Heath Brown.

22 Corsican file, Vol. I, p. 37. An abbreviated list is to be found in Costello and Tsarvev, op. cit., p. 77.

23 Leber, ed., *Conscience in Revolt*, p. 130.

24 Bennett, *Nemesis of Power*, p. 289.

25 Ibid., p. 339.

26 Bethge op. cit., p. 528. The list, when it was found by the Gestapo after July 20, 1944, had fatal consequences for Dohnanyi. As best I could determine, it has since disappeared.

27 Quoted in Johnson, *Modern Times*, p. 353.

28 Quoted in Kuckhoff, *Aufbau* (1948): "None of us wished a war. We were

not of the opinion that war was the only way to liberate Germany from the reign of terror. Anyone who was really interested in the true well being of his own people and other nations had to reject war or view it only as the last alternative. To us it seemed vital for the great powers to energetically halt the first attempts of Hitler to pursue his territorial expansionist policy. The firmness of their attitude would have given strength to the resistance fighters within Germany to continue the path perceived as right and, in spite of the high and unavoidable sacrifices, to coordinate the work of the different resistance groups."

29 Interrogation of Otto Donner, Summary no. 1755, p. 12, RG 238, NA.

30 Corsican file, Vol. I, p. 109, quoted in Costello and Tsarev, op. cit., pp. 81–82. The claim that there were sixty people in the Harnacks' group is perhaps optimistic. Although many were connected to the Harnacks socially and all were anti-Nazi, they scarcely shared the same political views. Among Harnack's sources were a few Ph.D's—Otto Donner and Egmont Zechlin for example, neither of whom were Communists—and also a number of Mildred's former students—Karl Behrens, Bodo Schlösinger, and Paul Thomas. While the NKVD hoped to gain a spy network, Harnack's purpose was to search for opponents of the regime who might become post-Hitler leaders. Many of Harnack's sources were just that, sources. In no way should they be presumed to have been part of a Communist spy apparatus.

31 Ibid.

32 Kuckhoff, Lüneberg, VIII, p. 131; in her interview with Lev Besymenski Kuckhoff says she was a year off in her previous statements and places the start of the contact in 1938. Greta Kuckhoff Papers, Besymenski interview, p. 20, GDW.

33 Kuckhoff, *Vom Rosenkranz zur Roten Kapelle*, pp. 211ff.

34 Ibid., p. 217.

35 Rudolf Behse, interview by David Dallin, February 10, 1953, p. 242, Dallin Archives, Ms Division, NYPL.

36 See Malek-Kohler, *Im Windschatten des Dritten Reich*, pp. 159ff.

37 Kuckhoff, *Vom Rosenkranz zur Roten Kapelle*, p. 215; and Malek-Kohler, op. cit., p. 183.

38 Each autumn the Kaiser's entourage gathered at Liebenberg for the all-male *Kaiserjagd*, the imperial hunt. As *eminence grise* of the "Liebenberg Round Table," Eulenburg played an important role in the Kaiser's life, that of pacifist counterweight to Wilhelm's bellicose personality. Accused by their enemies of being an "effeminate *camarilla*," the pacifist circle and its leader, Prince Eulenburg, were subsequently estranged from the kaiser by a homosexual scandal in 1906 involving the prince and Count Kuno von Moltke.

39 Griebel, Coburger, Scheel, eds., *Erfasst*, p. 66.

40 Johannes Haas-Heye, interview by author.

41 Höhne, op. cit., p. 108.

42 HS-B to his parents, January 26, 1936; quoted in Hans Coppi, *Harro Schulze-Boysen—Wege in den Widerstand*, p. 156.

43 LS-B to her parents, April 29, 1936; quoted in Coppi, ibid., p. 157.

44 HS-B to his parents, October 17, 1937; quoted in Coppi, ibid., p. 161.

45 LS-B to her parents, January 1936; quoted in Coppi, ibid., p. 156.

46 LS-B to the Reichsleitung of the NSDAP, Munich, in the Berlin Document Center, quoted in Coppi, "Harro und Libertas Schulze-Boysen," in Coppi et al., *Die Rote Kapelle im Widerstand gegen den Nationalsozialismus*, p. 193.

47 Scheel quoted in Krause, "Ein Mann wie eine Flamme: Eine Tagung über die 'Rote Kapelle' in der Gedenkstätte Deutscher Widerstand," *Frankfurter Allgemeine Zeitung*, November 16, 1981.

48 Marie-Luise Schulze, deposition of December 5, 1948, Lüneburg, quoted in Dallin, op. cit., p. 240.

49 HS-B to Chevalley, August 24, 1935; quoted in Coppi, *Harro Schulze-Boysen — Wege in den Widerstand*, p. 179.

50 HS-B to his parents, April 12, 1934; quoted in ibid., p. 142.

51 Irving, *The Rise and the Fall of the Luftwaffe*, p. 175.

52 See Weisenborn, "Harro und Libertas." In Griebel et al, op. cit., p. 278.

53 Alexander Kraell, August 6, 1948, quoted in Dallin, op. cit., p. 241.

54 Dulles, *Germany's Underground*, p. 100.

55 Niekisch, *Gewagtes Leben: Begegnungen und Begebnisse*, p. 354; quoted in Coppi, *Harro Schulze-Boysen*, p. 180.

56 Coppi, ibid., p. 183.

57 Quoted in Paul, *Ein Sprechzimmer der Roten Kapelle*, pp. 126–27.

58 Dissel, "Harro Schulze-Boysen: Freier, streitbarer Geist," *Junge Welt*, September 2–3, 1989; quoted in Coppi, op cit., p. 184.

59 Perrault, op. cit., pp. 209–10.

60 Buschmann, "De la resistance au defaitisme," *Les Temps Modernes*. 46–67 (1949); quoted in Höhne, op. cit., p. 142.

61 Weisenborn, *Memorial*, p. 3; quoted in Höhne, op. cit., p. 111.

62 Coppi, op. cit., p. 187.

63 Höhne, op. cit., p. 112.

64 Elfriede Paul, interview in Hanna Elling, *Frauen im deutschen Widerstand*, 1933–45, p. 140.

65 Ruth Andreas-Friedrich, *Berlin Underground*, p. xiii.

66 Coppi, op. cit., p. 185.

67 Griebel et al., op. cit., p. 66.

68 For the information about these arrests, I have drawn on the information contained in Griebel et al., op. cit.

69 Wilhelm Utech Protocol, Rote Kapelle Collection, GDW.

70 Clara Behrens Protocol, February 1969, Rote Kapelle Collection, GDW.

71 Corsican file, no 34118, Vol. I, pp. 57–61; quoted in Costello and Tsarev, op. cit., p. 80.

72 Quoted in Kuckhoff, "Rote Kapelle," *Aufbau* 1 (1948).

73 Utech, op. cit.

74 Ibid.

75 Behrens, op. cit.

76 For a discussion of Gestapo techniques, see Merson, *Communist Resistance in Nazi Germany*, pp. 52ff.

77 Utech, op. cit.

78 Wolfgang Havemann, op. cit.

79 During his stay, for example, in Sachsenhausen, Wilhelm Guddorf made

contacts with the Hamburg resistance circle formed around Robert Abshagen and Bernhard Bästlein.

80 Hugo Buschmann, "De la resistance au defaitisme," *Les Temps Modernes* 46–47 (1949): 265.

81 *Der Spiegel*, "Spionage: Das Geheimnis der V-Stoffe," 24 (1978): 90ff.

82 Paul, *Ein Sprechzimmer der Roten Kapelle*, pp. 115ff.

83 Griebel, et al., op. cit., pp. 166–67.

84 Behrens Protocol.

85 Tau, *Ein Flüchtling findet sein Land*, p. 175; and *Auf dem Weg zur Versöhnung*, p. 84.

86 Corsican file, Vol. I, p. 72. In the KGB files the person is called Matulski. A member of the BGA and of the German Communist Party (KPD), "with the help of Balt's wife" he obtained an entry visa to the United States and left Germany quietly. He became known as Arnold Motulski in the United States and appears again in the Harnacks' FBI files."

87 Wollheim, "Giessen zu Beginn der dreißiger Jahre." Ms. new series, 401, fol. 21, GU.

88 Bonnie Kime Scott, *Selected Letters of Rebecca West*, pp. 395–96. West was engaged at the time in writing *The New Meaning of Treason*. See also Dulles, *The Craft of Intelligence*, pp. 109–10.

89 Ibid.

90 Clara Leiser to William Ellery Leonard, February 1, 1939, Leiser Papers.

91 Kuckhoff, "Und ich habe Deutschland so geliebt . . . In memoriam Mildred Harnack-Fish—Lehrbeauftragte der Berliner Universität," in Gerald Wiemers, ed., *Ein Stück Wirklichkeit mehr: Zum 25. Jahrestag der Ermordung von Adam Kuckhoff*, p. 43.

92 Kuckhoff, *Vom Rosenkranz zur Roten Kapelle*, p. 188.

93 MH-F to Clara Harnack, November 1937, Falk Harnack Collection, GDW.

94 Otto Donner to Harriette Esch, September 5, 1945. Mildred Harnack War Crimes Files 12-2018, NA.

95 MH-F, "Durge Norge," p. 28; original in Harnack Archives, HU.

96 Elsa Boysen, op. cit., p. 17 (1947); quoted in Höhne, op. cit., p. 110.

97 Heath to Morgenthau, May 2, 1939, Roll 49, pp. 284–88, Morgenthau Diary, Franklin Delano Roosevelt Library, Hyde Park.

98 Ibid.

99 In the Feldurteil, the sentencing document from Harnack's case states: "He was also nationally oriented which is proven . . . by the fact that he had succeeded in the time before the war in getting German property from America to save it. He said he had also secured the German copper supply before the war." Quoted in Haase, op. cit., p. 109. Roeder in the CIA Rote Kapelle File (RG 319 ZA 020253), NA, p. 436, confirms this.

100 Falk Harnack interview by author, re the I. G, Farben case. Harnack's FBI file contains an article in the *Washington Evening Star*, December 4, 1947, which indicates that American government officials wished to interrogate Arvid.

101 Morley, *For the Record*, pp. 341ff. Also Christopher Sykes, *Troubled Loyalty*, pp. 293ff.

102 Martin Gilbert, review of *The Unnecessary War*, by Patricia Meehan, *Guardian Weekly*, August 9, 1992.

103 Harriette Esch to Clara Leiser, February 12, 1947, Leiser Papers.
104 Kuckhoff, *Vom Rosenkranz zur Roten Kapelle*, p. 227.
105 Utech Protocol, GDW.
106 Quoted in Shirer, *The Nightmare Years*, p. 433.
107 Malek-Kohler, op. cit., pp. 180ff.
108 Buschmann, op. cit., p. 264; translated in Perrault, op. cit., p. 217.
109 Elsa Boysen, op. cit., p. 17.
110 B. H. Liddell-Hart, ed., *The Soviet Army*, p. 265; quoted in Höhne, op. cit., p. 35; Volkogonov, *Stalin*, op. cit., p. 344.
111 Höhne, op. cit., pp. 40ff.
112 Kent Protocol, Russian Foreign Intelligence Service Archive (formerly the KGB Archive).

CHAPTER THIRTEEN

1 AH to CH, January 7, 1940, Falk Harnack Collection, GDW.
2 Bethge, "Bonhoeffers Familie und ihre Bedeutung für seine Theologie," *Beiträge zum Widerstand*, 1933–1945, no. 30, p. 3.
3 Falk Harnack, interview by author. Another family member recalled that once when Clara was arrested, she was brought before a judge who asked if she had called Hitler a "*Scheisskerl*" ("shitty fellow"). She replied, "A woman of my class would never use such a word."
4 Stanley Herman, interview by author.
5 Mildred's dissertation is all that remains of this contemplated work: five chapters devoted to Sherwood Anderson, Thornton Wilder, Thomas Wolfe, William Faulkner, Theodore Dreiser, an overview of American literature, and a conclusion. Omitted, upon her professor's suggestion, were a chapter on Dreiser and Sandburg, whose ties to international left-wing causes were too controversial.
6 Harnack File, Archives of the Guggenheim Foundation.
7 Memo from John V. van Sickle, November 30, 1937, RG (General Correspondence) Harnack File, Rockefeller Foundation Archive.
8 Clara Harnack to Riccarda Huch, July 31, 1946, IfZ, Munich.
9 Falk Harnack interview by author. The ticket is listed on the final inventory of her possessions, filed immediately before her death. It was confiscated by the Gestapo.
10 The Dutch comander in chief, General Winkelman, called Oster an "*erbärmlicher Kerl*," quoted in Klemperer, *German Resistance to Hitler: The Search for Allies Abroad, 1938–1945*, p. 6.
11 Graml, "Der Fall Oster," *Vierteljahrshefte für Zeitgeschichte* 14 (1966): 39; quoted in Hoffman, op. cit., p. 172.
12 Bethge, op. cit., p. 579.
13 She wrote, "Yes, Goethe slept here where I am sleeping. That makes him very human to me, and also shows me what great abilities, albeit not fully developed, each person has who lies down to sleep each night." Mildred Harnack to Clara Harnack, September 17, 1940, GDW.
14 Costello and Tsarev, op. cit., p. 79.
15 Ibid., p. 78. According to Costello and Tsarev, there were five so-called intelligence agents who were recalled and executed for treason. Harnack's initial contact had been Alexander Hirschfeld, who was recalled to Mos-

cow. Hirschfeld introduced Harnack to Boris Gordon, who became the NKVD's Berlin resident in 1935. Gordon gave Harnack the cover name "Balt." In 1938, Gordon was ordered back to Moscow, where he was arrested and sentenced to death in the purge trials. The contact to Harnack was taken over by Alexander Belkin and later by Nikolai Amajanz. However, Belkin was sent to Spain and Agajanz suddenly died (Corsican file, Vol. I, p. 92). The fifth was probably Bessonov.

16 Costello and Tsarev, op. cit., p. 80.

17 The sentencing document, Harnack's Feldurteil, gives the amount received from Erdberg shortly before the invasion of the Soviet Union as 8,000 marks. In the Corsican file, Vol. I, p. 194, it is stated that on June 24, Korotkov gave 20,000 marks to Elisabeth Schumacher for the group. Corsican file, Vol. I, p. 194, RFIS.

18 Harnack, Feldurteil. The author encountered repeated denials that an official sentencing document of the Rote Kapelle trial ever existed. However, in 1990, after the fall of the GDR, the document emerged from the Archives of the Institute of Marxism and Leninism. In 1993, Norbert Haase published the Feldurteils of the principal members of the Rote Kapelle in *Das Reichskriegsgericht und der Widerstand gegen die nationalsozialistische Herrschaft*, pp. 105ff.

19 Dr. Hans-Jürgen Finck, interview by David Dallin, in Dallin Papers, NYPL, p. 180. Finck was the investigator in the postwar war crimes case against Manfred Roeder. He told Dallin that "first conversations about anti-Fascism were held, but when, for example, Harnack refused to occupy himself with espionage, but only with resistance work, the Soviets told him, 'the Gestapo will be very interested.' "

20 Quoted in Edward Epstein, *Deception: The Invisible War between the KGB and the CIA*, p. 88.

21 Statement by Eugen Schmitt, Lüneburg, Vol. III, p. 510.

22 Corsican file, Vol. I, p. 112.

23 Ibid.

24 Ibid., p. 115. Korotkov's written report of his meeting with Harnack on January 17, 1941.

25 Costello and Tsarev, op. cit., p. 81.

26 This was the Brunswick libel trial against Major Otto Remer, a member of the Berlin guard battalion who was responsible for aborting the July 20 coup attempt.

27 Large, "A Beacon in the German Darkness: The Anti-Nazi Resistance Legacy in West German Politics," in Geyer and Boyer, eds. *Resistance against the Third Reich*, p. 245.

28 Klemperer, op. cit., p. 63.

29 Höhne, op. cit., pp. 246–47.

30 Höhne, ibid., p. 247.

31 Falk Harnack, interview by author.

32 Zechlin, "Erinnerung an Arvid und Mildred Harnack," *Geschichte in Wissenschaft und Unterricht*, p. 398.

33 The colleague was Albrecht Haushofer, later a July 20 conspirator. Hildebrandt, *Wir sind die Letzten: Aus dem Leben des Widerstandskämpfers Al-*

brecht Haushofer und seiner Freunde, p. 150. Harnack and Schulze-Boysen were influenced by Ernst Niekisch and his vision of a "national Bolshevism" that posited a bridge between the radical socialism of communism and German nationalism.

34 Zechlin, op. cit.

35 David Dallin, interview with Adolf Grimme, Notebook 2, p. 170, Dallin Papers, Ms Division, NYPL.

36 Corsican file, Vol. I, p. 62, quoted in Costello and Tsarev, op. cit., p. 82.

37 Wolfgang Havemann, interview by author.

38 "Einige Stichpunkte über Arvid Harnacks Leben entsprechende Aussprechen mit Falk" Greta Kuckhoff Papers, Bundesarchiv, Abteilungen Potsdam. Additional information provided in an interview with Falk Harnack by the author.

39 AH to CH, October 12, 1940, Falk Harnack Archives, GDW.

40 AH to CH, October, 1940, Falk Harnack Archives.

41 As far as the author was able to determine, this memo has never been found.

42 Corsican file, Vol. I, p. 99.

43 Corsican file, Vol. I, p. 75.

44 Corsican file, Vol. I, pp. 115–16.

45 Corsican file, Vol. I, pp. 108ff.

46 Corsican file, Vol. I, pp. 73ff.

47 Letter from Georg Lukács to Renate Dörner, Harnack Papers, HU; and Corsican file, Vol. I, p. 74. See also letter Georgi Dimitrov to P. N. Fitin, April 12, 1941 (495-74-27), Dimitrov Collection, Comintern Archive.

48 Under the pseudonym of Peter Tarin, Heinz Tietjens was the coauthor (with Adam Kuckhoff) of a mystery novel, *Strogany and the Missing Person (Strogany und die Vermissten).*

49 According to Donald Heath, Mildred had instructed the Heaths to put an ad in the newspaper for a tutor and Paul Thomas answered. Young Donald and Thomas went on hikes where they discussed Dos Passos and Knut Hamsun, Karl Liebknecht and Rosa Luxemburg. He disappeared in Breslau during World War II.

50 Korotkov reported meeting Karl Behrens in mid-April 1941: "The meeting with BEAMER took place in the apartment of Corsican with the latter present. Corsican recently renewed his contact with BEAMER, in order to find out what had changed in his life. BEAMER said that he had already been waiting a long time to resume his cooperation with us. He works as a design engineer at the military plant AEG Turbine. . . . In one section of the company, BEAMER heads a group consisting of five people. It includes a design engineer, a machinist and three laborers. It is not impossible that these might include Communists or former members of the KPD who have left the party because of the pressure. The work done in the group is essentially propagandistic, i.e. Karl holds conversations with each of the individuals in order to raise morale. BEAMER explained the limited nature of the group by saying that he is alone and cannot consult with anyone about how to pursue anti-fascist work. He is absolutely convinced of the necessity of this work. The members of the group do not know one another and are connected only via BEAMER. After further detailed study of the BEAMER group, the ques-

tion can be decided as to whether it is suitable for sabotage activities. Behrens himself, it seems to us, does not have informational possibilities available to him and can probably be further use as a helper, for example, as a radio operator. The question of a separation of CORSICAN and BEAMER, their isolation from one another, must in our opinion occur without unnecessary haste. Rushing this could negatively impact the morale of both and complicate our relationships with them. Quoted in Petscherski MS, pp. 145–56, Rote Kapelle Archive, GDW. The original is in the RFIS Archive, Moscow.

51 Corsican file, Vol. I, pp. 93–95, 97, and 113.

52 Interrogation of Otto Donner, April 1, 1947, by Paul Katscher: Summary no. 1755, RG 153, NA.

53 Corsican file, Vol. I, pp. 109–10.

54 Wilhelm Utech Protocol, December 1986, p. 16, AST/RK 43, GDW.

55 Corsican file, Vol. I, p. 206.

56 Ibid., p. 217.

57 Ibid., p. 206. Two charges have been made against the Red Orchestra: that their activities, like those of many other Communist groups ceased during the period of the Nazi–Soviet Pact—between September 1939 and May 1941—and that they failed to work with the West. Both assertions, we have seen, are false.

58 Corsican file, Vol. I, p. 217.

59 Ibid., p. 221.

60 Petscherski Ms., pp. 125–26. RFIS Archive.

61 Greta Kuckhoff, interview by Biernat, p. 27, Ast/RK 40, GDW.

62 CIA, "Rote Kapelle," Vol. I, p. 242, NA.

63 Interrogation of Otto Donner, April 1, 1947, by Paul Katscher, Summary no. 1755, RG 153, NA.

64 Interrogation of Otto Donner. Donner cites as proof in his interrogation a book by Undersecretary of State Summer Welles, *The Time for Decision*: "Welles reports on the sensational effect that the news transmitted to the State Department at the end of 1940/beginning of 1941 concerning a probable attack by Hitler on Russia had and discusses how the Russian Ambassador in Washington was then immediately informed." The KGB files also mention this information coming from Donner at the beginning of February 1941; see Coppi et al., op. cit., p. 113.

65 Corsican file, no. 34118, Vol. I, p. 107, a telegram from Berlin dated January 20, 1941.

66 Report of Korotkov to Foreign Intelligence Service, March 9, 1941; Corsican file, no. 34118, Vol. II, pp. 24–25; quoted in Coppi et al., op. cit., p. 114.

67 Ibid., Vol. II, p. 23; quoted in Costello and Tsarev, op. cit., p. 391.

68 Ibid., Vol. II, pp. 20ff., quoted in Costello and Tsarev, ibid.

69 Ibid., Vol. II, p. 23; quoted in Coppi et al., op. cit., p. 113.

70 Ibid., Vol. II, p. 32; quoted in Coppi et al., op. cit., p. 123.

71 April report from Korotkov: original in Moscow cited by Petscherski, "Tajna Krasnoi Kapelle," p. 88, quoted in Coppi, et al., p. 125. This message was delivered on April 10 by Merkulov to Stalin, Molotov, Timoschenko, and Beria.

72 Corsican file, Vol. I, pp. 183–84; quoted in Costello and Tsarev, op. cit., p. 85.

73 Corsican file, Vol. II, pp. 31–32. See Coppi et al., op. cit., p. 135; and Costello and Tsarev, op. cit., p. 393.

74 Ibid., Vol. II, p. 33; quoted in Coppi et al., p. 136.

75 Quoted in Gorodetsky, *Grand Delusion: Stalin and the German Invasion of Russia*, p. 296.

76 Corsican file, Vol. I, p. 223; quoted in Costello and Tsarev, op. cit., p. 86.

77 Full text published in *Isvestia* of the Central Committee of the CPSU, April 1990; quoted in Costello and Tsarev, op. cit., p. 86.

78 Baidakov, "Facts on Intelligence from the Archives of the Security Organs of the Soviet Union," *Pravda*, May 9, 1989; quoted in Andrew and Gordievsky, *KGB: The Inside Story*, p. 265.

79 Dimitrov's diary, February 20, 1941: quoted in Gorodetsky, op cit., p. 54.

80 Whaley in his book *Operation Barbarossa* (1973) estimated that Stalin received at least eighty-four warnings. Andrew and Mitrokhin, *The Mitrokhin Archive* (1999) quote KGB historians who have counted "over a hundred" intelligence warnings forwarded by Fitin to Stalin between January 1941 and June 1941.

81 Gorodetsky, op. cit., p. 184.

82 Ibid., pp. 180–81.

83 Report by "Starschina," May 9, 1941; quoted in ibid., p. 188.

84 Andrew and Gordievsky, op. cit., pp. 243ff.

85 Tschernjawski, *Neue Zeit* 33 (1991): 15–16.

86 Orlov, *Handbook of Intelligence and Guerilla Warfare*, p. 10.

87 Vladimi Petrov, ed., June 22, 1941, pp. 250ff: quoted in Whaley, *Codeword Barbarossa*, pp. 194ff.

88 G. K. Zhukov, *The Memoirs of Marshal Zhukov*, Vol. I, p. 229; quoted in Andrew and Gordievsky, op. cit., p. 269.

89 Trepper, *The Great Game*, p. 127.

90 Ibid.

91 Quoted in Whymant, *Stalin's Spy*, p. 158, who gives as his source the Russian archives and the date as June 19. Andrew and Gordievsky, op. cit., p. 264, give the date as May 19. The telegram is also paraphrased in Gorodetsky, op. cit., p. 182, who gives early June as the date.

92 Dementyeva, Agayants, and Yakovlev, *Tovarisch Zorge*; quoted in Andrew and Gordievsky, op. cit., p. 264.

93 Dallin, op. cit., pp. 132–33.

94 Andrew and Gordievsky, op. cit., p. 244.

95 Read and Fischer, *The Deadly Embrace: Hitler, Stalin, and the Nazi–Soviet Pact, 1939–1941*, p. 595.

96 Quoted in Andrew and Gordievsky, op. cit., p. 264.

97 Corsican file, Vol. II. p. 29; quoted in Costello and Tsarev, op. cit., p. 89. A slightly different version appears in Gorodetsky, op. cit., p. 186.

98 Costello and Tsarev, ibid.

99 Instruction of the NKVD to Korotkov, April 5, 1941. Corsican file, Vol. I, p. 223; quoted in Coppi et al., op. cit., pp. 124–25.

100 Gorodetsky, op. cit., p. 297.

101 Corsican file, Vol. II, p. 23.

102 Ibid., Vol. I, pp. 97–98.
103 Schulze-Boysen and Harnack held some discussions with the members of the July 20 group of resisters. A page from the Harnacks' FBI file states that "there was direct contact with the 20th of July people." We have seen that Harnack had significant familial links with Klaus Bonhoeffer and his cousin Ernst von Harnack, who were part of the circle around Julius Leber. Zechlin had also brought him together with Professor Albrecht Haushofer and diplomats Adam von Trott zu Solz and Hasso von Etzdorf. See Scheel, " 'Die Rote Kapelle' und der 20. Juli 1944," *Zeitschrift für Geschichtwissenschaft*, Vol. 4; and Hildebrant, op. cit., pp. 138ff.
104 Corsican file, Vol. II, p. 23.
105 Ibid.; quoted in Coppi et al., p. 114.
106 Corsican file, Vol. II, p. 29; quoted by Coppi et al., op. cit., p. 126.
107 Cited in Petscherski, "Tajna Krasnoi Kapelle," Ms. copy Rote Kapelle Collection, pp. 133–34, GDW; quoted in Coppi et al., p. 130.
108 Gorodetsky, op. cit., p. 247.
109 Costello, *Ten Days to Destiny*, pp. 435ff.
110 Quoted in Gorodetsky, op. cit., p. 268.
111 Read and Fisher, op. cit., p. 578.
112 Quoted in Beevor, *Stalingrad, the Fateful Seige: 1942–1943*, p. 5.
113 Corsican file, Vol. I, p. 393.
114 Ibid., p. 116.
115 Kuckhoff, interview by Biernat, p. 93.
116 Instructions from NKGB to Korotkov, April 12, 1941, Corsican file, Vol. I, p. 249; quoted in Coppi et al., op. cit., p. 126.
117 Corsican file, Vol. I, p. 385.
118 Ibid., Vol. II, p. 17.
119 Ibid, Vol. I, p. 345.
120 Trubetzkoi report, June 12, 1941; quoted in Coppi et al., op. cit., p. 133.
121 Excerpt from a letter of the Berlin *rezidentura* prepared by Trubetzkoi, June 17, 1941, quoted in Coppi et al., op. cit., p. 135.
122 Coppi et al., op. cit., p. 134.
123 Radó, *Dora meldet*, p. 453.
124 As Kuckhoff repeated this story many times there are different versions. For the most part I have drawn the story from the 1986 version of *Vom Rosenkranz zur Roten Kapelle*, pp. 262ff.
125 Kuckhoff letter, Lüneburg, Vol. VIII, p. 132.
126 Kuckhoff, *Vom Rosenkranz zur Roten Kapelle*, pp. 262ff. A version of Greta's story also appears in Höhne, op. cit., p. 128. He quotes Alexander Kraell, Lüneburg, Vol. XIII, p. 96 and Kuckhoff, Lüneburg, Vol. VIII, p. 131. He gives the date as June 14, 1941. Versions vary as to whether the radio worked or not and when it was broken.
127 Testimony of Ismail Ege, October 28, 1953. Hearings before the Senate Internal Security Subcommittee, 1006, quoted in Dallin, *Soviet Espionage*, pp. 134–35. Berezhkov, *Erlebte Geschichte, 1940 bis 1943: Dolmetscher und Diplomat gegen Faschismus und Krieg*, pp. 214ff.
128 Quoted in Andrew and Mitrokhin, op. cit., p. 94.
129 Whaley, op. cit., pp. 20ff.
130 Akhmedov, *In and Out of Stalin's GRU: A Tartar's Escape from Red Army*

Intelligence, pp. 146ff and Seweryn Bialer, *Stalin and His Generals,* pp. 214ff.

131 Bialer, op. cit., p. 583, n. 40.

132 Valentin Berezhkov, *Erlebte Geschichte 1940 bis 1943: Dolmetscher und Diplomat gegen Faschismus und Krieg,* pp. 91ff.

133 Kuckhoff, interview by Besymenski, pp. 31ff; the story also appears in the Biernat interview, pp. 90ff. Rote Kapelle Collection, GDW.

134 Petscherski, op. cit., p. 174; quoted in Coppi et al., op. cit., p. 137.

135 Information from exhibition "Rote Kapelle GDW, 1992–1993." The exhibition gave the date as June 21, 1941.

136 Letter of the Berlin *rezidentura* of June 17, 1941 prepared by Trubetzkoi, an employee of the NKGB Moscow; Coppi et al., op. cit., p. 135. A handwritten note (February 2, 1942) states: "The book is not in the 'Hans' file. *Der Kurier aus Spanien* is a novel by Hans Rabl (pseud. Hanns Kriesten) that was published in Berlin in 1939. Copies of it would have been readily available. Whether it was received by the Berlin rezidentura is uncertain.

137 Dallin (p. 245) says they were given 13,500 marks (at that time about $5,000). According to the Gestapo Final Report (RG 319 Z 0202253), p. 32, Korotkov gave Harnack 12,000 RM and 1,500 RM to Kuckhoff. Harnack distributed 2,000 to Grimme, 5,000 to Behrens, 3,000 to Skrzypczynski, and 1,000 to Rose Schlösinger. He kept the remaining 1,000 for himself. The exhibition "Rote Kapelle at the GDW" gave 8,000 as the figure. Corsican file, Vol. I, p. 386, says that Korotkov left 20,000 marks for expenses for Harnack and Schulze-Boysen as well as instructions for enciphering based on the number 19405 with Elisabeth Schumacher.

138 Corsican file, Vol. I, p. 385.

139 Petscherski, *Neue Zeit,* p. 174; quoted in Coppi, et. al., op. cit., p. 137. See also Blank and Mader, op. cit., pp. 221ff.

140 Report by Alexander Kraell, Lüneburg, August 6, 1948, Vol. III, p. 382, quoted in Höhne, op. cit., p. 129.

CHAPTER FOURTEEN

1 W. F. Flicke, *Spionagegruppe Rote Kapelle,* pp. 8–9.

2 Flicke, *Kreigsgeheimnisse in Aether,* translated as *War Secrets in the Ether,* SRH-002 AFSA-14; unpublished version in NA (RG 319, ZA 020253).

3 Höhne, op. cit., p. xv, credits the Abwehr with christening the Soviet circuit: "The word 'orchestra had long been part of the Abwehr's vocabulary. Admiral Wilhelm Canaris's officers described any enemy espionage circuit as an 'orchestra'; its short-wave transmitters were 'pianos,' its radio operators 'pianists' and its organisers 'conductors.' Roeder argues, p. 421 (RG 319 ZA 020259): "The name Red Orchestra was coined as a cover name during the investigation conducted by Amt IV of the Staatspolizei. It was customary to refer to radio operators as 'musicians' and to a group of 'musicians' as an 'orchestra.' Thus, the name indicated that the case involved the transmission of information via shortwave in behalf of the 'Reds.' " Schellenberg, *The Labyrinth,* p. 277, credits the Gestapo with naming the Red Orchestra. During the Cold War the term became inclusive, covering not only German, Swiss, French, Belgian, and Dutch but sometimes even British groups. The Rote Kapelle, or Red Orchestra, be-

came synonymous with Soviet espionage. By the 1970s, even members of
the resistance were calling themselves the Red Orchestra.

4 Gestapo Final Report, p. 5 (RG 319 ZA 020253), NA. Dallin says 120 messages, p. 252.

5 Kuckhoff interview with the Soviet journalist Lev Bezymenski, p. 22 (Ast/
RK35), GDW. See also her Biernat interview, pp. 39,93, GDW.

6 Gestapo Final Report, p. 21 (RG 319 ZA 020253).

7 Ibid., p. 36; Coppi, *Junge Welt*, December 22, 1967.

8 Kahn, *The Codebreakers*, p. 660.

9 All in all, the number of messages sent from Berlin seems to have been greatly
exaggerated. *Spiegel* journalist Heinz Höhne, basing his information on the
Gestapo Final Report, says that between June 14, 1941, and August 30,
1942, the Berlin group sent 500 radio messages to Moscow containing primarily military information (Höhne, op. cit., p. 240). One factor that would
account for the discrepancy between the number of messages stated in the
KGB and Gestapo archives would be that as the Russian front collapsed,
Soviet military intelligence also retreated and consequently the messages
reached the Funkabwehr but not the retreating Russians.

10 Kuckhoff interview: quoted in Blank and Mader, *Rote Kapelle gegen Hitler*,
p. 207; Biernat interview, pp. 28ff.

11 Blank and Mader, op. cit., p. 208.

12 Haveman describes Harnack's evening activities in March 1986: "Evenings
were devoted to the exchange of ideas and important information with comrades. He also needed to receive regular reports about the war situation on
the radio. And when night came he produced short, accurate, and absolutely
reliable analyses of the economic situation, then had to painstakingly encrypt
them, destroy the original, and send the message on its way. After the messages were sent, the enciphered messages were destroyed." Haveman "Erinnerung," SLD. Kuckhoff told Biernat (p. 103) that Arvid "considered it
proper to keep the technical side and the contents side of the material to be
transmitted as radically separate from each other as possible, in order to
incriminate the partner and the group itself as little as possible. During the
last nights, as far as I know, he worked day and night and was extraordinarily pressured, to the point of nervous exhaustion."

13 Gestapo Final Report, p. 35 (RG 319 ZA 020253).

14 This system was widely used by Soviet intelligence during World War II.
Thanks to David Kahn for his description of how it worked.

15 In her interview with Besymenski, Kuckhoff says that the group gave the
information on the order of battle and the dozen or so places that were
to be attacked first to Korotkov in June. As she had difficulty memorizing
the Russian names, Adam, who had a particularly good memory for places
and names, undertook the job. Besymenski, p. 29. In her interview with
Biernat, p. 42, she says that "Harro had knowledge of the operational plan
and Arvid of the delivery of supplies." Later she said that "when we saw
on our large map that in all of the places named there were few defensive
forces to be found, Arvid, Harro, and Adam, in my presence, expressed and
examined and rejected doubts and questions in connection with this, and
then still continued to brood about it" (Biernat, 90). In this second inter-

view she states Libertas went with Adam to the meeting: "Two people had to go, so that if possible nothing would be forgotten, and also, in particular, because a pair would be less conspicuous than a single person (Biernat, p. 91).

16 Many members of the Rittmeister group were alumnae of the Heilsher Evening School, where Eva had been a student.

17 "Exhibition Rote Kapelle," GDW, Berlin, 1992–1993, displayed the leaflet and investigative material of the Gestapo, including a daily report of the Federal Police (no. 9, February 23, 1942), which states: "On 18 and 19 February, 1942, a large number of six-page inflammatory pamphlets were written under the title 'Distress about Germany's Future runs through the Nation.' These typed flyers were sent to various Catholic dioceses and to a number of people in intellectual professions such as professors, doctors, engineers, etc. through the post office SW 21, NW 7, W8, and Charlottenburg 2 in closed envelopes. The envelopes showed the dispatch dates of 14, 15 and 16 February." It appears that a number were also mailed outside Berlin. The Gestapo eventually collected 288 examples of the pamphlet. It appears that besides the writer, Schulze-Boysen, his accomplices were Johannes Graudenz, Helmut Himpel, and Maria Terweil. All were executed.

18 Blank and Mader, op. cit., p. 112, say that there were about twenty issues over a two-year period but only one, from August 1942, remains. In it the authors warn that only the end of the war could save Germany and Europe from catastrophe.

19 Rosiejka, op. cit., p. 75.

20 Gestapo Final Report, p. 33.

21 Greta Kuckhoff, interview by Biernat, pp. 40ff.

22 Buschmann, "De la resistance au defaitisme," *Les Temps Modernes* 46–67 (1949) quoted in Höhne, p. 133.

23 Krauss, Lüneburg, Vol. X, p. 259, quoted in Höhne, p. 135.

24 Greta Kuckhoff, interview by Biernat, p. 55.

25 Malek-Kohler, op. cit., p. 199 and Alexander Spoerl, "Libertas Schulze-Boysen in Wiemers, ed., *Ein Stück Wirklichkeit Mehr*, p. 54.

26 Weisenborn, "Harro und Libertas," *Erfasst*, p. 279.

27 Kuckhoff, interview with Biernat, pp. 48–49; and *Vom Rosenkranz zur Roten Kapelle*, pp. 297ff.

28 Blank and Mader, op. cit., p. 111, Gestapo Final Report, p. 29. It was later said that Schulze-Boysen threatened the group with a loaded revolver (Gestapo Final Report, p. 29). To this, Kuckhoff replied (Biernat interview, p. 49): "I did not learn about the cocked pistol until later, and then in two versions: first, to protect those putting up the stickers, in case someone came, or possibly to fire into the air and cause a diversion. Our enemies then claimed that he had forced the people with a cocked pistol to carry out the sticker operation. . . . After Harro was dead, the defendants had every right to say this. It was not a public trial, but a trial in which the point was to mislead the judges as much as possible, and Harro was no longer alive. So nobody was hurting him or the cause. Based on my own experience prior to arrest, I can say nothing. My knowledge stems from conversations while in prison."

29 CIC Franz Six File (G8139007), NA.

30 SS Major Alfred Franz Six (1909–1976) was dean of the Foreign Studies Department of the University of Berlin and leader of the SD Amt VII (ideological research). Described by Adolf Eichmann as a "real eager beaver" on the Jewish question, he was a special favorite of Himmler's. One of Six's important projects was the Wannsee Institute, where he oversaw the collecting of intelligence on the Soviet Union. In the summer of 1941, as commander of the "Advance Party Moscow," he took part in the mass murder of Jews and partisans near Smolensk. In 1943, Six was transferred to the Foreign Office, where he helped plan a pan-European, anti-Semitic conference. After the war, together with Klaus Barbie, he was "rehabilitated" by the Americans and went to work for the intelligence specialist and former general Reinhard Gehlen. However, he was betrayed to the CIC by one of his former agents, convicted of war crimes in the *Einsatzgruppenprozess* and sentenced by the U.S. Military Court at Nuremberg to twenty years in prison. Four years later, in 1952, he was given clemency by the U.S. High Commissioner in Germany, John McCloy. He then rejoined his former SS and Gestapo colleagues in Gehlen's intelligence service, the BND, where he recruited agents from among former Soviet POWs. He also served as publicity manager for Porsche-Diesel as an advisor to both the West German and American governments. Vassiltchikov, *The Berlin Diaries*, p. 309; and Alfred Six CIC File, G8139007, NA.

31 Haase, *Das Reichskriegsgericht und der Widerstand gegen die nationalsozialistische Herrschaft*, pp. 113ff. and Hildebrandt, op. cit., pp. 138ff.

32 An account of this meeting and a reconstruction of the dialogue between Schulze-Boysen and Albrecht Haushofer about the Soviet Union occurs in Hildebrandt's book, op. cit., pp. 142ff., and Zechlin, "Erinnerung an Arvid und Mildred Harnack," *Geschichte in Wissenschaft und Unterricht*, pp. 398ff.

33 Griebel et al., op. cit., p. 64.

34 Gollnow Feldurteil, Haase, op. cit., pp. 110ff.

35 Jane Donner Sweeney, interview by author.

36 Gestapo Final Report, p. 40; Griebel et al., op. cit., p. 244.

37 Gollnow Feldurteil; quoted in Haase, op. cit., p. 110.

38 Ibid.

39 Gerhard Ranft, statement March 7, 1950, Lüneburg, Vol. XII, p. 87.

40 Falk Harnack, interview by author.

41 Strübing, statement January 18, 1950, Lüneburg, Vol. X, p. 197; Gollnow Feldurteil, Haase, op. cit., p. 111.

42 Haase, Ibid.

43 MH-F to CH, December 3, 1941. Falk Harnack collection, GDW.

44 MH-F to Ansa Harnack, Christmas 1941, Falk Harnack collection.

45 Stanley Herman, interview by author, and diary.

46 MH-F to Clara Harnack, December 3, 1941, and Christmas 1941. The stories were "Wie Foggeli eine Frau sucht" and "Der Notar in der Falle" by Gotthelf.

47 MH-F to Esches, August 14, 1942.

48 MH-F to Ursel Havemann, n.d., Wolfgang Havemann Archive, SBD.

49 MH-F to Clara Harnack, May 7, 1942.

50 Havemann interrogation, February 13, 1944.

51 This is an error. The Kuckhoffs lived at Wilhelmshöerstrasse 18.

52 During the summer of 1941 when Schulze-Boysen was stationed in Wildpark-West near Potsdam as a member of the Luftwaffe general staff, he kept a tent in nearby Marquardt where his friends met during the Whitsun holidays. Elisabeth Schumacher had acted as an intermediary between Schulze-Boysen and Korotkov during the spring of 1941.

53 Instructions from the military intelligence service (GRU) to Kent in Brussels, August 26, 1941. Cited in Petscherski, op. cit., pp. 193ff., no. 93621, Vol. I, p. 26. Another translation appears in Costello and Tsarev, op. cit., pp. 397ff. Flicke's version in *Spionagegruppe Rote Kapelle* differs from the telegram in the Moscow archive. Earlier writers, e.g., Höhne and Perrault, followed Flicke.

54 Pannwitz interrogation, quoted in *Rote Kapelle*, p. 485 (RG 319 ZA 020253), NA.

55 ss. Kent Protocol, November, 1953, copy provided to the author by Hans Coppi.

56 Ibid.

57 Ibid.

58 Ibid.

59 Gestapo Final Report, pp. 18–19. According to Costello and Tsarev (p. 398), he was unable to replace or repair the radio.

60 Mildred Harnack-Fish Feldurteil; Haase, op. cit., pp. 109–10; Kraell, Lüneburg, Vol. XII, p. 111.

61 Coppi et al., op. cit., pp. 139ff., lists messages in the Russian archive. See also Costello and Tsarev, op. cit., pp. 399–400.

62 Kent to GRU, November 15, 1941; Corsican file, Vol. II, p. 54.

63 For further details on the messages, see Coppi et al., op. cit., pp. 138ff; and Costello and Tsarev, op. cit., pp. 399ff.

64 Kent to GRU, November 21 1941; Corsican file, Vol. II, pp. 64–66, quoted in Costello and Tsarev, op. cit., p. 399.

65 Strübing testimony, statement January 18, 1950, Lüneburg, Vol. XII, p. 1.

66 Admiral Canaris quoted in Prittie, *Germans against Hitler*, p. 214.

67 Willi Weber letter to Höhne; quoted in Höhne, op. cit., p. 235.

68 Memorandum, November 25, 1941, Corsican file, Vol. II, pp. 64–66; quoted in Costello and Tsarev, op. cit., p. 400; and Petscherski, op. cit., p. 50.

69 Höhne devotes most of Chapter Eight to a discussion of the role played by espionage in the Russian campaign. Although much of the information in his book has been superceded by the release of the KGB files, his analysis that the group's information had little effect on Soviet military strategy is probably correct. But a more exhaustive analysis remains to be done.

70 Rohleder, statement July 2, 1950, Lüneburg, Vol. XII, p. 193. Rohleder attended the trial of the Harnacks and Schulze-Boysens and gave a deposition to the state attorney of Lüneberg after the war.

71 Ibid.

72 Ibid.

73 Gestapo Final Report, p. 5. Part of the problem with the number may have been that when the Gestapo presented members of the group with a stack of messages (e.g., Wolfgang Havemann and Greta Kuckhoff), they had no

firsthand idea about the number and content of the messages, and they may have confessed to sending them all.

74 Stahlmann to Dallin, pp. 214ff. Dallin Papers, Ms. Division, NYPL.
75 There are many accounts of the arrests: see CIA, op. cit., pp. 27ff.; Flicke, NA Document SRH-002 (English translation, pp. 108ff); Dallin, op. cit., pp. 152ff.; Höhne, op. cit., pp. 78ff.; Perrault, op. cit., pp. 86ff.; Trepper, op. cit., pp. 148ff.
76 Corsican file, Vol. II, p. 105ff.
77 Corsican file, Vol. II, p. 111.
78 Kuckhoff interview quoted in Blank and Mader, op. cit., p. 209.
79 Petscherski, *Novoe Vremia* (in Russian) "The Moscow Dossier: The Red Orchestra," November 13, 1994, p. 49; Costello and Tsarev, op. cit., pp. 402ff. Hössler and Bart were picked up by the Gestapo.
80 Flicke, writing in 1949, says the book was *Le miracle du Professeur Teramond* by Guy de Lecerf, and the code word was "proctor" (*Spionagegruppe Rote Kapelle*, pp. 147, 131). David Kahn (*The Codebreakers*, p. 1085, n. 658) believes that Flicke juggled the author and title of the book, which was called *Le miracle du Professor Lecerf*. However, in skimming the book, he never found the word "proctor." Schellenberg, p. 280, repeats the Flicke story. Höhne follows Perrault, who gives no source but repeats the Flicke account.
81 Trepper, op. cit., p. 181.
82 Perrault, op. cit., p. 132. Höhne, op. cit., pp. 90ff.
83 Höhne, op. cit., pp. 89ff.; Trepper, op. cit., pp. 160ff.; Kahn, op. cit., p. 658.
84 Schellenberg, *Memoiren*, p. 251: quoted in Coppi et al., op. cit., p. 146.
85 Pannwitz interrogation, Russian Foreign Intelligence Service Archives.
86 Heilmann Feldurteil: Haase, op. cit., p. 113.
87 Ibid.
88 Lüneburg, Finck Final Report, p. 61; Perrault, op. cit., pp. 203–4.
89 The letter bore a Swiss postmark. Otto Donner in a letter intercepted while he was in a "ministerial collecting center" that housed former German officials, mentioned mailing a letter and news from Sweden and Switzerland (September 5, 1945), NA.
90 She enclosed a verse from her translation of Goethe's "Wanderers Nachtlied":

> Thou that cometh from on high
> Stilling suffering and pain,
> Whom despair is doubly nigh
> Doubling quickening like rain,
> Ah, I long for pain to cease
> And for joy to give me rest!
> Lovely peace.

91 Mildred to her family, August 14, 1942.
92 Ingeborg Havemann, "Mildred Harnack: Eine Erinnerung," *Heute und Morgen* 2 (150): 77–78.
93 Falk Harnack, Berlin, 1947, Falk Harnack Archives, GDW.
94 Egmont Zechlin, op. cit., p. 401.
95 Ibid., pp. 395ff.
96 Ibid., p. 397.

CHAPTER FIFTEEN

1 Kuckhoff, interview by Besymenski, p. 48, GDW

2 I have taken this number from the list in *Erfasst*. Other sources give other numbers. The Gestapo report, December 22, 1942, for example, numbers the arrests at 119.

3 Scheel in Wiemers, ed., *Ein Stück Wirklichkeit mehr: Zum 25. Jahrestag der Ermordung von Adam Kuckhoff*, p. 12.

4 On December 3, 1942, Müller informed Himmler of the possibility of a "radio game" with Moscow. A short time later it was approved by Himmler (BA, NS 12/2002, December 12, 1942); quoted Tuchel, "Die Gestapo-Sonderkommission 'Rote Kapelle'" in Coppi et. al., op. cit., p. 158 n. 41.

5 Rürup ed., *Topography of Terror*, p. 70.

6 The Sonderkommission Rote Kapelle probably grew out of a 1942 agreement between Fritz Thiele, the chief of the Funkabwehr, Admiral Canaris of the Amt Ausland/Abwehr, Heinrich Müller, head of the Gestapo, and Walter Schellenberg, SS Brigadier. Under "Gestapo" Müller, a branch was formed in Berlin at the RSHA department IV A2 to counter and investigate the Red Orchestra. The story of the founding of the Sonderkommission Rote Kapelle is told in Schellenberg's memoirs, *The Labyrinth*. However, the information contained in this memoir is to be viewed with caution. Schellenberg told many different versions of his story both in print and to the Allies during his interrogations while he was in British and U.S. custody; see CIC, Schellenberg Files, XE 001752, NA.

7 Strübing, January 18, 1950, Lüneburg, Vol. X, pp. 192ff and XII, p. 7. Tuchel, "Sonderkommission Rote Kapelle," in Coppi, Danyel, and Tuchel, op. cit., pp. 145ff.

8 Strübing, Lüneburg, Vol X, p. 192.

9 Ina Ender; quoted in Molkenbur and Hörhold, *Oda Schottmüller*, p. 76.

10 Ibid.

11 Eva Rittmeister; quoted in Poelchau, op. cit., p. 73.

12 Kuckhoff, interview by Besymenski, p. 48.

13 Havemann interrogation, February 13, 1944, author's copy provided by Hans Coppi.

14 Weisenborn, *Memoiren*, quoted in Tuchel, "Die Gestapo-Sonderkommission 'Rote Kapelle,'" in Coppi et al., op. cit., p. 149. Through the efforts of the survivors of the Red Orchestra and July 20th trials, criminal proceedings were brought against Habecker. He hung himself in his Paderborn cell before he could be tried. For more on Habecker see Tuchel, pp. 148ff.

15 This album was published in 1992; see Griebel, Coburger, and Scheel, *Erfasst*. The impact of the photo album was summed up by an anonymous American: "Considering the great number of young, clean faces, it is a shocking document," p. 15, AFSA 254, Fort Meade.

16 Wolfgang Havemann interrogation.

17 Kuckhoff, Lüneburg, statement February 1, 1947, Vol. V, p. 628, quoted in Höhne, op. cit., p. 169.

18 Testimony of Carl Helfrich, September 1953, German Foreign Office Political Archives; quoted in Sahm, *Rudolf von Scheliha, 1897–1942; Ein deutscher Diplomat gegen Hitler*, p. 193. As of July 1942, the official guide-

lines pertaining to "intensified interrogations" had been rewritten. Under the new rules, rubber truncheons, riding whips, and clubs were routinely permitted against "Communists, Marxists, Seventh-Day Adventists, saboteurs, terrorists, members of resistance movements, parachute agents, asocials, Polish or Soviet Russian work refusers, and vagrants." When such punishment was prescribed, an SS medical officer was usually present to monitor the effect of torture on the prisoner's health, BA, R 58/243, fol. 337; quoted in Tuchel, "Die Gestapo-Sonderkommission 'Rote Kapelle'," in Coppi et al., op. cit., p. 149.

19   The term "Stalin room" appears in a report by Greta Kuckhoff dated February, 1947; quoted in Höhne, op. cit., p. 167: In Habecker's postwar interrogation (August 7, 1948) he elaborates on intensified interrogations: "I was given very clear orders to take vigorous action, if necessary, using intensified means. . . . I had brought the small rod and leg clamps with me from Berlin [to Hamburg where he was interrogating the parachutists Eifler and Fellendorf] and took them back with me. These methods—I don't know who invented them—were to be used instead of beatings. If they didn't work, then beatings with the stick would be used." Quoted in Coppi et al., op. cit., p. 149.

20   "Collective Report of Survivors," from p. 22 of a document entitled "USSR Military Intelligence: penetration of the German Government during World War II." AFSA 254, Fort Meade. The date is listed as October 11, implying that Sieg and Grimme were picked up as a consequence of Kuckhoff's torture. The information is probably from Greta Kuckhoff, who testified to the same. However, there is some disparity in the dates: Sieg was picked up on the 11th and Grimme on the 12th (see Griebel et al., op. cit., pp. 193, 203.)

21   Kuckhoff, Lüneburg, Vol. VIII, p. 132. Greta said that she was speechless when she heard of his confession, more shaken than when she heard of his death sentence.

22   Roeder interview with David Dallin, p. 157, Dallin Papers, Ms. Division, NYPL. Höhne, op. cit., p. 161, alleges that Libertas gave away John and Cato Bontjes van Beek, Hugo Buschmann, Wolfgang Havemann, Enka von Brockdorff, and Maria Terweil.

23   Eulenburg, *Erinnerungen an Libertas*, p. 30.

24   Quoted in Höhne, op. cit., p. 161.

25   Roeder interview by David Dallin, p. 157, Dallin Papers, Ms. Division, NYPL.

26   Although it was alleged that Gertrude Breiter died in Russian hands, she provided Höhne with an interview for his book in 1968. No charges were ever brought against her.

27   Tuchel, "Sonderkommission Rote Kapelle," in Coppi, Danyel, and Tuchel, p. 153.

28   Ibid., p. 153.

29   Ibid., p. 150.

30   Gestapo Final Report, p. 45.

31   Ibid.

32   Coppi et al., op. cit., p. 150.

33   Chawkin, Coppi, and Zorja, "Russische Quellen zur Roten Kapelle," in

Coppi et al., op. cit., p. 109 n. 8, give the date as November 9, 1942; Perrault, op. cit., p. 252, and Höhne, op. cit., p. 215, say November 12.

34 Pannwitz interrogation, CIA Rote Kapelle (RG 319 ZA 020253), Vol. I, pp. 485ff. Kent interrogation. The lives of Pannwitz and Kent would become inexorably entwined. Pannwitz would direct Kent in the *Funkspiel* and accompany him from Marseilles to Brussels, Paris, Berlin, and finally to Moscow at the end of the war.

35 Kent interrogation.

36 In an interview with the author, Falk Harnack admitted that he had been mistaken on the last charge. Mildred was not present at Arvid's execution.

37 MH-F to Frau Müller, September 19, 1942, GDW.

38 Falk Harnack, Lüneburg, statement Feruary 3, 1947, Vol. V, p. 635.

39 Maria Grimme, Lüneburg, Vol. VIII, p. 210.

40 Marie Louise von Scheliha, "Cell 25," quoted in Sahm, op. cit., pp. 197ff.

41 Kuckhoff, interview by Biernat, pp. 75–76.

42 Roeder, Lüneburg, Vol. VIII, pp. 12ff.

43 VVN Files, V 241/3/17, IML. The information appears to have been provided by Mildred's lawyer, Dr. Schwarz. Female prisoners were often engaged in sewing for the army. It is possible that is how Mildred obtained the pins.

44 GK to MD, July 3, 1946, in Martha Dodd Archive, Akademie der Kunste, East Berlin.

45 Strübing, Lüneburg, Vol. XII, p. 6.

46 Joy (Margarete) Weisenborn, July 31, 1949 deposition, Lüneburg, Vol. VIII, p. 19.

47 Quoted in Rürup, ed., op. cit., p. 164.

48 Erich Edgar Schulze, December 5, 1948, Lüneburg, Vol. VI, pp. 73ff; Boysen, op. cit. "Harro Schulze-Boysen: Das Bild eines Freiheitskämpfers," manuscript version; "Rote Agenten mitten unter uns," translated in Perrault, op. cit., pp. 300ff. Finck told Dallin that "intensified interrogation" was applied to Schulze-Boysen in relation to the Stockholm documents, p. 185, Dallin Papers. A fellow prisoner, Arnold Bauer, wrote admiringly of the care that Harro "gave to his body, soon to be destroyed." Harro kept fit through gymnastic exercises in order to be "in shape for his trial" (Arnold Bauer, "Reminiscences of Harro Schulze-Boysen, p. 133). USSR Military Intelligence Penetration of the German Government during World War II (Rote Drei and Rote Kapelle) AFSA-254 FOI, declassified December 17, 1991, NSA.

49 Axel von Harnack, *Die Gegenwart*, January 31, 1947, no. 26–27.

50 Ibid.

51 Falk Harnack to Clara and Ansa Harnack, October 26, 1942, Falk Harnack Archives, GDW.

52 Zechlin, "Erinnerung an Arvid und Mildred Harnack," *Geschichte in Wissenschaft und Unterricht*, p. 398; Falk Harnack in "Vom anderen Deutschland," Berlin, 1947, unpublished, Falk Harnack Papers, GDW.

53 Falk Harnack, "Vom anderen Deutschland."

54 Falk Harnack, "Besuch im Reichssicherheitshauptamt," in Tuchel and Schattenfroh, *Zentrale des Terrors*, pp. 240ff.

55 Kraell; quoted in Perrault, op. cit., p. 295.

56 Hassell; quoted in CIA, op. cit., pp. 161–62.

57 Krauss report; quoted in Günter Weisenborn, *Der lautlose Aufstand*, p. 256.

58 Puttkamer statement September 30, 1948, Lüneburg, Vol. IV, pp. 536ff.

59 Himmler, *Der Dienstkalender Heinrich Himmlers 1941/42*, pp. 577, 593, 645.

60 Taylor and Shaw, *The Third Reich Almanac*, p. 389.

61 Hassell, CIA, op. cit, pp. 161–62. In the published English version of his diaries for December 31, 1942, this exact quote does not appear, rather on p. 255. "A great Communist conspiracy has been uncovered in the Ministry for Air and other government offices. Apparently it is composed of fanatics filled with hatred for the system. They seem to have planned the creation of an interim organization that could function in case the Bolshevists won." In this version of his diary, von Hassell blames "the most brilliant strategist of all time," that is, "our megalomatic corporal," Hitler, for Stalingrad.

62 Gorlitz, ed., *The Memoirs of Field-Marshal Keitel*, pp. 177ff. Actually, the British had broken the German code.

63 Quoted in Perrault, op. cit., p. 296. Höhne (*Canaris: Hitler's Master Spy*, pp. 479ff.) says he was told this orally by Roeder in 1968. Höhne, however, gives the figure as 100,000. Terence Prittie, *Germans against Hitler*, p. 214, quotes Admiral Canaris as stating that the organization had "cost the lives of 200,000 German soldiers." Perrault (op. cit., p. 81) has also written that "the Red Orchestra, by its historic message of November 12, was giving the Soviet leaders nine months' notice of the crucial battle awaiting them—at Stalingrad, on the distant Volga. Trepper and his men made the victory of Stalingrad possible." Höhne takes him to task for this; see pp. 242ff.

64 Kraell, Lüneburg; quoted in Dallin, p. 258; also Roeder testimony in Dallin interview. See also Lüneburg, Vol. IV, p. 525.

65 Puttkamer, Lüneburg, Vol. IV, pp. 537ff.

66 Under paragraph 2, section 4 of the special wartime legal code.

67 Kraell, quoted in Sahm, op. cit., p. 203.

68 Roeder, statement June 30, 1949, Lüneburg, Vol. VIII, pp. 13ff. Lüneburg Final Report, pp. 67ff.

69 Höhne, op. cit., pp. 179ff.

70 Manvell and Fraenkel, *The Canaris Conspiracy*, p. 135.

71 Behse, statement February 20, 1950, Lüneburg, Vol. I, p. 154.

72 Kraell, statement March 14, 1950, Lüneburg, Vol. XII, p. 116; quoted in Höhne, op. cit., p. 179.

73 Eugen Schmitt statement September 22, 1948, Lüneburg, Vol. III, pp. 510ff; partially quoted in Höhne, op. cit., p. 179.

74 Axel von Harnack "Arvid und Mildred Harnack," *Die Gegenwart* 26–27 (1947).

75 Roeder, Lüneburg, Vol. VI, p. 810.

76 *Die Reichszeitung*, July 1, 1951; quoted in Höhne, op. cit., p. 185.

77 J. A. interview by author. *Landesverrat*, espionage, is a more serious crime with greater penalties. Sending radio messages to the Soviet Union, thereby aiding the enemy, was considered *Landesverrat*.

78 Falk Harnack, Lüneburg, Vol. X, pp. 4ff.

79   Haase, op. cit., pp. 133ff.

80   Axel von Harnack, op. cit.

81   Weisenborn, *Memorial*, p. 98.

82   Falk Harnack to Clara Harnack, December 5, 1942, and Falk to Clara and Ansa, December 7, 1942, Falk Harnack Collection GDW.

83   Paragraph 53, Deutsche Beamtengesetz; quoted in Sahm, op. cit., p. 204.

84   Paragraph 60 of the Deutsche Beamtengesetz; quoted in Sahm, op. cit., p. 205.

85   AH to MH-F, December 14, 1942, Falk Harnack Collection, GDW. "Du sollst immer darinnen sein" is from an anonymous twelfth-century German verse.

CHAPTER SIXTEEN

1   The proceedings against Colonel Erwin Gehrts were separated from the rest.

2   The scene is reconstructed from Kraell, statement March 14, 1950, Lüneburg, Vol. III, pp. 364ff.; and Güstrow, op. cit., pp. 57ff.; Blank and Mader, op. cit., p. 151; and Weisenborn, *Memorial*, pp. 98–99.

3   Kraell and two professional judges, Ranft and Schmitt, together with Generals Mushoff and Bertram and Vice Admiral Arps, composed the second senate. Final Report, Lüneburg, p. 75.

4   Alexander Kraell (1894–1964) became a member of the NSDAP in 1933. He joined the Wehmacht legal service in 1938 and was appointed president of the second chamber in 1942. In the literature that appeared on the Red Orchestra after the war, Kraell is portrayed as a man of high moral principle and sense of responsibility. This is belied, however, by his promotion to Senior Reich Judge Advocate on June 1, 1943 after the Führer directed that judges who were especially "soft" or "hesitant" be retired. Kraell was interrogated by the Americans at the end of the war. Although on the list of judges wanted for "war crimes," Kraell, like other members of the Third Reich judiciary, was never punished.

5   Although Kraell insisted that stenographers recorded the proceedings, the trial transcripts are missing, believed to have vanished at the end of the war. They were said to be added to Nazidom's funeral pyre in early summer 1945. According to a senior Gestapo official, their last hiding place was Gamburg Castle in the Taubertal, where SS-Hauptsturmführer and Kriminalrat Heinz Pannwitz, the head of the Special Commission Red Orchestra, "burnt and pulverised everything until there was nothing left" (Höhne, op. cit., p. xviii). A different version was given by Kraell; he claimed that the records were destroyed during an air attack while being shipped from Torgau, where the court had moved during the war's final days, to Freising in Bavaria (Kraell, RK document, CIA Rote Kapelle, p. 513 (RG 319 ZA 020253). Until 1990, essentially all that remained of the trial record was Hitler's confirmation of the sentences, available on microfilm in the U.S. National Archives. Then, in 1990, copies of the Feldurteils' sentencing documents of the main December 15–19 trials surfaced in the files of the Institute of Marxismus/Leninismus in East Berlin. Other documents turned up in the Military History Institute of the Czech army in Prague. (In the closing days of the war, Pannwitz preferred the Russians to the Americans and British, and he moved east.

Since other material from the trials has also surfaced in the Soviet Union, it is probable that Pannwitz, like General Gehlen in the West, took his files with him.)

6 Interrogation of Alexander Kraell, July 11, 1946, pp. 3–4, NA.

7 Haase, op. cit., pp. 127, 131. (I have used the trials of Greta Kuckhoff, Günther Weisenbom and Karl Behrens as sources.) Behrens wrote about his trial (January 18, 1943) to his wife, Clara: "Under the indictment presented by the prosecutor, the death sentence is certain. But this indictment is so blatantly fabricated, so obediently put together, that I have some hope of being able to fight against it . . . now I have an official defense lawyer . . . Unfortunately, I was not able to speak to him before my date in court. So now it's a matter of fighting for the bit of life or dying on the scaffold." On 28 January 1943, after his death sentence was pronounced, Behrens wrote: "The lawyer assigned to me did nothing, didn't defend me . . . evidently the sentences were set beforehand." Quoted in Haase, "Der Fall 'Rote Kapelle' vor dem Reichskriegsgericht," in Coppi et al., op. cit., p. 165.

8 Behse, statement February 20, 1950, Lüneburg, Vol. XII, pp. 71ff.

9 Kraell, statement March 14, 1950, Lüneburg, Vol. XII, p. 106.

10 Quoted in Haase, op. cit., p. 110.

11 Ibid., p. 109.

12 Kraell, Vol. III, p. 389; quoted in Höhne, op. cit., pp. 193–94.

13 Gollnow Feldurteil; quoted in Haase, op. cit., pp. 112–13.

14 Behse, Lüneburg, Vol. XII, p. 69.

15 Gollnow Feldurteil, quoted in Haase, op. cit., p. 111.

16 Telegram in Falk Harnack Collection, GDW.

17 Inge Havemann to Clara Harnack, December 20, 1942. Falk Harnack Collection.

18 Lehmann, statement September 28, 1948, Lüneburg, Vol. IV, pp. 525ff.

19 In various interviews she gave and letters she wrote, Clara Leiser asserted that "Hitler personally decided that her 'sentence of life imprisonment' was *zu mild für die verdammte Amerikanerin* ('too mild for the damned American woman')," but no other source for this quote has been found. See Clara Leiser to Bennett Cerf, July 18, 1951, Clara Leiser Papers.

20 On December 3, 1942 Müller informed Himmler of the possibility of a "radio game" with Moscow. A short time later it was approved. BA, NS 19/2002; see also Himmler notebooks for December 23, 1942.

21 Beevor, op. cit., pp. 239ff.

22 Notes of Kurt Rheindorf's conversation with Kraell, Rheindorf Collection, Vol. 305, p. 63, BA Koblenz.

23 Quoted in Scheel, "Mit ganzem Einsatz gegen den kriegsbesessenen Faschismus," *Neues Deutschland*, December 23, 1987.

24 Poelchau, op. cit., pp. 67–68.

25 Quoted in Scheel, *Vor den Schranken des Reichskriegsgerichts*, p. 316.

26 Poelchau, op. cit., p. 57.

27 Haase, op. cit., p. 14.

28 Poelchau, op. cit., p. 81. Conversation of Rheindorf with Kraell, Rheindorf Collection, p. 63. BA Koblenz.

29 Falk Harnack, *Über die Hinrichtung von Dr. Arvid Harnack*, pp. 63ff. Copy in RG 319 ZA 020259, NA.

30 In 1933, Goering reintroduced beheading into the German penal code. The guillotine was the usual method. It was thought to be more humane than hanging because death came more quickly.

31 Poelchau, op. cit., p. 81.

32 Falk Harnack, "Vom anderen Deutschland." Plans for the assassination of Hitler began to take shape during the winter of 1942–1943. Goerdeler went to Smolensk to discuss the matter with Kluge and Beck; Goerdeler, Olbricht, and Tresckow met in Berlin. In January the leaders of the resistance met at Yorck's house to outline the shape of the German constitution after the coup. In January, Adam von Trott met with Allen Dulles, the head of the OSS in Berne, to urge direct contact with the German resistance and the Allies.

33 Poelchau, op. cit., pp. 68–69.

34 Falk Harnack, "Über die Hinrichtung von Dr. Arvid Harnack." GDW. A slightly different version is in the FBI files.

35 Arvid's ashes were never released.

36 Falk Harnack, "Vom anderen Deutschland."

37 Falk Harnack, Lüneburg, Vol. I, pp. 115ff.

38 Zechlin, op. cit., p. 395.

39 Axel von Harnack, "Arvid und Mildred Harnack." *Die Gegenwart*, January 31, 1947.

40 Interview with Falk Harnack; a similar bill appears in Poelchau, op. cit., p. 27.

41 Inge Havemann memo, "World War II Underground Movements," Mildred and Arvid Harnack Folder, the Hoover Institution.

42 Gertrude Lichtenstein to Clara Harnack, October 8, 1952, Falk Harnack Collection, GDW.

43 Gertrude Lichtenstein to Clara Harnack, November 9, 1952, Falk Harnack Collection. Through a newspaper article Clara had written, Lichtenstein located her and returned the letter.

44 Heinrich Scheel, *Vor den Schranken des Reichskriegsgerichts: Mein Weg in den Widerstand*, p. 317.

45 Haase, "Der Fall 'Rote Kapelle' vor dem Reichskriegsgericht," in Griebel et al., pp. 167ff.

46 Bastien, statement July 14, 1949, Lüneburg, Vol. VIII, p. 20.

47 Schmauser, Lüneburg, Vol. XII, pp. 187ff.

48 Ibid.

49 Ibid.

50 Ibid.

51 Technically, Mildred held dual citizenship. Although she never gave up her American passport, under German law, as she was married to a German citizen, she automatically became a citizen of the Reich.

52 Schmauser, Lüneburg, Vol. XII, pp. 187ff.

53 Ibid.

54 Ibid. In order "to smooth the way for a pardon," Schmauser claimed that he had cited only the charge of aiding the enemy in his judicial instructions. According to his usual practice, he "did not have the Senate express itself on the question of a pardon as a whole," but instead had each individual judge express his view personally, in a sealed envelope, inaccessible even to me." There would be no appeal.

55 Kraell, Lüneburg, Vol. XII.

56 Interrogation of Kraell by Fehl, NA.

57 Schmauser, statement September 9, 1950, Lüneburg, Vol. XII, pp. 187ff.

58 Ibid.

59 Roeder interview by Dallin, p. 159, Dallin Papers, Ms. Division, NYPL.

60 Kraell, ibid.

61 Schmauser, op. cit., pp. 187ff.

62 Erika to her husband, Cay Gräf von Brockdorff, n.d. Copy in possession of author.

63 Ibid.

64 Puttkamer, Lüneburg, Vol. IV, pp. 187ff.

65 M. Domarus, *Hitler: Reden und Proklamation*, 1932–1945, Vol. II, p. 1985. English translation in Beevor, op. cit., p. 399.

66 When Schulze-Boysen's mother asked Roeder about the charges against her son, he replied: "Treason and treasonable activities on the largest scale. Your son will have to pay for it." Frau Schulze-Boysen all but shouted that this couldn't be true. Roeder replied with a threat: "I would draw your attention to the fact that you are speaking to a representative of the highest German court and that you will have to suffer the consequences of this insult" (Marie-Luise Schulze, Lüneburg, 6: 734; quoted in Höhne, op. cit., p. 181.) Roeder referred to the "wages of treachery," informing Schulze-Boysen's mother that her son had betrayed his fatherland for the price of a leather jacket, a "yacht," and a plot of ground in Teupitz. The leather jacket, in fact, had been a gift from his father, the "yacht" was the sailboat the Schulze-Boysens shared with the Weisenborns, and the plot of land was purchased with money Libertas had saved from her salary.

67 Marie-Luise Schulze, Lüneburg, XII, p. 57, quoted in Höhne, op. cit., p. 187.

68 Strübing, Lüneburg, Vol. X, p. 198.

69 Perrault, op. cit., pp. 208–9.

70 Strübing, op. cit., p. 198.

71 Ibid.

72 Lüneburg, Vol. VIII, p. 25.

73 *Die Reichzeitung*; quoted in Höhne, op. cit., p. 187.

74 Rudolf Behse, interview by David Dallin, February 10, 1953, Dallin Papers, Ms. Division, NYPL.

75 Herlemann, "Die Rote Kapelle und der kommunistische Widerstand" in Coppi et al., op. cit., pp. 84ff.

76 Kuckhoff, *Vom Rosenkranz zur Roten Kapelle*, p. 216.

77 Anna Beyer, 1982 interview; quoted in Herlemann, op. cit., p. 85.

78 Kuckhoff, *Vom Rosenkranz zur Roten Kapelle* (1979 ed.), p. 287, quoted in Herlemann, op. cit., p. 85.

79 Kamlah to Axel von Harnack, February 14, 1947, GDW.

80 Ingeborg Havemann, "Mildred Harnack, Eine Erinnerung," *Heute und Morgen* 2 (1950): 77–78.

81 MH-F, "Variations on the Theme: America," *Berliner Tageblatt*, December 2, 1934.

CHAPTER SEVENTEEN

1 Some of the files are concerned with the Schwarze Kapelle case or Depositenkasse, as it is sometimes called: the investigation of Abwehr members Dohnanyi and Bonhoeffer, and Joseph Müller. In 1942, an Abwehr agent, Dr. Wilhelm Schmidhuber, was arrested for smuggling currency into Switzerland. He implicated von Dohnanyi, who had assisted Jews by paying them considerable money illegally for confiscated property. In April 1943, Dohnanyi, Bonhoeffer, and Müller were arrested. Oster was forced to resign from the Abwehr and was placed under house arrest. Roeder was the original investigator.

2 Haase, "Der Fall 'Rote Kapelle'," in Coppi et al., p. 163.

3 Schulze-Boysen, November 1942, in "Gestapo Cell II"; Elsa Boysen, op. cit., *"Die letzten Argumente sind Strung und Fallbeil nicht und unsere heufgen Richter sind noch nicht das Weltgericht."* The poem was hidden in his cell and returned to his parents four years after his death.

4 Grimme, Lüneburg Final Report, p. 162.

5 Ibid., pp. 76, 82.

6 Falk Harnack, Lüneburg, Vol. I, p. 115. The allegation that Mildred was tortured came from Dr. Stieve, who examined Mildred's body after her death and reported it to Falk. The accusation that Mildred was made to watch Arvid's death was told to Falk Harnack by Christine von Dohnanyi. He said in an interview with the author that he later learned this was untrue. Hitler seems to have acted without pressure from Roeder to demand an additional trial. The exceptional cruelty that Roeder exhibited toward family members and the verbal abuse to which he subjected the defendants were found by Finck to be insufficient to bring charges against Roeder for crimes against humanity.

7 Kuckhoff, Lüneburg, Vol. VIII, pp. 131–32.

8 CIC document, Roeder File January 19, 1948, p. 387, NA.

9 The American investigation of Roeder was carried by Robert Kempner and Fred Rodell of the U.S. Office of the Counsel for War Crimes. Roeder was transferred to CIC Region 5 headquarters on December 23, 1947, and "exploited in the best interests of American intelligence." See p. 404 CIA Rote Kapelle files (RG 319 ZA 020253), NA.

10 CIA, Rote Kapelle, Vol. I, 1973, p. 166, RG 319 ZA 020253, NA.

11 Finck to Roeder, July 8–11, 1949, p. 35: excerpt from Lüneburg investigations in files in IfZ Munich. Kuckhoff, *Neues Deutschland*, April 12, 1947.

12 Finck Final Report, p. 622, quoted in Höhne, op. cit., p. xxii.

13 Sahm, pp. 296ff.

14 Ibid., p. 301.

15 Marie-Luise Schulze to Günther Weisenborn, June 11, 1951. Weisenborn File, Akademie der Kunste, (East) Berlin.

16 CIA Rote Kapelle files, Vol. 1, p. 166, RG 319 ZA 020253, NA.

17 Tuchel, "Die Gestapo-Sonderkommission 'Rote Kapelle'," Coppi et al., op. cit., p. 155.

18 Falk Harnack, interview by author.

19 Falk Harnack memo, Berlin, January 10, 1970, in possession of the author.

20 Letter from Richard Lloyd Jones to William Campbell, December 22, 1947, UWA.

21 Letter of W. J. Campbell to Lloyd Jones, December 26, 1947, UWA.

22 Senator Wiley to Frank Holt, director of public services, University of Wisconsin, January 8, 1948, UWA. See also C. G. Blakeney, Colonel, GSC, to Senator Wiley, December 30, 1947, UWA.

23 Memo to Captain Sloan, War Crimes Group U.S. Army from Albert Perry Jr., liaison officer. War Crimes File RG 153 12-2262 NA. It appears from the file that the only survivor who was interviewed was Günther Weisenborn, who had never met the Harnacks. Weisenborn stated that it was through the "little letters," *Kassiber*, that were passed between Libertas and Mildred in prison that exposed her as being more actively engaged than the Gestapo had originally suspected. It appears from Weisenborn's testimony that these were confiscated by the guards.

24 Memorandum dated December 13, 1946, to Captain H. H. Sloan, War Crimes Group, U.S. Army, from Albert R. Perry Jr., War Crimes liaison officer, RG 153 File 12-2262, NA.

25 CIA, Rote Kapelle, Vol. I, p. 247, NA.

26 Falk to Marion Dönhoff, January 8, 1963, Falk Harnack Collection, GDW.

27 Agnes von Harnack, in Gustav-Adolf von Harnack, ed., *Ernst von Harnack: Jahre des Widerstands, 1932–1945*, p. 242.

28 Letter from Lloyd A Wagener, State Commander Wisconsin American Legion, March 18, 1987 (in the files of Arthur Heitzer).

29 Hans Monath, "Statt Grotewohl Linden und Pappeln," *Die Tagezeitung*, February 17, 1993.

POSTSCRIPT

1 In Martha's FBI files there are wiretaps of conversations with Lillian Hellman. It is possible that because the story of Mildred was much on her mind at the time, Martha revealed it to Hellman who may have used it as background for "Julia."

2 Vanden Heuvel, "Grand Illusions," *Vanity Fair*, September, 1991, p. 248.

3 In this capacity Korotkov met Morros in Geneva in 1948. In discussing the Sterns, Korotkov is alleged to have said that he felt Martha was "a tremendous asset to them (the Soviets) and the Cause." Furthermore Korotkov is said to have exclaimed, "What a little recruiter! A thousand more like her and the battle will be won." Morros, op. cit., p. 82.

4 Sigrid Schulz to MD, March 9, 1970 LOC.

5 Chawkin, Coppi, Zorja, "Russische Quellen zur Roten Kapelle," in *Die Rote Kapelle im Widerstand gegen den Nationalsozialismus*, p. 109, fn. 8; Coppi, "Der Spion, der den Tod brachte" *Süddeutsche Zeitung*, July 13, 14, 1996, Sudoplatov, *Special Tasks*, pp. 143–44.

6 See Costello, Tsarev, op cit., p. 79; Chawkin, Coppi, Zorja, op cit, p. 110, fn 11; Murphy, Kondrashev, Bailey, op. cit, pp. 301ff.

ARCHIVES CONSULTED

Akademie der Kunste, Berlin (Martha Dodd Stem and Günther Weisenborn papers)
Archive of the President of the Russian Federation (material on Harnack and Schulze-Boysen)
Bundesarchiv Berlin-Lichterfelde, formerly Berlin Document Center (Harnack's NSDAP files and Greta Kuckhoff papers)
Bundesarchiv Koblenz (Rheindorf papers, Kopkow material)
Bundesarchiv, Potsdam (Kuckhoff files).
Central Intelligence Agency, Langley (Arvid Harnack, Mildred Harnack files)
City of Milwaukee Register, Milwaukee, Wisconsin
California Institute of Technology (Max Delbrück files)
Columbia University (Oral History [Majorie Nicolson and John White] Manuscript Collection, Knickerbocker papers)
Daughters of the American Revolution, Washington, D.C. (Harnack file)
Executive Committee of the Communist International (Comintern), Moscow (Dimitrov papers)
Federal Bureau of information, Washington. (Arvid Harnack, Mildred Harnack, Ernest L. Meyer, Martha Dodd Stern, Alfred Stern, Thomas Wolfe, Friedrich Lenz, Lillian Hellman files)
Franklin Delano Roosevelt Library, Hyde Park (Morgenthau papers and diary, Treasury Department Heath files)
Gedenkstätte Deutscher Widerstand (Rote Kapelle Collection, Falk Harnack papers and material formerly in the collection of the Akademie der Wissenschaften der DDR-Arbeitsstelle Schulze-Boysen/Harnack)
George Washington University Archives
Goucher College Archive
Guggenheim Foundation
Hans-Fallada-Archiv, Feldberg
Harvard, Houghton Library (Wisdom collection of Thomas Wolfe papers)
Heitzer Archives, Milwaukee Wisconsin
Hessischen Landesuniversität Gießen (Arvid and Mildred Harnack and Mona Wollheim files)
Hoover Institution, Stanford University (Inge Havemann material)

Humboldt University, Berlin (Mildred Harnack papers)
Institut für Zeitgeschichte, Munich (Rote Kapelle papers)
The Johns Hopkins University Archives
Leo Baeck Institute, New York
Library of Congress (Martha Dodd Stern and William Dodd Archives, Wilbur J. Carr papers, John Campbell White)
Milwaukee Historical Society (Mildred Harnack files)
Milwaukee School for the Arts (Archives of West Division High School)
National Archives, Washington
New York Public Library Manuscript Division (David Dallin papers)
Niedersächsische Hauptstaatsarchiv, Hanover (files of the public prosecutor, the proceedings against Dr. Manfred Roeder)
Politisches Archiv des Auswärtigen Amts, Bonn
Princeton University Library (Charles Scribner's Sons: Maxwell Perkins papers)
Rockefeller Foundation
Russian Foreign Intelligence Service (formerly KGB Archive, Moscow; Corsican, Senior, Beamer and Old Man and Martha Dodd files)
Russian Center for Preservation and Study of Records of Modern History (Dimitrov Papers, BGA, ARPLAN, Harnack's activities in the Economics Ministry)
Staatsbibliotek Berlin (Wallgora collection)
Sächsische Landesbibliothek Dresden (Wolfgang Havemann papers)
State of Wisconsin Historical Society (Louis Lochner, John R. Commons, Sigrid Schulz papers)
Stiftung Archiv der Parteien und Massenorganisationen der DDR im Bundesarchiv formerly SED archives (VVN collection and Rote Kappelle case)
Sumner Archives, Washington, D.C. (Western High Archives)
U.S. Intelligence and Security Command, Fort Meade
U.S.National Archives, Washington D.C. (Captured German documents, State Department, CIC, OSS files)
University of Wisconsin Archives (Mildred Harnack project, William Ellery Leonard, Marjorie Latimer, Oral History, German Department Archives)
Yale University, Beineke Rare Book and Manuscript Library (Thornton Wilder, Margery Latimer papers)

BIBLIOGRAPHY

Abshagen, Karl Heinz. *Canaris*. London, 1956.

Accoce, Pierre, and Pierre Quet. *A Man Called Lucy, 1939–45*. New York, 1966.

Akhmedov, Ismail. *In and Out of Stalin's GRU: A Tartar's Escape from Red Army Intelligence*. Frederick, 1984.

Amory, Cleveland. *Who Killed Society?* New York, 1960.

Andreas-Friedrich, Ruth. *Berlin Underground, 1938–1945*. New York, 1947.

Andrew, Christopher, and Oleg Gordievsky. *The KGB: The Inside Story of Its Foreign Operations from Lenin to Gorbachev*. New York, 1990.

Andrew, Christopher, and Vasili Mitrokhin. *The Mitrokhin Archive*. New York, 1999.

Auden, W. H. *W. H. Auden: Collected Poems*. New York, 1976.

Austin, H. Russell. *The Milwaukee Story: The Making of an American City*. Milwaukee, 1946.

The Badger. 1922–25 Yearbook of the University of Wisconsin.

Balfour, Michael. *Withstanding Hitler in Germany, 1933–45*. London, 1988.

Balzer, Karl. *Der 20. Juli und der Landesverrat: Eine Dokumentation über Verratshandlungen im deutschen Widerstand*. Göttingen, 1967.

———. *Verschwörung gegen Deutschland*. Oldendorf, 1976.

Beam, Jacob D. *Multiple Exposure*. New York, 1978.

Beck, Earl R. *Under the Bombs: The German Home Front, 1942–1945*. Lexington, 1986.

Beevor, Antony. *Stalingrad: The Fateful Siege, 1942–1943*. New York, 1998.

Benz, W., and W. H. Pehle. *Lexikon des deutschen Widerstandes*. Frankfurt am Main, 1994.

Bérard, Armand. *Un ambassadeur se souvient: Au temps du danger allemand*. Paris, 1976.

Berezhkov, Valentin. *Erlebte Geschichte, 1940 bis 1943: Dolmetscher und Diplomat gegen Faschismus und Krieg*. Frankfurt am Main, 1986.

Bergschicker, Heinz. *Deutsche Chronik, 1933–1945: Ein Zeitbild der faschistichen Diktatur*. Berlin, 1981.

Besymenski, Lev. *Zähmung des Taifuns*. Berlin, 1981.

Bethge, Eberhard. *Dietrich Bonhoeffer*. London, 1985.

Bethge, Eberhard, Renata Bethge, and Christian Grammels, eds. *Dietrich Bonhoeffer: A Life in Pictures*. London, 1986.

Beuys, Barbara. *Vergesst uns nicht. Menschen im Widerstand, 1933–1945.* Hamburg, 1987.

Bialer, Seweryn. *Stalin and His Generals.* New York, 1969.

Bielenberg, Christabel. *Ride Out the Dark: The Experiences of an Englishwoman in Wartime Germany.* New York, 1971.

Biernat, Karl Heinz, and Luise Kraushaar. *Die Schulze-Boysen/Harnack-Organisation im anti-faschistischen Kampf.* Berlin, 1970.

Billinger, Karl [Paul Massing]. *Fatherland.* New York, 1935.

Blackstock, Paul W. *The Secret Road to World War II: Soviet versus Western Intelligence, 1921–1939.* Chicago, 1969.

Blank, Alexander S., and Julius Mader. *Rote Kapelle gegen Hitler.* Berlin, 1979.

Bockmann, Vera. *Full Circle: An Australian in Berlin, 1930–46.* Netley, 1986.

Boehm E. *We Survived: The Stories of Fourteen of the Hidden and Hunted of Nazi Germany.* New Haven, 1949.

Bonhoeffer, Dietrich. *Gesammelte Schriften.* Munich, 1965–69.

———. *Letters and Papers from Prison.* New York, 1971.

Bonhoeffer, Karl. *Lebenserinnerungen: Für die Familievervielfältigt.*

Boveri, Margret. *Treason in the Twentieth Century.* New York, 1963.

———. *"Wir lügen alle: Eine Hauptstadtzeitung unter Hitler.* Olten, 1965.

———. *Verzweigungen: Eine Autobiographie.* Munich, 1977.

Boyle, Andrew. *The Climate of Treason.* London, 1979.

Boysen, Elsa. *Harro Schulze-Boysen: Das Bild eines Freiheitskämpfers.* 1947. Reprint, 1992.

Bracher, Karl Dietrich. *The German Dictatorship.* New York, 1971.

Bräutigam, Walter. *John Rittmeister: Leben und Sterben.* Ebenhausen, 1987.

Bridenthal, Renata, Atina Grossman, and Marion Kaplan, eds. *When Biology Became Destiny: Women in Weimar and Nazi Germany.* New York, 1984.

Broun, Heywood Hale, ed. *Collected Edition of Heywood Broun.* New York, 1941.

Brown, A. D., and C. B. MacDonald. *On a Field of Red: The Communist International and the Coming of World War II.* New York, 1981.

Brüning, Eberhard. *Mildred Harnack-Fish: Variationen über das Thema Amerika: Studien zur Literatur der USA.* Berlin, 1988.

Buber-Neumann, Margarete. *Kriegsschauplätze der Weltrevolution: Ein Bericht aus der Praxis der Komintern, 1919–1943.* Stuttgart, 1967.

———. *Under Two Dictators.* New York, 1949.

———. *Von Potsdam nach Moskau.* Stuttgart, 1957.

Bucholz, Arden. *Hans Delbrück and the German Military Establishment: War Images in Conflict.* Iowa City, 1985.

Bullock, Alan. *Hitler and Stalin: Parallel Lives.* New York, 1992.

Bulow, Bernhard Fürst von. *Memoirs.* Boston, 1931.

Carell, Paul. *Scorched Earth.* London, 1970.

Carpozi, George. *Red Spies in the U.S.* New Rochelle, 1963.

Carr, E. H. *The Comintern and the Spanish Civil War.* New York, 1984.

———. *Twilight of the Comintern, 1930–1935.* New York, 1982.

Cartarius, Ulrich. *Opposition gegen Hitler: Ein erzählender Bildband.* Berlin, 1984.

Caute, David. *The Fellow-Travellers: A Postscript to the Enlightenment.* New York, 1973.

Central Intelligence Agency. *The Rote Kapelle: The CIA's History of Soviet Intelligence and Espionage Networks in Western Europe, 1936–1945.* Washington, 1979.

Cerruti, Elisabetta. *Ambassador's Wife.* London, 1952.

Chickering, Roger. *Imperial Germany and a World without War: The Peace Movement and German Society, 1982–1914.* Princeton, 1975.

Childers, Thomas. *The Nazi Voter: The Social Foundations of Fascism, 1919–1933.* Chapel Hill, N.C., 1983.

Chowaniec, Elisabeth. *Der "Fall Dohnanyi" 1943–45: Widerstand, Militärjustiz, SS-Willkur.* Munich, 1991.

Clements, Barbara Evans. *Bolshevik Feminist: The Life of Aleksandra Kollontai.* Bloomington, 1979.

Commons, John R. *Myself.* New York, 1934.

Conquest, Robert. *The Great Terror: A Reassessment.* New York, 1990.

———. *Harvest of Sorrow.* New York, 1986.

———. *Inside Stalin's Secret Police: NKVD Politics, 1936–1939.* London, 1985.

Constantinides, George C. *Intelligence and Espionage: An Analytical Bibliography.* Boulder, 1983.

———. *Spy Trade.* New York, 1971.

Conrad, Will C., Kathleen Wilson and Dale Wilson. *The Milwaukee Journal: The First Eighty Years.* Madison, 1964.

Cookridge, E. H. [Edward Spiro]. *The Net That Covers the World.* New York, 1955.

Coppi, Hans. *Harro Schulze-Boysen—Wege in den Widerstand: Eine biographische Studie.* Koblenz, 1993.

Coppi, Hans, and Geertje Andresen. *Dieser Tod paßt zu mir.* Berlin, 1999.

Coppi, Hans, Jürgen Danyel, and Johannes Tuchel, eds. *Die Rote Kapelle im Widerstand gegen den Nationalsozialismus.* Berlin, 1994.

Costello, John. *The Mask of Treachery.* New York, 1988.

———. *Ten Days to Destiny.* New York, 1991.

Costello, John, and Oleg Tsarev. *Deadly Illusions.* New York, 1993.

Craig, Gordon. *Germany, 1866–1945.* Oxford, 1984.

Craig, Gordon, and Felix Gilbert, eds. *The Diplomats, 1919–1939.* Princeton, 1953.

Crepon, Tom. *Leben und Tode des Hans Fallada.* Halle, 1978.

Crossman, R. H. S., ed. *The God That Failed.* New York, 1950.

Curti, Merle, and Vernon Carstensen. *The University of Wisconsin: A History, 1848–1925.* Madison, 1949.

Dallek, Robert. *Democrat and Diplomat: The Life of William E. Dodd.* New York, 1968.

Dallin, David J. *Soviet Espionage.* New Haven, 1955.

Das Deutsche Führerlexikon, 1934/35. Berlin, n.d..

Davidson, Eugene. *Reaching Judgment at Nuremberg.* New York, 1977.

Deak, Istvan. *Weimar Germany's Left-Wing Intellectuals: A Political History of the Weltbühne and Its Circle.* Berkeley, 1968.

Deakin, F. W., and G. R. Storry. *The Case of Richard Sorge.* London, 1966.

Delmer, Sefton. *Trail Sinister.* London, 1961.

Denson, Robert Louis, and Michael Warnder, eds. *Venona.* Washington, D.C., 1996.

Deutsch, Harold C. *The Conspiracy against Hitler in the Twilight War*. Minneapolis, 1968.

Diels, Rudolf. *Lucifer ante Portas: Zwischen Severing und Heydrich*. Zurich, 1969.

Dippel, John V. *Two against Hitler*. New York, 1992.

Documents on German Foreign Policy, 1918–1945. Washington, 1983.

Dodd, Martha. *The Searching Light*. New York, 1955.

———. *Sowing the Wind*. New York, 1945

———. *Through Embassy Eyes*. New York, 1939.

Dodd, William E. Jr., and Martha Dodd, eds. *Ambassador Dodd's Diary*. New York, 1941.

Donald, David Herbert. *Look Homeward: A Life of Thomas Wolfe*. New York, 1987.

Duhnke, Horst. *Die KPD von 1933 bis 1945*. Cologne, 1972.

Dulles, Allen W. *Germany's Underground*. New York, 1947.

Dumbach, Annette E., and Jud Newborn. *Shattering the German Night*. Boston, 1986.

Dziak, John. *Chekisty: A History of the KGB*. New York, 1988.

Earle, Edward Mead, Gordon Craig, and Felix Gilbert. *Makers of Modern Strategy: Military Thought from Machiavelli and Hitler*. Princeton, 1943.

Eckardt, Wolf von. *Bertold Brecht's Berlin*. Garden City, 1975.

Effenburger, Hans. *Umriß der amerikanischen Kultur und Kunst*. Frankfurt am Main, 1937.

Ehrenburg, Ilya. *Memoirs, 1921–1941*. New York, 1963.

Elbe, Joachim von. *Witness to History: A Refugee from the Third Reich Remembers*. Madison, 1988.

Elling, Hanna. *Frauen im deutschen Widerstand, 1933–45*. Frankfurt am Main, 1981.

Elon, Amos. *Journey through a Haunted Land: The New Germany*. New York, 1967.

Engelmann, Bernt, *In Hitler's Germany: Daily Life in the Third Reich*. New York, 1986.

Enzensberger, Hans Magnus. *The Consciousness Industry*. New York, 1974.

Epstein, Edward. *Deception: the Invisible War between the KGB and the CIA*. New York, 1989.

Epstein, Leon D. *Politics in Wisconsin*. Madison, 1958.

Eulenburg, Thora zu. *Erinnerungen an Libertas*. n.d..

Felix, David. *Protest: Sacco-Vanzetti and the Intellectuals*. Bloomington, 1965.

Ferber, Edna. *Dawn O'Hara*. New York, 1911.

Fest, Joachim. *The Face of the Third Reich: Portraits of the Nazi Leadership*. New York, 1970.

———. *Hitler*. New York, 1974.

———. *Plotting Hitler's Death: The Story of the German Resistance*. New York, 1996.

Fischer, Ernst Peter, and Carol Lipson. *Thinking about Science: Max Delbrück and the Origins of Molecular Biology*. New York, 1988.

Fischer, Louis. *Men and Politics: An Autobiography*. New York, 1941.

Fischer, Ruth. *Stalin and German Communism*. Cambridge, 1948.

Fischer, Walther, ed. *Amerikanische Prosa vom Bürgerkrieg bis zur Gegenwart.* Leipzig, 1926.

———. *Die englische Literatur der Vereinigten Staaten von Nordamerika.* Wildpark-Potsdam, 1929.

FitzGibbon, Constantine. *20 July.* New York, 1956.

Fitzpatrick, Sheila. *The Russian Revolution.* Oxford, 1982.

Flannery, Harry W. *Assignment to Berlin.* New York, 1942.

Fleischhauer, Ingeborg. *Die Chance des Sonderfriedens: Deutsch-sowjetische Geheimgespräche, 1941–1945.* Berlin, 1986.

Flicke, Wilhelm F. *Agenten funken nach Moskau.* Munich, 1957.

———. *Die Rote Kapelle.* Hilden/Rhein, 1949.

———. *Spionagegruppe Rote Kapelle.* Kreuzlingen, 1958.

Focke, Harald, and Uwe Rainer. *Alltag unterm Hakenkreuz.* 3 vols. Hamburg, 1980.

Fogelmann, Eva. *Conscience and Courage.* New York, 1994.

Foote, Alexander. *Handbook for Spies.* Garden City, 1949.

Foster, Jane. *An Unamerican Lady.* London, 1980.

Francois-Poncet, Andre. *The Fateful Years.* New York, 1949.

Fraser, Kennedy. *Ornament and Silence: Essays on Women's Lives.* New York, 1996.

Freeman, Clive, and Gwynne Roberts. *Der Kälteste Krieg: Professor Frucht und das Kampfstoff-Geheimnis.* Berlin, 1982.

Friedrich, Otto. *Before the Deluge.* New York, 1986.

Fromm, Bella. *Blood and Banquets: A Berlin Social Diary.* New York, 1942.

Frucht, Maria, and Adolf Henning. *Briefe aus Bautzen II.* Berlin, 1992.

Gallin, Alice. *Midwives to Nazism: University Professors in Weimar Germany, 1925–1933.* Macon, 1986.

Gallo, Max. *Night of the Long Knives.* New York, 1973.

Gardiner, Muriel. *Code Name: Mary.* New Haven, 1983.

Gay, Peter. *Weimar Culture: The Outsider as Insider.* New York, 1970.

Gehlen, Reinhard. *The Service.* New York, 1972.

German Historical Institute. *Contending with Hitler: Varieties of German Resistance in the Third Reich.* Cambridge, 1991.

Geyer, Michael, and John W. Boyer, eds. *Resistance against the Third Reich, 1933–1990.* Chicago, 1992.

Giles, Geoffrey J. *Students and National Socialism in Germany.* Princeton, 1985.

Gilligan, Carol. *In a Different Voice: Psychological Theory and Women's Development.* Cambridge, Mass., 1982.

Gisevius, Hans Bernd. *To the Bitter End.* Boston, 1947.

Glanz, David M. *The Role of Intelligence in Soviet Military Strategy in World War II.* Novato, 1990.

Glanz, David. M., and Jonathan House. *When Titans Clashed: How the Red Army Stopped Hitler.* Lawrence, 1995.

Glees, Anthony. *The Secrets of the Service: A Story of Soviet Subversion of Western Intelligence.* New York, 1987.

Goddard, Donald. *The Last Days of Dietrich Bonhoeffer,* New York, 1976.

Goebbels, Joseph. *The Goebbels Diaries, 1939–41.* Edited by Fred Taylor. London, 1982.

———. *The Goebbels Diaries, 1942–43.* Edited and translated by Louis P. Lochner. New York, 1948.

———. *Tagebücher.* Munich, 1992.

Gorlitz, Walter, ed. *The Memoirs of Field-Marshall Keitel.* New York, 1977.

Gorodetsky, Gabriel. *Grand Delusion: Stalin and the German Invasion of Russia.* New Haven, 1999.

———. *Stafford Cripps' Mission to Moscow, 1940–42.* Cambridge, 1984.

Gostomski, Victor von, and Walter Loch. *Der Tod von Plötzensee: Erinnerungen-Ereignisse-Dokumente, 1942–1945.* Meitingen, 1969.

Grabowski, Stefan, and Valentin Tomin. *Die Helden der Berliner Illegalität.* Berlin, 1967.

Graml, Hermann, Hans Mommsen, Hans-Joachim Reichhardt, and Ernst Wolf. *The German Resistance to Hitler.* Berkeley, 1970.

Gramont, Sanche de. *The Secret War: The Story of International Espionage since World War II.* New York, 1962.

Gregory, Horace. *The House on Jefferson Street: A Cycle of Memories.* New York, 1971.

Griebel, Regina, Marlies Coburger, and Heinrich Scheel. *Erfasst? Das Gestapo-Album zur Roten Kapelle.* Halle, 1992.

Grimme, Adolf. *Briefe.* Heidelberg, 1967.

Gross, Babette. *Willi Münzenberg: A Political Biography.* East Lansing, 1974.

Grunberger, Richard. *The Twelve-Year Reich: A Social History of Nazi Germany, 1933–1934.* New York, 1971.

Grunfeld, Frederic. *Prophets without Honour: a Background to Freud, Kafka, Einstein, and Their World.* New York, 1996.

Gundel, H. G., Peter Moraw, and Volker Press, eds. *Giessener Gelehrte in der Ersten Hälfte des 20. Jahrhundert.* Marburg, 1982.

Haase, Norbert. *Das Reichskriegsgericht und der Widerstand gegen die nationalsozialistische Herrschaft.* Berlin, 1993.

Hachmeister, Lutz. *Der Gegnerforscher: Die Karriere des SS-Führers Franz Alfred Six.* Munich, 1998.

Haller, Johannes. *Philip Eulenburg: The Kaiser's Friend.* New York, 1930.

Hamerow, Theodore, S. *On the Road to the Wolf's Lair: German Resistance to Hitler.* Cambridge, Mass., 1997.

Hamilton, Richard. *Who Voted for Hitler?* Princeton, 1982.

Handbuch des Berliner Abendgymnasiums. Berlin, 1934.

Hanfstaengl, Ernst. *Unheard Witness.* Philadelphia, 1957.

Harnack, Arvid. *Die vormarxistische Arbeiterbewegung in den Vereinigten Staaten: Eine Darstellung ihrer Geschichte.* Jena, 1931.

Harnack, Axel von. *Ernst von Harnack 1888–1945: Ein Kämpfer für Deutschlands Zukunft.* Schwenningen, 1951.

Harnack, Clara. *An die Lebenden: Lebensbilder und letzte Briefe deutscher Widerstandskämpfer.* Bremen, 1960.

Harnack, Gustav-Adolf von, ed. *Ernst von Harnack: Jahre des Widerstands, 1932–1945.* Pfullingen, 1989.

Harrison, Gilbert. *The Enthusiast: A Life of Thornton Wilder.* New York, 1983.

Hart-Davis, Duff. *Hitler's Games: The 1936 Olympics.* New York, 1986.

Hartshorne, Edward. *The German Universities and National Socialism.* Cambridge, 1937.

Hassell, Ulrich von. *Die Hassell-Tagebücher, 1938–1944: Aufzeichnungen vom anderen Deutschland.* Berlin, 1988.
———. *The Von Hassell Diaries.* London, 1948.
Haushofer, Albrecht. *Moabiter Sonnette.* Berlin, 1975.
Hawthorne, Nathaniel. *Miscellanies: Biographical and Other Sketches.* Boston, 1900.
Haynes, John Earl, and Harvey Klehr. *Venona: Decoding Soviet Espionage in America.* New Haven, 1999.
Heideking, Jürgen, and Christof Mauch, eds. *American Intelligence and the German Resistance to Hitler.* Boulder, 1996.
Henderson, Sir Neville. *Failure of a Mission.* London, 1940.
Herf, Jeffrey. *Divided Memory: The Nazi Past in the Two Germanys.* Cambridge, 1997.
Herlemann, Beatrix. *Auf verlorenem Posten: Kommunistischer Widerstand im Zweiten Weltkrieg.* Bonn, 1986.
Herman, Stewart W. *The American Church in Berlin: A History.* Privately published, 1978.
Heym, Stefan. *Nachruf.* Munich, 1988.
Hildebrandt, Rainer. *Wir sind die Letzten: Aus dem Leben des Widerstandskämpfers Albrecht Haushofer und seiner Freunde.* Berlin, 1947.
Hilger, Gustav, and Alfred Meyer. *The Incompatible Allies: A Memoir History of German–Soviet Relations, 1918–1941.* New York, 1953.
Himmler, Heinrich. *Der Dienstkalender Heinrich Himmlers, 1941/42.* Hamburg, 1999.
Hodos, George. *Show Trials: Stalinist Purges in Eastern Europe, 1948–1954.* New York, 1987.
Hofer, Walther, et al. *Der Reichstagsbrand: Eine wissenschaftliche Dokumentation.* Berlin, 1972.
Höhne, Heinz. *Codeword: Direktor. The Story of the Red Orchestra.* New York, 1971.
———. *Der Krieg im Dunkel. Macht und Einfluss des deutschen und russischen Geheimdienstes.* Gütersloh, 1985.
———. *The Order of the Death's Head.* New York, 1971.
Höhne, Heinz and Hermann Zolling. *The General was a Spy.* New York, 1972.
Hoffmann, Peter. *The History of the German Resistance 1933–1945.* Cambridge, Mass. 1977.
———, *Stauffenberg. A Family History, 1905–1944.* Cambridge, 1995.
Housden, Martyn. *Resistance and Conformity in the Third Reich.* London, 1997.
Howarth, Stephen. *August '39.* San Francisco, 1989.
Hull, Isabel. *The Entourage of Kaiser Wilhelm II, 1888–1918.* Cambridge, 1982.
Institut für Marxismus-Leninismus beim ZK der SED, ed. *Deutsche Widerstandskämpfer, 1933–1945. Biographien und Briefe.* 2 vol. Berlin, 1970.
Irving, David. *Goering: A Biography.* New York, 1989.
———. *The Rise and Fall of the Luftwaffe.* Boston, 1973.
Isherwood, Christopher. *The Berlin Stories.* New York, 1954.
———. *Christopher and His Kind.* New York, 1976.
Italiaander, Rolf, and Willy Haas. *Berliner Cocktail.* Hamburg, 1957.
Jacobsen, Hans-Adolf. *July 20, 1944.* Bonn, 1969.
John, Otto. *Twice through the Lines.* New York, 1972.

Johnson, Paul. *Modern Times: The World from the Twenties to the Eighties.* New York, 1983.

Jones, Howard Mumford. *The Theory of American Literature.* Ithaca, 1965.

Kahn, David. *The Codebreakers.* New York, 1996.

———. *Hitler's Spies: German Military Intelligence in World War II.* New York, 1978.

Kaltenborn, Carl Jürgen. *Adolf von Harnack als Lehrer Bonhoeffers.* Berlin, 1973.

Kändler, Klaus, Helga Karolewski, and Ilse Siebert. *Berliner Begegnungen: Ausländische Künstler in Berlin 1918 bis 1933. Aufsätze-Bilder-Dokumente.* Berlin, 1987.

Kaplan, Justin. *Lincoln Steffens: A Biography.* New York, 1974.

Kaplan, Karel. *Dans les archives du Comité Central: Trente ans de secrets du bloc sovietique.* Paris, 1978.

Kegel, Gerhard. *In den Stürmen unseres Jahrhunderts: Ein deutscher Kommunist über sein ungewöhnliches Leben.* Berlin, 1983.

Keitel, Wilhelm. *The Memoirs of a Field Marshal.* London, 1965.

Kempowski, Walter, ed. *Das Echolot.* 4 vols. Munich, 1993.

Kempton, Murray. *Part of Our Time: Some Monuments and Ruins of the Thirties.* New York, 1955.

Kennan, George. *Memoirs: 1925–1950.* Boston, 1967.

Kennedy, Richard S., and Paschal Reeves, eds. *The Notebooks of Thomas Wolfe.* Chapel Hill, N.C., 1970.

Kern, Erich. *Verrat an Deutschland: Spione und Saboteure gegen das eigene Vaterland.* Göttingen, 1963.

Kershaw, Ian. *The "Hitler Myth": Image and Reality in the Third Reich.* Oxford, 1987.

———. *Hitler 1889–1936: Hubris.* New York, 1999.

Kessler, Count Harry. *In the Twenties: The Diaries of Harry Kessler.* New York, 1971.

Kiaulehn, Walther. *Berlin: Schicksal einer Weltstadt.* Munich, 1958.

Klemperer, Klemens von. *German Resistance to Hitler: The Search for Allies Abroad, 1938–1945.* Oxford, 1992.

Klemperer, Victor. *I Will Bear Witness: A Diary of the Nazi Years, 1933–1941.* New York, 1998.

Knight, Amy. *Who Killed Kirov? The Kremlin's Greatest Mystery.* New York, 1999.

Knightley, Phillip. *The Master Spy: The Story of Kim Philby.* New York, 1989.

Koch, Stephen. *Double Lives.* New York, 1994.

Koestler, Arthur. *Arrow in the Blue: An Autobiography.* New York, 1952.

———. *Darkness at Noon.* New York, 1941.

———. *The Invisible Writing: The Second Volume of an Autobiography.* New York, 1954.

———. *The Yoga and the Commissar and Other Essays.* New York, 1946.

Koonz, Claudia. *Mothers in the Fatherland.* New York, 1987.

Korolkow, Juri. *Die innere Front.* Berlin, 1974.

Kraushaar, Luise. *Berliner Kommunisten im Kampf gegen den Faschismus, 1936–1942.* Berlin, 1981.

Krivitsky, W. G. *In Stalin's Secret Service*. New York, 1939.

Kuckhoff, Greta. *Adam Kuckhoff zum Gedenken: Novellen, Gedichte, Briefe*. Berlin, 1946.

————. *Vom Rosenkranz zur Roten Kapelle—Ein Lebensbericht*. Berlin, 1986.

Kuczynski, Jürgen. *Dialog mit meinem Urenkel: Neunzehn Briefe und ein Tagebuch*. Berlin, 1983.

————. *Memoiren: Die Erziehung des J. K. zum Kommunisten und Wissenschaftler*. Berlin, 1983.

Kurtz, Peter. *American Cassandra: The Life of Dorothy Thompson*. Boston, 1990.

Laack-Michel, Ursula. *Albrecht Haushofer und der Nationalsozialismus*. Stuttgart, 1974.

Lamb, Richard. *The Ghosts of Peace, 1935–45*. London, 1987.

Lamphere, Robert J., and Tom Schachtman. *The FBI-KGB War: A Special Agent's Story*. New York, 1986.

Langer, Elinor. *Josephine Herbst*. Boston, 1984.

Laqueur, Walter. *Weimar: A Cultural History*. New York, 1975.

————. *Stalin: The Glasnost Revelations*. London, 1990.

Latimer, Margery. *Guardian Angel and Other Stories*. New York, 1932.

————. *This Is My Body*. New York, 1930.

Leber, Annedore, ed. *Conscience in Revolt*. London, 1957.

————. *Das Gewissen entscheidet: Berichte des deutschen Widerstandes von 1933–1945 in Lebensbildern*. Berlin, 1960.

Lehmann, Klaus, ed. *Widerstand im Dritten Reich I: Widerstandsgruppe Schulze-Boysen/Harnack*. Berlin, 1948.

Lenz, Friedrich. *Wirtschaftsplanung und Planwirtschaft*. Berlin, 1948.

Leonard, William Ellery. *The Locomotive God*. New York, 1927.

————. *Poems 1914–1916*. Privately published, 1916.

————. *Two Lives*. London, 1940.

Leonhardt, Wolfgang. *Child of the Revolution*. Chicago, 1958.

Lesy, Michael. *Wisconsin Death Trip*. New York, 1973.

Leverkuehn, Paul. *German Military Intelligence*. London, 1954.

Lewis, Flora. *Red Pawn: The Story of Noel Field*. New York, 1965.

Liebholz-Bonhoeffer, Sabine. *The Bonhoeffers: Portrait of a family*. London, 1971.

Liddell Hart, Basil Henry, Sir. *The Soviet Army*. London, 1956.

Lochner, Louis P. *Always the Unexpected*. New York, 1956.

————. *What about Germany?* New York, 1942.

Loring, Allison. *Frauen: German Women Recall the Third Reich*. New Brunswick, 1993.

Louis Ferdinand, Prince. *The Rebel Prince*. New York, 1952.

MacKinnon, Janice, and Stephen MacKinnon. *Agnes Smedley: The Life and Times of an American Radical*. Berkeley, 1988.

Maclean, Fitzroy. *Eastern Approaches*. London, 1951.

McKinsey, Elizabeth. *Niagara Falls: Icon of the American Sublime*. New York, 1985.

Magi, Aldo P., and Richard Walser, eds. *Thomas Wolfe Interviewed, 1929–1938*. Baton Rouge, 1985.

Maier, Charles S. *The Unmasterable Past: History, Holocaust, and German National Identity.* Cambridge, Mass., 1988.

Malek-Kohler, Ingeborg. *Im Windschatten des Dritten Reiches.* Freiburg, 1986.

Malone, Henry O. *Adam von Trott zu Solz: Werdegang eines Verschwörers, 1909–1938.* Berlin, 1986.

Mandell, Richard D. *The Nazi Olympics.* New York, 1971.

Mann, Golo. *Reminiscences and Reflections: A Youth in Germany.* New York, 1990.

Manvell, Roger, and Heinrich Fraenkel. *The Canaris Conspiracy.* New York, 1969.

Massing, Hede. *This Deception.* New York, 1951.

Masur, Gerhard. *Imperial Berlin.* New York, 1970.

Maxwell, Margaret. *Narodniki Women.* New York, 1990.

Meehan, Patricia. *The Unnecessary War.* London, 1992.

Mendelssohn, Peter de. *Zeitungsstadt Berlin: Menschen und Mächte in der Geschichte der deutschen Presse.* Berlin, 1959.

Merson, Alan. *Communist Resistance in Nazi Germany.* New York, 1984.

Metcalfe, Philip. *1933.* Sag Harbor, 1988.

Meyer, Ernest L. *Bucket Boy: A Milwaukee Legend.* New York, 1947.

———. *Making Light of the Times.* Madison, 1928.

Milwaukee Public Schools. *Our Roots Grow Deep.* Milwaukee, 1968.

Mitgang, Herbert. *Dangerous Dossiers.* New York, 1989.

Mitteilungen des Oberhessischen Geschichtsvereins Giessen. Vol. 65. Giessen, 1990.

Modin, Yuri. *My Cambridge Friends.* New York, 1994.

Molkenbur, Norbert, and Klaus Hörhold. *Oda Schottmüller: Tänzerin, Bildhauerin, Antifaschistin: Eine Dokumentation.* Berlin, 1983.

Mommsen, Hans. *From Weimar to Auschwitz.* Cambridge, U.K. 1991.

———. *The Rise and Fall of Weimar Democracy.* Chapel Hill, N.C., 1996.

Morley, Felix. *For the Record.* New York, 1979.

Morros, Boris. *My Ten Years as a Counterspy.* New York, 1959.

Moss, Noran. *Klaus Fuchs: The Man Who Stole the Atom Bomb.* New York, 1987.

Mosse, George. *The Crisis of German Ideology: Intellectual Origins of the Third Reich.* New York, 1964.

———. *Nazi Culture.* New York, 1966.

Mowrer, Edgar Ansel. *Germany Puts the Clock Back.* New York, 1939.

Mowrer, Lillian. *Journalist's Wife.* New York, 1939.

Muggeridge, Malcolm. *Chronicles of Wasted Time. Part I, The Green Stick.* London, 1972.

Müller, Ingo. *Hitler's Justice: The Courts of the Third Reich.* Cambridge, 1991.

Murphy, David, Sergei A. Kondrashev, and George Bailey. *Battleground Berlin: CIA vs. KGB in the Cold War.* New York, 1997.

Musser, Frederick O. *The History of Goucher Collage, 1930–1985* Baltimore, 1990.

Nicosia, Francis R., and Lawrence D. Stokes, eds. *Germans against Nazism.* New York, 1990.

Niekisch, Ernst. *Erinnerungen eines deutschen Revolutionärs.* 2 vols. Cologne, 1974.

Noakes, J., and G. Pridham, eds. *Nazism: The Rise to Power.* Vol I. Exeter, 1983.

Nollau, Günter, and Ludwig Zindel. *Gestapo ruft Moskau: Sowjetische Fallschirmagenten im 2. Weltkrieg.* Munich, 1979.

Nowell, Elizabeth, ed. *The Letters of Thomas Wolfe.* New York, 1956.

———. *Thomas Wolfe: A Biography.* Garden City, 1960.

Oliner, Samuel P, and Pearl M. Olimer. *The Altruistic Personality: Rescuers of Jews in Nazi Europe.* New York, 1988.

Orlov, Alexander. *A Handbook of Intelligence and Guerrilla Warfare.* Ann Arbor, 1962.

———. *The Secret History of Stalin's Crimes.* New York, 1954.

Overy, Richard J. *War and Economy in the Third Reich.* Oxford, 1994.

Pauck, Wilhelm. *Harnack and Troeltsch: Two Historical Theologians.* New York, 1968.

Paul, Elfriede. *Ein Sprechzimmer der Roten Kapelle.* Berlin, 1987.

Pechel, Rudolf. *Deutscher Widerstand.* Erlenbach, 1947.

Perrault, Gilles. *The Red Orchestra.* New York, 1967.

Persico, Joseph. *Piercing the Reich: The Penetration of Nazi Germany by American Secret Agents during World War II.* New York, 1979.

Petrov, Vladimir. *June 22, 1941: Soviet Historians and the German Invasion.* Columbia, 1968.

Peukert, Detlev J. K. *Inside Nazi Germany: Conformity, Opposition, and Racism in Everyday Life.* New Haven, 1987.

Picker, Henry, and Heinrich Hoffman. *Hitlers Tischgespräche im Bild.* Oldenburg, 1969.

Piekalkiewicz, Janusz. *Weltgeschichte der Spionage.* Munich, 1988.

Pincher, Chapman. *Their Trade Is Treachery.* London, 1981.

———. *Too Secret Too Long.* New York, 1984.

———. *Traitors: The Anatomy of Treason.* New York, 1987.

Poelchau, Harald. *Die letzten Stunden: Erinnerungen eines Gefängnispfarrers.* Cologne, 1987.

———. *Die Ordnung der Bedrängten: Autobiographisches und Zeitgeschichtliches seit den zwanziger Jahren.* Munich, 1965.

Porter, Katherine Anne. *The Never Ending Wrong.* Boston, 1977.

Prittie, Terence. *Germans against Hitler.* London, 1964.

Radó, Sándor. *Dora meldet.* Berlin, 1974.

Radzinsky, Edvard. *Stalin.* New York, 1966.

Rakosi, Carl. *The Collected Prose of Carl Rakosi.* Orono, 1983.

Read, Anthony, and David Fisher. *The Deadly Embrace: Hitler, Stalin and the Nazi-Soviet Pact, 1939–1941.* New York, 1988.

———. *Operation Lucy.* New York, 1981.

Rektorat der Martin Luther-Universität Halle-Wittenberg, ed. *Adam Kuckhoff.* Leipzig, 1967.

Regler, Gustav. *The Owl of Minerva: The Autobiography of Gustav Regler.* New York, 1960.

Reitlinger, Gerald. *SS: Alibi of a Nation, 1922–45.* New York, 1957.

Ribbentrop, Anneliese von. *Die Kriegschuld des Widerstandes: Aus britischen Geheimdokumenten, 1938/39.* Leoni am Starnbergersee, 1975.

Rickett, Peggy. *Sketches from My Life.* Privately printed, n.d.

Ringer, Fritz. *The Decline of the German Mandarins: The German Academic Community, 1890–1933.* Cambridge, 1969.

Ripley, LaVern J. *The German Americans.* Boston, 1976.

Ritter, Gerhard. *The German Resistance: Carl Goerdeler's Struggle against Tyranny.* London, 1958.

Robins, Nathalie. *Alien Ink: The FBI's War on Freedom of Expression.* New York, 1992.

Roeder, Manfred. *Die Rote Kapelle.* Hamburg, 1952.

Romerstein, Herbert, and Stanislav Levchenko. *The KGB against the Main Enemy: How the Soviet Intelligence Service Operates against the United States.* Lexington, 1989.

Roon, Ger van. *German Resistance to Hitler: Count von Moltke and the Kreisau Circle.* London, 1971.

Roon, Ger van. *Widerstand im Dritten Reich: Ein Überblick,* Munich 1985.

Roon, Ger van, ed. *Europäischer Widerstand im Vergleich: Die Internationalen Konferenzen Amsterdam.* Berlin, 1985.

Rosenbaum, Alan S. *Prosecuting Nazi War Criminals.* Boulder, 1993.

Rosiejka, Gert. *Die Rote Kapelle: "Landesverrat" als antifaschistischer Widerstand.* Hamburg, 1986.

Rositzke, Harry. *The CIA's Secret Operations.* New York, 1977.

Rovere, Richard. *Senator Joe McCarthy.* New York, 1959.

Rothfels, Hans. *The German Opposition to Hitler.* London, 1961.

Rückerl, Adalbert. *The Investigation of Nazi Crimes, 1945–1978: A Documentation.* Hamden, 1980.

Rürup, Reinhard, ed. *Topography of Terror.* Berlin, 1989.

Russell, Francis. *Sacco and Vanzetti: The Case Resolved.* New York, 1986.

Sahm, Ulrich. *Rudolf von Scheliha, 1897–1942: Ein deutscher Diplomat gegen Hitler.* Munich, 1990.

Salomon, Ernst von. *Fragebogen.* Garden City, 1955.

Sanford, Gregory. *From Hitler to Ulbricht: The Communist Reconstruction of East Germany, 1945–1946.* Princeton, 1983.

Schäfer, Hans Dieter, *Berlin im Zweiten Weltkrieg.* Munich, 1985.

Scheel, Heinrich. *Schulfarm Insel Scharfenberg.* Berlin, 1990.

———. *Vor den Schranken des Reichskriegsgerichts: Mein Weg in den Widerstand.* Berlin, 1993.

Schellenberg, Walter. *The Labyrinth: Memoirs.* New York, 1956.

———. *Memoiren.* Cologne, 1959.

Schlabrendorff, Fabian von. *The Secret War against Hitler.* New York, 1966.

Schmädeke, J., and Peter Steinbach, eds. *Der Widerstand gegen den Nationalsozialismus; Die deutsche Gesellschaft und der Widerstand gegen Hitler.* Munich, 1985.

Schneider, Ulrich. *Marburg, 1933–45.* Frankfurt am Main, 1980.

Schönemann, Friedrich. *Amerikakunde: Eine zeitgemäße Forderung.* Bremen, 1921.

Schramm, Wilhelm Ritter von. *Der Geheimdienst in Europa 1937 bis 1945.* Munich, 1974.

———. *Verrat im Zweiten Weltkrieg.* Düsseldorf, 1967.

Schröter, Heinz. *Stalingrad.* New York, 1968.

Scott, Bonnie Kime, ed. *Selected Letters of Rebecca West.* New Haven, 2000.

Sears, John F. *Sacred Places: American Tourist Attractions in the Nineteenth Century.* New York, 1989.

Shirer, William L. *Berlin Diary: The Journal of a Foreign Correspondent, 1934–1941.* New York, 1941.

———. *The End of a Berlin Diary.* New York, 1947.

———. *The Rise and Fall of the Third Reich.* New York, 1959.

———. *Twentieth-Century Journey: The Nightmare Years, 1930–1940.* Boston, 1984.

———. *Twentieth-Century Journey: A Native's Return, 1945–1988.* Boston, 1990.

Sieg, John. *Einer von Millionen spricht: Skizzen, Erzählungen, Reportagen, Flugschriften.* Berlin, 1989.

Simpson, Christopher. *Blowback.* New York, 1988.

Slaughter, Gertrude. *Only the Past Is Ours.* New York, 1963.

Slaughter, Jane, and Robert Kern, eds. *European Women on the Left. Socialism, Feminism, and the Problems Faced by Political Women, 1880 to the Present.* Westport, 1981.

Smith, Howard K. *Last Train from Berlin.* New York, 1942.

Smith, Truman. *Berlin Alert: The Memoirs and Reports of Truman Smith.* Stanford, 1984.

Spender, Stephen. *World within World.* New York, 1978.

Springer, Anne M. *The American Novel in Germany.* Hamburg, 1960.

Steinbach, Peter. *Widerstand: Ein Problem zwischen Theorie und Geschichte.* Cologne, 1987.

———. *Widerstand in Deutschland, 1933–1945: Ein historisches Lesebuch.* Munich, 1994.

Steinbach Peter, and J. Tuchel, eds. *Lexikon des Widerstandes, 1933–1945.* Munich, 1994.

Steinberg, Michael. *Sabers and Brown Shirts: The German Students' Path to National Socialism, 1918–35.* Chicago, 1977.

Stephenson, Jill. *Women in Nazi Society.* London, 1975.

Stern, Fritz. *Dreams and Delusions: The Drama of German History.* New York, 1987.

———. *Einstein's German World.* Princeton, 1999.

———. *The Politics of Cultural Despair: A Study in the Rise of German Ideology.* Berkeley, 1961.

Still, Bayrd. *Milwaukee: The History of a City.* Madison, 1948.

Sudoplatov, Pavel, and Anatoli Sudaplatov with Jerrold L. and Leona P. Schechter. *Special Tasks.* Boston, 1994.

Suvorov, Viktor. *Ice Breaker: Who Started the Second World War?* London, 1990.

———. *Soviet Military Intelligence.* London, 1986.

Sykes, Christopher. *Troubled Loyalty: A Biography of Adam von Trott zu Solz.* London, 1968.

Tarrant, V. E. *The Red Orchestra: The Soviet Spy Network inside Nazi Europe.* New York, 1995.

Tau, Max. *Auf dem Weg zur Versöhnung*. Hamburg, 1968.

———. *Ein Flüchtling findet sein Land*. Hamburg, 1964.

———. *Das Land, das ich verlassen mußte*. Hamberg, 1961.

Taylor, A. J. P. *The Origins of the Second World War*. New York, 1962.

Taylor, James, and Warren Shaw. *The Third Reich Almanac*. New York, 1987.

Tetens, T. H. *The New Germany and the Old Nazis*. London, 1962.

Thomas, Hugh. *The Spanish Civil War*. London, 1961.

Time-Life. *The Third Reich: The New Order*. Alexandria, 1989.

Tobias, Fritz. *The Reichstag Fire*. New York, 1964.

Tomin, Valentin, and Stefan Grabowski. *Die Helden der Berliner Illegalität*. Berlin, 1967.

Trepper, Leopold. *The Great Game*. New York, 1977.

Trevor-Roper, H. R., ed. and trans. *Hitler's Table Talks*. Oxford, 1988.

Tuchel, Johannes, and Reinhold Schattenfroh. *Zentrale des Terrors*. Berlin, 1987.

Tucker, R. C., and Stephen Cohen, eds. *The Great Purge Trials*. New York, 1965.

Tucker, Robert C. *Stalin in Power: The Revolution from Above, 1928–1941*. New York, 1990.

Turel, Adrian. *Ecce Superhomo*. Self-published, n.d.

Turner, Henry Ashby. *German Big Business and the Rise of Hitler*. New York, 1985.

———. *Germany from Partition to Reunification*. New Haven, 1992.

———. *Hitler's Thirty Days to Power*. Reading, Mass., 1996.

Vassiltchikov, Marie. *The Berlin Diaries*. New York, 1987.

Voegelin, Erich. *Über die Form des amerikanischen Geistes*. Tübingen, 1928.

Volkogonov, Dmitri. *Stalin: Triumph and Tragedy*. New York, 1992.

Wahl, Volker. *Jena als Kunststadt, 1900–1933*. Leipzig, 1988.

Waller, John. *The Unseen War in Europe*. New York, 1996.

Weinstein, Allen, and Alexander Vassiliev. *The Haunted Wood*. New York, 1999.

Weisenborn, Günther. *Der lautlose Aufstand: Bericht über die Widerstandsbewegung des deutschen Volkes, 1933–45*. Frankfurt am Main, 1953.

———. *Die Clowns von Avignon und Klopfzeichen*. Berlin, 1982.

———. *Die Illegalen*. Berlin, 1948.

———. *Memorial*. Frankfurt am Main, 1977.

Weisenborn, Günter, and Joy Weisenborn. *Einmal laß mich traurig sein: Briefe, Lieder, Kassiber, 1942–1943*. Zurich, 1984.

Weiss, Peter. *Die Ästhetik des Widerstands*. Frankfurt am Main, 1981.

———. *Notizbücher, 1971–1980* Frankfurt am Main, 1982.

Welles, Sumner. *The Time for Decision*. New York, 1944.

Wells, John. *This Is Milwaukee*. Garden City, 1970.

Werner, Ruth. *Sonya's Report*. London, 1991.

Werth, Alexander. *Russia at War, 1941–1945*. New York, 1964.

West, Rebecca. *The New Meaning of Treason*. New York, 1964.

———. *A Train of Powder*. London, 1955.

Whaley, Burton. *Codeword Barbarossa*. Cambridge, 1974.

Wheeler-Bennet, John W. *The Nemesis of Power: The German Army in Politics, 1918–1945*. New York, 1964.

Whitney, Craig R. *Spy Trader: Germany's Devil's Advocate and the Darkest Secrets of the Cold War*. New York, 1993.

Whymant, Robert. *Stalin's Spy: Richard Sorge and the Tokyo Espionage Ring.* New York, 1996.

Wiemers, Gerard, ed. *Ein Stück Wirklichkeit mehr. Zum 25. Jahrestag der Ermordung von Adam Kuckhoff.* East Berlin, 1968.

Williams, Robert Chadwell. *Klaus Fuchs, Atom Spy.* Cambridge, 1987.

Wilson, Edmund. *The American Earthquake.* Garden City, 1958.

———. *Red, Black, Blond and Olive. Studies in Four Civilizations: Zuni, Haiti, Soviet Russia, Israel.* New York, 1956.

———. *Travels in Two Democracies.* New York, 1936.

Winks, Robin. *Cloak and Gown: Scholars in the Secret War, 1939–1961.* New York, 1987.

Wolfe, Thomas. *Of Time and the River.* New York, 1935.

———. *The Web and the Rock.* New York, 1939.

———. *You Can't Go Home Again.* New York, 1942.

Wolton, Thierry. *Le grand recrutement.* Paris, 1993.

———. *Le KGB en France.* Paris, 1986.

WPA. *Wisconsin: A Guide to the Badger State.* New York, 1941.

Zahn-Harnack, Agnes von. *Adolf von Harnack.* Berlin, 1951.

Zeller, Eberhard. *Geist der Freiheit: Der zwanzigste Juli.* Munich, 1963.

Zoller, Albert. *Hitler privat: Erlebnisbericht seiner Geheimsekretärin.* Göttingen, 1964.

Zhukov, G. K. *Memoirs of Marshal Zhukov.* New York, 1971.

ARTICLES

Anderhub, Andreas. "Die Gießener Studenten in der Schlußphase der Weimarer Republik oder wie Mildred und Arvid Harnack zu Gegnern des Nationalsozialismus wurden." In *Mitteilungen des Oberhessischen Geschichtsvereins.* Vol. 65. Giessen, 1980.

Andrews, Dorothea. "Martyr Held Type of DAR 'Sterner Stuff.' Mildred F. Harnack, Nazi Victim, Is Paid Tribute at Services." *Washington Post,* April 24, 1948.

"Eine Armee stirbt durch Verrat."*Der Hausfreund in Stadt und Land,* November-December 1951.

Astor, David. "Why the Revolt against Hitler was Ignored: On the British Reluctance to Deal with German Anti-Nazis." *Encounter* 6 (1996).

Baum, Barbara. "Deutsche antifachisten im Widerstand. Funker machten die Nazis nervös. Rote Kapelle sandte geheime Nachrichten nach Moskau." *Berliner Zeitung,* March 28, 1985.

Baum, Marie. "Zum Gedächtnis von Arvid und Mildred Harnack." *Rhein-Main-Zeitung,* December 27-28, 1952.

Beck, Maria-Dorothea. "Erinnerungen an Mildred Harnack." *Die Andere Zeitung,* September 14, 1967.

Besymenski, Lew. "Geheimmission in Stalins Auftrag? David Kandelaki und die sowjetisch-deutschen Beziehungen Mitte der dreißiger Jahre." *Vierteljahrshefte für Zeitgeschichte* 40 (1992).

Bethge, Renate. "Bonhoeffers Familie und ihre Bedeutung für seine Theologie." In *Beiträge zum Widerstand,* 1933–1945. Lecture given at the Gedenkstätte Deutscher Wilderstand, November 1985.

Biernat, Karl-Heinz. "Kämpfer für eine neue Ordnung. Vor 25 Jahren wurden

Harro Schulze-Boysen und zehn Mitstreiter von den Faschisten ermordet." *Neues Deutschland*, December 22, 1967.

———. "Patriotischer Kampf in Liebe und Treue zur Heimat des Sozialismus." *Neues Deutschland*, December 28, 1969.

Brüning, Eberhard. "Berlin als persönliche Erfahrung und literarischer Gegenstand amerikanischer Schriftsteller (1890 bis 1940)." *Sitzungsberichte der Akademie der Wissenschaften der DDR* 2 (1988)

———. "Mildred Harnack-Fish als Literaturwissenchaftlerin." *Sitzungsberichte der Akademie der Wissenschaften der DDR*, 1983.

———. "Mildred Harnack—eine mutige Antifaschistin, die im Kampf für eine gerechte Sache ihr Leben liess." *Neuer Tag*, September 10, 1982.

———. "Zwei Professionen einer Frau. Mildred Harnack-Fish—Antifaschistin und Literaturwißenschaftlerin." *Spectrum* 2 (1982).

Brysac, Shareen Blair. "Die innere Front gegen Hitler." *Tagesspiegel*, February 2, 1993.

———. "She Spied, but Hitler Was the Traitor." *New York Times*, February 20, 1993.

———. "Mildred and Arvid Harnack: The American Connection." *Die Rote Kapelle im Widerstand gegen den Nationalsozialismus*, 1994.

Buschmann, Hugo. "De la resistance au defaitisme." *Les Temps modernes* 46–47 (August-September 1949).

Coolidge, Calvin. "Enemies of the Republic." *Delineator*, June 1922.

Coppi, Hans. "Das Gesicht des Helden." *Süddeutsche Zeitung*, April 20–21, 1996.

———. "Gespräche über die Rote Kapelle." *Die Weltbühne* 9 (1989).

———. "Die 'Rote Kapelle'—ein Geschichtsbild verändert sich." *Geschichte Erziehung Politik*, 7–8 (1994).

———. "Die 'Rote Kapelle,' im Spannungsfeld von Widerstand und nachrichtendienstlicher Tätigkeit, Der Trepper-Report vom Juni 1943." *Vierteljahrshefte für Zeitgeschichte* 44 (1996).

———. "Schokoreklame tarnte Flugblätter. Die Gestapo bezeichnete Schulze-Boysen/Harnack-Gruppe als 'Rote Kapelle.'" *Junge Welt*, December 22, 1967.

———. "Der Spion, der den Tod brachte." *Süddeutsche Zeitung*, July 13–14, 1996

Davies, Peter. "No Nameless Heroes." *Christian Century*, April 16, 1975.

"D.C. Woman Was Beheaded on Hitler's Order, Husband Executed on Christmas Eve of 1942." *Washington Times Herald*, December 3, 1947.

Dissel, Werner. "Harro Schulze-Boysen: Freier, streitbarer Geist." *Junge Welt*, September 2–3, 1989.

"Don't Write—Never Forget Me." *Wisconsin Alumnus*, December 1947.

Falkowski, Ed. "Berlin in Crimson." *New Masses*, March 1930.

"Frauen im roten Spiel." *Heidebote*, 1951.

Garson, Sandra. "Better Not Write but Don't Forget Me." *Wisconsin Alumnus*, May-June 1986.

"Das Geheimnis der Roten Kapelle." *Der Fortschritt* 45 (1950).

"Das Geheimnis der Roten Kapelle." *Norddeutsche Rundschau*, January 24, 1951.

"Geheimnisse der Kampfspionage: Mitwisser und Mittäter unter uns. Schweigsame Legion 'Rote Kapelle'—Musik für Moscow." *Die Reichszeitung* 4 (1951).

Gittler, L. F. "Ambassador Extraordinary: A Close-up Portrait of William E. Dodd." *Survey Graphic*, July 1938.

Graml, Hermann. "Der Fall Oster." *Vierteljahrshefte für Zeitgeschichte* 14 (1966).

Grimme, Adolf. "Rote Agenten mitten unter uns." Letter to the editor *Stern* 20 (1951).

Haase, Norbert. "Aus der Praxis des Reichskriegsgerichtes." *Vierteljahrshefte für Zeitgeschichte* 39 (1991).

Harnack, Axel von. "Arvid und Mildred Harnack." *Die Gegenwart*, January 31, 1947.

Harnack, Clara. "Unermüdlicher Streiter für die Menschenrechte: Die Mutter Arvid Harnacks über ihren Sohn und die Schwiegertochter Mildred." *Neues Deutschland*, December 1977.

Havemann, Ingeborg. "Mildred Harnack: Eine Erinnerung." *Heute und Morgen* 2 (1950).

Hayes, Elliot. "Harnack Deaths Covered Trail of German Hoard." *Washington Evening Star*, December 4, 1947.

"Hitler Beheaded American Woman as a Personal Reprisal in 1943." *New York Times*, December 1, 1947.

Hofmann, Hermann. "Kein Spionagering für die Sowjetunion." *Frankfurter Allgemeine Zeitung*, June 8, 1993.

Höhne, Heinz, and Gilles Perrault. "Ptx ruft Moskau": Die Geschichte des Spionage-Ringes 'Rote Kapelle.' " *Der Spiegel* 23–30 (1968).

Holborn, Hajo. "A Wilsonian in Hitler's Realm." *Yale Review*, Spring 1941.

Holman, C. Hugh. "Thomas Wolfe's Berlin." *Saturday Review*, March 11, 1967.

Hunter, John Patrick. "Germany Shouldn't Forget State Heroine." *Capital Times*, March 2, 1993.

Ihde, Horst. "Mildred Harnacks wissenschaftliches Erbe." *Neues Deutschland*, May 6, 1989.

Kappstein, Theodor. Review of *Adolf von Harnack*, by Agnes von Zahn-Harnack. *Die Literatur* 38, no. 11 (1936).

"Die Katze im Kreml." *Kristall* 25 (1950–1951).

Krause, Tilman. "Ein Mann wie eine Flamme; Eine Tagung über die 'Rote Kapelle' in der Gedenkstätte Deutscher Widerstand." *Frankfurter Allegemeine Zeitung*.

Kraushaar, Luise. "Als Kundschafter und Kämpfer im Widerstand." *Neues Deutschland*, May 23, 1981.

Kuckhoff, Greta. "Ein Abschnitt des deutschen Widerstandskampfes." *Die Weltbühne* 3–4 (1948).

———. "Arvid Harnack." *Die Weltbühne* 44 (1969).

———. "Jenseits der Front." *Neue Zeit* 22 (1965): 19.

———. "Meine Freundin Mildred: Einer tapferen Frau zum Gedächtnis." *Berliner Zeitung*, May 11, 1947.

———. "Rote Kapelle." *Aufbau* 1 (1948).

Lamb, Richard. "How Hitler Might Have Been Stopped." Review of *The Unnecessary War* by Patricia Meehan. *Spectator,* September 5, 1992.

Ledig-Rowohlt, H. M. "Thomas Wolfe in Berlin." *American Scholar* 22 (Spring 1953).

Leiser, Clara. "Wisconsin Writers IV: William Ellery Leonard." *Wisconsin Journal of Education,* February 1926.

———. "William Ellery Leonard: Some Memories and New Poems." *Tomorrow Magazine,* May 1, 1949.

Lietzmann, Hans. Gedächtnisrede auf Adolf von Harnack (*Sitzungsberichte der Preuss. Akademie der Wissenschaften*), January 22, 1931.

Lovett, Robert Morss. "Cassandra: Ambassador to the Third Reich." *New Republic,* March 3, 1941.

Mader, Julius. "Mildred from Milwaukee." *GDR Review* 20 (1978).

Martini, Winfried. "Deutsche Spionage für Moskau, 1939–1945." *Die Welt.* October 15, 17, 18, 27, 1966.

Mathieu, Gus. "And to Remind the Living." *OMGUS Observer,* September 27, 1946.

Meyer, Ernest L. "Glenn Frank: Journalist on Parole." *American Mercury,* February 1934.

———. "Twilight of a Golden Age." *American Mercury,* August 1933.

———. "William Ellery Leonard." *American Mercury,* July 1934.

Meyer, Helga. "Im Dienste des Friedens als Kundschafterin tätig, Mildred Harnack—Ein Leben für den Fortschritt." *Neues Deutschland,* September 18–19, 1982.

Monath, Hans. "Statt Grotewohl Linden und Pappeln: 400 ehemalige DDR-Schulen im Ostteil der Stadt müssen sich neue Name suchen. In Lichtenberg wurde gestern eine Schule erneut nach der Widerstandkämpferin Mildred Harnack benannt." *Die Tagezeitung,* February 17, 1993.

Mueller, Theodore. "Milwaukee's German Cultural Heritage." *Milwaukee History* 10, no. 3 (1987).

Myers, R. David. "The Wisconsin Idea: Its National and International Significance." *Wisconsin Academy Review,* Fall 1991.

"Nazis Confiscate Estate." *New York Times,* May 15, 1943.

"Nazi's Victim Has Kin Here. Her Sister Is Resident." *Milwaukee Journal,* May 18, 1943.

Nestler, Paul. "Wisconsin Must Not Honor Communist." *Milwaukee Journal,* September 29, 1986.

Norris, Tim. "Hard Lesson: Martyr of Nazi Period Recalled." *Milwaukee Journal,* December 17, 1990.

"Oberschule erhielt Namen "Mildred Harnack." *Neues Deutschland,* September 17, 1976.

Pampel, Joachim. Schule heißt wieder "Mildred Harnack." *Neues Deutschland,* February 17, 1993.

Paul, Elfriede. "Frauen aus der Widerstandsbewegung." *Aufbau* 2 (1947).

Petscherski, Vladimir. "Rasvetschik usnik Gestapo i EEK." *Sovetskaja Rossija,* December 16, 1990.

———. The Moscow Dossier: "Tajna Krasnoi Kapelle." *Novy Vremya* 12–13 (1994)

Piepe, Harry. "Ich jagte rote Agenten." *Der Mittag* February 11-March 15, 1953.

Pusey, William W., II. "The German Vogue of Thomas Wolfe." *Germanic Review* 23 (April 1948).

———. "William Faulkner's Works in Germany to 1940: Translations and Criticism." *Germanic Review*, October 1955.

Roeder, Manfred. Letter to the editor. *Stern* May 27, 1951.

Roper, Trevor. Review of *After Long Silence*, by Michael Straight. *New York Review of Books*, March 31, 1983.

"Rote Agenten mitten unter uns." *Stern* 18–26 (1951).

"Rote Kapelle, Kennwort Direktor." *Spiegel* 21 (1968).

Rybak, Timothy W. "Letters from the Dead." *New Yorker*, February 1, 1993.

Scheel, Heinrich. "Kampfbedingungen und Kunstlerfahrungen 'drinnen' und 'draußen.' Erinnerungen an Mitstreiter im antifaschistischen Widerstand." *Weimarer Beträge*, June 1979.

———. "Die 'Rote Kapelle' und der 20. Juli 1944: Die Widerstandsorganisation Schulze-Boysen/Harnack." *Evangelisches Akademie Berlin*, 1988.

———. "Ein Schulungsmaterial aus dem illegalen antifaschistichen Widerstand der Roten Kapelle." *Zeitschrift für Geschichtswissenschaft* 32 (1984).

———. "Mit ganzem Einsatz gegen den kriegsbesessenen Faschismus." *Neues Deutschland*, December 23, 1987.

———. "Vereint im Widerstand gegen den Faschismus: Aus der Geschichte der Roten Kapelle." *Spektrum* 5 (1975).

———. "Wesen und Wollen der Widerstandsorganisation Schulze-Boysen/Harnack." *Neues Deutschland*, June 19, 1968.

Schiff, Steven. "Leni's Olympia." *Vanity Fair*, September 1992.

Schulze-Boysen, Hartmut. "Ein Deutscher, der Patriotismus anders verstand als die Mehrheit."*Frankfurter Rundschau*, June 5, 1993.

Schumann, Frank. "Die Geheime Front: Widerstand in der Faschistenzentrale," *Junge Welt*, November 5, 1982.

Der Spiegel. "Spionage: Das Geheimnis der V-Stoffe." 24–28 (1978).

Soble, Jack, *New York Journal American.* November 10–20, 1957.

Steinbach, Peter. "50 Jahre danach." *Zeitschrift für Geschichtswissenschaft* 41 (1993).

———. "Widerstandsorganisation Harnack/Schulze-Boysen: die 'Rote Kapelle' ein Vergleichsfalls für die Widerstandsgeschichte." *Geschichte in Wissenschaft und Unterricht* 3 (1991).

Stover, Frances. "Albert Shong and West Division." *Historical Messenger*, March 1957.

Tschernjawski, Vitali. "Nato gegen 'Rote Kapelle.' *Neue Zeit* (Moscow) 5 (1981).

———. "Geheimdienste: Macht und Ohnmacht der sowjetischen Aufklärung." *Neue Zeit* (Moscow). 33 (1991).

Tuchel, Johannes. "Weltanschauliche Motivationen in der Harnack/Schulze-Boysen-Organisation" ("Rote Kapelle"). *Kirchliche Zeitgeschichte* 2 (1988).

Vanden Heuvel, Katrina. "Grand Illusions." *Vanity Fair*, August 1991.

Vesper, Karlen. "Als Kundschafterin im Dienste des Friedens: Vor 40 Jahren wurde Mildred Harnack ermordet." *Neues Deutschland*, February 16, 1983.

Vogel, Ursula. "Zeugnis eines reichen Lebens" (Mildred Harnack). *Für Dich* 36 (1976).

Voight, Frieda. "Kurt Baum: German Poet in Milwaukee." *Historical Messenger* 24 no. 3 (1968).

"Von Harnack's Son Slain." *New York Times*, April 11, 1943.

Ward, James J. "German Communist Efforts to Counter Nazis." *Central European History*, 14, no. 4 (1981).

Weisenborn, Günther. "Harro und Libertas." *Der gespaltene Horizont*, (1964).

———. "Letter to the editor. *Stern*, June 10, 1951.

———. "Letter to the editor. *Die Welt*, December 2, 1966.

Werres, Thomas. "In Liebenberg gingen Ulbricht und Mielke auf die Pirsch." *Der Tagesspiegel*, January 2, 1993.

"Wisconsin Girl Beheaded by Hitler, Magazine Says." *Washington Post* December 2, 1947.

Woehrmann, Paul. "Milwaukee German Immigrant Values: An Essay." *Milwaukee History*, Autumn 1987.

Wolfe, Thomas. "I have a Thing to Tell You." *New Republic*, March 10, 1937.

"Woman Dead, a Nazi Victim. Native of Milwaukee." *Milwaukee Journal*, October 6, 1943.

Yarbrough, Charles. "Victim of Nazi Ax Lived Here." *Washington Post*, December 3, 1947.

Yezhkov, Dimitry. "Vozrashchenie k Zhivym, Kto Predal 'Krasnuyu Kapellu?" (Return to the living, who betrayed 'the Red Orchestra?') *Sovershenno Secretno 9* (1993).

Zechlin, Egmont. "Erinnerung an Arvid und Mildred Harnack." *Geschichte in Wissenschaft und Unterricht. 7* (1982).

UNPUBLISHED SOURCES

Beam, Jacob. Unpublished ms.

Behrens, Clara. Protocol. Ast/RK 38, GDW.

Besymenski, Lev. Interview with Greta Kuckhoff, Ast/RK 35. GDW.

Biernat, Karl-Heinz. Interview with Greta Kuckhoff, Ast/RK 40. GDW.

Colwell, James Lee. "The American Experience in Berlin during the Weimar Republic." Ph.d. diss., Yale University, 1961.

Files of the public prosecutor against Dr. Manfred Roeder. Js 16/49, Lüneburg, 1951. Hanover.

Gurevich, Anatoli (KENT). Protocol. Copy in the GDW.

Gutmann, Henning. "A Conservative in the Third Reich: Hjalmar Schacht and the German Economy, 1933–39." M.A. Thesis, Harvard University, 1982.

Harnack, Falk. "Vom anderen Deutschland: Teilbericht über die Harnack/Schulze-Boysen-Widerstandsorganisation." Berlin, 1947.

Havemann, Inge. Material in Hoover institution on War, Revolution, and Peace, Stanford University.

Havemann, Wolfgang. "Erinnerung an Mildred und Arvid Harnack." March 1986. SLD.

———. "Über die notwendige Einheit von Theorie und Praxis bei der Anwendung des Marxismus-Leninismus (Erinnerungen an Arvid Harnack aus den Jahren 1931–1942) "Rote Kapelle" Collection, GDW.

Leiser, Clara. "The Atmosphere of Terror." Clara Leiser Papers, Anita Leiser, New York.

———, "Just Try Prison Visiting in Naziland!" Clara Leiser Papers, Anita Leiser, New York.

Rascher, Dr. Heinz. "Meine Freundschaft mit Arvid Harnack (1901–1942) im Jahre 1921. Hamburg, December 22, 1969. Copy in author's possession.

Schulze, Marie-Louise. "Warum ich im Jahre 1933 Parteigenossin geworden bin." N.d.

Smith, Katherine. Unpublished autobiography, Hoover Institution of War, Revolution, and Peace, Stanford University.

Stern, Martha Dodd. "In Memory." Memoirs of Mildred Harnack and Boris Vinogradov, LOC, Martha Dodd Stern Papers (LOC).

Trepper, Leopold. Protocol. Copy in the GDW.

U.S. Army (CIC) Interrogations: Otto Donner, Alexander Kraell, Louis Lochner, Heinz Pannwitz, Manfred Roeder. NA.

Utech, Wilhelm. Protocol. AST/RK 43, GDW.

Wollheim, Mona. "Giessen zu Beginn der dreißiger Jahre." MS New Series, 401, fol. 21. University Library, Giessen.

PUBLISHED WORKS OF MILDRED HARNACK-FISH

Harnack-Fish, Mildred. "The Fiend Has It." *Wisconsin Literary Magazine*, December 1922.

———. "In the Library." *Wisconsin Literary Magazine*, December 1922.

———. "Silver and Gold." *Wisconsin Literary Magazine*, February 1923.

———. "I Do Wander." *Wisconsin Literary Magazine*, June 1923.

———. "And Still You Weep." *Wisconsin Literary Magazine*, October 1923.

———. "Mechanism." *Wisconsin Literary Magazine*, October 1923.

———. "Superiority." *Wisconsin Literary Magazine*, October 1923.

———. "University Education." *Wisconsin Literary Magazine*, October 1923.

———. Brief Reviews (John Hampson, *Saturday Night at the Greyhound, O Providence*). *Berlin Topics*, November 12, 1933.

———. Brief Reviews (Albert Halper, *Union Square*. *Berlin Topics*, November 26, 1933.

———. Brief Reviews (Pearl Buck, *The First Wife*). *Berlin Topics*. December 24, 1933.

———. Brief Reviews (Kay Boyle, *Gentlemen I Address You Privately*). *Berlin Topics*, February 4, 1934.

———. Brief Reviews (Hervey Allen, *Anthony Adverse*). *Berlin Topics*, February 18, 1934.

———. Book Nook (Aldous Huxley, *Uncle Spencer and Other Stories*. *Berlin Topics*, January 21, 1934.

———. "Drei junge Dichter aus USA: Thornton Wilder, Thomas Wolfe, und William Faulkner." *Berliner Tageblatt*, August 5, 1934.

———. "Der Epiker der Südstaaten: William Faulkner." *Berliner Tageblatt*, August 23, 1934.

———. "Variationen über das Thema Amerika." *Berliner Tageblatt*, December 2, 1934.

———. "Amerikanische Schulmädchen." *Berliner Tageblatt*, April 10, 1934.

————. "Reifender Mais." *Berliner Tageblatt*, August 30, 1934.

————. "Der Mond und das Saxophon." *Die Dame* 7, (1935).

————. "Thornton Wilder, Idealist und Puritaner." *Berliner Tageblatt*, April 28, 1935.

————. "John Hampson: *Ein junger englischer Dichter.*" *Berliner Tageblatt*, February 17, 1935.

————. "Thomas Wolfe." *Berliner Tageblatt*, May 26, 1935.

————. "One of the Greatest of Younger American Authors in Berlin." Interview with Thomas Wolfe. *Continental Post*, May 12, 19, 1935.

————. "William Faulkner: *Ein amerikanischer Dichter aus großer Tradition.*" *Die Literatur*, November 1935.

————. "Im Wald von Arden." *Die Dame* 26 (1938).

————. "Sommersonnenwende." *Die Dame* 19 (1939).

Harnack-Fish, Mildred, and Wesley Repor [Martha Dodd]. Brief Reviews (Edna Ferber.) *Berlin Topics*, October 29, 1933.

TRANSLATIONS BY MILDRED HARNACK-FISH

Boyle, Kay. "Dein Leib ist ein Juwelenschrein." In *Neu Amerika: Zwanzig Erzähler der Gegenwart.* Ed. by Kurt Ullrich. (Berlin, 1937).

Baroness Orczy. *Ein Frau unter Tausenden.* Hamburg, 1938.

Edmonds, Walter D. *Pfauenfeder und Kokarde.* Berlin, 1936.

Sheridan, Clare. *Arabisches Zwischenspiel.* Berlin, 1938.

Stone, Irving. *Ein Leben in Leidenschaft.* Berlin, 1936.

Zugsmith, Leane. *Kein Platz in der Welt.* Berlin, 1937.

ACKNOWLEDGMENTS

Many people, with their generous help and unstinting interest, made this book possible. Two in particular stand out. My husband, Karl E. Meyer, never lost faith in the author or her book despite the delays, frustrations, and vicissitudes of the publishing process. The other indispensable colleague who stayed to the finish line is Beth Jackson Berman of Durham, North Carolina, the final authority for the German translations throughout the book. Her feel for the nuances of Third Reich bureaucratese was assured and illuminating.

I benefited at every point in exchanging documents, ideas, and criticism with Hans Coppi and Jürgen Danyel, German scholars whose involvement with the Harnack/Schulze-Boysen group is as informed as it is deeply felt. Samson Knoll, formerly of the Defense Language Institute at Monterey, California, not only read and commented on my manuscript in its early stages but shared with me his memories of Mildred as a teacher and recommended his former graduate student, Beth Jackson Berman, as translator. Larisa Gajdasic, Lisa Whitmore, and Christina Sickert provided early help with the German research. Unless otherwise noted, translations from the Russian were by Ann Dunnigan, Jürgen Danyel, and Hans Coppi. Irina Scherbakova of the University of Moscow and, Susan Heuman and George Feifer, Russian scholars, provided astute guidance on interpreting Soviet material.

Mildred's niece, Jane Donner Sweeney, provided copies of Mildred's letters and commented on the original versions of the manuscript. She was unstinting with her help and encouragement before her untimely death in 1994. Her son, Neal Donner, has sustained the family's interest in their aunt and uncle. Mildred's nephews, David Carlson and Robert Fish, and her niece, Marion Potter, were equally responsive. Sue Heath Brown and Donald Heath shared their invaluable recollections of Arvid and Mildred in Berlin. Dorothy Meyer's monologues in New York and Ernie Meyer's columns in the *Capital Times* recalled the special flavor of Madison, Wisconsin, during the 1920s. My sister-in-law, Susan Meyer, shared her material on her father and offered precious technical assistance on illustrations. Bercie Frohman provided books and photographs of Mildred that her mother, Grace Carlsruh, had saved over the years. Grace Yalkurt reminisced thoughtfully about her marriage to the Wisconsin scholar and poet William Ellery Leonard. Throughout, I owe a special debt to the many kindnesses, and the sympathetic ear, of Marion Greene in the editorial department of the *New York Times*.

Thanks are due to Milwaukee lawyer Arthur Heitzer, who maintains a clearinghouse and archives for those interested in the Harnacks. It was through his efforts that a bill was passed in Wisconsin designating September 16 as Mildred Harnack Day. Sandra Garson made available her earlier work on Mildred, and Gert Rosiejka in Berlin shared his research on the Red Orchestra. I followed the footsteps of Eberhard Brüning, a Leipzig scholar of American literature and early Harnack biographer, who had the daunting task of making sense of Mildred's scattered archives during the era of German division.

To the late John Costello and Oleg Tsarev I owe a special debt. Thanks to their help, I was able to obtain the original documents from Russian archives, pertaining to the Red Orchestra. Others providing primary source material include Stephen Koch, Herbert Mitgang, and Adrien Schriel. Timothy Naftali and Carl Rakosi kindly forwarded other information. Robert Ryley sent me the correspondence between Kenneth Fearing and Margery Latimer, Anita Leiser, custodian of the William Ellery Leonard and Clara Leiser papers, has been unfailingly generous. Philip Metcalfe, Katrina Vanden Heuvel, John Fox, and Douglas Wheeler assisted in the pursuit of elusive information about Martha Dodd Stern. Jacob Beam and Katherine Smith lent me drafts of their unpublished memoirs and shared their Berlin memories.

Among others who shared recollections with me I would like

to thank the following persons for their accounts of life in Milwaukee and Madison: John Patrick Hunter, Gertrude Bruns, the late Porter Butts, Dorothy Whipple Clague, Anne Campbell Davis, Lowell Frautschi, the late Mildred Gilman, Sender Garlin, Uta Hagen, the late Dorothy Knaplund, Stella Revell, Francesca Paratore, the late Gertrude Wilson, the late Peggy Rickett Ramsperger, the late Hazel Briggs Rice, Frank Zeidler, the late Leonard Silk, the late Clara Leiser, Leslie Fiedler, and Mark Perlman. Lorraine Obst remembered her favorite baby-sitter. The late Francis Birch remembered Washington days; Lucy Turner-High and Karl Heider briefed me on Mildred's first love; my Jena expert was Cornelia Cotton. Mrs. John C. White remembered her Dodd embassy days, and I benefited from a telephone conversation with Robert Dallek on Ambassador Dodd. Sylvia Crane, the late Letitia Ide, and the late Jürgen Kuczynski provided insights on Martha Dodd Stern, and Martha Turner and Stewart Herman were helpful on matters pertaining to the American Church in Berlin. During my various stays in Berlin I spoke with the late A. H. Frucht, the late Falk Harnack, Clarita von Trott, and Lillian Joachmczyk; in Dresden I met with Arvid's nephew Wolfgang Havemann; in Selent I spent a very enjoyable day listening to Anneliese and the late Egmont Zechlin and a very pleasant afternoon with the late Edith Reindl on the shores of Lake Constance. In Bonn, Hartmut Schulze-Boysen and Johannes Haas-Heye reflected on matters pertaining to the families of Harro and Libertas Schulze-Boysen. On a trip to Lousiana, I spoke with the late Franciska and Rudolf Heberle. During the early stages of the book, Inge Malek-Kohler likewise remembered her friends in the German resistance. Norbert Haase shared his expertise on the Third Reich's court-martial system; Herman Weiss and Robert Kempner proved to be experts on Manfred Roeder. Telephone conversations with George Fischer and Joe Gould provided useful background information. Eva Mekler generously gave me material she had collected on Mildred as well as an interview with Dorothy Meyer.

At the National Archives in Washington, John Taylor was for me, as for so many others, the indispensable guru and guide through the maze of intelligence documents. He made suggestions and offered encouragement, sometimes telephoning when new batches of material were declassified. I am indebted to his former colleague Robert Wolfe, who pointed me toward many World War II interrogations. Agnes Peterson, curator at the Hoover Institution at Stanford University, sent along material from Inge Havemann that I might not have discovered. Mrs. Max Delbrück generously gave permission for the copying of relevant documents from her husband's archives at the California Institute of Technology. Frank Cook, archivist at the University of Wisconsin Library, and the staffs of the Milwaukee County Historical Society, and the German History Society (London), and Faith Miracle of the Wisconsin Academy of Science, Arts, and Letters, assisted in the early days of research. Most crucially, Dr. Leerhoff of the Niedersächsisches Hauptstaatsarchiv in Hanover permitted access, unusual at the time, to documents pertaining to the postwar interrogations of Manfred Roeder. Thanks as well to Dr. M. Mühlner of the Sächsische Landesbibliothek in Dresden for granting access to the Wolfgang Havemann material in its collection. David Marwell, formerly of the Berlin Document Center, offered a helpful and colorful introduction to the history of his archive. I am also indebted to Ute Stiepani of the Gedenkstätte Deutsher Widerstand for help in finding and reproducing the photographs. I was additionally aided by Brian Harrington of the Johns Hopkins University archives and F. O. Musser at Goucher College. The office of Paul Gitlin Associates allowed access to the Thomas Wolfe Archives at Harvard. I also thank Ilona Kolb and Klaus Fuchs-Kittowski for allowing me to examine the Martha Dodd material in the Humboldt University Archives.

All writers blessed with a card to the Frederick Lewis Allen Room at the New York Public Library appreciate the benefits of having reserve books at hand. Two librarians, Danielle Carriera and David Cappiello at the Pequot Library, in Southport, Connecticut, cheerfully forwarded many interlibrary loan requests— and special thanks to their chief, Mary Freedman.

To various German diplomats—notably Hennecke Graf von Bassewitz, Karl Paschke, Hans Wiessmann, and Gisela Libal—a grateful salute for assistance in obtaining grants and hard-to-get books and in opening archives. Special thanks to my indefatigable Internationes guides, particularly Ilse Beck and Gert Rosiejka, and to Ursula Bender and Joachim Zepelin, who arranged and accompanied me to interviews in Berlin. A D.A.A.D. grant in 1989 allowed me to improve my German. I also benefited immensely from the year I spent in recently united Berlin as the spouse of a Fellow at the Wissenschaftskolleg zu Berlin (the Institute for Advanced Studies).

Thanks also to the late Heinrich Scheel, former chief of the Arbeitsstelle: Geschichte der Widerstandsorganisation Schulze-Boysen/Harnack. Thomas Simon and Ginga Eichler, formerly of the Liga für Völkerfreundschaft der DDR, assisted my work by introducing me to Erika and Martin Herzig, my accommodating hosts during visits to East Berlin. Dieter Weigert assisted me in the early stages of research, serving as a diplomatic chaperon on a memorable visit to Vera and Reiner Kuchenmeister.

The staff members of the Gedenkstätte Deutscher Widerstand, in what used to be West Berlin, were consistently helpful. Peter Steinbach and Johannes Tuchel bore my stream of questions and requests with courteous forbearance.

Hosts during my perambulations include Eve Joan and Jim Zucker, Joseph and Marilyn Hahn in Milwaukee; Diane Steffan and Scott Cutlip in Madison; Martha and Bob Lewis, Nikki Szulc, and Lucy Komisar in Washington; Inge and Henry Bondi in Princeton; Gillian Darley and Michael Horowitz, Jane Perlez, and Ray Bonner in London; Ingeborg Kruse in Hanover; the late Heinrich Maria Ledig-Rowohlt and his wife, Jane, in Lausanne; and finally, Barbara Gasch and June Erlick in Berlin.

A very grateful nod to Henry Bondi, Erika Herzig, David Kahn, Gabriel Gorodetsky, Arden Bucholz, Hartmut Schulze-Boysen, Dona Munker, Gwen Robyns, and the late Bruno Schachner, the late Ann Dunnigan, the late Peter Forbath, the late Peter Wyden, the late John Allenby, and the late Jo Kaufmann, who read all or part of the manuscript. I benefited greatly from their comments. Needless to add, I alone am responsible for any errors of fact or interpretation that remain.

This would have been a very different book if I had not been a member of the Women's Biography Seminar, which met first at New York University and then at the Graduate Center of the City University of New York. Throughout, I enjoyed the interest and support of Beatrice Steinmann-Smith and the Weston, Connecticut, "Kränzchen."

Finally, thanks are owed to my literary agents, Anne Engel and, at an earlier phase, Tom Wallace, who supported the project at its beginning. At Oxford University Press, let it be noted, my efforts were greeted with cheerful competence by Helen Mules and Rudy Faust. Peter Ginna has been the very model of the meticulous and caring editor, mistakenly assumed to be extinct.

* * *

Grateful acknowledgment is made for permission to reprint the following:

From *Deadly Illusions* by John Costello and Oleg Tsarev, permission © 1993 by Nimbus communications, Inc. and Oleg Tsarev. Reprinted by permission of Crown Publishers, a division of Random House, Inc.

From *The Haunted Wood* by Allen Weinstein and Alexander Vassiliev © 1998 by Alexander Vassiliev. Reprinted by permission of Random House, Inc.

From *You Can't Go Home Again* by Thomas Wolfe, permission granted by HarperCollins

From the unpublished papers of David J. Dallin, permission granted by Manuscripts and Archives Division, the New York Public Library, Astor, Lenox and Tilden Foundations

From the unpublished letters of Martha Dodd and the Dodd family, permission granted by Dr. S. Myslil, executor of the Martha Dodd Stern estate

From the unpublished letters and manuscripts of Mildred Harnack, permission granted by the late Jane Donner Sweeney and Marion Potter

For permission to quote from the unpublished material of the Harnack family, I am obliged to the late Käthe Braun-Harnack

From the unpublished letters of Franziska and Rudolf Heberle, permission granted by the late Rudolf Heberle

From the unpublished letters of Clara Leiser and William Ellery Leonard, permission granted by Anita Leiser

From the unpublished letter of Maxwell Perkins, permission granted by Charles Scribner III

From the unpublished letter of Thornton Wilder, with the permission of the Wilder Family LLC. All rights reserved.

Every effort has been made to secure permission for material quoted from the rightful copyright holders. We regret any inadvertent omission.

Shareen Blair Brysac
March 2000

INDEX

The notes are not included in the index.

481